OFFICIAL REPORT [HANSARD]

CENTENARY VOLUME

OFFICIAL REPORT [HANSARD]
HOUSE OF COMMONS

CENTENARY VOLUME
1909-2009

An anthology of historic and memorable
House of Commons speeches to
celebrate the first 100 years

COMPILED, WRITTEN AND EDITED BY
IAN CHURCH CBE
EDITOR OF THE OFFICIAL REPORT [HANSARD]
1989-2002

ISBN 978 0 11 8404631

ACKNOWLEDGEMENTS

We are grateful to the contributors to this volume, almost invariably busy people who have given freely of their time to research, and write their appreciations of, their chosen speeches. Those sentiments apply particularly to the Prime Minister, the party leaders and Mr Speaker Martin, all of whom contend with the relentless demands of more important matters.

The volume would have been incomplete without the photographs of the contributors, which were kindly donated by various organisations and persons. In particular, our thanks go to *The Daily Telegraph* for permitting use of the pictures of Professor Anthony King and Lord Deedes of Aldington, to Ben Schott for his picture of Trevor Kavanagh, and to Alex Folkes for his picture of Nick Clegg. Thanks to Terry Moore for his photograph of Mr Speaker in his ceremonial robes and to Deryc Sands, who took the cover photograph of the Chamber. My personal admiration goes to those contributors who bravely subjected themselves to the uncertainties and shortcomings of my own camera work.

A book such as this involves much toil that lies unseen. We are therefore indebted to three *Hansard* people – Portia Dadley, for her assistance with some of the biographies, and Brian Harrison and Bernard Hudson for their invaluable, unstinting and good humoured help in working through the dusty volumes to unearth the speeches that are the very core of the book. It would have been impossible to reproduce the pages of *Hansard* containing the selected speeches without the help and support of Amina Gual and Edward Wood in the House of Commons Department of Information Services. Finally, we wish to thank Catherine Bebbington of the Commons Media and Communications Service for devoting so much of her time to preparing the book for printing, and Dave Burchell of TSO for his impressive expertise.

Ian Church
March 2009

Contents

Foreword

I think that it was Tony Benn who described Hansard as the "only uncensored newspaper in Britain". I believe him to be right, and it is an excellent accolade for a publication that from inception until 1909 was privately owned. This year we celebrate its hundred years as the Official Report, under the ownership and control of the House itself, and its continued triumph in meeting such standards of quality and accuracy, expeditiously produced.

The success of, and the reliance we place upon, the document is achieved and justified only by the assiduousness of the reporters. Hansard is always present. Late at night, during the most insignificant of debates, when the Press and Public Galleries are empty, the reporters' and editors' concentration has to be as sharp as for the major parliamentary occasions, for what they produce is the only source of a complete and unbiased account of what has been said in the House.

The daily Hansard is best known to parliamentarians in its 'hard copy' form, but outside of the House, of course, computer technology has opened the door of the internet to a new audience Speeches are published to the worldwide web within four hours of having been given, and there, as in printed form, the report is a byword for precision and integrity.

Today, anyone anywhere in the world can access House of Commons Hansard either on the day of the debate itself or in archives going back to 1988, and at no charge. A project to digitise and make available every volume of Hansard ever produced since 1803 is well under way and it is true to say that this will broaden still further the material available to the millions of people who read Hansard every year, with plenty of evidence that they hold it in highest regard.

I believe we are more than fortunate to be supported by such an excellent publication and I know that I am not alone in wishing it further success for the next hundred years. This book does much to celebrate the achievements and standing of the official record of our proceedings, and to commemorate a selection of some of the finest and most memorable speeches made in the House.

Rt Hon Michael J. Martin MP,
Speaker of the House of Commons

From Newgate prison to byword for integrity – the history of Hansard

When Brass Crosby, Lord Mayor of London and the chief magistrate of the City, refused to convict two printers on a charge of breach of parliamentary privilege by having dared to print reports of the Commons proceedings, his action was to mark the beginning of the end of the secrecy that then surrounded the words and decisions of MPs.

Until that time, Parliament had rigorously kept secret from the people the proceedings of the two Houses. Anyone who ventured to publish Members' speeches was compelled to kneel in penitence before the House, which then imprisoned them for flouting the privilege that the Members so jealously guarded.

Infuriated by Crosby's conduct, the Commons dispatched the Serjeant at Arms to arrest him and bring him before them. As he stood at the Bar of the House, he was ordered to be detained in the Tower of London. But it was an action that sparked riot and dissent on the streets of the City. His courageous defiance of the Commons resulted, it is believed, in the birth of the maxim "As bold as Brass".

The year of these momentous events was 1771. In that same year, a young man left Norwich with a guinea in his pocket, determined to make his fortune in London. The journey by coach took him two days before, no doubt somewhat overwhelmed and bemused "I was set down in the middle of the second day in Bishopsgate street quite a stranger." The young man's name was Luke Hansard, and he was a printer.

The names of Crosby and Hansard were never associated, and the two men almost certainly never met, but their respective actions were to result in the name of Hansard becoming famous in Parliaments around the world, and, eventually, in the creation of the *Official Report* at Westminster almost 140 years later.

While Crosby cooled his heels in the Tower, public resentment at the treatment meted out to him grew. After several weeks, the Commons, realising that the public were against them, relented and ordered his release. He returned to the City in a triumphant procession, cheered by crowds lining the route.

So great had been the public outcry that the House never again sought to enforce its ban on the publication of its proceedings. In 1803 it surrendered to the will of the people and reluctantly allocated seats in the Public Gallery for the use of the press. The Press Gallery was born.

By this time, Luke Hansard was prospering. He had gone into partnership with John Hughs in his printing business and was heavily involved in parliamentary printing. He had established a sound reputation with no less a person than Samuel Johnson, who insisted that he wanted Hansard to print his work. In 1775, Luke had married Mary Curson, and within a year she had borne him their first son. His name was Thomas Curson Hansard, and he was destined to work in his father's printing firm.

One man who was keen to pursue the opportunities offered by the 1803 development was William Cobbett. He used the new freedom to found the first serious attempt to publish the proceedings of the Commons as a report of record. The first edition of *Cobbett's Parliamentary Debates* covered a five-month period starting on 22 November 1803.

Cobbett had been a soldier, but on discharge from the Army he had turned his attention to writing, with the principal aims of exposing corruption and scandal and advancing the interests of parliamentary reform. One of the causes he championed was the improvement of conditions for agricultural workers, which led him to embark upon and write "Rural Rides" later in his life.

His incessant agitation made him a thorn in the side of the Establishment, and when in 1809 he wrote a pamphlet condemning the flogging by German mercenaries of English soldiers who had mutinied at Ely over a knapsack allowance, those in authority seized their chance to bring him to book.

By now, Thomas, having left the family firm in 1803 to set up on his own, was a master printer. He had acquired a printing business in Peterborough court, off Fleet street. As a printer, he had gone into business with Cobbett, modernising the format of Cobbett's publications. Unfortunately for Thomas, it was he who had printed the controversial pamphlet about the flogging, and when Cobbett stood in the dock before the King's Bench judges in Westminster Hall charged with seditious libel, Thomas stood alongside him.

They were found guilty. Cobbett was sentenced to two years' imprisonment and went to Newgate. Hansard went to the King's Bench prison in Southwark for six months.

Luke was by now, because of his printing work for the two Houses, an eminent figure in parliamentary circles. He was devastated by the shame brought upon the Hansard name by Thomas's downfall, not least because he had financed Thomas in his printing venture. In his autobiography, he wrote of:

"the heart rending disgrace by Thomas's incarcerations".

It was to be many years before father and son were truly reconciled.

Thomas Curson Hansard at the age of 48, 12 years after he took over the publication from William Cobbet and some five years before the appearance of *Hansard's Parliamentary Debates.*

In Thomas's defence, it should be noted that in the whole affair he appears to have been something of an innocent bystander. He had had no hand in the content of the pamphlet, and, as the judge observed, he had made no profit from the libel. However, the court took the view that he had seen what was being printed, and he could and should have prevented its publication.

Good was to come of the whole sad affair, however. While in prison, Cobbett's finances reached a perilous state, and he needed money. TC, as Thomas was known, was to provide it by taking over the business from Cobbett in 1812. The title page of the *Debates* no longer bore the name Cobbett, proclaiming instead:

"Published under the superintendence of T. C. Hansard"

By 1829, the name Hansard was doubly respected in the corridors of Westminster. One Hansard was the Government printer, but a second Hansard – TC – was the source of the best reports of the proceedings, and in that year the publication was renamed *Hansard's Parliamentary Debates*. The name that is today synonymous around the Commonwealth with official parliamentary reporting was established. But TC did not enjoy a monopoly. One of his competitors was the *Mirror of Parliament*, a publication that was being produced by an uncle of Charles Dickens. Dickens knew and associated with TC, and eventually became a reporter for the *Mirror*.

Within four years of the change in the title, TC was dead and his son, also Thomas Curson Hansard, had taken over the business. The publication was yet to be produced by shorthand writers meticulously recording the words of all Members. It was largely compiled from press reports, which meant that, by and large, only the newsworthy speeches were reported. The transcripts of these were submitted to the Members for their confirmation or correction. Not all Members co-operated. Some refused to offer corrections in order to avoid being seen to endorse or confirm what they had said, and an Irish Member returned the proof unmarked except for the words "Do your own dirty work" scribbled across it.

However, while the methods were yet to be refined, first principles were being established. TC junior took the view that he owed the House a duty to be as accurate and impartial as circumstances would permit, and he refused to allow Members to make extensive changes that could not be justified.

On one occasion, a Member made an unfortunate remark about Queen Victoria that drew a reprimand from the Speaker and an angry response from William Gladstone. When the Hansard report was submitted to the Member for confirmation in the usual way, he returned it with the whole incident, including the Speaker's castigation, deleted. When TC reinstated the missing words, the Member became irate and threatened to take action. TC was undeterred. He printed the whole episode as originally reported.

The newspaper columns provided the principal source of material, and only a few speeches were reported by the Hansard man sitting in the Gallery. Nevertheless, TC's meticulous methods of checking meant that his publication became the preferred source of reports of debates. In 1855, the Chancellor of the Exchequer ordered that 100 sets of *Hansard's Parliamentary Debates* be purchased and distributed throughout Whitehall and around the colonies. The order was subsequently increased to 120 sets, and in 1878 the Treasury gave TC a grant of £3,000 a year to enable him to engage four reporters to produce a fuller report.

The grant was terminated in 1889 when the House of Commons asked the Stationery Office to put the contract for reporting out to tender. By now TC was 76 years old and he decided not to compete. Instead he sold the title to a company under the control of a certain Mr Horatio Bottomley, who then established the Hansard Publishing Union. Bottomley offered to provide the service without a subsidy. He also went after the lucrative parliamentary printing business being run by one of Luke's descendants, a cousin of TC named Henry Hansard. Henry, duped by the con man Bottomley, sold out but never received his money, and the Hansard Publishing Union crashed into bankruptcy. Again, the production of the *Debates* was looking for a new provider, and the Stationery Office was charged with finding one.

As the 19ᵗʰ century drew to a close, and as successive contractors failed satisfactorily to provide the House of Commons with accurate and reliable reports of its proceedings, Members returned to the question first raised some 20 years before of how to achieve that objective. In 1893, yet another Select Committee was charged with looking into the matter, but the question remained unresolved until 1907 when, on 26 March the House ordered the appointment of yet another Select Committee:

> "to Inquire and Report as to the Cost and Method of Reporting and Publishing the Debates and Proceedings in Parliament."

The Committee took evidence from a wide range of witnesses who included Members of Parliament, the Clerk of the House, the Controller of Her Majesty's Stationery Office, the chiefs of the parliamentary staffs of the Press Association and *The Times*, the parliamentary correspondent of the *Pall Mall Gazette*, contractors and printers. The Committee declared itself:

> "convinced that great dissatisfaction exists amongst Members of the House of Commons as to the present reporting of Debates, and that this dissatisfaction is justified."

One Member of Parliament who gave evidence was Mr Arthur H. Lee, who sat for Fareham. He had been the military attaché in the United States and Canada. In 1917 he would give his house to the nation to provide a weekend retreat for the Prime Minister. That house was Chequers.

He told the Committee of the Canadian system

> "which curiously enough they call Hansard, although there has never been any Hansard in Canada (it shows a sort of sentimental preservation of British institutions)".

It was, he said:

> "the best in existence; it is greatly superior to the American system, and I believe it is the best in the world."

Of the arrangements at Westminster, he stated:

> "I consider the present system of reporting our debates, at any rate the results, are quite unworthy of this Imperial Parliament."

The Committee went so far as to "condemn" the system of obtaining reports by contract and recommended that the House should set up its own report. It observed that the Parliament of the United Kingdom was almost the only legislature in the world that did not have its own reporting staff.

The response of the House was to agree to the establishment of the *Official Report* – in contrast to the unofficial reports that were then being produced – with reporters employed by the House under a figure to be known as the Superintendent of the Official Reporting Staff.

The House also accepted the recommendation that the new publication should operate under terms of reference first conceived by the 1893 Select Committee. Previous reports had been selective about which speeches would be reported in full. Some two-thirds were merely summarised, but the Committee decided that the practice should cease. For the future the report was to be a full report, which was defined as a report in the first person of all speakers alike:

> "which, though not strictly verbatim, is substantially the verbatim report with repetitions and redundancies omitted and with obvious mistakes corrected, but which, on the other hand, leaves out nothing that adds to the meaning of the speech or illustrates the argument."

Those terms of reference have stood the test of time. They still apply, unchanged, today, 100 years on. They demonstrated a canny appreciation of the problems facing Members when speaking in the Chamber. Members then, as now, were by a convention aimed at encouraging genuine debate, not permitted to read their speeches from a prepared text. They could refer to notes, but the words had to come from the heart and the head, not from the printed page. The members of the Committee will have known from personal experience that speaking in such

The first Editor from 1909, with his staff. James Dods Shaw is sixth from right. His deputy and successor, W. Turner Perkins is fourth from right.

circumstances, perhaps in the face of a noisy barrage from political opponents, was not conducive to the concise and grammatical printed rendition that would best serve the interests of the House.

When Members rambled as a means of gathering their thoughts, when they erroneously quoted inaccurate figures which the context showed to be obviously wrong, when they repeated themselves, not to reinforce a point but because they had lost their way, the Official Reporter would be there to set them straight.

The terms of reference, however, were as important for what they did not say as for what they did. True to the principles adopted by TC in the previous century, they did not allow for second thoughts born of mature reflection or the reaction to an unfavourable response. As many Members were to learn over the ensuing 100 years, the *Official Report* did not print the speech Members wished they had made.

The first volume of *The Official Report* covered the period 16 February to 5 March 1909, at the start of the 1909 Session. It was produced by 11 shorthand reporters. The Superintendent of the Official Reporting Staff was Mr James Dods Shaw, subsequently redesignated as the Editor, of whom there have been 13 in the 100 years. Mr Dods Shaw was given a knighthood by the King, the only one of the 13 to have received the honour.

Mr Dods Shaw, his deputy Mr W. Turner Perkins and the 11 reporters were not civil servants. They were servants of the House – completely independent of the Government and answerable directly to the Speaker, within whose department they came. Today, it is still the Speaker who has the final say on the content of the report, although on a day-to-day basis the judgment resides with the Editor, and the Speaker rarely has to get involved.

The Editor as the *Official Report* passes its centenary. Lorraine Sutherland in 2009.

When that first *Official Report* appeared, there was one sad omission. The name *Hansard* had been dropped from the title page. It may have been deleted from the publication, but it could not be removed from everyday use. Parliament – Members and staff – and the public who were familiar with it persisted in using the name *Hansard.*

The House bowed to the inevitable. In July 1943 the Publications and Reports Select Committee recommended reinstating the name and on 4 August 1943 Sir Francis Fremantle asked the Speaker what action he proposed to take on the recommendation.

The Speaker replied:

> "I propose that when the new Session of Parliament starts and the new series of the Official Report begins, the word "Hansard" should be printed below the words 'Official Report.'"

Since that time there have been other landmark changes. As the 1960s drew to a close, the pressure of work and the advance of technology resulted in the first major change in the working methods since the *Official Report* was created. An explosion in the number and duration of Standing Committees meant that there were insufficient shorthand reporters to cover them all, and a system of tape recording and tape transcription was introduced. Within five years, the use of shorthand in Standing Committees had been abandoned and tape recording had taken over.

In 1978, the House of Commons (Administration) Act created the Official Report as an autonomous department within the House administrative structure, with the Editor as its head joining the other five heads of departments as a member of the House of Commons Board of Management.

As the 1980s approached, technology began to apply its inexorable pressure for change. Since the 19th century, *Hansard's Parliamentary Debates* and, thereafter, the *The Official Report* had been printed in royal octavo size, latterly by Parliament's printers, Her Majesty's Stationery Office. HMSO had given the House notice, however, that the ageing printing presses would have to be replaced. It recommended moving *Hansard* to A4 size, which would accord with modern printing technologies.

Some Members were not happy at the prospect of change. They were unimpressed with arguments that the costs of production and the need to maintain or improve the quality of service to the House warranted a change to the new size. In four closely argued debates they fought a gallant rearguard action to retain the *Hansard* they had come to know and love. Horror of horrors, that dreaded word "metrication" seemed to be lurking somewhere at the root of the need for change.

They demanded to know how the proposed new, larger publication would get through letter boxes. How could one possibly slip the larger size into one's pocket in the way that successive generations of Members had been used to doing? For some Members, Mr David Crouch, the Conservative MP for Canterbury, clinched the argument. The new size, he said, would be much more difficult to read in bed.

When it came to a decision, 63 stalwarts could not hold back the tide of change, and they were outvoted. In November 1980, Norman St John Stevas, Leader of the House, announced to the Commons that the new size would be adopted when the House resumed in January after the 1980 Christmas recess. It was to be a miserable Christmas for 63 Members of Parliament.

A curious feature of the financial administration of the House of Commons was that although it employed and paid for the staff of the *Official Report*, the cost of producing the document was the ultimate responsibility of the Treasury. Her Majesty's Stationery Office was Parliament's printer. It managed the funds needed to produce Parliament's papers – the Bills, Order Papers, Select Committee reports and the *Official Report*. The Financial Secretary to the Treasury was the sponsoring Minister for HMSO, and it was to that Minister that HMSO would submit its requests for the money to print what Parliament demanded.

Prime Minister Margaret Thatcher, having not long settled into No 10 Downing street after her 1979 election victory, was to discover an even more curious aspect of this arrangement. It was for the Prime Minister of the day – also First Lord of the Treasury – to determine the cover price of *Hansard* when it was sold to the public. At that time some 4,000 copies a day were being bought.

When the Financial Secretary arrived in her office at No 10 to seek her decision, she was said to be astonished at the whole process. But she asked two questions in quick succession: how much was *Hansard* currently selling for? How much profit did it make? She did not like the answers. The first was 80p, and the second was none. In fact, the Minister told her hesitantly, far from making a profit, it required a substantial taxpayer subsidy to enable it to be sold at 80p.

Her reaction was one that might be regarded as typical of Mrs Thatcher. She told the Financial Secretary that he was to eliminate the subsidy during the then current Parliament by selling *Hansard* at an economic price. Within the required timescale, the price of the *Official Report* daily part was increased to £5 a copy. To obtain the hardback bound volume, the figure increased from £16.75 to £78. As the price rose, so the number of copies sold each day declined until barely 1,000 copies were being bought by the paying customer.

By the early 1990s, *Hansard* could no longer ignore the advantages to be gained from advances in technology, not least the considerable financial savings to be made in production costs. Computerised production methods had for some time been adopted by the newspaper industry, and it was time for *Hansard* to follow suit. Her Majesty's Stationery Office had moved its production of parliamentary papers on to computer typesetting, consigning to history the days of hot metal and the Linotype machine. When the new parliamentary Session began in 1992, the HMSO messenger carrying paper copy to the print works to be typeset was replaced with an electronic link. Instead of paper copy changing hands, the data containing Members' speeches were transmitted down a telephone line to be made up into pages on computer screens at the state-of-the-art Parliamentary Press.

Significant financial savings would be secured by the new technology, a matter that was by then of considerable interest to the House which, as a result of a review of administration, had assumed full financial responsibility for its printing budget. Service improvements were also available. With the old technology, the daily *Hansard* that appeared in the Vote Office at 7.30am and in the Stationery Office bookshops when they opened would carry all the proceedings up to 11.30pm the previous night. With the change, that deadline – known to the Hansard sub-editors as the cut-off – was extended to at least 1am. The Hansard that covered one subsequent all-night sitting contained all the proceedings up to 2.45am, with the 7.30am delivery to the Vote Office containing words uttered in the House less than five hours previously.

Today, as the *Official Report* marks its hundredth anniversary, much of what it does is made possible by computer technology. The major part of the production process is undertaken not by the printing contractor but within the House of Commons by staff of the *Official Report*. The most visible consequence of using the latest techniques is the availability of *Hansard* on the internet, free of charge to those who wish to see it. Every year millions of visits are made to the *Hansard* pages by those anxious to read precisely what was said in the House rather than rely on the versions that appear in the newspapers or on the television.

That same technology has brought the story of *Hansard* full circle, back to where it began. A digitisation project is in hand to make available on the internet the full collection of parliamentary reports starting with William Cobbett's *Parliamentary Debates* from 1803.

The heat of debate reflected in cold type – Hansard at work

Some years ago the then Prime Minister was invited to address a Foyle's literary lunch. He told the assembled guests of his reading habits:

> "Whatever time I go to bed, I read for at least half an hour. I am in the middle of reading a remarkable work – full of double-dealing, treachery, scorn and abuse. It is called *Hansard*."

For 100 years this unassuming and, to many, unremarkable publication has reported the nation's most remarkable events in what is arguably the most historic and almost certainly one of the busiest democratic legislatures in the world. Generations of *Hansard* reporters have witnessed Governments and Oppositions contending with war, financial crisis, and political drama and scandal, dispassionately committing to the record the words of the century's greatest politicians.

The reputation of House of Commons *Hansard* – the *Official Report* to use its formal title – has been built upon the dedication of people who, constantly working against the clock and often for long hours, have produced reports whose accuracy is regarded around the globe among those who understand such matters as the bench mark.

Matthew Parris, who has contributed to this volume, was once a Member of Parliament but today is renowned as a columnist for *The Times*. Earlier in his career he was the sketch writer for that newspaper. Sitting immediately behind the *Hansard* reporters in the Press Gallery, he could observe them at work and, the next day, read their report, comparing it to what he had heard coming up from the Floor of the House. On one occasion he wrote,

> "As we know, in the skilled hands of the parliamentary Hansard note takers, Monday's gibberish becomes Tuesday's classic English. The room in which the Official Report is compiled is the nation's top operating theatre for cosmetic surgeons in English prose. As a result, many MPs actually believe they talk sense. Today they strut their hour on the Commons stage, talking unintelligible rubbish. Tomorrow they read the report. From the report emerges a speech of passion and clarity, delivered in perfect English. 'Gosh,' they murmur over breakfast, 'did I really say that?' They didn't. They didn't say anything like that."

In theory, *Hansard's* editing function holds the greatest potential for dispute and controversy. In practice, the terms of reference that the House of Commons has decided shall govern how *Hansard* operates are rigidly adhered to and complaints rarely arise from the exercise of the discretion that *Hansard* is given by the House.

The extent of editing that is required varies considerably according to the Member's individual style, what he or she is saying, and the circumstances and atmosphere in which the speech is being made. In the heat of debate, with the distractions of noise and interruptions on all sides, Members may sometimes struggle to maintain the thread of their argument, even more to deliver it as the perfect prose that the *Official Report* aims to put on the printed page.

Members may refer to speaking notes, but, unless they are Front Benchers at the Dispatch Boxes, they are not permitted to read their speeches from a prepared text. In the circumstances, it may seem surprising that so many speeches are as good as they are. *Hansard's* task is to ensure that it produces a report that conveys concisely and grammatically the arguments and sentiments that the Member was seeking to advance, changing as little as possible, and then only to achieve that end.

While few Members can emulate Enoch Powell's pristine grammar and faultless delivery, the day-to-day reality is that the vast majority of speeches require only the lightest touch by the reporter in transferring the spoken word with its attendant emotion, intonation, and even body language – all the non-spoken components that are used to convey meaning – to the coldness of type on the printed page. The essence of successful *Hansard* reporting lies in knowing when it is right to change something and when it is wiser to leave well alone.

Harold Macmillan was the Housing Minister in Winston Churchill's 1951 Government. Speaking on the Committee stage of a Bill, he delivered an obscure and unintelligible response to an Opposition Member. He had been asked to give an undertaking that he would to make a concession on a particular point. Unusually, the *Hansard* reporter was baffled by Macmillan's reply. When the proceedings adjourned, the reporter approached him for help. "What you have said does not mean anything," the reporter explained. "No, my dear chap, and it was never meant to," Macmillan replied. His "undertaking" was printed as it was uttered, and it was for its recipient to work out exactly what, if anything, he had been promised.

The rules governing pre-publication access to the report have been changed recently in response to the advances in technology and the requirements of Members.

The most important rule, however, remains unchanged. It is that Members may not have second thoughts about what they have said. Once delivered, a speech becomes the property of the House, not of the Members, and *Hansard*, acting on behalf of the House and directly answerable to the Speaker, is the custodian of those words. Members who are unhappy with the report are entitled to "suggest" a change, but they have no right to demand it. Of course, if an error has been made it is corrected, but beyond that a Member, for good or ill, is saddled with what he or she has said.

Sir Robert Adley may be remembered in parliamentary circles for a memorable phrase. The Conservative MP for Christchurch was an ardent admirer of Britain's rail system and a vehement opponent of the 1992 Major Government's privatisation of the railways. He warned Ministers that if they went ahead with their plan they would be creating "the poll tax on wheels", harking back to what many regarded as probably Mrs Thatcher's least popular venture

In the *Hansard* office he is remembered for something else. In 1997, Britain handed Hong Kong back to China when the lease expired. The handover was preceded by protracted negotiations between Britain and China. A series of statements and debates from the late 1980s into the 1990s enabled the House to keep an eye on the progress of the talks.

Shortly after speaking in one of the debates, Robert Adley arrived in the *Hansard* sub-editors' room to check the transcript of his speech. He was given the transcript and took his place at one of the Members' tables. Sitting bolt upright and pen in hand, he screwed his monocle into his right eye and began to read. He reached page 3. "No, no, no no!" he stated, and began to cross out most of the page.

The astonished sub-editor asked him what he was doing. "I'm taking this passage out," he replied. "Why, did you not say it?" he was asked. "Yes, I said it but I should not have, and now I am retracting it." He was told that what he wanted was not possible. A discussion ensued in which he realised he was making no progress.

Grudgingly, he took the *Hansard* man into his confidence. He had been acting as an intermediary between Beijing and Whitehall. The offending passage contained information that he had been given in confidence at the highest level on his last trip to China. If the Chinese realised that he had breached that confidence – "there could be a diplomatic incident. Relations between the two countries could suffer a major setback at a very delicate time. At the very least, they will never trust me again. That is why you must allow me to delete it."

The sub-editor reluctantly shook his head. The deletion could not be permitted. Mr Adley was advised that only one person could authorise what he wanted – the Speaker. "I'll ask to see him immediately," Mr Adley said. He sat down to finish reading the transcript, and the sub-editor walked the short distance to the Press Gallery.

By the time the sub-editor returned to the room, the Member was putting on his coat and preparing to leave to see the Speaker. "You had better tell him that there are 22 Chinese and Asian journalists in the Press Gallery," said the sub-editor. "If your indiscretion was as important as you say, they will know. Do you want your words to be reported in China but not in *Hansard*?"

Faced with the inevitable, the forlorn Member abandoned his appeal to the Speaker. His words duly appeared in the *Official Report* the next morning. There was no diplomatic incident. Sino-British relations were unaffected by his revelations. And not long afterwards, her Majesty bestowed a knighthood on Robert Adley. Failing to breach *Hansard*'s determination to maintain the integrity of the report appeared to have done no harm.

The rules by which *Hansard* operates are the terms of reference drawn up initially by a Select Committee in 1893 and finally approved by the House on the report of another Select Committee in 1907. They are clearly set out in "Erskine May", but few Members have the time to take a close interest in what that book says about practice, procedure and precedent, including the paragraphs explaining *Hansard* and the rules by which it operates. It explains that while *Hansard* is not strictly verbatim, it is substantially verbatim with repetitions and redundancies omitted and with obvious mistakes corrected while leaving out nothing that adds to the meaning of the speech or illustrates the argument.

A new Member arrived in the *Hansard* office having delivered his maiden speech. A friendly inquiry from a sub-editor asking how it went was greeted with a grimace. "Not well, I'm afraid. In fact, I don't want you to print it. I have brought another speech to replace it which I want you to print instead." He produced a sheaf of typescript. His request was refused.

That was a one-off misunderstanding, but even Members with long service in the House have been known to express surprise when told that their words are not reported verbatim. When necessary, "Erskine May" is produced and the terms of reference – "a full report…not strictly verbatim…repetitions and redundancies omitted…obvious mistakes corrected" are pointed out.

Sir Rhodes Boyson, was a Conservative Member who was well regarded by Margaret Thatcher and who became a Minister in her Government in various Departments. Before entering the House as the Member for Brent, North he had been the headmaster of a north London school. He was a popular character with the *Hansard* reporters notwithstanding that his style of delivery made him very difficult to report. He spoke in a jumble of disconnected phrases and false starts, all delivered with the speed and force of a machine gun.

Like most fast speakers, he could not control or modify his speaking style. The reporters told him how difficult he was to report and asked him whether he could slow down. "I don't think that I can," he replied. "The thoughts just well up from inside and flow out as an ocean of words."

On one occasion, speaking from the Dispatch Box in his capacity as Social Security Minister, Sir Rhodes delivered the following memorable passage:

> "What I would say to the hon. Member for Eccles is this: I can give no undertaking that we will do something but we will look at it. We will definitely look at it and see – we will look at it before it arrives at the other place that has been referred to and I – what I mean by looking at it, looking at what exactly the hon Member said, whether it should be similar – be made a duty to the health authorities to acquaint the parents of local support organisations. I will give that assurance that we shall look at it before it goes to the other place, to the hon Member."

The reporter who took that passage in shorthand and rendered the spoken words to the printed page produced the slightly different version that appeared the next morning:

> "We shall consider the suggestion of the hon. Member for Eccles, before the Bill goes to the other place, to see whether health authorities should be required to inform parents in local support organisations, but I cannot say more than that."

Not all convoluted sentences, however, should be clarified. Some Members, particularly those with legal training, use a construction and vocabulary that, while not immediately apparent in meaning, must be reproduced as delivered. The following was uttered by former Labour MP Sir Lynn Ungoed-Thomas, who had been Solicitor-General under Clement Attlee, and subsequently became a High Court judge:

> "Therefore, one goes through a second psychiatric hoop. One then has to decide not only that he had reason to believe that permission would only be granted on the provisions which he had included, but one also has to decide what he might reasonably have been expected to have included if he did not include what he has in fact included. It is a fantastic proposition. It is not as though one did not have to envisage what the original plan would be without the provisions inserted for the purpose of obtaining the permission which he has reason to believe would not otherwise be granted. One has to go through the process of inserting in the plan what might reasonably have been in the plan if the applicant had not had reason to believe that the development would have been permitted only with the conditions which he has, in fact, inserted."

Hansard reports the proceedings according to the instruction of the House. The teams of people who are responsible for complying with that instruction occupy various locations around the parliamentary estate. The Committee reporters operate close to the Committee Rooms. The House reporting team of up to 16 reporters is conveniently situated in offices close by the Press Gallery. Each reporter's name appears on a rota, which gives the times of attendance in the Chamber. There will always be two reporters present in the seats in the Press Gallery, one taking the speech, the other there as a check and a back-up. Shorthand, which was the reporter's essential skill, is now very little used, with the technology of digital recording now the mainstay.

A reporter will be responsible for a five or 10-minute slice of the proceedings, depending upon the time of day, and will produce a transcript which is passed to sub-editors. While the reporters work in time slots, the sub-editors work on entire speeches, checking for continuity and consistency, as well as ensuring that the reporter has checked all relevant facts and complied with the rigid *Hansard* house style. It is the chief sub-editor who is responsible for authorising transmission of the final version of the copy to *Hansard's* internal page make-up unit. From there it is forwarded electronically to the Parliamentary Press for the final production process.

The operation throughout is under constant pressure of time. The requirement for overnight publication of the printed copy is enhanced by the demands of the internet. Speed of production allied with accuracy is the key. The Members have to meet a tight time limit by which to check the transcript, should they wish to do so. The reporters and sub-editors work to a constant rolling deadline. Every aspect of copy production and preparation must be completed to enable the print contractor to put the finished text on the internet within three hours of the Member having concluded his or her speech in the Chamber. The printing process contends with the most demanding of schedules to ensure that copies are delivered to the House by 7.30 the following morning.

When the House first broadcast its proceedings in 1978, Tam Dalyell raised with Mr Speaker Thomas a point of order about the status of the *Official Report* now that Members' precise words could be heard on the radio. Hitherto, there had been no reliable check on *Hansard*. Now, what was printed could be compared with what was said.

On the face of it, Tam Dalyell's point was a good one. If there was a discrepancy between the tape recording and what was printed in *Hansard*, *Hansard* must be wrong. The tape could not lie. The Speaker did not agree. The House had always relied on the *Hansard* reporter faithfully to record what he or she heard. The House would continue so to rely. The tape would not be accepted by the Chair as a check on *Hansard*, he ruled.

By definition, the tape, while being precisely a pure verbatim record of the proceedings, would often differ from *Hansard*, which might not be pure verbatim. Sir Rhodes Boyson's passage demonstrates why that is so, and the terms of reference – "not strictly verbatim" – justify the variation. Of course, if the tape threw up a factual error, *Hansard* would be shown to be wrong and a correction would be made. But in terms of the way in which Members' words were reported, the Speaker ruled that there was to be no electronic check.

A young man who was interested in pursuing a career with *Hansard* applied for a job. He was interviewed and tested in the usual way by being asked to transcribe a recording of a speech by a moderately difficult Member. The results showed that he had a basic ability that, with sufficient training, could be developed to enable him to do the job. He was then shown how an experienced reporter would have transcribed the test passage. Subsequently, the Editor offered him the post. His reply was a surprise. He wrote:

> "As a matter of principle, I cannot accept the offer. I cannot be part of an organisation that makes politicians look better than they are."

His response demonstrated a failure to understand *Hansard*'s purpose and what its terms of reference are designed to achieve, which is to convey clearly and concisely the arguments that Members are advancing on behalf of their constituents. What would be the point of printing a Rhodes Boyson jumble of words that left readers scratching their heads wondering what the Member was attempting to convey? Some of the great thinkers in the House have failed to match the best standards of oratory. *The Official Report* aims to ensure that their thoughts and ideas are not denied us by the barrier of a confusing verbatim rendition of their words.

There is, of course, a world of difference between judicious editing of a Member's words, more clearly to convey their meaning, and the outright dishonest rewriting of those words to change their meaning contrary to what was intended when they were uttered. Members very rarely attempt to import second thoughts into the transcript. They know, as Mr Adley found out, that what has been said cannot be unsaid.

Communication between the Official Reporters and the Members in the Chamber is a crucial factor in the process. The *Hansard* reporters occupy two seats in the Press Gallery directly above the Speaker's Chair. Sitting between the reporters from *The Times* on their left and the BBC correspondent on their right, they have the best seats in the House. The only person they cannot see is the one person to whom *Hansard* is directly answerable – the Speaker.

Most speeches give rise to requests from the reporters to the Members for clarification of points made, confirmation of the spelling of names, or any one of a number of other matters. To obtain the necessary information, the reporter will write a short note which is placed in a dumb waiter and lowered, by pulling on a rope, to the doorkeeper at the door to the Chamber. The doorkeeper will take the note into the Chamber and pass it to the Member, and a reply is sent back by the same means.

This process was used during a speech by Labour Back Bencher Tony Banks. Mr Banks was notable for two characteristics. He was very careful, though not ostentatious, about his attire and his appearance, choosing only the smartest clothes. He was also the master of the witty observation born of a searing sense of humour.

During a debate on the Arts, of which he was a passionate supporter, he was horrified to hear a Conservative denounce the subsidising of opera – "to enable people to hear an overweight Italian singing in a language that few understand." He responded: "The hon Gentleman is to the Arts what James 'Bonecrusher' Smith (at the time, a heavyweight boxer) is to lepidopterology."

He was much liked on both sides of the House, and he often provoked good-natured banter from his opponents. During one speech a Conservative shouted an intervention. Mr Banks responded: "I regard the hon Gentleman's observation as an insult." The reporter heard what was said but not who said it. Using the dumb waiter the reporter sent a note down to Mr Banks asking him who had intervened to call him a "Marxist-Leninist stooge".

Mr Banks wrote back with the name of the intervener, but added:

> "He didn't call me a Marxist-Leninist stooge. He said 'You're wearing a Marks and Spencer suit.'"

The system of notes is vital in ensuring the speedy contact with Members that is so crucial in the high pressure production of *Hansard*. In this instance it was essential for the reporter to identify the Member who intervened. Until the 1980s it was left to the discretion of the reporter whether to include seated interventions. The then Speaker, Bernard Weatherill, took the view that too many such interventions were being reported and ruled from the Chair that, henceforth, only seated interventions that were taken up by the Member who had the Floor were to be reported. Members soon learned that the way to prevent an opponent's unwelcome intervention disturbing the smooth flow of their speech as it appeared in *Hansard* was to ignore it.

It is understandable that, in the welter of words and emotion that constitute a busy Chamber, mishears will occur. Sometimes, they are understandable. On other occasions they are less so. Prime Minister Margaret Thatcher was reporting back to the House on her latest negotiations with her European Union counterparts, including German Vice-Chancellor and Foreign Minister Hans-Dieter Genscher. A Back Bencher called upon her to "give full credit to Herr Genscher." When the typescript reached the sub-editors it contained the memorable sentence:

> "Will the Prime Minister give full credit to her dentures?"

Such slips are, fortunately, very rare. The meticulous training that *Hansard* reporters are required to undergo teaches them to be acutely aware of the sense and context of what is said.

Members, however, are prone to a pitfall of parliamentary life. In their ardent desire to voice passionately held opinions on subjects about which they care deeply, they sometimes allow their words to run out of control. Embryo research is one such subject. It appears among selected speeches in this volume. Emotion took control when one Member stated:

> "The argument for the use of the human embryo as a guinea pig is nothing more than a red herring."

Sometimes it is simply an unfortunate choice of words, as in:

> "This is the start of a slippery slope and once one goes down it we will start to move into a vicious circle."

Or,

> "The number of firearms offences has shot through the roof."

Or,

> "They reacted in exactly the same way as the Greeks did to the bearer of bad news – they called for an immediate re-examination of the terms of reference of the Audit Commission."

Or,

> "The workplace nursery scheme, which has great potential, is being throttled before it has had time to blossom."

Or,

> "It took the trees some time to recover as they had been chopped down."

Or, after the Chernobyl nuclear disaster,

> "I have the misfortune to represent more irradiated sheep than any other hon. Member."

Or, in a debate on law and order,

> "Vandalism is running riot."

Then there was the case of the Member suffering a severe case of Spoonerism.

> "The Minister is making an estimistic over-optimation."

Second attempt:

> "I intended to say that the Minister is making an ostimistic over-eptimation."

Confusion reigned all around, accompanied by much shaking of head by the Member. Gathering his thoughts, he courageously persisted:

"The Minister is making an optimistic over-estimation."

Success at last, accompanied by cheers. Only the final version appeared in the *Official Report*.

Sometimes humour can be squeezed from a procedural nicety.

Sir Walter Bromley Davenport: I am not raising a point of order, Mr Speaker. I am raising a point of order on points of order which are not points of order.

Mr Speaker: Order. Points of order on points of order that are not points of order are not points of order."

The House was no doubt grateful for that clarification.

Notwithstanding the absence of clarity, the House would have greatly appreciated a reply by Roy Jenkins when he was Chancellor of the Exchequer to a question from Labour MP Arthur Lewis. Mr Lewis enumerated three problems and asked the Chancellor to say whether he would take action on each them. The Chancellor replied:

"The answer to my hon. Friend is yes, yes and no – but not necessarily in that order."

Members become experts in their particular areas of interest, perhaps assuming that everyone else shares their enthusiasm and their knowledge. Speaking about Soviet dissidents, one Member declared:

"Georgie Vins, Shcharansky, Orlov, Ratushinskaya, Senderov, Odnorodnikov, Yevdokimov, Chertkova and Vasili Shipilov have been released only because we in the west have made them household names."

The contents of this volume are a small sample of the fruits of 100 years of work of a succession of *Hansard* reporters and sub-editors and of speeches by Members across the generations. Many years ago, Lord Samuel described *Hansard* as "the ear of history".

Today, there is an abundance of sound bites and video clips of the proceedings of the House. But in their broadcasting, they add nothing to the sum of knowledge about the breadth of proceedings of the House or the immense amount of work, mostly in Committees, that the Members undertake. Viewers and listeners across the nation are in danger of being left with the impression that the only thing of interest or significance that happens in the House of Commons is when the Prime Minister and the Leader of the Opposition clash during half an hour on a Wednesday.

So, in a curious way, *Hansard* is today more important than ever. The broadcasting and print media, desperate for the next story to fill their 24-hour schedules, their news pages and their on-line services, are continually looking behind – or ignoring – the events in the Chamber.

Increasingly, they neglect the Floor of the House. The Press Gallery is almost empty more often than not, the only constant presence being the *Hansard* reporters, who are always there when the House is sitting. Yet the Chamber is where the laws are made. It is where the representatives of the people speak on behalf of the people. When it is important to know exactly what a Minister or Member said, that information, for the sake of democracy, must be available. It will only always ever be found in one place – the *Official Report – Hansard*.

A. P. Herbert was, until the university seats were abolished in 1950, the Independent Member for the University of Oxford. It is worth recalling his words extolling *Hansard's* significance to Parliament, for, although the facts and circumstances have changed, the sentiment of what he wrote remains valid.

In those days, *Hansard* cost sixpence in pre-decimal currency. The serious newspapers gave extensive coverage to the proceedings in the Chamber, but even they did not report every Member. Those whose speeches did not get printed were listed at the foot of the page under "Also spoke". Sir Alan wrote:

> Read *Hansard*. For the papers cannot tell
> The many things that Parliament does well.
> How many a Member labours many days
> To find his figures and perfect his phrase.
> And waits and waits, while many a meal goes by,
> Hungry and worn to catch the Speaker's Eye.
> Pours out his heart, his wisdom and his jokes,
> And is enrolled among the "Also Spokes"!
> You'll be surprised, good citizens, to see
> How right your representatives can be!
> It should be cheaper; sixpence is a shame,
> But it's a good sixpenny'orth all the same.

CONTRIBUTIONS

Robin Cook conducts ruthless interrogation over arms to Iraq

Michael Martin was elected Speaker of the House of Commons in October 2000, 21 years after becoming the Member for Glasgow, Springburn at the 1979 general election.

One of five children, he left school at the age of 15 to take up an apprenticeship as a sheet metal worker at the Springburn railway workshops. It was there that he subsequently became involved in trade union activities, and, as a result, pursued an interest in politics. At the age of 21 he joined the Labour party.

His work took him to the Rolls-Royce works at Hillington, where he became a shop steward for the Amalgamated Union of Engineering Workers. In the three years before he was elected to Parliament, he worked as a full-time trade union officer and, on election, he was sponsored by the Amalgamated Electrical and Engineering Union.

His political career began when he was elected as a councillor for Glasgow corporation in 1973. The memories of his childhood in which his mother, a school cleaner, worked hard to support her family, while his father was in the merchant navy, never left him. As a councillor, his passion was the provision of decent housing for the citizens of Glasgow. He played a significant role, as founder member, in the creation of a Glasgow housing association that became one of the biggest community-based associations in the city.

In 1983, four years after entering the House, he was appointed Parliamentary Private Secretary to Denis Healey as deputy leader of the Labour party, a post he held for three years before moving on to become a member of the Trade and Industry Select Committee.

In 1987, he was appointed to the Speaker's Panel of Chairmen, from whose ranks were drawn the Chairmen of Bill Committees. He became the Chairman of the Scottish Grand Committee. It was valuable experience which put him on the road to his present role.

In 1997, he was appointed the First Deputy Chairman of Ways and Means and a Deputy Speaker of the House. He was well regarded in the Chair, known for a quietly persuasive, but firm, approach that is now his hallmark. That stood him in good stead when Betty Boothroyd stepped down and the House set about choosing her replacement.

His election as Speaker was not straightforward. An unprecedented 12 candidates were nominated for the post, but he was the clear winner, the final vote mustering only eight votes against him.

Conscious that an apprenticeship had given him a trade, and aware of the many skilled trades that were required to maintain the fabric of the House, he introduced a scheme offering apprenticeships within the House to young people in schools in south London. He was anxious to provide young people with the advantage that he had received, but he also hoped that his action would encourage employers to follow his example.

Speaker Martin is a keen piper. He learnt to play the bagpipes as a boy soldier in the Territorial Army, and is a member of the College of Piping in Glasgow, the world's leading institution for the teaching of the bagpipes and for the preservation of the heritage of the Highland bagpipe.

Challenge encouraged and every intervention turned to brilliant advantage

BY RT HON MICHAEL J. MARTIN MP, SPEAKER OF THE HOUSE OF COMMONS

I feel very fortunate that I knew Robin Cook for more than 30 years. In my early days as Speaker I got to know him very well when he was Leader of the House and I learnt more about his eminence as a parliamentarian. In that context I recall a speech he made in early 1996.

In October 1992, three men from Coventry were charged with illegally exporting munitions to Iraq. The case collapsed. An inquiry followed under Lord Justice Scott, completing in 1996. Amongst many others, two Prime Ministers gave evidence. The report ran to 2,000 pages printed in five volumes and revealed the then Government's failure to disclose a decision to adopt a particular policy on defence sales.

The subject came up for debate on a Motion for the Adjournment on 26 February 1996. In preparation for the debate, Robin Cook shut himself away, having been given only four hours to study Scott's report before the debate began.

The result was probably the most statesman-like speech I witnessed in my time as a Back-Bench Member. It was Robin at his very best, and I set his performance that day against the strong competition of other speeches he made before and afterwards which may, I suppose, attract more lasting attention. He set out to encourage challenge to his arguments and then answered those challenges with generous aplomb. It was an extraordinary occasion.

I can only say that the atmosphere in the Chamber was charged, for this was the defining moment following years of intense public and press interest. It was early evening in winter, but it was as if the light energy diffused from him alone. Others had their moment, but he was centre stage. His voice was powerful, the emphasis and intonation perfect; he appeared to be tall but we know he was of small stature.

The result was as sharp and penetrating as a scalpel. He turned every intervention to brilliant advantage. It was intellectual incision of the highest quality – no weakness, no inaccuracy and ruthless interrogation buttressed by a confidence that he was calling the tune.

I got the impression from the quickness of his replies that he had no notes, so he must have known the five volumes better than any script. His speed of reading, his concentration and the calibre of his research were renowned, but this was the test of how good those qualities were. Most telling was his control of the debate. He built on intervention and he raised the tempo to the pedestal of his final words. It was about Government accountability to Parliament, which is the very strength of the House.

In looking back it seems to me that it mattered not which party was in government and which in opposition for this was an occasion when truth and the pursuit of justice were to the fore and the integrity of our democracy the prize.

sale of lethal weapons. It was not about the Government controlling such sales. Indeed, the Government helped to do the selling.

In 1966, the Ministry of Defence, under the then Secretary of State for Defence, Lord Healey, set up its own defence sales organisation tasked not with the control of overseas defence sales, as this Government's guidelines have sought to do, but with the specific purpose among others of organising sales, campaigns and presentations and of negotiating major deals—deals be it noted not in spare parts for microprocessors or field telephones, but in lethal weapons. At what countries did the Labour Government direct their sales campaign? I have done a little research and found that in 1975, 1976 and 1977, during the run-up to the Iran-Iraq war, British defence sales to Iran averaged more than £50 million a year, including the sale of lethal weapons.

Still more interesting is the previous Labour Government's record at the same time with another country: Argentina. I have discovered that the previous Labour Government helped to secure contracts to sell to Argentina—again, not a country renowned at the time either for its democracy or its human rights record—such choice consignments as 42 Sea Dart surface-to-air missiles, 120 Blowpipe surface-to-air missiles and two Lynx helicopters. Those are not spares for radar sales or metal detectors: they are weapons of war that were sold to the Argentine dictatorship.

If we go back a little further, we find that Labour Governments were selling to Argentina two type 42 destroyers and—direct, at their own hands—eight Canberra bombers. There we have it: destroyers, missiles, helicopters and bombers—it is a case of "Don't fly for me Argentina". Those lethal weapons were sold direct by a Labour Government. Is not the real contrast between Labour and ourselves that in the Gulf war against Iraq, British forces risked facing no British weapons in the hands of the enemy, but in the Falklands war against Argentina, they did? There can surely be no more sickening example of hypocrisy than that—Labour saying one thing and doing another. *[Interruption.]*

There remains the unfinished business of the hon. Member for Livingston (Mr. Cook), who has been shown by the Scott report to have systematically misled the House and the country over three years with the repeated charges that we secretly conspired to arm Saddam Hussein with lethal weapons and that we gagged the courts to suppress the evidence.

Mr. Kaufman: On a point of order, Madam Speaker. As I heard it, the right hon. Gentleman accused my hon. Friend the Member for Livingston (Mr. Cook) of having misled the House. If that is so, surely he is culpable.

Madam Speaker: If there were not so much noise, we could all hear precisely what is being said. Is it a fact that the Secretary of State used those words? *[Interruption.]* Order. I want to hear the Secretary of State, not the Opposition.

Mr. Lang: Yes it is, Madam Speaker, and if you rule that to be unparliamentary I shall withdraw the words "misled the House", but I shall leave in place the words "misled the country". I shall do so because for three years the hon. Gentleman went around the country accusing the

Government of secretly arming Saddam Hussein and of attempting to gag the courts. Those two serious charges are completely rejected by the report and the hon. Gentleman now tries, vindictively and contemptibly, to shift his ground in order to continue the odious smear campaign. He shows a standard of behaviour that renders him unfit to be trusted by either the House or any foreign country even in the shadow post of Foreign Secretary. The House continues to await and demand an apology.

The Government welcome their acquittal by the Scott report of the two serious charges that caused the inquiry to be set up. We accept, as I have said today—and, indeed, in my statement 10 days ago—that there have been mistakes. There have been shortcomings and there is a need for improvement in several areas. I have today mapped out a number of ways in which the House can proceed. I have done so in a positive and forward-looking spirit, recognising that long-established conventions and practices of the House and elsewhere need to be looked at in a fresh light. I invite the House to respond in that spirit and to support the Government in the Lobby tonight.

4.22 pm

Mr. Robin Cook (Livingston): I shall respond in a moment to the Secretary of State's purple peroration, but I shall first comment on the announcements that he has made today. That need not detain the House for long, because the length of the passage in the right hon. Gentleman's speech cannot conceal the shortness of the specifics in those proposals.

I shall respond on three counts. First, we welcome the fact that Customs is to have supervision of the prosecuting role. In the light of the grave criticisms by Sir Richard Scott of the conduct of the Matrix Churchill trial, it would have been astonishing if the right hon. Gentleman had not proposed changes to the prosecuting role of Customs.

Secondly, I agree with the Government that we require a review of ministerial accountability. After all, one of the key conclusions in the closing section of the report is that, during the inquiry, example after example has come to light of the failure of ministerial accountability. What I find surprising is that, having had 18 days to study the report, the right hon. Gentleman could still produce no proposal as to what might be done to strengthen ministerial accountability.

Today, the one initiative that the right hon. Gentleman announced was that the Government will give evidence if the Select Committee holds an inquiry into ministerial accountability. I would hope so—after all, it is their duty to give evidence to Select Committees if they are asked to do so. However, the initiative does not shed any light on what single proposal they will make in that evidence to avoid us ever again having to debate a report that, in its closing chapter, details seven specific cases in which ministerial accountability was broken.

Mr. Nicholas Budgen (Wolverhampton, South-West) *rose—*

Mr. Cook: I shall finish my point, and then give way to the hon. Gentleman.

Thirdly, we shall certainly consider the Government's paper on parliamentary questions on arms exports.

Mr. Budgen *rose—*

Mr. Cook: I will give way to the hon. Gentleman in a moment—he should relax; his time will come.

[Mr. Cook]

I have in front of me the paper that has been deposited in the Library, and I shall share its conclusion with hon. Members:

"This note summarises the position in relation to the release of information on defence related exports and has been prepared in order to assist further discussion on this subject."

Not a single proposal is contained in the document. We shall enter into the spirit of these discussions as fully as possible, but these discussions would have been assisted further if the paper had contained a single idea.

Mr. Budgen: Does the hon. Gentleman agree that it would be extremely difficult to lay down any rules for ministerial accountability, because, essentially, it is a question for the House, and a question as to how much the House wants information? For instance, as far as negotiations with the IRA were concerned before the ceasefire, the House came to a misunderstanding as to the state of discussions between the Government and the IRA. However, when my right hon. Friends the Prime Minister and the Secretary of State for Northern Ireland came to this House, it was pleased to accept a slightly changed expression of those relationships. Is that not an example of how the House decides what information it wants?

Mr. Cook: At a later stage in my speech, I shall return to the question whether it is justifiable at any stage not to share information with the House. I cannot accept for one moment the hon. Gentleman's claim that it is impossible to make any rules about ministerial accountability. Indeed, the Government keep issuing rules about ministerial accountability. In relation to those rules, Sir Richard Scott states in chapter 8 of section K:

"Paragraph 27 of Questions of Procedure for Ministers identifies as one of the facets of Ministerial accountability to Parliament 'the duty to give Parliament, including its Select Committees, and the public as full information as possible about the policies, decisions and actions of the Government, and not to deceive or mislead Parliament and the public'."

Then Sir Richard Scott—whom the Government appointed to judge on this point; he was their choice—said:

"In the course of the Inquiry example after example has come to light of an apparent failure of Ministers to discharge that obligation."

The right hon. Gentleman' commitment to openness was a lot less convincing when he ruled out a freedom of information Act. Secrecy made this scandal possible. The five volumes of the Scott report provide the firmest foundation yet of a case for a freedom of information Act. There were never better witnesses for a freedom of information Act than the long parade of officials and Ministers who queued up to explain to Sir Richard Scott that the public interest was best served by not letting the public know what they were deciding.

Mr. David Mellor (Putney): Does the hon. Gentleman accept that those who seek to hold Members of the Government accountable must expect to be held accountable themselves? The hon. Gentleman said:

"First, they armed Saddam; secondly, when he used those arms against a British ally, they covered up the fact that they had provided the arms; and thirdly, as the cover-up unravelled, rather than own up, they were willing to see three executives of Matrix Churchill go to prison."—[*Official Report*, 23 November 1992; Vol. 214, c. 638.]

Is the hon. Gentleman aware that not a word of that is true, and will he now withdraw it?

Mr. Cook: No. The right hon. and learned Gentleman is wrong on every single count, and I shall demonstrate that all those charges were justified.

The right hon. and learned Member for Putney (Mr. Mellor) has echoed the allegation made by the President of the Board of Trade. What made the latter's speech so remarkable was the absence of any acceptance by any Minister of any responsibility for the errors set out in the report.

Confronted with those errors and five volumes of supporting evidence, the President of the Board of Trade and the right hon. and learned Member for Putney have produced the novel constitutional principle that it is the Opposition's duty to accept responsibility and resign. Every time they produce it, a wave of hilarity crosses the nation and drowns them.

Hon. Members: Answer the question.

Mr. Mellor *rose—*

Mr. Cook: I will answer the question.

The Government are fond of lecturing the rest of the nation on its need to accept responsibility. Parents are held responsible for actions; teachers are held responsible for the performance of their pupils; local councillors are held legally and financially responsible; yet, when it comes to themselves, suddenly, not a single Minister can be found to accept responsibility for what went wrong.

Sir Peter Hordern (Horsham) *rose—*

Mr. Mellor *rose—*

Mr. Cook: I will not give way. I shall answer the right hon. and learned Gentleman, and he will not like the answer.

In the past week, several right hon. and hon. Gentleman, of whom he is only the latest, have expressed their version of Labour's charges against the Government. I have no doubt that they are trying to be helpful, and I am grateful for their assistance, but I hope that they will forgive me if I rely on the charges that the Opposition actually made. *[Interruption.]* Yes, they were all set out in the debate. They were in the motion that I moved three years ago, on the last occasion that the House debated the issue. There were four charges, not three. I shall deal with each of those four charges, and demonstrate how Sir Richard Scott's report convicts the Government on every one.

The first charge in the motion was that the Government had acted

"in clear breach of the Howe Guidelines of 1985".—[*Official Report*, 23 November 1992; Vol. 214, c. 631.]

Sir Richard returns a verdict of guilty. You can tell, Madam Speaker, the importance that he attaches to the conclusion, because, like all his key findings, it is expressed as a double negative:

"It is clear that policy and defence sales to Iraq did not remain unchanged."

Indeed, Sir Richard reserves the most scathing passages in his report for those witnesses who tried to argue that the guidelines had not changed. The Chief Secretary submitted that the guidelines were not changed, but were only interpreted more flexibly. Sir Richard dismisses his view as one that

"does not seem to me to correspond with reality".

For good measure, Sir Richard quotes a minute that says:

"Mr. Waldegrave is content for us to implement a more liberal policy on defence sales".

That minute was from what was then the private office of the Chief Secretary. It was signed by his private secretary. Sir Richard observed:

"Mr. Waldegrave did not find the expression jarring at the time. He did not do so for the reason that the words, 'a more liberal policy', describe in ordinary and simple language the reality of what he and his colleagues were discussing."

When he made his statement to the House, I asked the right hon. Gentleman whether the Government accepted—

Mr. Mellor rose—

Mr. Cook: I shall answer all three questions.

I asked the right hon. Gentleman whether the Government accepted all the conclusions of the Scott report, and he replied:

"Yes, the Government accept the conclusions".—[*Official Report*, 15 February 1996; Vol. 271, c. 1148.]

To avoid all doubt, I shall refer to the statement that he made to the House, which appears in the *Hansard*. Let us hear what he said one more time. I ask to hear it again because, while the right hon. Gentleman was telling me on the Floor of the House that the Government accepted the Scott report's conclusions, his information officers were in the Press Gallery handing out a press pack. It claimed that the Scott report exonerated Ministers, and it stated:

"There was no change of policy in 1989".

As a press guide to the conclusions of the Scott report, that was flatly untrue.

Can the President of the Board of Trade confirm whether the Government accept those conclusions? Do they accept the conclusions, or, when the right hon. Gentleman said, "Yes, we accept the conclusions," did he mean that the Government accept only those conclusions that support their position? If the right hon. Gentleman will not tell us, what about his boss?

Mr. Mellor rose—

Mr. Cook: I give the right hon. and learned Gentleman an undertaking that I shall give way towards the end of my speech, because, by then, every single one of his charges will be nailed. At the moment—[*Interruption.*]

Madam Speaker: Order.

Mr. Cook: At the moment, I am playing some bigger fish.

What about the right hon. Gentleman's boss? When he set up the inquiry, the Prime Minister wrote to me and said:

"Whether Ministers themselves breached their own guidelines is one of the things that will be established by the inquiry".

That fact has been established. Will the Prime Minister accept that Ministers broke their own guidelines? He told me that the inquiry was set up to investigate that issue, so will he now accept the result?

Upon reading the Scott report, I am unclear why an inquiry was needed to establish whether the guidelines were changed. In the week that the Prime Minister set up the inquiry, he was minuted by his private secretary, whose remarks appear in paragraph D4.51 of the report. He told him:

"as Chancellor of the Exchequer you knew that the Government had decided to change the guidelines".

In his evidence to the Scott inquiry, the Prime Minister said:

"One of the charges at the time"—

Mr. Lang: The hon. Gentleman may want to assist the House by pointing out that that occurred in July 1990, which was long after the time in question. It was a decision taken by a Committee presided over by the Foreign Secretary, about which my right hon. Friend, the then Chancellor and present Prime Minister, was subsequently told. That recommendation was not passed on to the Prime Minister for approval, because the imminent invasion of Kuwait by Iraq ruled it out. The matter was not proceeded with.

Hon. Members: Withdraw.

Mr. Cook: The right hon. Gentleman should listen to what he has just said: the month before Saddam Hussein invaded Kuwait, the Government were willing to relax the guidelines still further.

Mr. Kaufman: As the President of the Board of Trade has intervened inaccurately—to describe it in friendly terms—upon my hon. Friend, we should draw attention to the fact that Mr. Wall's statement to the Prime Minister—

"as Chancellor of the Exchequer you knew that the Government had decided to change the guidelines"—

was dated 13 November 1992. In that submission to the Prime Minister, his private secretary said:

"the Howe Guidelines of 1985 were amended by Ministers in December 1988 but the amendment was never announced to Parliament".

That is why, knowing those words, the President of the Board of Trade was too timorous to give way to me.

Mr. Cook: My right hon. Friend is absolutely right. The nub of the memorandum is: why did the Prime Minister and others feel able to tell the House that the guidelines had not been changed when they had that evidence?

I return to the right hon. and learned Gentleman's other charge, about the Government arming Saddam Hussein. It was in our motion, which said:

"British servicemen may have been exposed to fire from shells and rockets made in munitions factories equipped by Britain".

Sir Richard's report reveals that, three years before the Gulf war, there were intelligence reports that Iraq had placed multi-million pound orders with four British companies, including Matrix Churchill, to equip its armaments factories at Nassr. The same intelligence

[*Mr. Cook*]

reports warned that annual production targets for Nassr were 10,000 missiles, 150,000 artillery shells, 100,000 mortar shells and 300,000 fin-stabilised shells.

Mr. David Shaw (Dover): They were not British.

Mr. Cook: The hon. Gentleman says that they were not British. They were made on British machines. That is what I am reading out.

Mr. Shaw: That is not the same.

Mr. Cook: The hon. Gentleman says that it is not the same, but it was never our case that Saddam Hussein would shove the machine tools down gun barrels and fire them at his enemies. Our case was always that he would use those machine tools to turn out shells, some of which may well have been fired at British forces in the Gulf war.

Sir Richard paints a scandalous picture of the failure of intelligence reports by Whitehall to reach those who needed information—although, once again, no Minister will accept responsibility for that departmental failure—but enough information did reach Ministers to ring alarm bells, if they had wanted to hear them.

Mr. Phil Gallie (Ayr): Can the hon. Gentleman help me on this point? He said that British companies had sold machines to Iraq. I heard him make the statement that they had secretly sold arms to Saddam Hussein. It does not refer to anyone having secretly sold machines to Saddam Hussein. It referred to secretly selling arms. The hon. Gentleman has a reputation for propagating porkies, so will he answer that question?

Mr. Cook: I have to say to the hon. Gentleman that to claim that selling machine tools that produced the shells that went into those gun barrels was not arming Saddam Hussein is—to borrow a word from Sir Richard Scott—sophistry. Perhaps I should explain to the hon. Gentleman that sophistry means a plausible answer that, on further investigation, is plainly misleading.

Sir Timothy Sainsbury (Hove): Will the hon. Gentleman give way?

Mr. Cook: No. I must continue with my speech. [HON. MEMBERS: "Give way."] Perhaps I should give way to the right hon. Gentleman, as he was one of those who came to the Dispatch Box and repeatedly denied that there had been a change in guidelines.

Sir Timothy Sainsbury: Will the hon. Gentleman have the grace to admit that, if anything in the entire episode lacks credibility, it is his suggestion that, when he said that the Government had armed Saddam Hussein, he was trying to do anything other than give the impression that lethal weapons had been sold?

Mr. Cook: I have it here. The motion that I moved in the House three years ago stated:

"British servicemen may have been exposed to fire from shells and rockets made in munitions factories equipped by Britain".

That has consistently been our argument. Moreover, they knew where those machine tools were going as early as February 1989. The right hon. Gentleman shakes his head, but it is in paragraph D6.94.

In February 1989, when he was in the very act of negotiating change in guidelines with his colleagues, the Chief Secretary was given a minute that told him:

"The Iraqis intended to use"

Matrix Churchill

"to supply machinery for the new armaments and munitions factories of the Nassr and Hutteen State Establishments".

They knew what they were approving, and the knowledge went much higher than the Chief Secretary. It would be unfair if he were left to take the rap.

A year earlier, an intelligence digest warned the then Prime Minister that Matrix Churchill

"has been heavily involved [in the supply of equipment to Iraq for use in arms production]".

The problem was that Ministers kept turning a deaf ear to the alarm bells. When the Chief Secretary was warned that some of the machine tools might go into the Iraqi nuclear programme, he replied that screwdrivers are also required to make hydrogen bombs.

After the Gulf war, the International Atomic Energy Agency found 30 Matrix Churchill lathes in Iraqi nuclear plants. Faced with that evidence, how dare Ministers still claim that they did not arm Saddam Hussein?

The right hon. Gentleman played the trade card and justified the decision to equip Saddam's armaments factories on the commercial grounds that it was good for business. Perhaps one of the Conservative Members can help me. After all, they claim to be the party of business. Could one of them explain to me how it can be good for business to approve a contract for which one does not get paid?

That is what happened. Saddam did not pay for the machine tools that went into his factories—we did. The British taxpayer has been left with a bill for about £700 million for our total exports to Iraq. Incurring a bad debt of £700 million would surely be enough to get someone sacked from any organisation in Britain except the Conservative Government.

Mr. Bill Walker (North Tayside): Will the hon. Gentleman tell the House, on which weapons sales—and I mean weapons sales, including the destroyers sold by the former Labour Government—were debts not paid? Can the hon. Gentleman answer that? He should think very carefully before he does so.

Mr. Cook: As Ministers are for ever saying, not without notice. But one cannot find any example in the history of export credit guarantees of such a vast debt with one country. That debt was the direct result of ministerial decisions to increase export credit guarantees to Iraq, and to allocate one fifth of the total for defence sales.

The last of those decisions was in September 1988, when export credits to Iraq were increased by £340 million, despite mounting evidence that Iraq did not have the cash to service existing credits. Sir Richard notes:

"The Chief Secretary endorsed the proposed new offer".

The Chief Secretary in question is, of course, the current Prime Minister.

When Lord Howe gave evidence to the Scott inquiry, he explained that the decision to give no publicity to the change in guidelines was that the decision might appear cynical to the public. For once, I must defend Ministers. I would acquit them of the charge of cynicism. What I find striking about their attitude is its naivety and the innocence with which they believed that if they armed a brutal dictator, he would use his military capacity in manner consistent with HMG's foreign policy and would pay all invoices on time. Their policy was both a strategic blunder and commercial disaster. It is no wonder they wanted to keep it quiet.

Mr. Richard Needham (North Wiltshire): Will the hon. Gentleman give way?

Mr. Cook: I shall return to the points raised by the right hon. Member for Hove (Sir T. Sainsbury), as I have another of his charges to answer. I am glad that I have his support.

I come to the third charge that we laid against Ministers three years ago—that

"hon. Members were persistently misled by assurances that the Guidelines were being observed".

Sir Richard's conclusion is set out at the end of 600 pages in which he examines the Government's conduct of arms exports to Iraq. The final sentence records:

"Parliament and the public were designedly led to believe that a stricter policy . . . was being applied than was in fact the case."

In short, Parliament was misled, and was designedly misled.

Mr. Mellor: Will the hon. Gentleman give way?

Mr. Cook: Of course.

Mr. Dennis Skinner (Bolsover): Is he still here?

Mr. Mellor: I am still here, and I will be here for a long time yet.

The hon. Member for Livingston (Mr. Cook) has invented the third point. He has dealt with the question—typical of him—that arms are to be equated with multi-use machine tools. The third charge that I quoted from the hon. Gentleman's speech on 23 November 1992 was:

"as the cover-up unravelled, rather than own up, they were willing to see the three executives of Matrix Churchill go to prison."—[*Official Report*, 23 November 1992; Vol. 214, c. 638.]

That is an outrageous slur, and nothing in Scott gives the hon. Gentleman the right to maintain that accusation. He should withdraw it.

Mr. Cook: I hope that the right hon. and learned Gentleman will not be stretched too far if I ask him to count up to four. I said that there were four charges in our motion, and I will come to that charge. The right hon. and learned Gentleman did not do our charge sheet sufficient justice when he left out this charge, so let us make sure that we get it on the record.

Sir Richard concluded that the failure to inform Parliament of the truth was deliberate, and was the inevitable result of the agreement among three junior

Ministers that no publicity would be given to the decision. Let us try them out again. Will the Secretary of State tell us whether the Government accept that conclusion?

Perhaps the Prime Minister would like to answer. Three years ago, the Prime Minister told the House:

"The suggestion that Ministers misled the House is a serious and scurrilous charge and has no basis whatsoever in fact."—[*Official Report*, 17 November 1992; Vol. 214, c. 136.]

The suggestion does have a firm basis, in the five volumes beside me. I agree with the Prime Minister that it was a serious charge. Will he now accept that, far from being scurrilous, it was entirely accurate? [HON. MEMBERS: "Answer."] Suddenly, we have a row of limpets stuck to the Treasury Bench.

Where does that leave the Chief Secretary? In the six months after the guidelines were changed, the Chief Secretary signed not one or two, but 30, letters to Members of Parliament denying any change in the guidelines. The matter should concern not only Opposition Members, because 23 of those letters went to the Chief Secretary's colleagues on the Tory Benches—to each of them he refused to admit any change in the guidelines.

Sir Richard observed that the Chief Secretary

"knew, first hand, the facts that . . . rendered the 'no change in policy' statement untrue."

Of course the right hon. Gentleman was in a position to know at first hand—he was at the meetings at which the changes in the guidelines were changed.

Sir Richard's summing up is damning. He concluded:

"Government statements . . . consistently failed . . . to comply with the . . . Questions of Procedure for Ministers and, more important, failed to discharge the obligations imposed by the constitutional principle of Ministerial accountability."

The desk officer for Iraq who drafted those letters for the Chief Secretary knew that they were untrue, and he said so to the Scott inquiry. That desk officer resigned from the foreign service, rather than be obliged to continue drafting them. Tonight, the House must judge whether he is the only person who should resign over the misleading of Parliament.

I come to the last of the four charges in our motion of three years ago. We said that the Government were willing

"to see citizens put on trial for exports at which Ministers had connived and to put their liberty at risk by attempting to prevent the disclosure of documents crucial to their defence".—[*Official Report*, 23 November 1992; Vol. 214, c. 631.]

Section G, in which Sir Richard considers the conduct of the Matrix Churchill case, is one of the longest in his report. Anyone who has read it in its entirety will know that it is not we who should apologise in the light of Sir Richard's conclusions.

He concluded that the Matrix Churchill case should never have been brought to court, and that the claims of public interest immunity that were made in the course of it ought to have had no place in a criminal trial. Sir Richard sums up that the Government's attitude

"to disclosure of documents to the defence was consistently grudging. The approach ought to have been to consider what documents the defence might reasonably need and then to consider whether there was any good reason why the defence should not have them. The actual approach . . . seems to have been to seek some means by which refusal to disclose could be justified."

[Mr. Cook]

Not every means by which refusal was justified appears to have impressed Sir Richard. The claim by the then Minister of State, Foreign and Commonwealth Office, in his PII certificate that disclosure would cause "unquantifiable damage" to the public interest is dismissed by Sir Richard as "risible". Perhaps that is not surprising, as the Minister hardly helped himself at the inquiry by claiming that the word "unquantifiable" could have meant unquantifiably small, not necessarily unquantifiably large.

Mr. Donald Anderson: Does my hon. Friend agree that not only could the Attorney-General have stopped the prosecution at any time in the light of his knowledge of all the facts, but that the Government were quite prepared effectively to leave the guilt or innocence of the three Matrix Churchill executives to the robustness or otherwise of the trial judge? It happened that Judge Smedley was a robust judge and stood for justice. Another judge might have been less strong.

Mr. Cook: My hon. Friend draws attention to one of the Government's defences—that, in laying the public interest immunity certificates, they were only bringing the documents to the attention of the trial judge. However, there is the awkward matter of the second certificate, signed by the then Secretary of State for Trade and Industry. His first certificate contained a list of the documents covered by it. The second certificate, which was used at the trial, omitted that list. The minute to the Secretary of State that accompanied the doctored certificate stated that to retain the words

"might increase the risk that the judge will call for copies of the documents."

Having seen those documents, Sir Richard observed that it was "very obvious" that any defence counsel

"would give his (or her) eye teeth for them."

There is no need to ask the right hon. Gentleman whether he accepts those conclusions. From the moment of publication, the whole Government have been loud in their complaints that the Vice-Chancellor of Chancery Division does not understand the law. They were led by the right hon. Gentleman in his statement to the House that the Government's interpretation of the law was supported

"by such distinguished judges as Lord Scarman."—[*Official Report*, 15 February 1996; Vol. 271, c. 1141.]

The force of that argument was somewhat blunted, when Lord Scarman wrote to *The Times* five days later:

"The Attorney-General was wrong . . . the Attorney-General was under a duty to advise the Crown that in this case justice required immediate disclosure and an end to the prosecution."

Sir Ivan Lawrence (Burton): I know that the hon. Gentleman would not want to mislead the House about the effect of the contents of the documents in question. If they were so essential to the defence, can the hon. Gentleman explain why the trial did not stop immediately following their disclosure, but continued for five weeks, until the evidence given by Alan Clark was heard?

Mr. Cook: Anybody who has read the transcript of the trial knows that the prosecution case collapsed under the cross-examination of Alan Clark, when his evidence in chief was plainly inconsistent and unsustainable against the documents then obtained by the defence.

Sir Ivan Lawrence *rose—*

Mr. Cook: The hon. and learned Gentleman should read the transcript.

Sir Ivan Lawrence *rose—*

Mr. Cook: The hon. and learned Gentleman has lost his point, but he must not lose his rag.

There is a large problem with the Government's response. Sir Richard was the distinguished judge whose opinion the Government sought. Now that they do not like it, it is a bit rich to tell us that that opinion is not worth having, because Sir Richard is not distinguished enough.

The self-serving nature of this complaint can readily be understood if the House contemplates, just for a minute, what Ministers would be saying about Sir Richard Scott if he had told them what they wanted to hear. Then we would be told how conclusive his opinion was; how it was the product of three years' careful research and examination of all the legal judgments; how it was made on the authority of a long and respected career on the Bench.

Those facts are all still true. After three years' exhaustive research, Sir Richard concluded that there was no legal authority for the type of class claims for public interest immunity made in the Matrix Churchill trial. He also recommended that such class claims should never again be made in a criminal trial.

Mr. Stephen *rose—*

Mr. Cook: Not again; the hon. Gentleman has had his chance.

I note that there was one recommendation that the President did not endorse in his speech. I understand why. Although Sir Richard makes a compelling case in the interests of justice for his recommendation that class claims for PIICs should not be used again in criminal trials, the Government dare not announce that they accept it, because to do so would be to concede that they were wrong in the Matrix Churchill case.

Mr. Neil Hamilton (Tatton): May I take the hon. Gentleman back to the charge levelled by my right hon. and learned Friend the Member for Putney (Mr. Mellor), which the hon. Gentleman himself has described as the fourth charge in the Opposition's indictment, and from which he has moved somewhat in the course of his speech?

I do not know whether the hon. Gentleman's attention span faltered before he reached the last paragraph of volume III of Sir Richard Scott's report, but if I read it to him perhaps he would like to answer it:

"I must refer to the charges . . . that the Ministers who signed the PII Certificates were seeking to deprive defendants in a criminal trial of the means by which to clear themselves of the charges."

Sir Richard comes to this conclusion, in the very last sentence of volume 3:

"The charges to which I have referred are not, in my opinion, well founded."

Would the hon. Gentleman now withdraw his allegation?

Mr. Cook: I accept that paragraph in its entirety. Will the hon. Gentleman do likewise? Will he accept the passage in the middle of that paragraph which has been omitted from the central office crib sheet, but which states that the legal advice that Ministers received

"had no authoritative precedent in a criminal trial."

If Conservative Members are going to rely on the idea that Ministers acted only on legal advice, they must accept that that legal advice was wrong, and that it was given to them by another Minister.

Mr. Neil Hamilton *rose—*

Mr. Cook: No. The hon. Gentleman has had his chance—

Mr. Hamilton: On a point of order, Madam Speaker. The hon. Gentleman asked me a question. I now seek an opportunity to answer it.

Madam Speaker: The hon. Gentleman has been here long enough to know that the Member at the Dispatch Box is unlikely to give way now.

Mr. Cook: Not all Ministers acted on that legal advice. There was one shining example to all the rest of them. The Deputy Prime Minister has been very free in bandying my name around every studio that would let him in over the past week. I have given his comments careful consideration. I have concluded that what would hurt him most would be if I were to praise him. Let me now do so.

I praise the right hon. Gentleman willingly, because he was the first person to introduce the term "cover-up" to the discussion.

Two years before anyone else thought of the term, the Deputy Prime Minister objected to the attempt to withhold documents because

"it would look as though he had been engaged in an attempted cover-up".

I praise the right hon. Gentleman deservedly, because his reluctance to claim public interest immunity is praised by Sir Richard Scott as showing

"an instinct for the requirements of justice that was fully justified and corresponded with the legal principles correctly understood".

The right hon. Gentleman is a collector of titles. To his roll call of Deputy Prime Minister and First Secretary of State, perhaps we should now add Attorney-General-in-Chief. Certainly there should be a vacancy to fill. Some Conservative Members know that, even if they will not vote for it tonight. The hon. Member for Coventry, South-West (Mr. Butcher) illustrated their thinking with the helpful headline in the *Coventry Evening Telegraph*:

"Sack Lyell—but not yet".

It must be a comfort to the Attorney-General to know that he has that quality of support behind him.

The Deputy Prime Minister (Mr. Michael Heseltine): Why should anybody trust the hon. Gentleman's judgment against the views of the Attorney-General, when two of the defence counsel acting in the Matrix Churchill case thought that the Attorney-General was right?

Mr. Cook: I regret having to correct the Deputy Prime Minister while trying to achieve a spirit of unity with him,

but this is a debate based on the five volumes of the views of Sir Richard Scott. [HON. MEMBERS: "Answer."] That is the answer. Sir Richard Scott finds the Attorney-General personally at fault for failing to convey to the court the reservations expressed by the Deputy Prime Minister.

Mr. Nigel Evans (Ribble Valley): Stop dodging the question.

Mr. Cook: I am not dodging it. I am arguing closely from the five volumes in front of me. It is the Attorney-General who is dodging. Three years ago, on the day the inquiry was announced, the Attorney-General said:

"There could be no better way of examining whether ministerial responsibility should be pinned in any particular area".

Well, Sir Richard has certainly pinned ministerial responsibility in this area. He has concluded that the Attorney-General bears "major responsibility" for the inadequate instruction of the prosecuting counsel. Now that responsibility has been pinned on him by the inquiry that he appointed, will he accept it? Will he recognise that the Government should never have put on trial a man who was an agent of our security services and who had been the prime source of our intelligence on Iraq?

The Deputy Prime Minister: The Attorney-General advised me and my colleagues that the judge would consider the documents, and, if they were necessary for the defence, would order their release. The Attorney-General was proved right. Two of the defence counsel said that he was right. The hon. Gentleman has been attempting to wriggle out of the charges he originally made, but the hollow and synthetic allegations he has been publishing across the country for three years have now been exploded in his face.

Mr. Cook: I regret having to be combative with the Deputy Prime Minister, but at least we have got him to his feet. It would perhaps have been helpful if the Prime Minister had risen to his. May I remind the Deputy Prime Minister of what he told Sir Richard?

"I had been assured that my certificate would send a clear message to the judge."

The right hon. Gentleman was then asked:

"Do you think a clear message of the kind you were intending was sent to the judge?"

The Deputy Prime Minister replied:

"No, and it should have been."

It is this failure for which Sir Richard holds the Attorney-General personally at fault. Yet tonight, no one is going to accept responsibility—no one is going to go. As the Secretary of State said a week ago, there are to be no regrets, no resignations. This is not just a Government who do not know how to accept blame: they are a Government who know no shame. That is an appropriate judgment from which to approach how we should each vote tonight.

Last week, I again heard the Deputy Prime Minister on the "Today" programme, gently remonstrating with the presenter, as is his style. He said:

"You keep looking at it in terms of will the Government be defeated. That isn't the way to look at it. You ought to rejoice we live in a democracy."

[Mr. Cook]

I must confess that I was a bit surprised to hear that subconscious echo of his old opponent in the invitation to us all to rejoice—but, once again, I find myself in agreement. Conservative Members should heed his advice. They should not think of tonight's vote in terms of whether it is a defeat for the Government; they should look on it as a vote that will decide the quality of the democracy in which we live. They should remember Sir Richard's summing-up. In his final chapter, he said:

"A failure by Ministers to meet the obligations of Ministerial accountability undermines the democratic process".

The first function of Parliament is to hold the Government to account. The first duty of hon. Members is to defend the rights of Parliament against any Government who threaten those rights. That is why Parliament cannot allow the current Government to ignore the findings of the Scott report: hon. Members were designedly misled, and Ministers consistently failed in their duty of accountability to the House.

Of course the hon. Members on the other side of the Chamber were elected as Conservative Members, but that does not lessen their obligation to defend the rights of Parliament. On the contrary, there was a time when insisting on individual responsibility and upholding the sovereignty of Parliament would have been seen as conservative values.

Tonight Parliament has the opportunity to insist that Ministers must accept responsibility for their conduct in office and to assert that the health of our democracy depends on the honesty of Government to Parliament. That is what we shall vote for tonight. Of course Conservative Members have enough votes to defeat us. If they vote to reject those principles, however, they will demonstrate not only that the two Ministers who have been most criticised in the Scott report should leave office, they will convince the public that this is an arrogant Government who have been in power too long to remember that they are accountable to the people, and that the time has come when the people must turn them all out of office.

Several hon. Members *rose—*

Madam Speaker: Order. Before I call the next hon. Member to speak, I should say that the right hon. Member for Swansea, West (Mr. Williams) has asked me to inquire about a document in the Library that was said to be embargoed. I have made some inquiries about it. The document was sent over to the Library from the office of the Chancellor of the Duchy of Lancaster. There was no intention whatsoever to embargo that document; it was to be made available to hon. Members immediately, as the accompanying letter says.

Several hon. Members *rose—*

Madam Speaker: Will hon. Members allow me to finish, please?

"Embargo" was written on a brown paper envelope that was with the document. I believe that that word was written by someone who is not in a very high position— *[Interruption.]* I believe that there was no intention whatsoever to embargo the document.

5.13 pm

Mr. Douglas Hurd (Witney): The hon. Member for Livingston (Mr. Cook) has been telling the House about the Scott report for three years now. It sometimes seemed to us that he got not three hours' notice but about three years' notice of the Scott report. He seemed to have very extensive inside information about what it would contain. My right hon. and learned Friend the Member for Putney (Mr. Mellor), however, is quite right. What the hon. Gentleman has constantly predicted is not what has occurred.

The hon. Member for Livingston has constantly predicted that the Scott report would show a conspiracy of Ministers to do two indefensible things: to arm Saddam Hussein in secret; and, in that cause, to allow innocent men to be sent to prison. That is not what the Scott report has revealed. The hon. Gentleman has shown us an elegant sideways movement, so that he can claim that what he now alleges is what he has always alleged.

On the point about conspiracy to arm Saddam Hussein, what the hon. Member for Livingston said is wholly characteristic, because he omits—it is crucial—to say what Sir Richard Scott said about the conduct of my right hon. Friend the Chief Secretary. He said that if my right hon. Friend, when considering the licence for Matrix Churchill, had known the current intelligence about the destination of the lathes for export, he would not have approved the licence.

That movement is typical of what has happened to the accusations. What starts as an accusation of conspiracy becomes a criticism of the circulation of defence material. My right hon. Friend the President of the Board of Trade has acknowledged—as anyone would acknowledge—that there is a problem. The problem has already been addressed to some extent, and it can be further addressed. However, a problem about the circulation of intelligence material to Ministers of State is light years away from the accusation that the hon. Gentleman persists in making, that my right hon. Friend was in some way privy to a secret decision to arm Saddam Hussein. Exactly the same movement has occurred, as I shall seek to show, on the question of sending innocent men to prison.

I have no particular axe to grind in this matter. [Hon. Members: "Oh?"] No; Sir Richard Scott deals very reasonably with my difference of opinion with him about Jordan. He did the Home Secretary and me a favour by once more correcting the sloppy and inaccurate press reporting about the PII certificates that we signed on the Ordtech appeal, which once again showed that the certificates were upheld by the court and not repudiated by them.

Mr. Giles Radice (North Durham): Will the right hon. Gentleman give way?

Mr. Hurd: I do not wish to give way.

Nevertheless, I find the Scott report—I speak entirely for myself—a disappointing document. Sir Richard has been timid in one important matter in which he could have been bold and, in other passages, partly through ambiguity, he has allowed the Opposition and the press to convey to the country an impression of policy making that I know to be wrong.

Sir Richard makes an immense analysis of the PII certificates—I obviously do not have time to follow it— and I believe that there are three conclusions be drawn

Sir Edward Grey addresses the House on the outbreak of the first world war

Priscilla Baines was Librarian of the House of Commons for five years, but worked in the Library for 37 years, pursuing a career that might appear incongruous for someone with an interest in farming that had led her to study agriculture at Oxford.

However, her employment by the Commons in 1968 as an agriculture specialist was a reflection of the limitless range of topics upon which the Library has always been called to provide specialised information and advice. From the start, requests from Members for information about the farming industry landed on her desk.

Working for the Library in those days, however, required specialists to turn their hands to a wide range of topics, which in her case meant going far beyond agriculture and the related subjects of fishing and forestry.

Her appointment was also timely. Her specialisation proved invaluable at a time when the House was creating Select Committees to investigate specific subjects because they included a new Select Committee on Agriculture.

During her time in the Library, it evolved from a paper-based institution that relied primarily on an internal supply of information to one that embraced and exploited the astonishing changes brought about by the revolution in information technology and the access it allowed to worldwide sources of knowledge.

Computerisation coincided with a massive escalation in demand by Members for information and support as well as an expansion in their personal staff. It was a challenge that she was called upon to answer when, in later years, she assumed senior management roles that required her to reshape the Library to match changes in Members' requirements and to equip it with the means to respond to the growing flood of requests.

Being employed by the House had been an accident rather than a deliberate career choice. On leaving Oxford, she took a job as an administrator at Chelsea College, which became part of London University. Her responsibilities included student appointments. Among the notices of vacancies that passed through her hands were those from the Civil Service Commission. One was for a research post in the House of Commons Library. When she was told that the closing date was being extended, she decided that it was time for a change in her own life and she applied for and got the job – very much to her surprise.

Before she took on a senior management position, she served for over 10 years on the trade union side of the House. The First Division Association, the union that represents the top tiers in the Civil Service, formed a branch within the House, and she was asked to be its representative within the internal negotiating machinery. She served as both secretary and chairman of the branch and, subsequently, as secretary and chairman of the combined trade union side, the body that encompasses all the trade unions within the House.

In 1977 she was appointed Deputy Assistant Librarian and head of the economic affairs section of the Library's research division. In 1988, she was made head of the science and environment section, moving on in 1991 to take over as Assistant Librarian and head of the parliamentary division. In 1993 she became Deputy Librarian and Librarian in 2000.

She was awarded the CB in the 2004 Birthday Honours.

Power of persuasion skilfully deployed won over the waverers and took Britain to war

BY PRISCILLA BAINES CB

Sir Edward Grey served as Foreign Secretary from 1905 until 1916. For him, the weeks before 3 August 1914 had been a ceaseless round of intense and difficult negotiations during which it became increasingly obvious that war between Germany and France could not be averted. Left alone, France would be crushed.

Late on Sunday 2 August, Grey learnt that Germany was about to invade Belgium. Next morning, a divided Cabinet (two members resigned that day) sanctioned mobilisation of the Army to defend Belgian neutrality and endorsed the commitment to support France. That afternoon, Grey had to convince a still deeply sceptical House of Commons, including many in his own party, that it should support the Cabinet's decisions. Nobody, least of all Grey himself, could have failed to grasp the importance of the occasion or the magnitude of his task; it was undoubtedly one of the most important speeches ever made by a British Foreign Secretary.

Grey was no war-monger and was profoundly distressed at the failure of his efforts to preserve peace in Europe. He had had almost no time to prepare and was acutely conscious of the Government's "awful responsibility" but recalled that when the time came to speak, he did not feel nervous: "In a great crisis, a man who has to act or speak stands bare and stripped of choice. He has to do what is in him to do … and he can do no other."

Grey did not have a dramatic speaking style – some thought him boring – but he could be very persuasive, with a gift for finding the right words on difficult occasions. Even today, when speaking styles have changed greatly, the speech is remarkable for its lack of histrionics, its measured tone and appeals to reason rather than passion. The language was simple and the arguments clear and skilfully deployed, even where the case was weakest. One biographer commented that a "fairer speech was never made by a party to a quarrel, nor a more effective" and Grey succeeded in winning over virtually all the waverers in the House. Indeed, at several points towards the end he was loudly cheered.

Speaker Lowther spoke for many when he called it "the greatest and most thrilling occasion I ever witnessed in the House" while Lord Hugh Cecil (a Conservative and initially one of Grey's critics) said it was "the greatest example of the art of persuasion that I have ever listened to".

Grey was personally liked and admired but his foreign policies were criticised, then and since, for his preference for secret diplomacy and for getting Britain entangled in alliances that ultimately probably made war inevitable. On that occasion, however, he did what he had to do. It was one of the very few occasions when a Front-Bench speech changed not only minds but also the course of events.

GREAT BRITAIN AND EUROPEAN POWERS.

STATEMENT BY SIR EDWARD GREY.

The SECRETARY of STATE for FOREIGN AFFAIRS (Sir Edward Grey): Last week I stated that we were working for peace not only for this country, but to preserve the peace of Europe. To-day events move so rapidly that it is exceedingly difficult to state with technical accuracy the actual state of affairs, but it is clear that the peace of Europe cannot be preserved. Russia and Germany, at any rate, have declared war upon each other.

Before I proceed to state the position of His Majesty's Government, I would like to clear the ground so that, before I come to state to the House what our attitude is with regard to the present crisis, the House may know exactly under what obligations the Government is, or the House can be said to be, in coming to a decision on the matter. First of all let me say, very shortly, that we have consistently worked with a single mind, with all the earnestness in our power, to preserve peace. The House may be satisfied on that point. We have always done it. During these last years, as far as His Majesty's Government are concerned, we would have no difficulty in proving that we have done so. Throughout the Balkan crisis, by general admission, we worked for peace. The co-operation of the Great Powers of Europe was successful in working for peace in the Balkan crisis. It is true that some of the Powers had great difficulty in adjusting their points of view. It took much time and labour and discussion before they could settle their differences, but peace was secured, because peace was their main object, and they were willing to give time and trouble rather than accentuate differences rapidly.

In the present crisis, it has not been possible to secure the peace of Europe; because there has been little time, and there has been a disposition—at any rate in some quarters on which I will not dwell—to force things rapidly to an issue, at any rate, to the great risk of peace, and, as we now know, the result of that is that the policy of peace, as far as the Great Powers generally are concerned, is in danger. I do not want to dwell on that, and to comment on it, and to say where the blame seems to us to lie, which Powers were most in favour of peace, which were most disposed to risk or endanger peace, because I would like the House to approach this crisis in which we are now, from the point of view of British interests, British honour, and British obligations, free from all passion as to why peace has not been preserved.

We shall publish Papers as soon as we can regarding what took place last week when we were working for peace; and when those Papers are published, I have no doubt that to every human being they will make it clear how strenuous and genuine and whole-hearted our efforts for peace were, and that they will enable people to form their own judgment as to what forces were at work which operated against peace.

I come first, now, to the question of British obligations. I have assured the House—and the Prime Minister has assured the House more than once—that if any crisis such as this arose, we should come before the House of Commons and be able to say to the House that it was free to decide what the British attitude should be, that we would have no secret engagement which we should spring upon the House, and tell the House that, because we had entered into that engagement, there was an obligation of honour upon the country. I will deal with that point to clear the ground first.

There has been in Europe two diplomatic groups, the Triple Alliance and what came to be called the "Triple Entente," for some years past. The Triple Entente was not an Alliance—it was a Diplomatic group. The House will remember that in

[Sir E. Grey.]

1908 there was a crisis, also a Balkan crisis, originating in the annexation of Bosnia and Herzegovina. The Russian Minister, M. Isvolsky, came to London, or happened to come to London, because his visit was planned before the crisis broke out. I told him definitely then, this being a Balkan crisis, a Balkan affair, I did not consider that public opinion in this country would justify us in promising to give anything more than diplomatic support. More was never asked from us, more was never given, and more was never promised.

In this present crisis, up till yesterday, we have also given no promise of anything more than diplomatic support—up till yesterday no promise of more than diplomatic support. Now I must make this question of obligation clear to the House. I must go back to the first Moroccan crisis of 1906. That was the time of the Algeciras Conference, and it came at a time of very great difficulty to His Majesty's Government when a General Election was in progress, and Ministers were scattered over the country, and I—spending three days a week in my constituency and three days at the Foreign Office—was asked the question whether if that crisis developed into war between France and Germany we would give armed support. I said then that I could promise nothing to any foreign Power unless it was subsequently to receive the whole-hearted support of public opinion here if the occasion arose. I said, in my opinion, if war was forced upon France then on the question of Morocco—a question which had just been the subject of agreement between this country and France, an agreement exceedingly popular on both sides—that if out of that agreement war was forced on France at that time, in my view public opinion in this country would have rallied to the material support of France.

I gave no promise, but I expressed that opinion during the crisis, as far as I remember, almost in the same words, to the French Ambassador and the German Ambassador at the time. I made no promise, and I used no threats; but I expressed that opinion. That position was accepted by the French Government, but they said to me at the time—and I think very reasonably—"If you think it possible that the public opinion of Great Britain might, should a sudden crisis arise, justify you in giving to France the armed support which you cannot promise in advance, you will not be able to give that support, even if you wish to give it, when the time comes, unless some "conversations have already taken place between naval and military experts." There was force in that. I agreed to it, and authorised those conversations to take place, but on the distinct understanding that nothing which passed between military or naval experts should bind either Government or restrict in any way their freedom to make a decision as to whether or not they would give that support when the time arose.

As I have told the House, upon that occasion a General Election was in prospect. I had to take the responsibility of doing that without the Cabinet. It could not be summoned. An answer had to be given. I consulted Sir Henry Campbell-Bannerman, the Prime Minister; I consulted, I remember, Lord Haldane, who was then Secretary of State for War, and the present Prime Minister, who was then Chancellor of the Exchequer. That was the most I could do, and they authorised that on the distinct understanding that it left the hands of the Government free whenever the crisis arose. The fact that conversations between military and naval experts took place was later on—I think much later on, because that crisis passed, and the thing ceased to be of importance—but later on it was brought to the knowledge of the Cabinet.

The Agadir crisis came—another Morocco crisis—and throughout that I took precisely the same line that had been taken in 1906. But subsequently, in 1912, after discussion and consideration in the Cabinet it was decided that we ought to have a definite understanding in writing, which was to be only in the form of an unofficial letter, that these conversations which took place were not binding upon the freedom of either Government; and on the 22nd of November, 1912, I wrote to the French

Ambassador the letter which I will now read to the House, and I received from him a letter in similar terms in reply. The letter which I have to read to the House is this, and it will be known to the public now as the record that, whatever took place between military and naval experts, they were not binding engagements upon the Government:—

"My dear Ambassador,—From time to time in recent years the French and British naval and military experts have consulted together. It has always been understood that such consultation does not restrict the freedom of either Government to decide at any future time whether or not to assist the other by armed force. We have agreed that consultation between experts is not and ought not to be regarded as an engagement that commits either Government to action in a contingency that has not yet arisen and may never arise. The disposition, for instance, of the French and British Fleets respectively at the present moment is not based upon an engagement to co-operate in war.

"You have, however, pointed out that, if either Government had grave reason to expect an unprovoked attack by a third Power, it might become essential to know whether it could in that event depend upon the armed assistance of the other.

"I agree that, if either Government had grave reason to expect an unprovoked attack by a third Power, or something that threatened the general peace, it should immediately discuss with the other whether both Governments should act together to prevent aggression and to preserve peace, and, if so, what measures they would be prepared to take in common."

Lord CHARLES BERESFORD: What is the date of that?

Sir E. GREY: The 22nd November, 1912. That is the starting point for the Government with regard to the present crisis. I think it makes it clear that what the Prime Minister and I said to the House

of Commons was perfectly justified, and that, as regards our freedom to decide in a crisis what our line should be, whether we should intervene or whether we should abstain, the Government remained perfectly free and, *a fortiori*, the House of Commons remains perfectly free. That I say to clear the ground from the point of view of obligation. I think it was due to prove our good faith to the House of Commons that I should give that full information to the House now, and say what I think is obvious from the letter I have just read, that we do not construe anything which has previously taken place in our diplomatic relations with other Powers in this matter as restricting the freedom of the Government to decide what attitude they should take now, or restrict the freedom of the House of Commons to decide what their attitude should be.

Well, Sir, I will go further, and I will say this: The situation in the present crisis is not precisely the same as it was in the Morocco question. In the Morocco question it was primarily a dispute which concerned France—a dispute which concerned France and France primarily—a dispute, as it seemed to us, affecting France, out of an agreement subsisting between us and France, and published to the whole world, in which we engaged to give France diplomatic support. No doubt we were pledged to give nothing but diplomatic support; we were, at any rate, pledged by a definite public agreement to stand with France diplomatically in that question.

The present crisis has originated differently. It has not originated with regard to Morocco. It has not originated as regards anything with which we had a special agreement with France; it has not originated with anything which primarily concerned France. It has originated in a dispute between Austria and Servia. I can say this with the most absolute confidence—no Government and no country has less desire to be involved in war over a dispute with Austria and Servia than the Government and the country of France. They are involved in it because of their obligation of honour under a definite alliance with

[Sir E. Grey.]

Russia. Well, it is only fair to say to the House that that obligation of honour cannot apply in the same way to us. We are not parties to the Franco-Russian Alliance. We do not even know the terms of that Alliance. So far I have, I think, faithfully and completely cleared the ground with regard to the question of obligation.

I now come to what we think the situation requires of us. For many years we have had a long-standing friendship with France. [An Hon. MEMBER: "And with Germany!"] I remember well the feeling in the House—and my own feeling—for I spoke on the subject, I think, when the late Government made their agreement with France—the warm and cordial feeling resulting from the fact that these two nations, who had had perpetual differences in the past, had cleared these differences away. I remember saying, I think, that it seemed to me that some benign influence had been at work to produce the cordial atmosphere that had made that possible. But how far that friendship entails obligation—it has been a friendship between the nations and ratified by the nations—how far that entails an obligation let every man look into his own heart, and his own feelings, and construe the extent of the obligation for himself. I construe it myself as I feel it, but I do not wish to urge upon anyone else more than their feelings dictate as to what they should feel about the obligation. The House, individually and collectively may judge for itself. I speak my personal view, and I have given the House my own feeling in the matter.

The French fleet is now in the Mediterranean, and the Northern and Western coasts of France are absolutely undefended. The French fleet being concentrated in the Mediterranean the situation is very different from what it used to be, because the friendship which has grown up between the two countries has given them a sense of security that there was nothing to be feared from us. The French coasts are absolutely undefended. The French fleet is in the Mediterranean, and has for some years

been concentrated there because of the feeling of confidence and friendship which has existed between the two countries. My own feeling is that if a foreign fleet engaged in a war which France had not sought, and in which she had not been the aggressor, came down the English Channel and bombarded and battered the undefended coasts of France, we could not stand aside and see this going on practically within sight of our eyes, with our arms folded, looking on dispassionately, doing nothing! I believe that would be the feeling of this country. There are times when one feels that if these circumstances actually did arise, it would be a feeling which would spread with irresistible force throughout the land.

But I also want to look at the matter without sentiment, and from the point of view of British interests, and it is on that that I am going to base and justify what I am presently going to say to the House. If we say nothing at this moment, what is France to do with her Fleet in the Mediterranean? If she leaves it there, with no statement from us as to what we will do, she leaves her Northern and Western coasts absolutely undefended, at the mercy of a German fleet coming down the Channel, to do as it pleases in a war which is a war of life and death between them. If we say nothing, it may be that the French fleet is withdrawn from the Mediterranean. We are in the presence of a European conflagration; can anybody set limits to the consequences that may arise out of it. Let us assume that to-day we stand aside in an attitude of neutrality, saying, "No, we cannot undertake and engage to help either party in this conflict." Let us suppose the French fleet is withdrawn from the Mediterranean; and let us assume that the consequences—which are already tremendous in what has happened in Europe even to countries which are at peace—in fact, equally whether countries are at peace or at war—let us assume that out of that come consequences unforeseen, which make it necessary at a sudden moment that, in defence of vital British interests, we should go to war: and let us assume—which is quite possible—that

Italy, who is now neutral—[HON. MEMBERS: "Hear, hear!"]—because, as I understand, she considers that this war is an aggressive war, and the Triple Alliance being a defensive alliance her obligation did not arise—let us assume that consequences which are not yet foreseen—and which perfectly legitimately consulting her own interests—make Italy depart from her attitude of neutrality at a time when we are forced in defence of vital British interests ourselves to fight, what then will be the position in the Mediterranean? It might be that at some critical moment those consequences would be forced upon us because our trade routes in the Mediterranean might be vital to this country?

Nobody can say that in the course of the next few weeks there is any particular trade route the keeping open of which may not be vital to this country. What will be our position then? We have not kept a Fleet in the Mediterranean which is equal to dealing alone with a combination of other fleets in the Mediterranean. It would be the very moment when we could not detach more ships to the Mediterranean, and we might have exposed this country from our negative attitude at the present moment to the most appalling risk. I say that from the point of view of British interests. We feel strongly that France was entitled to know—and to know at once!—whether or not in the event of attack upon her unprotected Northern and Western Coasts she could depend upon British support. In that emergency, and in these compelling circumstances, yesterday afternoon I gave to the French Ambassador the following statement:—

"I am authorised to give an assurance that if the German Fleet comes into the Channel or through the North Sea to undertake hostile operations against the French coasts or shipping, the British Fleet will give all the protection in its power. This assurance is, of course, subject to the policy of His Majesty's Government receiving the support of Parliament, and must not be taken as binding His Majesty's Government to take any action until the above contingency of action by the German Fleet takes place."

I read that to the House, not as a declaration of war on our part, not as entailing immediate aggressive action on our part, but as binding us to take aggressive action should that contingency arise. Things move very hurriedly from hour to hour. Fresh news comes in, and I cannot give this in any very formal way; but I understand that the German Government would be prepared, if we would pledge ourselves to neutrality, to agree that its fleet would not attack the Northern coast of France. I have only heard that shortly before I came to the House, but it is far too narrow an engagement for us. And, Sir, there is the more serious consideration—becoming more serious every hour—there is the question of the neutrality of Belgium.

I shall have to put before the House at some length what is our position in regard to Belgium. The governing factor is the Treaty of 1839, but this is a Treaty with a history—a history accumulated since. In 1870, when there was war between France and Germany, the question of the neutrality of Belgium arose, and various things were said. Amongst other things, Prince Bismarck gave an assurance to Belgium that, confirming his verbal assurance, he gave in writing a declaration which he said was superfluous in reference to the Treaty in existence—that the German Confederation and its allies would respect the neutrality of Belgium, it being always understood that that neutrality would be respected by the other belligerent Powers. That is valuable as a recognition in 1870 on the part of Germany of the sacredness of these Treaty rights.

What was our own attitude? The people who laid down the attitude of the British Government were Lord Granville in the House of Lords, and Mr. Gladstone in the House of Commons. Lord Granville, on the 8th of August, 1870, used these words. He said:—

"We might have explained to the country and to foreign nations that we did not think this country was bound

[Sir E. Grey.]

either morally or internationally or that its interests were concerned in the maintenance of the neutrality of Belgium, though this course might have had some conveniences, though it might have been easy to adhere to it, though it might have saved us from some immediate danger, it is a course which Her Majesty's Government thought it impossible to adopt in the name of the country with any due regard to the country's honour or to the country's interests."

Mr. Gladstone spoke as follows two days later:—

"There is, I admit, the obligation of the Treaty. It is not necessary, nor would time permit me, to enter into the complicated question of the nature of the obligations of that Treaty; but I am not able to subscribe to the doctrine of those who have held in this House what plainly amounts to an assertion, that the simple fact of the existence of a guarantee is binding on every party to it, irrespectively altogether of the particular position in which it may find itself at the time when the occasion for acting on the guarantee arises. The great authorities upon foreign policy to whom I have been accustomed to listen, such as Lord Aberdeen and Lord Palmerston, never to my knowledge took that rigid and, if I may venture to say so, that impracticable view of the guarantee. The circumstance that there is already an existing guarantee in force is of necessity an important fact, and a weighty element in the case to which we are bound to give full and ample consideration. There is also this further consideration, the force of which we must all feel most deeply, and that is, the common interests against the unmeasured aggrandisement of any Power whatever."

The Treaty is an old Treaty—1839—and that was the view taken of it in 1870. It is one of those Treaties which are founded, not only on consideration for Belgium, which benefits under the Treaty, but in the interests of those who guarantee the neutrality of Belgium. The honour and interests are, at least, as strong to-day as in 1870, and we cannot take a more narrow view or a less serious view of our obligations, and of the importance of those obligations than was taken by Mr. Gladstone's Government in 1870.

I will read to the House what took place last week on this subject. When mobilisation was beginning, I knew that this question must be a most important element in our policy—a most important subject for the House of Commons. I telegraphed at the same time in similar terms to both Paris and Berlin to say that it was essential for us to know whether the French and German Governments respectively were prepared to undertake an engagement to respect the neutrality of Belgium. These are the replies. I got from the French Government this reply:—

"The French Government are resolved to respect the neutrality of Belgium, and it would only be in the event of some other Power violating that neutrality that France might find herself under the necessity, in order to assure the defence of her security, to act otherwise. This assurance has been given several times. The President of the Republic spoke of it to the King of the Belgians, and the French Minister at Brussels has spontaneously renewed the assurance to the Belgian Minister of Foreign Affairs to-day."

From the German Government the reply was:—

"The Secretary of State for Foreign Affairs could not possibly give an answer before consulting the Emperor and the Imperial Chancellor."

Sir Edward Goschen, to whom I had said it was important to have an answer soon, said he hoped the answer would not be too long delayed. The German Minister for Foreign Affairs then gave Sir Edward Goschen to understand that he rather doubted whether they could answer at all, as any reply they might give could not fail, in the event of war, to have the undesirable effect of disclosing, to a certain extent, part of their plan of campaign. I telegraphed at the same time to Brussels to the Belgian

Government, and I got the following reply from Sir Francis Villiers:—

"The Minister for Foreign Affairs thanks me for the communication, and replies that Belgium will, to the utmost of her power, maintain neutrality, and expects and desires other Powers to observe and uphold it. He begged me to add that the relations between Belgium and the neighbouring Powers were excellent, and there was no reason to suspect their intentions, but that the Belgian Government believe, in the case of violation, they were in a position to defend the neutrality of their country."

It now appears from the news I have received to-day—which has come quite recently, and I am not yet quite sure how far it has reached me in an accurate form—that an ultimatum has been given to Belgium by Germany, the object of which was to offer Belgium friendly relations with Germany on condition that she would facilitate the passage of German troops through Belgium. Well, Sir, until one has these things absolutely definitely, up to the last moment, I do not wish to say all that one would say if one were in a position to give the House full, complete, and absolute information upon the point. We were sounded in the course of last week as to whether if a guarantee were given that, after the war, Belgium integrity would be preserved that would content us. We replied that we could not bargain away whatever interests or obligations we had in Belgian neutrality.

Shortly before I reached the House I was informed that the following telegram had been received from the King of the Belgians by our King—King George:—

"Remembering the numerous proofs of your Majesty's friendship and that of your predecessors, and the friendly attitude of England in 1870, and the proof of friendship she has just given us again, I make a supreme appeal to the Diplomatic intervention of your Majesty's Government to safeguard the integrity of Belgium."

Diplomatic intervention took place last week on our part. What can diplomatic intervention do now? We have great and vital interests in the independence—and integrity is the least part—of Belgium. If Belgium is compelled to submit to allow her neutrality to be violated, of course the situation is clear. Even if by agreement she admitted the violation of her neutrality, it is clear she could only do so under duress. The smaller States in that region of Europe ask but one thing. Their one desire is that they should be left alone and independent. The one thing they fear is, I think, not so much that their integrity but that their independence should be interfered with. If in this war which is before Europe the neutrality of one of those countries is violated, if the troops of one of the combatants violate its neutrality and no action be taken to resent it, at the end of the war, whatever the integrity may be, the independence will be gone.

I have one further quotation from Mr. Gladstone as to what he thought about the independence of Belgium. It will be found in "Hansard," Volume 203, Page 1787. I have not had time to read the whole speech and verify the context, but the thing seems to me so clear that no context could make any difference to the meaning of it. Mr. Gladstone said:—

"We have an interest in the independence of Belgium which is wider than that which we may have in the literal operation of the guarantee. It is found in the answer to the question whether under the circumstances of the case, this country, endowed as it is with influence and power, would quietly stand by and witness the perpetration of the direst crime that ever stained the pages of history, and thus become participators in the sin."

No, Sir, if it be the case that there has been anything in the nature of an ultimatum to Belgium, asking her to compromise or violate her neutrality, whatever may have been offered to her in return, her independence is gone if that holds. If her independence goes, the independence of Holland will follow. I ask the House from the point of view of British interests, to consider what may be at stake. If France is beaten in a struggle

[Sir E. Grey.]

of life and death, beaten to her knees, loses her position as a great Power, becomes subordinate to the will and power of one greater than herself—consequences which I do not anticipate, because I am sure that France has the power to defend herself with all the energy and ability and patriotism which she has shown so often—still, if that were to happen, and if Belgium fell under the same dominating influence, and then Holland, and then Denmark, then would not Mr. Gladstone's words come true, that just opposite to us there would be a common interest against the unmeasured aggrandisement of any Power?

It may be said, I suppose, that we might stand aside, husband our strength, and that whatever happened in the course of this war at the end of it intervene with effect to put things right, and to adjust them to our own point of view. If, in a crisis like this, we run away from those obligations of honour and interest as regards the Belgian Treaty, I doubt whether, whatever material force we might have at the end, it would be of very much value in face of the respect that we should have lost. And do not believe, whether a great Power stands outside this war or not, it is going to be in a position at the end of it to exert its superior strength. For us, with a powerful Fleet, which we believe able to protect our commerce, to protect our shores, and to protect our interests, if we are engaged in war, we shall suffer but little more than we shall suffer even if we stand aside.

4.0 P.M.

We are going to suffer, I am afraid, terribly in this war whether we are in it or whether we stand aside. Foreign trade is going to stop, not because the trade routes are closed, but because there is no trade at the other end. Continental nations engaged in war—all their populations, all their energies, all their wealth, engaged in a desperate struggle—they cannot carry on the trade with us that they are carrying on in times of peace, whether we are parties to the war or whether we are not. I do not believe for a moment, that at the end

of this war, even if we stood aside and remained aside, we should be in a position, a material position, to use our force decisively to undo what had happened in the course of the war, to prevent the whole of the West of Europe opposite to us—if that had been the result of the war—falling under the domination of a single 'Power, and I am quite sure that our moral position would be such as to have lost us all respect. I can only say that I have put the question of Belgium somewhat hypothetically, because I am not yet sure of all the facts, but, if the facts turn out to be as they have reached us at present, it is quite clear that there is an obligation on this country to do its utmost to prevent the consequences to which those facts will lead if they are undisputed.

I have read to the House the only engagements that we have yet taken definitely with regard to the use of force. I think it is due to the House to say that we have taken no engagement yet with regard to sending an Expeditionary armed force out of the country. Mobilisation of the Fleet has taken place; mobilisation of the Army is taking place; but we have as yet taken no engagement, because I do feel that in the case of a European conflagration such as this, unprecedented, with our enormous responsibilities in India and other parts of the Empire, or in countries in British occupation, with all the unknown factors, we must take very carefully into consideration the use which we make of sending an Expeditionary Force out of the country until we know how we stand. One thing I would say.

The one bright spot in the whole of this terrible situation is Ireland. The general feeling throughout Ireland—and I would like this to be clearly understood abroad—does not make the Irish question a consideration which we feel we have now to take into account. I have told the House how far we have at present gone in commitments and the conditions which influence our policy, and I have put to the House and dwelt at length upon how vital is the condition of the neutrality of Belgium.

What other policy is there before the House? There is but one way in which the Government could make certain at the present moment of keeping outside this war, and that would be that it should immediately issue a proclamation of unconditional neutrality. We cannot do that. We have made the commitment to France that I have read to the House which prevents us from doing that. We have got the consideration of Belgium which prevents us also from any unconditional neutrality, and, without those conditions absolutely satisfied and satisfactory, we are bound not to shrink from proceeding to the use of all the forces in our power. If we did take that line by saying, "We will have nothing whatever to do with this matter" under no conditions—the Belgian Treaty obligations, the possible position in the Mediterranean, with damage to British interests, and what may happen to France from our failure to support France—if we were to say that all those things mattered nothing, were as nothing, and to say we would stand aside, we should, I believe, sacrifice our respect and good name and reputation before the world, and should not escape the most serious and grave economic consequences.

My object has been to explain the view of the Government, and to place before the House the issue and the choice. I do not for a moment conceal, after what I have said, and after the information, incomplete as it is, that I have given to the House with regard to Belgium, that we must be prepared, and we are prepared, for the consequences of having to use all the strength we have at any moment—we know not how soon—to defend ourselves and to take our part. We know, if the facts all be as I have stated them, though I have announced no intending aggressive action on our part, no final decision to resort to force at a moment's notice, until we know the whole of the case, that the use of it may be forced upon us. As far as the forces of the Crown are concerned, we are ready. I believe the Prime Minister and my right hon. Friend the

First Lord of the Admiralty have no doubt whatever that the readiness and the efficiency of those Forces were never at a higher mark than they are to-day, and never was there a time when confidence was more justified in the power of the Navy to protect our commerce and to protect our shores. The thought is with us always of the suffering and misery entailed from which no country in Europe will escape and from which no abdication or neutrality will save us. The amount of harm that can be done by an enemy ship to our trade is infinitesimal, compared with the amount of harm that must be done by the economic condition that is caused on the Continent.

The most awful responsibility is resting upon the Government in deciding what to advise the House of Commons to do. We have disclosed our mind to the House of Commons. We have disclosed the issue, the information which we have, and made clear to the House, I trust, that we are prepared to face that situation, and that should it develop, as probably it may develop, we will face it. We worked for peace up to the last moment, and beyond the last moment. How hard, how persistently, and how earnestly we strove for peace last week, the House will see from the Papers that will be before it.

But that is over, as far as the peace of Europe is concerned. We are now face to face with a situation and all the consequences which it may yet have to unfold. We believe we shall have the support of the House at large in proceeding to whatever the consequences may be and whatever measures may be forced upon us by the development of facts or action taken by others. I believe the country, so quickly has the situation been forced upon it, has not had time to realise the issue. It perhaps is still thinking of the quarrel between Austria and Servia, and not the complications of this matter which have grown out of the quarrel between Austria and Servia. Russia and Germany we know are at war. We do not yet know officially that Austria, the ally whom Germany is to support, is yet at war with Russia. We know that a good deal has

Vol. 65.   3 M

[Sir E. Grey.]

been happening on the French frontier. We do not know that the German Ambassador has left Paris.

The situation has developed so rapidly that technically, as regards the condition of the war, it is most difficult to describe what has actually happened. I wanted to bring out the underlying issues which would affect our own conduct, and our own policy, and to put them clearly. I have put the vital facts before the House, and if, as seems not improbable, we are forced, and rapidly forced, to take our stand upon those issues, then I believe, when the country realises what is at stake, what the real issues are, the magnitude of the impending dangers in the West of Europe, which I have endeavoured to describe to the House, we shall be supported throughout, not only by the House of Commons, but by the determination, the resolution, the courage, and the endurance of the whole country.

Mr. BONAR LAW: The right hon. Gentleman has made an appeal for support, and it is necessary I should say a word or two. They shall be very few. I wish to say, in the first place, that I do not believe there is a single Member of this House who doubts that, not only the right hon. Gentleman himself, but the Government which he represents, have done everything in their power up to the last moment to preserve peace, and I think we may be sure that, if any other course is taken, it is because it is forced upon them, and that they have absolutely no alternative. One thing only, further, I would like to say. The right hon. Gentleman spoke of the bright spot in the picture which only a day or two ago was a black spot on the political horizon. Everything he has said I am sure is true. I should like to say, further, that if the contingencies, which he has not put into words, but which are all in our minds as possible, arise, then we have already had indications that there is another bright spot, and that every one of His Majesty's Dominions beyond the Seas will be behind us in whatever action it is necessary to take. This only I shall add: The Government already know, but I give them now the assurance on behalf of the party of which I am Leader in this House, that in whatever steps they think it necessary to take for the honour and security of this country, they can rely on the unhesitating support of the Opposition.

Mr. JOHN REDMOND: I hope the House will not consider it improper on my part, in the grave circumstances in which we are assembled, if I intervene for a very few moments. I was moved a great deal by that sentence in the speech of the Secretary of State for Foreign Affairs in which he said that the one bright spot in the situation was the changed feeling in Ireland. In past times when this Empire has been engaged in these terrible enterprises, it is true—it would be the utmost affectation and folly on my part to deny it—the sympathy of the Nationalists of Ireland, for reasons to be found deep down in the centuries of history, have been estranged from this country. Allow me to say that what has occurred in recent years has altered the situation completely. I must not touch, and I may be trusted not to touch, on any controversial topic. By this I may be allowed to say, that a wider knowledge of the real facts of Irish history have, I think, altered the views of the democracy of this country towards the Irish question, and to-day I honestly believe that the democracy of Ireland will turn with the utmost anxiety and sympathy to this country in every trial and every danger that may overtake it. There is a possibility, at any rate, of history repeating itself. The House will remember that in 1778, at the end of the disastrous American War, when it might, I think, truly be said that the military power of this country was almost at its lowest ebb, and when the shores of Ireland were threatened with foreign invasion, a body of 100,000 Irish Volunteers sprang into existence for the purpose of defending her shores. At first no Catholic—ah, how sad the reading of the history of those days is!—was allowed to be enrolled in that body of Volunteers, and yet, from the very first day the Catholics of the South and West subscribed money and sent it towards the arming of their Protestant fellow countrymen.

John Smith's speech signals the end of the long Tory era

Margaret Beckett was the first woman in British political history to be appointed Secretary of State for Foreign and Commonwealth Affairs, but that was only one of a string of firsts in a political career that spans over 30 years.

She was also the first female President of the Board of Trade and the first woman to lead the Labour party – although only briefly after the death of John Smith. She chaired the first ever meeting of the UN Security Council to discuss climate security, and she was the first British Minister to address the Party School of the Chinese Communist party – China's foremost institution for the training of officials.

As Margaret Jackson, she entered Parliament as the Member for Lincoln, a seat she won from Dick Taverne in October 1974. Taverne had held the seat for Labour, but disagreement over his views on Europe led to him resigning from the party and successfully standing as an independent at a by-election in 1973.

In the aftermath of defeat, the Lincoln Labour party selected Margaret Jackson as its candidate and she stood against Taverne in the general election in February 1974. She lost by just under 1,300 votes, but then went to work as a special adviser to Judith Hart, the Overseas Development Minister until the second general election that year, when she defeated Taverne and took the seat.

She had graduated from Manchester College of Science and Technology as a metallurgist in 1961 and was taken on by AEI, the electrical engineering group, as an apprentice. It was at this time that she joined the Labour party, also joining the Transport and General Workers Union, of which she has remained a member. From 1970 to 1974 she worked at the party's Smith square headquarters as a researcher.

Once elected to the House of Commons, she became Parliamentary Private Secretary to Judith Hart, and after a year was promoted to Government Whip. In 1976, she was promoted again, this time to her first Front-Bench appointment, as Under-Secretary of State for Education and Science.

When Margaret Thatcher swept the board in the 1979 general election Margaret Jackson lost her Lincoln seat and went to work for Granada Television as a researcher. Now married, Margaret Beckett was elected in 1980 to the National Executive Committee of the Labour party. In the 1983 general election she won the seat of Derby, South, which she continues to represent.

For most of her time in the House of Commons she has been at the forefront of Labour politics, serving for 10 years in Tony Blair's Cabinets, and notching up 15 years on the Front Bench when Labour was out of office.

In Opposition, she was shadow Chief Secretary to the Treasury, shadow Leader of the House, shadow Secretary of State for Health, and shadow President of the Board of Trade. Under John Smith's leadership of the party, she was deputy Leader of the Opposition until his untimely death in 1994 when she took over as Leader and steered the party through that year's successful European elections.
In the ensuing leadership contest she came third after Tony Blair and John Prescott, the latter replacing her as deputy Leader. However, she remained in the shadow Cabinet.

In Government, her first post under Tony Blair was President of the Board of Trade and Secretary of State for Trade and Industry. It was in that capacity that she oversaw the introduction of the national minimum wage.

After a year she was moved on to become Leader of the House, where, in an atmosphere of modernisation, she implemented major reforms to the House's internal business procedures, including the historic innovation of the Westminster Hall debating chamber. She also spearheaded the Government's reform of the House of Lords, notably the abolition of hereditary peerages.

In 2001, she took over as Secretary of State for the Environment, Food and Rural Affairs. It was a new Government Department, which she was responsible for establishing from the amalgamation of the old Agriculture Ministry and the Department for the Environment. It was to be a busy time as she led for the United Kingdom in more than 15 major EU and international sets of negotiations on environmental and agricultural topics.

After five years, Tony Blair appointed her Foreign Secretary, she and Margaret Thatcher being the only women ever to hold one of the great offices of state. It was that post that she held when Gordon Brown took over as Prime Minister in June 2007. He replaced her with David Miliband and she returned to the Back Benches. Within months, however, he appointed her to chair the Intelligence and Security Committee, the non-parliamentary committee that reports direct to the Prime Minister on the activities of the British security services.

As the Labour Government's fortunes declined, however, the need for experienced campaigners became paramount and Margaret Beckett, one of the most experienced of all – she had served under Harold Wilson's premiership – was recalled to the Government as Minister for Housing, a position she has held since October 2008.

Sharp, penetrative and brilliant speech that rallied the troops

By Rt hon Margaret Beckett MP

John Smith had a very special way of connecting with people. Renowned for being straightforward, decent and trustworthy, he scored for projecting an image of the absolutely reliable bank manager or solicitor in whom voters could unhesitatingly put their trust.

But he was so much more than that. There are many examples of John speaking that I could have chosen; however I chose this particular exchange in the Commons as this is a classic example of how he brilliantly uses a news story that had been at the forefront of everyone's mind vividly to expose the way that the Major Government were falling apart.

John Major had been Chancellor of the Exchequer, Foreign Secretary and now had all the trappings of power as Prime Minister: national and international status; an impressive CV; and, in many ways, a likeable figure.

But his Government had a wafer-thin majority, were riven by internal tensions and, beneath the surface, were barely coherent.

John Smith's job as Leader of the Opposition was to expose that vulnerability.

This exchange from the Dispatch Box may not have had the same historical significance as Geoffrey Howe's withering attack on Thatcher in 1990 when he memorably castigated her leadership style as Prime Minister in his resignation speech ("It is rather like sending your opening batsmen to the crease only for them to find, the moment the first balls are bowled, that their bats have been broken before the game by the team captain") but, in its own way, John Smith's exchange was just as telling.

It rallied the Labour troops and gave a real sense that the Major Government were finished. That – like the houses that still stood firm on the cliff edge – the end was inevitable. It was still four years before the Major Government tumbled into the sea. And it fell to another Labour party leader after John was taken from us tragically early. But this Commons exchange told Labour Front Benchers like me – and the wider public – that the end of the long Tory era was surely in sight. And it was!

Re-reading John Smith's words here from 15 years ago, his oratorical skills shine through. It is the way that he could build a detailed case in a straightforward way, making sharp, penetrative, brilliant, contemporary references – and making it funny too. The lack of grandeur and pomposity lifts an otherwise ordinary exchange into the extraordinary.

Demolition of a Government in slow demise

Alastair Campbell was well-known as a journalist, but he moved centre stage and into the public spotlight with the Labour victory at the 1997 general election when he was appointed Prime Minister Tony Blair's official spokesman and chief press secretary.

As one of the principal participants in the creation of New Labour, he brought to the project his expertise in media communications and an awareness of the crucial importance of presentation in conveying the political message.

His new role was to bring him success and acrimony in equal measure as Labour's popularity soared but he was targeted by those who resented his management and control of information from No 10 Downing street and his unique position of access and influence to the Prime Minister.

In the heady days after the 1997 general election he had warned Tony Blair that the honeymoon would not last and that he should prepare for a media onslaught. It was something for which he had to prepare himself. He was at the Prime Minister's side throughout the crises and the scandals, culminating in a bitter row with the BBC over the intelligence dossier on weapons of mass destruction in Iraq. Eventually, family tensions, the death of Dr David Kelly and the pressures of the Hutton inquiry, at which his personal diary was presented in evidence, convinced him that his time at No 10 had run its course and he resigned in 2003.

He graduated from Gonville and Caius college, Cambridge with an MA in modern languages. After spending time busking with his bagpipes, he embarked on his journalistic career as a trainee with Mirror Group titles in the west country.

After two years he got a job as a reporter with the *Daily Mirror*, leaving three years later to work for Eddy Shah as news editor of the *Today* newspaper. After suffering a nervous breakdown, he subsequently returned to the *Mirror* as a reporter. In 1986 he was appointed political correspondent of the *Sunday Mirror* before moving up to the post of political editor. In 1989 while still writing a column for the Sunday paper, he rejoined the *Daily Mirror* as political editor and chief political columnist, a position he held for four years.

After a brief period as assistant editor and columnist for *Today*, by that time owned by Rupert Murdoch, he was asked by Tony Blair, then Leader of the Opposition, to work for him as his press secretary, a job he did for three years before Labour's stunning victory in the 1997 general election.

When Tony Blair moved into No 10, Alastair Campbell went with him. The job entailed co-ordinating Government communications and holding twice daily briefings of the press. After the second Labour election triumph in 2001, he became the Director of Communications and Strategy, a post he held until his resignation.

His main hobbies are running, playing the bagpipes and supporting Burnley football club. He actively supports the Leukaemia Research Fund, his best friend having died of the disease, and he has run the London marathon, the Great North Run and the Great Ethiopian Run, and has completed several full triathlons to raise money for the charity.

After leaving No 10, he returned to journalism, writing on sport for various newspapers and publications, presented television programmes, and, in 2007, published his diaries from his time with the Prime Minister in a book entitled "The Blair Years". It became a best seller.

Attack speech by a brilliant wit at his wittiest best

By Alastair Campbell

June 9 1993 was an important day in the slow demise of John Major's Government and the return of Labour to power. The combined effect of Norman Lamont's personal statement following his resignation as Chancellor, and Labour leader John Smith's brilliant opening of the Opposition day debate on Government economic and social policy, weakened Major substantially. Of course Lamont's speech took much of the coverage and comment at the time, but the significance of Smith's speech should not be underestimated.

As I know from my time with Tony Blair, even if Commons debates and exchanges no longer command the automatic attention of public and media in a way that, perversely, they did in the days of a smaller media, they remain strategically vital. They are a place to devise and refine and sharpen lines of attack and defence.

It was always a myth that Blair did not take Parliament seriously. To the very end, he fretted endlessly about how opponents would try to pick apart his arguments, and he was constantly analysing their strengths and weaknesses too. One after another, Tory leaders fell to the attacks he developed and executed in the House: Major's weakness and dithering; Iain Duncan Smith's opportunism; William Hague's strength turned into a weakness as in "good jokes but bad judgment"; Michael Howard's combination of opportunism and general unpleasantness; and with all of them the inability to unite their party. The beginnings of some of those attacks on the Tories in general and Major in particular are clear in Smith's speech.

John Smith, unlike his successor, never had to worry about being seen as a Parliament man. He so evidently excelled in debate, questioning and answering alike, and so evidently relished it, that nobody ever even tried to mount an attack upon the parliamentary side of his role. So an Opposition day debate, especially on such a high profile political day, was an important moment for him. He seized it.

I have sat through many debates, as journalist and press secretary. I cannot with any great accuracy recall the mood or reaction from many. But this one I can. I can recall the thin smile of Major's lips as one point after another was hammered home. It was thinnest of all when Smith said that Major had the lowest ratings of any Prime Minister since polling began. I can recall the laughter on the Labour Benches and the mirth in the Press Gallery. He was a wit, and he was at his wittiest best.

It was T S Eliot who said wit is the alliance of levity and seriousness by which the seriousness is intensified. That applied superbly to Smith's speech. He was making big serious points, about leadership, the economy, and society, but doing so in a way that brought the House down. His line, cruel and with enormous impact, that Major was the man with the non-Midas touch, was stinging enough. Add in the context – a few days earlier a farcical Grand National and a hotel on the east coast slipping into the sea, neither of them Major's fault but both somehow symbolic of his leadership at the time – and you have a demolition not just of Major, but of his Britain.

The wit was sharp from the word go, his praise of Lamont's speech laced with the observation that it was more effective than anything he did in office.

I can see Smith now, notes in front of him, used mainly as an aide memoire, Back Benchers behind him smiling, loving every minute, and he responding to their reaction with ever harsher and more colourful attacks. And I can see the Tories whispering to each other, "We have a problem."

There was a steady build up of invective, but never without little grace notes of humour, all building a big argument towards the final line – discredited Government, discredited Prime Minister.

There were only flavours of the forward looking policy agenda. This was largely an attack speech. Smith believed – much more than Blair or Gordon Brown – that Governments lost elections more than Oppositions won them. This speech was helping the Government to lose. I am sure that John Smith would have won a general election for Labour. Whether he would have led the party to the kind of landslide Blair delivered is less certain. But if it was all down to the ability to demolish an opponent in parliamentary debate, he was home and dry.

Orders of the Day

OPPOSITION DAY

[13TH ALLOTTED DAY]

Government Economic and Social Policy

Madam Speaker: I inform the House that I have selected the amendment standing in the name of the Prime Minister.

3.52 pm

Mr. John Smith (Monklands, East): I beg to move,

That this House condemns the Prime Minister's betrayal of election promises and commitments on economic and social policy; deplores the Government's intention to make the users of public services pay the price of Conservative economic and financial mismanagement; further deplores the failure to make changes in policies towards unemployment, industry and the skills revolution; and calls for new policies in these areas to strengthen British industry and the British economy, to end mass unemployment and to improve public services.

Before we embark on our debate, right hon. and hon. Members will have in their minds the statement that has just been made by the ex-Chancellor of the Exchequer. I had the opportunity to cross swords with him many times when he held the illustrious office from which he has so recently departed, and I commend him for the dignity of his statement. It was, if I may say so, as effective a speech as any he made when he was in office.

The right hon. Gentleman was wise to be wary in his endorsement of the Government's policies. What will no doubt be remembered by most of those who listened to his statement today was the revealing insight into the style and purposes of the Government from which he has so recently departed.

I must confess that it flicked across my mind when I was listening to the right hon. Gentleman that there might have been the odd political influence affecting him at the time of the 1992 Budget, especially if it is compared with the 1993 Budget—but let that pass. He was no doubt, as he constantly reminded us, acting on orders. The orders no doubt came from the pollsters and other people who appear to have such great influence on the Conservative party's policies. People will remember for some time his reference to being in office, but not in power.

When we think about the general election, we remember vividly that the Prime Minister and his colleagues made clear and specific promises to the electorate. It is reasonable to suppose that they were returned to power because people believed their promises. We now know how very few would vote for the right hon. Gentleman and his colleagues if there was an election today. There are reasons why the right hon. Gentleman has the lowest rating of any Prime Minister since polls began. The first and most important is that the right hon. Gentleman and his colleagues have cynically betrayed their pledges to the British people.

We heard a great deal about tax from the Tories at the general election. The Prime Minister promised tax cuts year on year. There were frequent promises of lower taxes from the Prime Minister, from the ex-Chancellor and from the present Chief Secretary to the Treasury. I do not know whether they meant them or whether they were told by the pollsters to say them, but they certainly said them. On 31 March, only 10 days before polling day, the right hon. Member for Kingston upon Thames (Mr. Lamont) said on Channel 4 news:

"We will not have to increase taxes. I cannot see any circumstances in which that will be necessary."

There were pledges on specific taxes as well. At an election press conference on 27 March, just a few days before polling day, the Prime Minister said:

"We have no plans and no need to extend the scope of VAT."

We know how sincere all that was. In this year's Budget, those promises were spectacularly overturned and those pledges were shamefully betrayed.

I need not remind a suffering public that, from next April, VAT will be imposed on household heating bills at 8 per cent. In the following year, it will be hiked to 17·5 per cent. Tax increases in that Budget amounted to a staggering £17·5 billion. So it is not tax cuts year on year; it is tax increases year on year.

What a shocking betrayal of the people. Millions of families will have to find those billions of pounds from their household budgets. I very much doubt whether those at the bottom of the scale—those on income support—will have their benefit properly increased to meet the full extra costs that they have to bear. I know even more clearly that there will be no relief for the millions of families and pensioners who are just above income support level. The stark truth is that every family in the land will have to foot the cost of this Government's perfidy.

Mr. Alan Howarth (Stratford-on-Avon): The right hon. and learned Gentleman referred to cynicism, and talked about style and purpose. It would be helpful to the House if he could comment on this. He has made it clear that a Labour Government would not reduce public spending. Indeed, his party is committed to policies that would increase public spending. At the same time, the shadow Chancellor has said that a Labour Government would not increase taxes. Will the right hon. and learned Gentleman therefore explain to the House how the Labour party, if it were in government, would pay for its policies?

Mr. Smith: The hon. Gentleman brings to our attention the parlous state of our public finances. What we need to do above all is to deal with public finances, bring down unemployment and get back on course for economic growth—*[Interruption.]*

Madam Speaker: Order. Hon. Members on both sides of the House must settle down—*[Interruption.]* Let us have order below the Gangway. I call Mr. Smith.

Mr. Smith: The hon. Member for Stratford-on-Avon (Mr. Howarth) knows perfectly well that the main reason why we have such a high public sector borrowing requirement is the cost of unemployment, which is the result of Government policies. It does not matter whether it is the fault of the right hon. Member for Kingston upon Thames (Mr. Lamont) or the Prime Minister, as the right hon. Member implied: the fault lies with the Conservative party.

Mr. John Townend (Bridlington): Does the right hon. and learned Gentleman really think that a deficit of £50 billion this year can be brought down by the reduction in unemployment that 2·5 or 3 per cent. growth would create? If he is opposed to public spending cuts, why does he not

[*Mr. John Townend*]

admit that the only alternative would be massive increases in taxation? His arguments today have justified the Government's public spending policy.

Mr. Smith: If that is so obvious, why did the Prime Minister say during the election campaign—when he knew the exact state of our public finances—that there was no need for increases in taxation? He said that there would be tax cuts and no cuts in public expenditure, which would be maintained. Of course, there is an explanation for that, to which I shall return. We were not told the full truth about our public finances at the last general election.

I shall now return to the promises made by the Conservative party. Incidentally, I hear that the Chancellor—the new Chancellor of the Exchequer—has been entertaining the Press Gallery at a lunch today, saying that it does not matter what one says during an election campaign: what matters is what is contained in the manifesto. His theory seemed to be that one could say whatever one liked during the campaign—if it was not in the manifesto, it did not matter. I hope that that will be repudiated.

The Chancellor of the Exchequer (Mr. Kenneth Clarke): I did not say that.

Mr. Smith: I am glad that the right hon. and learned Gentleman says that. I think that there are plenty of people who attended the Press Gallery lunch who are now in a good position to report it.

I am glad that we have achieved some degree of agreement—that someone is responsible for what he says during an election campaign. On 28 January 1992, not long before the campaign, the Prime Minister told the House:

"I have no plans to raise the top rate of tax or the level of national insurance contributions."—[*Official Report*, 28 January 1992; Vol. 202, c. 808.]

To be fair to the Prime Minister, he has kept one half of the promise—the half that applies to those at the top of the income scale.

How can the pledge that the Prime Minister made in the House possibly be squared with the increase of 1 per cent. in national insurance contributions that is to be imposed on every wage and salary earner in this country? What is the difference between 1 per cent. extra national insurance and another 1p on income tax? There is a difference, but a difference that adversely affects the lower-paid. Both policies are clearly taxes on income, but national insurance hits the lower-paid harder as it starts lower down the income scale than income tax and there are no allowances to be set against its liability.

What did Mr. Chris Patten—now Governor of Hong Kong, then chairman of the Conservative party—tell us about national insurance on 23 March 1992, during the election campaign? He said at a press conference:

"Raising national insurance contributions would be a back-door stealth tax."

We now know what the stealth was. It is the oldest trick in Tory politics to promise one thing and do another. That trick did not arrive with the pollsters during the past year or two; it has a much longer and more distinguished ancestry than that.

The Conservatives did not tell us in the election campaign that, in their first post-election Budget, they would freeze all personal allowances and bring 300,000 of

the lower-paid into the income tax net. There we have it: national insurance increases, soaring VAT and a freeze on personal allowances—not quite the double whammy that we kept hearing about from the Governor of Hong Kong. It turned out to be the Tories' triple whammy, perpetrated on the British taxpayer.

Now we see clearly what the Tory tax strategy is, as we can review the Tories' long period in office. During the 1980s, when they were flush with cash from North sea oil, the biggest and best handouts went to the rich. When the Government have come unstuck in the 1990s, it is the lower-paid and ordinary taxpayers who pay the price of their incompetence. It is like the old Victorian value: "It's the rich wot gets the pleasure, it's the poor wot gets the pain."

It is not only on tax that the Government have broken their word. Let us look at their pledges on public spending. Time and again, we were told during the election campaign that the Red Book set out the detailed plans of the Government's expenditure programme, and that it was based on sound public finances. The Government vehemently and continually denied that there would be any post-election cuts in public expenditure, a subject drawn to the public's attention occasionally by some of my percipient colleagues. The Prime Minister told us on 30 March, only 10 days before polling day, at a major election press conference:

"If we were going to cut public expenditure, we would have done it before and I don't believe it is economically right. I have said that in the past, and there is no need to do it whatsoever. So you can rule out any prospect of that."

Those words could not be much clearer: any prospect of public expenditure cuts emphatically ruled out—before the election.

We now know what a false prospectus that was, and I hope that everyone, especially those conned into voting Tory last year, will keep that clearly in mind as cuts in public service unfold in the months ahead. We also know that the Prime Minister and his colleagues, especially the former Chancellor, massaged the public borrowing figures downwards in the 1992 Red Book.

The *Financial Times* of 12 October 1992 told us that the former Chancellor had, in an internal Treasury note, instructed officials to recalculate projections for the public sector borrowing requirement in the five years to 1996-97, to pull them down if possible to zero by the end of the period. Despite—probably—valiant efforts inside the Treasury, its officials did not quite make it to zero, but they got the figure down to £6 billion at the end of the period. This was the projection for the PSBR before the election.

After the election, the £6 billion mysteriously jumped to £35 billion in the 1993 PSBR projection. The Government were correctly condemned by the Treasury and Civil Service Select Committee for what it called the former Chancellor's

"cavalier approach to massaging or falsifying statistics for political reasons."

Even the deputy editor of *The Spectator*—I do not think that he can be accused of left-wing scaremongering, which is the major objection to the Labour party at the moment —felt obliged to comment on the 1992 Budget in his issue of 20 March this year, as follows:

"The Budget executed a great deceit on the electorate. Since the election campaign of a year ago, honest dealing by the Tories has been rare. The first 1993 Budget provided evidence of the cynicism behind the smirks and mock sincerity on the faces of the First and Second Lords of the Treasury."

What is the consequence for the nation of all this? It has been signalled clearly enough, especially by the Chief Secretary to the Treasury. Public expenditure cuts are now being secretly planned; not only will they totally overturn all the solemn assurances given by the Prime Minister before the election, but they will gravely undermine the crucial public services which are vital to the security and well-being of millions of our fellow citizens.

Will the axe fall on pensioners entitled to exemptions from prescription charges, which are now at a record £4·25 an item? *[Interruption.]* That may be amusing for Conservative Members, but it is not for millions of people who are gravely worried that it might occur.

Will it be hotel charges of £30 a night for overnight stays in hospital? Will it be a payment for visits to GPs or, as predicted in *The Guardian* of 5 June, will there be savage cuts—*[Interruption.]* I do not always support *The Guardian* or agree with everything it says—it would be surprising if I did, given what it sometimes says—but it was right to refer to the internal memorandum from the Department of Social Security, which talked precisely about cuts in invalidity benefits. There will possibly be cuts in housing benefit and in invalidity and sickness benefits.

Mr. Tim Smith (Beaconsfield) *rose——*

Mr. John Smith: Perhaps the hon. Gentleman can clear up the matter.

Mr. Tim Smith: The Leader of the Opposition is indulging in the most disgraceful and irresponsible speech, and he knows it. He is frightening the most vulnerable people in our society. Is he aware that, as long as he fails to answer the questions that were put to him about the public sector borrowing requirement, the people of this country will conclude that he does not have the guts to tackle the most difficult economic question facing this country and that he is not fit to be Leader of the Opposition, let alone Prime Minister?

Mr. John Smith: Every time we refer to the Government's likely cuts, we are told that we are scaremongering. That allegation appears in the amendment to the Opposition motion. No doubt it has been drawn to the hon. Gentleman's attention that he might make that point during the debate. He has done it.

The hon. Gentleman used to be connected with a Conservative party organisation and, on the issue of scaremongering, I should like to draw his attention to a document with which he may be familiar—the Conservative campaign guide for 1992. I have been able to obtain one of the few remaining copies that has escaped the central office shredder. I am glad to have it, and I can make it available to hon. Members who want to consult it.

No doubt that guide was used by Conservative Members during the campaign. Page 12 states that there will be no increases in VAT. The material part states:

   "Following a series of unfounded and irresponsible scares from the Labour Party, the **Prime Minister**"—

the words "Prime Minister" are in bold letters, so at least he is given status in the campaign guide—

"has confirmed that the Government has no intention of raising VAT further."

The document also refers to a statement in the House, and says:

   "There will be no VAT increase. Unlike the Labour Party, we have published our spending plans and there is no need to raise VAT to meet them."

For good measure, the document quotes the right hon. and learned Member for Putney (Mr. Mellor), who, as Chief Secretary to the Treasury, said that the Government had no intention of widening the scope of VAT. Was it fair comment that the Labour party was scaremongering at the time of the last election?

Mr. David Shaw (Dover): Will the right hon. and learned Gentleman give way?

Mr. Smith: No. I am dealing with the last intervention.

I thought that Conservative Members might think that this was scaremongering. That nasty Labour party was once again maliciously misinterpreting the honest and decent intentions of these credible and straightforward Ministers. The public know exactly what happened when the Conservatives were returned to office, and they will not be fooled so easily again. VAT went up by 8 per cent., to 17·5 per cent., affecting every family in the land. Gosh, weren't we irresponsible to allege that? Weren't we wicked to make such scurrilous accusations against such honest and decent people?

Let me tell the Prime Minister that what scares the country is not what Labour predicts, because we are quite accurate in our predictions, but what the Government are capable of doing. The Government are prepared to promise anything to get elected and then to betray each and every promise afterwards.

Although the betrayal of election pledges is bitterly resented throughout the country, it is only one of the reasons for the contempt in which the Government are held. Since the general election, we have seen one catastrophe piled on another. Not even the most inventive or ruthless scaremongering among my hon. Friends would have had the audacity to allege that any Government could be so consistently incompetent, so hopelessly accident-prone and so foolishly inept.

I select but a few of the Prime Minister's recent triumphs: the billions of pounds lost in the panic and fiasco of black Wednesday; the grievous damage to our energy resources which the disastrous pit closure programme has inflected upon the country; the shady double dealing in the Matrix Churchill affair; the hopelessly bungled scandal of the education tests; and the disaster waiting to happen in the privatisation of our railways.

In response to the plummeting popularity of the Administration itself, revealed at Newbury and in the shire county elections, we have the Prime Minister's botched reshuffle. If we were to offer that tale of events to the BBC light entertainment department as a script for a programme, I think that the producers of "Yes, Minister" would have turned it down as hopelessly over the top. It might have even been too much for "Some Mothers Do 'Ave Them".

The tragedy for us all is that it is really happening—it is fact, not fiction. The man with the non-Midas touch is in charge. It is no wonder that we live in a country where the grand national does not start and hotels fall into the sea.

Mr. David Shaw: Will the right hon. and learned Gentleman give way?

Mr. Smith: No.

To be fair to the ex-Chancellor from whom we have heard today, he reminded us in his last public speech

[*Mr. Smith*]

before today that his biggest problems, one might say his major problem, had been inherited. It was a cruel twist of fate to have to succeed the right hon. Gentleman the Prime Minister. No doubt he is now reflecting that he is well out of it all.

There is proof abundant that this is a Government who are untrustworthy and incompetent—deeply untrustworthy, hopelessly incompetent. Perhaps their most defining characteristic is an aggressive, bullying and dogmatic obstinacy which assumes that they are entitled to control our affairs without the slightest recognition of the expertise of others or any opposing opinion.

The tragic farce of the education tests is a case in point. The Government are now a laughing stock as boxes of unopened test papers accumulate in schools all over the land. Of more than 4,000 secondary schools, only a handful took part. It is not that the Government were not warned; parents, teachers and head teachers unitedly told them they were wrong, but the expertise of the teaching profession is of no interest to the arrogant Secretary of State for Education.

Even the right hon. Gentleman's own advisers could not stay on the obviously sinking ship. The noble Lord Skidelsky attacked what he called "the Byzantine complexity" of the proposals:

"I was amazed,"

he said,

"at how insensitive they were to spending large sums of money on things that were no good."

He should not have been so surprised; they have a long record of doing just that. At a time when educational spending is under threat, perhaps it is worth remembering that the Government's own advisers tell us that this year's tests alone will cost £35 million.

It is of course interesting that the Government propose tests only for schools in the public sector. If they are such good news, why are the private schools to which most Conservative Ministers send their children not covered by the tests at all? Ministers know perfectly well that private schools do not want them, and they will not have to accept them—one role for schools that the Government favour and another for the rest. That is hypocritical as well as dogmatic.

Fresh from those triumphs, the Secretary of State for Education is on a collision course again with parents, teachers and head teachers, with his threats to end graduate status for primary school teachers—ideas much more associated with the last century than with the next. When will the Government learn that the teaching profession is the fundamental profession? It should be strengthened, supported and encouraged—not threatened, undermined and abused.

Dr. Robert Spink (Castle Point): What is the right hon. and learned Gentleman's view on testing? Would he abandon the three children in 10 who leave school still unable to read and write properly? How does he intend to drive up education standards? What is his education policy?

Mr. Smith: There is a perfectly good case for sensible tests agreed with the teaching profession and with parents —as is occurring in another part of this country which is not England or Wales, but which happens to be governed by the same Government. That is how the issue is being approached there, and there is no reason why the same cannot be done in England and Wales. It is not the principle of testing that is in question but the ham-handed, arrogant and foolish way in which this incompetent Government have handled it.

What possible justification can there be for the absurdities being proposed in the name of rail privatisation? What on earth makes the Government so determined to scorn the opinions of transport experts and of nearly every member of the travelling public? Hardly a day goes by without more evidence of the cost, folly and dangers of the Government's privatisation plans.

The latest assessment by Steer Davies Gleave, a transport consultancy that the Government themselves use, shows that the operating costs of a privatised rail network are likely to be £500 million more than the existing system. A Government in the grip of the privatisation virus appear immune to such compelling evidence.

Mr. David Tredinnick (Bosworth): Were not the same arguments deployed against bus privatisation, which has been an overwhelming success?

Mr. Smith: I do wonder about the Conservative party. One does not have carefully to prepare traps for it—it invents its own. Is the hon. Gentleman aware of what the people of this country think about bus privatisation? I dare say that he has not been on a bus for some time.

Even worse, this week ABB Transportation, better known as British Rail Engineering Ltd., announced 900 redundancies because of a shortage of new orders amid the uncertainties of rail privatisation. That company is the only British rolling stock manufacturer that makes all its components here in Britain. Thus is delivered a further blow to British manufacturing capacity and to the skills that are needed to sustain it.

We know from other privatisation examples that the principal victims of the process are British suppliers—whether it is coal equipment, buses or trains. If we lose manufacturing capacity at York, Crewe and Derby, the inevitable result is that future rolling stock, whether for the national railway system or for London Underground, will have to be purchased abroad, adding a further dangerous twist to our already serious balance of payments deficit.

We hear platitudes from the Prime Minister about his concern for manufacturing industry, but his policies do it the most deadly damage. Evidence of that is vividly shown not just in public finances, serous though they are, but in two other crucial aspects of economic performance—high and continuingly high unemployment, and a dangerous balance of payments deficit.

Britain has the worst deficit of the Group of Seven leading industrial countries. Most alarming of all, even after the last Tory record-breaking recession, there was a balance of payments surplus of £6·7 billion at the end of the cycle. This year, as we struggle for recovery, we face an enormous £17·5 billion deficit—which, according to the Budget, is forecast to be even worse in 1994, at £18·5 billion.

That simply reflects 14 years of neglect of Britain's manufacturing sector. In sector after sector, there really is no adequate British industrial capability. Our economy is too small to be able to create the wealth on which we need to rely. As Goldman Sachs commented in its latest economic review—it put it quite well—the British economy has suffered from

"an apparently permanent shift in the structure of the economy towards excess consumption and away from manufacturing, investment, exports and employment"—

all the things that really matter to a successful economy.

That is the key problem with the British economy. All the other depressing symptoms that we have to consider flow from that central cause. That is why we need a wholly new start in economic policies, not just a shuffle of personalities. It was deeply depressing that the need for a new approach was totally ignored by the Chancellor of the Exchequer when he breezily appeared on Radio 4 this morning.

What we need is what the Opposition have long argued for—an industrial policy that recognises that Britain's fundamental wealth creator is our manufacturing industry, and that supports it by the encouragement of sustained investment in new technology, research and development, regional policy and, above all the skills of our work force.

Dr. Spink: Will the right hon. and learned Gentleman give way?

Mr. Smith: I have given way already.

It is depressing that, as today's *Financial Times* reports, a Department of Trade and Industry study shows that United Kingdom companies spend significantly less than our competitors on research and development, and it is extremely worrying that the United Kingdom share of United States patents has fallen from 10 per cent. in 1980 to 6 per cent. in 1991.

No wonder that, when *Management Today,* in its latest issue, asked leading industrialists whether they felt that the Government had a clearly defined industrial policy, 90 per cent. said no. When they were asked whether they believed that the present Government's policy was the most effective for United Kingdom industry, again 90 per cent. said no. They understand that the purpose of an industrial policy is to co-ordinate to maximum effect investment, regional development, technological improvement and export performance. We believe that to be vital; it is, after all, what other successful countries do.

We need a new approach to tackle Britain's intolerable level of unemployment. Do not the Government yet realise that the biggest drain on our public finances is the cost of the unemployment that they have created—£9,000 a year for every person unemployed? It is the greatest misery in modern Britain—for individuals, families and whole communities—and, perhaps worst of all, a massive waste of invaluable human resources. We need action on unemployment, and we need it now.

I again ask the Government to act to help our beleaguered construction industry. Why do not the Government do what we and so many others have urged and allow local authorities to spend their own capital receipts on house building and house improvement programmes, helping both the homeless and the hundreds of thousands of unemployed construction workers? Once re-employed, those workers will start to pay taxes instead of drawing benefits, and companies will make profits on which they will pay taxes, rather than declaring losses on which they pay no tax at all.

This policy is backed by the construction industries, local authorities, the Institute of Housing and many City commentators. Midland Montagu has urged the Government

"to leap at the opportunity of adopting a policy full of common sense and compassion that efficiently targets the homeless, the housing market, the construction industry, and the South East."

All we have heard from the Government is the usual dogmatic and obstinate refusal.

It is no wonder that the Government have slumped in popularity. According to the front page of today's *Daily Telegraph*—on which I rely for my information about the Conservative party—senior Tories on the 1922 Committee executive are to hold an inquest on the failure of the ex-Chancellor's sacking to halt the biggest slump in morale since the Profumo affair 30 years ago. No doubt the Prime Minister will dismiss this too as scaremongering, but as a principal participant in the Profumo affair might have said, "He would say that, wouldn't he?"

But he knows, does he not, the menace of these men in grey suits? After all, he was the beneficiary of their deadly manoeuvres against his predecessor—although he no doubt reflects that, while it took 10 years to move against her, after only 12 months they have him in their sights. If I were he, I would worry most if they sought to reassure me. Most of all, I would worry if they sought to show their solidarity with a man in a spot of bother by giving him a present—perhaps a watch inscribed, "Don't let the buggers get you down." After all, it appears to be a coded message that it is time for an early and a swift departure.

The Prime Minister cannot complain about the giving of a watch. He himself says that it is not a hanging offence. What we know, from the botched reshuffle and the abrupt dismissal of the former Chancellor, is that a hanging offence in this curious Government is loyally to carry out the Prime Minister's own policies, especially to the accompaniment of effusive declarations of his support.

The British people deserve a better Government, for they dislike intensely the concoction of betrayal, incompetence and dogmatism which are the characteristics of the present occupants of the Treasury Bench. What people are beginning to dislike just as much is the low ambition that these people have for our country.

The people of Britain do not want the low-skill, sweatshop economy which is the miserable Tory response to the challenge of competiton from Europe and the wider world. What they want is for us to become a high-skill, high-tech, high-wage economy, able to compete with the best and to succeed on the basis of our ability and the quality of our products in the markets of the world.

Mr. David Shaw: What are you frightened about? Why will you not answer a question on the nepotism and corruption on Monklands district council? *[Interruption.]*

Madam Speaker: Order. Unless the hon. Gentleman resumes his seat and stays there, I shall take disciplinary action against him.

Mr. Smith: The people of Britain do not want any more years of high and debilitating unemployment, which destroys opportunity, squanders talent and wastes our resources. They want economic policies which support steady growth and rising employment, and which give our young people a chance to succeed.

The people of Britain do not want to see competition and dogma in the classroom. They want the best possible

[*Mr. Smith*]

education for their children in properly resourced schools from teachers whose vital contribution is valued, not scorned.

They do not want the ever-increasing commercialisation of their health service. They want once again to feel secure in the knowledge that, when it is needed, they will be able to obtain the care that they and their families need at the time that it is required.

The people of Britain do not want a Government who twist and turn, who betray their promises and dishonour their pledges. Above all, they want a Government that they can trust. No amount of reshuffling, repackaging or re-presentation can now disguise from the British people the stark reality of a discredited Government, presided over by a discredited Prime Minister.

4.33 pm

The Prime Minister (Mr. John Major): I beg to move, to leave out from 'House' to the end of the Question and to add instead thereof:

'welcomes the widespread indications of economic recovery in the United Kingdom at a time when many other major economies are in deepening recession; recognises that the interests of industry are at the heart of the Government's policy and acknowledges the comprehensive programme of training and employment opportunities for unemployed people that the Government has put in place; welcomes the Government's commitment to its Manifesto pledges including its commitment to improving the efficiency and effectiveness of public services through the Citizen's Charter; deplores the scare-mongering stories about public spending peddled by the Opposition; and applauds the Government for its determination to maintain low inflation, sound public finances and firm control over total public expenditure upon which a sustainable economic recovery depends.'.

As the right hon. and learned Member for Monklands, East (Mr. Smith) sits down, I have little doubt what is in his mind: "That'll keep John Edmonds quiet for a week or so."

Before I turn to the substance of the debate, I wish to say a word or two to my right hon. Friend the Member for Kingston upon Thames (Mr. Lamont) regarding his remarks at the commencement of today's debate. In his speech, my right hon. Friend spoke of a number of matters of very great importance, including the case that we have discussed on many occasions over the past two years for an independent central bank.

I share my right hon. Friend's loathing of inflation. That is an issue that we discussed frequently. We both saw the case for an independent central bank, able to take decisions on the implementation of monetary policy. There is a genuine case for that. I do not dissent from my right hon. Friend's remarks about it.

The very real concern that I have always faced is one that I believe is spread widely across the House: the need for accountability to Parliament for decisions on monetary policy matters. Were a way to be found to get the benefits of an independent central bank without the loss of parliamentary accountability, my views would be very close to those of my right hon. Friend, but I have to say to my right hon. Friend—I believe, from our many discussions, that it is a view he shares—that what is more important than the institutional arrangements is the underlying policy that is actually being followed. On that, I do not believe that an independent central bank would have brought down inflation any more rapidly than we

have been able to achieve. [*Interruption.*] That is something for which I am happy to pay tribute to my right hon. Friend.

Also, I entirely share my right hon. Friend's vision of the economic goals of this Government—[*Interruption.*]—and of the difficult path that we have had to follow to achieve and maintain low inflation and restore sustainable growth—[*Interruption.*]—and employment. My right hon. Friend and I—[*Interruption.*]

Madam Speaker: Order. The House must settle down. Hon. Members do not have to listen, but whoever is speaking has to be heard. There is a great distinction between those two statements. The Prime Minister.

The Prime Minister: My right hon. Friend and I faced crises both before and after September last year. We worked together towards objectives that we shared, and we were always agreed as to our main goals: low inflation, sustainable economic growth, an increase in prosperity for all our people as medium and long-term objectives. I believe that history will look favourably on my right hon. Friend's economic and financial skills, but a strong Government need political skills as well—[*Interruption.*]—when leading a democratic society and, in particular, when handling a lively House of Commons with a small majority.

Dealing with the problems of a small majority is a fundamental fact of democracy that no one dare or should even attempt to overlook. However, as we have shown in the battle over inflation and in our pursuit of European policy, against great difficulties in this House, we were not prepared in the Government to allow short-term difficulties to deflect us from what were the right long-term policies for this country. That was the position, and it is the position.

I am grateful to my right hon. Friend for his support and help throughout the past two and half difficult years. I acknowledge the difficulties that he has faced and the courage with which he has faced those difficulties, and I accept the support that he has offered to the Government for the future. I welcome the opportunity to debate economic policies at a time when output is up, exports are up, productivity is up, confidence is up and, as announced today, when business starts are up.

The right hon. and learned Member for Monklands, East has just made the speech that we expected of him. At the end of it, we are no better informed about his economic policies than we were at the beginning of it—or even about whether he has any economic policies or whether he has progressed beyond the sound bites that so frequently construct them.

We do know something about the right hon. and learned Gentleman. We know that he is the man who announced the biggest tax increase in peacetime history, just before the general election. He is the man who said confidence would carry on falling, just before the CBI announced the highest level of confidence in 10 years, and he is the man who calls for a debate on the economy just as the economy is recovering. I hope that, with timing like that, the right hon. and learned Gentleman never takes up boxing, because it would be very painful. Many things can be said about him, but "floats like a butterfly, stings like a bee" is clearly not among them.

What does seem right about the right hon. and learned Gentleman was said by the right hon. Member for

Richard Shepherd – a one-man awkward squad who put constituents first but did not become Speaker

After 35 years as a BBC journalist, **Martin Bell** had become one of the most familiar faces of television news. But he became the story not the conduit for it when only weeks before the 1997 general election he announced that he was standing as an Independent anti-sleaze candidate in the safe Conservative constituency of Tatton.

The Labour and Liberal Democrat parties declared that they would not field candidates against him. He took the seat from the sitting MP, Neil Hamilton, picking up over 60 per cent. of the vote, overturning a Conservative majority of over 22,000, and winning by 11,000 votes.

As a reporter he had worn a white suit. He had campaigned for election wearing a white suit, and when he made his maiden speech in the House of Commons, he wore a white suit. It had become his trade mark.

His intention as the MP for Tatton was to sit for only one Parliament. When the 2001 general election was called, he refused to stand again for the seat. However, with the campaign under way, he was back on the stump, again taking on the Conservatives but this time in the Essex seat of Brentwood and Ongar. It was suggested that a religious cult had infiltrated the local party there. In spite of winning nearly 32 per cent. of the vote, and seeing the Tory majority slump from over 9,600 to 2,821, he failed to dislodge the sitting MP.

His final foray into politics was in 2004 when he stood as an Independent in the European elections for the Eastern region of England, but he captured only a low percentage of the vote and failed to get elected.

Throughout his relatively brief political career, his personal manifesto was to champion honesty in politics and to fight corruption. During the cash for peerages controversy in 2006, he wrote to the Prime Minister, Tony Blair, asking him to suspend all appointments to the House of Lords.

Martin Bell began his career with the BBC in Norfolk in 1962. Three years later, he moved to the BBC in London, and was soon on his first foreign assignment, in Ghana. In the course of his career, he covered stories in more than 80 countries, but he was best known for his work as a war correspondent, reporting on 11 conflicts. After Ghana, he was sending news back from the war in Vietnam, and he went on to do the same in El Salvador, the Middle East, Nigeria, Angola and Rwanda, as well as Northern Ireland.

It was while he was delivering a bulletin in Bosnia in 1992 that he was hit by shrapnel from a mortar fired by the Serbian forces. As he lay in agony, badly wounded, viewers might have feared that they were witnessing the end of his reporting career. Not so. Back on his feet, he continued working for the BBC for the next five years, mainly in Bosnia, leaving the corporation only to fight the 1997 election and take his seat in Parliament.

During his career he won the Royal Television Society's award as reporter of the year, in 1977 and 1993. He was given the OBE in 1992.

He retired, describing himself as too old for politics and journalism, but he remains an ambassador for UNICEF, a role that, once again, has taken him around the globe.

Speech that expressed Commons ideals and traditions at their best

BY MARTIN BELL OBE

I had the honour to be elected in unusual circumstances and to represent the people of Tatton in the House of Commons for four years.

I entered the House, knowing little about it, with a certain reverence for it as an institution. I still feel that reverence, up to a point. It is the only expression of the will of the people that we have at the national level. But as time went by I became increasingly dismayed by the damage that in my view was being done to the House by its own Members, their willingness in too many cases to vote for measures they did not believe in and against those that they did, their acquiescence to the demands of party and the creeping surrender of their powers to the ever-encroaching Executive.

I was elected on an issue of public trust in public life. And concerns about that issue are as acute now as they were then — perhaps even more so.

I had no party, which was a great advantage; I voted for or against the Bills and clauses that came before us on what I perceived to be their merits, doubtless making many mistakes along the way; and I made friends on both sides of the House, chiefly among those MPs who are generally and loosely termed the "awkward squad".

Richard Shepherd, MP for Aldridge-Brownhills, is a one man "awkward squad" on the Conservative Benches. He does not flinch from voting against his party when he believes it is wrong – which has not exactly been a career enhancing practice – he puts the interests of his constituents first and is a truly honourable Member of the House: also, by his very presence, a standing reproach to those who are more obedient to the Whips. So when I was asked, as an Independent, to propose him for the Speakership in the election of October 2000, I had no hesitation in doing so. It was a privilege.

It was an excellent debate, un-whipped, mostly non-partisan and notable for the unusual presence of the Prime Minister, Tony Blair, throughout. In a short speech proposing the MP for Aldridge-Brownhills, I quoted Peter Wentworth, a great parliamentarian in the reign of Elizabeth the First, who criticised the subservience of the House to the power of the Executive, which then was represented by the Crown: "There is nothing so necessary to the preservation of the prince and the state as free speech, and without it, it is a scorn and a mockery to call it a Parliament House, for in truth it is none but a very school of flattery and dissimulation".

Tony Wright, the respected and free-spirited Labour MP for Cannock, seconded the nomination: "I commend my hon Friend to the House because I believe that the moment has arrived for a shock to the system...It is no good talking afterwards about the glories of Parliament and the need for reform, unless we are prepared now to administer the shock to the system".

Unfortunately, our fellow Members were not prepared to administer a shock to the system. They voted by a substantial majority for someone else. But Richard Shepherd, when he submitted his name for consideration, gave a speech to the House that seemed to me then, and seems to me still, to express the very best of its ideals and traditions. So it earns a place in the Hansard centenary volume.

[Mr. Martin Bell]

For that, the Queen had him locked up in the Tower of London the next day.

The cause is less conspicuous now, but the need is as urgent as it ever was to restore the dignity and reputation of the House. I believe that there is a man who, as Speaker, would be eminently well qualified to do the job. That man is the hon. Member for Aldridge-Brownhills and I commend his name to the House.

8.40 pm

Tony Wright (Cannock Chase): It gives me great pleasure to second the nomination of the hon. Member for Aldridge-Brownhills (Mr. Shepherd). If I may breach a parliamentary convention, I shall call him my hon. Friend, because we have campaigned together on causes that should engage everyone in the House. He is concerned about the rights of citizens, and he campaigns against official secrecy, to protect whistleblowers, and for the freedom of information.

I remember above all an occasion in the last Parliament when Sir Richard Scott had delivered his devastating report, alleging that Ministers had behaved as they should not have behaved. That produced a motion of censure in the House. It was a difficult moment because it required hon. Members to choose between Parliament, accountability, sovereignty—all those fine words that we use—and the pressures of party, Whips and discipline. On that day, two hon. Members in the Government party voted for Parliament, and one of them was the person whom I am seconding. He does not just talk about the rights of Parliament; he protects those rights and asserts them when it matters.

If one theme has been constant throughout the contributions, including those by all the candidates, it is that something is wrong with the House of Commons that must be put right. The question before the House is: how determined is it to put that right?

I commend my hon. Friend to the House because I believe that the moment has arrived for a shock to the system. Whatever else my hon. Friend would be, he would be a shock to the system. Either hon. Members believe that we have reached a point when a shock is required, or they believe that business as usual will do. That is the choice. This institution has arrived at that moment. It is no good saying that it will be the job of some future Speaker whom we may elect to put matters right. The job of putting them right rests with all of us in the House now. It is no good talking afterwards about the glories of Parliament and the need for reform, unless we are prepared now to administer the shock to the system that may produce that change.

I know that the person whom I am recommending is said to be an outsider. My goodness, he is. He is as far away from the usual channels as it is possible to get, and that is why I recommend him to hon. Members.

Sir Edward Heath: Mr. Richard Shepherd has been proposed and seconded. I now invite him to submit himself to the House if he so wishes.

8.44 pm

Mr. Richard Shepherd (Aldridge-Brownhills): In a sense, I am the least qualified of all the candidates who have stood in front of hon. Members today. In fact, my disqualifications fill a long sheet. I am one of the few Conservative Members to have lost the Whip. I have tried to vote against my party when I thought that it was wrong. It is claimed that I am emotional, and it is true that in Parliament I am emotional. I am emotional because I profoundly believe in the purpose of the House, and I think that that view is shared by many people. I hope that in that emotionalism I have used argument, reason, principle and conscience. Those are things that I think unite many Members.

In a sense, the House is experiencing a crisis. With the redevelopment of our constitution, we are in a remarkable state—a state in which the House of Lords, no less, is more vital and more vibrant, and checks authority and the executive power more meaningfully than is done here. How can it be that we, the elected representatives of the people, no longer effectively challenge Government? That is what we are asking people to reflect on.

I sense a great discontent among ourselves, on both sides of the House. We do not discuss measures that are timely, or matters that are important. We had only one Standing Order No. 24 emergency debate during the eight years in which the previous Speaker was Speaker. How can we be timely? How can we reflect the needs of those who sent us here?

I am mindful that I can stand in this House on equal terms with anyone—with a head of Government, with a Minister—because I, like such people, have been elected by an individual constituency. We should never forget that that is the first trust that sends us here.

To whom do we owe our allegiance? My party is very vigorous in trying to get rid of people, and a long time ago when it was trying to get rid of Winston Churchill, he was asked to whom he owed his allegiance. He said first to his country, then to his constituency, and thirdly to his party.

When party becomes so aggressive that it consumes our conscience—when we no longer discuss the politics that are the laws that form the way in which we live; when we accept that the House of Lords will now be dealing with legislation and the points that we raise with regard to that legislation, and that ultimately the Executive will deal not with us, the elected representatives, but with the appointees who now sit at the other end of this Parliament—there is a crisis, in a sense. We ought to assert and affirm that our first intent is to represent those who sent us here.

I have seen Members on both sides of the House in both Lobbies—I have been through more than one Lobby on occasions such as this—whose tears have flowed, and whose conscience has been sensitive; yet they have voted against issues that they have stood for during their parliamentary careers.

The right hon. Member for Chesterfield (Mr. Benn) said that he was leaving this place to take up politics. Most of us came here because we believed in politics. We believed that this was the fulcrum where we could dispose of the business of our country. If I am given the honour of representing this House, I want to ensure that each one of us—wherever we come from, and whomever we represent—is able to do just that.

Question put, That the amendment be made:—

The House divided: Ayes 136, Noes 282.

Division No. 309]   **[8.48 pm**

AYES

Ainsworth, Peter *(E Surrey)*
Arbuthnot, Rt Hon James
Atkinson, David *(Bour'mth E)*
Atkinson, Peter *(Hexham)*
Baker, Norman
Ballard, Jackie
Bell, Martin *(Tatton)*
Bercow, John
Blunt, Crispin
Body, Sir Richard
Boswell, Tim
Bradley, Peter *(The Wrekin)*
Brady, Graham
Brake, Tom
Brazier, Julian
Brooke, Rt Hon Peter
Browning, Mrs Angela
Bruce, Ian *(S Dorset)*
Burnett, John
Butterfill, John
Campbell, Ronnie *(Blyth V)*
Cash, William
Cawsey, Ian
Chapman, Sir Sydney
   (Chipping Barnet)
Chidgey, David
Chope, Christopher
Clappison, James
Clark, Rt Hon Dr David *(S Shields)*
Collins, Tim
Cooper, Yvette
Cotter, Brian
Curry, Rt Hon David
Dalyell, Tam
Davies, Rt Hon Denzil *(Llanelli)*
Davies, Quentin *(Grantham)*
Davis, Rt Hon David *(Haltemprice)*
Day, Stephen
Donaldson, Jeffrey
Duncan, Alan
Duncan Smith, Iain
Emery, Rt Hon Sir Peter
Faber, David
Fearn, Ronnie
Fisher, Mark
Flynn, Paul
Fraser, Christopher
George, Andrew *(St Ives)*
Gibb, Nick
Gill, Christopher
Gillan, Mrs Cheryl
Gorman, Mrs Teresa
Gorrie, Donald
Gray, James
Green, Damian
Grieve, Dominic
Hague, Rt Hon William
Hamilton, Rt Hon Sir Archie
Hayes, John
Horam, John
Howarth, Gerald *(Aldershot)*
Jackson, Robert *(Wantage)*
Jenkin, Bernard
Jones, Dr Lynne *(Selly Oak)*
Key, Robert

King, Rt Hon Tom *(Bridgwater)*
Kirkbride, Miss Julie
Lait, Mrs Jacqui
Lansley, Andrew
Leigh, Edward
Lewis, Dr Julian *(New Forest E)*
Lidington, David
Lilley, Rt Hon Peter
Lloyd, Rt Hon Sir Peter *(Fareham)*
Loughton, Tim
Luff, Peter
McCartney, Robert *(N Down)*
McIntosh, Miss Anne
MacKay, Rt Hon Andrew
Maclean, Rt Hon David
McLoughlin, Patrick
Major, Rt Hon John
Maples, John
Marshall–Andrews, Robert
Mawhinney, Rt Hon Sir Brian
Mitchell, Austin
Morgan, Alasdair *(Galloway)*
Mullin, Chris
Nicholls, Patrick
Oaten, Mark
Öpik, Lembit
Paterson, Owen
Pearson, Ian
Pickles, Eric
Prior, David
Radice, Rt Hon Giles
Randall, John
Robertson, Laurence
Robinson, Peter *(Belfast E)*
Rooker, Rt Hon Jeff
Ruffley, David
Russell, Bob *(Colchester)*
St Aubyn, Nick
Salmond, Alex
Sayeed, Jonathan
Sheerman, Barry
Sheldon, Rt Hon Robert
Shephard, Rt Hon Mrs Gillian
Shepherd, Richard
Simpson, Alan *(Nottingham S)*
Simpson, Keith *(Mid–Norfolk)*
Smyth, Rev Martin *(Belfast S)*
Spicer, Sir Michael
Steen, Anthony
Stunell, Andrew
Swayne, Desmond
Syms, Robert
Tapsell, Sir Peter
Taylor, Ian *(Esher & Walton)*
Taylor, John M *(Solihull)*
Thompson, William
Todd, Mark
Tonge, Dr Jenny
Townend, John
Tredinnick, David
Trend, Michael
Tyrie, Andrew
Walter, Robert
Waterson, Nigel
Wells, Bowen

Whittingdale, John
Widdecombe, Rt Hon Miss Ann
Wilkinson, John
Wilshire, David
Winterton, Mrs Ann *(Congleton)*
Winterton, Nicholas *(Macclesfield)*

Wright, Tony *(Cannock)*

Tellers for the Ayes:
  Sir Teddy Taylor and
  Mr. Eric Forth.

NOES

Adams, Mrs Irene *(Paisley N)*
Ainsworth, Robert *(Cov'try NE)*
Alexander, Douglas
Anderson, Janet *(Rossendale)*
Ashton, Joe
Banks, Tony
Barnes, Harry
Barron, Kevin
Bayley, Hugh
Beard, Nigel
Begg, Miss Anne
Benn, Hilary *(Leeds C)*
Benn, Rt Hon Tony *(Chesterfield)*
Benton, Joe
Bermingham, Gerald
Best, Harold
Betts, Clive
Blears, Ms Hazel
Blizzard, Bob
Boateng, Rt Hon Paul
Borrow, David
Bradley, Keith *(Withington)*
Brown, Rt Hon Gordon
  (Dunfermline E)
Brown, Rt Hon Nick *(Newcastle E)*
Brown, Russell *(Dumfries)*
Browne, Desmond
Bruce, Malcolm *(Gordon)*
Buck, Ms Karen
Burden, Richard
Burgon, Colin
Burstow, Paul
Byers, Rt Hon Stephen
Cable, Dr Vincent
Campbell, Alan *(Tynemouth)*
Campbell, Mrs Anne *(C'bridge)*
Campbell, Rt Hon Menzies
  (NE Fife)
Campbell–Savours, Dale
Canavan, Dennis
Casale, Roger
Caton, Martin
Chapman, Ben *(Wirral S)*
Chisholm, Malcolm
Clapham, Michael
Clark, Dr Lynda
  (Edinburgh Pentlands)
Clarke, Eric *(Midlothian)*
Clarke, Rt Hon Tom *(Coatbridge)*
Clarke, Tony *(Northampton S)*
Clelland, David
Clwyd, Ann
Coaker, Vernon
Coffey, Ms Ann
Coleman, Iain
Connarty, Michael
Cook, Rt Hon Robin *(Livingston)*
Corbyn, Jeremy
Corston, Jean
Cox, Tom
Crausby, David
Cummings, John
Cunningham, Jim *(Cov'try S)*
Darling, Rt Hon Alistair
Darvill, Keith
Davey, Edward *(Kingston)*

Davey, Valerie *(Bristol W)*
Davidson, Ian
Davies, Geraint *(Croydon C)*
Davis, Rt Hon Terry
  (B'ham Hodge H)
Dawson, Hilton
Dean, Mrs Janet
Denham, John
Dismore, Andrew
Dobbin, Jim
Dobson, Rt Hon Frank
Donohoe, Brian H
Doran, Frank
Dowd, Jim
Drew, David
Eagle, Angela *(Wallasey)*
Eagle, Maria *(L'pool Garston)*
Edwards, Huw
Efford, Clive
Ellman, Mrs Louise
Ennis, Jeff
Etherington, Bill
Fitzpatrick, Jim
Flint, Caroline
Foster, Don *(Bath)*
Foster, Michael Jabez *(Hastings)*
Foster, Michael J *(Worcester)*
Foulkes, George
Gapes, Mike
Gardiner, Barry
Gerrard, Neil
Gidley, Sandra
Gilroy, Mrs Linda
Goggins, Paul
Graham, Thomas
Griffiths, Nigel *(Edinburgh S)*
Griffiths, Win *(Bridgend)*
Grocott, Bruce
Hall, Mike *(Weaver Vale)*
Hall, Patrick *(Bedford)*
Hamilton, Fabian *(Leeds NE)*
Hancock, Mike
Hanson, David
Harman, Rt Hon Ms Harriet
Heal, Mrs Sylvia
Healey, John
Heath, David *(Somerton & Frome)*
Henderson, Doug *(Newcastle N)*
Henderson, Ivan *(Harwich)*
Hepburn, Stephen
Heppell, John
Hodge, Ms Margaret
Hood, Jimmy
Hope, Phil
Howarth, George *(Knowsley N)*
Hoyle, Lindsay
Hughes, Ms Beverley *(Stretford)*
Hughes, Kevin *(Doncaster N)*
Humble, Mrs Joan
Hutton, John
Iddon, Dr Brian
Illsley, Eric
Jamieson, David
Jenkins, Brian
Johnson, Miss Melanie
  (Welwyn Hatfield)
Jones, Rt Hon Barry *(Alyn)*
Jones, Mrs Fiona *(Newark)*

Winston Churchill announces that Britain will build the hydrogen bomb

Stuart Bell had at one time set his sights on a career in the House of Commons, but not as a Member of Parliament. An ambition was to become a Hansard reporter, and he learnt shorthand at Pitman's College where he attained a speed of 150 words per minute. He never did get a job reporting speeches in the House, but, having won the seat of Middlesbrough in the 1983 general election, he found himself making them instead.

He joined the Labour party in 1964, stood as parliamentary candidate at Hexham in 1979, and became a member of Newcastle City Council in 1980. He became a barrister in 1970 and specialised in international law. When elected to the Commons he was appointed Parliamentary Private Secretary to the deputy leader of the party, Roy Hattersley. He held a series of Front-Bench positions in Opposition, including being a spokesman on Northern Ireland and on Trade and Industry.

He comes from the pit village of High Spen in north-west Durham where his father worked as a miner. His first job on leaving grammar school was as a clerk in the Chopwell colliery office. He stayed there for nine months after which he joined the local *Blaydon Courier,* his first foray into the world of print. At the age of 18 he travelled south to London where he worked briefly as copytaker for *The Daily Telegraph.* Later he took a job as typist and shorthand-typist in a City of London employment agency. During his four years there he wrote freelance newspaper articles for *Weekend Mail* and *Reveille.*

His great ambition was to write, first as a newspaper reporter and then as an author. He studied shorthand at Pitman's college for 18 months but then left Britain to live in Paris. It was at that time that he wrote his first book of short stories and four novels. Like so many aspiring authors, he realised that the income from his work would enable him to starve so he took a job with an American attorney, first as a secretary and then as a collaborator. He read for the Bar in his spare time. Eventually, he joined Grays Inn and was called to the Bar in 1970. He then entered private practice in international law in Paris before returning to England in 1977 to pursue a full-time career in politics. He set aside his legal practice on becoming the Member for Middlesbrough.

He was knighted in the 2003 new year's honours list and is the Second Church Estates Commissioner, which involves representing the Church of England in the House of Commons and answering questions on the Floor of the House. He ranks as one of the longest serving holders of the post, having occupied it since 1997.

He is a member of the House of Commons Commission, the body that is chaired by the Speaker and oversees the non-political running of the House and its staff. He is also chairman of the Finance and Services Committee, a Select Committee of the House that keeps watch on behalf of the Commission on the administrative expenditure of the House departments. He is also a member of the Liaison Committee and the Members Estimate Committee.

His career as a writer has continued. He has published a series of novels and short story collections, amounting to nine books, as well as numerous political tracts and a political book on the European Union in the run up to the Lisbon Treaty 2008

He retains close links with France. He sits on the supervisory board of the Fondation pour l'Innovation Politique in Paris, has chaired many Franco-British conferences and is Chairman of the Franco-British Inter-Parliamentary Committee. In 2006, he was awarded the Legion d'Honneur, France's highest award for outstanding service to France.

Stirred by Churchillian prose on the bus from Chopwell

By Sir Stuart Bell MP

I left grammar school at 16 and went into the colliery office at Chopwell in north west Durham, locally known as Little Moscow because it had been the reddest village in England during the 1926 general strike. My ambition had not been to be a colliery clerk but a newspaper reporter and at the colliery institute I was able to read to such weighty newspapers as *The Manchester Guardian*.

On 2 March 1955 I was asked to take a bus to Durham to post a letter in the local post office. The office should have sent a letter for deadline arrival that day at the headquarters of the National Union of Mineworkers, but we were a day late and the senior clerk thought if I popped it in the post by midday in Durham it would be delivered that afternoon, such was the efficiency of the post in those days.

Durham is no more than 30 miles from Chopwell as the crow flies, but since I was not a crow I was required to take a bus to Consett and another to Durham. The bus stopped at every stop in every village and the journey took at least two hours, with a wait for the connection.

I armed myself with *The Manchester Guardian*, which carried almost the entire speech that Winston Churchill had made the day before when he introduced his defence budget. In fact, Churchill was announcing that Great Britain was to manufacture a hydrogen bomb: "a grave decision which forms the core of the defence paper which we are discussing this afternoon".

He declared that "the entire foundation of human affairs was revolutionised and mankind placed in a situation both measureless and laden with doom". In true Churchillian fashion, he finished his speech by declaring "never flinch, never weary, never despair".

The sentence that stayed in my mind was when he said it might well be "that we shall, by a process of sublime irony, have reached a stage where safety will be the sturdy shield of terror and survival the twin brother of annihilation".

Perhaps it was the cadence, the prose or the ability to intertwine two concepts that has held my attention all these years. This, however, was the last major speech Churchill would make in the Commons, since he resigned six weeks later to make way for Anthony Eden. He had nothing but kind words for the Russian people, admiration "for their bravery, their many gifts and their kindly nature", but few for communism.

When I reached Durham and enquired of the post office clerk when my duly-posted letter would arrive I was told it would be delivered next morning. My journey had been in vain – but for the rapt attention I had given to Churchill's speech. In later life, as a Labour MP, I would often visit the National Union Mineworkers at Durham and even make speeches surrounded by colliery banners. Each time I thought of the Churchill speech and often wondered if they received the letter.

DEFENCE

3.45 p.m.

The Prime Minister (Sir Winston Churchill): I beg to move,

That this House approves the Statement on Defence, 1955, Command Paper No. 9391.

This Motion stands in my name, and it is supported by my right hon. Friends the Foreign Secretary, the Chancellor of the Exchequer and the Minister of Defence.

We live in a period, happily unique in human history, when the whole world is divided intellectually and to a large extent geographically between the creeds of Communist discipline and individual freedom, and when, at the same time, this mental and psychological division is accompanied by the possession by both sides of the obliterating weapons of the nuclear age.

We have antagonisms now as deep as those of the Reformation and its reactions which led to the Thirty Years' War. But now they are spread over the whole world instead of only over a small part of Europe. We have, to some extent, the geographical division of the Mongul invasion in the thirteenth century, only more ruthless and more thorough. We have force and science, hitherto the servants of man, now threatening to become his master.

I am not pretending to have a solution for a permanent peace between the nations which could be unfolded this afternoon. We pray for it. Nor shall I try to discuss the cold war which we all detest, but have to endure. I shall only venture to offer to the House some observations mainly of a general character on which I have pondered long and which, I hope, may be tolerantly received, as they are intended by me. And here may I venture to make a personal digression? I do not pretend to be an expert or to have technical knowledge of this prodigious sphere of science. But in my long friendship with Lord Cherwell I have tried to follow and even predict the evolution of events. I hope that the House will not reprove me for vanity or conceit if I repeat what I wrote a quarter of a century ago:

" We know enough,"

I said,

" to be sure that the scientific achievements of the next 50 years will be far greater, more rapid and more surprising than those we have already experienced . . . High authorities tell us that new sources of power, vastly more important than any we yet know, will surely be discovered. Nuclear energy is incomparably greater than the molecular energy which we use today. The coal a man can get in a day can easily do 500 times as much work as the man himself. Nuclear energy is at least 1 m. times more powerful still. If the hydrogen atoms in a pound of water could be prevailed upon to combine together and form helium, they would suffice to drive a 1,000 horse-power engine for a whole year. If the electrons—those tiny planets of the atomic systems—were induced to combine with the nuclei in the hydrogen, the horse-power liberated would be 120 times greater still. There is no question among scientists that this gigantic source of energy exists. What is lacking is the match to set the bonfire alight, or it may be the detonator to cause the dynamite to explode."

This is no doubt not quite an accurate description of what has been discovered, but as it was published in the " Strand " Magazine of December, 1931—twenty-four years ago—I hope that my plea to have long taken an interest in the subject may be indulgently accepted by the House.

What is the present position? Only three countries possess, in varying degrees, the knowledge and the power to make nuclear weapons. Of these, the United States is overwhelmingly the chief. Owing to the breakdown in the exchange of information between us and the United States since 1946 we have had to start again independently on our own. Fortunately, executive action was taken promptly by the right hon. Gentleman the Leader of the Opposition to reduce as far as possible the delay in our nuclear development and production. By his initiative we have made our own atomic bombs.

Confronted with the hydrogen bomb, I have tried to live up to the right hon. Gentleman's standard. We have started to make that one, too. It is this grave decision which forms the core of the Defence Paper which we are discussing this afternoon. Although the Soviet stockpile of atomic bombs may be greater than that of Britain, British discoveries may well place us above them in fundamental science.

May I say that for the sake of simplicity and to avoid verbal confusion I use the expression " atomic bombs " and also " hydrogen bombs " instead of " thermo-nuclear " and I keep " nuclear " for the whole lot. There is an immense gulf between the atomic and the hydrogen bomb. The atomic bomb, with all its

[THE PRIME MINISTER.]

terrors, did not carry us outside the scope of human control or manageable events in thought or action, in peace or war. But when Mr. Sterling Cole, the Chairman of the United States Congressional Committee, gave out a year ago—17th February, 1954—the first comprehensive review of the hydrogen bomb, the entire foundation of human affairs was revolutionised, and mankind placed in a situation both measureless and laden with doom.

It is now the fact that a quantity of plutonium, probably less than would fill this Box on the Table—it is quite a safe thing to store—would suffice to produce weapons which would give indisputable world domination to any great Power which was the only one to have it. There is no absolute defence against the hydrogen bomb, nor is any method in sight by which any nation, or any country, can be completely guaranteed against the devastating injury which even a score of them might inflict on wide regions.

What ought we to do? Which way shall we turn to save our lives and the future of the world? It does not matter so much to old people; they are going soon anyway, but I find it poignant to look at youth in all its activity and ardour and, most of all, to watch little children playing their merry games, and wonder what would lie before them if God wearied of mankind.

The best defence would of course be *bona fide* disarmament all round. This is in all our hearts. But sentiment must not cloud our vision. It is often said that " Facts are stubborn things." A renewed session of a sub-committee of the Disarmament Commission is now sitting in London and is rightly attempting to conduct its debates in private. We must not conceal from ourselves the gulf between the Soviet Government and the N.A.T.O. Powers, which has hitherto, for so long, prevented an agreement. The long history and tradition of Russia makes it repugnant to the Soviet Government to accept any practical system of international inspection.

A second difficulty lies in the circumstance that, just as the United States, on the one hand, has, we believe, the overwhelming mastery in nuclear weapons, so the Soviets and their Communist satellites have immense superiority in what are called "conventional" forces—the

sort of arms and forces with which we fought the last war, but much improved. The problem is, therefore, to devise a balanced and phased system of disarmament which at no period enables any one of the participants to enjoy an advantage which might endanger the security of the others. A scheme on these lines was submitted last year by Her Majesty's Government and the French Government and was accepted by the late Mr. Vyshinsky as a basis of discussion. It is now being examined in London.

If the Soviet Government have not at any time since the war shown much nervousness about the American possession of nuclear superiority, that is because they are quite sure that it will not be used against them aggressively, even in spite of many forms of provocation. On the other hand, the N.A.T.O. Powers have been combined together by the continued aggression and advance of Communism in Asia and in Europe. That this should have eclipsed in a few years, and largely effaced, the fearful antagonism and memories that Hitlerism created for the German people is an event without parallel. But it has, to a large extent, happened. There is widespread belief throughout the free world that, but for American nuclear superiority, Europe would already have been reduced to satellite status and the Iron Curtain would have reached the Atlantic and the Channel.

Unless a trustworthy and universal agreement upon disarmament, conventional and nuclear alike, can be reached and an effective system of inspection is established and is actually working, there is only one sane policy for the free world in the next few years. That is what we call defence through deterrents. This we have already adopted and proclaimed. These deterrents may at any time become the parents of disarmament, provided that they deter. To make our contribution to the deterrent we must ourselves possess the most up-to-date nuclear weapons, and the means of delivering them.

That is the position which the Government occupy. We are to discuss this not only as a matter of principle; there are many practical reasons which should be given. Should war come, which God forbid, there are a large number of targets that we and the Americans must be able to strike at once. There are scores of airfields from which the Soviets could launch attacks with hydrogen bombs as soon as they have the bombers to carry them. It is essential to our deterrent policy and to our survival to have, with our American allies, the strength and numbers to be able to paralyse these potential Communist assaults in the first few hours of the war, should it come.

The House will perhaps note that I avoid using the word " Russia " as much as possible in this discussion. I have a strong admiration for the Russian people —for their bravery, their many gifts, and their kindly nature. It is the Communist dictatorship and the declared ambition of the Communist Party and their prose-lytising activities that we are bound to resist, and that is what makes this great world cleavage which I mentioned when I opened my remarks.

There are also big administrative and industrial targets behind the Iron Curtain, and any effective deterrent policy must have the power to paralyse them all at the outset, or shortly after. There are also the Soviet submarine bases and other naval targets which will need early attention. Unless we make a contribution of our own—that is the point which I am pressing—we cannot be sure that in an emergency the resources of other Powers would be planned exactly as we would wish, or that the targets which would threaten us most would be given what we consider the necessary priority, or the deserved priority, in the first few hours.

These targets might be of such cardinal importance that it would really be a matter of life and death for us. All this, I think, must be borne in mind in deciding our policy about the conventional forces, to which I will come later, the existing Services.

Meanwhile, the United States has many times the nuclear power of Soviet Russia—I avoid any attempt to give exact figures—and they have, of course, far more effective means of delivering. Our moral and military support of the United States and our possession of nuclear weapons of the highest quality and on an appreciable scale, together with their means of delivery, will greatly reinforce the deterrent power of the free world, and will strengthen our influence within the free world. That, at any rate, is the policy we have decided to pursue. That is what we are now doing, and I am thankful that it is endorsed by a mass of respon-

sible opinion on both sides of the House, and, I believe, by the great majority of the nation.

A vast quantity of information, some true, some exaggerated much out of proportion, has been published about the hydrogen bomb. The truth has inevitably been mingled with fiction, and I am glad to say that panic has not occurred. Panic would not necessarily make for peace. That is one reason why I have been most anxious that responsible discussions on this matter should not take place on the B.B.C. or upon the television, and I thought that I was justified in submitting that view of Her Majesty's Government to the authorities, which they at once accepted—very willingly accepted.

Panic would not necessarily make for peace even in this country. There are many countries where a certain wave of opinion may arise and swing so furiously into action that decisive steps may be taken from which there is no recall. As it is, the world population goes on its daily journey despite its sombre impression and earnest longing for relief. That is the way we are going on now.

I shall content myself with saying about the power of this weapon, the hydrogen bomb, that apart from all the statements about blast and heat effects over increasingly wide areas there are now to be considered the consequences of "fall out," as it is called, of wind-borne radio-active particles. There is both an immediate direct effect on human beings who are in the path of such a cloud and an indirect effect through animals, grass and vegetables, which pass on these contagions to human beings through food.

This would confront many who escaped the direct effects of the explosion with poisoning, or starvation, or both. Imagination stands appalled. There are, of course, the palliatives and precautions of a courageous Civil Defence, and about that the Home Secretary will be speaking later on tonight. But our best protection lies, as I am sure the House will be convinced, in successful deterrents operating from a foundation of sober, calm and tireless vigilance.

Moreover, a curious paradox has emerged. Let me put it simply. After a certain point has been passed it may be said, " The worse things get the better."

[THE PRIME MINISTER.]

The broad effect of the latest developments is to spread almost indefinitely and at least to a vast extent the area of mortal danger. This should certainly increase the deterrent upon Soviet Russia by putting her enormous spaces and scattered population on an equality or near-equality of vulnerability with our small densely-populated island and with Western Europe.

I cannot regard this development as adding to our dangers. We have reached the maximum already. On the contrary, to this form of attack continents are vulnerable as well as islands. Hitherto, crowded countries, as I have said, like the United Kingdom and Western Europe, have had this outstanding vulnerability to carry. But the hydrogen bomb, with its vast range of destruction and the even wider area of contamination, would be effective also against nations whose population hitherto has been so widely dispersed over large land areas as to make them feel that they were not in any danger at all.

They, too, become highly vulnerable; not yet equally perhaps, but, still, highly and increasingly vulnerable. Here again we see the value of deterrents, immune against surprise and well understood by all persons on both sides—I repeat " on both sides "—who have the power to control events. That is why I have hoped for a long time for a top level conference where these matters could be put plainly and bluntly from one friendly visitor to the conference to another.

Then it may well be that we shall by a process of sublime irony have reached a stage in this story where safety will be the sturdy child of terror, and survival the twin brother of annihilation. Although the Americans have developed weapons capable of producing all the effects I have mentioned, we believe that the Soviets so far have tested by explosion only a type of bomb of intermediate power.

There is no reason why, however, they should not develop some time within the next four, three or even two years more advanced weapons and full means to deliver them on North American targets. Indeed, there is every reason to believe that within that period they will. In trying to look ahead like this we must be careful ourselves to avoid the error of comparing the present state of our preparations with the stage which the Soviets may reach in three or four years' time. It is a major error of thought to contrast the Soviet position three or four years hence with our own position today. It is a mistake to do this, either in the comparatively precise details of aircraft development or in the measureless sphere of nuclear weapons.

The threat of hydrogen attack on these islands lies in the future. It is not with us now. According to the information that I have been able to obtain—I have taken every opportunity to consult all the highest authorities at our disposal—the only country which is able to deliver today a full-scale nuclear attack with hydrogen bombs at a few hours' notice is the United States. That surely is an important fact, and from some points of view and to some of us it is not entirely without comfort.

It is conceivable that Soviet Russia, fearing a nuclear attack before she has caught up with the United States and created deterrents of her own, as she might argue that they are, might attempt to bridge the gulf by a surprise attack with such nuclear weapons as she has already. American superiority in nuclear weapons, reinforced by Britain, must, therefore, be so organised as to make it clear that no such surprise attack would prevent immediate retaliation on a far larger scale. This is an essential of the deterrent policy.

For this purpose, not only must the nuclear superiority of the Western Powers be stimulated in every possible way, but their means of delivery of bombs must be expanded, improved, and varied. It is even probable, though we have not been told about it outside the N.A.T.O. sphere, that a great deal of this has been already done by the United States. We should aid them in every possible way. I will not attempt to go into details, but it is known that bases have been and are being established in as many parts of the world as possible and that over all rest the United States Strategic Air Force, which is in itself a deterrent of the highest order and is in ceaseless readiness.

The Soviet Government probably knows, in general terms, of the policy that is being pursued, and of the present United States strength and our own growing addition to it. Thus, they should be convinced that a surprise attack could not exclude immediate retaliation. As one might say to them, " Although you might kill millions of our peoples, and cause widespread havoc by a surprise attack, we could, within a few hours of this outrage, certainly deliver several indeed many times the weight of nuclear material which you have used, and continue retaliation on that same scale." " We have," we could say, " already hundreds of bases for attack from all angles and have made an intricate study of suitable targets." Thus, it seems to me with some experience of wartime talks, you might go to dinner and have a friendly evening. I should not be afraid to talk things over as far as they can be. This, and the hard facts, would make the deterrent effective.

I must make one admission, and any admission is formidable. The deterrent does not cover the case of lunatics or dictators in the mood of Hitler when he found himself in his final dug-out. That is a blank. Happily, we may find methods of protecting ourselves, if we were all agreed, against that.

All these considerations lead me to believe that, on a broad view, the Soviets would be ill-advised to embark on major aggression within the next three or four years. One must always consider the interests of other people when you are facing a particular situation. Their interests may be the only guide that is available. We may calculate, therefore, that world war will not break out within that time. If, at the end of that time, there should be a supreme conflict, the weapons which I have described this afternoon would be available to both sides, and it would be folly to suppose that they would not be used. Our precautionary dispositions and preparations must, therefore, be based on the assumption that, if war should come, these weapons would be used.

I repeat, therefore, that during the next three or four years the free world should, and will, retain an overwhelming superiority in hydrogen weapons. During that period it is most unlikely that the Russians would deliberately embark on major war or attempt a surprise attack, either of which would bring down upon them at once a crushing weight of nuclear retaliation. In three or four years' time, it may be even less, the scene will be changed. The Soviets will probably stand possessed of hydrogen bombs and the means of delivering them not only on the United Kingdom but also on North American targets. They may then have reached a stage, not indeed of parity with the United States and Britain but of what is called " saturation."

I must explain this term of art. " Saturation " in this connection means the point where, although one Power is stronger than the other, perhaps much stronger, both are capable of inflicting crippling or quasi-mortal injury on the other with what they have got. It does not follow, however, that the risk of war will then be greater. Indeed, it is arguable that it will be less, for both sides will then realise that global war would result in mutual annihilation.

Major war of the future will differ, therefore, from anything we have known in the past in this one significant respect, that each side, at the outset, will suffer what it dreads the most, the loss of everything that it has ever known of. The deterrents will grow continually in value. In the past, an aggressor has been tempted by the hope of snatching an early advantage. In future, he may be deterred by the knowledge that the other side has the certain power to inflict swift, inescapable and crushing retaliation.

Of course, we should all agree that a worldwide international agreement on disarmament is the goal at which we should aim. The Western democracies disarmed themselves at the end of the war. The Soviet Government did not disarm, and the Western nations were forced to rearm, though only partially, after the Soviets and Communists had dominated all China and half Europe. That is the present position. It is easy, of course, for the Communists to say now, " Let us ban all nuclear weapons." Communist ascendancy in conventional weapons would then become overwhelming. That might bring peace, but only peace in the form of the subjugation of the Free World to the Communist system.

I shall not detain the House very much longer, and I am sorry to be so long. The topic is very intricate, I am anxious to repeat and to emphasise the one word which is the theme of my remarks, namely, " Deterrent." That is the main theme.

[THE PRIME MINISTER.]

The hydrogen bomb has made an astounding incursion into the structure of our lives and thoughts. Its impact is prodigious and profound, but I do not agree with those who say, " Let us sweep away forthwith all our existing defence services and concentrate our energy and resources on nuclear weapons and their immediate ancillaries." The policy of the deterrent cannot rest on nuclear weapons alone. We must, together with our N.A.T.O. allies, maintain the defensive shield in Western Europe.

Unless the N.A.T.O. Powers had effective forces there on the ground and could make a front, there would be nothing to prevent piecemeal advance and encroachment by the Communists in this time of so-called peace. By successive infiltrations, the Communists could progressively undermine the security of Europe. Unless we were prepared to unleash a full-scale nuclear war as soon as some local incident occurs in some distant country, we must have conventional forces in readiness to deal with such situations as they arise.

We must, therefore, honour our undertaking to maintain our contribution to the N.A.T.O. forces in Europe in time of peace. In war, this defensive shield would be of vital importance, for we must do our utmost to hold the Soviet and satellite forces at arms' length in order to prevent short-range air and rocket attack on these islands. Thus, substantial strength in conventional forces has still a vital part to play in the policy of the deterrent. It is perhaps of even greater importance in the cold war.

Though world war may be prevented by the deterrent power of nuclear weapons, the Communists may well resort to military action in furtherance of their policy of infiltration and encroachment in many parts of the world. There may well be limited wars on the Korean model, with limited objectives. We must be able to play our part in these, if called upon by the United Nations organisation. In the conditions of today, this is also an aspect of our Commonwealth responsibility. We shall need substantial strength in conventional forces to fulfil our world-wide obligations in these days of uneasy peace and extreme bad temper.

To sum up this part of the argument, of course, the development of nuclear weapons will affect the shape and organisation of the Armed Forces and also of Civil Defence. We have entered a period of transition in which the past and the future will overlap. But it is an error to suppose that, because of these changes, our traditional forces can be cast away or superseded. The tasks of the Army, Navy and Air Force in this transition period are set forth with clarity in the Defence White Paper. The means by which these duties will be met are explained in more detail in the Departmental Papers which have been laid before the House by the three Service Ministers.

No doubt, nothing is perfect ; certainly, nothing is complete, but, considering that these arrangements have been made in the first year after the apparition of the hydrogen bomb, the far-seeing and progressive adaptability which is being displayed by all three Services is remarkable. [HON. MEMBERS: " Oh."] I understand that there is to be a motion of censure. Well, certainly, nothing could be more worthy of censure than to try to use the inevitable administrative difficulties of the transitional stage as a utensil of party politics and would-be electioneering. I am not saying that anyone is doing it ; we shall see when it comes to the vote.

The future shape of Civil Defence is also indicated in broad outline in the Defence White Paper. This outline will be filled in as the preparation of the new plans proceeds, but the need for an effective system of Civil Defence is surely beyond dispute. It presents itself today in its noblest aspect, namely, the Christian duty of helping fellow mortals in distress. Rescue, salvage and ambulance work have always been the core of Civil Defence, and no city, no family nor any honourable man or woman can repudiate this duty and accept from others help which they are not prepared to fit themselves to render in return. If war comes, great numbers may be relieved of their duty by death, but none must deny it as long as they live. If they do, they might perhaps be put in what is called " Coventry." [*Laughter.*] I am speaking of the tradition, and not of any particular locality.

The argument which I have been endeavouring to unfold and consolidate gives us in this island an interlude. Let us not waste it. Let us hope we shall use it to augment or at least to prolong our security and that of mankind. But how? There are those who believe, or at any rate say, "If we have the protection of the overwhelmingly powerful United States, we need not make the hydrogen bomb for ourselves or build a fleet of bombers for its delivery. We can leave that to our friends across the ocean. Our contribution should be criticism of any unwise policy into which they may drift or plunge. We should throw our hearts and consciences into that."

Personally, I cannot feel that we should have much influence over their policy or actions, wise or unwise, while we are largely dependent, as we are today, upon their protection. We, too, must possess substantial deterrent power of our own. We must also never allow, above all, I hold, the growing sense of unity and brotherhood between the United Kingdom and the United States and throughout the English-speaking world to be injured or retarded. Its maintenance, its stimulation and its fortifying is one of the first duties of every person who wishes to see peace in the world and wishes to see the survival of this country.

To conclude, mercifully, there is time and hope if we combine patience and courage. All deterrents will improve and gain authority during the next ten years. By that time, the deterrent may well reach its acme and reap its final reward. The day may dawn when fair play, love for one's fellow men, respect for justice and freedom, will enable tormented generations to march forth serene and triumphant from the hideous epoch in which we have to dwell. Meanwhile, never flinch, never weary, never despair.

4.30 p.m.

Mr. E. Shinwell (Easington): We shall all agree that the right hon. Gentleman has made an impressive speech—one which will undoubtedly make its impact on many millions of people in our country and throughout the world. With many of his sentiments those of us on this side of the House are in full accord. That we should make as our primary objective peace through disarmament has long been the policy of this party, and this policy, upon which the Government, with qualifications, have embarked, should be pursued with the utmost expedition.

Nor should we permit deep-seated prejudices or ideological differences to impede our progress, for it may well be, disliking Communist dictatorship as we all do, that there are some people—I should not say in our country; maybe in Europe and in Northern America and eleswhere—who, despite their intense dislike of totalitarianism, whatever form it assumes, may prefer Communist control to total extinction.

Prejudices must, therefore, be set aside and, in pursuance of our policy of total disarmament—because, as the Prime Minister has stated, nothing less will suffice—we must obviously be prepared to make concessions, as, indeed, the other side must be called upon to do. No rigid doctrinaire attitude, standing on points of punctilio, will do. Of course, we all recognise the difficulties which beset the search for this primary objective and the intransigence of the Soviet representatives at the Disarmament Conference early in the year. We all hope that the present conference will see a change of heart. But there may also be difficulties on our side, or, if not on the side of the United Kingdom, at any rate on the side of the United States of America, for there, as is natural, there is an intense hatred of Communism and all that it means.

I make these preliminary observations, first of all to indicate that we are with the Government in the search for disarmament, and also—I say this with all modesty—as a warning against intransigence on our side, whether from the United Kingdom representatives or from others.

Although the Prime Minister has made an impressive oration, I must say that there was nothing original in what he said. It has all been said before. We have on record the declarations of President Eisenhower. We have the record of the right hon. Gentleman's speeches in 1950, when he spoke from this side of the House about the frightful dangers which would beset the world if the atom bomb were unleashed. I recall that when he spoke to us on that occasion he talked about a speech which he had made in 1948, when he had referred to the same subject. No; there is nothing original in what the right hon. Gentleman said, nor is there anything particularly original——

Mr. David Logan (Liverpool, Scotland Division) *rose*——

Nye Bevan resigns in defence of the NHS, but offers a cold war warning

Tony Benn joined Parliament in 1950, when he won the seat of Bristol, South-East for Labour. He was the "Baby of the House", or youngest MP, at the age of 25. At that time he was known as Anthony Wedgwood Benn, but in 1973 he announced that he wished to be called Tony Benn and, eventually, by the 1980s that was how he came to be known.

He became what many regarded as the standard bearer for the left wing of the Labour party and, took an uncompromising view of what the Labour party stood for. He was Chairman of the party from 1971-72.

Both his grandfathers were Liberal MPs and his father, William, was created the first Viscount Stansgate by Winston Churchill. His parents were married in 1920 at St Margaret's church, Westminster, the parish church of the House of Commons. Herbert Asquith, who had been the Prime Minister at the outbreak of the first world war, witnessed the ceremony.

His mother was a deeply religious woman and a feminist, and in the 1920s, many decades ahead of her time, was a leading campaigner for the ordination of women. She was the first president of the Congregations Federation.

He met his wife Caroline while a student at Oxford and proposed to her nine days later on a park bench in the city. Subsequently, he bought the bench from the city council and relocated it to the garden of his home in London.

When his father died in 1960, Tony Benn inherited the title, his elder brother, Michael, having been killed during the second world war, and he was thus barred from membership of the House of Commons. He nevertheless stood at the ensuing by-election in May 1961 and won the seat, but an election court declared his victory invalid and proclaimed his Conservative opponent to have been elected.

Instrumental in the introduction of the Peerage Bill, he renounced his viscountcy on 31 July 1963—the day on which the Bill received Royal Assent. Before doing so, he had a sample of his blood taken ensuring that, technically, there is still a drop of blue blood in the Benn household.

He regained the seat in August of that year and held it for the ensuing 20 years until it was abolished by boundary changes. He stood for the new seat of Bristol, East, but was defeated. In 1984 he secured the candidacy of the Chesterfield constituency at the by-election when Eric Varley stood down. He represented the seat until he retired.

In the 1960s, he served as Postmaster General in the Wilson Government, before embracing the "white heat" of the technological revolution as Minister of Technology and overseeing Concorde's development. In the 1974-79 Government, he served briefly as Secretary of State for Industry.

After campaigning for a no vote in the referendum on Britain's entry to the EEC, he became Energy Secretary, and moved to the left of the party. His views were consolidated in Opposition in the 1980s and 90s with support for the NUM in the miners' strike and his anti-war stance on the Falklands, Kosovo and the Gulf.

In 2001 — by then, the longest serving Labour MP in the party's history — he retired from Parliament to "devote more time to politics". He opposed the Iraq war, and was elected the first president of the Stop the War coalition in February 2004.

Seven volumes of his diaries have been published, and he has enjoyed sell-out success with his one-man stage show. His second son, Hilary, was elected to represent Leeds, Central in 1999, serving as Secretary of State for International Development and, later, for the Environment.

Speech that was passionate, violent and right, but with a legacy of bitterness

BY RT HON TONY BENN

On 23 April 1951 Aneurin Bevan, then Minister of Labour, resigned from the Cabinet because he disagreed with the introduction of charges for the NHS that had been part of a package of measures in Chancellor of the Exchequer Hugh Gaitskell's budget.

I had been in Parliament for fewer than six months and had just passed my 26th birthday.

It had been clear for some days that there was serious trouble brewing and the possibility of Nye's resignation was much discussed.

At that time the Government had a majority of five following the election of 1950 and it was obvious that a major Cabinet resignation would have serious consequences in the election that was expected, and that did occur, in October 1951.

Nye made his resignation statement at the end of questions as is usual and the atmosphere was absolutely electric. As I wrote in my diary at the time:

> Monday 23 April 1951
> The resignation of Nye was announced this morning. Harold Wilson's position was uncertain though it was announced later today that he too intended to go. I arrived at the Commons at two and went up into the Members' Gallery. With the sunlight pouring through the windows opposite, the Chamber was suffused in a warm glow of light. Jennie Lee came in at about ten past three and sat, flushed and nervous, on the very back-bench, below the gangway. At twenty past three Nye walked in briskly and jauntily and went straight to his seat three rows back. He looked pale and kept shifting his position and rubbing his hands. The Front Benches on both sides were very full — Churchill, Eden and the Tories sat quietly.
>
> Morrison, Chuter Ede, Noel-Baker, Dalton, Gaitskell and the others sat unhappily together. Then the Speaker called Nye Bevan to make his resignation statement.

His rising was greeted by a few 'hear hears'. Not many. The Government Front Bench looked sicker and sicker as the speech went on and the violence of the attack intensified. Jennie Lee behind him sat forward and became more and more flushed. Every now and again he pushed back the lock of his iron-grey hair. He swung on his feet, facing this way and that and his outstretched arm sawed the air. He abused the Government, he threw in a few anti-American rernarks for good measure. He attacked the Treasury, economists, and the unhappy combination of an economist at the Treasury. Gaitskell showed clearly the contempt he felt. Dalton looked like death once warmed up and now cooled down.

The fact is that though there was substance in what he said Nye overplayed his hand. His jokes were in bad taste. I felt slightly sick.

He sat down, the hum of conversation started and the exodus began. Nye stayed put for a few moments. He rose to go, and Emrys Hughes shook his hand as he passed the Front Bench.

It has to be said that he has written the Tory Party's best pamphlet yet. I predict it will be on the streets in a week.

But when I look back on it now I realise that was a very important speech because Nye was not only defending the NHS, which has since then had many more charges imposed, but he was also warning against the cold war which had just emerged as a major issue following the Korean war.

Nye said three things about it which turned out to be true.

First, he said that the Soviet Union did not have the military strength to attack the West; secondly, that it did not wish to do so; and, thirdly, that this would inevitably lead to a witch-hunt against the left.

With the benefit of hindsight, all those predictions have come true. Weakened by the war, the Soviet Union did not have the strength to take on NATO and there is no evidence to believe that they ever intended it.

But the witch-hunt against the left proceeded at a terrifying rate, producing the McCarthy terror in America and very serious attacks in Britain on decent people who were thought to be fellow-travellers with the USSR when they were actually working for peace.

It was Gaitskell's budget which introduced a massive rearmament programme that we did not need, and which triggered inflation, split the Labour party, and cost Labour the election that year, ushering in 13 years of Conservative Government.

His speech, which was passionate and violent in language, may have sickened his colleagues and certainly led to great bitterness by the Bevanites and the right of the party, but Nye was right in what he said. And it was a brilliant parliamentary performance.

BRIXHAM TRAWLER
(LOSS)

Mrs. Middleton (*by Private Notice*) asked the Minister of Transport whether he has any information which he can give to the House concerning the loss of the trawler " Twilit Waters " off the coast of Cornwall between 11th and 20th April.

The Minister of Transport (Mr. Barnes): Yes, Sir. According to reports which have appeared in the Press the motor trawler " Twilit Waters," of 113 tons gross, left Brixham, her port of registry, with a crew of nine on 8th April to fish between Start Point, Devon, and Bishop's Rock. She was last heard of in Mount's Bay, Cornwall, on 11th April, when she communicated with her owners by radio. The " Twilit Waters " was due back at Brixham on 19th April ; on 20th April, widely scattered wreckage, including a lifebuoy bearing the ship's name, was found at sea in an area south and southwest of the Lizard. I have made arrangements for a preliminary inquiry to be held at once, and investigations are now proceding. The House would, I am sure, wish me to state on its behalf that they share the grave anxiety of the relatives and dependants of those who sailed in the ship.

Mrs. Middleton: While thanking my right hon. Friend for his sympathetic reply, which will be much appreciated by the relatives of these men in their grievous loss, may I ask if he will assure the House that, pending the results of the inquiry, he will take every step necessary to see that the dependants of the men whose lives have been in jeopardy, or are lost, are properly provided for?

Mr. Barnes: I am not sure that responsibility for the dependants rests upon myself. The preliminary inquiries are really to ascertain whether a formal and complete inquiry should follow.

NEW MEMBER SWORN

Sir Albert Newby Braithwaite, D.S.O., M.C., for Harrow, West.

PERSONAL STATEMENT

The Minister of Works (Mr. Stokes): With your permission, Mr. Speaker, I should like to express my regret for passing into the Division Lobby on Thursday night after the order had been given for the doors to be locked. Although I was in my room, I did not hear the first warning signals. I offer my sincere apologies both to you, Sir, and to the House. I have already made an explanation, and expressed my regret, to the Deputy-Chairman of Ways and Means.

Captain John Crowder: May I ask, Mr. Speaker, whether you could consider asking the Minister of Works to have a lever fitted on the double doors, so that they both shut together?

Mr. Speaker: That is a question which I suggest that the hon. and gallant Member should put on the Order Paper to the Minister of Works.

MR. ANEURIN BEVAN
(STATEMENT)

Mr. Aneurin Bevan (Ebbw Vale): Mr. Speaker, it is one of the immemorial courtesies of the House of Commons that when a Minister has felt it necessary to resign his office, he is provided with an opportunity of stating his reasons to the House. These occasions are always exceedingly painful, especially to the individual concerned, because no Member ought to accept office in a Government without a full consciousness that he ought not to resign it for frivolous reasons. He must keep in mind that his association is based upon the assumption that everybody in Government accepts the full measure of responsibility for what it does.

The courtesy of being allowed to make a statement in the House of Commons is peculiarly agreeable to me this afternoon, because, up to now, I am the only person who has not been able to give any reasons why I proposed to take this step, although I notice that almost every single newspaper in Great Britain, including a large number of well-informed columnists, already know my reasons.

The House will recall that in the Defence debate I made one or two statements concerning the introduction of a Defence programme into our economy, and, with the permission of the House, I should like to quote from that speech which, I assumed at the time, received the general approval of the House. I said:

"The fact of the matter is, as everybody knows, that the extent to which stockpiling has already taken place, the extent to which the

[MR. BEVAN.]

civil economy is being turned over to defence purposes in other parts of the world, is dragging prices up everywhere. Furthermore, may I remind the right hon. Gentleman that if we turn over the complicated machinery of modern industry to war preparation too quickly, or try to do it too quickly, we shall do so in a campaign of hate, in a campaign of hysteria, which may make it very difficult to control that machine when it has been created.

" It is all very well to speak about these things in airy terms, but we want to do two things. We want to organise our defence programme in this country in such a fashion as will keep the love of peace as vital as ever it was before. But we have seen in other places that a campaign for increased arms production is accompanied by a campaign of intolerance and hatred and witch-hunting. Therefore, we in this country are not at all anxious to imitate what has been done in other places."—[OFFICIAL REPORT, 15th February, 1951 ; Vol. 484, c. 738.]

I would also like to direct the attention of the House to a statement made by the Prime Minister in placing before the House the accelerated armaments programme. He said :

" The completion of the programme in full and in time is dependent upon an adequate supply of materials, components and machine tools. In particular, our plans for expanding capacity depend entirely upon the early provision of machine tools, many of which can only be obtained from abroad."—[OFFICIAL REPORT, 29th January, 1951 ; Vol. 483, c. 584.]

Those cautionary words were inserted deliberately in the statements on defence production because it was obvious to myself and to my colleagues in the Government that the accelerated programme was conditional upon a number of factors not immediately within our own control.

It has for some time been obvious to the Members of the Government and especially to the Ministers concerned in the production Departments that raw materials, machine tools and components are not forthcoming in sufficient quantity even for the earlier programme and that, therefore, the figures in the Budget for arms expenditure are based upon assumptions already invalidated. I want to make that quite clear to the House of Commons ; the figures of expenditure on arms were already known to the Chancellor of the Exchequer to be unrealisable. The supply Departments have made it quite clear on several occasions that this is the case and, therefore, I begged over and over again that we should not put figures in the Budget on account of defence expenditure which would not be

realised, and if they tried to be realised would have the result of inflating prices in this country and all over the world.

It is now perfectly clear to any one who examines the matter objectively that the lurchings of the American economy, the extravagant and unpredictable behaviour of the production machine, the failure on the part of the American Government to inject the arms programme into the economy slowly enough, have already caused a vast inflation of prices all over the world, have disturbed the economy of the western world to such an extent that if it goes on more damage will be done by this unrestrained behaviour than by the behaviour of the nation the arms are intended to restrain.

This is a very important matter for Great Britain. We are entirely dependent upon other parts of the world for most of our raw materials. The President of the Board of Trade and the Minister of Supply in two recent statements to the House of Commons have called the attention of the House to the shortage of absolutely essential raw materials. It was only last Friday that the Minister of Supply pointed out in the gravest terms that we would not be able to carry out our programme unless we had molybdenum, zinc, sulphur, copper and a large number of other raw materials and nonferrous metals which we can only obtain with the consent of the Americans and from other parts of the world.

I say therefore with the full solemnity of the seriousness of what I am saying, that the £4,700 million arms programme is already dead. It cannot be achieved without irreparable damage to the economy of Great Britain and the world, and that therefore the arms programme contained in the Chancellor of the Exchequer's Budget is already invalidated and the figures based on the arms programme ought to be revised.

It is even more serious than that. The administration responsible for the American defence programme have already announced to the world that America proposes to provide her share of the arms programme not out of reductions in civil consumption, not out of economies in the American economy but out of increased production ; and already plans are envisaged that before very long the American economy will be expanded for arms production by a percentage equal to the total British consumption, civil and arms.

And when that happens the demands made upon the world's precious raw materials will be such that the civilian economy of the Western world outside America will be undermined. We shall have mass unemployment. We have already got in Great Britain under-employment. Already there is short-time working in many important parts of industry and before the middle of the year, unless something serious can be done, we shall have unemployment in many of our important industrial centres. That cannot be cured by the Opposition. In fact the Opposition would make it worse—far worse.

The fact is that the western world has embarked upon a campaign of arms production upon a scale, so quickly, and of such an extent that the foundations of political liberty and Parliamentary democracy will not be able to sustain the shock. This is a very grave matter indeed. I have always said both in the House of Commons and in speeches in the country—and I think my ex-colleagues in the Government will at least give me credit for this—that the defence programme must always be consistent with the maintenance of the standard of life of the British people and the maintenance of the social services, and that as soon as it became clear we had engaged upon an arms programme inconsistent with those considerations, I could no longer remain a Member of the Government.

I therefore do beg the House and the country, and the world, to think before it is too late. It may be that on such an occasion as this the dramatic nature of a resignation might cause even some of our American friends to think before it is too late. It has always been clear that the weapons of the totalitarian States are, first, social and economic, and only next military ; and if in attempting to meet the military effect of those totalitarian machines, the economies of the western world are disrupted and the standard of living is lowered or industrial disturbances are created, then Soviet Communism establishes a whole series of Trojan horses in every nation of the western economy.

It is, therefore, absolutely essential if we are to march forward properly, if we are to mobilise our resources intelligently, that the military, social and political weapons must be taken together. It is clear from the Budget that the Chancellor of the Exchequer has abandoned any hope of restraining inflation. It is quite clear that for the rest of the year and for the beginning of next year, so far as we can see, the cost of living is going to rise precipitously. As the cost of living rises, the industrial workers of Great Britain will try to adjust themselves to the rising spiral of prices, and because they will do so by a series of individual trade union demands a hundred and one battles will be fought on the industrial field, and our political enemies will take advantage of each one. It is, therefore, impossible for us to proceed with this programme in this way.

I therefore beg my colleagues, as I have begged them before, to consider before they commit themselves to these great programmes. It is obvious from what the Chancellor of the Exchequer said in his Budget speech that we have no longer any hope of restraining inflation. The cost of living has already gone up by several points since the middle of last year, and it is going up again. Therefore, it is no use pretending that the Budget is just, merely because it gives a few shillings to old age pensioners, when rising prices immediately begin to take the few shillings away from them.

[HON. MEMBERS: " Hear, hear."]

It is no use saying " Hear, hear " on the opposite side of the House. The Opposition have no remedy for this at all. But there is a remedy here on this side of the House if it is courageously applied, and the Budget does not courageously apply it. The Budget has run away from it. The Budget was hailed with pleasure in the City. It was a remarkable Budget. It united the City, satisfied the Opposition and disunited the Labour Party—all this because we have allowed ourselves to be dragged too far behind the wheels of American diplomacy.

This great nation has a message for the world which is distinct from that of America or that of the Soviet Union. Ever since 1945 we have been engaged in this country in the most remarkable piece of social reconstruction the world has ever seen. By the end of 1950 we had, as I said in my letter to the Prime Minister, assumed the moral leadership

[MR. BEVAN.]
of the world. [*Interruption.*] It is no use hon. Members opposite sneering, because when they come to the end of the road it will not be a sneer which will be upon their faces. There is only one hope for mankind, and that hope still remains in this little island. It is from here that we tell the world where to go and how to go there, but we must not follow behind the anarchy of American competitive capitalism which is unable to restrain itself at all, as is seen in the stockpiling that is now going on, and which denies to the economy of Great Britain even the means of carrying on our civil production. That is the first part of what I wanted to say.

It has never been in my mind that my quarrel with my colleagues was based only upon what they have done to the National Health Service. As they know, over and over again I have said that these figures of arms production are fantastically wrong, and that if we try to spend them we shall get less arms for more money. I have not had experience in the Ministry of Health for five years for nothing. I know what it is to put too large a programme upon too narrow a a base. We have to adjust our paper figures to physical realities, and that is what the Exchequer has not done.

May I be permitted, in passing, now that I enjoy comparative freedom, to give a word of advice to my colleagues in the Government? Take economic planning away from the Treasury. They know nothing about it. The great difficulty with the Treasury is that they think they move men about when they move pieces of paper about. It is what I have described over and over again as " whistle-blowing " planning. It has been perfectly obvious on several occasions that there are too many economists advising the Treasury, and now we have the added misfortune of having an economist in the Chancellor of the Exchequer himself.

I therefore seriously suggest to the Government that they should set up a production department and put the Chancellor of the Exchequer in the position where he ought to be now under modern planning, that is, with the function of making an annual statement of accounts. Then we should have some realism in the Budget. We should not be pushing out figures when the facts are going in the opposite direction.

I want to come for a short while, because I do not wish to try the patience of the House, to the narrower issue. The Chancellor of the Exchequer astonished me when he said that his Budget was coming to the rescue of the fixed income groups. Well, it has come to the rescue of the fixed income groups over 70 years of age, but not below. The fixed income groups in our modern social services are the victims of this kind of finance. Everybody possessing property gets richer. Property is appreciating all the time, and it is well known that there are large numbers of British citizens living normally out of the appreciated values of their own property. The fiscal measures of the Chancellor of the Exchequer do not touch them at all.

I listened to the Chancellor of the Exchequer with very great admiration. It was one of the cleverest Budget speeches I had ever heard in my life. There was a passage towards the end in which he said that he was now coming to a complicated and technical matter and that if Members wished to they could go to sleep. They did. Whilst they were sleeping he stole £100 million a year from the National Insurance Fund. Of course I know that in the same Budget speech the Chancellor of the Exchequer said that he had already taken account of it as savings. Of course he had, so that the re-armament of Great Britain is financed out of the contributions that the workers have paid into the Fund in order to protect themselves. [HON. MEMBERS: "Oh! "] Certainly, that is the meaning of it. It is no good my hon. Friends refusing to face these matters. If we look at the Chancellor's speech we see that the Chancellor himself said that he had already taken account of the contributions into the Insurance Fund as savings. He said so, and he is right. [*Interruption.*] Do not deny that he is right. I am saying he is right. Do not quarrel with me when I agree with him.

The conclusion is as follows. At a time when there are still large untapped sources of wealth in Great Britain, a Socialist Chancellor of the Exchequer uses the Insurance Fund, contributed for the purpose of maintaining the social services, as his source of revenue, and I say that is not Socialist finance. Go to that source for revenue when no other source remains, but no one can say that there are no other sources of revenue in Great Britain except the Insurance Fund.

I now come to the National Health Service side of the matter. Let me say to my hon. Friends on these benches: you have been saying in the last fortnight or three weeks that I have been quarrelling about a triviality—spectacles and dentures. You may call it a triviality. I remember the triviality that started an avalanche in 1931. I remember it very well, and perhaps my hon. Friends would not mind me recounting it. There was a trade union group meeting upstairs. I was a member of it and went along. My good friend, " Geordie " Buchanan, did not come along with me because he thought it was hopeless, and he proved to be a better prophet than I was. But I had more credulity in those days than I have got now. So I went along, and the first subject was an attack on the seasonal workers. That was the first order. I opposed it bitterly, and when I came out of the room my good old friend George Lansbury attacked me for attacking the order. I said, " George, you do not realise, this is the beginning of the end. Once you start this there is no logical stopping point."

The Chancellor of the Exchequer in this year's Budget proposes to reduce the Health expenditure by £13 million—only £13 million out of £4,000 million. [HON. MEMBERS: " £400 million."] No, £4,000 million. He has taken £13 million out of the Budget total of £4,000 million. If he finds it necessary to mutilate, or begin to mutilate, the Health Services for £13 million out of £4,000 million, what will he do next year? Or are you next year going to take your stand on the upper denture? The lower half apparently does not matter, but the top half is sacrosanct. Is that right? If my hon. Friends are asked questions at meetings about what they will do next year, what will they say?

The Chancellor of the Exchequer is putting a financial ceiling on the Health Service. With rising prices the Health Service is squeezed between that artificial figure and rising prices. What is to be squeezed out next year? Is it the upper half? When that has been squeezed out and the same principle holds good, what do you squeeze out the year after? Prescriptions? Hospital charges? Where do you stop? I have been accused of

having agreed to a charge on prescriptions. That shows the danger of compromise. Because if it is pleaded against me that I agreed to the modification of the Health Service, then what will be pleaded against my right hon. Friends next year, and indeed what answer will they have if the vandals opposite come in? What answer? The Health Service will be like Lavinia—all the limbs cut off and eventually her tongue cut out, too.

I should like to ask my right hon. and hon. Friends, where are they going? [HON. MEMBERS: " Where are you going?"] Where am I going? I am where I always was. Those who live their lives in mountainous and rugged countries are always afraid of avalanches, and they know that avalanches start with the movement of a very small stone. First, the stone starts on a ridge between two valleys—one valley desolate and the other valley populous. The pebble starts, but nobody bothers about the pebble until it gains way, and soon the whole valley is overwhelmed. That is how the avalanche starts, that is the logic of the present situation, and that is the logic my right hon. and hon. Friends cannot escape. Why, therefore, has it been done in this way?

After all, the National Health Service was something of which we were all very proud, and even the Opposition were beginning to be proud of it. It only had to last a few more years to become a part of our traditions, and then the traditionalists would have claimed the credit for all of it. Why should we throw it away? In the Chancellor's Speech there was not one word of commendation for the Health Service—not one word. What is responsible for that?

Why has the cut been made? He cannot say, with an overall surplus of over £220 million and a conventional surplus of £39 million, that he had to have the £13 million. That is the arithmetic of Bedlam. He cannot say that his arithmetic is so precise that he must have the £13 million, when last year the Treasury were £247 million out. Why? Has the A.M.A. succeeded in doing what the B.M.A. failed to do? What is the cause of it? Why has it been done?

I have also been accused—and I think I am entitled to answer it—that I had already agreed to a certain charge. I

[MR. BEVAN.]

speak to my right hon. Friends very frankly here. It seems to me sometimes that it is so difficult to make them see what lies ahead that you have to take them along by the hand and show them. The prescription charge I knew would never be made, because it was impracticable. [HON. MEMBERS: "Oh!"] Well, it was never made.

I will tell my hon. Friends something else, too. There was another policy— there was a proposed reduction of 25,000 on the housing programme, was there not? It was never made. It was necessary for me at that time to use what everybody always said were bad tactics upon my part—I had to manœuvre, and I did manœuvre and saved the 25,000 houses and the prescription charge. I say, therefore, to my right hon. and hon. Friends, there is no justification for taking this line at all. There is no justification in the arithmetic, there is less justification in the economics, and I beg my right hon. and hon. Friends to change their minds about it.

I say this, in conclusion. There is only one hope for mankind—and that is democratic Socialism. There is only one party in Great Britain which can do it— and that is the Labour Party. But I ask them carefully to consider how far they are polluting the stream. We have gone a long way—a very long way—against great difficulties. Do not let us change direction now. Let us make it clear, quite clear, to the rest of the world that we stand where we stood, that we are not going to allow ourselves to be diverted from our path by the exigencies of the immediate situation. We shall do what is necessary to defend ourselves—defend ourselves by arms, and not only with arms but with the spiritual resources of our people.

Sir Waldron Smithers (Orpington): On a point of order. May ask whether it would be the duty of the Government now to announce the date of a General Election?

Mr. Speaker: That is not a point of order.

FIRE SERVICES [MONEY]

Resolution reported:

That, for the purposes of any Act of the present Session to amend sections twenty-six and twenty-seven of the Fire Services Act, 1947, it is expedient to authorise—

(a) the payment out of moneys provided by Parliament of any increase in the sums payable under any enactment out of moneys so provided which is attributable to provisions of the said Act of the present Session amending those sections—

(i) in respect of employment which is treated for the purposes of the Firemen's Pension Scheme as if it were employment as a member of a fire brigade maintained in pursuance of the said Act of 1947; or

(ii) in respect of the exclusion of statutory pension schemes other than the Firemen's Pension Scheme in relation to employment as, or treated as aforesaid as employment as, a member of a fire brigade maintained in pursuance of that Act;

(b) the payment into the Exchequer of any sums required by the said Act of the present Session to be so paid.

Resolution agreed to.

FIRE SERVICES BILL

Considered in Committee.

[Major MILNER in the Chair]

Clause 1 ordered to stand part of the Bill.

Clause 2.—(AMENDMENT OF S. 27.)

4.9 p.m.

The Under-Secretary of State for the Home Department (Mr. Geoffrey de Freitas): I beg to move, in page 2, line 27, to leave out "one month," and to insert "three months."

On the Second Reading, the hon. and learned Member for York (Mr. Hylton-Foster) asked me to consider whether one month's notice was long enough. In fact, the period would have been somewhat longer than a month and I believe we could have left the matter to the union and the fire authorities to see that everything was brought to the attention of the firemen concerned. To make it doubly sure, however, I have decided to accept the hon. and learned Gentleman's argument so that the notice will be of three months instead of one month.

Mr. R. V. Grimston (Westbury): Can the hon. Gentleman say anything about the other matters which have been raised?

Oswald Mosley offers radical thinking that might have prevented his descent into fascism

David Blunkett was blind at birth, was born into a poor family in one of the most deprived areas of Sheffield and became fatherless at the age of 12 through a horrific industrial accident. Notwithstanding, he became an MP at the age of 40, was promoted to the Opposition Front Bench after one year in the House, joined the shadow Cabinet after five, held top ministerial posts in Tony Blair's Cabinet, and was even spoken of as a possible successor to Mr Blair.

Throughout his political career, however, his forthright style surrounded him with controversy, and disastrous events in his private life made him the target of the media and eventually cost him his ministerial career.

He was educated at schools for the blind and attended night school and further education on day release. He won a place at Sheffield university where he took a BA in political theory and institutions. After securing a post-graduate qualification, he became a tutor in industrial relations at Barnsley college of technology, a position he held until he was elected the Member for Sheffield, Brightside in 1987.

His interest in and pursuit of politics began at an early age. He joined the Labour party when he was 16 and by the age of 22 he had been elected to Sheffield city council as its youngest ever member. In 1980 he became the council leader, and three years later he was on the National Executive Committee of the Labour party. He became the chairman in 1993.

Tony Blair had declared during the 1997 election campaign that his Government's three highest priorities would be "education, education, education", and it was to David Blunkett that he entrusted the job of Secretary of State for Education and Employment. He was in a powerful position within the Cabinet and he used his power to secure large increases in education funding. Controversially, he also announced the introduction of tuition fees for university students, a policy whose unpopularity was to outlast his ministerial career.

As a student at Sheffield university, he had listened to lectures from Bernard Crick, who later became an adviser to Labour leader Neil Kinnock. Now in office, David Blunkett also called on Professor Crick, in this case to chair the advisory group whose work resulted in citizenship becoming part of the core curriculum. He subsequently appointed the professor as a departmental adviser on citizenship.

When Labour returned to power in 2001, he realised a long-held ambition by being promoted to Home Secretary. Controversy was never far away. He downgraded the classification of cannabis, proposed the introduction of identity cards, introduced legislation to dispense with juries in certain trials, and proposed new powers to deal with illegal immigrants and bogus asylum seekers.

However, it was in his private life that the biggest controversies flared up. His relationship with a married woman and allegations about his part in securing a travel visa for the woman's nanny resulted in his resignation in December 2004.

When Labour won its historic third term in 2005, however, he was recalled to the Cabinet as Secretary of State for Work and Pensions. It was not to last. Within months, a fresh row had erupted over his directorship of and shareholding in a company that was bidding for work with his Department. They were matters on which he had failed to consult the Advisory Committee on Business Appointments.

Although he maintained throughout that he had done nothing wrong, his ministerial career came to an abrupt end. On 2 November 2005 he had been due to appear before a Commons Select Committee. Instead he was summoned to a meeting with Mr Blair in Downing street. He left the meeting to return to the Back Benches.

His constant companions during his years in the House of Commons were his guide dogs. During a speech by Conservative Front Bencher David Willetts, the guide dog, Lucy, which had been snoozing on the floor by the Dispatch Box suddenly vomited. Suggestions revolving around the content of Mr Willetts's speech and the dog's response were numerous. The immediate loser, however, was the Government Whip who, because House staff were not permitted to enter the Chamber during a sitting, was given the job of cleaning up.

Boldness of action and his new ideas could have offered a democratic alternative

By Rt hon David Blunkett MP

It may seem strange in the extreme for a former Cabinet Minister who had the privilege of overseeing employment policy not just once but twice, to choose a speech by Oswald Mosley – then Chancellor of the Duchy of Lancaster – whose subsequent history diverged so fundamentally from the Labour party as to put him beyond the normal bounds of current acknowledgement.

Yet, at this phase, prior to his decline into fascism via the New Party with which Aneurin Bevan certainly had a flirtation, he had much to say.

In fact, had his proposals, which were put to the Labour party conference later in the year, been accepted, the history of the 1930s including that of Mosley himself, might have been very different.

The opening of his speech on the floor of the House may not have been auspicious. It dealt with technicalities – although he made a very good point about the enormity of the challenge requiring more radical, rather than more cautious approaches.

But should his comments on administration strike us as odd? Not at all. It was only because of the radical modernisation of the Employment Service in 1997 that the New Deal programme devised between myself and Gordon Brown had any chance whatsoever of implementation. There was a transformation in attitude and action throughout the service but there was a total commitment to the reduction in unemployment – particularly for young people.

The clarion call for the Government to be in charge – for Ministers to lead – is one with which I accord entirely. Policies and programmes "captured" by existing thinking and administrative malaise are the road to disaster. It is clear from Mosley's speech that the MacDonald Government was indeed "captured".

What was interesting about this early part of the speech in historic terms was that you could also see, while in no way seeking to undermine his central point, the elements of his fascist thinking coming through. "Centralisation" was the hallmark. What the fascists came to know as "Autocracy with Science".

However, the reason I found the speech so interesting was his commitment to Keynesianism before Keynes. Here was radical thinking and articulate expression at a time when on economic and employment policy there was a dearth of both – which is of course why fascism became so attractive in first Italy, and then Germany.

No one would get away now with the kind of length of speaking that was acceptable in 1930, but, even so, the detail that was presented by Oswald Mosley was impressive. He both did his homework and had got a grasp of the significance of those facts in making a case for radical change.

At a time when we need now to face the enormity of rapid change and globalisation it was interesting, albeit at some considerable detail, to read the analysis of global change set out by Mosley in May 1930.

The programme of reconstruction – civil engineering and the like – which he sets out, became commonplace. It was not at the time. The impact that such a programme would have had not merely on reducing unemployment by a target of 800,000 but also in terms of the regeneration of the whole economy and the renewal of Britain would have been incalculable. It is this that makes the speech and his subsequent arguments over the year that succeeded it, of such interest.

His clarion call at the end of his speech that we should "not muddle through" was prescient. Had his programme and call for action rather than drift been accepted, the paradox may well have been that not only would there not have been the British Union of Fascists but the knock-on effect of economic growth and economic regeneration in Britain could well have had a dramatic impact in terms of condition in Europe as a whole, and a democratic beacon providing an alternative to fascism.

That is why I nominate this speech – because of its grasp of the global changes which were facing Britain, the understanding that dramatic action by government to lead economic recovery was necessary, and an appreciation that the machinery of government mattered. Above all, that politicians were not there simply to manage the existing machine, to oversee the departmental programme, but to shape, accelerate and deliver a radical programme of change.

Perhaps the House in Committee was not the place to deliver it, but in his efforts to win over the Labour party conference later that year he displayed some of his greatest oratorical skills – sadly deployed on the side of darkness in the years to come.

[Mr. Snowden.]

and therefore inflicting damage upon the industry. If that be so, then the greatest damage which is being done to British industry to-day is by remarks like those which the Leader of the Opposition made during his speech to-day. The proposal for Safeguarding is being advocated because—and this surely will not be denied—British industry is not able to compete successfully with the foreigner. I have heard the right hon. Gentleman the Member for Hillhead (Sir R. Horne) in this House very often talk about the depressed condition of our industries. Surely, is not that holding up to the world——

Sir R. HORNE: That is a totally different thing. There are other conditions that go with it, but, when you find firms spending vast sums of money in getting the most modern plant in the world, surely it is a shame to say to the world that those firms are inefficient.

Mr. SNOWDEN: I said I would not quote extracts from speeches or letters of our leading industrialists, but perhaps now I may change my mind. This is an address delivered quite recently, in November, 1929, by Sir Mark Webster Jenkinson who, I think, is a director of Vickers-Armstrong, and this is what he said:

" Since rationalisation was first advanced as a solution of our industrial difficulties there have been some amalgamations of individual units but certain works have been closed down, in isolated cases the managements have been merged, but, compared with Germany, practically few industries have taken any active steps to rationalise their productive capacity on a comprehensive and economical basis and to interpret the true meaning of rationalisation. We just ' muddle along,' hopeful that the sun of prosperity will shine again. . . . but unwilling to recognise that in the direction of merger modernisation, and management of our industrial undertakings lies the road we have to follow if we are to regain a position of pre-eminence in the markets of the world."

And, again, in a letter in the " Times," in November, 1927, signed " Arthur Colegate, Chairman, Robert Heath and Low Moor, Limited ":

" Many sections of the steel industry feel that no permanent improvement can be looked for unless their plant and methods are brought into line with the best practice of America and the Continent. . . . "

Sir KINGSLEY WOOD: What about the three firms that you have libelled ?

Mr. SNOWDEN: I have already said that I gave those three instances as illustrating my general argument.

Mr. MACQUISTEN: And your instances were all wrong.

Mr. SNOWDEN: I have already said that I hoped my remarks this afternoon, in which I expressed regret for the inaccurate figures, will be as widely circulated as my original statement. And as I rose only to correct and express my regret for the inaccuracy of the figures which I gave on that occasion, I think that it would be best, perhaps, to leave it there.

Sir O. MOSLEY: In the earlier stages of this debate to-day, to which I will return with the leave of the Committee, we have had from the Prime Minister an exposition of Government policy, and also some of the customary exchanges of debate from two great masters of that art. I do not propose to indulge in any form of dialectics, because I believe the purpose which this Committee desires can best be served if, as directly as possible, I proceed to the actual facts of the great administrative and economic issues which are involved. The Prime Minister, in his speech, pointed out a fact which none can deny, that world conditions have been vastly aggravated since the arrival in power of the present Government, and that no one can suggest that the Government are responsible for those conditions. None can deny that fact, but this I do submit, that the more serious the situation the greater the necessity for action by Government. We must, above all, beware, as the world situation degenerates, that we do not make that situation an excuse for doing less rather than a spur for doing more. That is the only comment on the general situation which I would permit myself before coming to the actual issues involved.

General surveys of unemployment I have always distrusted, because they are liable to degenerate into generalities which lead us nowhere. If we are to discuss this matter with any relation to realities, we must master the actual, hard details of the administrative problem, and to that problem I desire immediately to proceed. The first issue between the Government and myself arises in the purely administrative sphere of the machinery to be employed in dealing with the problem. I submit to the Committee that, if anyone starts in any business or enterprise, his first consideration must be the creation of a machine by which that business can be conducted; and, when a Government comes into power to deal with unemployment, its first business is the creation of an efficient and effective machine. That machine, in my view, does not to-day exist, and I will say why.

Under the late Government, the Ministry of Labour, with the assistance of various Cabinet Committees, was, as I understand, responsible for unemployment, and the staff of that office dealt both with the unemployment insurance aspect of the problem and with the provision of work and the reorganisation of industry. The only difference in the administrative procedure under the present Government is that the officials who were dealing with the constructive works side of the problem have been moved from the Ministry of Labour to the Treasury, and have been joined by a small staff gathered from other Departments. The actual central administrative machine is now as follows. An inter-departmental committee composed of the permanent chiefs of all Departments meet at irregular intervals under the chairmanship of the Lord Privy Seal. That is the main machine to secure co-ordination and liaison in the whole great attack upon unemployment. That committee has met nine times since the inception of the Government, and only twice during the present year. To the first two meetings of that committee, I and other advisory unemployment Ministers were not invited, and at those first two meetings every major decision on policy and administration was taken. I am not here to make any complaints, but to analyse the facts, and I suggest that a machine of that nature could not possibly grapple with the problem.

What was the result? The result was that all initiative tended to come from the Department, instead of from Ministers. I am not here to attack, and I certainly should not dream of making any attack upon the Civil Service. My admiration for the Civil Service has vastly increased since I have been in office. But to achieve a policy of this nature it is absolutely necessary that the whole initiative

and drive should rest in the hands of the Government themselves. The machine which I suggested—it is impossible to describe it in great detail on this occasion—was a central organisation armed with an adequate research and economic advisory department on the one hand, linked to an executive machine composed of some 12 higher officials on the other, operating under the direct control of the Prime Minister and the head of the Civil Service himself, and driving out from that central organisation the energy and initiative of the Government through every Department which had to deal with the problem. It is impossible really to expound such a scheme to the House in detail unless it is seen in the graph form in which I submitted it.

It is admittedly a complex organisation. I was told that to carry such an organisation into effect would mean a revolution in the machinery of government. My only comment is this. The machinery which I suggested may be right or may be wrong—after a very short administrative experience, it was probably wrong—but this I do suggest, that to grapple with this problem it is necessary to have a revolution in the machinery of government. After all, it was done in the War; there were revolutions in the machinery of government one after the other, until the machine was devised and created by which the job could be done. Unless we treat the unemployment problem as a lesser problem, which I believe to be a fallacious view, we have to have a change in the machinery of government by which we can get that central drive and organisation by which alone this problem can be surmounted.

That is all that I have to say for the moment upon machinery. May I now proceed to the nature of the problem which confronts us? I have always tried in the House, when speaking from the Treasury Bench, to divide the problem into two essential parts, the long-term reconstruction of the industries of this country, and the short-term programme to bridge the gulf before the fruition of the long-term programme. I think we can all agree, whatever our views upon the permanent re-construction of Britain, that it cannot be done in five minutes. It will be a matter of three years at least, and possibly five years, before you can arrive by long-term measures at an appre-

[Sir O. Mosley.]

ciable effect upon the unemployment figures. If that view be agreed to, it is evidently necessary, in addition, to have a short-term programme to deal with unemployment in the interval, which should at the same time contribute to the economic advantage of the country. I will come later to that short-term programme, and to an analysis in detail of the figures which the Prime Minister supplied to the House; but first of all may I address myself to the fundamental problem—the long-term problem—in the solution of which the Government and this House must decide the permanent economic basis of this country in the immediate future.

The Government throughout have pinned their hopes to rationalisation. For my part, I have always made it perfectly clear that, in my view, rationalisation was necessary and inevitable. It has to come in the modern world. Industries which do not rationalise simply go under. It is agreed among most people that rationalisation is necessary, but do not let us proceed, from our view that rationalisation is necessary, to the easy belief that rationalisation in itself will cure the unemployment problem. It is held, and it was submitted again this afternoon, that although at first rationalisation displaces labour, that very soon it so expands the market open to the industry that the labour displaced is absorbed, and more labour in addition, with the result that ultimately the unemployment problem is solved. The only criterion that we can apply to that belief is the evidence which exists in connection with trades which have already rationalised. I have been at some pains to examine the facts in trades which have at any rate partially rationalised, and I think we can take, as a criterion of a rationalised trade, those trades which, in a relatively short space of time, have greatly increased their production for a profitable market. I applied this criterion to trades of that character—four big groups of trades—and I found, between 1924 and 1929, an average increase in production of over 20 per cent., but an average decline in the insured workers in those trades of over 4 per cent. Over five years you have that immense increase in production—a very great achievement—and over the same long period a steady decline in the employment in those trades, which were ever increasing their efficiency and expanding their markets. It would appear, therefore, on the evidence which exists, that rationalisation in itself is at any rate no short and easy cut to the solution of the unemployment problem.

There is a further point. The whole emphasis in this matter of rationalisation is thrown by the Government on the export trade. I do not know if that fact will be challenged. The Lord Privy Seal put it very well on the 25th February, when he said:

"The problem, difficult in some respects, is boiled down to the simple proposition, how can the Government help our export trade?"

There are many other quotations of Government spokesmen to the same effect. I think it is beyond challenge that the Government believe that by the expansion of export trade through rationalisation our troubles are to be overcome. May we apply the evidence I have just adduced to the expansion of the export trade? The theory is that, if we can restore our export trade, by rationalisation, to its previous position in the markets of the world, we shall absorb our present unemployed. To win back our previous proportion of the export trade of the world means an increase of some £200,000,000 a year in our export trade or 25 per cent. of its present value. Supposing that is achieved by rationalisation, and that the same thing happens in the rationalisation of the export trade that has occurred in industries which have already been rationalised, to achieve that increase of 25 per cent. in our present volume of export trade would, if the same proportions hold good, mean an actual decrease of 5 per cent. in the men employed in those trades.

Let us set aside all existing evidence, and let us, in examining this problem, take a hypothesis altogether favourable —fantastically favourable—to the theory of the Government. Suppose that in the next four years we can expand our export trade by £200,000,000 a year, not by a rationalisation process which displaces labour, but by an ordinary expansion of world markets which takes more workers on the existing basis. We should, in that event, to achieve that increase of £200,000,000, employ, on the normal basis of production per head at the present time, something like 900,000 additional people. But during the next four years some 1,000,000 persons will be added to the working population, so that at the end of the process we should be back exactly where we began.

I submit that this hope of recovering our position through an expansion of our export trade is an illusion, and a dangerous illusion; and the sooner the fallacy is realised, the quicker can we devote ourselves to a search for the real remedy. There are innumerable factors beyond those which I have mentioned, militating against any increase of our export trade to that extent. There is the industrialisation of other countries for their own home markets; there is the industrialisation of countries which had no industries at all a few years ago. Take the position of our cotton trade on the Indian market. That market averaged for many years, I believe, according to the figures of the International Labour Office, about 5,600,000,000 yards of cotton a year. That was originally our exclusive market, but to-day India herself produces 1,000,000,000 yards, while Japan, which formerly only had one five-hundredth part of that Indian market, to-day has one-fifth. The intensified competition all over the world is making more and more illusory the belief that we can again build up in the world that unique position which we occupied many years ago.

I should be interested to hear if these figures and calculations can be challenged. If they cannot be challenged, we have to face a shift in the whole basis of the economic life of this country. I believe, and have always urged, that it is to the home market that we must look for the solution of our troubles. [HON. MEMBERS: " Hear, hear! "] I may come to a rather different conclusion from hon. Members opposite, but let us march together thus far. If our export trade on its pre-War basis is really no longer possible, we have to turn to the home market. We must always, of course, export sufficient to buy our essential foodstuffs and raw materials, but we need not export enough to build up a favourable trade balance for foreign investment of £100,000,000 a year, or to pay for the import of the so many manufactured luxury articles as to-day come into

6.0 p.m. the country. We have to get away from the belief that the only criterion of British prosperity is how many goods we can send abroad for foreigners to consume.

But whatever may be said for or against the recovery of the swollen export trade that we had before the War, the fact remains that it is most exceedingly difficult ever to restore that condition again, and facts have to be faced if we are to find any outlet for our present production. How can the home market be developed? Hon. Members opposite reply " Tariffs." They remind us, rightly, that Mr. Cobden is dead, but it is very often forgotten that the opponents of Mr. Cobden are dead as well. I believe both *laissez faire* and Protection are utterly irrelevant to the modern world. After all, what are the facts we have to face? We have to face fluctuations in the price level of basic commodities greater than we dreamt of before the War, for a variety of reasons, partly monetary, but still more, the mergence of great producers' organisations which have turned the struggle into a battle of giants in place of the day-to-day struggles of small merchants before the War. We have the struggle of these great organisations and in the event of the collapse of one of these great organisations in the struggle you have a downward rush in prices, or, in the event of their combination, you have an upward surge in prices which would frustrate and baffle any tariff wall that the wit of man could devise. Tariffs lead to the same fluctuations at higher price levels, while the organised and subsidised dumping that we are likely to meet in the not distant future can go over, or under, if the nation doing it so desires, or if the producers' organisations desire, any tariff barrier that was ever invented.

I do not want to-night to re-open that old controversy. I believe we can leave it to the ghosts of Cobden and his opponents to continue the discussions of long ago in whatever Elysian fields they frequent. We should get down to thrashing out the merits of the problem to meet the facts of the age in which we live. I have been driven more and more to the conclusion that the system of an import control board, long adopted as the policy

[Sir O. Mosley.]

of this party in the sphere of agriculture, and wheat in particular, is the only means by which the facts of the modern situation can be met, and many are daily coming to that conclusion. I have been astonished to find, during my period of office, big business men, whose association was altogether with the party opposite, saying that that policy was the only way to meet the agricultural situation. Some of them have advanced the claim that by that policy a price of some 10s. a quarter above the present world price could be given to the English farmer without any increase in the price of bread, and probably a decrease, owing to the savings that could be effected. I had an estimate put to me that 500,000 men could thereby be put on the land. I believe that to be an exaggeration, but I am confident that a good many could be put on the land. It would lead directly to the rationalisation of trades like milling and baking, diverting all the energies of those engaged in those trades from speculation in wheat to the efficiency of their own industrial processes, and by those economies, and economies in freight and insurance, which we can deal with in other and more detailed debates, I believe the basis of a great agricultural policy can be laid.

I want now to suggest that that policy of controlled imports can and should be extended to other trades, for this reason, that if we are to build up a home market, it must be agreed that this nation must to some extent be insulated from the electric shocks of present world conditions. You cannot build a higher civilisation and a standard of life which can absorb the great force of modern production if you are subject to price fluctuations from the rest of the world which dislocate your industry at every turn, and to the sport of competition from virtually slave conditions in other countries. What prospects have we, except the home market, of absorbing modern production? I have had put up to me so often the theory of the classical economists, which is held by many senior statesmen on all sides, that these things have all happened before. Men's labour has been replaced by machinery, only to be absorbed again later by an expansion of the market. That greater production was absorbed by the gradual raising of wages, by the shortening of hours, and, above all, by an expansion of the overseas market. I once heard it said, " Niggers did not ride bicycles when we were young. They ride bicycles now, and that has given employment." That theory is still held, that sooner or later world recovery will come and our rationalised industries will take advantage of it and so expand our home and overseas market and the problem will be solved. Apart from the effects of rationalisation, which I have already endeavoured to describe, we have to consider this great fact, that since the War there has been a tremendous spring of scientific invention. All through the last century it is true that these things happened, but they happened gradually. You had an adjustment of production to consumption over a long period of time, albeit with considerable suffering to the working-class and considerable dislocation of industry. Now you have this tremendous leap forward in a few years in your productive capacity which has absolutely upset the industrial equilibrium of the world and demands entirely different measures to deal with it.

A great scientist said to me only a few months ago, " In the last 30 years the scientific and industrial capacity of the world has increased more than it did in the previous 300 years," and rather unkindly he went on to add, " The only minds that have not registered that change are those of the politicians." We have in some respects to plead guilty to that charge, because many still believe that gradual automatic processes, as before the War, are going to absorb the great flood of goods which the modern scientific and industrial machine is throwing on to the markets of the world. That aspect of the problem that we have to consider could be elaborated indefinitely, but I have to pass to other subjects. I only suggest at this stage that there is, in the analysis which I have presented, and which many others have presented, some ground for disbelief in the current view that is now so widely accepted, and if there is any force in this analysis or in these arguments, the attempt to deal with unemployment by an intensification of the export trade is doomed to failure, and the belief that it can be done is a dangerous delusion which diverts the mind of the country from the problems which should be really considered and the things that really matter. But there is no machine of Government to-day thinking out and analysing these things. I had the advantage of very able and devoted civil servants preparing figures and facts for me but I have only been one Minister with a very small staff.

These things should be the subject of consideration and research by the most powerful economic machine that the country can devise. That is the point of my request at the beginning of my speech for a Government machine for governmental thinking. We have all done our thinking in our various political parties. Governments, officially at any rate, have never done any thinking. It is very difficult to analyse and get at the facts of the modern situation unless you have at your disposal the information and the research which Government Departments alone can supply. That is why it is so essential to have at the centre of things machinery that can undertake that work. What machine to-day is undertaking the great work of reorganising industry? Not the Government at all, but the banks. It is the Governor of the Bank of England who is doing this work. I admit at once that, in any effort of the Government in present conditions, the co-operation of the banks is very necessary and that efforts should be made to secure it, as the Lord Privy Seal has tried to do, but co-operation between the Government and the banks is a very different thing from abdication by the Government in favour of the banks, and we are perilously near that point.

But, putting aside all questions of general principle and facing purely the practical matter, I make this submission, that the banking machinery of this country is not equipped for the task of reorganising our industrial markets. On the purely practical point, if it was the banking system of Germany, you might say "Yes," because an entirely different practice has been followed by those banks. They have been industrial banks, always interwoven with industry, discovering and promoting new enterprise, putting their skilled, industrial directors on the boards of these new concerns, partners in their losses and in their successes. A vast industrial experience lies behind the German banks. Where is a similar experience in the banking system of this country, which has always repudiated any such conception as something immoral in financial doctrine? What is more, there is this danger. Our bank-

ing system has backed many losers. It is committed up to the hilt to many bad debts. As was powerfully brought out in the Balfour Report, industry has often been handicapped, not so much by the strictness of the banks as by ill-timed generosity in the promotion and the bolstering up of inefficiency.

Have we not to be very careful that this new banking enterprise is not an effort to salvage existing commitments rather than to reorganise the industrial life of the country. In all these facts there is a case for the Government taking a more effective control of the situation. The first duty of the Government is, after all, to govern. The worst thing that can happen to a Government is to assume responsibility without control. After all, the impression has been created in the country that in some way or other the Government is promoting the system and is responsible for the activity of these banking efforts, but effective control is absolutely lacking. Liaison and co-ordination do not exist except in the person of the Lord Privy Seal, and ceaseless as his activities are and hard as he works, no one man can in his own person act in co-ordination between all these diverse and great activities. When you are setting out on an enterprise which means nothing less than the reorganisation of the whole basis of the industrial life of the country, you must have a system. You must, in a word, have a machine, and that machine has not even been created.

I must now pass from the long-term side of the programme to the short-term side, and I will be as brief as possible. The Prime Minister this evening described the programme of the Government by which he hoped to provide immediate employment, and he said that that programme now amounted to £103,000,000. When he was asked how many years that programme was spread over he had not the information and could not say, in particular, how many years the £37,000,000 road programme was spread over. As I have been concerned with the details of this programme, possibly I may supply him with the information. The road programme is spread over five years. Its annual amount scarcely exceeds, if at all, the programme of the late Conservative Government. This is one of our major matters of dispute. The only difference is that instead of a one year programme

[Sir O. Mosley.]

this Government have a five years' programme, and an undertaking was given that if in any one year the revenue of the Road Fund was exceeded, the Treasury would arrange for a carry over by some means which has not been specified. But the actual dimensions of the programme per annum remain scarcely, if at all, in excess of the programme of the Conservative Government, and if that is challenged, then I shall challenge the publication of correspondence between the Minister of Transport and myself relative to my Memorandum, the publication of the Memorandum itself and detailed analyses of the figures which the Minister has never yet answered.

I want, if I can, to avoid controversy, but if any of my figures are challenged—my figures are not my own—I shall certainly challenge the publication of the official documents involved in order that the House itself may judge who is correct. That £100,000,000 programme as a whole is averaged over much the same period. It is impossible to say with absolute certainty how many years the rest of the programme is averaged over, but it is a great many, and I myself believe it to be not less than a five year programme as a whole. That means an expenditure of some £20,000,000 a year which, on the current computation, would only provide employment on the average for some 80,000 people a year. It is true that that programme will rise to a peak and then decline, and that it is not a steady average, but I very much doubt whether many men in excess of 100,000 will ever be employed by that programme. I very much doubt it, and I would like to see the Lord Privy Seal prove here in detail with facts and figures—I should be delighted if he could—that many more than 100,000 will ever be employed by the programme he is now adopting. I should like to see a detailed analysis in a White Paper, if it can be shown, which I doubt. That, as far as I can analyse it, is the programme of the Government. The greatest increase in that programme is an increase in Unemployment Grants Committee work from some £6,000,000 in the last two years of the late Government to a sum of £30,000,000 under the present Government, a very great increase, which was achieved by big administrative changes which we only got

through after a very hard fight. That is the biggest single increase in the programme of the Government.

May I proceed to advance very briefly the proposals which I submitted to the Government in their broad outline. I claimed that a programme could be adopted at a very small cost, as a budgetary charge—I will deal with the charge later—which would in a relatively short space of time provide work for at least 700,000 to 800,000 people. It was made up in the following way. The emergency retirement pensions plan would provide normal employment for some 280,000; the School Bill, which I am happy to know the Government are carrying through, should result in providing employment for some 150,000; while in constructive works, which I will later describe, I proposed the employment of some 300,000 per annum. I will go through the figures of these three proposals in very swift detail. The retirement pensions plan was an emergency measure offering to industrial workers at present over the age of 60 £1 a week pension, and 10s. a week for the wife, if the man is married, on the condition that within a specified and short time they retire finally from industry. The whole life of the scheme actuarially was only 15 years. I did in addition suggest that if the Government at that time desired another and a permanent scheme giving a pension at 65 might be provided, in respect of which, of course, no charge would fall for some five years.

Let me to-day deal with the emergency scheme to meet unemployment, with the facts and figures of that scheme and that alone, because the permanent scheme would be a matter for subsequent decision. The emergency scheme suggested a pension of £1 a week for a man and 10s. for the wife. The cost of it in the first year was £21,600,000 falling to some £10,000,000 at the end of five years, and it would be negligible at the end of 15 years. The direct economies to the Exchequer resulting from the reaction of the finance of that scheme upon the last additional contribution of the Exchequer to the Unemployment Insurance Fund reduced the charge from £21,500,000 to £13,000,000. There was an offset in economies in the contribution of the Government to the Unemployment Insurance Fund of some £8,500,000 if the retirement pension scheme was carried, so that the net cost to the Exchequer was £13,000,000 in the first year, and there were other less substantial economies in the Poor Law and other factors of that nature.

I went further and suggested that it would be right and proper in the case of an emergency scheme of this nature to average the cost of the scheme over the effective life of the scheme. If the cost be averaged over the 15 years of the scheme the cost averages £11,000,000 per annum, and in the first year in which the scheme was introduced you would have a cost to the Exchequer of £11,000,000 and an offset in economy to the Government's latest additional contribution to the Unemployment Insurance Fund of £8,500,000, so that the net extra burden to the Exchequer in the first year amounted to not more than £2,500,000 if the averaging expedient were adopted. This is held to be a very immoral suggestion because it might be necessary to borrow in the first few years. But what is borrowed in the first few years is repaid in the later years, and the whole duration of the plan is only 15 years, while it should be unnecessary to borrow at all if the ascending charges of the Budget can be set against the descending charges of the scheme, a very normal transaction, I understand, in balancing a Budget. Anyhow, I claim that if that averaging expedient be adopted the net cost to the Exchequer in the first year need not exceed £2,500,000.

Sir HERBERT SAMUEL: Does this only apply to people who are 60 now?

Sir O. MOSLEY: Yes. If those figures are challenged, then I shall challenge the publication of the retirement pensions report and the correspondence between the Government Actuary and myself on those figures. They are not my figures. I have claimed that 280,000 people could be set in normal employment by means of this retirement pensions scheme, and I should have mentioned, to be quite clear on all the figures, that those liable to the scheme, that is, those who would be offered the pension, numbered 677,000, that those who were estimated would accept amounted to 390,000, and that the replacements of those who accepted amounted to 280,000, so that by means

of that scheme we should put 280,000 to work. The only figure which I have given which is my own figure is the 280,000 who would be set to work. The official estimate was 230,000. My figure was 280,000 for very detailed reasons which I could not possibly enter under half an hour's exposition. But every other figure which I have given is not of my own calculation. The first item in the emergency programme was the retirement pensions scheme at a cost of £2,500,000. The next item was the raising of the school age, which is estimated to cost £4,500,000. I will not enter into the details of that scheme. It was outside my Department and it is to be discussed to-morrow, and other Ministers and the House as a whole are just as familiar with them.

Let me proceed to the question of the finance of the large constructive works schemes. I suggest that, apart from slum clearance and land drainage, with which I will only deal briefly in a few moments, a £100,000,000 programme of the Unemployment Grants Committee should be concentrated into three years, and £100,000,000 road programme should be concentrated into the same period. I will come to the administration and the method of handling the programme in a few moments. I will now deal with the finance. The extra £70,000,000 for Unemployment Grants Committee schemes, would, on a more generous basis of grant than that which prevails at present, be an Exchequer charge of about £3,000,000 a year. As for the road scheme, the necessary loan would be raised on the revenue of the Road Fund and no extra Exchequer charge would be incurred at all. Is it so wrong in days of depression to raise a loan on the revenue of the Road Fund for the provision of an emergency programme which in days of prosperity is repaid by a Sinking Fund from the Road Fund? There is nothing novel in the principle. Already the local authorities for the most part borrow large sums to meet their share of local expenditure. Why should not the State do the same in days of depression and repay in days of prosperity? That was the finance and the total finance of the emergency scheme—£2,500,000 for retirement pensions, £4,500,000 for raising the school age and £3,000,000 for the Unemployment Grants Committee, and the rais-

[Sir O. Mosley.]
ing of the loan for roads carried on the Road Fund. The whole proposal was a budgetary charge of £10,000,000, a £10,000,000 programme by which I believe some 700,000 to 800,000 people could be set to work on emergency measures.

That is a modest and a limited programme devised for the situation with which we are met. Fantastic rumours were circulated as to its cost, but it is a very limited and moderate programme designed to meet the actual facts of the situation with which we are faced. Of course, everybody must admit that the limits of taxation are very easily reached after several years of deflation. We all know that with such a situation the limits of taxation are easily reached, and that when you reach a certain point flight from the pound and disaster may ensue, but if that £10,000,000 programme had to be set against other charges which we have incurred, and are incurring, and if the number thereby to be set to work exceed 700,000, who would choose between that programme and the other charges? As long ago as last September I begged the Cabinet to make up its mind how much it was prepared to spend on unemployment, how much money it could find, and then allocate the money available according to the best objects which we could discover. As it is, no such system has ever been adopted. Departments have come crowding along, jostling each other with their schemes, and, like bookmakers on the race course, the man who can push the hardest, make the most noise and get through the turnstile first, gets away with the money. It is absolutely necessary to make up our minds in advance in any national reconstruction, what our resources are and how they are to be allocated.

Now I come to the actual administrative machinery of these big work plans. I have made the claim that £200,000,000 could be spent, and usefully spent, in Unemployment Grants Committee work, and roads alone, leaving for the moment slums and land drainage. To arrive at an understanding of the administrative machinery which I suggested, it is necessary for me briefly to analyse the relative breakdown of the present machine. We have greatly increased the output of the Unemployment Grants Committee's scheme by the modification of transferred conditions, and practically by that alone. I believe that the present Unemployment Grants Committee schemes could be trebled if we did away with transfer altogether. What happens? In order to maintain transfer you cannot give proper terms to the hard-hit areas of industry. Brighton or a seaside resort to-day can get more favourable financial terms from the Unemployment Grants Committee than the hardest hit mining area in South Wales, and, as a result, those areas, those depressed areas, cannot go ahead with schemes at all. They are burdened with rates, and even if they were prepared to raise fresh money the Ministry of Health would forbid them on financial grounds. Not only the depressed areas, but other areas with over 10 per cent. of unemployment get much less favourable financial terms, and they simply cannot go ahead with their schemes because they cannot put up the enormous share of the cost which falls upon them, while at the same time prosperous areas, with little or no unemployment, can get far more favourable financial terms, the details of which I described in the House of Commons last November.

What is the official defence of this? The defence is that these areas with under 10 per cent. of unemployment have to accept transfer from other areas. To make them do that they have to be given a premium in the shape of more favourable financial terms, otherwise transfer will appear as an obligation imposed rather than an obligation accepted in return for a reward. Therefore, if the transfer system is kept, the hard-hit areas are bound to get less favourable financial terms than the more prosperous areas. The result of that is that your schemes are hit in both ways. The depressed areas, the hard-hit areas cannot go ahead because the financial assistance is not good enough, and the prosperous areas will not go ahead because with any unemployment of their own they will not take transferred labour from other districts. Therefore, you catch it both ways. You are hit in every direction and your work is broken up and frustrated. What is the defence of all this? We are told that the hard-hit areas are economically dead, that they are finished, and that the only plan is to move the labour out from them. It may be true that those areas will never employ as many people as they did before, but it is a fallacy and overstatement to say that they are dead. Because less people will be employed in South Wales than before, is no reason for allowing its unclassified roads to fall to pieces or to deprive it of the ordinary amenities of financial assistance from the Exchequer which Brighton, Eastbourne or Worthing can obtain from the Exchequer. It is a most extraordinary doctrine.

Another way in which the Unemployment Grants Committee plans are held up is that the whole concentration is on works of magnitude, great wealthy corporations carrying out vast water schemes, and things of that kind. That is where you get delay and the necessity for Parliamentary powers. If you gave to all the small places more favourable financial terms, spreading your assistance all over Britain and letting them carry out schemes which they can do within their own boundaries, without Parliamentary powers of any kind, then not only would you enormously increase the aggregate of your schemes but you would diffuse and spread your relief all over Britain into every constituency and every town. Therefore, I suggested that transfer should be done away with as far as the Unemployment Grants Committee work was concerned, that the financial terms should be uniform throughout, and that in the depressed areas 100 per cent. grants should be made by the State. We have to face realities. In the depressed areas they cannot put up a penny. Either the work will not be done or the State must pay for it. If the State does not like to make a 100 per cent. grant to the local authorities in those areas, then let the State either do the work itself, employing the local authority as the contractor, or employ an actual contractor, if it must.

It is no good deluding ourselves that any formulas will get us round the depressed area problem. I was told to announce from that Box, in November, that a formula would be discovered to deal with South Wales. I made that announcement, in accordance with my instructions, but we failed absolutely with the Ministry of Health and the Treasury. They are still hunting for a formula, and they will never find it until

they face the reality that a 100 per cent. grant, and that alone, will get a move on in these areas. With these methods and the abolition of transfer I sincerely believe that the increase in work schemes which I have described could be achieved. With regard to transfer, we want, if we can, to draw men from the depressed areas to other parts of the country if and when useful jobs can be found for them and not to draw them away just to put men out of jobs in those areas. The only way to secure the transfer of labour is by national schemes, in which the State either does the work itself or puts up such a large proportion of money that it can impose its own terms. There are only three ways in which that can be done— slum clearance, land drainage and the roads. On slum clearance and land drainage I made this submission. They were right outside my Department, but I asked the Government whether they would consider a more direct intervention on the part of the State, with a view to short-circuiting the local delays. I believe that in such schemes something approximating to a mobile labour corps, under decent conditions of labour and wages, of course, could have been employed to deal with that problem. I make that submission for what it is worth, and proceed to the roads.

The road programme, as I have said, does not annually exceed the programme of the late Government. If you ask me: "Have you got the latest, the final engineering plans to build £100,000,000 worth of roads in this country?" I say, "No," and I say that it would be a great waste of time if any Department had worked out those plans before we knew if we could go ahead with them or not. I could not do it. My staff, one very able and devoted Treasury official, could not do it. The Ministry of Transport would not do it. I think they properly would not do it until they had settled in principle with the Treasury whether they could go ahead to that limit of money, if they were permitted to do it. If I am asked, "Can you define the administrative methods and procedure by which, in your belief, that achievement can be carried through?" I reply, "Yes," and I will go on to describe that administrative method and procedure, very briefly.

Our central difficulty in building roads quickly is the relationship of the State

[Sir O. Mosley.]

and the local authorities. On the one hand, you cannot ride rough-shod, and no one wants to ride rough-shod over the local authorities. On the other hand, the work has to be done. I am one of those who believe that the great main roads of this country should be national concerns, and that it is as much an anachronism to leave these roads in local hands as it would be to leave the railways in local hands. I admit that that raises a large controversy, but I try always to face reality and a practical situation, and I believe you can get round that difficulty and get agreement quickly in this way—leave the question of the nationalised roads until you settle the major question later, when you have to face the whole transport equilibrium of this country, as we have not begun to do. What matters in the building of roads quickly in relation to this problem is not the construction of the roads but the maintenance of the roads. Let the State construct and hand over to the local authority for subsequent maintenance. The local authorities would be something more than human or less than human if they objected very strongly to having their work done for them. This principle has been employed before, and in many cases the local authorities would do the work for you if your grant was anything approaching 100 per cent., or of such generous terms as to make a really tempting offer.

If you made it clear that this machinery was emergency machinery and formed no part of the permanent relationship between the State and the local authorities, then I believe that, without upsetting the existing relationship, you would get through that emergency programme on the basis of the State constructing and the local authority maintaining, until your whole system was decided upon. But before you launch out on any such programme you have to make up your mind, in broad outline, what the permanent transport equilibrium of this country is to be. On every turn when we want to build roads we are told that it will damage the railways. What is to be the relationship between railway, road and canal in the future? No research, no thinking beyond the Commission—which has been sitting for long, and is to report later —is going on in this country; no examination by Government; not faced up to by Government, and so at every turn your road programme and your immediate unemployment programme is thwarted because it is said any great development of the roads will injure the railways. That matter has to be decided.

Further, we have to face this fact that to get things done quickly the State has to put up a large share of the cost. If you put up more generous terms under Unemployment Grants Committee work and road work for the emergency programme, and give the local authorities a now-or-never position, and say to them, " Here is your chance to get jobs done which are necessary to do. This is not the permanent problem of unemployment. We are merely bridging the gulf before the fruition of our long-term measures. Directly our permanent reconstruction is achieved this emergency programme will come to an end, at the end of three years or more, and you local authorities will have missed your chance ; you will not for ever be getting assistance from the State to do your job." In those circumstances, you would get every local authority coming forward with schemes, if you face them with a " now-or-never " position and urge them forward with machinery of Government, which must be rather similar to the machine of the right hon. Member for Carnarvon Boroughs (Mr. Lloyd George) under the National Health Insurance Act, when I believe he had machinery going into every constituency and to every local authority, explaining it and gingering up the locality. Such a machine is needed in this work, because nothing is so astonishing as the ignorance of many local authorities, and even their paid officials, as to the conditions offered by the Government. Have your emergency programme, have your now-or-never position, and then, with a great drive of Government machinery behind it, you will easily treble the work of the Unemployment Grants Committee programme.

I am coming now to my conclusion. I am sorry to have detained the Committee so long, but it is amazingly difficult to cover such a vast field as this in a short time. We have to face up to this fact, that if men are to be employed on any large scale that employment has to be paid for either by the State or by local authorities. There is a tremendous struggle, an incessant struggle, going on in every Government department to put every penny they can off the taxpayer and on to the ratepayer. What holds up these plans for months is the struggle for these pennies, these minor details. What does it matter? What is the use of shifting the burden from the taxpayer to the ratepayer? What is the use of lifting the burden from the right shoulder to the left? It is the same man who has to carry it, and the economic fact is this, as the Colwyn and every other authoritative inquiry upon the economic side has said, that the burden on the ratepayer is more onerous upon industry than the burden upon the taxpayer. If this burden has to be carried, need we struggle and waste time in deciding whether it is to be carried by the taxpayer or by the ratepayer?

Further, it must be remembered that to set many men working for a year costs a great deal of money. It costs £1,000,000 to employ 4,000 men at work for a year, and £100,000,000 to employ 400,000 men for a year. Therefore, if you are going to do this work on any large scale large sums of money will have to be raised by the State or local authorities to carry it out. How is it to be raised, out of revenue or out of loan? £100,000,000 out of revenue! Who will suggest it in the present situation? It is 2s. on the Income Tax. It must be raised by loan. If the principle of a big loan is turned down then this kind of work must come to an end. It has been suggested that I advocated the raising of large loans and spending the money afterwards on any programme we could find. Nobody would be so mad as to suggest anything of the kind. This money, under a three years programme, would be raised as and when required to pay for that programme over a period of three years. It is not a question of raising £100,000,000 right away. It would be spread over at least three years, or even longer as there is always a big lag between the work and payment.

If this loan cannot be raised then unemployment, as an emergency and immediate problem, cannot be dealt with. If we are told that we cannot have the money let us confess defeat honourably and honestly; let us run up the white flag of surrender if we cannot have the money to pay for unemployment. If we are to deal with unemployment then the money, by revenue or by loan, has to be found. I advocate the method of a loan, and in my programme the amount which would fall upon the Exchequer would be the small charge of £10,000,000 a year. I have no doubt that we shall hear from the right hon. Member for Epping (Mr. Churchill) in answer to this latter part of my case, what he has so often described as the Treasury view: the view that any money loans raised by the Government must be taken from other industrial activities and will put out of employment as many men as are put in employment. The right hon. Gentleman in powerful expositions has often put forward that case. How far is that case supported by the present Government? I should like to have the views of the Chancellor of the Exchequer, for every argument with which I have been met seems to support that case. I admit that there is some force in that view in a period of acute deflation. If you are pursuing a deflation policy, restricting the whole basis of credit, there is some force in what is known as the Treasury view, that it is difficult to raise large loans for such purposes as this. The "Financial Times" on 14th April said:

"The policy of deflation is apparently proceeding apace,"

and it went on to observe that it was no use having a low bank rate if the whole basis of credit was restricted and charged the Chancellor of the Exchequer in his action in regard to Treasury Bills with a large share of the responsibility. I am not going into that subject on this occasion because there will be other opportunities for doing so, but I agree that if you are pursuing a policy of deflation you are lending force to the Treasury view. Given, however, a financial policy of stabilisation, that Treasury point of view cannot hold water. It would mean that every single new enterprise is going to put as many men out of employment as it will employ. That is a complete absurdity if you pursue that argument to its logical conclusion. If it is true it means that nothing can ever be done by the Government or by Parliament. It means that no Government has any function or any purpose; it is a policy of complete surrender. It has

[Sir O. Mosley.]

been said rather curiously, in view of the modesty of my programme, that it is the policy of the " red flag." I might reply that what is known as the Treasury view is the policy of the " white " flag. It is a policy of surrender, of negation, by which any policy can be frustrated and blocked in this country.

Hanging all over that policy is the great conception of conversion. There are two ways of achieving conversion. One through the inherent financial strength of your position, leading to a strengthening of Government credit. The other is by the simple process of deflation to make all industrial investments unprofitable, and drive your investor into Government Securities because he has no other profitable outlet. But there may be another effect of that policy; that the money goes abroad, and then you get the logical effect of that policy suggested by the President of the Board of Trade as the only means of solving our industrial problems, when he said on the 14th May:

" During the past fortnight alone £16,000,000 of new capital has been authorised or raised for overseas investment, and so I trust the process will continue."

Why? Why is it so right and proper and desirable that capital should go overseas to equip factories to compete against us, to build roads and railways in the Argentine or in Timbuctoo, to provide employment for people in those countries while it is supposed to shake the whole basis of our financial strength if anyone dares to suggest the raising of money by the Government of this country to provide employment for the people of this country? If those views are passed without examination or challenge the position of this country is serious indeed. In conclusion let me say that the situation which faces us is, of course, very serious. Everybody knows that; and perhaps those who have been in office for a short time know it even better. It is not, I confidently believe, irreparable, but I feel this from the depths of my being, that the days of muddling through are over, that this time we cannot muddle through.

This nation has to be mobilised and rallied for a tremendous effort, and who can do that except the Government of the day? If that effort is not made we may soon come to crisis, to a real crisis. I do not fear that so much, for this reason, that in a crisis this nation is always at its best. This people knows how to handle a crisis, it cools their heads and steels their nerves. What I fear much more than a sudden crisis is a long, slow, crumbling through the years until we sink to the level of a Spain, a gradual paralysis beneath which all the vigour and energy of this country will succumb. That is a far more dangerous thing, and far more likely to happen unless some effort is made. If the effort is made how relatively easily can disaster be averted. You have in this country resources, skilled craftsmen among the workers, design and technique among the technicians, unknown and unequalled in any other country in the world. What a fantastic assumption it is that a nation which within the lifetime of every one has put forth efforts of energy and vigour unequalled in the history of the world, should succumb before an economic situation such as the present. If the situation is to be overcome, if the great powers of this country are to be rallied and mobilised for a great national effort, then the Government and Parliament must give a lead. I beg the Government tonight to give the vital forces of this country the chance that they await. I beg Parliament to give that lead.

Mr. LLOYD GEORGE: We have listened to a very remarkable and powerful speech from the hon. Member for Smethwick (Sir O. Mosley). He has put his case with remarkable lucidity and force, and he certainly need not have apologised for the time he occupied. I am perfectly certain that it is the feeling of every hon. Member that he did not waste any words and that he could not have compressed the case he was bound to put into fewer words. I profoundly agree with his final sentence, and, with such powers as I have, I want to drive that appeal home to the Prime Minister. The proposals of the hon. Member for Smethwick were good in parts. Some of them I found quite palatable; there were others which were a little high. When he came to his long-term programme, I thought I detected some of the heresies which he must have imbibed in the party in which he was brought up. It is perfectly true that his conclusions are different from those of hon. Members above the Gangway, but his fundamental argu-

Leo Amery exercises Back-Bench power to help change the course of history

Monday 27 April 1992 was a remarkable day in parliamentary history. It was the day that the House of Commons elected its first woman Speaker. After 154 men had held the position for some six centuries, **Betty Boothroyd** was elected to the Chair at the start of eight impressive years that were to end with her becoming Baroness Boothroyd of Sandwell.

The other outstanding event of the day for those whose memory of the House went back decades was the spontaneous applause that erupted from the crowded green Benches when, in the formal terminology of the *Official Report,* she took her place "on the upper step" – one step away from the Chair itself – to express her thanks for having been elected.

The Chamber had never before heard the sound of clapping. It was a time not to break the rules, but to change them. One of her first decisions was not to wear the Speaker's wig. Since that time, applause has again been heard, and the Speaker's wig remains on its stand, unused.

In the debate that preceded her election, the House inevitably had been excited and fascinated at the prospect of a woman Speaker. But in her speech accepting the nomination, she had directed her fellow MPs to what she considered to be a matter of greater substance – to ensure that the House voted the right person into the job. The worst possible result, both for the House and for the cause of women, would be a bad woman Speaker, she told them. "Elect me for what I am, not for what I was born," she said.

Her supporters had little doubt about her suitability or capabilities. They had seen her in action as Deputy Speaker for the preceding five years, and they knew, too, that she had acquired a hard edge as a Government Whip.

Speakers always bring their own style to the Chair, and Madam Speaker Boothroyd was no exception. Her no-nonsense manner and the firm grip she always maintained on a House that had shown that it could be boisterous verging on riotous won her admiration from across the world as television pictures of her were beamed into millions of homes.

But while she would brook no misbehaviour from Back Benchers, she was passionate in her defence of their rights in the face of the power of the Executive. It was a stance that she regarded as incumbent on any occupant of the Chair. Some of her sternest reprimands, usually behind the scenes, were reserved for Ministers who had shown what she considered to be disrespect for the House by making announcements to the media before giving the information to Back Benchers in the Chamber.

She was born in Dewsbury, West Yorkshire, where her parents worked in the local woollen mills. She joined the Labour party as a teenager, won a national speaking award, and began her career at Westminster as a personal assistant to leading Labour party figures. In 1960 she took a year off to work in the United States, first as a volunteer in the John F. Kennedy presidential campaign and then as a full-time secretary for a Congressman on Capitol Hill.

She became an MP at her fifth attempt when in May 1973 she won the midlands seat of West Bromwich at a by-election. She represented the constituency until she retired from the House in 2000 when she was made a life peer with the title Baroness Boothroyd of Sandwell. She sits in the House of Lords as a Cross Bencher – the Lords title for an Independent.

During her time as Speaker she welcomed many foreign leaders to Westminster including Boris Yeltsin, Bill Clinton and Nelson Mandela, with whom she addressed a distinguished audience in the historic setting of Westminster Hall. She was also invited to address the Russian Duma, and she attended the 50th anniversary of Indian independence as the overseas guest.

In 2005, the Queen recognised her services to the nation by making her one of the only 24 holders of the Order of Merit.

Her other awards include freedom of the City of London and honorary degrees from the Universities of Oxford, Cambridge and St Andrews. As Speaker, she was voted Parliamentarian of the Year, Personality of the Year and Communicator of the Year.

When she retired from the Chair, she told MPs:"Rejoice in your inheritance, defend your rights and remember always that the privileges the House enjoys were dearly won and must never be squandered."

Ferocious attack that spelt the end for Chamberlain and opened the way for Churchill

By Rt hon Baroness Boothroyd of Sandwell OM

Back Benchers come into their own when the ruling party is divided and Governments have to fight for every vote. It happened during my time as Speaker when John Major failed to persuade his party's Eurosceptics to accept the Maastricht treaty. I used my casting vote, as the rules required, to defeat an Opposition amendment that would have changed the treaty. The atmosphere was electric. Party lines were blurred. Britain's future in Europe hung in the balance.

But the stakes were nothing compared with those that faced the House on 7 May 1940. Hitler had occupied Norway and Denmark in a daring operation that caught Britain totally unprepared. An ill-equipped, disorganised expeditionary force was sent to Narvik, but was being forced to withdraw as the House began a two-day debate.

The Government's 240 plus majority seemed impregnable until Leo Amery, Conservative Member for Birmingham, Sparkbrook, and a former Minister, attacked Neville Chamberlain's handling of the war with such ferocity that his premiership was fatally undermined and Winston Churchill emerged to lead a national coalition. Amery, by elevating patriotism above party, showed the Back Bencher's power to help change the course of history.

Harold Macmillan said it was the most formidable attack he ever heard by a former Minister against a lifelong friend and colleague. Rejecting Chamberlain's appeal to his friends to support him, Amery replied in words that echo down the decades: "There are no loyalties today except to the common cause" – to win the war. "It is Parliament itself that is on trial in this war," Amery declared. "If we lose this war, it is not this or that ephemeral Government, but Parliament as an institution that will be condemned for good and all."

Churchill listened from the Government Front Bench. Chamberlain had made him First Lord of the Admiralty, the position he held in 1914, when the war broke out. He and Amery had known each other since they were schoolboys at Harrow. They had both opposed Chamberlain's appeasement of Hitler in the 1930s, but it was left to Amery to deliver the hammer blows that destroyed was little was left of Chamberlain's credibility. He spoke for 41 minutes and was heard without interruption, an astonishing feat.

He succeeded, I think, because he appealed to the deepest instincts of the House in a national crisis. He led no faction and sought no personal advantage. He used his experience as a former Minister to good effect. He disclosed that Whitehall had known of German ambitions to seize the Norwegian ports four months earlier, but nothing had been done to prevent it.

He recalled Chamberlain's boast that Hitler had "missed the bus" in not attacking the west earlier. Now they had gained "the whole of Scandinavia" by occupying Norway and Denmark and enclosing Sweden. Amery's solution was stark and unanswerable. "We cannot go on as we are. There must be a change." Above all, war had to be waged on military principles by a united people.

It could not be won by "shirking risks" and relying on policies based on the "feeblest common denominator". The country needed a "supreme war directorate" supported by the Labour party and the trade union movement. "The next blow may fall at any moment," he said. "It may be Holland." He was proved right three days later when Germany attacked the Low Countries and the western front began to crumble.

Amery did not call for Churchill to replace Chamberlain on 7 May. However, first Chamberlain had to go. "Somehow or other, we must get into the Government men who can match our enemies in fighting spirit, in daring, in resolution and in thirst for victory," Amery declared. He closed by quoting Cromwell's dismissal of the moribund Long Parliament, which served as Chamberlain's epitaph, too. "You have sat too long here for any good you have been doing. Depart, I say, and let us have done with you. In the name of God go."

Chamberlain resigned on 10 May, when Hitler unleashed his blitzkrieg against the Low Countries and France. That same day the Labour party agreed to serve under Churchill, and Amery, the Empire man, became Secretary of State for India. United at last in a common purpose, Parliament finally went to war with its honour intact.

[Captain Bellinger.]

satisfied with the Government, I am certain that many of those serving in the Army to-day are not.

As a Minister who recently represented the War Office is here at the moment, I would like in passing to bring to his notice what may seem a small matter but which, I am sure, is not. If it were an isolated case, I would have brought it to the notice of the War Office by a letter. I have a letter from one of my constituents who tells me about a brother of his who is in Norway. He belongs to the Sherwood Foresters, which is one of the regiments that were engaged in this operation. It is now common knowledge that it was, and as it has appeared in the Press I am not divulging any military secret. My correspondent asks me whether I can find out what has happened to his brother, and he says:

" Of course, since the 8th Foresters are recruited from this district there are literally hundreds of your constituents whose anxiety and suffering are no less than our own."

I would appeal to the War Office to give some reassuring information to the parents of those men who are abroad. If there have been casualties, let them know it. In the last war casualties were promptly notified, quite often by telegram, and the parents or relations were not kept in suspended anxiety. If those men are safe, why is it not possible to say so? That is all I ask the War Office to do, to relieve the anxiety which many of those parents and relations are suffering.

I would only say, in conclusion, that it is no good the Opposition criticising the Government—which is one of their essential functions—unless they are prepared to make some constructive proposal. It is not the slightest use the Prime Minister throwing across the Table, as he did this afternoon, some sort of suggestion that his mind is always open to proposals. We know only too well that the Prime Minister can be a very obstinate man, and if his proposal is that certain Members of the Opposition should take office under him, I for one would say that it would be impossible. We have criticised the policy of the Prime Minister in this House and outside it so often, and it is impossible for us at the present time, when we believe that the Prime Minister is mainly responsible for not choosing a Government which can carry out this job properly, to serve under him. I think,

and I suggest to my hon. and right hon. Friends on these benches, that the time is not far distant—it may even have arrived —when the Opposition should accept its responsibility before the nation and say openly whether it is prepared to take part in any Government. I, personally, believe—my views may not be in accord with those of my hon. Friends, but I occupy a somewhat detached position at the present moment—that it is not sufficient for us to have a sort of critical acquiescence in Government policy, or the lack of it, at the present time. If we believe that the times are so critical, we should say openly—if we believe it, and many of us do—that the Government should make place for one of a different character and a different nature. I believe, at any rate I hope, because the times are so critical, that if there were a possibility of forming that Government —and it rests mainly with hon. Members on the other side of the House—we should play our part, as we so often say, " in the public interest."

8.3 p.m.

Mr. Amery (Birmingham, Sparkbrook): May I say that I agree wholeheartedly with what just fell from the lips of the hon. Member for Bassetlaw (Mr. Bellenger) as to the responsibility of the Opposition in playing a constructive part at this critical moment? The whole of Parliament has a grave responsibility at this moment; for, after all, it is Parliament itself that is on trial in this war. If we lose this war, it is not this or that ephemeral Government but Parliament as an institution that will be condemned, for good and all. I fully realise that this is not an easy Debate. There is much that ought to be said which cannot well be said in public. After listening to some of the speeches to-day, not least the profoundly impressive speech made by my hon. and gallant Friend the Member for North Portsmouth (Sir R. Keyes), it seems to me that the whole of recent events—not only in Norway, but the whole conduct of the war up to date—calls for searching inquiry, not for one stray private sitting, but for a series of private sittings in which all that Members of Parliament can contribute of their private knowledge should be put into the common stock and frankly discussed.

Meanwhile, even to-day there is plenty that can be said, that ought to be said, and that must be said frankly; for there are no loyalties to-day except to the common cause. This afternoon, as a few days ago, the Prime Minister gave us a reasoned, argumentative case for our failure. It is always possible to do that after every failure. Making a case and winning a war are not the same thing. Wars are won, not by explanations after the event but by foresight, by clear decision and by swift action. I confess that I did not feel there was one sentence in the Prime Minister's speech this afternoon which suggested that the Government either foresaw what Germany meant to do, or came to a clear decision when it knew what Germany had done, or acted swiftly or consistently throughout the whole of this lamentable affair. I am not going to discuss the reasons for the actual evacuation. They may well have been conclusive in the circumstances. But the circumstances should never have arisen; and it is the story of those events —of the decisions, of the absence of decisions, of the changes of decisions which brought about those circumstances— which call for our inquiry and raise many questions which have yet to be answered.

We were told by the Prime Minister on 2nd May that all except a relatively small advance guard of the Expeditionary Force which was earmarked for Finland had gone elsewhere and that the ships had been taken for employment for other purposes. Even the small, inadequate nucleus that was kept in being had no transports except warships. Why was this done? For months we had been aware that the Germans had been accumulating troops and transports and practising embarkation and disembarkation against somebody. It is perfectly true that they could spare the ships better than we could. But was there any reason which would make us believe that they were sending the men elsewhere? Obviously the danger was there and might develop into actuality at any moment. The Prime Minister suggested that we could not know which of many objectives it might be. Surely we had some good reasons for suspecting which one it might be. The Finnish war had focussed the interest of the whole world on Scandinavia. Within a week of its termination the Prime Minister declared, speaking of Norway and Sweden, that the danger to them—from Germany—" stands upon

their very doorstep." The Altmark affair had before that showed clearly the illegal uses which Germany was prepared to make of Norwegian neutrality. What is more, within a few days of that statement we ourselves decided deliberately to challenge Germany over her use of Norway's territorial waters. All the world knew that that was the main theme of the deliberations of the Supreme War Council which met, I think, on 28th March. To make that perfectly clear to the whole world, including Germany, the Prime Minister said, on 2nd April: " We have not yet reached the limit of our effective operations in waters close to the German bases." That was sufficient warning. On 8th April we laid our mines.

What did we expect to follow? Did we know Hitler and his merry men so little as to think that their rejoinder would be slow or half-hearted, or that it would follow the lines of " too little and too late " with which we have been so familiar here? However, it was not a question of a German rejoinder at all, but of Germany making our half-hearted intervention an excuse for measures far greater in scope and far more daring than we seem even to have envisaged. My hon. and gallant Friend the Member for Bournemouth (Sir H. Croft) was congratulating ourselves upon Hitler's strategic folly in going to Norway. Does he realise that, from the moment we were in the war, Admiral Raeder insisted that this time the German Navy could not afford to be confined to the existing German coastline, but that, for the purposes of his air and submarine warfare, he must have not only egress from the Baltic but the whole of the indented, deep-water coastline of Norway?

I understand that information as to this reached our Departments early in January. Was that aspect of the strategic situation considered? Again, it was known everywhere that Hitler had designs on Scandinavia. Was it not obvious that the first stroke must be directed against Denmark and Norway, not only because they were weaker, but because once Hitler had seized them, Sweden was automatically within his power without the need for conquest? I would ask another question: Is it not a fact that the most direct warnings of Germany's designs against Norway were sent from both Stockholm and Copen-

[Mr. Amery.]
hagen in the first few days of April? I am afraid that what really happened was that, while we thought we were taking the initiative, our initiative, such as it was, only coincided with a far more formidable and far better planned initiative of the enemy.

I remember that many years ago in East Africa a young friend of mine went lion hunting. He secured a sleeping car on the railway and had it detached from the train at a siding near where he expected to find a certain man-eating lion. He went to rest and dream of hunting his lion in the morning. Unfortunately, the lion was out man-hunting that night. He clambered on to the rear of the car, scrabbled open the sliding door, and ate my friend. That is in brief the story of our initiative over Norway. In any case, even if we did not realise that the Germans were acting at the same time, why were we not prepared to meet their inevitable counter-stroke? We had only this inadequate little force, without transports, of which the Prime Minister has told us, in readiness to occupy Norwegian western ports if there were German action against Southern Norway. There was no plan to meet the contingency that Germany might seize the western ports as well or to meet any really serious attack by Germany upon Norway. As we know now, the German detachments for the more distant ports, Trondheim and Narvik, were despatched more than a week before, in readiness for the zero hour when all the German forces were to strike.

On 8th April we laid our mines. That time happened to be just before Germany's zero hour. On the morning of that day a great German convoy sailed up the Kattegat and into the Skagerrak on its highly dangerous mission. To cover this daring manoeuvre the Germans sent a large part of their fleet, 48 hours before, away up the West coast of Norway towards Narvik. That action was duly reported to us, and the Prime Minister has told us that the Navy went off in hot pursuit after that German decoy. Rarely in history can a feint have been more successful. The gallantry of our officers and men in the blizzards of the Arctic, and the losses of the German fleet, serious as they were, do not alter the fact that the main German expedition to Norway took place without any interference from the Fleet, except from our submarines. With amazing courage and resolution, our submarines inflicted heavy losses on the Germans. How much heavier would those losses have been if the Fleet or any substantial portion of it had been there then, or, at any rate on subsequent days. That raises very formidable questions to which answers will have to be given sooner or later.

However, let me come to the next stage. What was our reaction when we learned that Oslo and all the main ports were in German hands? If we had any hope of retrieving the situation in Norway even partially, or of relieving the Norwegian forces, our obvious move was to retake one or other of those ports without a moment's delay. We now know that the Germans seized them with only the tiniest handful of men. Only by seizing such a port would it have been possible to obtain landing facilities for our artillery and tanks, and above all, aerodromes, without which no operation could be conducted with any hope of success. The port clearly indicated by the circumstances was Trondheim, because it was farthest removed from the main German base at Oslo—which gave us time and the opportunity of maintaining railway connection with Sweden. We could have constructed a defensive line across the waist of Norway, behind which the Norwegian forces could have rallied, and from which we could have advanced, if necessary, to the reconquest of the country. That was the obvious plan.

The Prime Minister's statements, however, make it clear that such forces as we had were at once sent off to Narvik, and not to their original destination of Trondheim or Bergen. Why Narvik? If we had held Trondheim, the isolated German force at Narvik would have been bound to surrender in time, and it could have done no mischief to us in the meantime. If we had ever contemplated retaking Trondheim at the start, there could have been no more crass instance of the dispersion, the frittering away, of forces. It is clear, however, from what the Prime Minister said to-day that the decision to send troops to Trondheim to try and retrieve that position was an afterthought, taken only after a number of days, and only at the urgent request of the Norwegians. How was it carried out? We have listened to the impressive speech of my hon. and gallant Friend the Member for North Portsmouth. It is common knowledge that the original plan accepted by the Government for the taking of Trondheim was that the Navy should force its way into Narvik fiord while subsidiary landings took place to North and South. Once in the fiord our ships could command the whole of its vast coastline, with its roads and railway and its aerodrome. What we are entitled to ask is a very serious question: By whom and on whose authority was the indispensable hammer blow at Trondheim itself countermanded? Of course, there were risks. War is not won by shirking risks. Once the linch pin of the Trondheim operations was withdrawn, the rest was bound to fail precisely as it has failed.

As to those operations, there are many stories that reach us which cannot be discussed here. Our men did their best in impossible conditions, and one can only be glad that they got away. At the same time there is something which I feel bound to say. The Prime Minister, both the other day and to-day, expressed himself as satisfied that the balance of advantage lay on our side. He laid great stress on the heaviness of the German losses and the lightness of ours. What did the Germans lose? A few thousand men, nothing to them, a score of transports, and part of a Navy which anyhow cannot match ours. What did they gain? They gained Norway, with the strategical advantages which, in their opinion at least, outweigh the whole of their naval losses. They have gained the whole of Scandinavia. What have we lost? To begin with, we have lost most of the Norwegian Army, not only such as it was but such as it might have become if only we had been given time to rally and re-equip it. It goes to one's heart to think of the Norwegian forces trapped in southern Norway and forced to surrender after their bitter protest against that withdrawal. I am glad that the right hon. Gentleman the Leader of the Liberal Opposition paid the tribute which he did to the gallantry of the Norwegian troops under adverse circumstances. What we have lost, above all, is one of those opportunities which do not recur in war. If we could have captured and held Trondheim, and if we could have rallied the Norwegian forces, then we might well have imposed a strain on Germany which

might have made Norway to Hitler what Spain was once to Napoleon. All we can hope for now is that we may hang on to Narvik, and that will not be too easy, till the tide of war turns against Germany elsewhere. So much for the Norwegian chapter. It is a bad story, a story of lack of prevision and of preparation, a story of indecision, slowness and fear of taking risks. If only it stood alone. Unfortunately, it does not. It is only of a piece with the rest of it, of a piece with our hesitation and slowness in responding to Finland's appeals for arms, in our handling of economic warfare and the re-organisation of industry, of our re-training of our workers, of the production of the essential munitions of war, of agriculture —in fact, the whole of our national effort, which, according to the Chancellor of the Exchequer, is apparently to be at most 10 per cent. higher in the course of this year than it is to-day.

The right hon. Gentleman the Prime Minister—I fully understand the good reason for his absence—in a digression explained why he used a certain unlucky phrase about Hitler missing the bus. He explained that what he meant was that during these eight months of war Hitler had lost the opportunity which he had at the beginning of the war because we had been catching up on Germany's preparations. Believe me, that is very far from the truth. While we may catch up on her presently if only we do what we ought to, there is no doubt that during these eight months, thanks to Germany's flying start and our slowness off the mark, the gap between the German forces and ours has widened enormously as far as troops, their equipment, tanks, guns and all the paraphernalia of land war are concerned. It has widened in the air, even if we reckon in things which may be " accruing " to us. That is a curious phrase, the precise meaning of which is difficult to determine. I remember that on the very morning of that speech I was reading the financial statement of a company which among its prospects included interest accruing to it from a mine in which gold had not yet been discovered.

We cannot go on as we are. There must be a change. First and foremost, it must be a change in the system and structure of our governmental machine. This is war, not peace. The essence of peace-time democratic government is

[Mr. Amery.]

discussion, conference and agreement; the Cabinet is in a sense a miniature Parliament. The main aim is agreement, the widest possible measure of agreement. To secure that it is necessary to compromise, to postpone, to rediscuss. Under those conditions there are no far-reaching plans for sudden action. It is a good thing to let policies develop as you go along and get people educated by circumstances. That may or may not be ideal in peace. It is impossible in war. In war the first essential is planning ahead. The next essential is swift, decisive action.

We can wage war only on military principles. One of the first of these principles is the clear definition of individual responsibilities—not party responsibilities or Cabinet responsibilities—and, with it, a proper delegation of authority. What commander-in-chief attempts to command 20 or 30 divisions in the field? He delegates the task to a number of army corps commanders responsible to him alone, and with authority over the divisional commanders underneath them. The last thing such a commander-in-chief would ever dream of doing is to make some of his army corps commanders divisional commanders as well. What is our present Cabinet system? There are some 25 Ministers, heads of Departments, who have no direct chief above them except the Prime Minister. How often do they see him? How often can they get from him direct advice, direct impulse, direct drive? Who is to settle disputes between them? There should be someone, not chairmen of innumerable committees, but someone with authority over these Ministers and directly responsible for their efficiency.

There is another cardinal principle of warfare: that is, the clear separation of the framing and execution of policy and the planning of operations, from administration. That is why every Army, Navy and Air Force has its General Staff. It is well known that the same man cannot do the work of administration and also frame and execute policy. How can you get either policy or administration from a Cabinet in which the two are mixed up hugger-mugger as they are at the present time? The next blow may fall at any moment. It may be in Holland; it may be in the Mediterranean. How many hours has any of the three Service Ministers been able to give during the last three weeks to the innumerable preparations required for that contingency? With the present organisation, there is not the slightest chance for them to consider these matters properly.

The Prime Minister has told us to-day of the change that he has made in at last giving a director and guide to the Chiefs of Staff Committee. He said that this struck him as being a good idea. For four years or more, ever since the Chiefs of Staff Committee was first spoken of in this House, some of us have said that it was impossible to produce adequate plans from a committee of men representing three separate Services, and each concerned to guard the interests of his own Service, without a chief over them. The result has inevitably been what I might call plans based on " the feeblest common denominator." Now at last something is done to place the responsibility for framing and deciding plans clearly upon my right hon. Friend. The Prime Minister tells us that this has no connection with recent events in Norway; it is just a happy new idea. It is curious how we have for years now so effectively been locking the stable door always after we have discovered the loss of the horse. Anyhow, if those are the right functions for my right hon. Friend, how can he also carry on the tremendous tasks of the First Lord of the Admiralty? The Leader of the Opposition said that it was not fair to him. It is not fair to his colleagues; it is not fair to the nation.

Believe me, as long as the present methods prevail, all our valour and all our resources are not going to see us through. Above all, so long as they prevail, time is not going to be on our side, because they are methods which, inevitably and inherently, waste time and weaken decisions. What we must have, and have soon, is a supreme war directorate of a handful of men free from administrative routine, free to frame policy among themselves, and with the task of supervising, inspiring, and impelling a group of departments clearly allocated to each one of them. That is the only way. We learned that in the last war. My right hon. Friend the Member for Carnarvon Boroughs (Mr. Lloyd George) earned the undying gratitude of the nation for the courage he showed in adopting what was then a new experiment. The experiment worked, and it helped to win the war. After the war years, the Committee of Imperial Defence laid it down as axiomatic that, while in a minor war you might go on with an ordinary Cabinet, helped perhaps by a War Committee, in a major war you must have a War Cabinet—meaning precisely the type of Cabinet that my right hon. Friend introduced then. The overwhelming opinion of this House and of the public outside has been demanding that for a long while. We are told that there would be no particular advantage in it at the present time. I ask, Is this or is this not a major war?

We must have, first of all, a right organisation of government. What is no less important to-day is that the Government shall be able to draw upon the whole abilities of the nation. It must represent all the elements of real political power in this country, whether in this House or not. The time has come when hon. and right hon. Members opposite must definitely take their share of the responsibility. The time has come when the organisation, the power and influence of the Trades Union Congress cannot be left outside. It must, through one of its recognised leaders, reinforce the strength of the national effort from inside. The time has come, in other words, for a real National Government. I may be asked what is my alternative Government. That is not my concern: it is not the concern of this House. The duty of this House, and the duty that it ought to exercise, is to show unmistakably what kind of Government it wants in order to win the war. It must always be left to some individual leader, working perhaps with a few others, to express that will by selecting his colleagues so as to form a Government which will correspond to the will of the House and enjoy its confidence. So I refuse, and I hope the House will refuse, to be drawn into a discussion on personalities.

What I would say, however, is this: Just as our peace-time system is unsuitable for war conditions, so does it tend to breed peace-time statesmen who are not too well fitted for the conduct of war. Facility in debate, ability to state a case, caution in advancing an unpopular view, compromise and procrastination are the natural qualities—I might almost say, virtues—of a political leader in time of peace. They are fatal qualities in war. Vision, daring, swiftness and consistency of

decision are the very essence of victory. In our normal politics, it is true, the conflict of party did encourage a certain combative spirit. In the last war we Tories found that the most perniciously aggressive of our opponents, the right hon. Member for Carnarvon Boroughs, was not only aggressive in words, but was a man of action. In recent years the normal weakness of our political life has been accentuated by a coalition based upon no clear political principles. It was in fact begotten of a false alarm as to the disastrous results of going off the Gold Standard. It is a coalition which has been living ever since in a twilight atmosphere between Protection and Free Trade and between unprepared collective security and unprepared isolation. Surely, for the Government of the last 10 years to have bred a band of warrior statesmen would have been little short of a miracle. We have waited for eight months, and the miracle has not come to pass. Can we afford to wait any longer?

Somehow or other we must get into the Government men who can match our enemies in fighting spirit, in daring, in resolution and in thirst for victory. Some 300 years ago, when this House found that its troops were being beaten again and again by the dash and daring of the Cavaliers, by Prince Rupert's Cavalry, Oliver Cromwell spoke to John Hampden. In one of his speeches he recounted what he said. It was this:

" I said to him, ' Your troops are most of them old, decayed serving men and tapsters and such kind of fellows.' . . . You must get men of a spirit that are likely to go as far as they will go, or you will be beaten still."

It may not be easy to find these men. They can be found only by trial and by ruthlessly discarding all who fail and have their failings discovered. We are fighting to-day for our life, for our liberty, for our all; we cannot go on being led as we are. I have quoted certain words of Oliver Cromwell. I will quote certain other words. I do it with great reluctance, because I am speaking of those who are old friends and associates of mine, but they are words which, I think, are applicable to the present situation. This is what Cromwell said to the Long Parliament when he thought it was no longer fit to conduct the affairs of the nation:

" You have sat too long here for any good you have been doing. Depart, I say, and let us have done with you. In the name of God, go."

Edward Heath deploys forensic skill to thwart bid to reinstate death penalty

Gordon Brown became Chancellor of the Exchequer with the Labour party's sensational 1997 general election victory. He went on to run Britain's economy for the next decade until he took over as Prime Minister from Tony Blair.

His period in office of a little over 10 years made him the longest serving Chancellor in modern times. He was ranked by many as among the country's most successful Chancellors, based not least on the claim that he had given Britain its longest sustained period of economic growth in its history.

One of his first acts in office was to make the historic change of granting the Bank of England independence of Government in setting interest rates. He went on during his time at the Treasury to ensure that record sums were invested in Britain's public services, including health and education. He maintained Labour's promise not to increase income tax, although his political opponents accused him of taxing by stealth in order to raise the huge sums needed for the programmes of regeneration.

With Tony Blair and Peter Mandelson he had created New Labour. His partnership with Tony Blair over 10 years in Government was a key ingredient in securing an unprecedented three consecutive general election victories for his party. However, behind the scenes there were tensions in their relationship which led to media speculation of a rift between Labour's two most significant figures and rivalry between Blairite and Brownite factions in the party.

When the Blair premiership ended in 2007, Gordon Brown was elected party leader unopposed and moved into No 10 Downing street amid euphoria in the Labour ranks. The honeymoon was not to last. Stories of an election threatened but then not called and the unintended consequences for the lowest paid of his abolition of the 10p rate of income tax were among factors that severely dented his popularity and his party's standing in the opinion polls.

With the international banking crisis of 2008, however, he appeared to many to be in his element. He took the lead on the world stage in devising measures designed to stave off banking failures and the most severe effects of what commentators were describing as the worst catastrophe to hit world finances certainly since the 1929 crash, and possibly ever.

He had been criticised for being "too serious", but at the Labour party conference in 2008 he told his followers that serious times required a serious man. His popularity as a leader began to rise, and some opinion polls implied that the lead they had shown for the Conservatives had been narrowed.

He had entered Parliament in 1993 when he took the seat of Dunfermline, East at the age of 32. However, his political activities had started many years before. At the age of 12, he was distributing Labour party leaflets around his home town of Kirkcaldy.

Academically gifted, he was at the time the youngest student to attend Edinburgh university since the second world war. There, in addition to his academic career, he had two passions – sport and politics. In the former he suffered an injury that left him without the sight of one eye, but that did nothing to diminish his determination to pursue the latter.

He became the editor of the student magazine, which he used to propagate his political beliefs. He was careful to ensure that his political activities were not detrimental to his studies, and he secured a first class degree, then an MA and finally a PhD. After a vigorous campaign, he became the youngest-ever rector of the university, which put him in the chair of the its governing body. When he moved on, it was to take a job as a lecturer in politics at Glasgow college of technology. Meanwhile he was working hard to establish his position in the Scottish Labour party.

In the 1974 general election, he stood unsuccessfully against Michael Ancram at Edinburgh, South. There followed a job as a television journalist with Scottish Television, which he gave up when he won the Dunfermline, East seat.

Once in the Commons, he struck up a friendship with another new MP with whom he shared an office – Tony Blair. Between them they resolved that with the party at an all-time low it desperately needed to change if it was ever to get back into power. The idea of New Labour was born.

Labour leader Neil Kinnock recognised the obvious talent of these two young men. He promoted them both to the Opposition Front Bench, giving Gordon Brown the job of shadow Chief Secretary to the Treasury.

When Neil Kinnock resigned after the defeat of the 1992 general election, John Smith took over and he appointed Gordon Brown shadow Chancellor.

John Smith's tragic death meant a leadership contest. Gordon Brown backed Tony Blair. In return, Tony Blair made him his shadow Chancellor with the promise that he would head the Treasury should Labour be returned to power. The formidable team that was to spearhead Labour's achievement of that objective in 1997 was established.

Eloquence of a timeless contribution that put Members to the test and swung the debate

BY RT HON GORDON BROWN MP, PRIME MINISTER

In the 25 years I have been a Member of Parliament, the House of Commons has always in my view been at its best when challenged and aroused by the great ethical questions of our time.

The narrow partisanship and smallness of many of the day-to-day political debates we have in the House contrasts directly with the wisdom and eloquence that flows when, as recently on human embryology or down the years on capital punishment, issues of conscience inspire debates which reach the highest of standards.

I entered Parliament in June 1983. Just a month later, I sat in a packed House and saw what I still regard as one of the finest debates I have seen since.

A Tory party buoyed by election victory was looking forward to a party conference expected to be dominated by calls to bring back hanging. Mrs Thatcher and her new Home Secretary, Leon Brittan, decided to head off the issue by allowing a full debate and a free vote on the issue in the House of Commons.

Memories of the Hyde Park and Regent's Park bombings were fresh in the memory, as were the serial killings by Peter Sutcliffe and Dennis Nilsen. On the very day of the debate, four members of the Ulster Defence Regiment were murdered by the IRA in Tyrone.

Newspapers speculated that – with public opinion in their favour – the pro-hanging MPs would win the day, at least on amendments to restore the death penalty for murderers of police officers or for terrorist killers.

The debate started late in the afternoon, with dozens of MPs due to speak. Leon Brittan made a much-criticised speech, arguing against the deterrent value of the death penalty, but then announcing his support for the hanging of terrorist killers to express his particular repugnance at their crimes. By contrast, Roy Hattersley, the shadow Home Secretary, expressed his unequivocal opposition to all forms of capital punishment, and praised *The Sun* for its strong and influential opposition to the death penalty.

Then, from his familiar seat, rose Edward Heath.

Before the second world war, Heath had been preparing for a career at the Bar, and it was with the forensic skill of a lawyer that he dismantled the arguments of the pro-hanging lobby, emphasising all the while that it was for them to prove the case to change the status quo.

With dry humour, he skewered a Tory colleague who had told an interviewer that if no one else was prepared to hang people he would happily do it himself. "I ask him a rather different question. Because of his views, is he prepared to be hanged by mistake?"

For me, it was a speech for the ages. That is not just because it provides a timeless contribution to one of history's great moral and ethical debates. It is also because Heath captured the eternal dilemma for parliamentary representatives whose conscience and principles stand at odds with the views of their constituents.

With the authority of his own 33 years in the House, he urged that new MPs like me should "feel free to use their judgment."

His speech was representative of the very high standard of debate that day. Roy Jenkins memorably told the House: "The finality of the punishment is too great for the frailty of human judgment." And a series of MPs from Northern Ireland spoke with raw emotion about the impact that capital punishment would have on terrorism in the province.

But it was my sense that after Edward Heath's intervention, the mood of the House had changed, and no MP on the pro-hanging side of the debate was able to pass Heath's test by proving the case to change the status quo.

Late at night, when the Divisions came, half the Cabinet – including Mrs Thatcher – voted for at least one of the amendments to restore the death penalty, but each one was soundly defeated.

In America, which had itself restored capital punishment seven years previously, the quality of the debate won plaudits, and the *Washington Post* told its readers: "In the best traditions of British debating societies, when the votes were called, the side with the greater eloquence won the day."

And there was no more eloquent contribution than Edward Heath's.

that when we debate terrorist murders in the House and outside, by and large we think of Northern Ireland and the effects on Northern Ireland. Therefore, I ask the Home Secretary two questions: is he really coming to the House to propose, and vote for, executing men who have not been convicted by the jury system? Is that what he proposes should happen in Northern Ireland? Perhaps, as the afternoon goes on, the Home Secretary will tell us whether in 1983, in a civilised, democratic society, he is proposing that men who have not been convicted by their peers should be executed. Merely to describe the proposition is to show that it is wholly unacceptable.

I wish to make three further points, all of them concerning Northern Ireland. Having asked the Home Secretary one rhetorical question and received not so much an inadequate answer as no answer at all, I must ask him a second question. Does the Home Secretary realise that by introducing such a proposal he will concede one of the IRA's most passionate demands — that its crimes be treated differently from other people's crimes? It is a long-established principle in this country that the man who shoots a soldier should not be treated in any different way from the man who knifes a bookie's runner and steals his cash. We have always argued that two horrible crimes cannot be given different legal or judicial treatment because the man who commits one of the crimes claims that he is doing it for some special reason or from some special motive.

The IRA wants that distinction to be made. If the Home Secretary has his way, we will for the first time in our law distinguish between terrorists and common criminals. That is madness in terms of the Northern Ireland prospect. Hanging such men will mean that by their deaths they will make a far greater contribution to the cause of Republican violence than they would have made by their lives. In the eyes of thousands of Irishmen who now despise terrorism and detest the killings, suddenly the British Government will become the instrument of violence and the oppressor.

When I last said that to the House, one Conservative Member said that the martyrs would be not the hanged IRA terrorists, but their dead victims. The problem is that it will not be seen that way in the IRA recruiting areas. Nor will it be seen as a deterrent among the IRA. The Northern Ireland terrorist has virtually no concern for human life, the lives of his opponents, the lives of innocent bystanders, or even the lives of his own supporters. Terrorists have persuaded men to die on hunger strike — indeed, they have terrorised them with threats against their families if they abandon the hunger strike. In future they will organise, glory in and, worst of all, benefit from the execution of their members. It is absolute madness to provide them with such a weapon.

The Home Secretary warned us about various visions of terrorism and asked us not to accept the terrorist on his own definition of his character and conduct—and nor do I. But I ask the Home Secretary not to take comfort in the sentimental notion that all bullies are always cowards. The people with whom we are dealing in Northern Ireland are certainly vile, but weak and undetermined they are not. We must not pretend that they are something out of a *Boy's Own Paper* story. They must be dealt with in the most effective way, and judicial execution would be to play into their hands.

I conclude as I began, by making it absolutely clear——

Mr. Norman St. John-Stevas (Chelmsford) *rose*——

Mr. Hattersley: No. I am sorry, but I must conclude so that the right hon. Gentleman and others can make their speeches.

I conclude as I began. Were all the practical or pragmatic arguments against capital punishment not to apply, I should still resist its reintroduction. Supporters of capital punishment insist on comparing the crime rates before and after abolition, as though abolition itself had created a more violent society. The truth is something different. Violence has grown within our society during the past 25 years for many reasons. To legalise violence in the way proposed would make Britain not a more peaceful nation, but one in which violence had been accepted and institutionalised.

I very much regret the misuse of statistics that we have heard during the past six weeks, and will undoubtedly hear again today, but there is one other point that I regret even more—indeed, almost resent—and that is the suggestion that abolitionists think only of the perpetrators of crime and not of the crime victims. The victims, the potential victims and the relatives of the victims are, like the rest of us, men and women who will benefit most by living in a decent society where violence is loathed and rejected. That loathing must be directed against all violence—by the state as well as by individuals. By killing murderers we become too like the murderers themselves. The whole community is lowered to their standards. For that reason I shall vote against the motion and all the proposed amendments. For that reason I say with great pride that I believe that all right hon. and hon. Members in the Labour party will do the same.

4.45 pm

Mr. Edward Heath (Old Bexley and Sidcup): I wish initially to address myself to the general question of capital punishment. I think that my position is well known to all hon. Members. For more than 20 years I have been opposed to capital punishment for all crimes of homicide, and I have always voted against it. I intend to do so tonight. My position is not only as strong as it ever was; it has been confirmed in recent years.

For nearly 20 years capital punishment has been abolished in this country. My hon. and learned Friend the Member for Fylde (Sir E. Gardner), who moved the resolution with great restraint and wisdom, wishes to change the status quo. He and those who support him must prove that it is necessary, in fact vital, to change the status quo. The onus of proof rests with him and his friends. When the House judges the issue and votes tonight, it should ask itself whether the proposer of the resolution and his supporters have proved beyond any shadow of doubt that it is vital to change the status quo.

In my judgment—and I say this with great respect for my hon. and learned Friend whom I have known for many years—he has not proved his case. He said quite frankly that he did not intend to rely on statistics. The Home Secretary rightly said the same. If they did, they would have to explain why the increase in homicides began long before the abolition of the death penalty and why the increase in ordinary crimes of violence has been many times greater than the increase in homicides. It is that factor which has produced attention in the public mind. The growth of lesser crimes of violence has been so great that the public has deduced that the only answer is

461

[Mr. Edward Heath].

to deal with homicide by capital punishment. That is a confusion in the public mind. A great deal rests upon us to remove that confusion.

My hon. and learned Friend did not introduce the question of retribution and revenge, although it was mentioned by the right hon. Member for Birmingham, Sparkbrook (Mr. Hattersley). I was saddened to hear murmurs in some parts of the House that appeared to support retribution and revenge. Quite frankly, from any moral viewpoint, I find revenge completely unacceptable. I do not believe that it is for the House to decide whether there should be revenge—*[Interruption.]* If some of my hon. Friends want revenge, I hope that they will say so and also state their position on other issues that they consider require revenge. It is not for the House or for Parliament to decide retribution either. That lies elsewhere at other times. That is why I cannot accept either of the arguments of revenge or retribution.

My hon. and learned Friend said that our purpose must be to secure the safety of the people of this realm to the greatest possible extent. That is the task of Government both externally and internally, and I agree with him entirely. The question at issue is whether the restoration of capital punishment will improve the security of the people of this realm. That issue remains unproven.

My hon. and learned Friend said that that is a matter of judgment. It is. Others would say that it is a matter of instinct—indeed that has already been said—but in my view the judgment, if it is in favour of restoration, is wrong. This is far too great a matter to rest on instinct. We need more substantial reasons than just instinct for changing the status quo.

I come next to the point which in recent years I have found more and more worrying and more and more impressive. I refer to condemnation by mistake. I find it impossible to accept a penalty that is irreversible when it is so apparent that a number of mistakes have been made. One of my hon. Friends said on the radio that if no one else is prepared to hang people he is quite prepared to do the job himself—[Hon. Members: "Which one?"] I ask him a rather different question. Because of his views, is he prepared to be hanged by mistake? I am not asking my hon. Friend to reply on the spur of the moment. I shall let him give due consideration to the problem before he finally makes up his mind.

I wish now to deal with the specific amendments on the Order Paper about the restoration of capital punishment in particular cases. In this respect, I emphasise what was said by the right hon. Member for Sparkbrook and in great detail by my right hon. and learned Friend the Home Secretary about the Homicide Act 1957. I agree with everything that my right hon. and learned Friend said about that. The Homicide Act 1957 was largely shaped by Viscount Kilmuir as Lord Chancellor. I was involved as the Chief Whip of the Government of the day in trying to bring together those who felt strongly about capital punishment and the abolitionists. The Government wanted to lift the problem out of the constant battle in the House of Commons and try to get public support for a final position. That Act lasted for only eight years. It failed, as the Home Secretary said. It failed because the general public was not prepared to support an Act—nor was the judiciary for that matter—which said that one kind of murderer was worthy of the death penalty and that another

kind was not; that if a public figure was shot crossing Trafalgar Square that was a matter for the death penalty, but that if a man poisoned his wife that was a matter between the two of them and did not deserve the death penalty.

There is a basic lesson here about trying to pick out particular aspects of homicide for the death penalty. I believe that the public would quickly say "Yes, if there is to be a death penalty, is not such and such a case also worthy of it?" That is the fundamental argument of principle against trying to select particular aspects of homicide as justifying the death penalty.

If there is to be a selection, I regard the case for the selection of terrorism as the weakest. If murder of the police or prison warders were to be selected, I think that the public would say that those people have a rather better chance of looking after themselves than they, the innocent public. Terrorists present great problems. I think that the Home Secretary is underestimating the determination of terrorists in Northern Ireland and elsewhere, quite regardless of death, to carry through their purposes. Even if one is dealing with Arab terrorists, one finds that very few of them are paid marksmen. If they are paid marksmen, they will weigh up the risks against the penalties. If money is what they want they will take the risk. Therefore, I cannot see that the argument for capital punishment for terrorists is a powerful one.

I come now to the definition of terrorism, the importance of which I hope my right hon. and learned Friend will not underestimate, as he glossed over it this afternoon. If there is to be the final capital penalty for terrorism, there is the problem of judges and juries deciding whether a person is a political terrorist. There has been criticism in the Province of attempts to deal with the IRA on the basis that its members should, when arrested, be treated as political prisoners, and it has been said that that is an immense mistake. Exactly this definition, as has so rightly been pointed out, would have to be made permanently for capital punishment if the amendment were agreed. I do not believe that one can gloss over the issue of defining terrorism or of how a jury and the judge would handle it.

Even more important — as the Home Secretary emphasised—is that there is no hope of returning to jury verdicts in Northern Ireland. One will not persuade a jury to convict if there is the death penalty. My right hon. and learned Friend then referred to a judge and perhaps two assessors. But is the Northern Ireland judiciary in favour of dealing with IRA terrorism by a judge and two assessors? I cannot believe for one moment that the judiciary would accept that. I lived through all the problems of 1970 to 1974 and have been back to Northern Ireland many times since. I know the views of the people there and, leaving aside the impact on the IRA, I cannot believe that our judiciary or the Northern Ireland judiciary would be prepared to deal with these cases with an assessor sitting on each side.

Therefore, as my right hon. Friend the Secretary of State for Northern Ireland has already said, it is out of the question for practical reasons to apply capital punishment there. But we cannot punish terrorist murderers on the mainland by imposing the death penalty if we do not do so in Northern Ireland. The number of cases here is comparatively few—a few Arab and other terrorists—but from the public's point of view, let alone all the other considerations, it is impossible to deal with an Arab terrorist who shoots the Israeli ambassador in one way but to deal with the same crime differently in Northern Ireland, which most people consider to be the home of terrorism. Amendment *(e)* therefore is entirely impractical.

I am astonished—I must not say that—I was taken unawares by the fact that my right hon. and learned Friend the Home Secretary argued as he did. His argument did not seem to deal with any of the basic problems of making terrorism a separate capital crime. Other European countries have had great problems with terrorism—for example, the Federal Republic of Germany and the Italian Republic. They have dealt with those problems not by bringing back capital punishment, but in other ways, largely by effective police action and by reducing the status of the terrorists so that they could not gain public support. The same is true of the Netherlands. I do not support the argument that we of all European countries should have to reintroduce capital punishment to deal with terrorism.

I conclude with these points. First, we must consider what changes there have been over the past 20 years. One change has been the immense growth of the media— television, radio and the press — and the almost complete removal of privacy. The media's impact in rousing public feeling on the occasion of an execution would be many times what it was in the days before the abolition of capital punishment. One cannot encourage a deeper feeling for the spirituality of man when he is being influenced all the time by the media dealing with executions in that way. That in itself is a powerful argument against capital punishment.

When one considers what has happened in the few states of the United States that have restored capital punishment, one realises the growth in the influence of the media over the past 20 years. It is seen in the horrifying stories that appear before, during and after an execution, especially when men plead for death, which shows that death is not for them a deterrent. I believe that the impact on people is terrible.

Secondly, I am sure, having listened to these debates for 30 years, that the constant emphasis on capital punishment is preventing us from giving real attention and real resources to the problems of crime in a modern democracy. The Government have done a great deal. At one stage criminals had much greater resources than the police. They had better radio facilities, modern communications, such as the use of motorways and other technical devices as well as more up-to-date firearms. The police have now caught up a great deal. We must recognise that if we really are to tackle the penal problems of the country we must turn our attention to that, instead of automatically saying that the answer is hanging and flogging.

I hope, therefore, that this debate can settle it for this Parliament and for many years to come. If my hon. and learned Friend the Member for Fylde is right about that — he said that it might be the last time Parliament would vote on the issue—then I warmly support the fact of him having put the motion forward—though I want to see it defeated—I hope for the last time.

I can claim to speak with a certain amount of experience. When one first comes into the House, one faces many pressures in relation to the way in which one should vote. This has therefore become an early test for many of the victors in the recent general election. My career in the House, covering 33 years, has not been entirely without controversy. I think back to debates on Suez, the abolition of resale price maintenance, the European negotiations, the war in the Middle East, the whole reform of the trade union movement and, for more than 20 years, the abolition of capital punishment.

I can say with honesty to every person who has had the privilege of entering the House that, having said clearly where I stood, and having explained to my constituents why I took up the position that I did, they have accepted that as being the right of their Member of Parliament. I hope that that will always be the case. It is the basis of the British constitution; we are not mandated, we cannot be mandated, by a selection committee, by a constituency committee or by the public as whole.

This is the occasion, above all, when we must use our own judgment. I hope that tonight every hon. Member, and particularly new hon. Members, will feel free to use their judgment. I do not believe that the case for the reintroduction of the death penalty has been proved and I therefore urge the House to reject the motion and all the amendments.

5.3 pm

Mr. Roy Jenkins (Glasgow, Hillhead): The speech of the Home Secretary—a speech similar to two on this subject which I delivered from the same position during the 1970s—left me bewildered. He began by setting out the good, clear, reasonable test of saying, "Let us judge the issues by the test of public safety. Let us, in a way, put old prejudices behind us and look at it afresh from that criterion"—and on the whole I would be prepared to go along with him on that—but he then proceeded, coolly and rationally—and to me persuasively—to destroy the case for capital punishment on all the amendments but one —and then he came to terrorism.

As soon as the right hon. and learned Gentleman did that, he galloped through — as a sort of tribute to differing views in the Cabinet—a catalogue of the case put forward by the Secretary of State for Northern Ireland, and proceeded to face none of the issues involved in that case. He elided off into some general asseverations in which he completely deserted the test of public safety and the rational approach which he had previously applied. He went on to say that terrorist crimes had to be viewed with such repugnance, because they were crimes against the state, that we should not apply those rational tests but should use the final supreme penalty without regard to whether it would work or increase public safety.

There are enormous dangers in that approach. It implies that other crimes, however bestial they may be, are not regarded with the same repugnance. That is a dangerous view to take. It also means that we are moving away from looking at the matter clearly and cooly, as the right hon. and learned Gentleman started by doing. He made a good speech to begin with, but it was fatally flawed and so it became a sorry performance at the end of the day.

The right hon. and learned Gentleman cannot get away with not answering the questions to clarify his position which were put to him by the right hon. Member for Birmingham, Sparkbrook (Mr. Hattersley) and which I shall repeat, because, if he does not answer them, I must tell him, as somebody who has twice occupied his office and spoken from the Dispatch Box in very similar circumstances, that he will be neglecting his duty to the House as Home Secretary.

105

Aneurin Bevan indicts the Eden Government over Suez

James Callaghan – popularly known as Jim, and in due course to become Lord Callaghan of Cardiff – was the only politician to have come to the office of Prime Minister having held the three other great offices of state, Chancellor of the Exchequer, Foreign Secretary and Home Secretary.

He won the leadership of the Labour party and became Prime Minister on the retirement of Harold Wilson in 1976, holding the post until he lost a vote of confidence in the House of Commons in 1979. At the ensuing general election Margaret Thatcher led the Conservatives to victory, and he faced her across the Dispatch Box for 18 months before he stepped down and returned to the Back Benches.

His father was a chief petty officer in the Royal Navy who died when James was nine years old. He left school at 14 and worked, among other things, as a tax officer and for the Trades Union Congress. His links with the trade unions were a constant feature of his political life.

During the second world war he served in the Royal Navy, and when the general election was called in 1945 he stood for Labour in Cardiff, South and won the seat. He represented the constituency, subsequently Cardiff, South-East, for over 40 years before he retired from the Commons in 1987.

He made his maiden speech within weeks of the new Parliament, speaking in the debate on the Loyal Address on the subject of the situation in the Pacific after the Japanese surrender. Within two years he was given his first Front Bench appointment as Parliamentary Secretary to the Minister of Transport. In 1950, he moved to the Admiralty as Parliamentary and Financial Secretary.

Labour left office after the defeat of the 1951 general election and he spent the next 13 years of Opposition building his status and position in the party. On the return to power in October 1964 Harold Wilson appointed him Chancellor of the Exchequer, but his time in the job was to end in the controversy of the 1967 devaluation of sterling, after which he resigned. His position was taken by Roy Jenkins, but Wilson immediately made him the Home Secretary, which position he held until the election defeat in 1970.

During his time at the Home Office, he ordered the deployment of troops to Northern Ireland as the situation in the Province deteriorated. He was also responsible for bringing in the Bill that was to become the Race Relations Act which outlawed discrimination in housing, education and employment on the grounds of ethnic origin.

In February 1974, Labour were returned to power when Prime Minister Ted Heath went to the country over his dispute with the miners and lost. James Callaghan was made Foreign Secretary and as such was responsible for renegotiating Britain's membership of the Common Market. He told Parliament that the new terms were acceptable, and in the 1975 referendum he campaigned for a Yes vote.

In March 1976 Harold Wilson announced his retirement. The Labour party elected James Callaghan leader, and he took over in No 10 Downing street on 5 April 1976. It was not to be a comfortable tenure of office. He was destined to preside over a sterling crisis, spending cuts and pay restraint.

In what may have seemed a painful repeat of the position after the 1964 general election, Labour's majority in the Commons after going to the country for a second time in 1974 had been wafer thin. It disappeared in 1977, which left Prime Minister Callaghan dependent on the minority parties to remain in office. The Liberals withdrew their support, but he decided to soldier on. With what in hindsight may be seen as an error of judgment, he chose not to call an election in the autumn of 1978, but to hold on until the following year.

It was a mistake. Faced with a hostile trade union movement and widespread strikes over his policy of pay restraint, he was forced to endure the now famous "Winter of Discontent". The trade union movement, to which he had always been so close, was to become the cause of his downfall. Images of uncollected refuse piling up in the streets, and stories of people unable to bury their dead spelled the end of the Labour Government.

On 28 March 1979, his Commons majority having evaporated, he lost a vote of confidence by one and called a general election. Mrs Thatcher swept into Downing street with an agenda of labour reform that was to marginalise the trade unions and strip them of any meaningful political involvement.

James Callaghan retired from the Commons in 1987 and took his place in the House of Lords. He died on 26 March 2005 at his farm in East Sussex on the day before his 93rd birthday.

Temperate and restrained speech that dissolved the bitterness of failure

By Rt hon Lord Callaghan of Cardiff

Aneurin Bevan's speech on Suez came shortly after an attack had been launched on Egypt by Israel, followed by a joint Anglo-French invasion of Egypt, which the two Governments claimed was for the purpose of separating the combatants.

It was widely believed that there had been collusion with Israel before the attack was launched and that, in reality, the intention of the Anglo-French force was to expel Nasser and regain control of the Suez Canal, which had been taken over by him.

These events drew down worldwide condemnation from Arab states, the United States, the Commonwealth and the United Nations. The Anglo-French force was obliged to end its attack and to withdraw without gaining any of its objectives.

The House of Commons was debating the outcome in a tense atmosphere. Anthony Eden, the Prime Minister, had withdrawn, through exhaustion, to Jamaica. Bevan had been appointed as shadow Foreign Secretary only a few days before.

The Conservative Government had no leader. The Labour Opposition were genuinely and deeply angry. Ministers had produced a number of different reasons for their actions, whose lack of coherence was obvious. Many of their Conservative supporters felt humiliated by these events.

Bevan's speech was as remarkable for the effect it had on the tone of the debate as it was for its content. He could have made a slashing attack on a wounded Government, and, indeed, he set out fully the indictment, the errors and the inconsistencies. But not only was his language temperate and restrained, it also looked beyond the immediate rebuff suffered by the Government in being forced to withdraw, and instead set out a number of ideas about Britain's long-term future role.

His 50-minute speech – they were longer in those days – held the attention of the whole House. It was not all grave and serious. At one point he indulged in playful imagery, casting the Anglo-French collusion on the Israeli attack in the form of John Bull and Marianne warming hands together at a small fire – Suez – discussing whether to put it out, and Marianne perhaps even seducing John Bull.

At this passage, Bevan lowered his voice to a conversational tone, the words coming in a caressing Welsh lilt. The Labour Benches began to chuckle, then the Conservative Back Benchers joined in. Eventually the whole House was laughing, even Ministers.

For a moment Bevan had dissolved the bitter feelings felt by Members on both sides, and the complete speech left a great impression on nearly everyone. Harold Macmillan, himself shortly to become Prime Minister, did not withhold his praise, when the debate continued, of Bevan's "very brilliant speech ... made in a parliamentary style which is all his own and worthy of the best of all his predecessors".

Many others – friends, opponents and the press, joined in the congratulations. Bevan had spoken in such a way that not only lowered the temperature on both sides of the House, but also reached out and across to the Government's Back Benches. In doing so, he served the national interest and greatly added to his own reputation.

[MR. LLOYD.]
the Arab countries and who, I think, will be as anxious as anyone to see that the Bagdad Pact should develop and strengthen. I believe that what the hon. Gentleman has drawn attention to is a purely temporary phase.

I have been in close contact with the member Governments of the Bagdad Pact. I believe that this statement of the United States is of major importance, and I think that better service would have been done to the cause of restoring the situation of friendship between the Arab countries and ourselves if the hon. Gentleman had welcomed what I said without pointing out the other matter.

I believe that the Bagdad Pact will grow in strength with our membership, and, as I was going on to say, I hope that the United States will pass on from its membership of the Economic Committee, beyond its declaration to which I have referred today, to full membership of that Pact.

There is another matter, and that is the question of closer association between the countries of Western Europe. There is, I think, another line of development which becomes clear in consequence of what has happened in the Middle East and in consequence of the present situation in the United Nations. That is the need for a more efficient basis for co-operation between the nations of Western Europe. I believe that this can be achieved without impairing either our association with the Commonwealth or our alliance with the United States, and without creating new institutions. I go at the weekend to the meetings of the Western European Union and the North Atlantic Treaty Organisation with those considerations very much in mind.

I maintain—it has been my belief throughout and it is still my conviction —that out of this situation certain definite advantages have been achieved. [*Laughter.*] I really do not think that right hon. and hon. Members opposite do their country a service in seeking to make out that this whole business has been a disastrous failure, as in the words of their Amendment. I believe that what we did was right. I believe that we stopped a war. I believe—and, for once, an extraordinary fact, hon. Members opposite were almost reduced to silence

—that I proved, by my quotation from the Egyptian Commander-in-Chief, that we stopped the war from spreading in the Middle East.

I believe that we have now given this United Nations Force a task of the greatest responsibility. Those who criticise us so vocally and glibly——

Mr. William Ross (Kilmarnock): Which side?

Mr. Lloyd: —forget what would have been the consequences of inactivity. They forget completely the dangers which are existent in the area. They forget completely the steady deterioration which was taking place. They forget completely the mounting risk of war between Israel and the Arab States. They shut their eyes to all those things. We have shown in this country our will to act in a situation of crisis, and it is now for us all, I suggest, to bend our energies to see that the United Nations grasps this opportunity.

4.36 p.m.

Mr. Aneurin Bevan (Ebbw Vale): I beg to move, to leave out from " House " to the end of the Question and to add instead thereof:

" recognising the disastrous consequences of Her Majesty's Government's policy in the Middle East, calls upon Her Majesty's Government to take all possible steps to restore Commonwealth unity, recreate confidence between our allies and ourselves and strengthen the authority of the United Nations as the only way to achieve a lasting settlement in the Middle East."

The speech to which we have just listened is the last of a long succession that the right hon. Gentleman the Secretary of State for Foreign Affairs has made to the House in the last few months and, if I may be allowed to say so, I congratulate him upon having survived so far. He appears to be in possession of vigorous health, which is obviously not enjoyed by all his colleagues, and he appears also to be exempted from those Freudian lapses which have distinguished the speeches of the Lord Privy Seal, and therefore he has survived so far with complete vigour.

However, I am bound to say that the speech by the right hon. Gentleman today carries the least conviction of all.

Mr. Cyril Osborne (Louth): The right hon. Gentleman wrote that before he heard the speech.

Mr. Bevan : I have been looking through the various objectives and reasons that the Government have given to the House of Commons for making war on Egypt, and it really is desirable that when a nation makes war upon another nation it should be quite clear why it does so. It should not keep changing the reasons as time goes on. There is, in fact, no correspondence whatsoever between the reasons given today and the reasons set out by the Prime Minister at the beginning. The reasons have changed all the time. I have got a list of them here, and for the sake of the record I propose to read it. I admit that I found some difficulty in organising a speech with any coherence because of the incoherence of the reasons. They are very varied.

On 30th October, the Prime Minister said that the purpose was, first,

" to seek to separate the combatants " ;

second,

" to remove the risk to free passage through the Canal."

The speech we have heard today is the first speech in which that subject has been dropped. Every other statement made on this matter since the beginning has always contained a reference to the future of the Canal as one of Her Majesty's Government's objectives, in fact. as an object of war, to coerce Egypt. Indeed, that is exactly what hon. and right hon. Gentlemen opposite believed it was all about. [*Interruption.*] Hon. Members do not do themselves justice. One does not fire in order merely to have a cease-fire. One would have thought that the cease-fire was consequent upon having fired in the first place. It could have been accomplished without starting. The other objective set out on 30th October was

" to reduce the risk . . . to those voyaging through the Canal."—[OFFICIAL REPORT, 30th October, 1956 ; Vol. 558. c. 1347.]

We have heard from the right hon. and learned Gentleman today a statement which I am quite certain all the world will read with astonishment. He has said that when we landed in Port Said there was already every reason to believe that both Egypt and Israel had agreed to cease fire.

The Minister of Defence (Mr. Antony Head) *indicated dissent.*

Vol. 561

Mr. Bevan : The Minister shakes his head. If he will recollect what his right hon. and learned Friend said, it was that there was still a doubt about the Israeli reply. Are we really now telling this country and the world that all these calamitous consequences have been brought down upon us merely because of a doubt? That is what he said.

Surely, there was no need. We had, of course, done the bombing, but our ships were still going through the Mediterranean. We had not arrived at Port Said. The exertions of the United Nations had already gone far enough to be able to secure from Israel and Egypt a promise to cease fire, and all that remained to be cleared up was an ambiguity about the Israeli reply. In these conditions, and against the background of these events, the invasion of Egypt still continued.

In the history of nations, there is no example of such frivolity. When I have looked at this chronicle of events during the last few days, with every desire in the world to understand it, I just have not been able to understand, and do not yet understand, the mentality of the Government. If the right hon. and learned Gentleman wishes to deny what I have said, I will give him a chance of doing so. If his words remain as they are now, we are telling the nation and the world that, having decided upon the course, we went on with it despite the fact that the objective we had set ourselves had already been achieved, namely, the separation of the combatants.

As to the objective of removing the risk to free passage through the Canal, I must confess that I have been astonished at this also. We sent an ultimatum to Egypt by which we told her that unless she agreed to our landing in Ismailia, Suez and Port Said, we should make war upon her. We knew very well, did we not, that Nasser could not possibly comply? Did we really believe that Nasser was going to give in at once? Is our information from Egypt so bad that we did not know that an ultimatum of that sort was bound to consolidate his position in Egypt and in the whole Arab world?

We knew at that time, on 29th and 30th October, that long before we could have occupied Port Said, Ismailia and

X 2

[MR. BEVAN.]
Suez, Nasser would have been in a position to make his riposte. So wonderfully organised was this expedition—which, apparently, has been a miracle of military genius—that long after we had delivered our ultimatum and bombed Port Said, our ships were still ploughing through the Mediterranean, leaving the enemy still in possession of all the main objectives which we said we wanted.

Did we really believe that Nasser was going to wait for us to arrive? He did what anybody would have thought he would do, and if the Government did not think he would do it, on that account alone they ought to resign. He sank ships in the Canal, the wicked man. What did hon. Gentleman opposite expect him to do? The result is that, in fact, the first objective realised was the opposite of the one we set out to achieve ; the Canal was blocked, and it is still blocked.

The only other interpretation of the Government's mind is that they expected, for some reason or other, that their ultimatum would bring about disorder in Egypt and the collapse of the Nasser regime. None of us believed that. If hon. Gentleman opposite would only reason about other people as they reason amongst themselves, they would realise that a Government cannot possibly surrender to a threat of that sort and keep any self-respect. We should not, should we? If somebody held a pistol at our heads and said, " You do this or we fire ", should we? Of course not. Why on earth do not hon. Members opposite sometimes believe that other people have the same courage and independence as they themselves possess? Nasser behaved exactly as any reasonable man would expect him to behave.

The other objective was
" to reduce the risk . . . to those voyaging through the Canal."

That was a rhetorical statement, and one does not know what it means. I am sorry the right hon. Gentleman the Prime Minister is not here. I appreciate why he is not here, but it is very hard to reply to him when he is not in the House, and I hope hon. Members opposite will acquit me of trying to attack him in his absence.

On 31st October, the Prime Minister said that our object was to secure a lasting settlement and to protect our nationals. What do we think of that? In the meantime, our nationals were living in Egypt while we were murdering Egyptians at Port Said. We left our nationals in Egypt at the mercy of what might have been merciless riots throughout the whole country, with no possibility whatever of our coming to their help. We were still voyaging through the Mediterranean, after having exposed them to risk by our own behaviour. What does the House believe that the country will think when it really comes to understand all this?

On 1st November, we were told the reason was
" to stop hostilities "
and
" prevent a resumption of them."—[OFFICIAL REPORT, 1st November, 1956 ; Vol. 558, c. 1653.]

But hostilities had already been practically stopped. On 3rd November, our objectives became much more ambitious—
" to deal with all the outstanding problems in the Middle East."—[OFFICIAL REPORT, 3rd November, 1956 ; Vol 558, c. 1867.]

In the famous book " Madame Bovary " there is a story of a woman who goes from one sin to another, a long story of moral decline. In this case, our ambitions soar the farther away we are from realising them. Our objective was,
" to deal with all the outstanding problems in the Middle East."

After having outraged our friends, after having insulted the United States, after having affronted all our friends in the Commonwealth, after having driven the whole of the Arab world into one solid phalanx, at least for the moment, behind Nasser, we were then going to deal with all the outstanding problems in the Middle East.

Mr. Gilbert Longden (Hertfordshire, South-West) : As this is going on the record, and as the Prime Minister is not here, I hope that the right hon. Gentleman will be fair enough not deliberately to mislead the House, as I am sure he would not wish to, but the Prime Minister never said that we alone could deal with all the problems of the Middle East. What the Prime Minister said on 1st November was :

" We do not seek to impose by force a solution on the Israel-Egypt dispute, or the Suez Canal dispute, or any other dispute in the area."—[OFFICIAL REPORT, 1st November, 1956 ; Vol. 558, c. 1653.]

He said that if the United Nations would send forces to relieve us no one would be better pleased than we.

Mr. Bevan : The hon. Gentleman need not worry ; I will deal with that quite soon ; I am coming to that quite quickly. This is a new alibi. It was only a few weeks ago in this House that hon. and right hon. Gentlemen opposite sneered at every mention of the United Nations. We will deal with that.

The next objective of which we were told was to ensure that the Israeli forces withdrew from Egyptian territory. That, I understand, is what we were there for. We went into Egyptian territory in order to establish our moral right to make the Israelis clear out of Egyptian territory. That is a remarkable war aim, is it not? In order that we might get Israel out, we went in. To establish our case before the eyes of the world, Israel being the wicked invader, we, of course, being the nice friend of Egypt, went to protect her from the Israelis, but, unfortunately, we had to bomb the Egyptians first.

On 6th November, the Prime Minister said :

" The action we took has been an essential condition for . . . a United Nations Force to come into the Canal Zone itself."—[OFFICIAL REPORT. 6th November, 1956 ; Vol. 559, c. 80.]

That is one of the most remarkable claims of all, and it is one of the main claims made by right hon. and hon. Members opposite. It is, of course, exactly the same claim which might have been made, if they had thought about it in time, by Mussolini and Hitler, that they made war on the world in order to call the United Nations into being. If it were possible for bacteria to argue with each other, they would be able to say that of course their chief justification was the advancement of medical science.

As *The Times* has pointed out, the arrival of the United Nations Force could not be regarded as a war aim by the Government ; it called it, " an inadvertance." That is not my description : it is *The Times.* It was a by-product of the action not of Her Majesty's Government but of the United Nations itself.

Let me ask hon. Members opposite to listen to this case. The right hon. and learned Gentleman was spending most of his time in America trying to persuade the United States—that is after we were

in Egypt—to make the control of the Canal one of the conditions of our withdrawal. On Thursday last he himself said here :

" I mention these facts to the House because, obviously, the build-up of this force must have an important relationship to a phased withdrawal of our own and the French troops. There are, however, other important matters to be considered, such as the speedy clearance of the Canal, and negotiation of a final settlement with regard to the operation of the Canal."—[OFFICIAL REPORT. 29th November, 1956 ; Vol. 561, c. 582.]

On every single occasion—and hon. Members opposite expected this—when he went upstairs to tell his hon. Friends that he had come back empty-handed, what did they say? Why did we start this operation? We started this operation in order to give Nasser a black eye —if we could to overthrow him—but, in any case, to secure control of the Canal.

Viscount Hinchingbrooke (Dorset, South): To stop the war.

Mr. Bevan : I have been dealing with that ; the hon. Gentleman must catch up.

The United Nations Force was in Egypt as a result of a Resolution of the United Nations for the purposes of the Charter. All along, the United States and all the other nations attached to the United Nations resolutely refused to allow the future of the Canal to be tied up with the existence of the Force. But the right hon. and learned Gentleman, in order to have some trophy to wave in the faces of his hon. Friends, wanted to bring from across the Atlantic an undertaking which would have destroyed the United Nations, because if the United Nations had agreed that the future of the Canal should also be contingent upon the withdrawal of British troops, then the United Nations Force would no longer have been a United Nations Force but an instrument of the rump of the United Nations, that is, the Western Powers.

I put it again to the right hon. and learned Gentleman that if hon. Members opposite had succeeded in what they wanted to do, they would have ruined the United Nations, because the very essence of the United Nations Force is that it is not attempting to impose upon Egypt any settlement of the Canal.

Mr. Anthony Fell (Yarmouth): It is a police force.

Mr. Bevan : I hope that hon. Members opposite will realise that the argument is a really serious one. It was seen to be so serious by the United States that, despite what I believe to be the desire on the part of a very large number of Americans to help us in these difficulties, it was clear to President Eisenhower, as it should be clear to anybody, that a settlement of that sort was bound to be resented by the whole of the Arab world and Egypt. It was bound to be resented by the Commonwealth because it would make it appear that Her Majesty's Government were using the United Nations to obtain an objective that we set ourselves as far back as last August. Therefore, if the right hon. and learned Gentleman had succeeded, if the future of the Canal had been tied up with our withdrawal, the United Nations Force in Egypt would no longer have been a police force for the world, but would have been a means of coercing Egypt to accept our terms about the Canal.

Mr. Fell : Surely the right hon. Gentleman would find it very difficult to imagine a United Nations Force that could, in fact, be a successful police force unless under certain circumstances it had the right to infringe——

Mr. Bevan : The hon. Member is not meeting my point. The point that the Government spokesmen are making here and in the country is that they have been responsible for calling the United Nations Force into existence. My answer is that by attaching to the United Nations Force a persistent attempt to secure the future of the Canal in order to satisfy hon. Members opposite they are, in fact, sabotaging the United Nations.

Mr. K. Zilliacus (Manchester, Gorton): Is it not a fact that the Government voted against the Security Council Resolution calling the General Assembly and then abstained on the vote creating the United Nations Force?

Mr. Bevan : This, of course, is known to hon. Members in all parts of the House. They may have their own explanations for it, but I was not anxious to add to the burden of my argument. That fact is known. Of course, the Government did not support the United Nations Force—we all know that. Nevertheless, in this retrospective exercise that we are having from the other side of the House, it is possible for us to deal with the seriousness of the whole case.

The right hon. and learned Gentleman is sufficiently aware of the seriousness of it to start his speech today with collusion. If collusion can be established, the whole fabric of the Government's case falls to the ground, and they know this. It is the most serious of all the charges. It is believed in the United States and it is believed by large numbers of people in Great Britain that we were well aware that Israel was going to make the attack on Egypt. In fact, very few of the activities at the beginning of October are credible except upon the assumption that the French and British Governments knew that something was going to happen in Egypt.

Indeed, the right hon. and learned Gentleman has not been frank with the House. We have asked him over and over again. He has said, " Ah, we did not conspire with France and Israel." We never said that the Government might have conspired. What we said was that they might have known about it. The right hon. and learned Gentleman gave the House the impression that at no time had he ever warned Israel against attacking Egypt. Even today, he hinged the warning we gave to Jordan on the possibility of the other Arab States being involved in any attack on Jordan.

We understand from the right hon. and learned Gentleman that at no time did the Government warn Israel against an attack on Egypt. If we apprehend trouble of these dimensions—we are not dealing with small matters—if we apprehend that the opening phases of a third world war might start or turn upon an attack by Israel on anyone, why did we not make it quite clear to Israel that we would take the same view of an attack on Egypt as we took of an attack on Jordan?

The fact is that all these long telephone conversations and conferences between M. Guy Mollet, M. Pineau and the Prime Minister are intelligible only on the assumption that something was being cooked up. All that was left to do, as far as we knew from the facts at that time, was to pick up negotiations at Geneva about the future of the Canal, as had been arranged by the United Nations. But all the time there was this coming and going between ourselves and the French Government.

Did the French know? It is believed in France that the French knew about the Israeli intention. If the French knew, did they tell the British Government? We would like to know. Did M. Guy Mollet, on 16th October, tell the British Prime Minister that he expected that there was to be an attack on Egypt? Every circumstantial fact that we know points to that conclusion. For instance, Mr. Ben Gurion, the Israeli Prime Minister, had already made it clear in the *Knesset* on several occasions that Israel regarded Egypt as the real enemy, and not Jordan. Therefore, a warning not to attack Jordan was not relevant. At the same time, many Israelis were saying that at last Israel had got a reliable friend.

What happened? Did Marianne take John Bull to an unknown rendezvous? Did Marianne say to John Bull that there was a forest fire going to start, and did John Bull then say, " We ought to put it out," but Marianne said, " No, let us warm our hands by it. It is a nice fire "? Did Marianne deceive John Bull or seduce him?

Now, of course, we come to the ultimate end. It is at the end of all these discussions that the war aim of the Government now becomes known. Of course, we knew it all the time. We knew where they would land. After this long voyaging, getting almost wrecked several times, they have come to safe harbour. It was a red peril all the time. It was Russia all the time. It was not to save the Canal. The hon. Member who interjected has been deceived all the time. It was not the Canal, it was the red peril which they had unmasked. The Government suspected it before, said the right hon. and learned Gentleman, about the arms to Egypt. We on this side knew it— we did not suspect it—but the right hon. and learned Gentleman suspected it, so he said, at the very time when he was informing the House that he thought there was a proper balance of arms between Egypt and Israel.

What will the Israelis think of this when they read the right hon. and learned Gentleman's words, or are we to understand that the Israelis have got as many arms as the Egyptians have? We understand that they were fully armed all the time, because the right hon. and learned Gentleman suspected that the Egyptians had these arms.

I am not in the least surprised by this situation. That the Russians have provided these arms to the Egyptians we accept—of course they did. It is a curious thing—I may be frivolous, but I am not frightened by it—and I will tell the House why. The Russians have a habit, curiously enough, it seems to me, of not knowing what is happening in other nations. They do not even know what is happening in Poland or Hungary, and it does not seem to have occurred to the Russians that there was no military advantage in providing weapons that the Egyptians could not use.

The fact of the matter is that these great modern weapons are practically useless in the hands of backward nations. [HON. MEMBERS: " There were the volunteers."] But there were no volunteers. Do not, however, let hon. Members push the argument too far. I am not for one moment seeking to justify the Russian supply of arms to Egypt. I think it was a wicked thing to do and I think it is an equally wicked thing for us to supply arms. That area is much too combustible, far too inflammatory. This is now the end of 1956, when very many things have happened in the Middle East, when it is more dangerous than ever. I think that the Russians ought not to have done it and I will say further that I think that Nasser ought not to have invited them.

It seems to me—and here I probably shall carry hon. Members opposite with me—that Nasser has not been behaving in the spirit of the Bandoeng Conference which he joined, because what he did was not to try to reduce the temperature of the cold war: what he did was to exploit it for Egyptian purposes. Therefore, Nasser's hands are not clean by any means. I have said this before. I said it in Trafalgar Square. We must not believe that because the Prime Minister is wrong Nasser is right. That is not the view on this side of the House.

What has deeply offended us is that such wrongs as Nasser has done and such faults as he has have been covered by the bigger blunders of the British Government. That is what vexes us. We are satisfied that the arts of diplomacy would have brought Nasser to where we wanted to get him, which was to agree about the free passage of ships through the Canal, on the civilised ground that a riparian

[MR. BEVAN.]
nation has got no absolute rights over a great waterway like the Canal. That is a principle which has been accepted by India and by America and by most other nations. We have never taken the position that in the exercise of sovereign rights Egypt has the right to inflict a mortal wound upon the commerce of the world.

Mr. Osborne : Will not the right hon. Gentleman agree that six years of patient negotiation had not caused Nasser to allow the passage of Israeli ships?

Mr. Bevan : Do not let hon. Members now bring to the forefront of the argument the fact that Egypt had not been allowing Israeli ships to go through the Canal. If they thought so much of the seriousness of that, why did they not even invite Israel to the conference? It is not good enough to bring these things forward all the time as though they were the main objectives. Of course, we take the view that Egypt should permit the ships of all nations to pass through the Canal, and we hope that that objective will still be insisted upon. We are satisfied that those objectives could have been realised by negotiation. Not only have they not been realised by the action taken by the Government, but the opposite has been realised.

It has been clear to us, and it is now becoming clear to the nation, that for many months past hon. Members opposite have been harbouring designs of this sort. One of the reasons why we could not get a civilised solution of the Cyprus problem was that the Government were harbouring designs to use Cyprus in the Middle East, unilaterally or in conjunction with France. Whenever we put in this House Questions to the right hon. Gentleman asking him why he did not answer whether he wanted a base on Cyprus or Cyprus as a base, he answered quite frankly that we might want to activate the base on Cyprus independently of our allies. That was the answer. Well, we have activated it—and look at us. We have had all these murders and all this terror, we have had all this unfriendship over Cyprus between ourselves and Greece, and we have been held up to derision in all the world merely because we contemplated using Cyprus as a base for going it alone in the Middle East.

And we did go it alone. Look at the result.

Was it not obvious to hon. Members opposite that Great Britain could not possibly engage in a major military adventure without involving our N.A.T.O. allies? Was it not very clear, if we did contemplate any adventure at all, that it would have to be in conjunction with them? No. It is a sad and a bitter story. We hope that at least one beneficial by-product of it will be a settlement of the Cyprus question very soon indeed.

Now I would conclude by saying this. I do not believe that any of us yet—I say any of us yet—have realised the complete change that has taken place in the relationship between nations and between Governments and peoples. These were objectives, I do beg hon. Members to reflect, that were not realisable by the means that we adopted. These civil, social and political objectives in modern society are not attainable by armed force.

Even if we had occupied Egypt by armed force we could not have secured the freedom of passage through the Canal. It is clear that there is such xenophobia, that there is such passion, that there is such bitter feeling against Western imperialism—rightly or wrongly: I am not arguing the merits at the moment—among millions of people that they are not prepared to keep the arteries of European commerce alive and intact if they themselves want to cut them. We could not keep ships going through the Canal. The Canal is too easily sabotaged, if Egypt wants to sabotage it. Why on earth did we imagine that the objectives could be realised in that way in the middle of the twentieth century?

Viscount Hinchingbrooke : Would the right hon. Gentleman apply the same argument to Germany at the end of the last war? It seems to me that the Germans showed great willingness to open the Kiel Canal.

Mr. Bevan : That is not really a parallel at all. The noble Lord does not face the argument. We should be imposing our will upon Egypt against the bitter opposition of the whole population there.

Viscount Hinchingbrooke : Not necessarily.

Mr. Bevan : It is necessarily so. If the noble Lord does not understand that, then he is in the eighteenth and not even the nineteenth century.

Exactly the same thing is true of the Russians in Hungary. The Russians in Hungary are attempting to achieve civil, social and political objectives by tanks and guns, and the Hungarian people are demonstrating that it cannot be done.

The social furniture of modern society is so complicated and fragile that it cannot support the jackboot. We cannot run the processes of modern society by attempting to impose our will upon nations by armed force. If we have not learned that we have learned nothing. Therefore, from our point of view here, whatever may have been the morality of the Government's action—and about that there is no doubt—there is no doubt about its imbecility. There is not the slightest shadow of doubt that we have attempted to use mehods which were bound to destroy the objectives we had, and, of course, this is what we have discovered.

I commend to hon. Members, if they have not seen it, a very fine cartoon in *Punch* by Illingworth and called " Desert Victory." There we see a black, ominous, sinister background and a pipeline broken, pouring oil into the desert sands. How on earth do hon. Members opposite imagine that hundreds of miles of pipeline can be kept open if the Arabs do not want it to be kept open? It is not enough to say that there are large numbers of Arabs who want the pipeline to be kept open because they live by it.

It has been proved over and over again now in the modern world that men and women are often prepared to put up with material losses for things that they really think worth while. It has been shown in Budapest, and it could be shown in the Middle East. That is why I beg hon. Members to turn their backs on this most ugly chapter and realise that if we are to live in the world and are to be regarded as a decent nation, decent citizens in the world, we have to act up to different standards than the one that we have been following in the last few weeks.

I resent most bitterly this unconcern for the lives of innocent men and women. It may be that the dead in Port Said

are 100, 200 or 300. If it is only one, we had no business to take it. Do hon. Members begin to realise how this is going to revolt the world when it passes into the imagination of men and women everywhere, and in this country, that we, with eight million here in London, the biggest single civilian target in the world, with our crowded island exposed, as no nation in the world is exposed, to the barbarism of modern weapons, we ourselves set the example.

We ourselves conscript our boys and put guns and aeroplanes in their hands and say, " Bomb there." Really, this is so appalling that human language can hardly describe it. And for what? The Government resorted to epic weapons for squalid and trivial ends, and that is why all through this unhappy period Ministers —all of them—have spoken and argued and debated well below their proper form —because they have been synthetic villains. They are not really villains. They have only set off on a villainous course, and they cannot even use the language of villainy.

Therefore, in conclusion, I say that it is no use hon. Members consoling themselves that they have more support in the country than many of them feared they might have. Of course they have support in the country. They have support among many of the unthinking and unreflective who still react to traditional values, who still think that we can solve all these problems in the old ways. Of course they have. Not all the human race has grown to adult state yet. But do not let them take comfort in that thought. The right hon. Member for Woodford (Sir W. Churchill) has warned them before. In the first volume of his *Second World War*, he writes about the situation before the war and he says this:

" Thus an Administration more disastrous than any in our history saw all its errors and shortcomings acclaimed by the nation. There was however a bill to be paid, and it took the new House of Commons nearly ten years to pay it."

Mr. Charles Ian Orr-Ewing (Hendon, North): Was not that after appeasement?

Mr. Bevan : No, this was before. In any case, the words are apposite. It will take us very many years to live down what we have done. It will take us many years to pay the price. I know that tomorrow evening hon. and right hon.

[MR. BEVAN.]
Members will probably, as they have done before, give the Government a vote of confidence, but they know in their heart of hearts that it is a vote which the Government do not deserve.

5.25 p.m.

Mr. R. Brooman-White (Rutherglen): The right hon. Member for Ebbw Vale (Mr. Bevan) has made a speech which in skill of debating in the House rates undoubtedly very high. I am glad to follow him because, during the early exchanges in these discussions, and during some of the chronology of events which he recited to the House, I was myself in the Middle East. On reflection, I think the right hon. Gentleman will realise that the language of debate which is so effective in this Chamber sounds very different among the nations and looks very different in relation to the course of events out there when seen from the Middle East.

Before I come to the main burden of what I have to say about the Middle East, I should like to make one or two comments on certain points in the right hon. Gentleman's remarks which I noted while he was speaking. He said that my right hon. Friends on the Front Bench might not be happy with the type of language they have been using. No one would accuse the right hon. Gentleman of being deficient in linguistic abilities. He said that we had been unconcerned about the loss of life, that we had shown a lack of concern about the casualties suffered.

Mr. Bevan : I really was referring to the original decision to send out bombers at all, because one cannot send bombers out without killing people, which seems to me to show a lack of concern for ordinary men and women.

Mr. Brooman-White : I am glad that the right hon. Gentleman bears out that point, to which I wanted to refer. This House has been sitting, perhaps concerned, but utterly impotent, as the United Nations and the world have been sitting, during a long category of incidents and a long list of casualties mounting steadily during the weeks, months and years which preceded this episode. The right hon. Gentleman has been in Israel; I do not know whether he has also been in Jordan. He has probably seen the burned villages and the dead, as so many of us have. We heard from the Foreign Secretary of the casualties in even the most recent border raids—50 here and 40 there. If I had had the time to check the facts before being called so early in the debate, I should have liked to total up the number of casualties along the Arab-Israeli frontiers in the few weeks immediately preceding our operation and compare them with the casualties occasioned at Port Said.

One of the justifications in the long run of our actions will be if, by the casualties regrettably but inevitably incurred in our operations in Port Said, that long, lamentable, melancholy toll of suffering and of loss of life between the Arabs and Israeli States should have at last been brought to a close.

The second point, on which the right hon. Member for Ebbw Vale was perhaps not doing himself full justice was in his reference to the British attitude to the original Israeli incursion. This was possibly, or so one hopes, a last shot fired at a target of collusion which is rapidly vanishing into a mirage. [HON. MEMBERS: "No."] If hon. Members opposite hope to find something more substantial, the right hon. Gentleman's argument is even weaker. He was implying that we had in some sinister way tended to condone or encourage Israeli action against Egypt because we did not speak against it in exactly the same phraseology that we had used in relation to possible action against Jordan.

The right hon. Gentleman should make allowance for the difference of language customary in diplomacy and in the House of Commons. With all his great experience, the right hon. Gentleman has not yet perhaps delved deeply into the affairs of official diplomacy, but no doubt he is doing some homework on it now.

Mr. Bevan : We can all see how wonderfully the experts have been performing on the subject.

Mr. Brooman-White : The right hon. Gentleman cannot ride out of it that way. The implication of his remarks was that we had gone to the Israelis and said, "If you take action against Jordan this will be an unfriendly act against a Power with which we are in treaty relations." That was a perfectly clear point, and we would have been bound to intervene. We then said, "If you take action against Egypt we must urge restraint in that

Duff Cooper resigns with the warning to Chamberlain not to trust Hitler

When **David Cameron** was elected leader of the Conservative party and Leader of the Opposition in 2005, he took the job telling his followers that the party would have to change and that he would change it.

After an unprecedented three Labour general election victories beginning with the defeat of John Major in 1997, he was the fourth Tory leader to be entrusted with what at the time was the uphill task of taking his party back to power.

He aimed to bring to the position an approach that promised to rejuvenate the Conservative camp with something different and something new. He was 39 years old, and one of his key aims was to win over the support of new voters by offering "a modern and compassionate Conservatism" more in tune with their attitudes and beliefs. By-election and local election results implied that he was enjoying more success against his Labour opponents than did his three predecessors.

He was educated at Eton College and when he left, before going to university, he acquired his first experience of the House of Commons by doing a short stint as a researcher for Conservative MP, Tim Rathbone. He also worked briefly in Hong Kong before returning to Britain to attend Brasenose College, Oxford, where he took a first class degree in philosophy, politics and economics.

On leaving university in 1988, he worked for the Conservative research department for four years, becoming head of the political section and a member of the team tasked with briefing John Major for Prime Minister's Questions.

During the 1992 general election, he helped John Major to prepare for the daily press conferences and when, against expectations, the Conservatives were returned to power, Chancellor Norman Lamont invited him to join his team at the Treasury as a special adviser. Difficult times lay ahead. In September that year, Britain was unable to maintain the value of sterling and on so-called Black Wednesday Norman Lamont was forced to announce that he was taking it out of the European exchange rate mechanism.

Precisely six months after Black Wednesday, he presented his 1993 Budget. It was to be his last. In May he was sacked. David Cameron left the Treasury shortly afterwards to work as a special adviser to Michael Howard, the Home Secretary. He stayed for a year before leaving to take the job of director of corporate affairs at Carlton Communications, the media group that held the London commercial television franchise.

In 1996 he was selected as the candidate for the newly created constituency of Stafford, but the Labour landslide at the following year's general election meant that the seat went to Labour. He attempted unsuccessfully to secure the candidacy of other safe Conservative seats until Tory MP Shaun Woodward, who held Douglas Hurd's old seat of Witney, stunned his constituents by defecting to Labour in December 1999.

David Cameron was chosen as the candidate to succeed Shaun Woodward, and at the 2001 general election he increased the Tory share of the vote by 2 per cent. and the majority by almost 1,000. The Conservatives generally failed to make much impact. Tony Blair was swept back into power, albeit with a slightly reduced majority, and the Conservative leader William Hague stepped down, to make way, in due course, for Iain Duncan Smith.

Once in the Commons, the new MP was appointed to the Home Affairs Select Committee where he took an active part, pushing for an inquiry by the Committee on drugs law. The following year, he and George Osborne were recruited by Iain Duncan Smith to advise on how to improve his handling of Prime Minister's Question Time.

The following year, he was given his first Front-Bench appointment, as deputy to Eric Forth, shadow Leader of the House. In November 2003, Iain Duncan Smith was ousted as leader and replaced by Michael Howard. He immediately appointed David Cameron as a deputy chairman of the party, and, again, he and George Osborne were brought in to brief the new leader on handling Prime Minister's Question Time. In 2004, Michael Howard appointed him Front-Bench spokesman on local government finance. He also became head of policy co-ordination, a role he filled until the 2005 general election.

After the third election defeat in a row, Michael Howard announced his intention to stand down and, once more, the leadership race was on. It was to be a prolonged campaign. In the meantime, David Cameron was appointed shadow Education Secretary.

The favourite to take over from Michael Howard was David Davis, but a strong performance by David Cameron at the Conservative party conference boosted his chances. In the first leadership ballot of MPs in October, David Davis came top, but David Cameron was only six votes behind. On the second ballot, he took the lead, and it was he and David Davis whose names went before the party in the country for the final endorsement. David Cameron won with nearly double the votes of his opponent.

As Leader of the Opposition, he was appointed to the Privy Council.

Resignation over Munich was a brave and principled stand

By Rt hon David Cameron MP, Leader of the Opposition

Duff Cooper's speech following the Munich agreement in 1938 was outstanding for two reasons: he was brave; and he was right.

Two days earlier he had resigned as First Lord of the Admiralty. As he was to explain in his speech, it was a painful decision which left him feeling isolated – in the Cabinet, in his party, and in the country as a whole.

He did have his supporters. Lord Mountbatten, then a serving naval officer, wrote to express admiration at his courage. Winston Churchill spoke of a "shining example of firmness of character" and, in a private note, described the speech as one of the finest parliamentary performances he had ever heard.

But that was certainly not the general reaction – either in Parliament, where his speech was said to have been regarded as pretty unimpressive, or beyond it. Memories of the great war were all too fresh, and Duff Cooper described in his diaries the general mood of euphoria when Munich was agreed, and another war with Germany had apparently been averted:

> "The Prime Minister arrived [at Cabinet] at about twenty past seven amid scenes of indescribable enthusiasm. He spoke to the mob from the window. I felt very lonely in the midst of so much happiness that I could not share".

No one else resigned. And many in his own constituency party shunned him. His autobiography recalls great bitterness, and recounts one old friend cancelling a meeting at his house "rather than allow me to cross the threshold".

Defending his stance, he told the House that foreign policy required clarity – especially when dealing with dictators. Yet the messages sent to Hitler had been uncertain; couched in the guarded language of diplomacy; and "with at least three qualifying clauses". Sending mixed signals was precisely the wrong approach.

While praising Neville Chamberlain's negotiating skills, he warned him against continuing to believe, contrary to all the evidence, in the good will and in the word of Hitler.

Duff Cooper was later to be reappointed to government under Winston Churchill. But that was not something he foresaw at the time. He ended the speech by noting he had "forfeited a great deal" – an office he loved, relations with friends and colleagues, the privilege of serving a leader he still regarded with the deepest admiration and affection:

> "I have ruined, perhaps, my political career. But that is a little matter; I have retained something which is to me of great value – I can still walk about the world with my head erect".

When I visited the Czech Republic in November 2007, the Government presented me with a treasured letter Duff Cooper had sent to the former President, Edvard Benes, in exile in 1940.

Duff Cooper was a distant relative of mine – he was my grandmother's uncle – and it was an honour to see at first hand the lasting impact which a brave and principled stance can have.

HOUSE OF COMMONS.

Monday, 3rd October, 1938.

The House met at a Quarter before Three of the Clock, Mr. SPEAKER *in the Chair.*

PERSONAL EXPLANATION.

2.50 p.m.

Mr. Duff Cooper: The House will, I am sure, appreciate the peculiarly difficult circumstances in which I am speaking this afternoon. It is always a painful and delicate task for a Minister who has resigned to explain his reasons to the House of Commons, and my difficulties are increased this afternoon by the fact, of which I am well aware, that the majority of the House are most anxious to hear the Prime Minister and that I am standing between them and him. But I shall have, I am afraid, to ask for the patience of the House, because I have taken a very important, for me, and difficult decision, and I feel that I shall have to demand a certain amount of time in which to make plain to the House the reasons for which I have taken it.

At the last Cabinet meeting that I attended, last Friday evening, before I succeeded in finding my way to No. 10, Downing Street, I was caught up in the large crowd that were demonstrating their enthusiasm and were cheering, laughing, and singing; and there is no greater feeling of loneliness than to be in a crowd of happy, cheerful people and to feel that there is no occasion for oneself for gaiety or for cheering. That there was every cause for relief I was deeply aware, as much as anybody in this country, but that there was great cause for self-congratulation I was uncertain. Later, when I stood in the hall at Downing Street, again among enthusiastic throngs of friends and colleagues who were all as cheerful, happy, glad, and enthusiastic as the crowd in the street, and when I heard the Prime Minister from the window above saying that he had returned, like Lord Beaconsfield, with " peace with honour," claiming that it was peace for our time, once again I felt lonely and isolated; and when later, in the Cabinet room, all his other colleagues were able to present him with

bouquets, it was an extremely painful and bitter moment for me that all that I could offer him was my resignation.

Before taking such a step as I have taken, on a question of international policy, a Minister must ask himself many questions, not the least important of which is this: Can my resignation at the present time do any material harm to His Majesty's Government; can it weaken our position; can it suggest to our critics that there is not a united front in Great Britain? Now I would not have flattered myself that my resignation was of great importance, and I did feel confident that so small a blow could easily be borne at the present time, when I think that the Prime Minister is more popular than he has ever been at any period; but had I had any doubts with regard to that facet of the problem, they would have been set at rest, I must say, by the way in which my resignation was accepted, not, I think, with reluctance, but really with relief.

I have always been a student of foreign politics. I have served 10 years in the Foreign Office, and I have studied the history of this and of other countries, and I have always believed that one of the most important principles in foreign policy and the conduct of foreign policy should be to make your policy plain to other countries, to let them know where you stand and what in certain circumstances you are prepared to do. I remember so well in 1914 meeting a friend, just after the declaration of war, who had come back from the British Embassy in Berlin, and asking him whether it was the case, as I had seen it reported in the papers, that the Berlin crowd had behaved very badly and had smashed all the windows of the Embassy, and that the military had had to be called out in order to protect them. I remember my friend telling me that, in his opinion and in that of the majority of the staff, the Berlin crowd were not to blame, that the members of the British Embassy staff had great sympathy with the feelings of the populace, because, they said, " These people have never thought that there was a chance of our coming into the war." They were assured by their Government —and the Government themselves perhaps believed it—that Britain would remain neutral, and therefore it came to them as a shock when, having already

[Mr. Cooper.]

been engaged with other enemies, as they were, they found that Great Britain had turned against them.

I thought then, and I have always felt, that in any other international crisis that should occur our first duty was to make it plain exactly where we stood and what we would do. I believe that the great defect in our foreign policy during recent months and recent weeks has been that we have failed to do so. During the last four weeks we have been drifting, day by day, nearer into war with Germany, and we have never said, until the last moment, and then in most uncertain terms, that we were prepared to fight. We knew that information to the opposite effect was being poured into the ears of the head of the German State. He had been assured, reassured, and fortified in the opinion that in no case would Great Britain fight.

When Ministers met at the end of August on their return from a holiday there was an enormous accumulation of information from all parts of the world, the ordinary information from our diplomatic representatives, also secret, and less reliable information from other sources, information from Members of Parliament who had been travelling on the Continent and who had felt it their duty to write to their friends in the Cabinet and give them first-hand information which they had received from good sources. I myself had been travelling in Scandinavia and in the Baltic States, and with regard to all this information—Europe was very full of rumours at that time—it was quite extraordinary the unanimity with which it pointed to one conclusion and with which all sources suggested that there was one remedy. All information pointed to the fact that Germany was preparing for war at the end of September, and all recommendations agreed that the one way in which it could be prevented was by Great Britain making a firm stand and stating that she would be in that war, and would be upon the other side.

I had urged even earlier, after the rape of Austria, that Great Britain should make a firm declaration of what her foreign policy was, and then and later I was met with this, that the people of this country are not prepared to fight for Czechoslovakia. That is perfectly true, but I tried to represent another aspect of the situation, that it was not for Czechoslovakia that we should have to fight, that it was not for Czechoslovakia that we should have been fighting if we had gone to war last week. God knows how thankful we all are to have avoided it, but we also know that the people of this country were prepared for it—resolute, prepared, and grimly determined. It was not for Serbia that we fought in 1914. It was not even for Belgium, although it occasionally suited some people to say so. We were fighting then, as we should have been fighting last week, in order that one great Power should not be allowed, in disregard of treaty obligations, of the laws of nations and the decrees of morality to dominate by brutal force the Continent of Europe. For that principle we fought against Napoleon Buonaparte, and against Louis XIV of France and Philip II of Spain. For that principle we must ever be prepared to fight, for on the day when we are not prepared to fight for it we forfeit our Empire, our liberties and our independence.

I besought my colleagues not to see this problem always in terms of Czechoslovakia, not to review it always from the difficult strategic position of that small country, but rather to say to themselves, " A moment may come when, owing to the invasion of Czechoslovakia, a European war will begin, and when that moment comes we must take part in that war, we cannot keep out of it, and there is no doubt upon which side we shall fight. Let the world know that and it will give those who are prepared to disturb the peace reason to hold their hand." It is perfectly true that after the assault on Austria the Prime Minister made a speech in this House—an excellent speech with every word of which I was in complete agreement—and what he said then was repeated and supported by the Chancellor of the Exchequer at Lanark. It was, however, a guarded statement. It was a statement to the effect that if there were such a war it would be unwise for anybody to count upon the possibility of our staying out.

That is not the language which the dictators understand. Together with new methods and a new morality they have introduced also a new vocabulary into Europe. They have discarded the old diplomatic methods of correspondence. Is it not significant that during the whole of this crisis there has not been a German Ambassador in London and, so far as I am aware, the German Chargé d'Affaires has hardly visited the Foreign Office? They talk a new language, the language of the headlines of the tabloid Press, and such guarded diplomatic and reserved utterances as were made by the Prime Minister and the Chancellor of the Exchequer mean nothing to the mentality of Herr Hitler or Signor Mussolini. I had hoped that it might be possible to make a statement to Herr Hitler before he made his speech at Nuremberg. On all sides we were being urged to do so by people in this country, by Members in this House, by Leaders of the Opposition, by the Press, by the heads of foreign States, even by Germans who were supporters of the regime and did not wish to see it plunged into a war which might destroy it. But we were always told that on no account must we irritate Herr Hitler; it was particularly dangerous to irritate him before he made a public speech, because if he were so irritated he might say some terrible things from which afterwards there would be no retreat. It seems to me that Herr Hitler never makes a speech save under the influence of considerable irritation, and the addition of one more irritant would not, I should have thought, have made a great difference, whereas the communication of a solemn fact would have produced a sobering effect.

After the chance of Nuremberg was missed I had hoped that the Prime Minister at his first interview with Herr Hitler at Berchtesgaden would make the position plain, but he did not do so. Again, at Godesberg I had hoped that that statement would be made in unequivocal language. Again I was disappointed. Hitler had another speech to make in Berlin. Again an opportunity occurred of telling him exactly where we stood before he made that speech, but again the opportunity was missed, and it was only after the speech that he was informed. He was informed through the mouth of a distinguished **English** civil servant that in certain conditions we were prepared to fight. We know what the mentality or something of the mentality of that great dictator is. We know that a message delivered strictly according to instructions with at least three qualifying clauses was not likely to produce upon him on the morning after his great oration the effect that was desired. Honestly, I did not believe that he thought there was anything of importance in that message. It certainly produced no effect whatever upon him and we can hardly blame him.

Then came the last appeal from the Prime Minister on Wednesday morning. For the first time from the beginning to the end of the four weeks of negotiations Herr Hitler was prepared to yield an inch, an ell perhaps, but to yield some measure to the representations of Great Britain. But I would remind the House that the message from the Prime Minister was not the first news that he had received that morning. At dawn he had learned of the mobilisation of the British Fleet. It is impossible to know what are the motives of man and we shall probably never be satisfied as to which of these two sources of inspiration moved him most when he agreed to go to Munich, but wo do know that never before had he given in and that then he did. I had been urging the mobilisation of the Fleet for many days. I had thought that this was the kind of language which would be easier for Herr Hitler to understand than the guarded language of diplomacy or the conditional clauses of the Civil Service. I had urged that something in that direction might be done at the end of August and before the Prime Minister went to Berchtesgaden. I had suggested that it should accompany the mission of Sir Horace Wilson. I remember the Prime Minister stating it was the one thing that would ruin that mission, and I said it was the one thing that would lead it to success.

That is the deep difference between the Prime Minister and myself throughout these days. The Prime Minister has believed in addressing Herr Hitler through the language of sweet reasonableness. I have believed that he was more open to the language of the mailed fist. I am glad so many people think that sweet reasonableness has prevailed, but what actually did it accomplish? The Prime Minister went to Berchtesgaden with many excellent and reasonable proposals and alternatives to put before the Fuhrer, prepared to argue and negotiate, as anybody would have gone to such a meeting. He was met by an ultimatum. So far as I am aware no

[Mr. Cooper.]

suggestion of an alternative was ever put forward. Once the Prime Minister found himself in the atmosphere of Berchtesgaden and face to face with the personality of Hitler he knew perfectly well, being a good judge of men, that it would be a waste of time to put forward any alternative suggestion. So he returned to us with those proposals, wrapped up in a cloak called " Self-determination," and laid them before the Cabinet. They meant the partition of a country, the cession of territory, they meant what, when it was suggested by a newspaper some weeks or days before, had been indignantly repudiated throughout the country.

After long deliberation the Cabinet decided to accept that ultimatum, and I was one of those who agreed in that decision. I felt all the difficulty of it; but I foresaw also the danger of refusal. I saw that if we were obliged to go to war it would be hard to have it said against us that we were fighting against the principle of self-determination, and I hoped that if a postponement could be reached by this compromise there was a possibility that the final disaster might be permanently avoided. It was not a pleasant task to impose upon the Government of Czechoslovakia so grievous a hurt to their country, no pleasant or easy task for those upon whose support the Government of Czechoslovakia had relied to have to come to her and say " You have got to give up all for which you were prepared to fight "; but, still, she accepted those terms. The Government of Czechoslovakia, filled with deep misgiving, and with great regret, accepted the harsh terms that were proposed to her.

That was all that we had got by sweet reasonableness at Berchtesgaden. Well, I did think that when a country had agreed to be partitioned, when the Government of a country had agreed to split up the ancient Kingdom of Bohemia, which has existed behind its original frontier for more than 1,000 years, that was the ultimate demand that would be made upon it, and that after everything which Herr Hitler had asked for in the first instance had been conceded he would be willing, and we should insist, that the method of transfer of those territories should be conducted in a normal, in a civilised, manner, as such transfers have always been conducted in the past.

The Prime Minister made a second visit to Germany, and at Godesberg he was received with flags, bands, trumpets and all the panoply of Nazi parade; but he returned again with nothing but an ultimatum. Sweet reasonableness had won nothing except terms which a cruel and revengeful enemy would have dictated to a beaten foe after a long war. Crueller terms could hardly be devised than those of the Godesberg ultimatum. The moment I saw them I said to myself, " If these are accepted it will be the end of all decency in the conduct of public affairs in the world." We had a long and anxious discussion in the Cabinet with regard to the acceptance or rejection of those terms. It was decided to reject them, and that information, also, was conveyed to the German Government. Then we were face to face with an impossible position, and at the last moment —not quite the last moment, but what seemed the last moment—another effort was made, by the dispatch of an emissary to Herr Hitler with suggestions for a last appeal. That emissary's effort was in vain, and it was only, as the House knows, on that fateful Wednesday morning that the final change of policy was adopted. I believe that change of policy, as I have said, was due not to any argument that had been addressed to Herr Hitler—it has never been suggested that it was—but due to the fact that for the first moment he realised, when the Fleet was mobilised, that what his advisers had been assuring him of for weeks and months was untrue and that the British people were prepared to fight in a great cause.

So, last of all, he came to Munich and terms, of which the House is now aware, were devised at Munich, and those were the terms upon which this transfer of territory is to be carried out. The Prime Minister will shortly be explaining to the House the particulars in which the Munich terms differ from the Godesberg ultimatum. There are great and important differences, and it is a great triumph for the Prime Minister that he was able to acquire them. I spent the greater part of Friday trying to persuade myself that those terms were good enough for me. I tried to swallow them—I did not want to do what I have done—but they stuck in my throat, because it seemed to me that although the modifications which the Prime Minister obtained were important and of great value—the House will realise how great the value is when the Prime Minister has developed them—that still there remained the fact that that country was to be invaded, and I had thought that after accepting the humiliation of partition she should have been spared the ignominy and the horror of invasion. If anybody doubts that she is now suffering from the full horror of invasion they have only to read an article published in the " Daily Telegraph " this morning, which will convince them. After all, when Naboth had agreed to give up his vineyard he should have been allowed to pack up his goods in peace and depart, but the German Government, having got their man down, were not to be deprived of the pleasure of kicking him. Invasion remained; even the date of invasion remained unaltered. The date laid down by Herr Hitler was not to be changed. There are five stages, but those stages are almost as rapid as an army can move. Invasion and the date remained the same. Therefore, the works, fortifications, and guns on emplacements upon which that poor country had spent an enormous amount of its wealth were to be handed over intact. Just as the German was not to be deprived of the pleasure of kicking a man when he was down, so the army was not to be robbed of its loot. That was another term in the ultimatum which I found it impossible to accept. That was why I failed to bring myself to swallow the terms that were proposed—although I recognised the great service that the Prime Minister had performed in obtaining very material changes in them which would result in great benefit and a great lessening of the sufferings of the people of Czechoslovakia.

Then he brought home also from Munich something more than the terms to which we had agreed. At the last moment, at the farewell meeting, he signed with the Fuhrer, a joint declaration. [An Hon. Member: " Secret."] I do not think there was anything secret about the declaration. The joint declaration has been published to the world. I saw no harm, no great harm and no very obvious harm, in the terms of that declaration, but I would suggest that for the Prime Minister of England to sign, without consulting with his colleagues and without, so far as I am aware, any reference to his Allies, obviously without any communication with the Dominions and

without the assistance of any expert diplomatic advisers, such a declaration with the dictator of a great State, is not the way in which the foreign affairs of the British Empire should be conducted.

There is another aspect of this joint declaration. After all, what does it say? That Great Britain and Germany will not go to war in future and that everything will be settled by negotiation. Was it ever our intention to go to war? Was it ever our intention not to settle things by communication and counsel? There is a danger. We must remember that this is not all that we are left with as the result of what has happened during the last few weeks. We are left, and we must all acknowledge it, with a loss of esteem on the part of countries that trusted us. We are left also with a tremendous commitment. For the first time in our history we have committed ourselves to defend a frontier in Central Europe.

Brigadier-General Sir Henry Croft: It is what you have been asking for.

Mr. Cooper: We are left with the additional serious commitment that we are guaranteeing a frontier that we have at the same time destroyed. We have taken away the defences of Czechoslovakia in the same breath as we have guaranteed them, as though you were to deal a man a mortal blow and at the same time insure his life. I was in favour of giving this commitment. I felt that as we had taken so much away we must, in honour, give something in return, but I realised what the commitment meant. It meant giving a commitment to defend a frontier in Central Europe, a difficult frontier to defend because it is surrounded on all sides by enemies. I realised that giving this commitment must mean for ourselves a tremendous quickening-up of our rearmament schemes on an entirely new basis, a far broader basis upon which they must be carried out in future.

I had always been in favour of maintaining an army that could take a serious part in Continental war. I am afraid I differed from the Prime Minister, when I was at the War Office and he was at the Treasury two years ago or more, on this point, but if we are now committed to defend a frontier in Central Europe, it is, in my opinion, absolutely imperative that we should maintain an Army upon

[Mr. Cooper.]

something like a Continental basis. It is no secret that the attitude maintained by this Government during recent weeks would have been far stiffer had our defences been far stronger. It has been said that we shall necessarily now increase both the speed at which they are reconditioned and the scale upon which they are reconditioned, but how are we to justify the extra burden laid upon the people of Great Britain if we are told at the same time that there is no fear of war with Germany and that, in the opinion of the Prime Minister, this settlement means peace in our time? That is one of the most profoundly disquieting aspects of the situation.

The Prime Minister has confidence in the good will and in the word of Herr Hitler, although when Herr Hitler broke the Treaty of Versailles he undertook to keep the Treaty of Locarno, and when he broke the Treaty of Locarno he undertook not to interfere further, or to have further territorial aims, in Europe. When he entered Austria by force he authorised his henchmen to give an authoritative assurance that he would not interfere with Czechoslovakia. That was less than six months ago. Still, the Prime Minister believes that he can rely upon the good faith of Hitler; he believes that Hitler is interested only in Germany, as the Prime Minister was assured. Well, there are Germans in other countries. There are Germans in Switzerland, in Denmark and in Alsace; I think that one of the only countries in Europe in which there are no Germans is Spain and yet there are rumours that Germany has taken an interest in that country. But the Prime Minister believed—and he has the advantage over us, or over most of us, that he has met the man—that he can come to a reasonable settlement of all outstanding questions between us. Herr Hitler said that he has got to have some settlement about colonies, but he said that this will never be a question of war. The Prime Minister attaches considerable importance to those words, but what do they mean? Do they mean that Herr Hitler will take " No " for an answer? He has never taken it yet. Or do they mean that he believes that he will get away with this, as he has got away with everything else, without fighting, by well-timed bluff, bluster and blackmail? Otherwise it means very little.

The Prime Minister may be right. I can assure you, Mr. Speaker, with the deepest sincerity, that I hope and pray that he is right, but I cannot believe what he believes. I wish I could. Therefore, I can be of no assistance to him in his Government. I should be only a hindrance, and it is much better that I should go. I remember when we were discussing the Godesberg ultimatum that I said that if I were a party to persuading, or even to suggesting to, the Czechoslovak Government that they should accept that ultimatum, I should never be able to hold up my head again. I have forfeited a great deal. I have given up an office that I loved, work in which I was deeply interested and a staff of which any man might be proud. I have given up associations in that work with my colleagues with whom I have maintained for many years the most harmonious relations, not only as colleagues but as friends. I have given up the privilege of serving as lieutenant to a leader whom I still regard with the deepest admiration and affection. I have ruined, perhaps, my political career. But that is a little matter; I have retained something which is to me of great value —I can still walk about the world with my head erect.

———

EUROPEAN SITUATION.

PRIME MINISTER'S STATEMENT.

Motion made, and Question proposed, " That this House do now adjourn."—[*Captain Margesson.*]

3.31 p.m.

The Prime Minister (Mr. Chamberlain): It has been my lot to listen to more than one speech by a Minister who came to this House to explain the reasons why he had felt it necessary to resign his office in the Government. I have never been able to listen to such speeches without emotion. When a man gives up, as my right hon. Friend has so eloquently described, a great position, and association with friends in the pursuit of work in which he takes a pride and interest, and gives up these things for conscience' sake, everybody must listen to him with respect. One must feel, too, sympathy for a man struggling to explain the reasons which have separated him from his colleagues conscious that among them at any rate, he has been in a minority. But

Edmund Morel, a long forgotten humanitarian hero, warns of the dangers of the Versailles peace

Ian Church served as the Editor of *Hansard* from 1989 until his retirement in 2002 at the age of 61. He worked for the Department of the Official Report for more than 30 years, having been recruited as a reporter in 1972.

He began his working life as a journalist. Leaving school, he joined D. C. Thompson as an editorial assistant on the Dundee *Courier and Advertiser*, subsequently working as a reporter on that and other Thompson titles including the Dundee *Evening Telegraph, The Sunday Post* and *The Weekly News*. At one time he wrote scripts for the comic adventures portrayed in *The Hotspur* and *The Rover*.

As part of his training, he learnt shorthand and became sufficiently fast to get a job with the Press Association as a reporter in the Press Gallery. That was in 1964 when Alec Douglas-Home was Prime Minister.

After two years he moved on to become the Gallery correspondent for *The Scotsman*, and two years after that he joined the parliamentary staff of *The Times*. It was an uncertain time for newspapers. The Eddie Shah and Rupert Murdoch revolutions were some years in the future, but the labour troubles and financial torments that beset the newspaper industry at that time would hasten the technological change that came to be associated with those two proprietors.

With the disputes with the print unions threatening the very existence of *The Times*, it was apparent that Roy Thomson, benevolent owner though he was regarded, did not have bottomless pockets endlessly to finance the mounting losses. So, when Ian Church was offered the job of a reporter on *Hansard* he took it. He was to remain with the *Official Report* for the rest of his working life.

As the Editor he was responsible for a House department employing some 100 staff. It was a job that, in spite of the title, took him away from the Press Gallery and editorial work. In his new role he devoted his time to modernising *Hansard's* production processes with the introduction of information technology. In 1997 he was given an award by the Freedom of Information Campaign for having been instrumental in making *Hansard* available free on the internet. He received a CBE in 2002.

Shipping clerk who challenged a king and exposed a bloody regime of cruelty and greed

By Ian Church CBE

Edmund Dene Morel's maiden speech merits inclusion in any list of great parliamentary speeches not so much for its content, chillingly prescient though it was, or for its oratory but more because of the man who delivered it. He ranks as one of the great heroes of the humanitarian cause whom history has forgotten and of whom the public now know nothing.

By the time that Morel came to the House of Commons as a Labour MP, having beaten Winston Churchill at Dundee in the 1922 general election, King Leopold II of Belgium, whom Morel had successfully campaigned so hard to bring down, was long dead and the Congo was a Belgian colony.

The expression "reign of terror", is usually associated with Stalin or Hitler or, more recently, ethnic cleansing in the Balkans or Saddam Hussein. But the bloodstained regime of torture, mutilation, abduction, rape and murder for which Leopold was responsible in the Congo, and which Morel worked so hard to expose, puts him in a league of his own, probably for its scale but also for the greed that was its motivation.

As he enslaved and slaughtered the people of the Congo to plunder its riches of ivory and rubber for his personal gain, Leopold protested that he was embarked upon a philanthropic crusade to protect the primitive inhabitants of the "dark continent". His guile enabled him to hoodwink the then most powerful nations and take over the Congo as his private fiefdom. His "philanthropy" made him one of the richest men in Europe. Morel was not taken in.

The world is familiar with the horror of the holocaust in which 6 million Jews died. Stalin was responsible for untold millions of deaths in the Soviet Union. But, while a duped world looked on, Leopold chalked up a death toll estimated at up to 10 million among an indigenous population of 20 million as he ripped apart a country at the heart of Africa – the "Heart of Darkness" as Morel's friend, Joseph Conrad, entitled the novel he wrote based on his experiences working there.

Morel discovered what was going on and told the world. He did more than any other man to expose Leopold's cruelty. He uncovered the horrific truth of what was happening in the Congo around 1900 while working as a clerk for Elder Dempster, the Liverpool-based shipping line. Leopold had awarded it the exclusive contract to carry cargo to and from the Congo. Thereafter, Morel worked tirelessly, writing, addressing public meetings, lobbying politicians and even establishing his own newspaper to publicise the evil being perpetrated and to secure international action to stop Leopold.

His work behind the scenes resulted in a Commons resolution calling for humane treatment for the people of the Congo. The Foreign Office accordingly ordered its consul in the Congo to investigate. His name was Roger Casement, and he became Morel's staunchest ally and friend. Between them they created the Congo Reform Association, which was to become the backbone of the anti-Leopold movement.

In November 1908 Leopold eventually handed the Congo over to Belgium, pocketing millions in the process. He died a year later. In 1913 Morel accepted that his objectives had been achieved and the Congo Reform Association was wound up.

But as one cause was won, the next was not long coming. Morel was passionately opposed to the first world war. He was instrumental in establishing the Union of Democratic Control, whose objective was parliamentary control of foreign policy and the ending of secret deals between nations, such as those with France and Russia that he blamed for what he regarded as an unnecessary war, and which he again attacks in this speech.

Amid the jingoistic fervour to which Britain's youth marched to the mud and slaughter of the trenches, his crusade alienated those who had admired him for his work on the Congo. He was attacked, physically as well as verbally; he was denounced in the press as pro-German; he was ousted from the Liberal party; and he followed Casement into Pentonville prison, convicted on flimsy charges related to the defence of the realm.

Unlike Casement, he came out alive, but his stance was undiminished. Welcomed into the Labour party, he transformed his opposition to the war into opposition to the peace – at least the peace that resulted from Versailles. With great foresight he warned, as he does in this speech, that it contained the seeds of the next war – in a later Commons speech he spoke of the "cannon fodder" that would be its result.

Morel was probably neither a pacifist nor an anti-colonialist. He certainly believed in the just and humane treatment of his fellow man. He died aged 51 within a few days of the second anniversary of the speech that is here reproduced.

home and creates unemployment in this country. We plead, therefore, for a policy of enlightened self-interest, and for all nations to live and let live, so that the animosities which war has engendered can be wiped out and that people, not only here but abroad, can face the future with that degree of confidence and hope which all nations desire.

Passing from that subject, the Gracious Speech also referred to the League of Nations scheme and stated that the loan to Austria is to be engineered and carried through by the organisation and under the direction of the League of Nations. We hope that that foreshadows a new policy and that our whole foreign policy will be animated and directed through the League of Nations. During the last few years the assistance of the League of Nations has frequently been invited when the Supreme Council were unable to secure agreement. We hope that the spirit of the League of Nations will be put in the forefront of the foreign policy of His Majesty's Government, so that all nations represented there may gather together in friendly conference, and, at Geneva or elsewhere, may consider and effect an ultimate cure of the difficulties due to the warring interests between one nation and another.

Mr. MOREL: In rising to participate in this Debate, I beg to ask the indulgence which, I understand, the House always accords to a new Member, particularly when he makes his first speech, even when, as in this case, the particular Member who has the honour to address the House now is one who, when he was not a Member, has had the rather curious experience, during the last few years, of hearing himself, from the gallery, both praised and blamed. It has been remarked by hon. Members opposite that a somewhat new spirit has been introduced into the House in connection with our domestic affairs, and a new spirit has been introduced into the House on this side in connection with our foreign affairs. One thing to which the Labour party has become more and more alive during the last two years is that our foreign affairs and domestic affairs are inextricably intertwined and we can no longer in the future as we have in the past allow our foreign affairs to be conducted under a veil of secrecy, and allow interests of the most vital importance to the nation to be decided behind closed doors, without the knowledge of the people, and I believe that I am voicing the views of all my friends behind me when I say that we shall in this Parliament press unrelentingly until we have secured that full democratic control over our foreign affairs which the Labour party demands.

We are all agreed that the European situation, with which we are faced, is one of extreme gravity, but it seems to me that, unless we are prepared also to face the causes of that situation which brought that situation about, we cannot possibly hope to cope with it effectively. The situation with which we are faced in the world to-day is the direct result of the so-called peace treaties signed after the War, and those peace treaties themselves are but the outcome of the secret treaties and arrangements made behind the back of this House and of the country by the Liberal Government during the War. All that I shall say with regard to the Near Eastern question is this: I agree with the Under-Secretary of State for Foreign Affairs that perhaps the least said about the negotiations now proceeding at Lausanne the better, but there are at least two points which I think can and ought to be made without incurring the charge of wishing in any way to embarrass those negotiations. One is this—we are bound to make it here as we have made it in the country. An error of a magnitude which can hardly be measured now has been made by excluding Russia from the Conference. How can the Near Eastern question ever be solved, or how can any real attempt ever be made to solve it, if you omit the people who, more than any other, are interested in the question? And I earnestly beg His Majesty's Government to consider, even now at the last moment, inviting the Russian Government to the Lausanne Conference. Apparently from what one reads in the press, Signor Mussolini, the head of the present Italian Government, is of the same opinion. The other point made in connection with the Near Eastern question is this. At this stage it does seem a pity to indulge in strong attacks upon one of the negotiating Powers at the Conference. I do not think that any of us on these benches can fairly be called Turcophile; I certainly cannot but those of us who have read the Report of the Carnegie Commission on the Balkan wars will be very chary in

[Mr. Morel.]

imputing all tendency to massacre to the Turk.

May I return for a moment to the point which I made at the beginning of my remarks—that the present situation is the outcome of the errors and the follies committed at Versailles four and a half years ago, and that that situation cannot be remedied until those errors and follies themselves are remedied? What an immeasurable opportunity lay before the Government of this country and of the Allied and Associated Governments four and a half years ago, and especially before the Government of this country! Surely at that time we were, without challenge, the most influential Power in the world. Our influence to direct policy into the right channels, our power to have completely reversed the bad policy of the past, were unlimited. We had the ball at our feet. What was done? The country was told that Germany would pay for the War, and there was something said about conducting the Kaiser to the scaffold. Well, the Kaiser has since been conducted to the altar, and it is for hon. Members who are married to declare which is the worse sentence. As for making Germany pay, it was the greatest bluff ever put forward, and it was put forward, in my belief, largely by those influences which dreaded being taxed for the profits which they had made out of the War. If Members of the Coalition Government really believed that Germany could be made to pay the cost of the War a special educational penitentiary ought to be built for them.

What was the great moral purpose put before the people of this country during the years of the War? What was the ideal for which hundreds of thousands of the youth of this country perished on the battlefield, the ideal which, in my own personal knowledge, animated some 15 or 16 young officers and privates whom I knew personally and whom I shall know no more? They were fighting, as the hon. and gallant Member for Limehouse (Major Attlee) stated in an eloquent speech, for something even greater than King or country; they were fighting to make a better world. That was the great moral purpose which permeated the terms upon which the Armistice was signed. I do not think hon. Members opposite, who, perhaps, are somewhat scandalised by some of the speeches they have been hearing from these benches, can realise what it means to my hon. Friends and to myself—that infinitely greater scandal of millions of men of the working classes who went into the War with that high and noble aim, and who to-day see their country spending twice as much as it spent before the War that was to end war, and find themselves abandoned and many of them starving. What was not to be done for the miners toiling in the bowels of the earth below the level of the sea? What was not to be done for them when they took off their khaki? Yet we have in South Wales to-day thousands of miners' families in such a state of utter destitution that the women have not a change of raiment and the children cannot be sent out of the house because they have not enough rags to cover them.

We are faced with a Europe rent and shattered, a Europe over which is creeping economic paralysis, a Europe in which the seeds of war are floating from one end to the other as a result of the disastrous errors committed four and a half years ago. How are these errors to be repaired? We have had an interesting speech from the Under-Secretary for Foreign Affairs. Perhaps some of my hon. Friends are blessed with more intelligence than myself, but I sought in vain for any light or guidance in that speech. The one thing in his statement that seemed to be definite appeared to be also of a very bad augury. He practically defended the group system of nations. The alternatives are the group system or the League of Nations. There is no room for the two. It is the group system of nations which was responsible for the horrible holocaust of 1914-1918. Does it mean that, after all that has been said in favour of the League of Nations, the Government's opinion is that we are to go back to the old system of partial alliances, of two great rival groups, to the old system of the balance of power, denounced in such eloquent language by John Bright in this House many years ago? The Under-Secretary for Foreign Affairs said that hon. Members could not be expected to be praising the League of Nations all the time. There is all the difference between trying to make the League of Nations a vital mechanism and blocking the League at every turn. What we complained of in the last Government, and what we hope that we shall not have to complain of in this Government, is that that policy was followed.

The hon. Member for Greenock (Sir G. Collins) indicated a desire for further discussion on foreign affairs, and another hon. Member suggested that we should have a day for the discussion of reparations. Apparently we are not to be allowed that, and I therefore take this opportunity of saying a few words on this question of reparations—so-called. The first thing to be noted about it is that the whole system of calculating reparations has proved to be a most monstrous and ludicrous absurdity. We began with a figure of £24,000,000,000. Then we came down to £11,300,000,000, then to £6,600,000,000 and now apparently there is a difference of opinion between right hon. Gentlemen opposite and others who held prominent positions in the Coalition Government as between the figures of £2,500,000,000, £2,000,000,000 and £1,100,000,000. If we want to reconstruct Europe and to re-open our markets, how is it possible to do so in these circumstances? How is it posible that the mark can be stabilised unless and until Germany knows what she has got to pay? It is this uncertainty which is paralysing the whole European situation. Make it £2,500,000,000, make it £1,100,000,000; make it what you like, but as long as you have this great nation in a state of despair and uncertainty, how can it borrow? You do not lend money to a man until you know what are his liabilities. Many of us on this side of the House take the view—I do so myself—that apart from the restoration of the devastated areas in France, upon which we are all agreed, we ought to wipe out reparations altogether as a mere cash transaction. Trying to enforce reparations has already cost us more than we have got. I have not the figures before me, but I think I am right in saying that after tempestuous bullying, we have succeeded in screwing £54,000,000 sterling out of the German working class and lower middle class, and we have spent £56,000,000 sterling in keeping a British Army eating its head off in idleness on the Rhine. As a mere cash transaction, this whole reparation question is a myth. Apart from that the country is beginning to realise that the claim which has been enforced

for 4½ years to screw money out of Germany has acted, as far as we are concerned, like a boomerang. It has destroyed our trade; it is this very question of reparations, it is these ridiculous and absurd economic fetters put upon this great industrial nation of Central Europe, which is blasting our whole economic life and the whole economic life of Europe to-day.

I ask the Prime Minister what is the policy of His Majesty's Government on this question? Whatever aspirations the Government may have after tranquillity—and one sympathises with them to an extent—it is perfectly ridiculous to suppose that there will be any tranquillity in Europe as long as the great festering cancer of these Treaties is eating into it. I am reminded that some of us have been stating for years what many hon. Members are prepared to admit to-day, and we were accused of unimaginable crimes for doing so. I could not help thinking of that when I heard the hon Member for Greenock putting before the House what I may call the argument of the clean slate, which I and hon. Members with whom I am associated have been putting before the country for four years. What have we been called for so doing? "Lunatics" was the mildest term applied to us. "Traitors" and "pro-Germans" were the worst. I was much struck by a statement of the Under-Secretary for Foreign Affairs and also of the hon. Member for the Scotland Division of Liverpool (Mr. O'Connor). It is the statement made almost every day and everywhere, that the Entente must continue to be the basis of British foreign policy or the whole house will fall to pieces. I ask the Government, what is the Entente to-day, what does it mean, and in what does it involve us? I do not think there is a single Member on this side of the House who would not regard it as an absolute tragedy if our relations with France should cease to be of a friendly character, but the question arises: What France? There are two Frances. There is a great change coming over France to-day and the France of two years hence will not be the France of to-day. The France of two years hence will be a far more democratic France. The question which causes grave anxiety to many of my Friends is how far we are going to be led along the road of those elements in France from which we absolutely dissociate ourselves.

[Mr. Morel.]

Everybody knows that if Germany is not going to follow Austria into bankruptcy, bringing a further decrease of our trade and further unemployment here, Germany will have to be given a moratorium. Some very alarming statements have recently been made in France by high authorities. What is the position of His Majesty's Government going to be if at Brussels next month or the month after, you are faced with this statement. " We agree to a moratorium provided that we may keep the Ruhr or provided that we may separate the Rhine Provinces from Germany to form an autonomous State "? What reply is His Majesty's Government going to make if a proposal of that kind should be made? If such a proposal were accepted. the signature would have been put to the declaration of the next war. Any attempt to separate the Rhine Provinces from Germany is bound to lead to war and, without venturing in any way to arrogate to myself a position other than that of a humble Member of my party, I believe I express the views of all my Friends when I say the Labour party will associate itself with no policy of further military occupation. Our policy is one making for peace. We are against any policy that leads to war, and we should oppose, I believe, and strongly oppose, any policy calculated to extend the area of French military occupation, with black troops or other, in Germany.

I thank the House for the courtesy it has extended to me. All I want to say in conclusion is that we on these benches believe that an absolutely different spirit has got to be introduced into our foreign policy and that an absolutely different spirit has got to be introduced into the present conditions based upon the Peace Treaties, which are ruining Europe. We stand for a revision of the Peace Treaties —not a mere change, but a revision of them out of all recognition. not only the Treaty of Versailles, but the Treaty of Neuilly and the other Treaties. The basis of our belief is that foreign policy must now be founded upon that living fact, the inter-economic dependence of peoples, and that it must be directed in the interests, not of particular classes, but of the whole people. The peoples, we believe, insist upon peace, and the peoples will get it, but they must have a framework within which they can act, and that is the complete abrogation of the secret diplomacy which has brought us to this pass, and as far as our country is concerned a breath of democratic air sweeping through these old, musty, fusty channels.

BRITISH TRADE, BRAZIL.

Lieut.-Colonel Sir PHILIP RICHARDSON: I ask the indulgence of the House in making a few brief remarks as a first effort in speaking. There are many more competent than I to deal with large questions, but there are those who would draw attention to matters which are relatively smaller, and I wish to draw the attention of the Under-Secretary of State for Foreign Affairs to the state of our trade with Brazil. Brazil, I need hardly remind Members of this House, is the fourth greatest country in the world, and has a large population of some 30,600,000. It is a country of great possibilities in the matter of mining, agriculture, and other things, and it is a country that buys from us a great number of British goods. During the last few months some Gentlemen who were Members of the late House and who are Members of the present House had the privilege of visiting Brazil and the opportunity of studying trade relations between this country and Brazil, being afforded the greatest assistance by all with whom we came in contact, and I have to express our appreciation of the honour paid to us by the President of the Republic, by the Senate, and by the Chamber of Deputies in receiving us, and in giving us every facility to know that which we desired to know. I also wish to render testimony to the efficacy of the British Chambers of Commerce. Both in Rio de Janeiro and in San Paulo, there are Chambers which look after British interests and take every care of them. While we were there we learned, in relation to our trade, that it was less than it was before the War, as we should expect, because the volume of trade throughout the world is smaller than it used to be, but we were distressed to find that the proportion of British trade had fallen in relation to the trade of other nations.

I should like to give some figures in relation to some of the principal headings. British exports to Brazil, which in 1913 were over £16,000,000 had dropped in 1921 to £12,000,000, but whereas that drop might not appear to be very important in view of the general diminution of trade, the British proportion of the total

Geoffrey Howe makes a spellbinding attack to change the course of history

Kenneth Clarke, regarded by many as one of the most popular of the senior Conservative politicians with the general public, has been a Member of the House of Commons since 1970, is a barrister and a QC, and has pursued a successful business career. The less formal side of his character displays a liking for jazz, bird watching, brown suede shoes, cigars and real ale.

He was born in 1940 and was educated at Nottingham High School and Gonville and Caius College, Cambridge. It was at Cambridge that his political life began when he became chairman of the Cambridge University Conservative Association and of the Federation of Conservative Students. He was also President of the Cambridge Union.

By profession he is a lawyer, having been called to the Bar by Grays Inn in 1963. He became a QC in 1980.

He stood unsuccessfully at the 1964 and 1966 general elections in the safe Labour seat of Mansfield, but at the general election in 1970 he overturned a Labour majority to take the south Nottingham seat of Rushcliffe. He has retained it at every election since, putting him among the longest continuous serving MPs.

In 1971 he was appointed Parliamentary Private Secretary to the Solicitor-General, Sir Geoffrey Howe. That was followed by a stint working with Sir Geoffrey on the Industrial Relations Bill and then on the enabling legislation on the European Community. Appointment as a Whip followed until the Conservatives were ousted from office in 1974. In Opposition he became a Front-Bench spokesman first on social services and then on industry.

When Margaret Thatcher took the Tories back into office in 1979, she appointed him a junior Transport Minister. It was the start of 18 unbroken years of ministerial office. He was made a privy counsellor in 1984 and moved into the Cabinet the following year as Paymaster General and Minister for Employment.

He was appointed Chancellor of the Duchy of Lancaster and Minister for Trade and Industry after the June 1987 general election. From July 1988 to November 1990 he was Secretary of State for Health, and from November 1990 to April 1992 he was Secretary of State for Education and Science.

After the Tories' unexpected election victory in 1992, Prime Minister John Major appointed him Home Secretary, a position he held until, in 1993, he moved up to become Chancellor of the Exchequer. He remained in charge of the Treasury until Tony Blair returned the Labour Party to power in 1997. He is credited by some as having laid the foundation for the economic stability that characterised Tony Blair's decade in Downing street.

In Opposition he stood unsuccessfully for the leadership of his party three times – in 1997 when William Hague won, in 2001 when Eurosceptic Iain Duncan Smith was elected, and in 2005 when David Cameron became the leader. During a period when Europe had dogged and divided the Conservative party, his pro-Europe stance was thought to have been a significant factor in the outcome on at least one occasion.

He was a vociferous critic of Tony Blair for taking the country to war in Iraq in 2003.

In his business life, he has held board positions with a number of companies, including as non-executive deputy chairman both of British American Tobacco and Alliance Unichem. He was also non-executive chairman of the tobacco company's motor racing sponsorship business, British American Racing.

In January 2009, as the Conservative party geared up for the forthcoming general election, David Cameron, Leader of the Opposition, recalled Kenneth Clarke to the Tory Front Bench. He was given the job of shadowing another recall to front-line Westminster politics – Peter Mandelson, who had returned from his post as trade commissioner in Brussels to enter Gordon Brown's Cabinet as the Secretary of State for Business, Enterprise and Regulatory Reform.

Barbed criticism and condemnation as the verbal daggers fly

By Rt hon Kenneth Clarke QC MP

I was sitting on the Front Bench in the House with about two Cabinet colleagues between me and Margaret Thatcher as I listened to Geoffrey Howe's personal statement following his resignation from Mrs Thatcher's Cabinet.

I was a friend and follower of Geoffrey, and I expected him to make a polite and regretful statement, which would contain the usual thanks for the privilege of serving in the Government, and conclude with expressions of continuing support in the future.

I sat as spellbound as everyone else as it quickly became clear that Geoffrey was giving a very passionate explanation of the reasons for his resignation, with the clearest possible condemnation of the conditions under which he was working in the Government that he had eventually decided were intolerable.

It was quite obvious that the course of political events was being dramatically changed with every sentence that he spoke. Each sentence was carefully constructed, with some very barbed criticism, and it was delivered with clear and calculated effect to a silent House.

I looked towards Margaret as verbal dagger after verbal dagger was going into her, and saw that she was sitting motionless and expressionless, riveted to her seat. Geoffrey's timing in his delivery, and the quiet purposefulness of his speech, were exactly right for the purpose of making the whole statement an extremely dramatic event.

When he concluded, I remarked to my neighbour that this left Michael Heseltine, who was still undecided about a challenge, with no choice but to stand for the leadership if he was to continue to be taken seriously as a leadership contender. I did not add, but I thought, that there was a distinct possibility that Mrs Thatcher would not survive the resulting crisis. She had broken her political relationship with the man who had been her most important colleague and supporter throughout all the early years of her Government.

He was voicing growing concern about the style and conduct of the Government in a way that was bound to chime with a very large number of Back Benchers.

One of her entourage was unwise enough to make a witty attack on the speech shortly afterwards, suggesting that it must have been written by Geoffrey's wife, Elspeth, whose cool relationship with Margaret Thatcher over the years was quite notorious.

I actually knew, and still know, one of the team of three people who had been consulted by Geoffrey, and had helped him with the drafting – one of whom was one of Margaret's closest leading colleagues. My friend continues to be adamant that the three of them had played little actual part in the drafting. The principal author, who had carefully put it together, was Geoffrey Howe himself.

I cannot remember any speech in the House of Commons which not only achieved a great dramatic effect on the day, but which probably changed the course of history.

Twenty electric minutes that were to write history and end the Thatcher years

Regarded by many as one of the most flamboyant politicians of his era, **Michael Heseltine** ascended to the highest levels in both politics and business.

A member of Margaret Thatcher's Cabinet from the time she came to power in 1979, he was described by her as one of the most talented people in politics. But she also said that her relations with him had never been easy, and it was their falling out that led him to resign from the Cabinet, to which he was not to return until she had been replaced.

He came close to, but never attained, his great ambition of being Tory leader and, possibly, Prime Minister, but his charismatic style won him strong support among the Conservative rank and file. His speeches to the party conference were the highlight of the week for which the conference hall was always packed to capacity.

His business career made an uncertain start, but an eye for publishing opportunities led him to help create the Haymarket organisation, now one of Britain's largest independent magazine companies with over 100 titles and employing more than 2,500 people at home and abroad.

Business took a back seat to politics in 1970 when he stepped down as chairman of Haymarket Press to concentrate on his political career. He was first elected to Parliament for Tavistock in 1966, having stood unsuccessfully at Gower in 1959 and Coventry, North in 1964. After boundary changes, he moved from Tavistock to Henley for the 1974 general election. He was to represent the seat until he left the Commons in 2001.

By 1970 he was a full-time politician with his foot on the threshold of a ministerial career. Prime Minister Ted Heath appointed him Parliamentary Secretary, Ministry of Transport, but within months he was promoted to Under-Secretary of State for the Environment. Eighteen months later he was promoted again, to Minister for Aerospace and Shipping.

With the 1974 general election defeat, Heath appointed him shadow Secretary of State for Industry. In 1976, the Labour Government narrowly and controversially won a crucial vote on the aircraft and shipbuilding nationalisation Bill. As the result was announced, the House descended into turmoil. It was to be a memorable night for Michael Heseltine. As MPs of all parties milled and jostled noisily on the Floor of the House and jubilant Labour MPs sang "The Red Flag" to celebrate their win, he picked up the Mace from the Table and thrust it towards the jeering Labour Benches. It was an action that was to earn him the epithet Tarzan, a name that was to follow him for the rest of his Commons career

For two and a half years leading up to Margaret Thatcher's 1979 election victory, he was shadow Environment Secretary. In her first Cabinet he became Secretary of State for that Department and a Privy Counsellor.

In late 1985, a crisis blew up for Westland, the helicopter manufacturer. It was to be a major source of friction with Mrs Thatcher. As Defence Secretary, he negotiated to fend off an offer from the US manufacturer Sikorsky. Matters came to a head in January 1986 when he spectacularly walked out of a Cabinet meeting and resigned as a protest over the Prime Minister's refusal to allow the Cabinet to discuss a rival bid.

Nearly five years on, Nigel Lawson having resigned over his differences with Mrs Thatcher, Sir Geoffrey Howe also went, no longer able to work with her. Michael Heseltine challenged her for the leadership and secured sufficient votes to go through to a second ballot. She calculated that she could not win and resigned. The Thatcher era was over. In the second ballot, John Major came within a whisker of an overall majority. Michael Heseltine conceded and John Major moved into No 10. He appointed Michael Heseltine to his Cabinet as Secretary of State for the Environment.

After the Conservative victory in the 1992 general election, he was appointed President of the Board of Trade, and in 1995 he became First Secretary of State and Deputy Prime Minister.

With the defeat of the 1997 Labour landslide, he returned to the world of business. He stood down as an MP at the 2001 general election. But the man who described politics as a gripping "life sentence" declared that although he was leaving the Commons, he was not leaving politics and he remained active, taking his seat in the House of Lords as Lord Heseltine of Thenford in 2001.

At his home at Thenford he has devoted time to his arboretum, developing it into one of the best collections in the country.

Massive impact of speech that marked the end of temperamentally difficult relationship

By Rt hon Lord Heseltine of Thenford CH

I heard of Geoffrey Howe's resignation as I arrived to speak at a local Conservative meeting on the south coast. I had no idea what he had in mind to say in his personal statement, which tradition dictates is made following such a resignation.

However, his speech has to have been the one that made the biggest impact on the fortunes of the country, of my party and of my life.

The House of Commons is a place of moods. Television reporting has revealed to an international audience the rapidity with which the comedy show turns to serious documentary and then to bear garden. A careless phrase, a chance word can precipitate disproportionate reaction. Survivors rely on the antennae of experience and a nimbleness of mind to lead and ride one of the most merciless – but sometimes most forgiving – forums in the world.

A resignation speech, by tradition, is heard in silence. So the House was reminded by the Speaker, Bernard Weatherill, as he called Geoffrey Howe to deliver his historic utterance on 13 November 1990. Such silence in that packed Chamber – unsure of what would follow, gripped by high drama – was electric.

Re-reading Geoffrey's words a generation later, one cannot avoid the familiarity of arguments that have been central to British foreign and domestic policy from the end of the second world war right through to today.

Anyone who has read and, even more revealing, listened to the taped interviews with the leading politicians and civil servants of the 1950s correlated by Michael Charlton for his book, "The Price of Victory", will recognise that Geoffrey's experience, in his growing disenchantment with the Prime Minister's conduct of European affairs, largely reran the arguments heard from the late 1940s on.

Although a member of the war's victorious partnership, Britain's world was changing at bewildering speed. We may have prevented the future envisaged by our former enemies, but the world we had fought to preserve had gone. The Europeans, their countries ravaged by military conflagration, had every reason to search for a new order based on the overarching determination that such conflict must never happen again. The acceptance of a sovereignty-sharing partnership was a central assumption. Indeed it offered a vision of an enhanced, more effective sovereignty in the new world order.

It was fitting that in his speech Geoffrey made reference to the decisive influence of Harold Macmillan in clearly setting out the realities of Britain's changed position in the world. He was the first of Britain's Conservative Prime Ministers to cross a line from Empire and Commonwealth to a primarily European destiny. Others gave form and structure but the vision and the courage to articulate it must be his.

As Geoffrey summed it up "He saw it as essential then, as it is today, not to cut ourselves off from the realities of power; not to retreat into a ghetto of sentimentality about our past and so diminish our own control over our own destiny in the future."

My friendship with Geoffrey stretches back a half century to our early activities in the Bow Group and the weekly meetings at my parents' house in Swansea during the 1959 election campaign. The Tory candidates for Aberavon, Swansea West, Swansea East and Gower – Geoffrey Howe, Hugh Rees, and Humphrey Crum-Ewing and I plotted the overthrow of Labour's monopoly in South Wales. Hugh Rees actually won.

No one brought up in the shadow of the Welsh steel companies and coalfields could be indifferent to the contrast between the extremes of wealth and poverty that 200 years of industrialisation around the local ports had created. Geoffrey certainly was not and his Conservatism is firmly implanted in the one nation tradition.

Yet in the stormiest Thatcher years it was Geoffrey who was the rock on which her Government's fortunes depended. The very qualities of determination and integrity that enabled him to weather the economic storms of the early 1980s would have been tested to the extreme by his abiding concerns for those who suffered as a consequence of the harshness of the policies he believed to be necessary.

But, however loyal he undoubtedly was, no one could believe that temperamentally the relationship between Margaret Thatcher and Geoffrey Howe could be easy. Geoffrey moved cautiously, courteously but relentlessly towards his objective, marshalling his arguments, poring over his facts. The impatience of the Prime Minister, her hectoring and her baser instincts make it difficult to understand how the relationship lasted so long rather than cause any surprise that it ended as it did.

I had resigned from the Cabinet four years before Geoffrey, and I know no more of the deterioration in relations between them than other observers with limited access to insider comment and to media coverage, with all the doubts that attend it.

As time passed, it was as if there were two European policies – the Government's and Mrs Thatcher's. Increasingly frustrated by the realisation that, for all the rhetoric, her Government consolidated British sovereignty within a shared Europe on a scale never achieved by any of her predecessors, the Prime Minister resorted to a running commentary set quite apart from the practical decision-taking of her Government.

Let Geoffrey speak for himself: "I realise now that the task has become futile: trying to stretch the meaning of words beyond what was credible, and trying to pretend that there was a common policy when every step forward risked being subverted by some casual comment or impulsive answer".

Geoffrey's speech ended after 20 electric minutes with the words that were to write history: "The time has come for others to consider their own response to the tragic conflict of loyalties with which I have myself wrestled for perhaps too long".

There was no room to doubt that high on that nameless group of "others" mine would have featured.

As I left the Chamber I passed Michael Jopling, who had been Chief Whip in the early years of the Government. "What on earth do I do now?" I said to him. "You do nothing" he replied. "You will be Leader of the Opposition in 18 months." But I did not want to be Leader of the Opposition.

Geoffrey's resignation precipitated the second challenge to Margaret Thatcher's leadership. In 1989 Sir Anthony Meyer, the member for Flint, East had revealed the growing discontent on the Government's Back Benches. The 33 votes that he gained should have been seen for the warning it clearly was. A year later the poll tax had eroded even more support.

In the 1990 contest, Margaret Thatcher won the first round with 204 votes to my 157. We knew the names of virtually every one of them. The stark conclusion, if the loyalty of members of the Government permits them to be put to one side, was that a majority of backbenchers voted for change. They achieved their purpose.

A resignation speech that transfixed the House and toppled a Prime Minister

John Major's entry to the House of Commons in 1979 was followed by a meteoric rise to the top when, less than 12 years after first taking his seat, he became Prime Minister after the fall of Margaret Thatcher.

The combination of the speed of his ministerial progress and the seniority of the posts he held was unparalleled in recent British political history.

After his election for Huntingdonshire in May 1979 he made steady progress. He became Parliamentary Private Secretary to Home Office Ministers within two years. He then moved into the Whips Office in 1983, was Under-Secretary of State for Social Security in 1985, and, in 1986, became the Minister of State. It marked his admission to the select group seen as possible Cabinet material.

He did not have long to wait. A year later, he was in the Thatcher Cabinet as Chief Secretary to the Treasury. As one of Mrs Thatcher's favourites he was destined for great things, but no one would have dared to predict that within three years he would replace her.

In the July 1989 reshuffle, in a humiliating demotion, Mrs Thatcher moved Sir Geoffrey Howe from Foreign Secretary to the more mundane role of Leader of the House of Commons. She made John Major, in his fourth promotion in four years, the new Secretary of State for Foreign and Commonwealth Affairs – a job he described as a "glittering prize."

However, he barely had time to unpack. Three months later, Nigel Lawson, whose relations with Thatcher had finally broken down, resigned as Chancellor and returned to the Back Benches. Margaret Thatcher sent John Major back to the Treasury from which he had so recently come, but this time as Chancellor, a job he had coveted, but not one he would have sought in the circumstances that prevailed.

A year later, Sir Geoffrey Howe finally decided that, like Nigel Lawson, he could no longer work with the Prime Minister and he, too, resigned. His speech, as Sir John observes here, transfixed the House, but it also spelt the end of the Thatcher era. Michael Heseltine challenged Margaret Thatcher for the leadership and won sufficient votes to go through to a second ballot. She realised that she might not defeat him and she resigned.

Douglas Hurd and John Major had been prepared to propose and second her, but when she withdrew they felt free to stand, challenging Michael Heseltine. In the vote, John Major fell short of the required majority by only two. Michael Heseltine and Douglas Hurd conceded, and he moved into No 10 at the age of 47.

It was to be a bumpy ride. On the economy, the consequences of the 1980s boom were hitting hard. Inflation was nearing 10 per cent., interest rates were well into double figures, unemployment was rising, house prices were on the slide, and recession loomed. On the domestic front, the conflict in Northern Ireland showed no signs of abating, and abroad, Iraq refused to relinquish its brutal occupation of Kuwait and the first Gulf war was only weeks away. The corrosive influence of Europe continued to eat away at party unity, and he had only 18 months before he had to call a general election.

In the following year, victory was secured in the Gulf, he abolished the poll tax and replaced it with the council tax, and the IRA mortar bombed No 10. A disillusioned Margaret Thatcher — who had said when he became Prime Minister that she would be "a back-seat driver" who would keep him on course — felt that he was betraying her legacy. He was showing that he was his own man who would choose which of her policies to keep and which he would ditch. Ditching the poll tax was among those that caused her greatest offence.

One of the most enduring issues facing John Major, however, was Europe in general and the Maastricht treaty in particular. He had successfully negotiated Britain's position on the treaty in late 1991, and it was signed in February 1992. But the trouble that lay ahead as the enabling legislation passed through the House was to place severe strains upon his leadership.

The general election was held in April that year, and a Major victory was far from certain. In the event, he held on, but with a reduced majority of 21. The ensuing five years were to see Britain dramatically withdraw from the European exchange rate mechanism on so-called Black Wednesday, economic recovery, continuing and persistent rebellion by Eurosceptic Conservative Back Benchers, and him resigning in a direct challenge to the rebels. They were routed in the resulting leadership election, which saw him returned with overwhelming support.

In Northern Ireland, he was to be frustrated and disappointed at the failure to secure peace, but his painstaking work, in spite of the setbacks, laid the foundations for his successor, Tony Blair, to negotiate the Good Friday agreement and all that eventually flowed from it.

After defeat in 1997, he resigned as party leader. In 1999 he was awarded the Companion of Honour, and in 2005 the Queen bestowed upon him a knighthood of the Order of the Garter.

Every deadly word heard in tomb-like silence

By Rt hon Sir John Major KG CH

On 13 November, 1990, in the Chamber of the House of Commons, I sat beside Margaret Thatcher, then Prime Minister, as Geoffrey Howe delivered his resignation statement. No one in that packed Chamber could possibly have imagined that Geoffrey, ever the gentleman, ever the man to understate than over-egg, was about to make a speech that would transfix the House, topple a Prime Minister and change the course of politics.

There were no histrionics. No ringing declarations. No great historical allusions. It was delivered calmly to a House which – although tradition requires that such statements are heard without interruption – was positively tomb-like in its silence. Every word was weighed, targeted, precise – and deadly.

The fact of Geoffrey's resignation was in itself high drama. When Margaret Thatcher had come to power, 11 years earlier, Geoffrey Howe became her long-term Chancellor and then Foreign Secretary. The ideology that became known as "Thatcherism" owed as much to Geoffrey's own courage and intellect, as it did to Keith Joseph and Nigel Lawson, for it was they who had devised the political philosophy that Margaret advocated to such great effect. But, by 1990, Keith Joseph had left the Commons and Nigel Lawson – having had his authority as Chancellor of the Exchequer repeatedly undermined by one of Margaret's economic advisers – had resigned from the Government.

Margaret had sacked Geoffrey as Foreign Secretary following their disagreements over European policy. She had offered him the less influential post of Leader of the House with the *title* of Deputy Prime Minister, but with no power attached to the Office. Geoffrey smouldered, but soldiered on – even when targeted and undermined by some of Margaret's over-enthusiastic allies. Members of Cabinet were dismayed and often shocked by the cavalier way in which Margaret treated one of her oldest allies. A clash seemed pre-ordained.

It came – inevitably – over Europe, when Margaret once again cut herself adrift from her European partners and, in so doing, undermined the carefully constructed policy consensus that held together her own Government. It was too much, even for the stoical Geoffrey, and the House – packed full with anticipation and pin-drop silent – waited to hear how he would explain his disillusion.

Geoffrey's low-key delivery was expected. So, too, was his innate courtesy, and his pride – both personal and political – at what he and Margaret had achieved together. But then, with words sharper than a disembowelling knife, he turned to a cumulative number of policy differences that many had suspected, but only few had witnessed at close quarters.

At the beginning of the statement, Geoffrey dismissed those detractors who had claimed his resignation was a matter of style as opposed to substance, with the remark that, if this were so, he "must be the first Minister in history who has resigned because he was in full agreement with Government policy". From that moment, the House was rapt.

He set out profound disagreements on economic policy noting that if we had joined the ERM some years before "higher rates of inflation would have been avoided" (it was nearly 10 per cent at the time). So, as the House well knew, would have been Nigel Lawson's resignation.

He then turned to a second substantive policy disagreement. On Europe, Geoffrey and Margaret disagreed on style *and* substance. Margaret, he claimed, "sometimes seems to look out upon a Continent positively teeming with ill-intentioned people, scheming, in her words, to extinguish democracy".

He went on. Her attitude damaged business. She isolated Britain. She undermined her own Government's policy and "people throughout Europe see our Prime Minister's finger wagging and hear her passionate 'No, No, No' .... It is too easy [for Europe] to believe we all share her attitudes; for why else has she been our Prime Minister for so long?"

Each of these assertions was a hammer-blow and, sitting beside Margaret, it was clear she felt their weight. She was hurt and angry: she had not anticipated that Geoffrey would deliver such a devastating critique. Nor had she believed that someone who – for two decades – had been one of her most loyal lieutenants, could conclude his statement with what colleagues widely perceived as a call to arms: "The time has come", he stated, "for others to consider their own response to the tragic conflict of loyalties with which I have myself wrestled for perhaps too long."

On return to her room, Margaret sought reassurance – from me and from others – that the attack was not personal but political. Although I could not deny the personal damage it had done, I did manage to reassure her that Geoffrey's motives were driven by the latter. This, I believe, drew some of the sting from it.

But the fall-out was much wider and far-reaching. The following day, Michael Heseltine challenged Margaret for the leadership. It began a chain of events which ended, 15 days later, with her resignation and – following a leadership contest with Michael Heseltine and Douglas Hurd – my appointment, as Prime Minister. The Conservatives won the ensuing general election, but the divisions, exacerbated by her violent political death, festered and grew, dividing the party for a generation.

The lead-up to the speech, the speech itself and the long, painful aftermath had all the ingredients of political tragedy. It was, without question, the most influential parliamentary speech of the last few decades.

Personal Statement

Mr. Speaker: I remind the House that a resignation statement is heard in silence and without interruption.

4.19 pm

Sir Geoffrey Howe (Surrey, East): I find to my astonishment that a quarter of a century has passed since I last spoke from one of the Back Benches. Fortunately, however, it has been my privilege to serve for the past 12 months of that time as Leader of the House of Commons, so I have been reminded quite recently of the traditional generosity and tolerance of this place. I hope that I may count on that today as I offer to the House a statement about my resignation from the Government.

It has been suggested—even, indeed, by some of my right hon. and hon. Friends—that I decided to resign solely because of questions of style and not on matters of substance at all. Indeed, if some of my former colleagues are to be believed, I must be the first Minister in history who has resigned because he was in full agreement with Government policy. The truth is that, in many aspects of politics, style and substance complement each other. Very often, they are two sides of the same coin.

The Prime Minister and I have shared something like 700 meetings of Cabinet or shadow Cabinet during the past 18 years, and some 400 hours alongside each other, at more than 30 international summit meetings. For both of us, I suspect, it is a pretty daunting record. The House might well feel that something more than simple matters of style would be necessary to rupture such a well-tried relationship.

It was a privilege to serve as my right hon. Friend's first Chancellor of the Exchequer; to share in the transformation of our industrial relations scene; to help launch our free market programme, commencing with the abolition of exchange control; and, above all, to achieve such substantial success against inflation, getting it down within four years from 22 per cent. to 4 per cent. upon the basis of the strict monetary discipline involved in the medium-term financial strategy. Not one of our economic achievements would have been possible without the courage and leadership of my right hon. Friend—and, if I may say so, they possibly derived some little benefit from the presence of a Chancellor who was not exactly a wet himself.

It was a great honour to serve for six years as Foreign and Commonwealth Secretary and to share with my right hon. Friend in some notable achievements in the European Community—from Fontainebleau to the Single European Act. But it was as we moved on to consider the crucial monetary issues in the European context that I came to feel increasing concern. Some of the reasons for that anxiety were made very clear by my right hon. Friend the Member for Blaby (Mr. Lawson) in his resignation speech just over 12 months ago. Like him, I concluded at least five years ago that the conduct of our policy against inflation could no longer rest solely on attempts to measure and control the domestic money supply. We had no doubt that we should be helped in that battle, and, indeed, in other respects, by joining the exchange rate mechanism of the European monetary system.

There was, or should have been, nothing novel about joining the ERM; it has been a long-standing commitment. For a quarter of a century after the second world war, we found that the very similar Bretton Woods regime did serve as a useful discipline. Now, as my right hon. Friend the Prime Minister acknowledged two weeks ago, our entry into the ERM can be seen as an

"extra discipline for keeping down inflation."—[*Official Report*, 30 October 1990; Vol. 178, c. 888.]

However, it must be said that that practical conclusion has been achieved only at the cost of substantial damage to her Administration and, more serious still, to its inflation achievements.

As my right hon. Friend the Member for Blaby explained:

"The real tragedy is that we did not join the exchange rate mechanism . . . at least five years ago."

As he also made clear,

"That was not for want of trying."—[*Official Report*, 23 October 1990; Vol. 178, c. 216.]

Indeed, the so-called Madrid conditions came into existence only after the then Chancellor and I, as Foreign Secretary, made it clear that we could not continue in office unless a specific commitment to join the ERM was made.

As the House will no doubt have observed, neither member of that particular partnership now remains in office. Our successor as Chancellor of the Exchequer has, during the past year, had to devote a great deal of his considerable talents to demonstrating exactly how those Madrid conditions have been attained, so as to make it possible to fulfil a commitment whose achievement has long been in the national interest.

It is now, alas, impossible to resist the conclusion that today's higher rates of inflation could well have been avoided had the question of ERM membership been properly considered and resolved at a much earlier stage. There are, I fear, developing grounds for similar anxiety over the handling—not just at and after the Rome summit—of the wider, much more open question of economic and monetary union.

Let me first make clear certain important points on which I have no disagreement with my right hon. Friend, the Prime Minister. I do not regard the Delors report as some kind of sacred text that has to be accepted, or even rejected, on the nod. But it is an important working document. As I have often made plain, it is seriously deficient in significant respects.

I do not regard the Italian presidency's management of the Rome summit as a model of its kind—far from it. It was much the same, as my right hon. Friend the Prime Minister will recall, in Milan some five years ago.

I do not regard it as in any sense wrong for Britain to make criticisms of that kind plainly and courteously, nor in any sense wrong for us to do so, if necessary, alone. As I have already made clear, I have, like the Prime Minister and other right hon. Friends, fought too many European battles in a minority of one to have any illusions on that score.

But it is crucially important that we should conduct those arguments upon the basis of a clear understanding of the true relationship between this country, the Community and our Community partners. And it is here, I fear, that my right hon. Friend the Prime Minister increasingly risks leading herself and others astray in matters of substance as well as of style.

It was the late Lord Stockton, formerly Harold Macmillan, who first put the central point clearly. As long ago as 1962, he argued that we had to place and keep ourselves within the EC. He saw it as essential then, as it is today, not to cut ourselves off from the realities of power; not to retreat into a ghetto of sentimentality about our past and so diminish our own control over our own destiny in the future.

The pity is that the Macmillan view had not been perceived more clearly a decade before in the 1950s. It would have spared us so many of the struggles of the last 20 years had we been in the Community from the outset; had we been ready, in the much too simple phrase, to "surrender some sovereignty" at a much earlier stage.

If we had been in from the start, as almost everybody now acknowledges, we should have had more, not less, influence over the Europe in which we live today. We should never forget the lesson of that isolation, of being on the outside looking in, for the conduct of today's affairs.

We have done best when we have seen the Community not as a static entity to be resisted and contained, but as an active process which we can shape, often decisively, provided that we allow ourselves to be fully engaged in it, with confidence, with enthusiasm and in good faith.

We must at all costs avoid presenting ourselves yet again with an over-simplified choice, a false antithesis, a bogus dilemma, between one alternative, starkly labelled "co-operation between independent sovereign states" and a second, equally crudely labelled alternative, "centralised, federal super-state", as if there were no middle way in between.

We commit a serious error if we think always in terms of "surrendering" sovereignty and seek to stand pat for all time on a given deal—by proclaiming, as my right hon. Friend the Prime Minister did two weeks ago, that we have "surrendered enough".

The European enterprise is not and should not be seen like that—as some kind of zero sum game. Sir Winston Churchill put it much more positively 40 years ago, when he said:

"It is also possible and not less agreeable to regard"
this sacrifice or merger of national sovereignty
"as the gradual assumption by all the nations concerned of that larger sovereignty which can alone protect their diverse and distinctive customs and characteristics and their national traditions."

I have to say that I find Winston Churchill's perception a good deal more convincing, and more encouraging for the interests of our nation, than the nightmare image sometimes conjured up by my right hon. Friend, who seems sometimes to look out upon a continent that is positively teeming with ill-intentioned people, scheming, in her words, to "extinguish democracy", to
"dissolve our national identities"
and to lead us
"through the back-door into a federal Europe".
What kind of vision is that for our business people, who trade there each day, for our financiers, who seek to make London the money capital of Europe or for all the young people of today?

These concerns are especially important as we approach the crucial topic of economic and monetary union. We must be positively and centrally involved in this debate and not fearfully and negatively detached. The costs of disengagement here could be very serious indeed.

There is talk, of course, of a single currency for Europe. I agree that there are many difficulties about the concept —both economic and political. Of course, as I said in my letter of resignation, none of us wants the imposition of a single currency. But that is not the real risk. The 11 others cannot impose their solution on the 12th country against its will, but they can go ahead without us. The risk is not imposition but isolation. The real threat is that of leaving ourselves with no say in the monetary arrangements that the rest of Europe chooses for itself, with Britain once again scrambling to join the club later, after the rules have been set and after the power has been distributed by others to our disadvantage. That would be the worst possible outcome.

It is to avoid just that outcome and to find a compromise both acceptable in the Government and sellable in Europe that my right hon. Friend the Chancellor has put forward his hard ecu proposal. This lays careful emphasis on the possibility that the hard ecu as a common currency could, given time, evolve into a single currency. I have of course supported the hard ecu plan. But after Rome, and after the comments of my right hon. Friend the Prime Minister two weeks ago, there is grave danger that the hard ecu proposal is becoming untenable, because two things have happened.

The first is that my right hon. Friend the Prime Minister has appeared to rule out from the start any compromise at any stage on any of the basic components that all the 11 other countries believe to be a part of EMU—a single currency or a permanently fixed exchange rate, a central bank or common monetary policy. Asked whether we would veto any arrangement that jeopardised the pound sterling, my right hon. Friend replied simply, "Yes." That statement means not that we can block EMU but that they can go ahead without us. Is that a position that is likely to ensure, as I put it in my resignation letter, that
"we hold, and retain, a position of influence in this vital debate"?
I fear not. Rather, to do so, we must, as I said, take care not to rule in or rule out any one solution absolutely. We must be seen to be part of the same negotiation.

The second thing that happened was, I fear, even more disturbing. Reporting to this House, my right hon. Friend almost casually remarked that she did not think that many people would want to use the hard ecu anyway—even as a common currency, let alone as a single one. It was remarkable—indeed, it was tragic—to hear my right hon. Friend dismissing, with such personalised incredulity, the very idea that the hard ecu proposal might find growing favour among the peoples of Europe, just as it was extraordinary to hear her assert that the whole idea of EMU might be open for consideration only by future generations. Those future generations are with us today.

How on earth are the Chancellor and the Governor of the Bank of England, commending the hard ecu as they strive to, to be taken as serious participants in the debate against that kind of background noise? I believe that both the Chancellor and the Governor are cricketing enthusiasts, so I hope that there is no monopoly of cricketing metaphors. It is rather like sending your opening batsmen to the crease only for them to find, the moment the first balls are bowled, that their bats have been broken before the game by the team captain.

The point was perhaps more sharply put by a British business man, trading in Brussels and elsewhere, who wrote to me last week, stating:
"People throughout Europe see our Prime Minister's finger-wagging and hear her passionate, 'No, No, No', much more clearly than the content of the carefully worded formal texts."
He went on:
"It is too easy for them to believe that we all share her attitudes; for why else has she been our Prime Minister for so long?"

[*Sir Geoffrey Howe*]

My correspondent concluded:

"This is a desperately serious situation for our country." And sadly, I have to agree.

The tragedy is—and it is for me personally, for my party, for our whole people and for my right hon. Friend herself, a very real tragedy—that the Prime Minister's perceived attitude towards Europe is running increasingly serious risks for the future of our nation. It risks minimising our influence and maximising our chances of being once again shut out. We have paid heavily in the past for late starts and squandered opportunities in Europe. We dare not let that happen again. If we detach ourselves completely, as a party or a nation, from the middle ground of Europe, the effects will be incalculable and very hard ever to correct.

In my letter of resignation, which I tendered with the utmost sadness and dismay, I said:

"Cabinet Government is all about trying to persuade one another from within".

That was my commitment to Government by persuasion —persuading colleagues and the nation. I have tried to do that as Foreign Secretary and since, but I realise now that the task has become futile: trying to stretch the meaning of words beyond what was credible, and trying to pretend that there was a common policy when every step forward risked being subverted by some casual comment or impulsive answer.

The conflict of loyalty, of loyalty to my right hon. Friend the Prime Minister—and, after all, in two decades together that instinct of loyalty is still very real—and of loyalty to what I perceive to be the true interests of the nation, has become all too great. I no longer believe it possible to resolve that conflict from within this Government. That is why I have resigned. In doing so, I have done what I believe to be right for my party and my country. The time has come for others to consider their own response to the tragic conflict of loyalties with which I have myself wrestled for perhaps too long.

Orders of the Day

Debate on the Address

[Fifth Day]

Order read for resuming adjourned debate on Question [7 November].

That an humble Address be presented to Her Majesty, as follows:

Most Gracious Sovereign, We, Your Majesty's most dutiful and loyal subjects, the Commons of the United Kingdom of Great Britain and Northern Ireland, in Parliament assembled, beg leave to offer our humble thanks to Your Majesty for the Gracious Speech which Your Majesty has addressed to both Houses of Parliament.—[*Mr. Younger.*].

Question again proposed.

Education and Training

Mr. Speaker: I must announce that I have selected the first amendment in the name of the Leader of the Opposition and that furthermore today, because of the large number of right hon. and hon. Members who wish to participate in the debate, I propose to put a 10-minute limit on speeches between 7 pm and 9 pm. I should have liked to put the limit on somewhat earlier, but we have two maiden speeches today and that would have been unnecessarily harsh and perhaps unfair to those hon. Members. Therefore, I ask hon. Members who are called before 7 pm to bear it in mind that I should be most grateful and the whole House would applaud them if they could keep their speeches to approximately 10 minutes in length.

4.38 pm

Mr. Jack Straw (Blackburn): I beg to move, at the end of the Question, to add:

But humbly note the increasing anxiety of parents and employers that the education and training policies of Her Majesty's Government have seriously undermined choice and opportunity and placed standards at risk; express anxiety and concern that Britain's investment and achievement in education and training is leaving the country further behind its major European and other competitors; condemn Her Majesty's Government for its incompetence towards, and mismanagement of, the education service and its profound failure to fulfil its proper and necessary role in improving and upgrading the skills base of the nation; and believe that standards will only be raised and opportunities increased by a change of administration to a government committed to serious investment in the nation's future.

It is customary to congratulate a new Secretary of State on his appointment to office, and that I do. The presence of a new Secretary of State at the Dispatch Box results from the deep political crisis that faces this broken-backed Administration. It is not only a crisis about the future role of Britain in Europe but a crisis of confidence in the Government's ability—indeed, their inability—to provide the standards of education and training enjoyed by our major competitors in Europe and beyond. Never has public anxiety about the state of Britain's education system been greater. Never has public confidence in the Government's ability to deliver a decent standard of education been lower.

In last week's Gallup poll in *The Daily Telegraph*, 82 per cent. of respondents said that Britain was not giving

Jeremy Thorpe shows remarkable foresight in cool and reasoned speech on EEC application

Nick Clegg became leader of the Liberal Democrat party in 2007 with the resignation of Sir Menzies Campbell. He was elected to the House of Commons in 2005 when he won the seat of Sheffield, Hallam, having previously worked for the European Union and then having been elected to the European Parliament.

He began his working life as a journalist. After graduating from Cambridge, where he studied archaeology and anthropology, he won a scholarship to the University of Minnesota. On leaving, he took a job as a trainee journalist at *The Nation,* a left-wing magazine in New York. He won the *Financial Times* David Thomas prize for first-time writers in 1993 and was sent to Hungary to write about the privatisation of former state enterprises.

The next move was to Brussels where he worked for the European Union, initially in a training capacity but subsequently as an expert on development aid and trade for the European Commission.

In 1996, Leon Brittan, vice-president of the Commission and the EU trade commissioner, offered him a job in his private office as a policy adviser and speech writer. In his new capacity, he was in charge of the EU team that was negotiating with China and Russia on their accession to the World Trade Organisation.

He resisted the suggestion from Leon Brittan that he should join the Conservative party, and, while still working for the vice-president, he was adopted in 1998 as the lead Liberal Democrat candidate for the East Midlands seat in the European Parliament. At the Euro elections the following year, he won the seat. Once in the Parliament, he was appointed the trade spokesman for the Liberal Democrat and Reform group of MEPs, leading on a programme of deregulation and competition in European telecommunications. Among the campaigns he mounted were opposition to illegal logging and greater transparency and accountability in the payment of expenses to MEPs.

He stood down from the European Parliament in 2004 and took up part time lecturing in politics at Sheffield and Cambridge universities. He also devoted his energies to campaigning for the Liberal Democrats in the East Midlands. When Liberal Democrat MP Richard Allen announced that he would not be contesting the Sheffield, Hallam seat at the 2005 general election, Nick Clegg secured the candidacy.

He won the seat convincingly, taking more than 50 per cent. of the vote. The party he joined in the Commons was led by Charles Kennedy, who made him the spokesman on Europe and deputy to Sir Menzies Campbell on Foreign Affairs. When Charles Kennedy stood down in 2006 as a result of his personal problems, Nick Clegg declared his support for Sir Menzies, who went on to win the ensuing leadership contest.

The new leader promoted him to be shadow Home Secretary. He used his new position to mount a defence of civil liberties, to campaign for prison reform and to urge a more liberal approach to immigration.

When Sir Menzies stood down after a year and a half in the post, Nick Clegg put his name forward, standing in a two-way contest against Chris Huhne. He won, but it was a narrow victory. He was declared the new leader with a majority of marginally more than 1 per cent.

His declared aim for the party was that it should become the party of the family, concentrating on social justice, education and opportunity. He also proposed tax cuts for low and middle income families and pledged to double the Liberal Democrat representation at Westminster within two Parliaments.

Appeal to abandon half-hearted commitment and become enthusiastic Europeans

By Rt hon Nick Clegg MP

Jeremy Thorpe is usually remembered in British politics for the controversies of his personal life. But forgetting his extraordinary contribution to political thought and debate is a huge mistake. At a time when being a Liberal was unfashionable almost to the point of extinction, he chose the Liberal party despite a family tradition of Conservatism, and led it with great dynamism and foresight.

Jeremy Thorpe was both in line with liberal traditions of internationalism and ahead of his time when he gave this powerfully-argued response to the United Kingdom's second application for EEC membership. The speech covered the broad range of British foreign policy; it also showed that he understood how important it was that we committed ourselves to the European project and that our partners believed us – that we became "enthusiastic Europeans", as he put it.

What is remarkable, too, is the foresight of Thorpe's remarks. He predicted that Europe would one day create a reserve currency, that the European Parliament would be directly elected, that Europe would need to play a growing role in foreign affairs, and that excessive subservience to the United States would give the UK the "political status of Porto Rica".

Thorpe's humour emerges mischievously too, notably when he appears to invent a quote by Reginald Maudling arguing against entry into the EEC because it would "sell the Commonwealth down the river and bankrupt the housewife". Maudling, duly goaded, challenges Thorpe to justify the quotation but gets little satisfaction.

The debate took place, of course, in the shadow of General de Gaulle's dramatic and imperious rejection of Britain's first bid to join the EEC in 1963. Whilst Thorpe made it clear he didn't like De Gaulle's decision, he was unflinching in accusing successive British Governments of being too half hearted in their commitment to Europe to overcome French doubts. In Thorpe's view, we had not persuaded the French Government that we could join the EEC without undermining it; and we paid the price – in exclusion.

Some great parliamentary speeches stir the emotions of those who listen; others arouse anger against injustice; and still others set out the difficult questions facing Parliament and the country in a cool, reasoned fashion. This speech is of the third sort, and its arguments are still relevant.

For Thorpe, the political lesson of the 1950s and 1960s was simple: "For too long we had men in control (Thatcher came later) who had no vision of what was happening on the other side of the Channel". Given the internal splits and shrill anti European hostility of the Thatcher and Major administrations, and the muted commitment to Europe from the Blair and Brown Governments, his allegation is just as strong today as it was 40 years ago. As I know only too well, Europe retains an unusual power to divide opinion between and within political parties at Westminster.

There is a clarity and a simplicity to this speech which may seem out of date, almost quaint, when compared to the convoluted recent debates about Europe in the House of Commons. In truth, Thorpe identified a simple truth which has not wavered in 40 years: no British Government can deliver safety and prosperity to the British people in a borderless age without a wholehearted commitment to our place in Europe. Pro-Europeans could do a great deal worse than keeping Jeremy Thorpe's words in mind.

[MR. CALLAGHAN.]
in developing its institutions and influence. We cannot take a static view of developments in the Community or in the world.

Much of the argument about the consequences of joining is conducted on the basis of the world's affairs standing still. It is not given to any of us to look too far into the future, but I would hazard my own guess that, 10 years from now, if Britain becomes a member of the Community, it will be healthier for Britain, advantageous for Europe and a gain for the whole world. I do not know of many economic or political problems in the world which will be easier to solve if Britain is outside rather than inside the Community.

From outside—[*Interruption.*]—yes, I do not think that it makes it any easier to solve the problems because we are outside. From outside, we should need to maintain and develop this network of separate relationships. If we are compelled to do that—this is a problem for Europe as well as for Britain—we shall certainly survive and, indeed, we may prosper, but it would be at the expense of fragmenting the world instead of uniting it and we should have to build up barriers instead of tearing them down.

I understand and share the strong desire to develop the Community so that the voice of Europe speaking together is heard throughout the world. There are other paths for our future if this venture should fail, but I do not believe that the other alternatives offer, either to us or to Europe, advantages comparable to those presented by a negotiated membership of the Community.

5.24 p.m.

Mr. Jeremy Thorpe (Devon, North): This debate is a cause for celebration by Liberals ; I congratulate the Government on their decision to apply for membership of the European Economic Community and I wish them success in that application. I believe that today, whatever may be the past, both the Prime Minister and the Foreign Secretary are now accepted on the Continent as committed and enthusiastic Europeans. I hope to touch on one or two matters which I think may be relevant to the successful outcome of the negotiations, and I will refer only briefly to the past —first, as it is relevant to the future, and, second, as it is necessary to avoid certain pitfalls.

I must confess that the history of the post-war Europe as understood by the Leader of the Opposition had some astonishing gaps. I found only slightly more astonishing his new nuclear deterrent policy on which there appeared to be some difference as to what he was saying. No one really seemed to know what he was saying—least of all, perhaps, the right hon. Gentleman himself.

If the right hon. Member for Kinross and West Perthshire (Sir Alec Douglas-Home) and the Leader of the Opposition thought that we were in difficulties today because we were late entrants, how right they were. But if that is the only reason in their view, they have failed to take into account the reason that General de Gaulle, on 14th January, 1963, decided to exercise his veto because he said that this country was not ready for membership. Whether he was right or wrong— and I believe that he was wrong—it is vital to assess why he came to that view, so that we should not fall into that position again.

The reason that we were held in that position was that the hypercritical in Europe thought that we were bad Europeans, and even our closest colleagues in Europe thought that we were almost insensitive to trends on the Continent. It is perfectly true that the Atlee Government cold-shouldered the Iron and Steel Community whilst the European Defence Community, which was the one way of including a German Army within a European force, was thrown out by the French Assembly, only after the Eden Government refused to have any British participation in that force.

Indeed, perhaps the monumental understatement of this debate was when the Leader of the Opposition talked of the Messina talks in 1955, and said that we had some small part in them. Indeed we did. We walked out after a couple of days and boycotted them. One can only suppose, from the attitude of the Government of the day, that they suspected the Messina Powers to have some connection with the brothers of the same name.

I well remember the lack of enthusiasm in the 1959 election, when candidates like myself advocated that we should join the Common Market. But when one looks at the election addresses, not only of the Prime Minister and the Foreign Secretary but of the Leader of the Opposition himself, one finds not a single reference to the Continent of Europe and still less to the Common Market in their individual election addresses.

It is, of course, true that the right hon. Member for Barnet (Mr. Maudling) was more aware of the situation. That was why he made his speech in October, 1959:

> "We never dreamed of entering the Common Market. If we joined, we would have to abolish all tariff protection for agriculture and horticulture and give up control of our own agricultural policy."

We would sell the Commonwealth down the river and bankrupt the housewife, and this was why the Tory Government could never support what the Liberal Party was advocating——

Mr. Maudling: Is that an exact quotation, may I ask?

Mr. Thorpe: In regard to the first section—

> "We never dreamed of entering the Common Market. If we joined, we would have to abolish all tariff protection for agriculture and horticulture"—

I am delighted to give the right hon. Gentleman this added opportunity of refreshing his memory—

> "and give up control of our own agricultural policy"   .

that was verbatim. The reference to the housewife and to the British Commonwealth, he will find not only in this speech, which he made outside the House, but in the first speech which was made in the House of Commons——

Mr. Maudling *rose*——

Mr. Thorpe: I will answer the right hon. Gentleman. To be fair to him— the words relating to agriculture are verbatim and I am sure that he would agree with that—the reference to the housewife and selling the British Commonwealth down the river——

Lord Balniel (Hertford): No.

Mr. Thorpe: If the noble Lord would just exercise *noblesse oblige* for a moment, I should be grateful. I believe that I have given a wholly correct paraphrase of what the right hon. Gentleman said. If, in my references to his remarks about the Commonwealth and his comments about it adversely affecting the housewife, I have in any way misrepresented his argument, I will willingly amend my remarks.

Mr. Maudling: I gather that the right hon. Gentleman was using a mixture of a quotation, which I accept, and a paraphrase, which I do not accept. Is he aware that that is not the normal way of conducting a debate in this House?

Mr. Thorpe: As I said, if I have misquoted the right hon. Gentleman I will be happy to withdraw the section of my remarks which, he claims, misrepresent his views. I am sure that he will agree that he took the view then that adverse effects would flow not only for the Commonwealth but for the British housewife. He does not intervene, so I take it that that was his view.

I also remember two occasions in this House—14th December, 1959, and 25th July, 1960—when we Liberals divided the House on the need to join the Common Market. On the first occasion the then Conservative Government voted us down, while the Opposition abstained. On the second occasion the then Conservative Government had the added assistance in the Lobby of the present Prime Minister, Secretary of State for Defence, President of the Board of Trade and the Secretary of State for Commonwealth Affairs. Perhaps that added Labour support was fortunate, because the present Leader of the Opposition was not able to be present.

Being late entrants, let us realise that one of the reasons for our late entry is that we have given the impression, not only by words but by actions, that we were not anxious to become part of the Community. I believe that the Prime Minister's success lies in the fact that he and the Foreign Secretary have convinced our European colleagues that we are anxious to join and are enthusiastic Europeans. The Prime Minister said:

> ". . . if we do not succeed, the House will . . be able to judge at the end of the day that it was not our fault."—[OFFICIAL REPORT, 2nd May, 1967; Vol. 746, c. 316.]

I believe that if we are not successful it will be largely the fault that for too long we had men in control who had no vision of what was happening across the Channel

[MR. THORPE.]

and whose horizon was bordered either by the Channel Isles or by the Isles of Scilly. Thus, as late entrants, we have in my view no more than a fifty-fifty chance of success.

Because of the undertakings that will be needed for the transitional period—concerning our commitments to agriculture and the Commonwealth ; and not being a founder member it is difficult for us to negotiate these matters—it will probably take three or four years, even if we are successful, before our application has been signed and we are a member of the Community.

Having said that, the first point I wish to make about the application is that if it is to be a long haul of three or four years, we must guard against public opinion in Britain going sour and becoming impatient. If that were to happen, people would search after alternatives, one of which is the Atlantic Community —and, in my view, the North American Community as an alternative would give us the economic benefits but would also give us the political status of Porto Rica. We therefore need patience.

In the Government today are four senior Ministers who have, up to the very last moment, been passionately opposed to the idea of our joining the E.E.C. What will be their position if there is a long haul of three or four years? It is an interesting acrobatic sight to see senior Ministers standing on their heads. I have great respect for the Secretary of State for Commonwealth Affairs, but I have seldom seen a Minister putting forward an argument with less enthusiasm such as that which the right hon. Gentleman was asked to put forward last night. One can at least say of the Minister of Agriculture, who has not yet spoken in favour of the Common Market, that his previous speeches have been totally consistent throughout.

The Prime Minister would be in a much stronger position if those who are hostile to the Common Market gave practical expression to their hostility now and were not seen lurking like Trojan horses so that, in three or four years' time, their patience was found to have become exhausted.

The Chancellor of the Exchequer speaks with great knowledge about ster-ling. However, the view of the Leader of the Opposition about the need for a European reserve currency is a matter to which greater attention should be given. The fear in Europe is not the present weakness of sterling but its potential vulnerability, which is a very different thing. When the Prime Minister said, on his return from Luxemburg, that we had given assurances under Article 108 that we would not co-ordinate the assistance of Europe if sterling came under pressure —not external but only internal pressure —I sought to make him realise that we had to distinguish between external and internal pressure on a reserve currency.

We are now in the position in which nearly one-third of the world's trade is financed by sterling. Some of us believe that this places an intolerable burden on the economy of this country. Indeed, many of the countries for which we act as banker are not even members of the Commonwealth and have no ties of kinship with Britain. The possibility of a new European reserve currency will, I believe, arise when we are a member of the E.E.C. Instead of the Prime Minister saying, as he did in reply to a Question from me, that this cannot or would not be ruled out after we were in, he should agree that it is a matter that should be ruled in now for discussion so that we really are intent on there being a real Common Market.

After all, we cannot have a Common Market in the fullest sense if one member is acting as banker with an external currency while the others are acting in a different capacity. The speech of Giscard D'Estaing on 4th May to the Federal Trust in London made this point clear when he said that, whether or not we liked it, sterling would be one of the great question marks and worries in Europe during the negotiations. Whatever may be the position of sterling today, a European reserve currency would be very much stronger in future than sterling could be on its own.

Sir Richard Glyn (Dorset, North): Is the right hon. Gentleman arguing that sterling should cease to be a reserve currency?

Mr. Thorpe: No. I am suggesting that sterling should continue to be a European reserve currency but that when we are in the Community we should be able to expand and fuse sterling into a European reserve currency ; to interleave it so that in perhaps 10 or 15 years' time we might be able to transform sterling into a new European reserve currency. That would place less of a burden on this country and would make it a strong world currency.

Indeed, the position of sterling is such that, in terms of politics, it has created a weakness. Some people are so cynical and uncharitable—and I am one of them —as to believe that most of our attitude towards Vietnam has been dictated by our attitude towards sterling. I consider this to be true. A new reserve currency is, therefore, a matter which we should be prepared to discuss.

Politically, the Prime Minister has always maintained that one of the main reasons why the Common Market negotiations broke down in 1963 was because of the Nassau Agreement which followed the talks at Rambouillet ; that it was an effort to keep up a special relationship with America. If that view was right in 1963, it is equally right to say that the continuation of our Polaris programme and the possibility that we shall buy another generation of nuclear missiles in the form of Poseidon is an indication of our intention to keep up some form of special relationship. I should have thought that, again, some criticism could be levelled against us by our prospective European colleagues.

With regard to the idea of the Leader of the Opposition of a new European deterrent, I believe that Britain should give up the pretence of being an independent nuclear Power. I believe that with as much conviction as did the Prime Minister before the 1964 election, although I am less likely to change my views than he is. First of all, we have to renegotiate N.A.T.O., because N.A.T.O. has been shaken to the foundations by the attitude of the French. But we may well see a European defence community evolving from the Common Market. It should be non-nuclear. We must realise that the two nuclear Powers are, should be, and, indeed, will remain, Russia and the United States of America.

I believe that if we get in we shall, having been the most frightened of political involvement, become one of the most political members of the Community ; and that we shall probably insist in the

European political assembly that there should be far closer control over the Commission. In 10 or 15 years' time we may be pressing for the direct election of members to the European Parliament.

The Prime Minister mentioned that the Commission has proposed that by 1969 the added value tax as operated in France shall be at the same level throughout the whole of Europe, but I should like us to introduce this tax here before we get in. I had hoped that this would have been done in this Budget, but it may well be in the autumn Budget— nowadays we always have at least two every year, so we may not have as long to wait. If we are going in, we must prepare our physical fiscal system to match that in Europe, but I believe that, even if we are not successful, this fiscal change would release the technical energies of our people.

Technologically, whether we go in or not, the more co-operation we have with Europe the better. I am sure that the House would take comfort to learn of the comparative success of the recent discussions which the Secretary of State for Defence had in France. One of the possible reasons for the change in attitude of President de Gaulle was, I believe, his surprise when he woke up to find that an American company, G.E.C., had a commanding position in the French computer industry by the purchase of a very substantial shareholding in the computer machinery firm of Machine Bull. Technologically, and from the tax point of view, there is much we could do now to prepare the country for entry into Europe.

I do not believe that the Commonwealth position—particularly in the case of the tropical countries—presents insuperable difficulties. Nigeria has applied for associate membership and so have some East African countries. In Canada, from which country I returned last week, the possible short-term effects on aluminium, pulp and wheat are appreciated. The long-term prospect of Britain's being within the Community, and therefore having greater power of capital investment, is that the Canadians feel they could have diversified investment and so get relief from the enormous economic pressures from the United States.

New Zealand presents perhaps the most difficult of the Commonwealth problems.

[MR. THORPE.]
We have read the speech in Auckland by Mr. Leslie O'Brien, Governor of the Bank of England, in which he says that Britain's position is broadly understood. This is helpful. I see no reason why we should not be able to negotiate outlets for New Zealand.

I believe that our agricultural industry is already suffering from the effect of our exclusion from the Common Market. When farmers complain about bacon being exported from Denmark and about the increase in beef exports from Ireland, this is one of the prices we have to pay for our exclusion from the Common Market, because these are exporting countries which cannot export for the Community and so turn to Britain as the softest port of entry.

But even though we are outside the Common Market, British agriculture is greatly affected by the position in Europe. I do not know the position in other constituencies, but I know that in my division the price in the beef market is very largely affected by the extent to which in any particular week we are exporting to the Continent. The question is asked: what is happening in the German market? What is the price there? We are already greatly affected by fluctuations in Europe itself. I have always wanted to see a managed market. I believe that Harold Woolley, as he then was, was quite right in saying that it was lunacy to have a managed home market in this country and a totally unplanned import policy. But, of course, I was howled down on that score in this House six weeks before we announced that we intended to try to join the Common Market; for advocating precisely this for agriculture.

Very great care must be given to the position of our production grants to hill cow and hill sheep farmers. We must see that if there is to be some variation in support, their position is not worsened, because I believe that here we have very great scope for expansion of British agriculture.

Since I understand, Mr. Deputy Speaker—and perhaps this will be some relief to the House—that only one Liberal Member is likely to catch your eye, for which reason I make no apology for having spoken at some length—I wanted to work off my euphoria at the conversion of the very many sinners—I have to say that my Scottish colleagues are very disappointed to know that the Secretary of State for Scotland will not be speaking in the debate. It may well be that his outlook is not sufficiently favourable, or perhaps not sufficiently unfavourable, to the Common Market for him to be put in to bat, but it is certainly hoped that the right hon. Gentleman will make clear the position for Scotland, possibly in the Scottish Grand Committee, at an early moment——

Mr. Emrys Hughes: When the right hon. Gentleman says that, can he assure us that his Liberal colleagues in Scotland will vote for the Common Market?

Mr. Thorpe: My colleagues are perfectly prepared to vote for themselves and to make up their own minds. If the hon. Gentleman is here tomorrow night his anticipation will be answered and he will see exactly what we shall do—[An HON. MEMBER: "A three-line Whip."] Obviously, a party that believes in the very old-fashioned doctrine that hon. Members should vote according to their conscience and not according to the dictates of the party Whips would not, on an issue like this, have a three-line Whip. Neither did we think it necessary to have one on such a great political issue as decimal currency.

I want to hear what the Minister for Agriculture believes about the transitional period. I expect he would like 50 years, but we will need at least three or four years to bring about the transition, and possibly slightly more. If we get in—and I still think that we have only a fifty-fifty chance, it will be our opportunity to make the Community an outward-looking body. In many ways the external tariff is very much lower than the system we already operate here, with the exception of our Commonwealth partners.

There are very great dangers if we are out of the E.E.C. and, frankly, I do not believe that we have any other practical option but to go in. It is because there are no other practical options that the Prime Minister has been so decisive. He is only really decisive when there are no other options available.

I believe that not only economically but politically we have a duty to go in. The last thing I want to do is to try to inflame the feelings one might have about

Germany, a country which has, in many ways, had a remarkable record in democracy since the war, but we see the Germans' present disinclination to sign a non-proliferation treaty, which is interpreted by some as a wish to reserve to herself a possible right to independent nuclear manufacture. We see the emergence of the N.D.P., which frightens people in Germany just as much as it frightens them here.

I believe that, politically, the presence of Britain would have a very steadying effect, not only on Germany but on the possibilities of East-West relations. It is very significant that whatever else Soviet Russia may have said in recent years in her criticisms of the Common Market, although she may pay lip-service to current anti-capitalist slogans, the Common Market has not been regarded by Russia as a menace and threat to her own integrity and security.

If it is an outward-looking Community, if it continues with its very impressive record of development, of investment in developing countries—I think Germany has invested more in India's Five Year Plan than this country—because of its economic potential—this can be an expanding Community and a force for world peace, but it will be a long haul. We must be careful not to revive the fears of our being bad Europeans which we did so much to create in the years immediately after the war. If we can convince them that we are good Europeans and that we can make the Community work as a territorially expanding Community, not only this country but Europe has one of the greatest contributions to make to the world in the whole of her long history.

5.51 p.m.

Mr. Stanley Orme (Salford, West): I am sure that the right hon. Member for Devon, North (Mr. Thorpe) will forgive me for not following the train of his thought and his conclusions, because mine lie in the opposite direction. I make one comment, however. He should be very careful before criticising members of the Government who might have an opposite point of view to his and then talking about the freedom which the Liberal Party has saying that Liberal hon. Members do not have any three-line Whips. It does not lie with him to take that attitude.

Mr. Thorpe: Liberal Members are free. The Government are imposing a three-line Whip.

Mr. Orme: The points in the Amendment signed by my hon. Friends and me appear in the policy of the Labour Party and in the manifesto on which we fought the General Election. The Amendment clearly suggests that the safeguards which we undertook in 1963 still stand so far as we are concerned, but those five conditions have not been written into the negotiations which are about to take place with the European Community. Those conditions, which cover E.F.T.A., foreign policy, national planning and agriculture, we believe, have not been eroded away. We were told only the other day that the E.F.T.A. position was possibly one issue which was eroded more than any other, but if we read the reports of the E.F.T.A. conference, recently held in London, we find that there was far from unanimity among the E.F.T.A. countries represented here at that time. That position is still exceedingly valid.

I turn, first, on the economic side to the European Economic miracle we hear so much about and its relationship to Britain's economy and what the Chancellor was dealing with this afternoon. There is a real contradiction here about the 3 per cent. growth rate which was talked about in the Budget prior to the decision to apply to join the Common Market. It was necessary for this country if we were to be outside the Community. Surely with added commitments a 3 per cent. growth will not be sufficient, if we are to attain membership, because of the additional adverse effects on balance of payments, capital, and so forth. This needs to be cleared up. My hon. Friend the Member for West Stirlingshire (Mr. W. Baxter) made this point in April. Is it 3 + 3 or just 3 per cent.? This should be answered.

Following the destruction suffered in the war by Germany, Italy and France, and the build-up which started in their economies when they were redeveloped with new plant and modern industry, the economic miracle we hear so much about —the yearly increase in productivity— was quite large over a number of years. I maintain that this had nothing to do with the Economic Community as such.

Winston Churchill establishes the ethos and structure of the new Commons Chamber

When **Michael Cummins** retired from the service of the House of Commons in 2004 he had been the Serjeant at Arms for five years, having joined the Serjeant's department in 1981 on leaving the Army.

The public image of the Serjeant may be a figure attired in an antiquated uniform of court dress complete with black stockings, brightly buckled shoes and carrying a sword. However, a superficial assessment that concluded that the Serjeant was simply a ceremonial adornment that linked the House to its illustrious past would be badly misconceived.

Michael Cummins held one of the most demanding posts in the administration of the House, one that required first-class organisational and leadership skills, firmness when necessary, diplomacy in dealing with difficult people and circumstances, and quick reactions that provided the correct response in an emergency. He was the head of a department that employed over 400 staff and provided vital support services for some 650 Members and their staffs in one of the busiest Parliaments in the world.

As the Serjeant at Arms he was responsible for the smooth running of a bewildering array of services. To him and his team fell the task of providing everything from notepaper to computer systems, from overseeing multimillion pound building contracts to being personally accountable for the security of the House itself and an estate of nine buildings, and ensuring that, should the worst happen, MPs would have an immediate alternative venue in which to meet.

Within the confines of Parliament's self-contained community, the Commons part encompasses over 4,000 people – Members, Members' staff and staff of the House. They all require offices and facilities, which have to be sourced, organised and provided. It was to him as Serjeant and his people that the demands were usually made. By common consent, it was a job he performed with unfailing courtesy and good humour.

His high profile role, however, was in the seat in the Chamber, just by the Bar of the House, where he passed many hours. There he was available to Members, ready to deal with any one of a range of requests, one of the most common of which was the issue of orders to enable constituents to visit the Public Gallery – another area of responsibility that came within his remit.

In the event of trouble, he was there to do the Speaker's bidding, and that could have involved escorting from the Chamber a Member who was reluctant to comply with an order from the Chair that he or she should leave for having transgressed the rules of the House.

His 23 years with the House of Commons followed a military career that spanned 24 years. He attended the Royal Military Academy, Sandhurst, and graduated from the staff college in 1972. He saw overseas service in Germany, Norway, Denmark, Aden and Kuwait, and did numerous tours of duty in Northern Ireland, including in South Armagh, the predominantly nationalist border area known as "bandit country" for its violent hostility to the British Army.

He was knighted by the Queen in 2003.

Tradition and practice of centuries enshrined in a Chamber for all occasions

By Sir Michael Cummins

Shortly after my arrival in the House as a junior Serjeant in 1981, the then Serjeant at Arms, Sir Peter Thorne, drew my attention to Churchill's speech of 28 October 1943 on the rebuilding of the House of Commons. Its relevance soon became apparent to me since on almost every sitting day for 24 years I occupied the Serjeant's Chair in the Chamber for part of the proceedings.

By the end of my service to the House in 2004 I had probably accumulated a longer period of duty in the Chamber than even the most assiduous attending Member. I was present not only on some of the most intense and emotive occasions, but also during many more sparsely attended debates lasting often after midnight and sometimes into the following day.

I was able to measure and absorb the effects of Churchill's words and found them to have been based on the tradition and practice of many centuries; it was clear that he had spoken not only for himself but on behalf of the vast majority of Members who had occupied the then recently destroyed Victorian Chamber.

It was from the Chamber of the House of Lords that Winston Churchill made his speech. The Lords had given up their Chamber to the Commons shortly after the bombing of 10 May 1941, just as they had done following the Great Fire of 1834. Churchill spoke with deep feeling. He supported continuing the configuration of former Chambers: the clear physical separation of Government and Opposition and with it the determination required ever to "cross the Floor", a feat which he had performed twice; he spoke of the advantage of a crowded, overflowing Chamber on great occasions and of the need for a more intimate setting for the many less well attended debates.

Churchill's words confirmed both the ethos and the structural blueprint for the rebuilding of the Chamber; opened in 1950, it contained the physical elements which would allow its Members to carry forward a form of democratic government begun some seven centuries earlier.

The present Chamber of the House of Commons is the fourth "permanent" home of the House in over six centuries. The first, taken into use in the late fourteenth century, when the Commons formally separated from the Lords, was the Chapter House of Westminster Abbey, to be followed in 1547 by the use of St Stephen's Chapel of the Palace of Westminster, allocated to the Commons by King Edward VI after the Reformation.

The configuration of St Stephen's Chapel, in both shape and size, was significant: Members occupied the stalls left behind by the monks, and the opposing parties addressed each other across the width of the Chapel; the Speaker's chair was placed on the altar steps, where he could both see and be seen. Doorways in the ecclesiastical screen, at the opposite end of the Chapel to the Speaker, led to areas to which he directed Members to vote – "Ayes to the Right, Noes to the Left" - just as he or she does to this day. The House conducted its business in the modified Chapel for 278 years until it was destroyed, along with much of the old Palace of Westminster, by the Great Fire of 1834.

There followed a fiercely fought architectural competition to design and build a new Palace of Westminster, a suitably prestigious building to accommodate both Houses of Parliament. This was won by the architect Charles Barry; Augustus Welby Pugin was engaged as the interior designer. Conscious of the need to recognise the size and shape of the destroyed chamber, Barry and Pugin, under the eye of the Royal Fine Arts Commission, built and furnished a new Chamber which was finally taken into use in 1852.

The new Chamber, of a similar size to the old, again contained seating for Government and Opposition, who faced each other down the length of the Chamber. The Speaker's chair was raised above floor level as before. On the night of Saturday 10 May 1941, in one of the last major air raids of the "Blitz", the Chamber was destroyed. Winston Churchill, in his first year of office as Prime Minister, visited the site of destruction on the morning of Monday 12 May. The Victorian Chamber had been his stage for 40 years.

The House approved the Report of the Select Committee on House of Commons (Rebuilding) in January 1945. In opening the debate, Churchill made a further proposal which was well received: he drew attention to the badly bomb-damaged arch which had led from Members' Lobby to the old Chamber and suggested that the arch should remain in its damaged state as "a monument of the ordeal Westminster has passed through in the Great War ..." Now known as the Churchill Arch, it stands at the Chamber entrance, flanked by bronze statues of the two great wartime Prime Ministers, David Lloyd George and Winston Churchill.

ORDERS OF THE DAY

REGENCY BILL [*Lords*]

Considered in Committee; reported, without Amendment; read the Third time, and passed, without Amendment.

HOUSE OF COMMONS REBUILDING

The Prime Minister (Mr. Churchill): I beg to move,

" That a Select Committee be appointed to consider and report upon plans for the rebuilding of the House of Commons and upon such alterations as may be considered desirable while preserving all its essential features."

On the night of 10th May, 1941, with one of the last bombs of the last serious raid, our House of Commons was destroyed by the violence of the enemy, and we have now to consider whether we should build it up again, and how, and when. We shape our buildings and afterwards our buildings shape us. Having dwelt and served for more than 40 years in the late Chamber, and having derived very great pleasure and advantage therefrom, I, naturally, would like to see it restored in all essentials to its old form, convenience and dignity. I believe that will be the opinion of the great majority of its Members. It is certainly the opinion of His Majesty's Government and we propose to support this resolution to the best of our ability.

There are two main characteristics of the House of Commons which will command the approval and the support of reflective and experienced Members. They will, I have no doubt, sound odd to foreign ears. The first is that its shape should be oblong and not semi-circular. Here is a very potent factor in our political life. The semi-circular assembly, which appeals to political theorists, enables every individual or every group to move round the centre, adopting various shades of pink according as the weather changes. I am a convinced supporter of the party system in preference to the group system. I have seen many earnest and ardent Parliaments destroyed by the group system. The party system is much favoured by the oblong form of Chamber. It is easy for an individual to move through those insensible gradations from Left to Right but the act of crossing the Floor is one which requires serious consideration. I am well informed on this matter, for I have accomplished that difficult process, not only once but twice. Logic is a poor guide compared with custom. Logic which has created in so many countries semi-circular assemblies which have buildings which give to every Member, not only a seat to sit in but often a desk to write at, with a lid to bang, has proved fatal to Parliamentary Government as we know it here in its home and in the land of its birth.

The second characteristic of a Chamber formed on the lines of the House of Commons is that it should not be big enough to contain all its Members at once without over-crowding and that there should be no question of every Member having a separate seat reserved for him. The reason for this has long been a puzzle to uninstructed outsiders and has frequently excited the curiosity and even the criticism of new Members. Yet it is not so difficult to understand if you look at it from a practical point of view. If the House is big enough to contain all its Members, nine-tenths of its Debates will be conducted in the depressing atmosphere of an almost empty or half-empty Chamber. The essence of good House of Commons speaking is the conversational style, the facility for quick, informal interruptions and interchanges. Harangues from a rostrum would be a bad substitute for the conversational style in which so much of our business is done. But the conversational style requires a fairly small space, and there should be on great occasions a sense of crowd and urgency. There should be a sense of the importance of much that is said and a sense that great matters are being decided, there and then, by the House.

We attach immense importance to the survival of Parliamentary democracy. In this country this is one of our war aims. We wish to see our Parliament a strong, easy, flexible instrument of free Debate. For this purpose a small Chamber and a sense of intimacy are indispensable. It is notable that the Parliaments of the British Commonwealth have to a very large extent reproduced our Parliamentary institutions in their form as well as in their spirit, even to the Chair in which the Speakers of the different Assemblies sit. We do not seek to impose our ideas on others; we make no invidious criticisms of other nations. All the same we hold, none the less, tenaciously to them ourselves. The vitality and the authority of the House of Commons and its hold upon an electorate, based upon universal suffrage, depends to no small extent upon its episodes and great moments, even upon its scenes and rows, which, as everyone will agree, are better conducted at close quarters. Destroy that hold which Parliament has upon the public mind and has preserved through all these changing, turbulent times and the living organism of the House of Commons would be greatly impaired. You may have a machine, but the House of Commons is much more than a machine; it has earned and captured and held through long generations the imagination and respect of the British nation. It is not free from shortcomings; they mark all human institutions. Nevertheless, I submit to what is probably not an unfriendly audience on that subject that our House has proved itself capable of adapting itself to every change which the swift pace of modern life has brought upon us. It has a collective personality which enjoys the regard of the public and which imposes itself upon the conduct not only of individual Members but of parties. It has a code of its own which everyone knows, and it has means of its own of enforcing those manners and habits which have grown up and have been found to be an essential part of our Parliamentary life.

The House of Commons has lifted our affairs above the mechanical sphere into the human sphere. It thrives on criticism, it is perfectly impervious to newspaper abuse or taunts from any quarter, and it is capable of digesting almost anything or almost any body of gentlemen, whatever be the views with which they arrive. There is no situation to which it cannot address itself with vigour and ingenuity. It is the citadel of British liberty; it is the foundation of our laws; its traditions and its privileges are as lively to-day as when it broke the arbitrary power of the Crown and substituted that Constitutional Monarchy under which we have enjoyed so many blessings. In this war the House of Commons has proved itself to be a rock upon which an Administration, without losing the confidence of the House, has been able to confront the most terrible emergencies. The House has shown itself able to face the possibility of national destruction with classical composure. It can change Governments,

and has changed them by heat of passion. It can sustain Governments in long, adverse, disappointing struggles through many dark, grey months and even years until the sun comes out again. I do not know how else this country can be governed other than by the House of Commons playing its part in all its broad freedom in British public life. We have learned—with these so recently confirmed facts around us and before us—not to alter improvidently the physical structures which have enabled so remarkable an organism to carry on its work of banning dictatorships within this island and pursuing and beating into ruin all dictators who have molested us from outside.

Mr. Tinker (Leigh): Will the right hon. Gentleman allow me——

The Prime Minister: I think I might be allowed to proceed. I shall not be very long, and then perhaps my hon. Friend can make his own speech. His Majesty's Government are most anxious and are indeed resolved to ask the House to adhere firmly in principle to the structure and characteristics of the House of Commons we have known, and I do not doubt that that is the wish of the great majority of the Members in this the second longest Parliament of our history. If challenged, we must take issue upon that by the customary Parliamentary method of Debate followed by a Division. The question of Divisions again relates very directly to the structure of the House of Commons. We must look forward to periods when Divisions will be much more frequent than they are now. Many of us have seen 20 or 30 in a single Parliamentary Sitting, and in the Lobbies of the Chamber which Hitler shattered we had facilities and conveniences far exceeding those which we are able to enjoy in this lordly abode. I am, therefore, proposing in the name of His Majesty's Government that we decide to rebuild the House of Commons on its old foundations, which are intact, and in principle within its old dimensions, and that we utilise so far as possible its shattered walls. That is also the most cheap and expeditious method we could pursue to provide ourselves with a habitation.

I now come to some of the more practical issues which are involved. It is said that we should wait until the end of the

G* 2

[The Prime Minister.]
war, and I think perhaps that was the point my hon. Friend opposite wished to put. Certainly we must do nothing which appreciably detracts from the war effort, but what we have to do in the first instance is to make up our minds and have a plan and have the preliminary work and survey effectively done, so that at the end of the war, if not earlier, we can start without delay and build ourselves a House again. All this will be a matter for the Committee, which will certainly have more than 15 Members of the House, representative of the different parties and different points of view. I am, however, not entirely convinced that it may not be found possible to make definite progress with this work even during the course of the war. The First Commissioner of Works has submitted a scheme which would enable the old House of Commons to be reconstructed with certain desirable improvements and modernisations affecting the ventilation, lavatories, accommodation for the Press, the ladies' gallery and other prominent features. This scheme would take only 18 months, but it would be prudent—and those concerned with building houses would, I think, feel that it would be prudent—to count on double that period, because everything must be fitted in with war needs and also because it is the habit of architects and builders usually to be more sanguine when putting forward their plans than is subsequently found to be justified by the actual facts. The last House of Commons, the one which was set up after the fire in 1834, was promised in six years and actually took 27 years——

Mr. Maxton (Glasgow, Bridgeton): We had not a bricklayer Prime Minister then.

The Prime Minister: —and so, when I speak of rebuilding the House of Commons in 18 months, it is, of course, without panelling or carving, which can be added as the years pass by. It is simply a Chamber for us to dwell in and conduct our Business as we require to do. The timber must be set aside now if it is to be properly seasoned. The Clipsham Quarry, from which the stone was procured for the maintenance and replacement of the Houses of Parliament, is temporarily closed. It would have to be reopened. We must then consider very carefully the strain upon our labour resources. The First Commissioner informs me that for the first six months after the plan has been started, after the word " Go " has been given, only 46 quarrymen and demolition men would be required, of which half would be over 40 years of age and the other half over 50 years of age. In the second six months 185 men would be required over 40 and an equal number over 50. But of those over 50 years of age 60 would be masons, whose trade has so little work at the present time. In the third six months—and we shall be getting on by then—we shall require 170 men, not additional, over 40 and an equal number over 50. All the 170 over 50 would come from the building trade; the 170 over 40 and under 50 would come from the engineering trade. This last is a much more serious consideration. But there is no need for us, even when the whole scheme is approved and the work has begun, to commit ourselves to the rate of reconstruction. We can fit it in as a stand-by job. It might well be that in a year's time, when we require men from the engineering trade, our affairs might be in such a posture that we should be looking for jobs rather than for men.

However, the House is not asked to commit itself to any decisions of this kind. On the contrary, the Committee has first of all to make its decisions of principle and then the execution of these decisions must be a matter for the Government to carry out as and when the public interest requires and strictly within the limits of the war effort. All the same, I must tell you, Mr. Speaker, that it would be a real danger if at the end of the war we find ourselves separated by a long period from the possibility of obtaining a restored and suitable House of Commons Chamber. We are building warships that will not be finished for many years ahead, and various works of construction are going forward for war purposes. But I am bound to say that I rank the House of Commons—the most powerful Assembly in the whole world—at least as important as a fortification or a battleship, even in time of war. Politics may be very fierce and violent in the after-war days. We may have all the changes in personnel following upon a General Election. We shall certainly have an immense press of Business and, very likely, of stormy controversy. We must have a good, well-tried and convenient place in which to do our work. The House owes it to itself, it owes it to the nation, to make sure that there is no gap, no awkward, injurious hiatus in the continuity of our Parliamentary life. I am to-day only expressing the views of the Government, but if the House sets up the Committee and in a few months' time the Committee give us their Report, we shall be able to take decisions together on the whole matter, and not be caught at a disadvantage in what must inevitably be a time of particular stress and crisis at the end of the war, from a Parliamentary point of view. Therefore, I ask that the Committee should be set up, and I feel sure that it will be able to make a good plan of action leaving the necessary latitude to the Government as to the time when this action can be taken and the speed at which it can be carried into effect having regard to the prime exigencies of the war.

We owe a great debt to the House of Lords for having placed at our disposal this spacious, splendid hall. We have already expressed in formal Resolution our thanks to them. We do not wish to outstay our welcome. We have been greatly convenienced by our sojourn on these red benches and under this gilded, ornamented, statue-bedecked roof. I express my gratitude and appreciation of what we have received and enjoyed, but

" Mid pleasures and palaces though we may
    roam,
    Be it ever so humble, there's no place
    like home."

Mr. Arthur Greenwood (Wakefield): I am sure the House has enjoyed the Prime Minister's speech fully as much as he obviously enjoyed making it. It was the Prime Minister in the genial mood in which some of us prefer to see him. This is not a party question. It is a question that affects all of us. I remember that Sunday morning. I was the first member of the Government to see the blazing Chamber. I found it very difficult to express my feelings at that time. I felt a sense of personal loss, which I knew would be shared by all Members of the House, and, I am bound to say, an intensified sense of bitterness against the author of the damage. I am not by nature a conservative, though some of my friends think I am, but on these matters conservatism shows itself at its best. I should myself have felt most unhappy if we had had to live for long in what we called the annexe. We were grateful for the habitation at the time, but one felt that it was not a Chamber consonant with the dignity of this House. It looked rather like an attempt at cheap fiction.

I think myself the Government are right in trying as far as possible, and having regard to efficiency, to restore the old Chamber. At the same time I feel that there are improvements which could obviously be made in all kinds of ways. I believe that our Assembly after the war will be a focus for people from all parts of the world. I am certain that the great newspapers of the world will come to be more strongly represented in our Chamber, in the Press Galleries, and, if we could somehow or another improve the ventilation, which I have always heard defended, though I never met any Member of the House who thought it was any good, that would be to the good. If we could modernise the building, in as far as we can, without in any way altering its historical character, if we could make further provision for the public and for the Press—I admit that is difficult—I think that would be all to the good. I think the Select Committee ought to get to work fairly quickly. I share the Prime Minister's view that a long hiatus, gradually outstaying our welcome, would be losing something of the spirit of the old place, which will go in time unless we get back, would be a national loss and a loss to the Chamber, and I hope, therefore, the House will accept the Motion and that the Select Committee will be appointed, and then, I think, will be the time to talk at greater length on the proposals put before us.

Mr. Maxton (Glasgow, Bridgeton): May I ask you, Sir, whether you are proposing to call any of the Amendments on the Paper?

Mr. Speaker: I did not propose to call any of these Amendments.

Mr. Maxton: I regret that very much. The Prime Minister knows that I am not hostile to the proposal that a Select Committee should be set up to consider the matter. I think he is also aware that I had very great fondness for the other Chamber. I have the same sort of nostalgia as he expressed it in his well-chosen peroration. I think he is giving his Select Committee much too narrow a mandate. I do not know whom he is proposing to put

Alf Morris introduces his Bill to ease the plight of chronically sick and disabled people

When **Tam Dalyell** asked for a private meeting with Margaret Thatcher at the time of the Falklands conflict, she greeted him with the words "I always have time for the awkward squad." He did not take kindly to her observation, but Prime Ministers and Ministers alike down the years might have seen him in that light. He was in his 43 years in the House arguably its most assiduous and persistent campaigner on a wide range of issues. Five times he was ordered to leave the Chamber for calling Mrs Thatcher a liar, and he risked having the whip withdrawn over his vocal opposition to the 2003 invasion of Iraq.

Tam Dalyell inherited a baronetcy from his mother and has the title Sir Thomas Dalyell of the Binns, one that he has never used. It is a lineage that descends directly from Black Tam, the 17th century royalist general, and it relates him distantly to Harry S. Truman.

He was elected to represent West Lothian in 1962, the seat he held – later redrawn as Linlithgow – until he retired at the 2005 general election.

Hugh Gaitskell's death in 1963 resulted in Richard Crossman taking a Front-Bench role and he asked Tam Dalyell to become his shadow Parliamentary Private Secretary, a job that he held in the more substantial form when, with Labour back in office, Crossman was appointed Minister of Housing, the Lord President of the Council and then Secretary of State for Social Services. However, Tam Dalyell progressed no further up the promotion ladder, should he have wished to do so, perhaps because of his relentless campaigning and the stance he adopted on so many issues that put him at odds with his own Government. When Sir Edward Heath retired in 2001, Tam Dalyell became the Father of the House.

His campaigns began shortly after he arrived in Parliament. The first, in 1965, was against the war in Borneo and the confrontation with Indonesia. He moved on to fight against the Anglo-French variable geometry aircraft that was seen as part of the replacement of the cancelled TSR2. He then called for the introduction of drug testing for schoolchildren, which he abandoned when initial support from colleagues faded and he was quietly advised to drop it.

That did not deter him from pursuing other issues. In 1967, in pursuit of his opposition to Britain's continued military presence East of Suez, he undertook what Denis Healey, then Defence Secretary, described as a "brilliant campaign of parliamentary questions" against the proposal to turn the idyllic Indian Ocean atoll of Aldabra into an airbase. Allied to this proposal was a similar scheme in respect of Diego Garcia. When Healey announced the abandonment of the Aldabra project, Tam Dalyell was cheered from all sides of the House for the persistence that was to become his defining characteristic.

It was as a result of his questioning of his Government's proposals for Scottish devolution that he earned enduring parliamentary recognition. He pointed out that under devolution, with specified powers reserved to the Scottish Assembly, Scottish MPs at Westminster could pronounce on matters in England while English MPs would be prohibited from pronouncing on those same matters in respect of Scotland. It meant that as the MP for West Lothian he could vote on certain matters relating to West Bromwich but not on those same matters as they related to West Lothian. It was a point he hammered home at every opportunity. Enoch Powell coined the expression "the West Lothian question", and the phrase has passed into the parliamentary lexicon for ever to be associated with Tam Dalyell.

His vehement opposition to the Falklands war led him to question the veracity of Margaret Thatcher's account of the circumstances of the sinking of the Argentine warship the General Belgrano. His questions were a constant feature of the House of Commons Order Paper.

His longest and most persistent campaign was on the bombing of PanAm flight PA103, which crashed on Lockerbie on 21 December 1988, killing 270 people. In the course of his quest for answers he initiated 17 Adjournment debates, thought to be some five times as many as any MP on a single subject. It was an issue he continued to pursue after he left the House.

Minister's volcanic fury fails to counter Back Bencher's passion and obstinacy

By Tam Dalyell

I have chosen the Second Reading speech of my then Back-Bench chum, later distinguished and long-term Minister for the Disabled, Alf Morris, now Lord Morris of Manchester, introducing his ground breaking Chronically Sick and Disabled Persons Bill. Part of the reason is that he sponsored a lasting, not an ephemeral, piece of legislation, born of a passionate concern which has lasted not four weeks, not four months, not even four years, but 40 years.

On issues of disablement I voted, not according to the Whips, but as Alf Morris and his and my friends Jack Ashley (now Lord Ashley of Stoke) and the late Lewis Carter-Jones, MP for Eccles, suggested that I should. I took the view that they were more conversant with the issues than I ever could be, and knew more about the chronically sick than I – or the Government – did.

What I admired above all was Alf Morris's sheer bloody obstinacy in refusing to succumb to the blandishments of Government Ministers who tried to persuade him to drop his proposals in favour of a "proper Government Bill", which, in my opinion had fat chance of being produced for a decade.

In the early spring of 1963 Hugh Gaitskell unexpectedly died, and, equally unexpectedly, Dick Crossman became a major Front-Bench spokesman, a position to which fellow Wykehamist Gaitskell would never have appointed him. Thus he cast around for a parliamentary aide. Since his brief included science, and since, in my first six months of membership of the House, I had been asking a series of pointed questions on science policy, he chose me.

When Labour won the 1964 election Crossman became Minister of Housing, then Leader of the House and, in 1968, Secretary of State for Social Services. I was appointed his parliamentary private secretary. Staying in his house, as I was, and making his breakfast every morning in 9 Vincent Square, I am in the unique position among the living to recall the facts.

In the Ballot for Private Members' Bills, after the Queen's Speech in 1969, Alf Morris had the good luck to come out as number one. Bluntly, most MPs have little notion what to do with such good fortune. Personally, I never came in the first 20 in 43 years of putting my name in! Most MPs who do strike lucky simply snap up some ready-made Bill, presented to them on a proverbial plate by some interest group. Not so Morris. He knew precisely what he wanted to do – an unusual situation.

When told of Morris's intention, Crossman, whom I liked and admired, behaved abominably. He "did his nut". Crossman stormed at me: what did a Labour Back-Bencher think he was up to in pre-empting major Government legislation? His volcanic temper had hardly improved when I opined that the Labour party might warm more to a Bill put forward by a colleague who had fought his way to Oxford via elementary school, Manchester evening classes and Ruskin College rather than the philosophy tutor of Winchester and New College, the son of a distinguished Chancery Judge. I pointed out that the Morris brothers – Charles, MP for Openshaw had been Harold Wilson's PPS – were the sons of a chronically disabled father.

Fortunately for Morris he had not only the goodwill of the Prime Minister but the support of Fred Peart, the Leader of the House. He had been Parliamentary Private Secretary to Fred at the Ministry of Agriculture as well as to Home Secretary James Callaghan. Callaghan told me with his sardonic grin that he had chuckled at how upset I (Eton and King's College, Cambridge) had made Dick Crossman over contrasting New College with Ruskin.

When that crucial Friday of the debate arrived, Crossman was off sick. I was deputed to go to the Chamber and report back what Morris had said. Hearing of the painstaking detail of Morris's speech, Crossman expressed his respect for this "cussed young Labour MP". Morris's cause was greatly helped by the fact that the Tory who followed him was Neil Marten. Since Crossman spent his weekends at his home, Prescot Manor, Cropredy, which meant that they both used the same train, he would often invite Marten to join him in the compartment reserved for the Secretary of State. Marten's glowing account of Morris's effort made an impression on Crossman, helping to give Morris and his Bill the crucial "favourable parliamentary wind".

In my opinion, had it not been for Morris and his speech, the chronically sick and disabled would have had to wait much longer.

HOUSE OF COMMONS

Friday, 5th December 1969

The House met at Eleven o'clock

PRAYERS

[MR. SPEAKER *in the Chair*]

ORDERS OF THE DAY

CHRONICALLY SICK AND DISABLED PERSONS BILL

Order for Second Reading read.

11.5 a.m.

Mr. Alfred Morris (Manchester, Wythenshawe): I beg to move, That the Bill be now read a Second time.

The Bill deals with many problems, all of them intensely human, but has a single intention. This intention is to increase the welfare, improve the status and enhance the dignity of the chronically sick and of disabled persons.

I am told that it is a big Bill, but then it deals with a big and important subject. The House will recall that the principal Private Member's Bills in recent Sessions have all been concerned with subjects of major social importance, such as capital punishment, abortion and homosexuality and divorce law reform. Thus one need hardly apologise for the size and scope and purpose of this Bill.

The Bill was conceived scarcely more than three weeks ago as an essay in helping the disabled. Clearly, there may be imperfections of phrasing in parts of the essay which will require careful study if, as so many people profoundly hope, it receives a Second reading today. There are points, too, which may not entirely please, nor even survive, the assessors in Standing Committee when we reach the stage, as it were, of *viva voce* examination.

The Bill is a collective essay to which hon. Members on both sides of the House, and countless organisations and individuals outside, including Mr. Clifford Hilditch, Chief Welfare Officer of the

City of Manchester, and his colleagues in other towns and cities, have contributed proposals for helping the very sick, the halt, the blind, the deaf and many other groups of chronically sick and disabled people.

I warmly acknowledge the extremely generous help I have had in preparing the Bill. I should also like to thank my brother, my hon. Friend the Member for Manchester, Openshaw (Mr. Charles R. Morris), who entered my name in the Private Member's Ballot and who, therefore, more than anyone else, with the possible exception of you, Mr. Speaker, is responsible both for my success in winning the first place in the Ballot and for my having the opportunity to introduce the Bill today. I know that no subject is nearer to his heart than this one.

It has been put to me, of course, that good ideas, even good ideas for helping the disabled, cease to be good if they cost money. This is neither humane nor imaginative. In discussing the welfare of the disabled, can we not at least agree to talk less of cost and more of net cost? There are many distinguished experts who argue that, for example, increased domiciliary care can lead to a net saving of public expenditure.

Again, it has been impressed upon me by some very experienced administrators in this field that even a modest improvement in the standard of welfare services provided by the less progressive local authorities could well relieve much of the present strain on the hospital service. Increasing the mobility and employment opportunities of disabled people could also very well lead ultimately to a net saving of public money, as well as relieve the pressure on their families and reduce the health risks to which they in consequence become exposed.

What most disabled people want more than anything else is to lessen their dependence on other people, to get on with living their own lives as normally as they can in their own homes amongst their own family, and, wherever possible, to have the opportunity of contributing to industry and society as fully as their abilities allow. Investment in people, disabled people no less than fit and strong and fortunate people, is much the best of all investments.

But what if it is still insisted that initial outlay is more important even than the possibility of ultimate net savings? My reply is that there are provisions in the Bill which will require very little public expenditure and which in terms of priority are wholly admissible on grounds both of social justice and priority. Under the present Government, the hospital building programme has nearly doubled in the past five years and is now five times as great as it was ten years ago. New projects to the value of £116 million are in hand for the current year, while the average for the 16 years to 1964 was only £17 million.

Five years ago, £270 was spent on the social services for every £100 spent on defence. This year, £370 is being spent on the social services for every £100 spent on defence. The number of qualified nurses and midwives has risen by 32,000, or 30 per cent., in the last five years and there have been other impressive achievements in health and social welfare.

Yet, even with a Government who have done so much to improve the social services, we still live in a society where more is heard of the complaints of the affluent and the strong than of the legitimate claims of those in special need. While there are millions of people, including many of the most vocal critics of increased public expenditure on health and welfare, whose main problems are trying to diet and knowing where to park their second car, there is still a shortage of hospital beds for the young chronic sick, many of whom even now have to spend the final years of their young lives in geriatric wards.

For those who believe in the ideal of:

" From each according to his ability, to each according to his needs "

it is distressing that less than a tithe of what is spent by the affluent on their pleasures would be more than enough to meet all the legitimate and pressing claims of the chronically sick and disabled. As the Pearson Commission puts it in another context,

" . . . it is only right for those who have to share with those who have not."

There is a near consensus among the organisations working to help those who are disabled that the maintenance of a register of the names of disabled persons, regardless of whether they apply for assistance, should be mandatory upon the local authorities, subject only to a person's willingness to have his name included and the assurance of a reasonable degree of confidentiality. This already applies to the registration of blind persons and I see no reason why it should not be extended to all disabled persons, so that the information available to the public authorities on the extent of disablement is both accurate and uniform.

Schemes submitted by local authorities under the provisions of Section 29 of the National Assistance Act, 1948, usually contain the following :

" The . . . Council shall keep a register of handicapped persons who apply for assistance and whom the Council assist under this scheme and shall include therein such particulars as they think fit, including any which the Minister may from time to time direct ".

At first glance this appears to be mandatory, but the important words are " persons who apply for assistance ". If the authority is not anxious to assist the disabled, it can obviously fail to advertise its services, and this inevitably limits the number of persons who apply for assistance. Thus, the keeping of uniform registers with the safeguards to which I have referred is a matter of central importance in terms of improving the welfare of disabled persons.

Mr. John M. Temple (City of Chester) : The hon. Gentleman knows that I support him wholeheartedly, but there is a point which is worrying the local authority associations and myself. It is that there is no definition in the Bill of chronically sick and disabled persons. Would it be the hon. Gentleman's intention at a later date to introduce a definition? That would be of great assistance.

Mr. Morris : In Clause 20(3) I attempt to define the younger chronic sick. I am deeply conscious of the need for further definitions as we proceed, as I hope we shall, to more detailed consideration of the Bill in Standing Committee.

The hon. Member for Moray and Nairn (Mr. Gordon Campbell), who has consistently stressed the urgency of the need to compile a full and meaningful register, has written to me to say how sorry he is not to be able to be with us today.

[MR. MORRIS.]

The House knows of his sincere and abiding interest in the aims of the Bill and, in particular, the provisions of Clause 1, and of the part he has played in emphasising the importance of registration.

The reference in Clause 1 and in other Clauses to the local health authority is not, of course, intended to mean that the duties should be the responsibility of the local authority's medical officer of health, or of the health committee. These duties would normally be the responsibility of the welfare services committee, or its equivalent, and my hope is that all the provisions of the Bill will soon become the responsibility of new social service committees.

Clause 2 sets out the information that should be available to the chronically sick and the disabled and emphasises the importance of communicating this information, in whatever form may be appropriate to the individual. This cannot be done unless we know where the disabled are, and the register is therefore of primary, not to say crucial, importance.

That local authorities are not providing adequate information at present is well evidenced by a letter sent to me by Mr. Marsh Dickson, the well respected President of the National Campaign for the Young Chronic Sick. He writes:

"My wife, Dorothy, suffers from advanced multiple sclerosis and is unable to read, write, feed herself or stand, and her vision is very much impaired. She has available aids such as Possum, Ripple Mattress and a battery operated Ripple Cushion for her chair."

Mrs. Dickson was entitled to the possum and her general practitioner was asked to arrange a visit to the consultant at the Middlesex Hospital. I am told that the Middlesex Hospital did not realise the entitlement and was most discouraging, saying that people with her disease to the best of its knowledge were not entitled. Mr. Marsh Dickson writes:

"Fortunately, I knew this not to be true and we fought on, eventually gaining the support of the Consultant and obtained the Possum . . . Again, when we discovered about the Ripple Mattress and the Ripple Cushion our G.P. immediately got on to the local authority who then proceeded to obtain them for us. It is interesting that the Social Workers concerned had never heard of a battery operated Ripple Cushion."

It will be seen from the above that Mrs. Dickson was not informed either by the hospital or the local authority about any of these important aids. And there must be many other sufferers from advanced multiple sclerosis who still know nothing of their entitlements.

Mr. Dickson's letter goes on:

"In the boroughs of Kensington and Chelsea there are three Possums. In no case has the information about Possums come from either the hospital or the local authority . . . Moreover it is interesting that the three Possum users are all of middle-class background with access to information from campaigns or voluntary organisations. My wife knew of these aids through the National Campaign for the Young Chronic Sick. How many people in North Kensington need these things? How are they to get to know about them—especially those who, because of lack of education or background, have no way of finding out for themselves?".

One need hardly say more on the need for adequate communication between local authorities and those who need their help.

Under Clause 3, subsections (1), (2) and (3), provisions for the disabled which are now permissive would be mandatory upon local authorities. The whole Clause is intended to standardise local provision on the basis of the best existing practice. None of its requirements would be resisted by any self-respecting local authority. Indeed, such an authority would already be doing all, or almost all, that is required by the Clause. But there are still far too many local authorities whose provisions for their disabled citizens are both nebulous and ineffectual.

I should like to read from a letter sent to me on 19th November by the head occupational therapist of a hospital management committee in Lancashire, who said:

"Again, depending on the local authority, it can take many months and quite a lot of 'nagging' from the consultant and from me to provide aid which may in itself cost very litle. One patient was assessed in January, 1968, for a raised lavatory seat at a cost of £2 10s. After much nagging, the local authority supplied this in April, 1968, only to take it way again the following March in order to give it to an older person."

That is just not good enough, even by the lowest standards, and it points to the importance of Clause 4, where I refer to the housing needs of the disabled and the need for adaptations, as well as of Clause 3.

I have received comments even more derisive than that which I have just quoted. With some bitterness in its phraseology, one letter informs me that the local authority of a very well-known Lancashire seaside resort spends more on its annual end-of-season illuminations than on its disabled citizens.

At present the services and facilities available to the disabled, both medical and others, depend on geographical luck. Again, this is just not good enough. Why should the father of a disabled child be forced to reject promotion in another town or city because the facilities available to his child would be so poor compared with those in his existing local authority? This often happens now, and the purpose of Clause 3 is to stop it happening in the future.

The city of Manchester provides a very good example of concern for the disabled, in the provision it makes for mentally recovered patients in welfare homes like "Weylands" in my constituency of Wythenshawe. That home was the first of its kind built in this country. Fortunately, there are now three in the city of Manchester. They are places where mentally recovered patients can adjust to normal living. Such places show how much the less progressive local authorities can learn from those local authorities which have been leading the way in this so important field of helping the chronically sick and the disabled.

Subsections (2) and (3) of Clause 3 are no less important than subsection (1). The permissive schemes for handicapped persons other than the blind operated by the local authorities usually include the following provision for sheltered workshop employment:

"The . . . Council may provide such sheltered workshops as the Minister may approve in which handicapped persons may be employed in suitable work or may be trained in pursuance of the Disabled Persons Employment Acts, 1944 and 1958."

The Bill seeks to make that function mandatory.

As the House knows, the Government's Remploy scheme caters for many thousands of handicapped persons, but there are handicapped people who are so disabled that they are unacceptable to Remploy. Therefore, unless the local

authority operates a sheltered workshop scheme, either directly or through an agency, there is always the possibility that there are still disabled persons who could undertake useful productive work but who lack local opportunities for such work. In Manchester, in the sheltered workshops for the disabled, there is a good number of men who are rejects of Remploy but who are now engaged in useful productive work. What is more, these so-called rejects now have a higher basic minimum wage than their erstwhile colleagues in Remploy.

Another facility which appears in most councils' schemes relates to home employment. The usual phraseology is as follows:

"The . . . Council, in consultation with the Minister, may assist under supervision handicapped persons who are capable of earning at least such reasonable weekly sums as the council may determine, by the production of saleable goods or the tendering of useful services, to engage in activities to that end in their own homes or elsewhere other than in sheltered workshops."

I know from contact with administrators concerned that home employment, which is usually called outwork, is difficult to operate. But that should be a secondary consideration, as these administrators themselves concede, because the interests of disabled persons should count for more than administrative difficulties. A vast amount of work is not necessarily needed to keep numerous disabled people in out-work, for there is a statutory limit of £2 a week placed on their earnings before their National Insurance benefit is reduced. But the satisfaction gained by the disabled employee makes the administrative problems involved so very well worth while.

I have naturally been in conversation recently with Miss Mary Greaves, who now leads the Disablement Income Group, succeeding in her present office a lady whose memory is revered and cherished by so many right hon. and hon. Members on both sides of the House. I refer, of course, to the late Megan du Boisson. I must emphasise a point that was put to me strongly by Mary Greaves in talking of the importance of employment opportunities for those who are disabled. She told me that the disabled person who becomes a worker experiences a great thrill, the thrill of joining industrial society. She emphasised also,

[MR. MORRIS.]
of course, that this is so important to the attitude of mind of disabled people, for if one is told that there is no job life can lose its meaning. Perhaps I hardly need speak further about the importance of the need for all of us who are active in public life to give much more emphasis to the importance of helping the disabled in the matter of employment opportunities.

Clause 4 refers to the housing needs of the disabled. The first action of an owner-occupier whose wife becomes, say, a rheumatoid arthritic, is likely to be to adapt the home to save his wife avoidable pain and suffering. But tenants of local authorities rely on enlightened policies from those authorities to save members of their families who are disabled from preventable suffering and distress.

I have a letter from Mr. A. G. Morren, who is a member of the North Cheshire Multiple Sclerosis Society, who says that a lot more could be done to provide two-room bungalows for people suffering from multiple sclerosis, for such people have

" to contend with stairs which they are not fit to manage and this causes untold falls. There has just recently been a little estate of these built in Chorlton, Manchester, but the cash was all raised by the Society. The joy of those moved in has to be seen to be believed at not having any steps to contend with."

I pay warm tribute to all those dedicated people who work in the voluntary organisations. Without their help, the problems throughout the whole field covered by this Bill would be very much greater.

There are tens of thousands of families in this country who, because of the severe disability of the man or wife, seek transfers from one council house to another or, more usually, from a council flat to a council house. Clause 4 suggests that local authorities should adapt the homes of the disabled in every possible case. There are hon. Members present, including the hon. Member for Lowestoft (Mr. Prior), who have emphasised the importance of provisions similar, not to say in some respects identical, to the provisions I am now proposing. In the City of Manchester, disabled families are sometimes preselected for houses that are in the process of being built so that the houses can be adapted to meet their needs. This also could be emulated by other authorities.

Clauses 5 and 6 deal with another important aspect of this problem. In Clause 5 I refer to the need for toilet facilities to be signposted and publicised and for improved access for the disabled. The City of Norwich leads local authorities throughout this country in the provision which it makes in this respect. I commend to the leaders of other local authorities the idea of making a journey to Norwich to see the practical concern which is taken there in the problem of giving disabled people access to public buildings.

The Co-operative Party, with which I am very proud to be associated, passed a very important resolution at its annual conference this year on giving disabled people easier access to public buildings. I am very pleased to be able to acknowledge the important contribution made to thinking about this in the Labour Movement by the Co-operative Party. There have been resolutions on caring for the aged, including the elderly disabled, not just recently, but at one annual conference after another of the Co-operative Party.

In Clause 9 I refer to young people under the age of 18 suffering from severe visual defects. This Clause has its origins in a case in my constituency concerning a young person with very severe visual defects who found it extremely difficult even to continue her education after the age of 16. I should like to quote a letter from my constituent, Mr. Frank Greaves, who refers to a girl of 16 and a boy of 12 years in the same family who is also semi-blind. Their father is a civil servant at Ringway Airport with a take-home pay of £13 10s. Mr. Greaves says that

" . . . she has to walk in all weathers in inadequate clothing two miles to her school in Barlow Moor Road from 29 Kenworthy Lane, Northenden, and two miles back again . . .".

My local newspaper, the *Wythenshawe Express* has said that:

" The decision is not only causing a great deal of financial hardship, but it is also putting the blind girl's education in jeopardy. If she has to give up attending Braille classes and the other special sessions, she will not be able to teach. That is what she wants to do, if she finishes her course."

I know that my right hon. Friend the Minister of Transport will give every possible consideration to the proposition in Clause 9 and the case of my unfortunate young constituent and her family.

Other right hon. and hon. Members have specialised in various subjects dealt with in the Bill. The hon. Member for Banbury (Mr. Marten) and my hon. Friends the Members for Caerphilly (Mr. Fred Evans) and Eccles (Mr. Lewis Carter-Jones) and others will speak about the importance of Clauses 17, 18 and 19. Motoring for the disable is not a luxury. It is a necessity if they are to have contact with the rest of society. Moreover, haemophiliacs, in particular, may suffer further injury if they travel in the wrong kind of vehicles. I hope this debate will enable both sides of the argument about vehicles for disabled people to be fully deployed.

Clause 20 has caused me much the deepest concern. I refer to the admission of the younger chronic sick to geriatric accommodation. I appreciate that if geriatric accommodation is the only accommadation available the younger chronic sick must be admitted to it. But there are some very distressing cases. There are young people languishing in wards where the average age of the other patients is over 80 and who, in the phrase of one of them, are learning to grow up in geriatric accommodation. I very much hope that the Minister, in replying to the debate, will accept that there is very deep concern on both sides of the House about the problems of geriatric accommodation.

I should have liked to deal with other Clauses. My hon. Friend the Member for Stoke-on-Trent, South (Mr. Ashley) and my hon. Friend the Member for Willesden, West (Mr. Pavitt) than whom there are no two greater experts in this House on the problems of the deaf and the hard of hearing, will speak about the Clauses which refer to the problems of the deaf and the problems of deaf-blind children. As my hon. Friend the Member for Stoke on Trent, South has pointed out on other occasions, children who suffer the dual handicap of being deaf and blind may in some cases be taught as deaf children or as blind children. They have the dual handicap and need special provision. There are the problems also of the autistic children.

I read recently that there are 21 units to help autistic children, 18 of them being in the South-East of England. The other three cover the rest of the country.

I must, however, refer to Clause 25, which will be of considerable help to disabled children. The purpose of this Clause is to allow certain types of slow-moving invalid carriages to be used on the footway without being subject to the requirements of the Road Traffic Acts concerning the use of motor vehicles on roads. In particular, it will allow these invalid carriages to be used by child invalids who would normally be under the minimum age for driving a motor vehicle.

It is hoped that the Clause will be of particular help to the thalidomide children, who have been provided with small battery-driven cars, not unlike children's pedal cars, which hitherto have not been allowed to be used outside the children's own homes. The Clause should also help handicapped children suffering from a variety of other disabilities, such as muscular dystrophy, who are also able to propel themselves about in small specially coverted powered chairs.

The Clause will be of assistance to certain adult invalids, often elderly, who also have the use of power-driven wheel chairs which, at present, can be used only on the roads and not on pavements and which must be controlled by a pedestrian who is licensed to control this kind of vehicle.

The Clause gives the Minister of Transport power to make regulations about the vehicles which may take advantage of this concession and about the way in which they are to be used. Clearly, the the Minister has responsibility for the safety of other pedestrians as well as for the invalids themselves. If the Bill is passed, the Minister will be able to make regulations concerning, for example, the maximum weight of the vehicles and their maximum speed. This will ensure that only vehicles which are suitable for use on pavements will be able to take advantage of the concession. The Minister will also be able, if he thinks fit, to specify a minimum age at which invalid children can use these vehicles or to require that if a child is below a certain age, a pedestrian should accompany the vehicle. The Clause should do

[MR. MORRIS.]

a great deal for certain disabled people, particularly children, without imposing serious risk on other road users.

Mr. Speaker, if we could bequeath one precious gift to posterity, I would choose a society in which there is genuine compassion for the very sick and the disabled ; where understanding is unostentatious and sincere ; where needs come before means ; where, if years cannot be added to the lives of the chronically sick, at least life can be added to their years ; where the mobility of disabled people is restricted only by the bounds of technical progress and discovery ; where the handicapped have the fundamental right to participate in industry and society according to ability ; where socially preventable distress is unknown ; and where no man has cause to be ill at ease because of disability.

Several Hon. Members *rose——*

Mr. Speaker : As the House will know, there are many aspects of this very human problem which hon. Members with experience and special knowledge seek to canvass. If speeches are reasonably brief, I would hope that we should have a wide-ranging debate on the various problems of disability as raised in the Bill.

11.44 a.m.

Mr. Neil Marten (Banbury) : I am sure that we would all wish to congratulate the hon. Member for Manchester, Wythenshawe (Mr. Alfred Morris) on his good fortune and to congratulate his brother, the hon. Member for Manchester, Openshaw (Mr. Charles R. Morris), on fixing it so well that he should get top of the list with this Bill. I do not mean "fixing" in any wrong way ; I am sorry if I have, perhaps, used the wrong word. It is extremely good that the hon. Member should have chosen this subject, because when one thinks of all the subjects in our life that he might have chosen, I am very glad that he has chosen a Bill to deal with human beings and not chosen animals, much as I like them, as the most important subject for attention.

There is one point that the hon. Member might refer to his right hon. Friend the Leader of the House, with whom he works so closely. It is an unfortunate situation that a person who draws top place in the list and whose Bill is likely to get through—we hope, in some form at least—has the shortest time in which to prepare it. I know that the hon. Member has been under great pressure. It would be rather nice if we could give thought to this matter so that a little more time might be allowed for the preparation of a Bill which, I hope, will find its way on to the Statute Book. I congratulate the hon. Member on his speech and all the work that he has devoted to this subject. We are likely to have a fairly lengthy time in Committee and for my part I foresee certain Amendments and discussions about cost and other matters, with which I will not waste the time of the House this morning.

As the hon. Member for Wythenshawe said, I wish to confine my remarks to a limited front and to speak for a very short time on the question of vehicles for disabled drivers. I am, however, glad that Clause 6, which deals with access to buildings, has been included in the Bill. This matter is getting more and more important. Indeed, we had better look at our own House as well. I doubt whether many disabled people have been able to get in upstairs. I know that when we have meetings downstairs with the Disabled Drivers' Association, an all-party group, there are substantial difficulties in getting people in. I am glad, therefore, that Clause 6 has been included.

I would like to say a word about Clause 17 and the haemophiliacs. I do this with a certain sense of modesty because I see opposite me two practising or ex-practising doctors and a former junior Minister of Health. I would like to remind the House about haemophilia because it is an extraordinary illness. It is a lifelong illness, a hereditary bleeding disorder due to the lack of protein in the blood plasma which is necessary to cause the blood to clot.

Probably everybody knows that haemophiliacs get substantial bleeding, which continues for a long time, from an open wound, but the experts tell me that the chief disability of haemophiliacs is from repeated internal haemorrhages, particularly in muscles and joints, and that these can arise from a sudden twist

Aneurin Bevan uses his masterful oratory to present Government defence policy

Lord Deedes of Aldington, Bill to anyone who knew him and to many who did not, was a remarkable man in most respects, not least in having uniquely been both a Cabinet Minister and the Editor of a national newspaper, *The Daily Telegraph*. He died on 18 August 2007 at the age of 94, only two weeks after having written his final column for the paper.

He became a journalist almost by accident. While at school at Harrow the 1929 crash put paid to the family's fortunes, and he was compelled to leave and find work. An uncle put in a word for him at the *Morning Post*, and he was taken on as a reporter.

Staffing at the paper was minimal and he was paid only for what he got printed, so young Bill was compelled to turn his hand to whatever came along. It was the beginning of a distinguished career that took him to all parts of the world, and resulted in him being named Reporter of the Year when he was 84. He could claim the unique distinction of having been both a Lobby correspondent while Ramsay MacDonald was still on the scene and an observer of the Blair years.

In 1935 he was sent to cover Mussolini's military actions against Abyssinia, where he met Evelyn Waugh, and the model for William Boot in Waugh's novel "Scoop" was conceived. Back home, the *Morning Post* was absorbed into *The Daily Telegraph*. Bill Deedes moved over to the paper on which he was to remain for the rest of his life.

In the second world war, he served in the King's Royal Rifle Corps and won the Military Cross in 1944 as a result of his courage in an action at a bridge near Arnhem. After advancing under enemy fire, he was ordered to pull his men back. They took many casualties in what he described as a "rough day."

With the war over, he returned to the *Telegraph* but was inexorably drawn into politics. One of his forebears had served in the Long Parliament and three of them, all named William, had been elected to Parliament in the 19th century.

In 1947 he beat Edward Heath for the candidature of the parliamentary constituency of Ashford in Kent, the part of the world that had been represented both by his grandfather and great grandfather. He won the seat at the 1950 general election and held it until he retired from the House in 1974. During that time he was a junior Minister in Housing and the Home Office under Churchill and served in the Cabinet as Macmillan's media expert from 1962-64.

His personal friend and golfing partner of many years was Denis Thatcher, and Bill Deedes became known almost as well as for most of his achievements as the "Dear Bill" of the satirical Denis Thatcher letters in *Private Eye* magazine.

When he left Parliament, he became the editor of *The Daily Telegraph*, a position he held for 12 years. When Conrad Black took over the paper, his days at the helm were over. He was given a peerage as Lord Deedes of Aldington and, although in his 70s, he resumed his career as a reporter, which he was to continue until his death.

Provocative yet serious – the best speech by one who was among the best

BY RT HON LORD DEEDES OF ALDINGTON KBE, MC

I have chosen Aneurin Bevan's speech on the Labour Government's defence policy on three main counts. It was the best of many I heard him make in Parliament as a Minister – and he was always among the best.

It was almost the last big speech we would hear from him, for his resignation came in 1951, and after the general election of that year, the Conservatives governed for 13 years. He died in 1960, four years before Labour returned to office. Finally, as c. 737 testifies, Churchill knew it was a good speech – and said so, although during world war two Bevan had been a parliamentary thorn in his flesh.

The serious content is to be found from c. 732 onwards. Bevan was entering his views about Russia, not as Foreign Secretary or Minister for Defence, but as Minister of Labour – yet he delivered his analysis almost extempore, with barely a note in front of him. That requires enormous confidence.

It was also a debating speech, with sallies at Churchill and the Tory party, which courted interruption. The peroration about giving mankind another breathing space made a marked impression.

I remember thinking, while I sat on the Benches opposite and listened to it and enjoyed it, what a great parliamentary gift it was to be able to make such a provocative speech, yet one with serious content, and also one that held the attention of both sides of the House.

That was Nye Bevan's gift – to make you want to listen to what he was saying, no matter how rude it was; and to do it almost invariably with the minimum of notes in front of him. It is because I think he was the outstanding parliamentary debater of his time – and this was an example of him at his best – that I have selected it.

[SIR D. MAXWELL FYFE.]

Again, and more important, we should know what steps they have taken to deal with stock-piling by the United States and others so that it will not adversely affect us. Again, as I understood the Chancellor of the Exchequer—and he was speaking only in outline—said that the labour force would come first from existing factories turned over to re-armament and where there was at the moment a shortage in some cases; secondly, it would come from where the effects of raw materials would show themselves.

I was happy to note that the Chancellor of the Exchequer did not say it was intended to apply any direction of labour at this time. I should like to get an assurance from the Minister of Labour, whose particular province it is, that that omission was deliberate and correct. The other three points are so clear that I want to put them on record. I am surprised that we have not had more consideration given to them. The Chancellor mentioned the danger of inflation, but he did not relate the question of inflation and dis-inflation to the problem of mobility of labour. I am sure we ought to know the Government's view on this point—and it is obviously one of the most important—of how mobility of labour is to be obtained.

I turn to my last point, and I promise that I will then conclude. [HON. MEMBERS: "Hear, hear."] Well, I have had one or two interruptions. This point concerns restrictive practices. The right hon. Gentleman knows that a long time ago—I think it was two years ago—a committee started inquiring into that subject. We have several times asked about it in the House but we have had no satisfaction. That is a matter which I think ought to be considered when the vital question of this aspect is how we are to keep our production and output going on.

Hon. Gentlemen opposite have challenged us again and again about why we have put down this Amendment. [HON. MEMBERS: "No."] We have been challenged over and over again; I have been listening to the debate. It is quite true that the hon. Member for Preston, South (Mr. Shackleton), not only challenged but put the answer himself, because he said it was quite clear that our reason was that we wanted to get hon. and right hon. Gentlemen opposite out, while they would vote against us because they wanted to keep hon. and right hon. Gentlemen in. He was quite blunt about it.

I want to make the position quite clear, because it would be wrong to speak to this Amendment without saying it. We have said that we have no confidence in the Ministers who are in charge of this programme. With regard to the Minister of Defence, we are bound to look back —and who would not look back?—to the fuel crisis of 1947. When the right hon. Gentleman gave his undertaking to the Z Reservists yesterday that they would not be called up next year, we remembered rather bitterly the undertakings which he gave to industry and the country that there would be no cuts.

Here is one of the most intricate economic and administrative problems ever put before the country. It is in the hands of the right hon. Gentleman the Secretary of State for War, whose claim to administrative fame is just in the word "groundnuts." But it does not really stop there. This is the point: in a short time we shall hear the result from Bristol, West, and the result is, of course, perfectly obvious; but suppose it were the other way round. Suppose the winner were Mr. Lawrance, who says, as he is reported in today's papers, "I do not believe in re-armament but if I am returned I will vote for this Motion." The Government are attempting to bring in their programme on the strength and by the votes of those who disagree with their programme and have not the slightest confidence in any proposal which has been put forward. That is a mockery of Parliamentary democracy. The hon. Member for Preston, South spoke the one correct word—that they are voting only to keep us out. [*Interruption.*] When a great idealist party of the past has come down to that cynical view of the present, the country will judge, and judge soon.

9.20 p.m.

The Minister of Labour (Mr. Aneurin Bevan): The right hon. and learned Gentleman will forgive me if I spend a few moments in reducing the temperature. I have to make a reply to one or two of the things he said which have a Departmental significance before I follow him into the stratosphere. The right hon. and learned Gentleman asked me one or two questions concerning the mobility of labour. I have discussed this matter already with the representatives of the trade unions and of the employers, and we have come to the conclusion that it would be premature to reach a decision about the direction of labour, if it becomes necessary at all, until we see how the impact of the re-armament programme develops.

I am bound to say to the right hon. and learned Gentleman that if it becomes necessary to control the engagement of labour it will also be necessary to discuss with the employers how far their activities also are to be restricted in employing workers in non-essential industries. There is such a matter as the direction of employers as well as the direction of workers. If it becomes necessary to do so we shall deal equitably with both; but we do not think it is necessary to reach any such Draconic decision because, as the Chancellor of the Exchequer said today, in a speech which, I think, will repay close reading, the weight of the re-armament programme falls on a comparatively narrow sector of the economy, and until we see how far the impact has reached it will not be possible for us to find out what steps may be necessary to secure the greater mobility of labour.

With regard to restrictive practices, I deplore them on both sides—on both sides. There is as much Ludditism amongst employers today as there is amongst the workers. However, it is no use, I have found—in fact, it is quite infertile—to ask representatives of trade unions and representatives of employers to meet together for the purpose of considering the abolition of restrictive practices. It is far too negative a form of approach, and what I asked them to do when I last met them was to consider how they could concert together in order to reach optimum production—to take a very much more positive line in the matter; because all that happens when we start talking about restrictive practices is that old memories are revived, old fears are restored, and, before we know where we are, we are fighting traditional battles all over again; whereas if we can get people to sit down and look at the contemporary scene unhampered as far as possible by ancient quarrels and rivalries, and think only of increasing production there is a chance of getting some that way.

Let me say also under this heading that I do hope that organised labour in the country will realise the very serious times through which the country is passing. There have been a number of unofficial strikes recently, and some more are threatened. There is in this country at the moment plenty of conciliation machinery that can be used; it is ready; it is available all the time. In fact, we have a more highly organised system of industrial conciliation than any other nation in the world, and people are only inflicting unnecessary losses upon themselves in not making use of it. At the same time, I should like to say that there is a responsibility resting upon managements to try to develop good personal relations. It very often happens that some of these disputes occur because modern managements have not realised that in the absence of the whip of unemployment, common sense must be applied more frequently.

May I say in passing that it is not enough always to look for Communists under the bed. That can be an awfully lazy habit. I remember when I was connected with the coal mining industry; whenever there was an explosion there was always an inquiry, and the inquiry used to be directed wearisomely to the cause of ignition. We always used to say, "Look for the cause of the gas." There are lots of people going about trying to ignite inflammable material, but we must also ask ourselves: Why is the material so inflammable? It very often happens that many of these disputes would never occur if they had not been festered and fostered by personal relationships which could quite easily be, if I may use the term, anodyned.

I have to say something here which perhaps will not be so pleasant to some hon. Members. As hon. Members in all parts of the House know, the size of the Armed Forces fell below expectations because of the manpower position, and it has been found necessary to make a decision that the "blanket" shall be removed from agriculture. [HON. MEMBERS: "Feather bed."] I prefer to call it a blanket. I am trying to use as soft a word as possible. Deferment was granted to the agricultural industry because it was at that time an under-manned industry. That is not now the case. It is no more under-manned than other industries, and therefore it must

[Mr. Bevan.]

take its place in providing National Service men. However, farmers will have made their plans for their sowing and this year's harvest on the basis of the previous position. It is not, therefore, thought wise and prudent to start the call up until after the next harvest, which will be 1st November. In the meantime, I shall be consulting with the Minister of Agriculture and the two sides of the agricultural industry on how the call-up can be made with the least damage to agriculture.

Mr. Churchill : How many does this involve?

Mr. Bevan : It involves about 15,000 out of nearly a million, taking farm workers and farmers together. Nevertheless, there are some instances where there are remote farms, and farms with very few engaged upon them, where some hardship may occur unless machinery were provided for the purpose.

Mr. Emrys Hughes : Will the farm workers be allowed to volunteer for the mines?

Mr. Bevan : There is no Control of Engagement Order for agriculture or the mines. They can do and are doing it.

Mr. Hughes : This is a very important point in my constituency. Does it mean that these men who are called up as Z men will be allowed the alternative of going into the mines?

Mr. Bevan : We are not talking about the Z Reserve at the moment. We are talking about the National Service men.

There is also one point of considerable importance that I want to deal with. It has been mentioned in the course of the debate that a statement ought to be made concerning Yugoslavia. His Majesty's Government are alive to the potential threat to Yugoslavia from the swollen armed forces of the satellites which has been emphasised by hostile Soviet and satellite propaganda. Any threat to Yugoslavia, who played a heroic part in resistance to Hitler aggression, is naturally of concern to His Majesty's Government, and we are in touch with other Governments on this. I am sure that the House would not expect me to say more than this at the moment.

The right hon. Gentleman the Leader of the Opposition made a speech today to which, I am bound to say, I find it very difficult to reply. It is like trying to climb up a smooth, flat surface ; I can get no hold on it at any point whatsoever. He went from generalisation to generalisation with hardly a concrete noun from beginning to end. It is really quite difficult to understand what is the nature of the indictment. The right hon. and learned Gentleman who wound up the debate did not give us any more illumination. Of course, he threw a few gibes across to the Front Bench here, and said how incompetent we were. I could reply in similar terms. All that I would need to do is to quote from the right hon. Gentleman's speeches before the war about his present colleagues, and I must say that he was much more concrete then than he is now. He has lost his genius for particularity. But I am not going to do it.

The right hon. Gentleman should have seen the faces of his followers when he was speaking today. When I last had the honour of replying to the right hon. Gentleman, I described him as the decoy of the Tory Party. When I saw the faces today, I knew that he had had a transfiguration ; he is now the Jonah. They looked like a glum and apprehensive crew, seeing their ship going nearer and nearer the rocks, in charge of a captain who appeared to be witnessing the scene with increasing enthusiasm.

The charge against the Government is that they have been dilatory, inefficient and irresolute, and that they have not made proper preparation for the security of the country. I have been looking at some of the figures. In mid-1939, just a few months before the war, there were 1,300,000 unemployed in Great Britain, and there were, upon our present calculations, at least another 800,000 female workers who would have been mobilised at that time if the economy then had been managed like it is now.

So we have brought into production since then and held in production 1,800,000 people who in 1939 had not been mobilised either for the Armed Services or for the civil economy. That is the first point. I should point out the significance of this. Since the war and since 1945 we have altered the pattern of distribution so that now we have a wider technical base than ever we had before, because there are 400,000 fewer people in the distributive industries than in 1939, and nearly one million more in the engineering and manufacturing industries.

No one knows better than the right hon. Gentleman that the essential prerequisite for a modern war machine is the technical basis of civil industry. Indeed, it will be found that one of the weaknesses of the Soviet armed forces is the narrowness of their industrial base. Far too little attention is given to it. I know that the Soviet Union has accumulated since the war a very formidable striking power, but I am always encouraged by the knowledge that behind that striking power is a very narrow technical foundation. Modern war machines are only kept going by the technicians behind them. Therefore, I am not as much frightened as many people are. I do not under estimate the danger, but nevertheless when we are adding up the figures on the balance sheet let us look at the assets as well as the liabilities.

I am not frightened by the situation, because after all Russia claims—and I think she exaggerates quite considerably here—to have a production of 28 million tons of steel per year. I know she has not got that. She has not got 25 million tons yet. Modern steel power is the best possible expression of arms strength if mobilised, but it is the mobilising that is the question, because so long as steel is consumed by civil industry the technical basis for armed power is there. I do not believe that a nation, however large its manpower, coldly contemplates launching 25 million tons of steel per annum against the combination of 140 million tons per annum.

For Heaven's sake do not let us have so much bogy man talk. I am speaking about those evil people in many parts of the world who are talking as if the third world war had already begun. We deny that. The fact of the matter is that the Tory Party is as old-fashioned as the Communist Party. They are both living in a world that has gone. One has only to read the Communist thesis today to see that it has not changed in the last 100 years since Karl Marx wrote it—and I am a considerable student of Karl Marx.

The Soviet thinking has not adjusted itself to the fact that the most revolutionary power in the world is political democracy. She has not adjusted herself to the fact that progress can only be made in modern complicated industrial civilisation on the basis of peace. She still clings to the notion that war is a revolutionary opportunity, and she does so because the Soviet Union was born in war and because she knows that some nations tried to destroy her by war. Therefore she thinks in those terms. But the fact of the matter is that in the last five years not only has the Soviet Union been able to achieve a number of victories but she has also sustained a number of quite formidable defeats.

It has always been assumed that Soviet Marxism would gain its first and easiest victories in the heavily industrialised nations. That was always the assumption. It was because the theory of Marxism was born in Brussels, London, Paris, and New York and not in the agrarian areas. As a consequence of that, she expected to find easy allies. But I am convinced, as I have said before, that the only kind of political system which is consistent with a modern artisan population is political representative democracy.

As the Soviet Union pushes further West she gets more and more theoretical defeats. She has been able under the protection of the Red Army to clamp the satellite States to her breast in the last five years, but the interesting thing is to see the growing hostility to Soviet propaganda in Western Europe and its failure to establish any foothold in Great Britain and in America. This forms the background of the Defence debate, and very important conclusions follow from it, conclusions not drawn by the Opposition at all in the course of the debate.

The curious thing is that the Soviet Union has won its victories in those agrarian parts of the world where poverty is her chief ally. She has not won them, and she will not win them, in modern industrial communities. Therefore, we on this side of the House say that we must put ourselves in the position of armed preparedness, not to tempt her into seeking an easy victory, but, on the basis of that armed strength, to realise that the earliest opportunity must be taken to bring

[MR. BEVAN.]

about not appeasement but the pacification of the tensions of the world.

There is all the difference in the world in that. The right hon. Gentleman the Member for Woodford said in his speech that only one thing restrained Russia from attack—it was repeated from the Opposition Benches—and that was fear of the atom bomb. Do hon. Members really believe that? The Russians are very brave people. They are as brave as we are. All right; then would we be restrained by fear of the atom bomb?

Mr. Churchill : The Russian people will not have much to say to it. They are governed by the oligarchy of the Kremlin.

Mr. Bevan : If there is one thing of which the Russian people are aware it is the existence of the atom bomb. Therefore, if there is fear of the atom bomb, it is a mutual fear, and out of that mutual fear, mutual sense may be born. Therefore we ourselves consider—we have always considered on this side of the House—that every opportunity must be eagerly sought in order to try to bring about an alleviation of international tension. But there was little evidence of that on the opposite side of the House.

I really was shocked, because the right hon. Gentleman in the course of his speech said not only was the Soviet Union restrained by the existence of the atom bomb, but it was restrained by the formidable preparations that were being made by the United States at the present time. The shocking thing about the right hon. Gentleman is that he never gives any credit to this nation at all.

Mr. Churchill : Oh!

Mr. Bevan : Never. At least, he never has except when it is under his own leadership. The right hon. Gentleman for the last five years has been talking as if we were flat on our backs. He has been speaking of the nation as being down and out.

The fact of the matter is that in the last three to four years Great Britain has made a greater contribution to defence than any other nation in the world in proportion to her size. Take the expenditures in terms of a national income in 1949. [Hon. Members: " Oh! "] Let us have at this stage of the debate some sense of responsibility. The United Kingdom spent in 1949 7.2

per cent. of its national income on defence, Canada 2.9 per cent., Australia 6 per cent., the U.S.A. 5.9 per cent., France 4.2 per cent., New Zealand 2.2 per cent. We were spending all the time although we were building up our resources. Yes, and we have today about 730,000 people in the Defence Forces as compared with about 480,000 in May, 1939. And we have had to sustain garrisons all over the world in different parts.

The right hon. Gentleman talks about the necessity of injecting the re-armament programme with greater energy and greater drive in the economic system——

Mr. Churchill : I never used those words.

Mr. Bevan : Well, I may have given the right hon. Gentleman far better ones than he himself selected, but that, after all, was what he meant. If he means anything at all by the Amendment, that is what he means. The fact of the matter is, as everybody knows, that the extent to which stockpiling has already taken place, the extent to which the civil economy is being turned over to defence purposes in other parts of the world, is dragging prices up everywhere. Furthermore, may I remind the right hon. Gentleman that if we turn over the complicated machinery of modern industry to war preparation too quickly, or try to do it too quickly, we shall do so in a campaign of hate, in a campaign of hysteria, which may make it very difficult to control that machine when it has been created.

It is all very well to speak about these things in airy terms, but we want to do two things. We want to organise our defence programme in this country in such a fashion as will keep the love of peace as vital as ever it was before. But we have seen in other places that a campaign for increased arms production is accompanied by a campaign of intolerance and hatred and witch-hunting. Therefore, we in this country are not at all anxious to imitate what has been done in other places.

My right hon. Friend the Chancellor of the Exchequer said today that I would have to call upon the resources of a Celtic imagination to find some arguments in reply to the right hon. Gentleman. I listened to the right hon. Gentleman and I thought that he displayed a sort of Anglo-Saxon naïveté in quoting from the election programme of the Tory Party, because he has told us that that party does not take its own programme seriously. We had from him in the steel debate a description in his own inimitable language of the profundity of his own cynicism. He said:

" I do not admit as democratic constitutional doctrine that anything that is stuck into a party manifesto "—

" stuck in "—I say!

" thereupon becomes a mandated right if the electors vote for the party who draw up the manifesto. [*Interruption.*] We are all allowed to have our opinions about constitutional matters. If that principle is accepted, why not shove a dozen more items in? One can always leave them out if there is not time, or circumstances change."—[OFFICIAL REPORT, 7th February, 1951 ; Vol. 483, c. 1752.]

Really, my youthful innocence is shocked by this.

When, therefore, my right hon. Friend the Chancellor of the Exchequer called attention to the inconsistencies of the Tory Party's last election programme, it did not abash the right hon. Gentleman at all because he has first and second class items in his programme, as the Nazis had first and second class citizens in their country.

Mr. Churchill : I had nothing to do with the Nazis. Do not spoil a good speech now.

Mr. Bevan : I certainly will be the very last person to try to make any resemblance between the right hon. Gentleman and the Nazis, but he is falling into evil ways here ; because when the right hon. Gentleman goes to the country next time, what can we believe? He has already told us that he does not leave all the items in. Would he then be good enough to accent those in which he believes?

And so with the right hon. Gentleman now. The fact of the matter, we know very well, is that this Vote of Censure has not been put down for any other purpose than to hurry up and exacerbate the political situation as much as possible so that the right hon. Gentleman can get into Downing Street as early as possible if he can. It is not the war menace or the Soviet which the right hon. Gentleman fears. That is not his enemy—his enemy is time ; and when he goes there, he will leave—[*Interruption.*] Hon. and right

hon. Gentlemen opposite do not like to take it at all ; they always like to give it. The fact of the matter—and I have said so before—[*Interruption.*] It is not for the right hon. Member for Bromley (Mr. H. Macmillan) to work up that synthetic indignation. We have heard his Gladstonian asperities on too many occasions.

What the right hon. Gentleman is seeking to do at the moment and what hon. Members behind him are seeking to do is to hurry things up. I must say I can imagine no greater disservice to this country at the moment than to have the hon. Members on the other side of the House sitting on this side of the House. I believe that it is possible for us—I have always expressed some doubts about it, because I am convinced the task we are trying to do is a very heavy one—to reconcile the principles of Parliamentary democracy with these great exertions we all have to make. The right hon. Gentleman is not in tune with the times.

Mr. Godfrey Nicholson (Farnham) : He is in tune with the people.

Mr. Bevan : Hon. Members opposite thought that in 1945. They thought it last year. They will discover when they have read this debate that all the party opposite is concerned with is to exploit every international difficulty for party purposes, and they will discover I believe, as I said, that hon. Members opposite, like the Communist Party, have fallen behind the times.

It is a fact, a fact that stands out, that one of the most important contributions that have been made to the pacification of the world at the present time was the behaviour of my right hon. Friend the Prime Minister in securing the friendship of India and Pakistan, whereas the right hon. Gentleman would have still faced that situation with early 19th Century conceptions. We think that the things happening in Asia at the present time are not only the consequences of malignant plottings by the Soviet Union. Do not let us get it wrong. It is certain, of course, that the Soviet Union are doing their very best to work these things up, but the events taking place in Asia at the present time are under the influence of historical compulsions which do not have their seat in the Kremlin at all. We shall deal with them.

[MR. BEVAN.]

That is the reason we do beg that we shall not have all these jeers about the re-armament that we are putting under way. We shall carry it out; we shall fulfil our obligations to our friends and Allies, and at the same time we shall try to prevent such an exacerbation of the world atmosphere as makes it impossible for the nations to come together in peace and harmony and give mankind another breathing space.

Question put, "That the words proposed to be left out stand part of the Question."

The House divided: Ayes, 308; Noes, 287.

Division No. 37.]   AYES   [10.0 p.m.

Acland, Sir Richard
Adams, H. R.
Albu, A. H.
Allen, Arthur (Bosworth)
Allen, Scholefield (Crewe)
Anderson, Frank (Whitehaven)
Attlee, Rt. Hon. C. R.
Awbery, S. S.
Ayles, W. H.
Bacon, Miss Alice
Baird, J.
Balfour, A.
Barnes, Rt. Hon. A. J.
Bartley, P.
Bellenger, Rt Hon. F. J.
Benn, Wedgwood
Benson, G.
Beswick, F.
Bevan, Rt. Hon. A. (Ebbw Vale)
Bing, G. H. C.
Blenkinsop, A.
Blyton, W. R.
Boardman, H.
Booth, A.
Bottomley, A. G.
Bowden, H. W.
Bowles, F. G. (Nuneaton)
Braddock, Mrs. Elizabeth
Brockway, A. F.
Brook, Dryden (Halifax)
Brooks, T. J. (Normanton)
Broughton, Dr. A. D. D.
Brown, George (Belper)
Brown, Thomas (Ince)
Burke, W. A.
Burton, Miss E.
Butler, Herbert (Hackney, S.)
Callaghan, L. J.
Carmichael, J.
Castle, Mrs. B. A.
Champion, A. J.
Chetwynd, G. R.
Clunie, J.
Cocks, F. S.
Coldrick, W.
Collick, P.
Collindridge, F.
Cook, T. F.
Cooper, Geoffrey (Middlesbrough, W.)
Cooper, John (Deptford)
Corbet, Mrs. Freda (Peckham)
Cove, W. G.
Craddock, George (Bradford, S.)
Crawley, A.
Crosland, C. A. R.
Crossman, R. H. S.
Cullen, Mrs. A.
Daines, P.
Dalton, Rt. Hon. H.
Darling, George (Hillsborough)
Davies, A. Edward (Stoke, N.)
Davies, Ernest (Enfield, E.)
Davies, Harold (Leek)
Davies, Stephen (Merthyr)
de Freitas, G.
Deer, G.
Delargy, H. J.
Diamond, J.
Dodds, N. N.
Donnelly, D.

Driberg, T. E. N.
Dugdale, Rt. Hon. John (W. Bromwich)
Dye, S.
Ede, Rt. Hon. J. C.
Edelman, M.
Edwards, John (Brighouse)
Edwards, Rt. Hon. Ness (Caerphilly)
Edwards, W. J. (Stepney)
Evans, Albert (Islington, S.W.)
Evans, Edward (Lowestoft)
Evans, Stanley (Wednesbury)
Ewart, R.
Fairhurst, F.
Fernyhough, E.
Field, Capt. W. J.
Finch, H. J.
Fletcher, Eric (Islington, E.)
Follick, M.
Foot, M. M.
Forman, J. C.
Fraser, Thomas (Hamilton)
Freeman, John (Watford)
Freeman, Peter (Newport)
Gaitskell, Rt. Hon. H. T. N.
Ganley, Mrs. C. S.
George, Lady Megan Lloyd
Gibson, C. W.
Gilzean, A.
Glanville, James (Consett)
Gooch, E. G.
Granville, Edgar (Eye)
Greenwood, Anthony (Rossendale)
Greenwood, Rt. Hon. Arthur (Wakefield)
Grenfell, D. R.
Grey, C. F.
Griffiths, David (Rother Valley)
Griffiths, Rt. Hon. James (Llanelly)
Griffiths, W. D. (Exchange)
Grimond, J.
Gunter, R. J.
Haire, John E. (Wycombe)
Hale, Joseph (Rochdale)
Hale, Leslie (Oldham, W.)
Hall, John (Gateshead, W.)
Hall, Rt. Hon. Glenvil (Colne Valley)
Hamilton, W. W.
Hardman, D. R.
Hardy, E. A.
Hargreaves, A.
Harrison, J.
Hastings, S.
Hayman, F. H.
Henderson, Rt. Hon. Arthur (Tipton)
Herbison, Miss M.
Hewitson, Capt. M.
Hobson, C. R.
Holman, P.
Holmes, Horace (Hemsworth)
Houghton, D.
Hoy, J.
Hudson, James (Ealing, N.)
Hughes, Emrys (S. Ayrshire)
Hughes, Hector (Aberdeen, N.)
Hughes, Moelwyn (Islington, N.)
Hynd, H. (Accrington)
Hynd, J. B. (Attercliffe)
Irvine, A. J. (Edge Hill)
Irving, W. J. (Wood Green)
Isaacs, Rt. Hon. G. A.
Janner, B.

Jay, D. P. T.
Jeger, George (Goole)
Jeger, Dr. Santo (St. Pancras, S.)
Jenkins, R. H.
Johnson, James (Rugby)
Johnston, Douglas (Paisley)
Jones, David (Hartlepool)
Jones, Frederick Elwyn (West Ham, S.)
Jones, Jack (Rotherham)
Jones, William Elwyn (Conway)
Keenan, W.
Kenyon, C.
Key, Rt. Hon. C. W.
Kinghorn, Sqn. Ldr. E.
Kinley, J.
Kirkwood, Rt. Hon. D.
Lang, Gordon
Lee, Frederick (Newton)
Lee, Miss Jennie (Cannock)
Lever, Harold (Cheetham)
Lever, Leslie (Ardwick)
Lewis, Arthur (West Ham, N.)
Lewis, John (Bolton, W.)
Lindgren, G. S.
Logan, D. G.
Longden, Fred (Small Heath)
McAllister, G.
MacColl, J. E.
Macdonald, A. J. F. (Roxburgh)
McGhee, H. G.
McGovern, J.
McInnes, J.
Mack, J. D.
McKay, John (Wallsend)
Mackay, R. W. G. (Reading, N.)
McLeavy, F.
McNeil, Rt. Hon. H.
MacPherson, Malcolm (Stirling)
Mainwaring, W. H.
Mallalieu, E. L. (Brigg)
Mallalieu, J. P. W. (Huddersfield, E.)
Mann, Mrs. Jean
Manuel, A. C.
Marquand, Rt. Hon. H. A.
Mathers, Rt. Hon. G.
Mellish, R. J.
Messer, F.
Middleton, Mrs. L.
Mikardo, Ian
Mitchison, G. R.
Moeran, E. W.
Monslow, W.
Moody, A. S.
Morgan, Dr. H. B.
Morley, R.
Morris, Percy (Swansea, W.)
Morrison, Rt. Hon. H. (Lewisham, S.)
Mort, D. L.
Moyle, A.
Mulley, F. W.
Murray, J. D.
Nally, W.
Neal, Harold (Bolsover)
Noel-Baker, Rt. Hon. P. J.
O'Brien, T.
Oldfield, W. H.
Oliver, G. H.
Orbach, M.
Padley, W. E.

Leslie Hale tells the story of Mr Malloy during a debate on capital punishment

Joe Haines describes himself as having been born "in a Rotherhithe slum, with gas, but no electricity", but he was destined to bring influence to bear at the highest level of Government, in No 10 Downing street, as Harold Wilson's press secretary. He arrived there having been a political correspondent for several popular newspapers and subsequently became a director of what at one time had been the biggest of them all.

At Harold Wilson's side he experienced tempestuous and difficult times, but he was fortified by having had a tough upbringing, having carved out a successful career against all the odds, and by an unwavering political commitment.

He was born into a staunch Labour family. His mother was a member of the party and his aunt was a councillor. His formal education came to an abrupt halt after the outbreak of the second world war when the ARP – the air raids civil defence – commandeered the schools that the Luftwaffe's bombs had failed to demolish. He became an avid reader of anything political – including *Mein Kampf* when he was 11 – and subsequently taught himself, among other things, shorthand, which in those days was the journalist's most indispensable tool.

At the age of 14, he started work in Fleet street as a messenger for the Associated Press. Sacked for answering back, he joined the *Glasgow Herald* three months later where he became, successively, messenger, lift operator, telephone operator, advertising accounts clerk, counter staff selling newspapers, copy boy for the Commons reporters, copy taker, sub-editor, and, eventually, parliamentary correspondent.

He moved on to a Glasgow tabloid newspaper, *The Bulletin*, where, until it folded, he was the political correspondent. Next, to the Scottish *Daily Mail* from which he resigned in 1964, at odds with the paper's politics. *The Sun*, five years before it was owned by Rupert Murdoch, rose from the dying embers of the once great *Daily Herald*, and he joined it as political correspondent after the 1964 general election.

The next move was in 1969 to Downing street as deputy press secretary to the Prime Minister with the promise of the top job once he had learned the ropes and had resigned his position as a Labour councillor. The promotion came within months. He intended to stay in the post for two years, but he was there for seven.

With Harold Wilson's surprise resignation in 1976, he also left Downing street, facing a year during which he had no job but wrote his first book "The Politics of Power". Over 20 years later he wrote "Glimmers of Twilight". Between them the books provide a frank and detailed description of life and events inside No 10 during Harold Wilson's premiership and are required reading for any study of that fascinating period in British political history.

In 1977 he took on a clutch of roles at the *Daily Mirror* – first, feature writer, then chief leader writer, assistant editor, political editor and director. He retired for the first time in 1990 but was back in print four years later with the *Today* newspaper. After two years it closed and he retired to his home in Kent.

Passion, humour and an unforgettable speech

By Joe Haines

When I first went to the House of Commons Press Gallery in 1954, Winston Churchill was Prime Minister, in the late autumn of his days, but still with the grandeur of distant thunder.

On the Front Benches sat Anthony Eden, Harold Macmillan, R. A. Butler, Edward Heath, Clement Attlee, Herbert Morrison, Hugh Gaitskell, Harold Wilson and James Callaghan.

On the Back Benches were Enoch Powell, Iain Macleod, Quintin Hogg, Aneurin Bevan, Denis Healey, Roy Jenkins and many who were still to make their names.

They flourished in an Indian summer of oratory before new technology and new technocrats condemned the Chamber to a featureless winter.

Yet, for all the great speeches among the thousands I heard, one by a little known Back Bencher, Leslie Hale, a rotund solicitor from Oldham, West, still stands out. His oratorical style was Niagaran, a torrent delivered at a speed approaching 300 words a minute and rarely with the assistance of a prepared note. His pendulous lower lip would quiver, a child-like naivety would set his face aglow, and tears would moisten his eyes as he stood there, baffled by the inability of others to share the passions that aroused him.

He was the funniest politician I ever heard: when Sir Gerald Nabarro, a much moustachioed Back Bencher, interrupted him, he flashed back, without a pause, the torrent of his delivery unrelenting: "Just because the hon. Gentleman has a Jimmy Edwards moustache it doesn't make him a comedian."

During a debate on the Homicide Bill, speaking from his accustomed place below the Gangway, he questioned whether murder by bow and arrow was included in the definition of shooting liable to the death sentence. An old opponent and former Attorney General, Sir Lionel Heald, interrupted: "If I had a bow and arrow, I would shoot the hon Gentleman." "Yes," retorted Hale, "and if you did it with your usual accuracy, you'd hit the Speaker."

The speech I have chosen was during the Committee stage of that Bill, on a Conservative Back-Bench amendment designed to add poisoning to the category for which death would be the punishment. In style, delivery and content, it was unforgettable. It also had an unintended consequence. Many years later, when I was Harold Wilson's press secretary, he asked me for names who could add life to Labour's strength in the House of Lords. "Leslie Hale," I said, and so it was. As Lord Hale, he brought a much-needed merriment to the Upper House.

This is the legendary story of Michael Malloy, as told by Mr Hale, to the Commons on 23 January 1957.

Mr. Hale: I personally agree with much of what the right hon. and learned Gentleman the Member for Chertsey (Sir L. Heald) has said. He pointed out, perfectly fairly and with his usual logic, some of the difficulties produced in this kind of legislation. Certainly if one uses the word " poisoning " for the moment in the sense in which it is normally understood by average members of the public and if one thinks of arsenic or strychnine and of the pain they cause, very often resulting in an alarming and lingering and miserable death, one feels a bitterness and hostility towards such secret, calculating, rather cold criminals, and it is extremely difficult to say what argument there can be for asserting that the penalty to be applied to a young man who uses a revolver shall be greater than that applied to a criminal who uses a deadly and painful poison. But the right hon. and learned Gentleman himself will have observed already that this argument can lead us into a dilemma. It can lead us either to impose the death penalty for the use of poisoning or it can lead us to abolish it for shooting. I prefer the latter method, and I hope to give some reasons why I do so.

I had hoped to give a modest word of welcome to the Home Secretary, but now that there have been some cheers which had in them an element of the facetious, I want to congratulate the right hon. Gentleman seriously, because it is of great value to the Committee to have a man of his acknowledged ability and experience in this difficult situation. I hope that we shall be able to approach the Home Secretary and talk to him seriously about some of the real and serious problems of penal reform which remain to be dealt with. Therefore, I say to the right hon. Gentleman seriously that we are grateful to see him in his present position. Whether he is keeping the seat warm for someone else, or not, we are sure that while he occupies it we shall have reason to appreciate his ability and his sincerity at the Home Office.

The right hon. Gentleman's predecessor, for whom I had a personal regard, and of whom I do not wish my remarks to imply any criticism, used to listen to us in the course of these debates with a slight air of wonder and seemed to think that we were manufacturing all sorts of obscure possibilities and all sorts of doubtful crimes as illustrations to reinforce an argument which he seemed to regard as somewhat technical.

Consequently, I will today take a precise case in detail as exemplifying some of the doubts in my own mind about the Amendment. There is a case made famous to the reading public by the brilliant pen of Mr. Edmund Pearson, who, in American writing on criminology, ranks with our own favourite, William Roughead. He dealt, perhaps rather more cheerfully than is usual with murder cases, with the case of Mr. Mike Malloy which occurred in the Bronx in New York State in 1932.

The circumstances were as follows. It could have been called in a sense a gang murder ; perhaps more appropriately a club murder. Mr. Mike Malloy was a customer of what is, I believe, technically known there as a speakeasy, where he spent the greater part of his time, and, indeed, pursued most of his endeavours. The landlord of the speakeasy, with one or two of his friends, felt that there were opportunities for exploiting the law relating to insurance, and that insurance would provide a profitable investment provided that one eliminated the element of uncertainty which the average life insurance policy involves.

It was thought that as Mr. Malloy was rapidly drinking himself to death it could hardly be regarded as a very exceptional crime if they were to speed the parting guest. They were able to insure Mr. Malloy for 1,788 dollars. The principal members of the club were, with singular appropriateness, the owner of the speakeasy, an undertaker and a taxi driver, and the view was taken that each would be able to contribute to the enterprise his various forms of activity and knowledge which might be required or desirable to help Mr. Malloy on his way.

Mr. Malloy, beyond any doubt, was drinking himself to death. It was felt that the addition of a considerable quantity of free alcohol to his diet would bring about the desired result even if the overcrowded side-streets of New York in the early hours did not contribute somewhat fortuitously to what was hoped would happen. I pause to ask the right hon. and learned Gentleman to consider the case as far as we have got, because there are varying definitions of alcohol which come to us in our correspondence. I remember having long discussions with the Ministry of Transport which laid down that to say that "Guinness is good for you" is a perfectly proper and uncontroversial statement, but to say "It is bad for you" is political and that phrase cannot be exhibited upon the bridges or hoardings of British Railways. We are entitled to say that alcohol is good but not that it is bad, but there are people who think it is bad. Whether the administration of a constant supply of alcohol to Mr. Malloy in the form of free whisky, free brandy or other free drinks could be regarded as using a noxious thing would itself have presented a very difficult problem even to the ability of a New York jury, even if the motive were admittedly a criminal one.

However, that problem did not arise in this case because Mr. Malloy flourished on the alcohol. His cheeks grew redder. His self-confidence increased. He came along to the speakeasy every day asking for more alcohol. The club realised that Mr. Malloy was what might be called, in the language of a balance sheet, a wasting asset and that he would probably cost them more in alcohol than the insurance policy was likely to yield.

I am sorry to add, but it is very relevant to the argument, that the club decided to debase the currency of the murder and to replace the perfectly good alcohol by some very bad alcohol. They commenced to use wood alcohol, turpentine and methylated spirits in the form of a mixture, and it was felt that this might secure the desired result. The Minister will appreciate that all this might be regarded as a question of something in the imagination of the drinker and that so long as one thinks it is Romanèe Conti, or Berncasteler, or Chateau Yquem it does not much matter what it is. As the great Dr. Johnson once said, one can, but for imagination, be as happy in the arms of a chambermaid as in the arms of a duchess. But subsequent commentators have suggested that there is less formalism and, indeed, some advantages in the more plebian embraces, and the mixing of the strawberry leaf with the fig leaf involves a formality which might well be avoided.

5.45 p.m.

In fact, however, Mr. Malloy rejoiced in the alteration to his liquor. He said there was much more kick in the new

form of drink, and he spent some considerable time profiting by this while the insurance moneys, in perspective, were being diminished and the club's hopes of revenue were going down. The right hon. and learned Gentleman ought to be able to tell us whether wood alcohol is a noxious thing in that connection and whether an attempt to kill a man by a mixture of wood alcohol, turpentine and methylated spirits would fall within the purview of the provisions before us.

Sir L. Heald : Would the hon. Gentleman allow himself to be used as an experiment in that way?

Mr. Hale : If Parliamentary salaries continue at their present level, that might be something for consideration.

There was then a meeting of the club, and it was felt that more direct action was necessary. On a very cold night in January the members took Mr. Malloy out in a slightly insensible condition. The undertaker was in charge, and the taxi driver was driving. They laid him out in the cold, and covered him reverently with snow, and then they poured cold water over him in 10 degrees of frost and left the body there, confident that nature would do the rest. Their confidence was misplaced. In fact, the undertaker contracted a severe attack of tonsilitis and was ill in bed for some time. Mr. Malloy arrived for his drinks as usual and made some apparently irrelevant comment about a change in the weather.

The right hon. Gentleman will still have to consider whether in these circumstances water could be a noxious thing. With his considerable knowledge of history, he will recall that at one time water was used as a form of torture. It was certainly so used in France for a long time. It will be recalled that the innocent Jean Calas and the guilty Madame de Brinvilliers had to absorb a very large amount of water in circumstances which left them in peril. Frozen water could, in itself, be deleterious to most people except Mr. Malloy.

There is no question that now there was a certain amount of despondency in the club. So depressed were they at the time that I am sure that if the Prime Minister had come along and offered to make them all viscounts if they would give up their activities, they would have accepted, even with some pleasure.

E

[MR. HALE.]

They decided to sublet the contract, and a couple of gangsters were employed. They also tried the effect of attempting to kill somebody else with Mr. Malloy's card in his pocket. Both ventures, unhappily, failed. Finally, Mr. Malloy was taken out and laid on a kerb, and the taxi, which was ever handy, was run over him several times fracturing most of the bones in his body, and the club members returned to await the payment of the insurance money. Before the insurance money came in, Mr. Malloy came out of hospital, said that hospital was a very thirsty place, and asked what could be done about it.

At that stage—perhaps it was at a slightly earlier stage in the proceedings —someone with medical knowledge came along and made some comments about botulism, ptomaine poisoning and so on. By reference to a handy encyclopaedia one will find that if sardines are left in a tin long enough they reach the stage of becoming a noxious thing. For some time the club caused sardines to be left in the open on various window sills, and they awaited the time when they could tell from the temperature, or the odour which arose, that the sardines could be put into sandwiches for Mr. Malloy.

At the end, those lacking confidence in the expertise of their scientific advisers suggested the addition of a few tintacks and bits of broken glass. These were added and Mr. Malloy eat this for some considerable time and grew thirstier every time. He said that there was something about sardines which gave one an appetite, and when Mr. Malloy said " appetite ", he meant thirst.

That was the position when in desparation they took him upstairs, put a tube in his mouth, attached it to the gas and filled him full of gas to the extent that he went to a place from which normally no man ever returns. Nor did he, although he was brought back as a corpse for the inquest. The insurance companies having expressed some little dubiety about it, there was an inquest and then a trial in which all of these complicated questions should have been considered.

Although, let us say at once, we would all deprecate all this, nevertheless there was in the course of it something of the spirit of Samuel Smiles, something of the lessons one draws from Robert Bruce. Having put their hands to the plough, they ploughed the furrow to the end. In the end they found themselves keeping a seat warm, to use the modern terminology.

There it was. What were the noxious things? At what stage of the proceedings would they have come within the purview of the Amendment? Had Mr. Malloy's unhappy demise taken place at an earlier period, would they have come within the Amendment or not? It is absolutely impossible to incorporate in an Act of Parliament, when the matter with which we are dealing is the sentence of death, words which have so little meaning and which have so much application.

My hon. and learned Friend the Member for Northampton (Mr. Paget) made one of the most interesting, most constructive and most able speeches which I have ever heard him make. He raised some issues of importance to the Committee. He raised the issue of certainty. It is true that in criminal cases—and at some time the Committee might well consider it—we leave these questions to a jury of 12 men on the principle that the unanimity of 12 men, even when expressing only a fairly casual certainty, will be sufficiently convincing to produce the probability of certainty.

But judges still warn juries that it is very desirable that they should agree. Minorities on juries are still put under some pressure to agree with the majority. It is not unknown for juries to be sent back when they have disagreed time after time and to be told that it will cause great public inconvenience if the public is put to the expense of a second trial. Juries so rarely disagree that we are entitled to question what really does happen in a jury room and whether the unanimity is so readily arrived at as we are sometimes called upon to believe.

My hon. and learned Friend mentioned a case to which I do not intend to refer, but a whole series of cases of poisoning have become famous in the last 50 or 60 years and almost every one has raised the same problem. My hon. and learned Friend referred to the conflict of medical evidence. In every famous case there has been a great conflict of medical evidence. Those who practise in the criminal courts know perfectly well that when Sir Bernard Spilsbury went into the box, it was possible to call the Scottish forensic expert to contradict him. When the case was in Scotland, Spilsbury went north of the Border and gave evidence for the defence.

That happened not only in this country, but abroad. The most famous case is that of Madame La Farge, when Orfila, the most famous of all French poison experts, came into conflict with experts on the other side. My hon. and learned Friend referred to the practice in France of referring these matters to experts for advice, a very desirable and important practice, because in so many of these cases there is a conflict.

One does not want to quote controversial cases and I shall therefore refer to the case of Mr. Maybrick and the flypapers when so much evidence for the defence was not called, so much evidence which was available and which by some mistake or lack of care was not called in time to be put before the court. Here was a case of a man using arsenic as an aphrodisiac, a man who had been consuming arsenic for years and there was evidence that he had ordered it. The lady who bought the flypapers said she was making cosmetics. She was convicted and sentenced to death, but finally kept in prison by the Home Office on a charge on which she had never been tried. Because of doubts of her guilt on the charge on which she was tried, the Home Office intervened and said there were doubts about whether Maybrick had died of poison, but she was to be imprisoned because there was no question that she had administered poison to him.

Mr. Ede (South Shields): She was kept there by the Home Secretary and not by the Home Office. It is an important distinction.

Mr. Hale : I am very grateful and on such a matter I am perfectly certain that my right hon. Friend has attained that high degree of accuracy which we expect from him. The Home Secretary announced that there was doubt about the murder, but no doubt about the administration of poison. Presumably she was kept in prison on a charge of attempted murder on which she had never been tried.

There is the famous case of Dr. Smethurst, when one of the greatest of all the medical experts, Dr. Alfred Swaine Taylor,

author of a great book on medical jurisprudence, went into the box at the assizes and said that the arsenic which he thought he had found in the body had actually come from the materials which he had used in the test, that in precipitating the arsenic on to gauze in Marsh's test he precipitated arsenic from the materials which he himself had provided. Yet that evidence had been given on oath at the petty sessions and it is to his credit that he had the courage to come forward and make so frank and free an admission of error. Had he not done so, the situation might have been more serious, though Dr. Smethurst was still convicted.

In the area of the greatest possible uncertainty the Amendment suggests introducing provisions for imposing an irrevocable sentence. Although I said that I agreed with the right hon. and learned Member for Chertsey about shooting, the case fails if one applies to it the test of brutality.

> " Lizzie Borden took an axe,
>   And gave her mother 40 whacks,
>   And when she saw what she had done,
>   She gave her father forty-one."

She was, in fact, acquitted though criminologists have since raised doubts about the verdict of the Boston jury. If she had given them sleeping tablets when they went to bed, would that have been more serious? Would the giving of barbiturates be more criminal, a more punishable crime?

Some hon. Members have appreciated this point and have tried to put down Amendments which will cover this particular matter, which will say that mercy murders should be exempted from the more severe penalty. We will come up against another matter of great difficulty, we will meet problems which the Committee might one day find it necessary to have to face. I deplore the sentence for murder in these cases, cases where the sentence has been passed on a poor, harassed, overworked mother who has tried to put out of the way some deeply suffering, incurable, deformed child, deformed mentally or physically.

It is a rather shocking thing that we should have to go through all this panoply of threat and intimidation——

Mr. Fell *indicated dissent.*

Mr. Hale : The hon. Member shakes his head. He shakes his head at so

[MR. HALE.]

many simple propositions. How many judges have said this! Sir Henry Hawkins was regarded as a very tough judge and yet he said that he detested having to go through the wretched procedure of passing a sentence which he knew would never be imposed on some unhappy woman after she had been dragged through her misery on a charge of infanticide or mercy killing. We abolished it for infanticide.

Mr. Fell *indicated dissent.*

Mr. Hale: The hon. Member shakes his head. We abolished it for infanticide.

Mr. Fell: I shake my head only because I wonder just where we shall arrive if we start upon this expedition. It is very difficult to know at what point mercy killing is more than condoned.

6.0 p.m.

Mr. Hale: I agree; that is exactly what I am saying. All these considerations are difficult. Every definition creates difficulty. But the voice which says, " How far are you going? If you start on the right road you may reach the wrong road " is the voice of Ellenborough—of the 1830s. This was the argument put forward against every judicial reform and every measure which was intended to bring some decency into our criminal laws and some sense and responsibility into our penal system. It has always been the argument.

I suggest that the Amendment moved by the right hon. and learned Gentleman is impracticable and must be rejected. I rather gathered from what he said at the end of his speech that he himself had some doubts whether or not to press the matter to a Division. I would say that one would have to vote against the Amendment if it were pressed to a Division, because it would introduce into our system a responsibility which juries would be unable to bear; a difficulty for judges which would make trials far more complex and, as my hon. and learned Friend has said, an additional element of uncertainty in trials which already have quite sufficient of that element. In those circumstances I urge the Committee to reject the Amendment and say that it is prepared to leave this part of the Clause as it stands.

Mr. W. R. Rees-Davies (Isle of Thanet): I want to follow straight away the point which has been made by the hon. Member for Oldham, West (Mr. Hale). The Amendment standing in my name, which is also being considered now, goes a great deal further than the Amendment which has been moved, and tries to meet the point set out in the speech of the hon. Member for Oldham, West, namely, the question of mercy killing. The Amendment which I invite the Committee to consider is one which I feel will command the respect and, I hope, the support of many hon. Members. In part, it should command the support of those who are in favour of abolition and in part the support of those who favour retention.

This is designedly so, because the Bill is in the nature of a compromise. I should like to point out how the Clause will read if the Amendment is accepted. The liability for the death penalty would then be covered in the following terms:

" the following murders shall be capital murders "—

that is to say, murders in respect of which the death penalty will be retained—

(a) any murder done in the course or furtherance of theft;

(b) any murder by shooting or by causing an explosion; or by administration of poison or of any other noxious matters,"—

with this proviso:

" provided that the murder shall not be a capital murder if the jury is satisfied having regard to all the circumstances of the case that the accused committed the murder with the dominant motive and in the belief that he was acting from a sense of mercy or with intent to save the person murdered from suffering."

One can summarise the position by saying that the types of murder to which I have just referred will be capital murders only when they are deliberate and evil murders; in other cases, the proviso will apply. It will not be a capital murder

" if the jury is satisfied having regard to all the circumstances of the case that the accused committed the murder with the dominant motive and in the belief that he was acting from a sense of mercy or with intent to save the person murdered from suffering ".

The latter part of the Amendment follows largely along the lines of a new Clause which has been tabled in the names of the hon. Member for Oldham, West and others. I agree with his argument that it is not right in these days that someone who has put away a mentally

Lloyd George presents his "People's Budget" to relieve distress and wage war on poverty

Roy Hattersley was elected to Parliament in 1964 as the Labour MP for Birmingham, Sparkbrook, but his political activities had started many years before when, at the age of 13 in Sheffield, he worked in campaigns for Labour both for his local MP and for city councillors. His mother was a Sheffield city councillor and, in later years, when he was an MP, she became the Lord Mayor of Sheffield.

In 1956 he, too, was elected a Sheffield councillor, but his ambition was to get to Westminster. He stood unsuccessfully against Geoffrey Lloyd at Sutton Coldfield in the 1959 general election. Determined to secure a candidacy, he applied for 25 seats in a period of three years, eventually succeeding at Sparkbrook. When the election came, he turned a Conservative majority of 900 into a Labour win by 1,254 votes. At the next general election in 1966 he pushed his majority up to 6,398, and for the ensuing seven general elections, he held the seat comfortably for Labour.

His ministerial career began as a junior to Ray Gunter in the Department of Employment in 1966. In 1969, he was promoted to Minister of Defence, and signed the order which resulted in the deployment of troops to Northern Ireland. Denis Healey was the Secretary of State, but he was in hospital undergoing a hernia operation at the time of the crisis. He is on record as saying that Roy Hattersley "showed exceptional flair" in dealing with Northern Ireland, and he happily left him to manage the defence aspects of the Province thereafter.

Following Labour's defeat in the 1970 election, he became foreign affairs spokesman for his party. He went on to serve as Minister of State for Foreign Affairs in the Wilson Government of 1974, renegotiating British membership of the EEC, which the UK had joined in 1973. He was appointed a Privy Councillor in 1975 and joined the Cabinet in 1976 as Secretary of State for Prices and Consumer Protection, a position he held until the Labour defeat of 1979.

In opposition, he helped to found Labour Solidarity, a movement aimed at tackling the problems posed by the hard left and the defections that resulted in the creation of the SDP in 1981. He was elected deputy Labour leader in 1983 and worked with leader Neil Kinnock to make the party electable, but it was defeated again in 1992 and both men resigned from their positions. He left the Commons at the 1997 election – he received a peerage in the dissolution honours list – and went on to become a critic of new Labour in the media.

Roy Hattersley enjoys a distinguished reputation as a prolific writer and journalist, and became a fellow of the Royal Society of Literature in 2003. His work includes fiction such as "The Maker's Mark", several volumes of autobiography, and biographies of John Wesley, and of William and Catherine Booth. In 1987 he wrote "Choose Freedom: the future of Democratic Socialism". "Buster's Diaries", penned after he was fined £75 when his Staffordshire bull terrier, Buster, killed a goose in St. James's park, became a best seller. Buster now has his own website, on which he claims that while much has changed, "Those who say that I bark more because I am a bit deaf are wrong – I just have a lot to say."

He is and has been a frequent contributor to various newspapers, writing columns and features for the *Guardian*, the *Daily Mail*, *The Sunday Times*, the *Daily Express*, *The Listener*, *The Spectator* and *Punch*.

He broadcasts regularly on radio and television, having appeared in a wide range of programmes including "Have I Got News for You", "Any Questions?", "The News Quiz", "Quote Unquote", and Arts, current affairs and political programmes. He has been Granada Television's "What the Papers Say" columnist of the year.

Fortified by beef tea, the Chancellor brooks no criticism and erects a milestone in political history

BY RT HON LORD HATTERSLEY

Hilaire Belloc, then a Liberal Member of Parliament, called it the worst speech ever made in the House of Commons. Some of David Lloyd George's colleagues were more kind and described it as only the worst in living memory. It lasted for just over four and a half hours – not including a 30 minute Adjournment which Arthur Balfour, the Leader of the Opposition, suggested was necessary to protect what was left of the Chancellor of the Exchequer's voice. Lloyd George drank a cup of warm beef tea. and, thus revived, completed his Budget statement.

After 554 Divisions, the Finance Bill which followed was sent by the Commons to the Lords – thus bringing to a head the historic constitutional struggle between the two Houses. But more than the cry "Who shall rule, peers or people?" made 29 April 1909 a major milestone in British political history. After the tentative steps of the previous year, Lloyd-George was advancing into "the still unconquered territory of social reform". That is why he called his proposals "The People's Budget."

Lloyd George planned for expenditure to rise, year on year, by £16,112,000 – a vast amount by the standards of the time. Not all of it was for welfare policies. Much against his will, he had to finance an extended Dreadnought building programme and he created the "road fund" to improve the condition of Britain's highways. But as well as meeting the cost of the first full year of the national old-age pension, he needed £100,000 to pay for Winston Churchill's new labour exchanges and twice as much to invest in railway and port improvements.

He found it by increasing income tax, death and estate and stamp duties, and alcohol licences, and by introducing all the land taxes that he was able to persuade his Cabinet colleagues to support. He would have taxed development land more heavily. Some of his supporters thought that even his reduced proposals went too far.

Astonishing though it now seems, Austen Chamberlain, leading for the Opposition, replied to the Chancellor's statement with the admission that "with a good deal and with a great number of the objects which he has set before the House, I heartily agree." The bi-partisan approach did not last. Balfour described the Budget as "arbitrary and unjust" and gave the warning that all progressive Chancellors are told they must heed. "You have given a shock to confidence and credit which will take a long time to recover." The judgment turned out to be as faulty as the grammar.

Lloyd George was not in a mood to listen to such criticism. He saw his task as more than providing a balance sheet of national income and expenditure. "This... is a War Budget. It is for raising money to wage implacable warfare against poverty and squalidness. I cannot help hoping and believing that before this generation has passed away we shall have advanced a great step towards that good time when poverty and wretchedness and the human degradation which always follow in its camp, will be as remote to the people of this country as the wolves which once infested its forests."

It might have been a bad speech, but it was a splendid peroration

Mr. ASHLEY: If it has not been customary to specify the particular Powers, why was the United States specifically left out the last time?

ORDER OF BUSINESS.

Sir ALEXANDER ACLAND-HOOD: I desire to ask the Prime Minister what business he intends to take next week; secondly, with regard to his Motion for the Suspension of the Eleven o'clock Rule, and presume he does not intend to keep the House to a later hour than is necessary for getting the Resolutions; and, thirdly, I wish to ask whether we shall have a full opportunity of discussing the Budget proposals on some subsequent Resolution?

The PRIME MINISTER (Mr. Asquith): With regard to next week we propose on Monday, Tuesday and Wednesday to take the Budget Resolutions, with the suspension of the 11 o'clock Rule on these nights. On Thursday we shall take Supply. With regard to the last question put by the right hon. Gentleman it will be necessary before the House adjourns to-night to get three Resolutions. On Monday, with the assent of the Chair, in accordance with the usual practice, we suggest that the general Debate should be continued on the next Resolution.

PRESENTATION OF BILLS.

The following Bills were presented and read the first time :—

Earl of RONALDSHAY—Easter Offerings.—Bill to exempt voluntary Offerings to clergymen and ministers from taxation. (To be read a second time to-morrow.)

Viscount MORPETH—Clerks of the Peace and County Councils (No. 2).—Bill to amend the Law with regard to the appointment of Clerks of the Peace and County Councils (To be read a second time to-morrow.)

BUSINESS OF THE HOUSE (WAYS AND MEANS).

Ordered, "That the Committee of Ways and Means have precedence this day of the business of Supply."—[*The Prime Minister.*]

Ordered, "That the proceedings of the Committee of Ways and Means, if under consideration at Eleven o'clock this night, be not interrupted under the Standing Order (Sittings of the House)."—[*The Prime Minister.*]

WAYS AND MEANS.

CONSIDERED IN COMMITTEE.

[Mr. EMMOTT in the chair.]

(IN THE COMMITTEE.)

BUDGET STATEMENT.

The CHANCELLOR of the EXCHEQUER (Mr. Lloyd-George) rose, at six minutes after Three of the clock, to submit the Annual Financial Statement.

At the close of my right hon. Friend's last Budget speech the right hon. Gentleman, the Member for East Worcestershire, condoled with me upon having to follow such a master of lucid exposition. I confess that even if my task had been a comparatively easy one, I should have felt sorry for myself to have to follow such a predecessor as my right hon. Friend. But seeing that my difficulties are abnormally great and the burden which I have to carry is a very heavy one, I can only throw myself upon the kind sympathy and indulgence of the House. I have departed from precedent in one respect, which I hope will command the general assent of the House. I caused to be circulated with the Votes this morning a full statement showing the position last year, and showing what the position would be this year, assuming that taxation remained in its present form. I circulated that statement not merely because it lightened my task in delivering my speech, and lightened the task of the House in having to listen to it, but because I think it is fairer to Members.

It is exceeding difficult to follow these figures, even if you have time to go through them. They are very complicated, they are very perplexing, and they are apt to be very elusive, and therefore I thought the better plan would be to give hon. members full time to go through these figures in order thoroughly to appreciate what the position is. I have no doubt that hon. Members perhaps were slightly disappointed with the figure of the anticipated deficit, but on the whole I am sure there was a great sense of relief at the figure of the realised deficit. There is a realised deficit, as will be seen from the statement, amounting to £714,000, and the Exchequer balance, which stood on 31st March, 1908, at £8,919,000—an exceptionally large amount arising by reason of the very considerable old Sinking Fund of 1907-8—is accordingly depleted by the amount of this deficit. That is how I propose to deal with that. I do not propose to add it to the taxation of the year, but I propose to deal with it by taking it out of the Exchequer balance. I will give a full explanation later on of these arrangements. They are rather complicated, and I do not want to take up too much time. Now I come to the consideration of the anticipated deficit for the coming year.

REVENUE AND EXPENDITURE FOR 1909-10.

I now turn to a brief consideration of the Revenue and Expenditure of 1909-10, the main details of which are already in the hands of hon. Members. It will be seen that on the basis of existing taxation and of the estimates of expenditure already presented to Parliament, there is an anticipated deficit of £15,762,000. This amount is perhaps even larger than some Members may have anticipated, but this is attributable in part, at any rate, to the fact that the true revenue of this year from Customs and Excise has been largely anticipated. Towards the end of last year there were unusually heavy withdrawals of all dutiable commodities, particularly of spirits, owing to a not unnatural apprehension of increased taxes. The sum that was thus added to the revenue of last year must be taken away from the revenue for the present year and therefore has to be counted twice in the comparison. This to a great extent accounts for the very large and otherwise inexplicable drop in our estimate of the Excise of the year.

When we come to Customs, the apparent decline of one million pounds is due entirely to the same cause—the transference of £550,000 which properly belongs to the present year to the receipts of 1908-9, since the normal increase in the consumption of sugar, of tea and of tobacco will, in the opinion of my advisers, more than make up for a probable decline in the consumption of foreign liquor. I ought to observe that apart altogether from forestalments there was, I will not say an alarming, but an encouraging, diminution in the consumption of alcoholic liquors observable during last year. This was partly due to the very bad trade from which we suffered. But the figures of the last few years justify me in assuming that it was also attributable to the steady growth in the habits of sobriety amongst the masses of the people.

Although there is every prospect that before the end of this financial year there will be considerable improvement in the trade of the country—the symptoms are all distinctly favourable—still I shall have to reckon upon a continuation of that steady growth in the habits of self-restraint amongst the people in the matter of indulgence in alcoholic liquors which has been such a very marked feature of the national liquor bill during the past few years, which is so gratifying to the reformer and so discouraging to the revenue. The Committee will bear in mind that a comparatively small decrease in the consumption of a certain class of highly alcoholised liquor would account for a considerable drop in the revenue. These elements taken altogether, forestalments and increased temperance—account for the considerable diminution which I anticipate in this branch of the revenue for the coming year, and which adds greatly to my difficulties.

Before I leave this brief and cursory examination of the revenue side of my balance sheet I should like specially to call the attention of the Committee to the wonderful steadiness in the yield of the income tax. In spite of one of the worst years of bad trade which this country has experienced for many a year, the income tax has surpassed every prediction and realised nearly a million pounds in excess of the Budget Estimate. No tax could possibly be put to a more severe test, no tax could possibly rise from it more triumphantly than the income tax has during the past year. Whatever else may be said about our fiscal system, there is this to be said for it, that it stands the strain much better than any other system in time of trade depression as far as producing revenue is concerned. So much for the revenue side.

EXPENDITURE.

Now I come to the expenditure side of my balance sheet, and it is to this, after all, that must mainly be ascribed the exceptionally heavy deficit. Were I dealing with a shortage due only to a temporary cause like forestalments I might have resorted to some temporary shift which would have carried me over until next year, when the revenue would resume its normal course. But, unfortunately, I have to reckon not merely with an enormous increase in expenditure this year, but an inevitable expansion of some of the heaviest items in the course of the coming years. To what is the increase of

[Mr. Lloyd-George.]

expenditure due? It is very well known that it must be placed to the credit of two items and practically two items alone. One is the Navy and the other is Old Age Pensions. Now, I have one observation which I think I am entitled to make about both, and I think that now I am about to propose heavy increased taxation it is an observation that I am entitled to make on behalf of the Government. The increased expenditure under both these heads was substantially incurred with the unanimous assent of all political parties in this House. There was, it is true, a protest entered on behalf of hon. Members below the Gangway against increased expenditure in the Navy, but as far as the overwhelming majority of Members in this House are concerned the increase has received their sanction and approval. I am entitled to say more. The attitude of the Government towards these two branches of increased expenditure has not been one of rushing a reluctant House of Commons into expense which it disliked, but rather of resisting persistent appeals coming from all quarters of the House for still further increases under both heads.

As to the Navy, we are now in the throes of a great agitation to double and even treble the cost of our Construction Vote this year; and as to old age pensions, the responsibility was cast upon me of piloting that Bill through the Committee, and the one difficulty I experienced was to persuade the House of Commons not to press Amendments which would enormously augment the very heavy bill we were incurring under the original proposals. I had constantly to appeal to the party loyalty of the supporters of the Government to resist Amendments which commended themselves to hon. Members, and which we ourselves should like to have seen carried, in order to confine within something like reasonable limits the Bill which we were encouraged to pass. And these were not Amendments moved by small sections of the House; on the contrary, they were moved from all quarters and almost invariably received the official sanction and support of the Opposition. I say that in order to show that, in the main, the two great items of expenditure which are responsible for this deficit are items which a vast majority of the Members of the House of Commons have not merely sanctioned, but in regard to which they brought a con-

siderable amount of pressure to bear upon the Government to increase.

I made a calculation the other day as to what these Amendments would have cost us in the aggregate if we had assented to them, and I am sure the Committee will be surprised to find that Amendments which received the support of the official Leaders of the Opposition, if they had been carried, would have left me to-day to find not £9,000,000, but £14,000,000. The Amendments received the official sanction of the Leaders of the Opposition. I am not complaining of that. On the contrary, I think that many were Amendments which represented the extensions of the principle which I think are inevitable, but for the time being our attitude was to restrict expenditure rather than extend it. There were a few hon. Members who opposed the Bill altogether. There was my hon. Friend the Member for Preston and the hon. Baronet for the City. They represented a very small party, although no doubt a very intelligent party. I am not mentioning these matters by way of reproach to any section, nor with any desire to divest the Government of any share of its responsibility, but merely in order to show that the deficit in respect of which I have to suggest such heavy imposts to-day is not, as has been hinted in many quarters, one which the Government has landed the country in by wild and extravagant socialistic proposals, but rather an expenditure in which the Government represented the minimum demands and in which its proposals were more moderate from the point of view of expenditure than those which emanated from any other section of the House.

Before I dismiss this question of the expenditure for this year, I think I am entitled to answer a criticism from another quarter. We are told that we ought not to have touched old age pensions—at least, not at the present moment, when heavy liabilities were in sight in connection with the defence of the country. I may point out that when we introduced our Old Age Pensions Bill the emergency had not arisen. But, apart altogether from that, we had no honourable alternative left. We simply honoured a cheque drawn years ago in favour of the aged poor, which bore at its foot the signature of all the leaders of political parties in this country. They had all promised pensions at election after election, and great political parties have no right to make promises to poor people in return for political support, which is all these people had to give, and then—time after time—return the bill with "No assets" written across it. It was time this measure should be carried for the fair fame of British politicians as a whole. I am glad we have done it. I am not here on behalf of the Government to apologise for having done it. On the contrary, I think all political parties ought to be pleased that this thrice defaulted obligation has at last been discharged.

FINANCIAL OUTLOOK.

Before I come to explain the proposals which I shall submit to the Committee for the liquidation of this deficit I must invite hon. Members to join me in taking a wider survey of our financial responsibilities at this moment. It must be patent to everyone cognisant of the facts that fresh liabilities must be incurred next year in connection with the Navy and with social reform. These are commitments to which we are pledged, and from which no Government can honourably escape, and if I were to ignore these liabilities altogether in arranging my finance for this year I might, it is true, lighten my burden very considerably, but I should be guilty of an unbusinesslike short-sightedness which would be highly culpable.

I cannot conceive anything which would be more disturbing to trade than the uncertainty which must ensue if it were thought that in addition to the taxes for the year new and unknown taxes were looming in the near future. It is far better, as well as bolder, therefore, that we should frankly examine the financial outlook and make provision not merely for the ascertained needs of the year, but for the further and increased liabilities which are not merely in sight, but to which the Government and Parliament are definitely and irrevocably committed. Prudence seems to me to dictate such a policy, and although it may seem as if we were needlessly anticipating troubles of the morrow, still those troubles are inevitable, and it is therefore better to provide against them without delay. This is the course which would be adopted in any commercial undertaking conducted on ordinary business lines. Whenever an exceptional effort has to be made to raise money for the discharge of liabilities already incurred stock is generally taken of all further liabilities which must necessarily be incurred in the immediate future, and the financial provision made generally covers both present and future indebtedness. That is the course I propose to

follow in the financial operations which I shall submit to the judgment of the Committee.

NAVAL PROBLEM.

Let us, therefore, examine our commitments. First of all comes the Navy. Up to the present we have been considering the Naval problem from the point of view of merely spending money.

An HON. MEMBER on the Opposition side: Speak up.

Mr. LLOYD-GEORGE: I hope hon. Gentlemen will extend to me their indulgence. I am afraid that I shall have to try their patience by speaking at considerable length, and I do not want to strain my voice. I will do my very best. I shall now have to invite hon. Members and the country to consider the Naval problem from the equally essential but less agreeable standpoint of paying. Spending is pleasant, paying is irksome; spending is noble, paying is sordid. And it is on me falls the labour of making the arrangements for the less attractive part of the Naval programme. Let us see what it means. The building of two "Dreadnoughts" represents nearly a penny a year on the income tax during the two years of construction. The construction of four "Dreadnoughts" therefore, represents nearly 2d., and of eight "Dreadnoghts" nearly 4d., added on to the income tax. It is my business as Finance Minister to consider all these programmes which add to the expenditure of the country in the terms of new taxes. In estimating what the Naval programme is likely to cost the Chancellor of the Exchequer next year I must, of course, premise that it is quite impossible with even approximate accuracy to forecast twelve months' ahead what the expenditure in any Department of the Government is likely to be, at least so I am assured.

But there are one or two facts which lead to the inevitable conclusion that we must look forward to a considerable increase in our Naval expenditure next year. Let us, first of all, examine the prospect, if the programme this year is confined to four "Dreadnoughts." Then I will examine what it will mean if we have eight "Dreadnoughts." The Vote taken this year in respect of building these four "Dreadnoughts" will cover building operations in the case of two "Dreadnoughts" for nine months, in the case of the second instalment for only six months, and the first few months' ex-

[Mr. Lloyd-George.]

pense upon these huge machines is, I am told, the least burdensome. But next year the Treasury will have to find money for paying the whole cost of construction of four "Dreadnoughts" during an unbroken period of 12 months. This, in addition to an eleven months' building on the two "Dreadnoughts" which were laid down some time ago, will bring up the Estimates of the year for Naval construction to a figure which is considerably above even the increased estimate of this year. But if, in addition to these four "Dreadnoughts," we are to have a 12 months' expenditure upon still four more, the Naval bill for the year will attain very serious and grave dimensions indeed, at which the taxpayer may well shudder. It is quite impossible to say in advance what the Naval Estimates will be next year, because there are other items in those estimates, but on construction alone the increase will be something gigantic. I am not putting these considerations forward in any sense as reasons why we should not incur this expenditure. Whatever be the cost, no great country can afford to shirk its responsibilities for the defence of its coasts against every possible invader, and I am not dwelling on the magnitude of the burden which is cast upon us in order to suggest that we should in the slightest degree lighten the load by evading any part of our obligations. I have simply invited the Committee to consider the prospect in front of them, not with a view to urging them to run away from the imperative duty which is thrust upon them of providing for the defence of the country, but rather in order that they might follow me in facing that prospect, and make beforehand all the provision which wise and resolute forethought shall deem adequate for the occasion. We all value too highly the immunity which this country has so long enjoyed from the horrors of an invaded land to endanger it for lack of timely prevision. That immunity at its very lowest has been for generations, and still is, a great national asset. It has undoubtedly given us the tranquillity and the security which has enabled us to build up our great national wealth. It is an essential part of that wealth. At the highest it means an inviolable guarantee for our national freedom and independence. Nay, more. Many a time in comparatively recent history it has been the citadel and the sole guarantee which has saved the menaced liberties of Europe from an impending doom. I can

assure hon. Members if they still have any suspicion lurking in their minds that any Member of this Government or of this party proposes in any ill-judged fit of parsimony to risk even for an hour so precious a national treasure they can dismiss those unworthy suspicions entirely from their minds. Such a stupendous act of folly would, in the present temper of nations, not be Liberalism, but lunacy. We do not intend to put in jeopardy the naval supremacy which is so essential not only to our national existence, but, in our judgment, to the vital interests of Western civilisation.

"DREADNOUGHT" BUILDING.

But, in my judgment, it would also be an act of criminal insanity to throw away £8,000,000 of money which is so much needed for other purposes on building gigantic flotillas to encounter mythical Armadas. That is why we propose only to incur this enormous expenditure when the need for it arises. We must ensure the complete security of our shores against all real dangers, but, rich nation as we are, we cannot afford to build navies against nightmares. It is much too expensive an operation. To throw away millions of money when there is no real need for it purely to appease an unreasoning panic would be to squander resources essential to our safety in time of real danger, and it is the business of a Government to follow with calmness, as well as with courage, the medium path between panic and parsimony, which is the only safe road to national security. However, as it may be necessary to make arrangements for laying down all the eight "Dreadnoughts" on 1st April, 1910, so as to complete them by April, 1912, the financial proposals which I shall submit to the Committee will be of such a character that we can pay for them without resorting either to additional taxation or to the vicious expedient of a loan. Should it on the other hand be discovered that our fears are groundless, and this precipitate "Dreadnought" building is unnecessary, then the money will find its uses either in further endowment of our social programme for the benefit of the masses of the people or in giving the much-promised relief to the local ratepayer. He is entitled to consideration in respect of the increased expenditure imposed upon him both by the late Government and by the present Government, more especially in educational matters. He has also been very hard pressed owing to the increased costliness of maintaining the roads, attributable to the development in mechanical traction. I am not sure that it is altogether a fiscal question. It has almost become a great social question, for the municipalities are at the end of their resources, and their work is almost at a standstill in many of these areas because they cannot afford to spend what is absolutely necessary on their development. The local ratepayer has been promised consideration by successive Governments, and he is surely entitled to get it. I think I can safely say more; the financial proposals which I shall lay before the House will enable me to make good that promise.

URGENT SOCIAL PROBLEMS.

Now I come to the consideration of the social problems which are urgently pressing for solution—problems affecting the lives of the people. The solution of all these questions involves finance. What the Government have to ask themselves is this: Can the whole subject of further social reform be postponed until the increasing demands made upon the National Exchequer by the growth of armaments has ceased? Not merely *can* it be postponed, but ought it to be postponed? Is there the slightest hope that if we deferred consideration of the matter, we are likely within a generation to find any more favourable moment for attending to it? And we have to ask ourselves this further question: If we put off dealing with these social sores, are the evils which arise from them not likely to grow and to fester, until finally the loss which the country sustains will not be infinitely greater than anything it would have to bear in paying the cost of an immediate remedy? There are hundreds of thousands of men, women, and children in this country now enduring hardships for which the sternest judge would not hold them responsible; hardships entirely due to circumstances over which they have not the slightest command; the fluctuations and changes of trade—even of fashions; ill-health and the premature breakdown or death of the breadwinner. Owing to events of this kind, all of them beyond human control—at least beyond the control of the victims—thousands, and I am not sure I should be wrong if I said millions, are precipitated into a condition of acute distress and poverty. How many people there are of this kind in this wealthy land the figures of old age pensions have thrown a very unpleasant light upon. Is it fair, is it just, is it humane, is it

honourable, is it safe to subject such a multitude of our poor fellow-countrymen and countrywomen to continued endurance of these miseries until nations have learnt enough wisdom not to squander their resources on these huge machines for the destruction of human life? I have no doubt as to the answer which will be given to that question by a nation as rich in humanity as it is in store. Last year, whilst we were discussing the Old Age Pensions Bill, all parties in this House recognised fully and freely that once we had started on these lines the case for extension was irresistible. The Leader of the Opposition, in what I venture to regard as the most notable speeches he has probably delivered in this Parliament — I refer to his speech on the third reading of the Old Age Pensions Bill and the speech he delivered the other day on the question of unemployment—recognised quite boldly that whichever party was in power provision would have to be made in some shape or other for those who are out of work through no fault of their own and those who are incapacitated for work owing to physical causes for which they are not responsible. And there was at least one extension of the Old Age Pensions Act which received the unanimous assent of the House and which the Government were pressed to give, not merely a Parliamentary but a Statutory pledge to execute. I refer to the proposal to extend the pension to the meritorious pauper.

REMOVAL OF PAUPER DISQUALIFICATION FROM OLD AGE PENSIONS.

During the discussion on the Old Age Pensions Bill in the House of Commons, several Amendments were moved with a view to extending the benefits of the Act to the septuagenarian pauper, and I think it was generally felt in all quarters of the House that it was rather hard upon those who had managed up to a ripe old age by a life of hard work to keep off the poor law, and who only finally resorted to parochial relief when their physical powers utterly failed them, it was rather hard they should be still kept to their miserable and pauper-tainted allowance of 2s. 6d. a week, while their more fortunate, but not more deserving, neighbours were in receipt of an honourable State pension of 5s. a week, and often of 10s. a week. That cannot possibly stand. It was condemned by all, and could only be defended by the Government on the ground of stern financial necessity. With

Q

[Mr. Lloyd-George.]

the unanimous assent of the House of Commons a purely provisional character was given to the pauper disqualification, and unless something is done, it automatically comes to an end on the 1st January, 1911, and all these poor old people, numbering between 200,000 and 300,000, will become chargeable to the Pension Fund. I cannot recommend Parliament to undertake the whole financial burden of putting such a transaction through. It would put too heavy a charge upon the Exchequer, and there is no reason why it should fall entirely upon Imperial funds. At the present moment these paupers cost something like £2,000,000 to the local rates of the country. If we received a contribution from local funds which would be substantially equivalent to the relief which would be afforded by withdrawing such a large number of paupers from the rates, then something can be done to remove this crying hardship. My right hon. Friend the President of the Local Government Board and I have entered into negotiations with some representatives of local authorities with a view to effecting an arrangement on this basis, and although we have not yet arrived at any decision as to the amount of the national contribution, we are very hopeful of being able to enter into a bargain which will be satisfactory to all parties concerned. I do not think it would be desirable for me at this stage to give any figures—otherwise it might embarrass us in the negotiations—but it is my intention in the financial proposals which I shall submit to the House, I am afraid not this year, but probably next year, to make provision which will enable us with the assistance of the local authorities to raise over 200,000 old people from the slough of pauperism to the dignity and the comparative comfort of State pensioners. That is a contingent liability which I am bound to take full note of in arranging for my finance, because it is perfectly clear we cannot impose taxation this year and next year impose new taxation for proposals of which at the present moment we have full cognisance.

But still, all those who have given any thought and study to this question must realise that the inclusion of the septuagenarian pauper is but a very small part of the problem which awaits solution — a problem of human suffering which does not become any easier of solution by postponement. On the contrary, the longer we defer the task of grappling with it the more tangled and the more desperate it becomes. We are pledged, definitely pledged, by speeches from the Prime Minister given both in the House and outside, to supplementing our old age pensions proposals. How is that to be done? It has been suggested that we should reduce the age limit. I am emphatically of opinion that that is the most improvident and ineffective method of approaching the question, and that it would be the line upon which advance would be slowest and most difficult, and which would achieve the least hopeful results. For the moment it is financially impracticable.

REDUCTION OF AGE LIMIT IMPOSSIBLE.

A reduction of the age limit to 65 would cost an additional 15 or 20 millions a year to the Exchequer. I will not say that is beyond the resources of a rich country like this, but it is much the most wasteful way of dealing with the question, for whilst it would afford relief to many thousands and hundreds of thousands probably who neither need nor desire it, and whose strength is probably more happily and profitably employed in labour, it would leave out of account altogether far and away the most distressing and the most deserving cases of poverty. What are the dominating causes of poverty amongst the industrial classes? For the moment I do not refer to the poverty which is brought about by a man's own fault. I am only alluding to causes over which he has no control. Old age, premature breakdown in health and strength, the death of the breadwinner, and unemployment due either to the decay of industries and seasonable demands, or the fluctuations or depressions in trade. The distress caused by any or either of these causes is much more deserving of immediate attention than the case of a healthy and vigorous man of 65 years of age, who is able to pursue his daily avocation, and to earn without undue strain an income which is quite considerable enough to provide him and his wife with a comfortable subsistence. When Bismarck was strengthening the foundations of the new German Empire one of the very first tasks he undertook was the organisation of a scheme which insured the German workmen and their families against the worst evils which ensue from these common accidents of life. And a superb scheme it is.

It has saved an incalculable amount of human misery to hundreds of thousands and possibly millions of people who never deserved it.

INSURANCE AGAINST INVALIDITY, ETC., IN GERMANY.

Wherever I went in Germany, north or south, and whomever I met, whether it was an employer or a workman, a Conservative or a Liberal, a Socialist or a Trade Union Leader—men of all ranks, sections and creeds of one accord joined in lauding the benefits which have been conferred upon Germany by this beneficent policy. Several wanted extensions, but there was not one who wanted to go back. The employers admitted that at first they did not quite like the new burdens it cast upon them, but they now fully realised the advantages which even they derived from the expenditure, for it had raised the standard of the workman throughout Germany. By removing that element of anxiety and worry from their lives it had improved their efficiency. Benefits which in the aggregate amounted to 40 millions a year were being distributed under this plan. When I was there the Government were contemplating an enlargement of its operation which would extend its benefits to clerks and to the widows and orphans of the industrial population. They anticipated that when complete the total cost of the scheme would be 53 millions a year. Out of the 40 millions the Government contributes something under three millions a year. Out of the 53 millions they were looking forward to having to find five millions. I know it is always suggested that any approval of the German scheme necessarily involves a condemnation of the Act of last year. That is not so. The Act of last year constitutes the necessary basis upon which to found any scheme based on German lines. It would be quite impossible to work any measure which would involve a contribution from men who are either already 70 years of age or approaching the confines of that age as a condition precedent to their receiving any benefits. It was therefore essential that people who had attained this great age should be placed in a totally different category. But that is not a reason why the young and vigorous who are in full employment should not be called upon to contribute towards some proposals for making provision for those accidents to which we are all liable, and always liable.

At the present moment there is a network of powerful organisations in this country, most of them managed with infinite skill and capacity, which have succeeded in inducing millions of workmen in this country to make something like systematic provision for the troubles of life. But in spite of all the ability which has been expended upon them, in spite of the confidence they generally and deservedly inspire, unfortunately there is a margin of people in this country amounting in the aggregate to several millions who either cannot be persuaded or perhaps cannot afford to bear the expense of the systematic contributions which alone make membership effective in these great institutions. And the experience of this and of every other country is that no plan or variety of plans short of an universal compulsory system can ever hope to succeed in adequately coping with the problem. In this country we have trusted until recently to voluntary effort, but we found that for old age and accidents it was insufficient. In Belgium they have resorted to the plan of granting heavy subsidies to voluntary organisations, and they have met with a certain amount of success. But whether here or in Belgium, or in any other land, success must be partial where reliance is absolutely placed upon the readiness of men and women to look ahead in the days of abounding health and strength and buoyancy of spirit to misfortunes which are not even in sight, and which may be ever averted.

The Government are now giving careful consideration to the best methods for making such a provision. We are investigating closely the plans adopted by foreign countries, and I hope to circulate Papers on the point very soon. We have put ourselves into communication with the leaders of some of the principal friendly societies in the country with a view to seeking their invaluable counsel and direction. We could not possibly get safer or more experienced advisers. We are giving special attention to the important reports of the Poor Law Commission, both Majority and Minority, which advise that the leading principle of poor law legislation in future should be the drawing of a clear and definite line between those whose poverty is the result of their own misdeeds and those who have been brought to want through misfortune. All I am in a position now to say is that, at any rate, in any scheme which we may finally adopt we shall be guided by these leading principles or considerations. The first is that no plan can hope to be really comprehensive or conclusive which does

Q 2

[Mr. Lloyd-George.]

not include an element of compulsion. The second is that for financial as well as for other reasons, which I do not wish to enter into now, success is unattainable in the near future, except on the basis of a direct contribution from the classes more immediately concerned. The third is that there must be a State contribution substantial enough to enable those whose means are too limited and precarious to sustain adequate premiums to overcome that difficulty without throwing undue risks on other contributors. The fourth, and by no means the least important, is that in this country, where benefit and provident societies represent such a triumph of organisation of patience and self-government, as probably no other country has ever witnessed, no scheme would be profitable, no scheme would be tolerable, which would do the least damage to those highly beneficent organisations. On the contrary, it must be the aim of every well-considered plan to encourage, and, if practicable, as I believe it is, to work through them. That is all I propose to say on that particular subject at this juncture. I have gone into it at this length merely to indicate that here also is a source of contingent liability which I am bound to take into account in my financial scheme. In this country we have already provided for the aged over 70. We have made pretty complete provision for accidents. All we have now left to do in order to put ourselves on a level with Germany—I hope our competition with Germany will not be in armaments alone—is to make some further provision for the sick, for the invalided, for widows and orphans. In a well-thought out scheme, involving contributions from the classes directly concerned, the proportion borne by the State need not, in my judgment, be a very heavy one, and is well within the compass of our financial capacity without undue strain upon the resources of the country.

PROBLEM OF UNEMPLOYMENT.

The Government are also pledged to deal on a comprehensive scale with the problem of unemployment. The pledges given by the Prime Minister on behalf of the Government are specific and repeated. I do not wish to encourage any false hopes. Nothing that a Government can do, at any rate with the present organisation of society, can prevent the fluctuations and the changes in trade and industry which produce unemployment. A trade decays, and the men who are engaged in it are thrown

out of work. We have had an illustration within the last few days, to which Lord Rosebery has so opportunely called our attention, in the privation suffered by the horse cabdriver owing to the substitution of mechanical for horse traction. That is only one case out of many constantly happening in every country. Then there are the fluctuations of business which at one moment fill a workshop with orders which even overtime cannot cope with, and at another moment leave the same workshops with rusting machinery for lack of something to do. Trade has its currents, and its tides, and its storms and its calms like the sea, which seem to be almost just as little under human control, or, at any rate, just as little under the control of the victims of these changes, and to say that you can establish by any system an absolute equilibrium in the trade and concerns of the country is to make a promise which no man of intelligence would ever undertake to honour. You might as well promise to flatten out the Atlantic Ocean. But still, it is poor seamanship that puts out to sea without recognising its restlessness, and the changefulness of the weather, and the perils and suffering thus produced. These perils of trade depression come at regular intervals, and every time they arrive they bring with them an enormous amount of distress. It is the business of statesmanship to recognise that fact, and to address itself with courage and resolution to provide against it.

INSURANCE AGAINST UNEMPLOYMENT.

Now, I have a word to say about the proposals of the Government to meet this state of things. The Poor Law Commission has recently called attention to the importance of endeavouring to devise some effective scheme of insurance against unemployment. The question is one which bristles with difficulties, and the Commission put forward no definite scheme of their own, but they expressly approved the principle, and recommended that immediate steps should be taken to devise a workable scheme. My right hon. Friend the President of the Board of Trade has anticipated this recommendation, and the Board of Trade have been closely engaged for the last six months in endeavouring to frame and develop a scheme which, while encouraging the voluntary efforts now being made by trade unions to provide unemployment benefit for their members, will extend the advantage of insurance to a very much larger circle of workmen, including unskilled labourers. I do not now speak of the unemployment due to infirmity or personal failings or of unemployment due to labour disputes, but to that unemployment, by far the larger part of the evil, which occurs as a regular feature, varying with seasons and cycles, in important groups of trades; which renders the position of the worker in such trades unusually precarious; and which can only be dealt with, and ought clearly to be dealt with, by a process of spreading wages and of averaging risks and fluctuations. I do not propose to enter into the details of the Board of Trade scheme, which is, however, far advanced, and for which the national system of labour exchanges promised in the King's Speech will afford the necessary machinery. We recognise in this matter that we must walk with caution, and that it will be best to begin with certain groups of trades peculiarly liable to the fluctuations I have referred to, and in other respects suitable for insurance rather than to attempt to cover the entire area of industry. The Royal Commission were emphatic in recommending that any scheme of unemployment insurance should have a trade basis, and we propose to adopt this principle. Within the selected trades, however, the scheme will apply universally to all adult workers. Any insurance scheme of this kind must necessarily require contributions from those engaged in the insured trades, both as employers and employed; but we recognise the necessity of meeting these contributions by a State grant and guarantee. We cannot, of course, attempt to pass the necessary Bill to establish unemployment insurance during the present Session. But the postponement will not involve any real delay, for the establishment of labour exchanges is a necessary preliminary to the work of insurance, and this will occupy time which may also be advantageously employed in consulting the various interests upon the details of the scheme and in co-ordinating its financial provisions with the machinery of invalidity and other forms of insurance.

DEVELOPMENT SCHEME.

So much for the provision which we hope to be able to make for those who, under the changing conditions which are inevitable in trade and commerce, are temporarily thrown out of employment. We do not put this forward as a complete or an adequate remedy for all the evils of unemployment, and we do not contend that when this insurance scheme has been set up and financed that the State has thereby done all in its power to help towards solving the problem. After all, it is infinitely better, in the interests both of the community and of the unemployed themselves, that the latter should be engaged on remunerative work, than that they should be drawing an allowance from the most skilfully-contrived system of insurance. This country is small—I suppose it is the smallest great country in the world—but we have by no means exhausted its possibilities for healthy and productive employment. It is no part of the function of a Government to create work; but it is an essential part of its business to see that the people are equipped to make the best of their own country, are permitted to make the best of their own country, and, if necessary, are helped to make the best of their own country. [Cheers.] I am glad that that statement has been received with such general assent. A State can and ought to take a longer view and a wider view of its investments than individuals. The resettlement of deserted and impoverished parts of its own territories may not bring to its coffers a direct return which would reimburse it fully for its expenditure; but the indirect enrichment of its resources more than compensates it for any apparent and immediate loss. The individual can rarely afford to wait, a State can; the individual must judge of the success of his enterprise by the testimony given for it by his bank book; a State keeps many ledgers, not all in ink, and when we wish to judge of the advantage derived by a country from a costly experiment we must examine all those books before we venture to pronounce judgment.

Any man who has crossed and recrossed this country from north to south and east to west must have been perplexed at finding that there was so much waste and wilderness possible in such a crowded little island. There are millions of acres in this country which are more stripped and sterile than they were, and providing a living for fewer people than they did even a thousand years ago—acres which abroad would either be clad in profitable trees or be brought even to a higher state of cultivation. We want to do more in the way of developing the resources of our own country. [Cheers.] Hon. Members opposite cheer, and I am sure they will help me to find the money. There is much to be done for the re-settlement of neglected and forgotten areas in Britain. We have been spending for the last two or

[Mr. Lloyd-George.]

three years £200,000 to £300,000 a year upon work which I would not like to discourage. I have no doubt that it has relieved a great deal of distress, and that it is the best thing that could be done as a temporary shift and expedient, and all thanks and gratitude are due to the people who have devoted their time, leisure, and labour in expending the money in the most profitable way possible, but still it is a wasteful expenditure. Sometimes I have no doubt some good is done, but it is wasteful whenever you create work for the sake of creating it. We think that the money could be spent much more usefully and profitably, and with better direction, so long as we take a wider view of our responsibility in this matter.

AFFORESTATION.

This brings me straight to the question of afforestation. There is a very general agreement that some steps should be taken in the direction, I will not say of afforesting, but of reafforesting the waste lands of this country. Here, again, we are far behind every other civilised country in the world. I have figures here on this point which are very interesting. In Germany, for instance, out of a total area of 133,000,000 acres, 34,000,000, or nearly 26 per cent., are wooded; in France, out of 130,000,000 acres, 17 per cent.; even in a small and densely populated country such as Belgium 1,260,000 acres are wooded, or 17 per cent., out of a total area of 7,280,000 acres. Again, in the Netherlands and Denmark, out of total areas of 8 and 9½ million acres respectively, over 600,000 acres, or between 7 and 8 per cent., are wooded. In the United Kingdom, on the other hand, out of 77,000,000 acres, only 3,000,000, or 4 per cent., are under wood.

Sir Herbert Maxwell, who has made a study of this question for a good many years, and whose moderation of statement is beyond challenge, estimates that, in 1906, "eight millions were paid annually in salaries for the administration, formation and preservation of German Forests, representing the maintenance of about 200,000 families, or about one million souls," and that, "in working up the raw material yielded by the forests, wages were earned annually to the amount of 30 millions sterling, maintaining about 600,000 families, or three million souls."

Anyone who will take the trouble to search out the Census Returns will find out that the number of people directly employed in forest work in this country is only 16,000. And yet the soil and the climate of this country are just as well adapted for the growth of marketable trees as that of the States of Germany. I am disposed to agree with those who contend that afforestation is not particularly well adapted to the provision of employment on any large scale for the kind of labourer who is thrown out of work by the fluctuations of trade in the towns, and that its real utility will be rather found (to use the phrase of the hon. Member for Merthyr) "in the extension of the area of employment." It will be serviceable in providing employment in the rural districts during that inclement season of the year when work is least abundant. It would also afford an excellent adjunct to a system of small holdings and allotments.

Recently we have been favoured with a striking Report of a Royal Commission very ably presided over by my hon. Friend the Member for Cardiff. A perusal of the names attached to that Report will secure for it respectful and favourable consideration. It outlines a very comprehensive and far-reaching scheme for planting the wastes of this country. The systematic operation which the Commission recommend is a gigantic one, and, before the Government can commit themselves to it in all its details, it will require very careful consideration by a body of experts skilled in forestry. I am informed by men whom I have consulted, and whose opinion on this subject I highly value, that there is a good deal of preliminary work which ought to be undertaken in this country before the Government could safely begin planting on the large scale indicated in that Report I am told that experiments ought to be made, so as to test thoroughly the varying conditions of climate and soil and the best kind of trees and methods of planting to meet those variations. I am also told that we cannot command the services in this country of a sufficient number of skilled foresters to direct planting. I am advised, and, personally, I am disposed to accept that counsel as the advice of prudence, that the greater haste in this matter will mean the less speed, and that to rush into planting on a huge scale, without first of all making the necessary experiments, organising a trained body of foresters, and taking all other essential steps to secure success when you advance, would be to court disaster, which might discourage all future attempts.

ENCOURAGEMENT OF AGRICULTURE.

I will tell the Committee how I propose that this subject should be dealt with ; but, before I do so, I have something more to say about proposals for aiding in the development of the resources of our own country. The State can help by instruction, by experiment, by organisation, by direction, and even, in certain cases which are outside the legitimate sphere of individual enterprise, by incurring direct responsibility. I doubt whether there is a great industrial country in the world which spends less money on work directly connected with the development of its resources than we do. Take, if you like, and purely as an illustration, one industry alone—agriculture—of all industries the most important for the permanent well-being of any land. Examine the Budgets of foreign countries—we have the advantage in other directions—but examine and compare them with our own, and hon. Members will be rather ashamed at the contrast between the wise and lavish generosity of countries much poorer than ours and the short-sighted and niggardly parsimony with which we dole out small sums of money for the encouragement of agriculture in our country.

We are not getting out of the land anything like what it is capable of endowing us with. Of the enormous quantity of agricultural and dairy produce and fruit, and of the timber which is imported into this country, a considerable portion could be raised on our own lands. There, hon. Members opposite and ourselves will agree. The only difference is as to the remedy. In our opinion, the remedy which they suggest would make food costlier and more inaccessible for the people ; the remedies which we propose, on the other hand, would make food more abundant, better, and cheaper. What is it we propose ?—and, let the Committee observe, I am only dealing with that part of the problem which affects finance.

NATIONAL DEVELOPMENT GRANT.

I will tell the House therefore, briefly, what I propose doing in regard to this and all kindred matters I have dwelt upon. There is a certain amount of money—not very much—spent in this country in a spasmodic kind of way on what I call the work of national development—in light railways, in harbours, in indirect but very meagre assistance to agriculture. I propose to gather all these grants together into one Development Grant, and to put in this year an additional sum of £200,000.

Legislation will have to be introduced, and I will then explain the methods of administration and the objects in greater detail, but the grant will be utilised in the promoting of schemes which have for their purpose the development of the resources of the country. It will include such objects as the institution of schools of forestry, the purchase and preparation of land for afforestation, the setting up of a number of experimental forests on a large scale, expenditure upon scientific research in the interests of agriculture, experimental farms, the improvement of stock—as to which there have been a great many demands from people engaged in agriculture, the equipment of agencies for disseminating agricultural instruction, the encouragement and promotion of co-operation, the improvement of rural transport so as to make markets more accessible, the facilitation of all well-considered schemes and measures for attracting labour back to the land by small holdings or reclamation of wastes. Every acre of land brought into cultivation, every acre of cultivated land brought into a higher state of cultivation, means more labour of a healthy and productive character. It means more abundant food —cheaper and better food for the people.

The sum which I propose to set aside for these large and diverse purposes may seem disproportionate, especially as a good deal of capital expenditure will necessarily be invested in the carrying out more especially of the experiments. For the purpose of afforestation schemes, at any rate at the earlier stages, when the expenditure will be particularly heavy, I propose that borrowing powers should be conferred upon the Commission directing the distribution of the grant, though I intend to avoid the necessity of resort to loans in connection with the capital expenditure required for other parts of the scheme.

Mr. JOHN REDMOND: Does this include Ireland?

Mr. LLOYD-GEORGE: Oh, yes. I should hope to retain a great deal of money spent in Ireland for the purposes of which I have spoken. I should hope to attain this end by what may at first sight appear a proposal of a more drastic character. Hitherto all surpluses due either to unexpected accessions to the revenue or savings upon the Estimates have passed automatically into the old Sinking Fund for the liquidation of debt. I propose that all these unanticipated accretions and economies shall in future pass into the Development Fund, so as to constitute a re-serve for the purpose of money spent on the recommendations of the Commissioners, but under the direction of Parliament, on such objects as I have too compendiously sketched. The days of surpluses are not quite gone, and I sincerely hope, although the omens are for the moment bad, that the days of economising in public Departments are not over. Last year the various Departments saved over two millions, and I feel confident that we shall not look in vain for a similar spirit of cautious and conscientious dealing with public money in the course of the coming years.

We have more especially during the last 60 years in this country accumulated wealth to an extent which is almost unparalleled in the history of the world, but we have done it at an appalling waste of human material. We have drawn upon the robust vitality of the rural areas of Great Britain, and especially of Ireland, and spent its energies recklessly in the devitalising atmosphere of urban factories and workshops as if the supply were inexhaustible. We are now beginning to realise that we have been spending our capital, and at a disastrous rate, and it is time we should make a real concerted, national effort to replenish it. I put forward this proposal, not a very extravagant one, as a beginning.

MOTOR TRAFFIC AND ROAD MAINTENANCE.

It would be better that I should in this connection inform the House of another project which I shall have to submit in detail to its judgment later on in the course of the Session, but as it involves a substantial addition to the financial burdens of the year, I have to outline its general character in my Budget statement. It also has an indirect, but important, bearing on the question of providing useful and not purposeless employment in times of depression. I propose that a beginning should be made this year with a scheme for dealing with the new, but increasingly troublesome, problem of motor traffic in this country. We are far ahead of all other European countries in the number of motor vehicles upon our roads. We have at least three times as many as France and more than four times as many as Germany. And I am informed by those best able to judge, that to-day among the products of our factories are some of the best cars procurable in the world, both as regards the compara-tive perfection of the more costly vehicles and the value given for the prices asked for those designed for popular use.

I therefore look forward to a great future for this industry, and I am the last to wish to hinder its development or be responsible for proposals which would be in any way hostile to its interests. Quite the reverse. I am anxious to be helpful to its growth and prosperity. But I cannot help feeling that this problem is urgent, and calls for immediate attention. Any man who takes the trouble to consider the damage which is done to the roads of this country, often by men who do not contribute—or perhaps I ought to put it in another way, who have not been given the opportunity of contributing to the upkeep of the roads they help so effectively to tear up—the consequent rapid increase in the expense of road maintenance, the damage done, if not to agriculture, at least to the amenities of rural life by the dust clouds which follow in the wake of these vehicles, above all, the appalling list of casualties to innocent pedestrians, especially to children, must come to the conclusion that this is a question which demands immediate notice at the hands of the Central Government. The question of road construction, which was at one time deemed to be part of the essential development of the country, seemed to have been almost finally disposed of by the railways, but the advent of the motor has once more brought it to the front. It is quite clear that our present system of roads and of road-making is inadequate for the demands which are increasingly made upon it by the new form of traction. Roads are too narrow, corners are too frequent and too sharp, high hedges have their dangers, and the old metalling, admirably suited as it was to the vehicles we were accustomed to, is utterly unfitted for the motor-car.

If there be any truth at all in Ruskin's sweeping assertion that "all social progress resolves itself into the making of new roads," it must be admitted that we have been lamentably deficient. The State has for a very long period done nothing at all for our roads. I believe that no main road has been made out of London for 80 years. We have no central road authority. The roads of England and Wales are administered by 30 metropolitan borough councils (including the London County Council and City of London), 61 county councils, 326 county and non-county borough councils, and 1,479 urban and rural district councils. The great North Road, our greatest historic and national highway from London to Carlisle, is under no fewer than 72 authorities, of whom 46 are actually engaged in maintaining it. Among those are such authorities as the Kirklington Urban District Council, which controls one mile, and the Thirsk Rural District Council, which is responsible for 1 mile 1,120 yards in one place and 2 miles 200 yards in another! Both the general public and motorists are crying out for something to be done, and we propose to make a real start. How the funds will be raised for the purpose it will be my duty later on to explain; the only indication I shall give now is that the brunt of the expense at the beginning must be borne by motorists, and to do them justice they are willing, and even anxious, to subscribe handsomely towards such a purpose, so long as a guarantee is given in the method and control of the expenditure that the funds so raised will not merely be devoted exclusively to the improvement of the roads, but that they will be well and wisely spent for that end. For that reason we propose that the money shall be placed at the disposal of a central authority, who will make grants to local authorities for the purpose of carrying out well-planned schemes which they have approved for widening roads, for straightening them, for making deviations round villages, for allaying the dust nuisance, and I should also propose that power should be given to this central authority to set aside a portion of the money so raised for constructing where they think it necessary and desirable, absolutely new roads. Power will be given them not merely to acquire land for that purpose, but also for the acquisition of rights over adjoining lands, which will enable them eventually to bring into being new sources of revenue by taking full advantage of the increment and other benefits derived from the new easements they will be creating for the public. That is all I have to say with regard to expenditure, and I now come to the question of how I have got to meet it.

Once more I want to make it clear before I dismiss this part of the subject that the expenditure undertaken out of the fund must be directly referable to work done in connection with the exigencies of the motor traffic of the country. Although this is expenditure which will be incurred in the course of the present year, and is, therefore, not in the same category as the prospective liabilities which I have hitherto sketched, I do not think it incumbent on me to add this new liability to the ordinary deficit for the year, and I think the House will see that I have a sufficient reason for not doing so. I propose to deal with this expenditure by raising a special fund for the purpose, and it is therefore not quite in the position of being part of the current expenditure of the year. The expenditure will be strictly limited by the revenue we succed in raising.

SUMMARY OF LIABILITIES.

I have outlined what I deem to be some of our more pressing requirements in the near future. I have now to consider in what way my proposals will affect the balance sheet of the current year. For this purpose I shall leave out of account for the moment the expenditure upon motor roads since it will, as I have indicated, be covered by and limited to the produce of certain special sources of revenue. Liabilities in respect of schemes of insurance against unemployment and other contingencies affecting the working classes will not mature within the current year, but for labour exchanges £100,000 will be required mainly for the provision of buildings. Under the head of development £200,000 will, as I have explained, be set aside for the first year's grant to the proposed fund. These two items together give a total of £300,000, to which must be added a sum of £50,000 for a purpose which will shortly become apparent, making a total addition of £350,000 to the estimated expenditure. If this is added to the estimated deficit of £15,762,000 on the basis of present taxation, and of the Estimates already presented to Parliament, the amount which must be found, either by further taxation or other means, is increased to £16,112,000, or (allowing a margin for contingencies) to, say, 16½ millions.

NATIONAL DEBT AND SINKING FUND.

It is important that the Committee should recollect that during the first three years of the present administration taxes amounting in the aggregate to something over 7½ millions a year were taken off. In addition to that, provision has been made for a net reduction of dead-weight debt to the extent of no less than 47¼ millions, and of our aggregate capital liabilities to the extent of 42¼ millions. This means a saving to the country in respect of interest of over a million pounds a year, which, if it had been directed to relieving the taxpayers' burthens instead of to increasing the Sinking Fund, would

[Mr. Lloyd-George.]

have enabled the total remission of taxation to have been raised to 8½ millions—a sum practically equivalent to the annual cost of the Old Age Pensions measure of the Government.

Another satisfactory element in our Capital Account is to be found in the fact that under the head of "Other Capital Liabilities" the repayments will, in the present financial year, for the first time since the introduction of the system of naval and military works loans, exceed the new borrowings. The estimated borrowings on capital account for 1908-9 were £2,785,000. The actual borrowings were £2,636,000, of which £1,300,000 was for telephone purposes, £859,000 for naval works, and £270,000 for military works, while the amount applicable in the year to repayment of principal was £2,279,000. The estimated borrowings for the current year are only £1,795,000, of which £1,300,000 will be required for telephone works, while the amount applicable to repayment of principal is estimated at £2,497,000. The borrowings under the Naval and Military Works Acts are now limited to works actually in progress, and have practically come to an end. The proposal which I now have to make was foreshadowed and justified by the Prime Minister when he opened the Budget last year, and I need now scarcely say more than that the amount by which I propose that the fixed debt charge should be reduced is three millions pounds.

The dead-weight debt on the 1st of April last was £702,688,000, a decrease of £8,788,000 as compared with the amount on the 1st of April, 1908. The reduction would have been considerably larger but for the fact that I did not deem it advisable, having regard to the state of the market towards the close of the year, to lay out the whole of the moneys available for debt reduction. The unexpended balance of Sinking Fund moneys in the hands of the National Debt Commissioners at the end of 1908-9 was no less than £7,667,000, as compared with £1,132,000 a year ago. This additional £6,500,000, or £5,750,000, if we assume that the realised deficit is met out of these moneys, represents a debt-redeeming capacity in terms of Consols at current prices amounting to £6,750,000. If we add this amount to the previous figure of £8,788,000 we arrive at the real reduction of dead-weight debt which is properly attributable to the finance of last year—£15,538,000. When this is brought to

account the dead-weight debt will stand at approximately £696,000,000, or somewhat less than its amount twenty years ago (£697,043,000), when the late Lord Goschen reduced the ·debt charge to 25 millions a year. There is, however, an important difference between a fixed debt charge of 25 millions in 1899-90 and a fixed debt charge of the same amount now. The rate of interest on Consols 20 years ago was in process of reduction from 3 to 2¾ per cent., now it is 2½ per cent. While, therefore, in 1889-90 20 millions in round figures of the total provision was applied to the payment of interest and management expenses, leaving little more than 5 millions, or about three-fourths of 1 per cent. of the amount of the debt available for repayment of principal, interest and management will in the current year absorb only about 18 millions, leaving nearly 7 millions (or more than 1 per cent.) for Sinking Fund purposes. This figure is £300,000 more than the average annual provision made for the repayment of principal in the ten years immediately preceding the South African War, and only three quarters of a million less than the amount estimated to be available in 1899-1900, before the adoption of Lord St. Aldwyn's proposal to reduce the fixed debt charge from 25 millions to 23 millions, and whereas in 1899-1900, and the years immediately preceding and following it, we incurred a net increase of our other liabilities in respect of naval, military, and other works by an average of more than £3,500,000, there will this year be a net surplus of moneys applicable to repayment of principal over new borrowings of about £700,000. In view of these facts, and more particularly as we are spending so much out of current revenues upon Naval construction which less provident finance might have found an excuse for charging upon a future generation, I think the time has come when, without any failure in our duty to posterity, we can reduce the fixed debt charge from 28 to 25 million pounds. The adoption of this proposal will mean a reduction of the amount to be found by new taxation from 16½ to 13½ millions.

DIFFICULTIES OF THE ECONOMIST.

How am I to obtain the necessary money for the settlement of this very heavy account? I dismiss borrowings. One way, of course, to balance the account would be to effect a saving of expenditure, and the other is by raising taxes. I should like to say one word on the first before I come to the second question. The path of the economist is hard. His is not a very attractive or popular role in any Government. One might infer that the first object of a finance minister who has to face a heavy deficit would be to inquire as to possible economies, with a view, if not of obviating new imposts altogether, at all events lightening them as far as possible. Last summer, when there was a suspicion that I might possibly do my level best to seek out economies and make a beginning in that respect, what was the result? I saw paragraphs in responsible Opposition journals accusing me of impertinence in instituting a search into possible economies in some of our most expensive services. What happened? Merely because I proposed to inquire, merely because I sought investigation, myself and my colleagues were subjected to such persistent abuse, insults, and scurrility as few Ministers have ever been subjected to, merely for desiring inquiry. I am still of opinion that it is worth this country's while to inquire thoroughly into its affairs, but I am equally clear that until public opinion is educated up to the point of assenting to the institution of that inquiry, and therefore giving the necessary support, no substantial results will be achieved in that way. Therefore I fall back upon the other resource of raising taxes and of so meeting and liquidating the demand.

PRINCIPLES OF TAXATION.

Now what are the principles upon which I intend to proceed in getting those taxes? The first principle on which I base my financial proposals is this—that the taxation which I suggest should be imposed, while yielding in the present year not more than sufficient to meet this year's requirements, should be of such a character that it will produce enough revenue in the second year to cover the whole of our estimated liabilities for that year. And, moreover, that it will be of such an expansive character as to grow with the growing demand of the social programme which I have sketched without involving the necessity for imposing fresh taxation in addition to what I am asking Parliament to sanction at the present time. The second principle on which I base my proposals is that the taxes should be of such a character as not to inflict any injury on that trade or commerce which constitutes the sources of our wealth.

My third principle is this, that all classes of the community in this financial emergency ought to be called upon to contribute. I have never been able to accept the theory which I have seen advanced that you ought to draw a hard-and-fast line at definite incomes and say that no person under a certain figure should be expected to contribute a penny towards the burden of the good government of the country. In my judgment all should be called upon to bear their share. No voluntary association, religious or philanthropic or provident, has ever been run on the principle of exempting any section of its membership from subscription. They all contribute, even to the widow's mite. It is considered not merely the duty, but the privilege and pride of all to share in the common burden, and the sacrifice is as widely distributed as is the responsibility and the profit. At the same time, when you come to consider whether the bulk of the taxation is to be raised by direct or indirect means, I must point out at this stage—I shall have a little more to say on this subject later on—that the industrial classes, in my judgment, upon a close examination of their contributions to local and Imperial finance, are paying more in proportion to their incomes than those who are better off. Their proportion to local finances especially is heavier, because, although nominally the rates are not paid by them, as everyone knows, they are really. For that reason the burden at the present moment of new taxation bears much more heavily in proportion to their income on that class than it does upon the wealthier and better-to-do classes.

NEW TAXATION—MOTOR CARS.

I now come—and I trust that the Committee will not think that I have delayed too long—to the most interesting and the most difficult part of my task, the explanation of the various proposals for fresh taxation which I have to lay before them. I think it will be to the convenience of the Committee if I deal first with motor cars, and so dispose at once of a source of revenue from which, as I have explained, I, as Chancellor of the Exchequer, shall derive no advantage. In Great Britain, private cars, as distinct from hackney carriages (*i.e.*, taxicabs and motor omnibuses) at present pay £2 2s. carriage tax if under one ton in weight, with an additional £2 2s. if between one and two tons in weight, and an additional £3 3s. if between two and three tons, while motor-cycles pay 15s. In Ireland there is at present no tax on motor-

[Mr. Lloyd-George.]

cars. I propose to remove that Irish grievance. These duties brought in for the year 1908-9 the sum of £150,569.

I propose to substitute for this a new and increased scale, with graduations, which will come into force next January, for the whole of the United Kingdom, and I have decided to base the scale on the power of the cars and not on the weight. The horse-power will be determined in accordance with regulations made by the Treasury, and in the case of petrol cars with reference to the bore of the cylinders. It will no doubt be somewhat more difficult to ascertain the power than it is to ascertain the weight, but I believe that the plan I am adopting will be on the whole the fairest method of distributing the tax.

The scale I propose will be as follows :—

Under	6½	horse-power,	tax	£2	2s.
,,	12	,,	,,	£3	3s.
,,	16	,,	,,	£4	4s.
,,	26	,,	,,	£6	6s.
,,	33	,,	,,	£8	8s.
,,	40	,,	,,	£10	10s.
,,	60	,,	,,	£21	0s.
Above	60	,,	,,	£42	0s.

It will be seen that the tax rises rapidly when we get to cars over 40 horse-power—a provision with which I think the Committee will not quarrel.

Doctors' cars I propose to charge at one-half these rates.

Motor cycles I would charge at the uniform rate of £1.

No additional duties will be placed on hackney carriages, and the existing exemptions to trade vehicles will be continued. The new duties on private cars and motor cycles I estimate to yield, in the aggregate, this year £410,000, or an increase of £260,000 over last year's figures; but such an estimate must be to a large extent guess-work, for, though I am able to say with fair certainty that the number of private cars is about 55,000 and of motor cycles 40,000, the number of the former in each category of power is of course entirely a matter of conjecture. I need hardly say that, in accordance with the Prime Minister's undertaking in his Budget Speech in 1907, arrangements will be made so that the local authorities will continue to obtain a sum equivalent to the old duties.

DUTY ON PETROL.

I now come to a second proposal that I have to make in this connection. I have already explained to the Committee that one of the chief reasons for imposing additional taxation on motor cars is the fact that the increase in their numbers necessitates a reorganisation of our main-road system, and it will be obvious that, were I to confine taxation to a mere re-adjustment of the scale of licence duties, the burden would be imposed with absolutely no relation to the extent that the car might use the roads. Some cars are out four or five hours a day all the year round, others are used but rarely, and I believe that, were I to obtain anything like adequate contribution from motor cars entirely by direct taxation, I might hinder to some extent the development of the motor industry by discouraging persons from keeping a motor, or an additional motor, should they only want it for occasional use.

I, therefore, propose to put a tax of 3d. per gallon on all petrol used for motor vehicles. This small tax, very small compared with what hon. Gentlemen would have to pay if they were motoring in France, where they would be compelled to pay 1s. 8d.—[HON. MEMBERS: "They have got protection," and "No, no."] I worked it out, and the hon. Member is absolutely wrong. It varies very much, but in the principal towns you also pay an octroi duty. This small tax will fall on motorists in proportion both to the distance travelled and also to the power of the car, for the Committee knows that a high-powered car will consume considerably more petrol per mile run. In order to meet the case of commercial vehicles and vehicles such as motor cabs and omnibuses which will not perhaps profit to so great an extent by the improvement in our roads, I propose to give a rebate of half the duty on the quantity consumed in their propulsion. There will, of course, be a rebate of the whole duty on petrol used for all purposes other than propelling motor cars—though the amount used for such other purposes is comparatively small.

I estimate the yield of this tax to be about £340,000 for the 11 months of the current financial year, and to be about £375,000 for a full year. The total sum, therefore, available for that part of my development scheme which bears on road improvement from these two sources (after allowing for the payment to the local authorities of a sum equivalent to the old licence duties) will be some £600,000—a figure which should rapidly increase in succeeding years. I propose that the proceeds of these duties should be issued from the Exchequer to a separate account under statutory arrangements similar to those applicable to the estate duties grant, and the local taxation grant. Now that disposes of motors, and gets them out of the road.

DIRECT TAXATION.

Now I come to my direct taxation. It must be obvious that in meeting a large deficit of this kind I should be exceedingly unwise if I were to trust to speculative or fancy taxes. I therefore propose, first of all, to raise more money out of the income tax and estate duties. Income tax in this country only begins when the margin of necessity has been crossed and the domain of comfort and even of gentility has been reached. A man who enjoys an income of over £3 a week need not stint himself or his family of reasonable food or of clothes and shelter. There may be an exception in the case of a man with a family, whose gentility is part of his stock in trade or the uniform of his craft. Then, I agree, often things go hard.

Then when you come to estate duties what a man bequeaths, after all, represents what is left after he has provided for all his own wants in life. Beyond a certain figure it also represents all that is essential to keep his family in the necessaries of life. The figure which the experience of 70 years has sanctified as being that which divides sufficiency from gentility is £150 to £160 a year. A capital sum that would, if invested in safe securities, provide anything over that sum ought to be placed in a different category from any sum which is below that figure.

There is one observation which is common to income tax and the death duties, more especially with the higher scales. What is it that has enabled the fortunate possessors of these incomes and these fortunes to amass the wealth they enjoy or bequeath? The security ensured for property by the agency of the State, the guaranteed immunity from the risks and destruction of war, ensured by our natural advantages and our defensive forces. This is an essential element even now in the credit of the country; and, in the past, it means that we were accumulating great wealth in this land, when the industrial enterprises of less fortunately situated countries were not merely at a standstill, but their resources were being ravaged and destroyed by the havoc of war. What, more, is accountable for this growth of wealth? The spread of intelligence amongst the masses of the people, the improvements in sanitation and in the general condition of the people. These have all contributed towards the efficiency of the people, even as wealth-producing machines. Take, for instance, such legislation as the Education Acts and the Public Health Acts: they have cost much money, but they have made infinitely more. That is true of all legislation which improves the conditions of life of the people. An educated, well-fed, well-clothed, well-housed people invariably leads to the growth of a numerous well-to-do class. If property were to grudge a substantial contribution towards proposals which ensure the security which is one of the essential conditions of its existence, or towards keeping from poverty and privation the . old people whose lives of industry and toil have either created that wealth or made it productive, then property would be not only shabby, but short-sighted.

INCOME TAX.

Now what do I propose? When it is remembered that the total yield of income tax on its present basis amounts to little more than five years' normal growth of the aggregate income upon which income tax is payable (which increased from £607,500,000 in 1901-2 to £640,000,000 in 1906-7), it will be seen that our present reserve of taxable capacity is as great at the present moment with the existing rate of the tax as it would have been five years ago if there had been no tax at all. If the tax were doubled in the present year income tax payers would, in the aggregate, after payment of the double rate, be in the enjoyment of almost exactly the same net income as five years ago. A careful consideration of these figures ought to convince the most sceptical that the maximum rate of the tax may be retained at 1s., or even increased, without seriously encroaching upon our available reserves for national emergencies. The time, however, has gone by when a simple addition of pence to the poundage of the tax, attractive as the simplicity of that expedient is, can be regarded as a satisfactory solution of a financial difficulty.

As the Prime Minister so well pointed out two years ago, inequalities which might be tolerated in a tax designed for the purpose of meeting a temporary emergency are intolerable in a permanent part

[Mr. Lloyd-George.]

of our fiscal machinery. The income tax, imposed originally as a temporary expedient, is now in reality the centre and sheet anchor of our financial system. The principles of graduation and differentiation, the apportionment of the burden as between different classes of taxpayers, according, on the one hand, to the extent, and, on the other hand, to the nature of their resources, are in the lower stages of the income tax scale already recognised by abatements and allowances. It remains to complete the system by extending the application of these principles, and in regard to differentiation by taking account to some extent, at any rate, not only of the source from which income is derived, but also of the liabilities which the taxpayer has contracted in the discharge of his duties as a citizen, and of the other burdens of taxation borne by him by virtue of those responsibilities.

Notwithstanding the relief given by the Finance Act of 1907, the burden of the income tax upon earnings is still disproportionately heavy. While, therefore, I propose to raise the general rate at which the tax is calculated, I propose that the rates upon earned income in the case of persons whose total income does not exceed £3,000 should remain as at present, namely, 9d. in the pound up to £2,000, and 1s. in the pound between £2,000 and £3,000. In respect of all other incomes now liable to the 1s. rate I propose to raise the rate from 1s. to 1s. 2d.

ABATEMENT ON CHILDREN.

In the case of incomes not exceeding £500, the pressure of the tax, notwithstanding the abatements at present allowed, is sorely felt by taxpayers who have growing families to support, and although a comparatively trifling additional burthen will be imposed upon them by the increased rate, since the aggregate income of this class is to the extent of at least four-fifths exclusively earned income, I think that even upon the present basis they have a strong claim to further relief. Even from the purely fiscal point of view there is this essential difference between the position of a man with a family and that of the taxpayer who has no such responsibilities. The family man is, generally speaking, a much heavier contributor to that portion of the revenue which is derived from indirect taxation and inhabited house duty, so that in comparison with the bachelor he is taxed not so much in proportion to his income as in proportion to his outgoings.

There is no class of the community which has a much harder struggle or a more anxious time than that composed of the men whose earnings just bring them within the clutches of the income tax collector. On a small income they have not merely to maintain themselves, but to exhaust a large proportion of their limited resources in that most worrying and wasteful of all endeavours known as "keeping up appearances." They are often much worse off and much more to be pitied than the artisan who earns half their wages. If they have only themselves to think about they do well, but when they have a family dependent upon them the obligation to keep up the appearance of respectability of all their dependants is very trying. I am strongly of opinion that they deserve special consideration in the rearrangement of our finances. Continental countries recognise their claim, and I propose that for all incomes under £500, in addition to the existing abatements, there shall be allowed from the income in respect of which the tax is paid a special abatement of £10 for every child under the age of 16 years. Take the case of the widow with a family, which is always cited in reference to proposals to tax income or property: she will in most cases be better off with this abatement, should her family be of average numbers, even though she is rated at 1s. 2d., than she was before. The new abatement will, like the existing abatements, be allowed irrespective of the source from which the income is derived, and earned incomes, upon which no new burthen is to be imposed, as well as unearned incomes, will enjoy the advantage of the concession. The addition of 2d. to the rate upon all incomes in excess of £2,000, and upon unearned income enjoyed by persons whose total income does not exceed that amount, would yield in a full year £4,700,000, and in the year of imposition £3,760,000. But from this source I must deduct £160,000 in respect of the retention of the 1s. rate upon earned income enjoyed by persons whose total income is between £2,000 and £3,000, and £600,000 for the costs of the new abatements. This reduces the estimated net receipts from the additional 2d. in 1909-10 to £3,000,000.

The rate of income tax under the present law is absolutely uniform upon all incomes in excess of £2,000 a year; between that rate and £700 the allowance in respect of earned income operates to relieve the less wealthy taxpayer, and thus to introduce the principle of graduation. Below £700 the system of abatements produces a regular graduation by descending stages. The introduction of a complete scheme of graduation, applicable to all incomes, besides raising questions of general principle, which it is not necessary now to discuss, would require an entire reconstruction of the administrative machinery of the tax, including in all probability the abandonment to a very large extent of the principle of collection at the source upon which the productivity of the tax so largely depends. It would create for the administrative Department a series of problems which, if not insoluble, could at any rate scarcely hope to obtain a satisfactory solution in a year where other taxation of a novel character must necessarily claim a large part of its attentions.

INCOME (SUPER) TAX.

The imposition of a super-tax, however, upon large incomes on the lines suggested by the Select Committee of 1906 is a more practicable proposition, and it is upon this basis that I intend to proceed. Such a super-tax might take the form of an additional poundage charged at a uniform rate upon the whole income of persons whose total income exceeds the maximum above which the tax is to be applied, or the poundage might be varied according to the amount of the income to be taxed. A third, and I think preferable, alternative is to adopt a uniform poundage, but to charge the tax not upon the total income, but upon the amount only by which the income exceeded a certain fixed amount which would naturally, but need not necessarily, be the amount of the minimum income which attracts the tax. We might begin, say, at £3,000, and levy the new tax upon all income in excess of £3,000, or at £5,000, and levy the tax upon income in excess of £5,000. In the former case some 25,000 assessments would be required, in the latter only 10,000—from the point of view of administration a very strong argument in favour of the adoption of the higher figure at any rate in the first instance. On the other hand, a general abatement of £5,000 per taxpayer would be extremely costly, and though it would have the effect of largely reducing the actual as compared with the nominal rate of the tax except in the case of very large incomes indeed, the nominal rate necessary to produce an adequate revenue—though in reality no measure of the general burthen—would

tend to appear somewhat alarming. While therefore I propose to limit the tax to incomes exceeding £5,000, I propose to levy it upon the amount by which such incomes exceed £3,000, and at the rate of 6d. in the £ upon the amount of such excess. An income of £5,001 will thus pay in super-tax 6d. in the £ on £2,001, the equivalent of an addition to the existing income tax of rather less than $2\frac{1}{2}$d. in the £, and an income of £6,000 the equivalent of an additional 3d. The equivalent of an extra 4d. (or a total income tax of 1s. 6d. in the £) will only be reached when the total income amounts to £9,000 and 5d. not until £18,000. Assessments to the new tax will be based upon the Returns of total income from all sources, which will be required from persons assessable. The machinery will be, in the main, independent of the machinery of the existing income tax, but the assessments will be made by the special Commissioners appointed under the Income Tax Acts, and assessable income will be determined according to the rules laid down in the income tax schedules. Total income for the purposes of the tax will be ascertained in the manner prescribed by Statute for determining total income for the purposes of the present income tax exemptions and abatements, that is to say, deductions will be allowed for interest upon loans and mortgages and any other payments made under legal obligation, while in the case of real property assessed to property tax under schedule A, a special 5 per cent. allowance will be made for cost of management, as well as the allowances of one-sixth and one-eighth for repairs at present made in collection of the property tax under that schedule. Sir Henry Primrose, in his evidence before the Select Committee in 1906 estimated the number of persons in receipt of incomes over £5,000 a year to be 10,000, and their aggregate income to be £121,000,000. From this it will be seen that the amount of income liable to a super tax would be £90,000,000. The yield of the super-tax in a full year is estimated at £2,300,000, but as new machinery has to be set up and as returns have to be obtained from taxpayers, examined, and assessments made upon them, I should be sanguine if I anticipated that more than a small proportion of the first year's income will reach the Exchequer before 31st March next. In these circumstances I have not felt justified in including more than £500,000 in my Estimate for the current year.

[Mr. Lloyd-George.]

RESTRICTION OF ABATEMENTS.

My last proposal relating to the income tax is the restriction of the exemptions and abatements to persons resident in the United Kingdom. The income of a person resident abroad only comes within the scope of the income tax in so far as it is derived from sources within the United Kingdom. Whatever may be his total actual income, his total income from all sources within the meaning of the Income Tax Acts comprises only such receipts as accrue to him from sources in this country. A foreign millionaire, who draws anything between £160 and £400 from English investments, can obtain £8 from the Commissioners of Inland Revenue. If his dividends exceed £400 but do not exceed £700 he can recover a sum which varies from £7 10s. to £3 10s. in accordance with the abatement scale. If they are £701 or upwards he can recover nothing. There is reason to suppose that by far the greater part of the money paid to persons outside the United Kingdom in respect of these abatements goes to people who, if they were resident here, would not be entitled to it. The claims are, besides, from an administrative point of view, very difficult to deal with, and the difficulty will be greatly increased if my proposal to grant special abatements to the fathers and mothers of families are adopted. The claims themselves are received in the main through income tax repayment agencies, which absorb in commission a large percentage—often, I believe, as much as 50 per cent.—of the amount recovered. In these circumstances I am satisfied that the abolition of this concession, which was recommended by Lord Ritchie's Committee of 1904, will give rise to no appreciable hardship. The consequent saving to the revenue will be something like £250,000, to which must be added a considerable saving in respect of the salaries of the staff at present employed in the troublesome business of dealing with the claims. As, however, the repayments take place in a year subsequent to that in which the tax is collected, and I do not propose to make the alteration retrospective, no part of the saving will accrue to the revenue of the present year.

DEATH DUTIES.

The proposals I have to make with regard to the death duties are of a very simple character. The great reconstruction of these duties in 1894, which will always be associated with the name of Sir William Harcourt, has given us a scheme of taxation which is at once logical and self-consistent as a system, and a revenue-producing machine of very high efficiency. Apart, therefore, from one or two minor changes in the law, which experience has shown to be desirable, I intend to confine my attention to adjusting the rates with a view to increasing the yield without altering the basis on which the duties are levied.

The estate duties upon small estates of which the net principal value does not exceed £5,000 will remain at one, two or three per cent., according to value, as at present; but between £5,000 and £1,000,000 I propose to shorten the steps and steepen the graduation. I do not propose to increase the maximum of 15 per cent., but I propose it should be reached at £1,000,000 instead of £3,000,000. An estate of £10,000 belongs to a different category, and represents a greater taxable capacity, than an estate of £1,001, yet both alike pay three per cent.; and the same is true of an estate of £25,000 as compared with one of £10,001, both of which now pay four per cent. Under the new scale, estates from £5,000 to £10,000 will pay four per cent., and those from £10,000 to £20,000 five per cent. The next step will be £20,000 to £40,000, and the rate six per cent.; the next £40,000 to £70,000, with seven per cent., while estates of £70,000 to £100,000 will pay 8 per cent.; from £100,000 to £150,000, the rate will be 9 per cent.; from £150,000 to £200,000 it will become 10; the rate from £200,000 to £400,000 will be 11 per cent.; from £400,000 to £600,000, 12; from £600,000 to £800,000, 13; from £800,000 to £1,000,000, 14; and above £1,000,000, 15 per cent. upon the whole of the estate. The new rates, if chargeable, as I propose they should be, in respect of all estates passing upon deaths occurring on or after to-morrow, are estimated to yield an additional revenue of £2,550,000 in 1909-10, increasing to £4,200,000 in the following year, and ultimately to £4,400,000.

SETTLEMENT ESTATE DUTY.

As a consequence of these increases, added to the increases made in the higher steps of the estate duty scale two years ago, it becomes necessary to deal with the settlement estate duty, which has remained unaltered since its original imposition in 1894. Non-settled property is chargeable with estate duty according to scale every time the interest in the property passes on death upon the full corpus of the property. Settled property, on the other hand, if settled by will, is so chargeable only upon the death of the testator, or, if settled otherwise than by will, only upon the death of the first tenant for life, and, unless a subsequent life tenant is competent to dispose, escapes any further payment of estate duty until the expiry of the settlement, however many life tenants may intervene. For example, a non-settled estate left to a son, by him to a brother, and by the brother to his son would pay estate duty three times, whereas, if it took the same course under a settlement made by the will of the original testator, it would pay once only—at the original testator's death. By way of set-off to this preferential treatment of the settled estate it was provided by the Finance Act of 1894 that an additional rate of 1 per cent., called settlement estate duty, should be paid in addition to the estate duty, at the rate appropriate to the estate, on the first occasion of its passing at death under the settlement. The duty must therefore be regarded as a sort of composition for future payments of estate duty to which the property would become subject in the absence of a settlement. Sir William Harcourt's intention, as expressed in the Budget speech of 1894, was to secure by means of this duty absolute equality of treatment as between settled and non-settled property. "In this manner," he said, "we levy the same amount from the estate as if it were left absolutely, but each beneficiary will contribute according to the extent of his interest by the reduction of his income resulting from the original diminution of the capital."

The proposition that an immediate payment at the rate of 1 per cent. is an adequate composition for a future payment, or possibly several future payments, according to the character of the disposition and the course of events, at rates varying from 1 to 8 per cent. (the then limits of the Estate Duty Scale) is at first sight somewhat startling. On the other hand, when we remember that the expedient of settling a whole estate is often adopted as an alternative to dividing it in the first instance, that the average age at which a life tenant succeeds is probably much higher than that of the average beneficiary taking free property, and last, but not least, that the difference in value between the fee simple of the property and the life interest or life interests of the tenant or tenants for life passes, in theory at any rate, directly from the settler to the

remainderman, it is not unreasonable that a substantial abatement should be made from the present value (calculated on a strictly actuarial basis) of what would probably be the future liability in respect of estate duty, in the event of the whole estate being charged in full every time it passed upon death under the settlement. When, however, every allowance has been made for difference of circumstances, I think there can be no doubt, especially when regard is had to the fact that settlement estate duty is not chargeable where the only life interest is that of a spouse, that the 1 per cent. additional duty was not, even in 1894, when the average rate of estate duty was approximately 5 per cent., anything like the full equivalent for the immunity from further charge enjoyed by the property during the remainder of the settlement. The alterations in the estate duty scale made in 1907 and those which I now propose will together have the effect of raising the average rate of estate duty from about 5 to approximately 7 per cent., and the charge of only 1 per cent. settlement estate duty, which was not in fact a full equivalent for the privilege granted even on the basis of the 1894 rates, clearly cannot be defended in conjunction with the new scale. I propose, therefore, to increase the rate from 1 to 2 per cent. Although the effect of this alteration will ultimately be to double the yield of the present 1 per cent. duty (about £500,000) I can only reckon on £50,000 extra revenue from this source in 1909-10 and £375,000 in 1910-11, since these duties are in most cases not collected until some time after the death.

ANOMALY CORRECTED.

I propose at the same time to correct a small anomaly, introduced as an—I believe—accidental effect of the legislation of 1894, which gives rise to a very considerable loss of revenue every year. Where property subject to a life interest does not fall into possession until after the death of the prospective beneficiary, only one estate duty is payable, namely, as in respect of settled property. But where it falls into possession in his lifetime, two estate duties are payable, namely, one on the transmission of the property to him, and one on the transmission of the property from him. It is, of course, a matter of indifference to the ultimate taker whether the decease of the life tenant is prior or subsequent to the decease of his own testator; yet, in the former case, it

R

[Mr. Lloyd-George.]

comes to him charged with two duties, and, in the latter, charged with one duty only. My proposal is that such property should be treated, as before 1894, in the same way in the latter as in the former contingency. The estimated advantage of this alteration to the revenue of the current financial year is £250,000, and £375,000 in 1910-11 and future years.

LEGACY AND SUCCESSION DUTIES.

The rate of legacy and succession duties, where the beneficiary is a brother or sister or a descendant of a brother or sister of the deceased, will be raised from 3 per cent. to 5 per cent. ; while the other legacy and succession duties, which at present vary from 5 to 10 per cent., according to the degree or absence of relationship, will be charged at the uniform rate of 10 per cent. ["Oh, oh."] Most of them are charged 10 per cent. at present. [An Hon. Member: "Not at all."] It is so. The present exemptions from the 1 per cent. legacy and succession duties now chargeable, where the beneficiary is a lineal ancestor or descendant of the deceased, will be abolished, and the duty extended to the case where a husband or wife takes the legacy or succession. In the cases of spouses and lineals, however, I propose to exempt from the new and reimposed duties all legacies and successions of whatever value in cases where the aggregated property passing on the death of the deceased does not exceed £15,000.

Exemption will also be allowed, whatever may be principal value of the aggregated property, wherever the amount of the legacy or succession itself does not exceed £1,000, or, if the person taking the legacy or succession is the widow of the deceased or a child under the age of 21 years, wherever the amount of such legacy or succession does not exceed £2,000. The changes will, like the new estate duty scale, operate only in the case of persons dying on or after the 30th instant ; but as these duties are not as a rule payable until the end of the executor's year, I cannot count on receiving any additional revenue until 1910-11. I estimate the amount which the alterations will produce next year at £1,370,000, and that the yield will in course of time increase to £2,150,000.

VALUATION FOR PURPOSES OF ESTATE DUTIES.

Apart from the question of rates, the method of valuation adopted for the purposes of the death duties has necessarily a very important influence on the revenue.

Under the present law, agricultural property enjoys the somewhat peculiar privilege that, whatever may be its value in the market, its valuation for death duty purposes cannot exceed 25 years' purchase of the net rental after allowing for expenses of management. I propose to abolish this limitation, and to deal with the class of property to which it applies on the basis applicable to all other property passing upon death—namely, the actual price which would be paid by a willing buyer to a willing seller as on the date upon which the property becomes chargeable to duty.

Further, the law as to the valuation of large blocks of stocks and shares is not sufficiently clear. It is sometimes contended that, if the whole property were placed on the market on the date of the deceased's death, a "slump" would take place in the value of the securities Of course, no executor would be so imprudent as to take this course. There is no reason why it should not be definitely laid down that stocks and shares are in all cases to be valued at the market price, without any reference to the size of the holding, and I propose to amend the law accordingly. From these two changes in the law relating to valuation, I hope ultimately to derive a considerable accession of revenue, but the effect of the changes will only be felt gradually, and the advantage to be derived from the alteration in the current financial year is scarcely likely to be appreciable.

DISPOSITIONS INTER VIVOS.

I now come to the period within which gifts made during the lifetime of the deceased are reckoned as part of the estate for the purposes of estate duty. The loss to the revenue arising from voluntary dispositions *inter vivos*, made with the purpose of avoiding the death duties, cannot be precisely ascertained ; but it is probably very considerable, and I fear that resort to this expedient may become still more common when the rate of duty is raised. I therefore propose to substitute five years for one year, as the period within which property so alienated shall remain liable to duty. I am not sanguine that this reform will do more than operate to check what at present is thought to constitute a considerable leakage of revenue ; and I do not therefore feel justified in estimating any positive increase of revenue from the alteration.

FREE ESTATES.

My last proposal is to extend to free estates the concession made by section 20 of the Finance Act, 1896, which grants exemption from estate duty in respect of objects of national, scientific, or historic interest forming part of a settled estate. The estate duty in respect of such objects, whether forming part of a free or settled estate, will only become chargeable in future if and when they are actually sold. This concession will, I hope, result in keeping together many collections whose owners are, from various reasons, unable to take advantage of the privilege afforded by the present law, and so keep in the country many national treasures which would otherwise, more especially in view of the prospective change in the United States customs tariff upon such objects, tend to find a home on the other side of the Atlantic.

STAMP DUTIES.

Under the head of stamp duties I propose to increase the duty upon conveyances on sale from 10s. to 20s. per cent., an exemption from the increased rate being made in favour of conveyances of stock or marketable securities which, by reason of the greater frequency with which they change hands, in comparison with other kinds of property, bear a disproportionate burthen under the present uniform scale. The greater part of the additional revenue under this head will be derived from transfers of real property. As such property will benefit largely from the decrease of the poor rate, which must necessarily follow as a result of the adoption of a State system of old age pensions and other schemes of social reform, it is equitable that it should be called upon to contribute to the Exchequer expenditure for these purposes. [Some cries of "Speak up."] I am afraid I shall have to appeal to the indulgence of the House. I cannot go right through as I thought, but I will just say what I have to say with regard to stamps. Even after my proposed addition, the transfer duty upon such property will still be low as compared with the rates charged in other communities. In Germany, there are both State and municipal taxes which, in towns like Cologne and Frankfort, at any rate, together amount to not less than 3 per cent. ; while, in France, the rates are still higher.

Conveyances or transfers operating as a voluntary disposition, *inter vivos*—an expedient largely resorted to as a method of avoiding the death duties—will in future attract, instead of the present fixed duty of 10s., an *ad valorem* duty calculated on the worth of the property transferred, at the same rate as is applicable to a con-veyance on sale of property of a similar description, and the same rates will apply to certain instruments chargeable at present with stamp duty as settlements. The rates upon marriage settlements will remain unaltered. As a corollary to the increase of the conveyance duties, duties upon leases will be doubled, except in the case where the 1d. rate is chargeable, which will remain as at present.

BONDS TO BEARER.

My next proposal relates to bonds to bearer and other securities transferable by delivery. The duty in these cases is the counterpart of the stamp duty upon the conveyance necessary to transfer securities transferable by deed; but, whereas the latter covers only a single transaction, the duty upon bearer securities covers all the transactions taking place during the life of the bond. It is therefore an anomaly that under the existing law this valuable privilege should be given at the cost of a single transfer. I, accordingly, propose to increase the duty upon such bonds (not being bonds issued by a Colonial Government, upon which the rate will remain as now at 2s. 6d. per cent.) from 10s. to 20s. per cent. of the nominal value, the duty upon bonds issued in lieu of existing bonds being concurrently raised from 2s. 6d. to 5s. per cent.

STOCK TRANSFERS.

This completes the list of my proposals relating to stamp duties, with one important exception. The transfer duty upon stocks and shares is at the rate of 10s. per cent. *ad valorem*, leviable upon the conveyance by which the transfer is effected. There are, however, many transactions in securities which, for one reason or another, are never followed by an actual conveyance. A block of shares may be sold and resold several times in the course of passing from one permanent holder to another, and the whole of these transactions may be covered by a single transfer from the first seller to the final purchaser. In such cases the intermediate transactions escape taxation altogether, except for the stamp duty chargeable upon the broker's contract note—1d. upon transactions between £5 and £100, and 1s. upon larger transactions irrespective of amount, and they may, I think, reasonably be required to make a moderate contribution to the Exchequer.

Such transactions, being mainly of a speculative character, and worked upon

R 2

[Mr. Lloyd-George.]

narrow margins, will clearly not bear a rate of duty in any way comparable with that charged upon an actual conveyance. Such an impost would, in the first place, from the point of view of the revenue, defeat its object by rendering the greater portion of such transactions impossible, while, in the second place, it would, in my opinion, be opposed to the public interest as calculated to curtail that free circulation of securities which is a necessary condition of steady prices and an open market. For, although these transactions are in the main speculative, and do, at times, like all speculative transactions, degenerate into mere gambling, it is a mistake to suppose that this is their essential or pervading characteristic. In their proper place they form part of the legitimate machinery for discounting fluctuations in value, necessary, not only to the Stock Exchange, but to every sphere of commercial activity, and the imposition of a penal tax designed to curtail the mischievous developments of the system could scarcely attain its object without inflicting irretrievable damage upon the marketability of securities as a whole.

The same objections do not, however, apply to a small *ad valorem* tax, which would operate to check business, if at all, only in the case of operations undertaken upon infinitesimal margins, in which, as a rule, the purely gambling element is most prominent, and which can be dispensed with without seriously endangering the stability of the market. I propose, therefore, that the rate between £5 and £100 should be 6d., instead of 1d.; from £100 to £500 1s. (as at present); from £500 to £1,000 2s., with a further 2s. for every additional £1,000 To prevent those rates affecting what are known as "carry-over" operations with undue severity, a single duty will be charged upon the two transactions involved therein, instead of, as now, the full duty upon each transaction.

"OPTION NOTES."

"Option notes" will be charged at similar rates, calculated upon the value of the securities to which the option relates. When a substantive contract follows upon the option and involves the payment of stamp duty upon the contract note, there will be a return of the duty already paid in respect of the option contract. Brokers who are not members of the Stock Exchange, whether acting as agents or principals, will be required to issue similar notes to their clients and such notes will

be chargeable with the same duties. The preferential treatment now enjoyed by the so-called "bucket shops"—institutions whose principal object is the encouragement of gambling—in the matter of stamp duties will thus be removed. These additional stamp duties may be expected to yield about £1,450,000 in a full year—of which conveyances, deeds of gift, settlements and leases will account for £850,000, bonds to bearer and other marketable securities for £350,000, and contract notes for £250,000. They will not, however, come into force until the Finance Bill has received the Royal assent. The greater part of the first half-year's revenue will thus be lost, while, in the case of most of the duties, a considerable amount of "forestalment" has to be reckoned with, since transactions will no doubt be expedited wherever possible to secure the advantage of the lower rate of duty. I cannot, therefore, safely calculate upon receiving more than £650,000 in 1909-10.

[Sitting suspended for half an hour.]

FURTHER TAXATION OF LICENCES.

Mr. LLOYD-GEORGE [resuming at 23 minutes past six of the clock]: I am exceedingly obliged to you, Sir, and to the House for the indulgence extended to me. I now come to the question of licences. I think I may fairly say that further taxation of licences has been anticipated for some time. It has been generally felt that the State has not received a fair return for the valuable monopoly which it has granted to the trade. If a comparison is instituted with the amount charged for this privilege in a community like that of the United States, one cannot help feeling amazed that the trade has been let off so lightly in this country. Land and licences have this in common, that where they have a value at all it is a monopoly value. No one would pay rent for a plot of land if he could secure an equally valuable piece of ground in the same neighbourhood for nothing; nor would anyone give the slightest consideration for an existing licence if a new licence could be got for the asking. The State for reasons of public utility limits the number of licences in a given neighbourhood, with the result that the holder of one of the licences is able to enjoy the exceptional rate of profit which the possession of the privilege permits him to earn. This point was very effectively put in the able circular issued by the brewers themselves during the passage of the Licensing Bill through this House. I shall quote the words they use, as argument could not have been more forcibly or more fairly put. These are the words which the brewers used in stating their case:—

"Now, with the exception of that portion of the trade which is done by delivery to private houses and clubs, and that which is done through off-licences, the only channel through which the consumption of excisable liquor can take place is through the licensed houses. Parliament has provided that it shall not be sold in any other way, and as a consequence the existing licensed houses, being in possession of a practical monopoly, have acquired a very high value."

That is the statement of the case of the brewers themselves. As to the extent of that value I shall be able to afford the Committee some statistical enlightenment in the course of a few minutes, but I should like to premise that during recent years there have been two or three elements which have added very considerably to the value of this monopoly. The first is the growing disinclination of benches of magistrates to issue fresh licences and the steady effort made by benches of magistrates rather to reduce the numbers. The reduction which has been made under the Bill of the right hon. Gentleman in 1904 has undoubtedly contributed to the increase in the value of licences. All this has endowed old licences with a special value, which did not attach to them in the days when new licences were more readily granted. The second element in the enhancement of value has undoubtedly been the tied-house system; and the third has been the conversion of what was an annual licence, determinable by the magistrates on evidence as to the necessities of the neighbourhood, into an interest—I will not call it a freehold—determinable only on misconduct.

By the Act of 1904 a valuable public right or property was parted with without any commensurate return being obtained. Is the market value of this privilege conferred by the State a sufficiently substantial one to justify a considerable increase in the very light licence duties which are now levied on these houses? Fortunately, we are not left to conjecture in appraising the money worth of this privilege. We have three important tests of its value. The first is that claimed by the trade itself. The trade has repeatedly assured the House of Commons through its well authenticated spokesmen that it assesses the value of the monopoly thus conferred upon it by the State at the enormous sum of 150 millions. I am not sure that this does not apply to licences in England and Wales alone, and that Scotland and Ireland are left out of account in the computation. At 10 years purchase this would mean the annual value of 15 millions conferred by a State monopoly. In return for this the public receive by way of licence duties upon public-houses, beer-houses, and hotels in the United Kingdom, an annual rent of £1,809,000. If all the freeholds of the Kingdom were farmed out on these light and easy terms what fortunes our farmers and farm labourers would divide between them. A farmer's profits are assessed for income-tax purposes at a third of his rent. One ready proof of the difference which the granting of this privilege of exclusive trading makes in the value of a business is to be found in the fact that an ordinary business is generally bought and sold at two and three years' purchase of the profits, whereas the value of a public-house licence is always appraised at from 10 to 12 years' purchase, the difference being attributable entirely to the greater certainty, both as regards turnover and rate of profit, which arises from the restriction upon competition afforded by the licensing system. Another test of value has been supplied by the working of the Act of 1904, where compensation is afforded to the owner of the licence when it is forcibly withdrawn by the action of the magistrates. These houses do not afford, perhaps, the best criterion of the real value of a prosperous public-house. Licences are generally withdrawn from the poorer type of public-house because the licensing magistrates have come to the conclusion that they are not required, and therefore, if the value of a house of that kind is high, what must be the price which would be put upon a house which is required by the neighbourhood, and which is, therefore, doing a good trade. However, let us take this, the least favourable illustration which is available, and here again I quote from the brewers' circular. It gives the cases of 126 houses of this kind spread over London, Essex, and Hertfordshire, and we are assured that these houses must be taken as a fair sample of the whole of the houses valued for compensation in that district. The result, according to this document, was that in these 126 cases the total value of the premises with a licence was £280,870; the value of the premises without the licence was £59,071, or, in other words, the value of the premises without the licence amounted only to 21 per cent. of the value of the same premises with a licence. So much for the value of a licence in a house which is not required by a neighbourhood, a thoroughly pernicious and poisonous influence as a

[Mr. Lloyd-George.]

rule, which ought not to be tolerated a single day after its superfluous character has become evident to the authorities.

Now let us take the case of the thriving house, or rather of the house whose trade proves that it is required by its neighbours. I have had before me a list of 141 licensed premises which have been acquired by the London County Council in connection with street and other improvements between March, 1889, and February, 1907. The total premium value attaching to the sites by reason of the licences has been estimated at £344,550, or an average of £2,443 per site. The acquisition of such sites in connection with the Kingsway and Aldwych has been estimated to have cost the Council in respect of the premium value attaching to the sites of the public-houses acquired, a sum of £132,300. In another instance, the premium value of a public-house site required for the improvement of the northern approach to the Tower Bridge is estimated at £20,000. I might multiply these instances, but I think I have furnished the House with sufficient evidence of the enormous value which this monopoly has created. Anyone who impartially investigates the figures may come to the conclusion that the rent or toll exacted by the public is ludicrously inadequate, and that in the interests of good management of public property that rent ought to be brought up to a figure which, without reaching anything like the proportions of a rack rent, will at any rate be commensurate with that which would be charged by a fair-minded and tolerant landlord, who, without doing himself a gross injustice, still at the same time wishes to afford his tenant not only a reasonable but even a generous margin within which to make a living out of his trade. And when a country requires revenue to provide for the defence of its shores and to supply the urgent social need of its people, that seems to be just the moment when, before imposing fresh taxes on its citizens, it ought to look round and see whether it has farmed its property to the best advantage.

INADEQUATE ASSESSMENTS.

Now the legislature has long ago fixed what it considers as a reasonable toll in the case of the little village inn. For a house assessed under Schedule A at £9 a licence of £4 10s. is charged, that is, 50 per cent. of the nominal annual value. As I shall point out later on, this bears no relation to the real value; in the vast majority of cases the assessment is probably less than one-half of what it ought to be on the basis acknowledged by the trade itself, in all its business transactions, so that the real charge imposed upon the licensee of the village inn amounts to something like 25 per cent. of the value. The principle which has been considered good enough for the small village publican we think ought to be extended to the proprietors of the prosperous liquor palaces of our great towns, and our rates of duty will be based generally on that principle. But before I actually give the figures I should like to say a few words on the question of valuation. We realise that by keeping the present assessable value as the basis of computation for our licences there will be a good many anomalies and inequalities. Any man who looks at the list of compensated public-houses, and compares the amount of the compensation given in each case with the annual value, will realise how unequally the present principle of licensing bears upon public-house owners. Here is one house, with an annual value which could hardly exceed £40, receives in compensation money £3,246. Here is another house, with an annual value of nearly £300, receives in compensation money £731. We have therefore come to the conclusion that it is essential, in order to ensure fair treatment as between one publican and another, that there should be a valuation based upon the principles on which publicans for the time being receive compensation, and therefore generally accepted by the trade as an equitable basis for appraising the value of their monopoly. This assessment, when it is complete, will be translated into terms of annual value, and the licence will be levied accordingly. The burdens of some publicans may be lightened, that of others may be increased, but on the whole justice will be done, as each man will be called upon to pay according to the value which he receives from the privilege which the State confers upon him.

It may well be, however, that it will have the effect of so considerably raising the whole level of the contribution required of the publican as to make it appear oppressive. In that case we undertake, when the valuation is complete, to reconsider the whole scale in the light of the more accurate and scientific figures which will have been secured by the operation of this new assessment. This new valuation will, however, take some months to complete, and meanwhile we propose to levy our duties upon the basis of the valuation upon which the present duties are chargeable.

PUBLICANS' LICENCES.

My new scale of duties for the full publican's licence begins, as I have already indicated, like the existing scale, at 50 per cent. of annual value; but, instead of following the existing scale—by gradually diminishing the percentage as the value increases until upon houses having an annual value of £700 the charge amounts to no more than 8½ per cent., above which figure, thanks to the cessation of the scale at that point, the decrease in the rate of the charge in proportion to annual value proceeds with still greater velocity, until, in the case of the highest values, it becomes almost insignificant—we propose to charge an uniform 50 per cent. of annual value throughout, subject to a minimum. The minimum rate in rural districts and in urban areas having a population of less than 2,000 will be £5, which, although only 10s. in excess of the present minimum charge, is, I think, a sufficient duty to exact from the small country inn, which satisfies the legitimate social needs of a scattered population, and whose volume of trade is in many cases not more than sufficient to provide the inn-keeper with a decent subsistence. The same considerations do not, however, apply to the poorer class of premises in the larger urban areas. A very large part of the mischief resulting from the liquor traffic is associated with the small, and often disreputable, house of this kind, which, in fact, ought never to have been licensed. Such houses are, indeed, in many cases, mere survivals from the period before 1872, since which date new licences have not, in fact, been granted, at any rate in England and Wales, to any premises in towns containing a population of not less than 100,000 inhabitants, of a lower annual value than £50; and in other towns, containing a population of not less than 10,000, of a lower annual value than £30. Such houses, where they do exist, have often a turnover quite out of proportion to the character of the premises, and make large profits. We think, therefore, that no hardship will be created by the charge of a minimum duty of £10 in urban areas of between 2,000 and 5,000 inhabitants; £15 between 5,000 and 10,000; £20 between 10,000 and 50,000; £30 between 50,000 and 100,000; and £35 in London and other towns having a population in excess of 100,000.

BEER RETAILERS' LICENCES.

So much for the full "on" licences. The next point in importance is the beer-retailers' "on" licence, commonly known as the "beer-house" licence. The same conditions as regards the enjoyment of a monopoly value attach to these licences as to the publicans' licences. The trade done in a beer-house is frequently as extensive and as profitable as the trade done in fully licensed premises, though, of course, as the privilege granted by the licence is a more restricted one, this is not invariably the case. The present fixed charge of £3 10s. for a beer-house licence, without regard to the value of the premises to which it is attached or to the profits which it enables the owner to earn, is, if judged by the standard of what would form a fair and reasonable consideration for so valuable a privilege, absurdly inadequate.

I propose, therefore, to introduce for this class of licence rates graduated on the same basis as that which is to be made applicable to full "on" licences, the rate being in each case two-thirds of the amount chargeable for a publican's licence in respect of similar premises—that is to say, one-third of the annual value of the premises. The principle of a minimum rate according to the size of the place in which the house is situated will be applied to this as to the public-house licence. The scale will be: For rural districts having a population of under 2,000, £3 10s.; between 2,000 and 5,000, £6 10s.; between 5,000 and 10,000, £10; from 10,000 to 50,000, £13; 50,000 to 100,000, £20; and above 100,000, £23 10s.

HOTELS AND RESTAURANTS.

The distinction made by the existing law between hotels and ordinary public-houses works in a very unsatisfactory and arbitrary manner, both from the point of view of the revenue and from the point of view of hotel-keepers. The charge for the hotel licence, properly so-called, is, on the one hand, an extremely low one; but, on the other hand, it is so difficult for the average keeper of a *bonâ fide* hotel to comply with the conditions laid down for the grant of this licence that the great majority of such hotel-keepers in fact find it necessary to take out the full publican's licence.

This latter licence, even at the rates at present charged, constitutes in the case of small hotels, at any rate, whose receipts from the sale of liquor are sometimes insignificant compared with the total business done, an undue burden, and it would

[Mr. Lloyd-George.]

clearly be inequitable to apply the new scale without qualification to this class of house. I therefore propose to make special concessions to *bonâ-fide* hotels, inns, and restaurants. I am anxious to draw a deep and clear line for purposes of taxation between the house which supplies all the best traditional objects of the inn and the mere drinking establishment which lives and thrives on "swilling" and "tippling." Under the new system, therefore, a distinction will be drawn between houses whose receipts from the sale of stimulants do not exceed one-third of their total receipts from all sources, and those in the case of which that proportion is exceeded. I have made careful inquiries, as a result of which I am satisfied that the proportion of one-third, at which I suggest the line should be drawn, will cover the case of practically all establishments whose business primarily consists in supplying food and lodging, facilities for recreation, or other services only incidentally connected with the consumption of alcohol. Hotels and restaurants which are mainly drinking places will thus be, as they ought to be, chargeable with the full publican's licence duty, but where the bulk of the business consists in the satisfaction of public requirements in directions other than the supply of stimulants, the rate of duty applicable to the publican's licence will be reduced in proportion as the receipts from the sale of intoxicating liquor diminish. It must, of course, be remembered in this connection that the possession of a licence gives an advantage not only as respects the sale of liquor, but also as respects the other business of a hotel, higher price being obtainable both for food and lodging in licensed premises than in premises not enjoying a licence. This value, no less than the profit directly derived from the sale of liquor itself, is part of the monopoly value of the premises and ought to be taken into account in assessing the duty. I propose to recognise this principle by making the reduction dependent on the proportion which the receipts from intoxicants bear, not to the whole, but to one-half of the total receipts from all classes of business. Thus, a house whose receipts from the sale of liquor amount to one-quarter of its total receipts will pay only one-half, and one whose liquor receipts amount to one-sixth only one-third of the full rate. The effect of this reform will be to tax hotels on a logical basis and to put large hotels for the first time into their proper place as

contributors to the revenue. A provision is inserted in the Bill under which the increase in duty will not, in the case of tied houses, fall on the publican. Payments in respect of monopoly value of new licences under the Licensing Act of 1904 will, in future, be taken for the Exchequer, thus removing the temptation to local justices to grant such licences for the sake of the profit accruing to the local authority, which, in some parts of the country at any rate, has resulted in the grant of licences in excess of legitimate public requirements.

CLUBS.

The case of clubs remains to be dealt with. The sale of intoxicating liquor in a club is not legally "sale," but "supply," and this method of distribution is under the present law entirely untaxed. Clubs in which liquor is supplied, at present compete to a large extent directly with the ordinary public-house, and this competition of an alternative and untaxed method of distribution is not only unfair to the holders of publican's licences, but likely, in the long run, seriously to encroach on the revenue derived from licence duties. In some cases, particularly where licences have been suppressed under the Act of 1904, clubs have sprung up which are mere public-houses in disguise, some of them financed by the very persons who have received compensation for the trade supposed to be lost by the withdrawal of the licence, but really transferred, with the added privilege of exemption from licence duty, to the house in which the club has been established. A scheme of licence duties for clubs, however, based upon annual value, would be both inequitable and impracticable. The better class of club, from whatever social rank its members may be drawn, possesses, as a rule, much better premises than a club which is mainly a drinking club. A tax upon annual value would, therefore, in all probability, vary almost inversely with the amount of liquor consumed, and it would penalise a club for increasing its accommodation for other than drinking purposes. I therefore propose that the duty should take the form of a poundage upon the amount of the receipts from the sale of liquor. Under this proposal clubs will not be licensed, that is to say. they will not be put in the same position as licensed premises; but an obligation will be imposed upon them to keep an account of the receipts from the sale of liquor, and a duty of three-pence in the £ will be imposed on every £ of those receipts. The effect will be that clubs will not be taxed as clubs, but will simply be taxed as drinking clubs.

REVISION OF EXCISE LIQUOR LICENCES.

These are, from the point of view of the Revenue, and of public interest, the most important of my proposals relating to licence duties; but I propose to take the opportunity of revising the whole system of Excise liquor licences—a system which is at present full of confusion and anomalies, both in law and practice, and to place it upon a simple and intelligible basis. These licences are divided into three main classes: (1) manufacturers' licences, (2) wholesale dealers' licences, (3) retailers' licences. Speaking generally, no licence of the first two classes requires a justices' licence; but, with a few minor exceptions, all the licences of the third class require such a licence. The considerations to which I have referred relating to monopoly value are, therefore, applicable only to licences of the third class, but this does not, of course, mean that a further contribution to the revenue by way of taxation cannot properly be required from the holders of the other classes of licences. Under the head of manufacturers' licences I propose to substitute for the present fixed duties of £1 and £10 10s. for brewers for sale and distillers of spirits respectively, graduated scales of duty according to the amount produced. In the case of the brewer's licence, the present payment of £1 will cover a production of 100 barrels only, and 12s. additional will be charged for every 50 barrels or fraction of 50 barrels above that quantity. The distiller's licence will be £10 for any quantity not exceeding 50,000 proof gallons, with an additional £10 for every additional 25,000 or fraction of 25,000 proof gallons. For the other manufacturers' licences the duties will still be charged at fixed rates, but I propose to increase the licence for rectifiers of spirits from £10 10s. to £15 15s., and that for makers of sweets—a term which in this case does not, of course, mean confectionery, but British-made wines—from £1 to £5 5s. Makers of cider or perry will likewise pay a duty of £5 5s., except when they manufacture solely from fruit which they themselves produce, in which case the duty will not be chargeable. The system of taxing wholesale dealers' licences will be the same as that at present in force, namely, a fixed duty, but the duty will be increased. There is, however, one important change, namely, that these wholesale dealers' licences will not in any case authorise retail sale, and the licences for wholesale dealing and retail sale are kept absolutely distinct. Subject to this qualification, the rates for wine (including sweets) and sweets will remain at £10 10s. and £5 5s. as at present. That for beer will be raised from £3 6s. 1d. to £10 10s., and spirits from £10 10s. to £15 15s. A licence to deal by wholesale in cider and perry will cost £5 5s.

The existing additional licences for retail trade, issued in connection with some of the wholesale dealers' licences, will be abolished, and wholesale dealers who desire to engage in retail trade will be required to take out the ordinary retailer's off-licence, subject, however, to a reduction of 25 per cent. in the scheduled rate for that licence. A separate retailer's off-licence will be introduced in the case of spirits, and the spirit retailer will accordingly be relieved from the necessity under which he at present labours, of taking out a wholesale licence which he does not require. The manufacturer's licence will cover the sale by wholesale of his own product, and dealers' licences will not require to be taken out by manufacturers unless they desire to engage in independent business as dealers.

RETAILERS' LICENCES.

I now come to retailers' on-licences. With the public-house and beerhouse licences I have already dealt, as also with hotels, restaurants, and clubs, which come under the same category. Theatres will, as at present, pay the same rates as public-houses, but with a maximum of £50 instead of £20. In the case of wine, sweets, and cider, I propose to substitute for the present fixed duties (£3 10s. in the case of wine (including sweets), and £1 5s. in the other cases), a scale according to annual value in four sections, the steps being at £20, £50, and £100. The respective rates for wine will be £4 10s., £6, £9, and £12, and for sweets and cider one-half these rates. Under retailers' off-licences the same principle will be adopted, the rates for spirits will be £14 for premises under £20 annual value, £20 between £20 and £50, £30 between £50 and £100, and £50 above £100. The scale for the off beer licence (including cider and perry) will be £3 10s., £5, £7, or £10, according to the value of the premises, and for wine (including sweets) the same, but off-licences

[Mr. Lloyd-George.]

for cider alone or sweets alone will cost only £2 irrespective of annual value. The new rates will be applicable to the whole of the United Kingdom, and the anomalies at present existing as between England, Ireland, and Scotland, as regards this class of licence, will be removed. As regards Scotland, there are various minor points in which the adoption of a uniform system throughout the United Kingdom will make a certain amount of difference, but the point which will attract attention is the modification of the conditions under which the retailers' off-licence for spirits is granted. In Scotland, at present, the holder of a grocer's spirit licence can sell wholesale, and can also sell in open vessels and in small quantities, whereas the English grocer can only sell in quart bottles or larger quantities. A great deal of business at present done by the holders of grocers' spirit licences in Scotland is really publican's business, that is to say, they sell small quantities of spirit in little glass noggins which are drunk outside the house and the glass noggin is left on the pavement outside. There is no doubt that a business of this sort is an abuse of the retailer's off-licence, and constitutes an abuse which ought to be suppressed. The present combined beer and wine licences will be abolished, and persons desirous of selling both beer and wine will in future have to take out two separate licences. The rate for passenger vessels will be increased from £5 to £10, the daily rate being raised from £1 to £2, while railway restaurant cars, which do not at present pay any licence duty will pay £1. The charge for occasional licences will be raised from 2s. 6d. to 10s. a day for a full licence, and from 1s. to 5s. a day for beer or wine only. I propose that the new rates should come into force on 30th September next, subject to the necessary adjustments with respect to unexpired existing licences, and I estimate that the effect of the changes will be to increase the revenue of the year from licence duties by £2,600,000.

Mr. AUSTEN CHAMBERLAIN: Is that for the full year?

Mr. LLOYD-GEORGE: For the full year. As a matter of fact, I should rather anticipate a reduction than an increase in the second year. This will be probably a maximum year. As payment of these duties is made for the whole year in advance the full effect of the charge will be felt in the year in which it takes place.

Against this, however, must be set the prejudicial effect upon the yield of the spirit duties which may be expected to be produced should an effort be made (and I am not sufficiently sanguine to think that it will not be made) to shift the new burden to the shoulders of the consumer by reducing the quantity or quality of the spirits supplied. On this aspect of the question I shall have more to say at a later stage.

TAXATION OF LAND.

Now I come to the question of land. The first conviction that is borne in upon the Chancellor of the Exchequer who examines land as a subject for taxation is this: that in order to do justice he must draw a broad distinction between land whose value is purely agricultural in its character and composition, and land which has a special value attached to it owing either to the fact of its covering marketable mineral deposits or because of its proximity to any concentration of people. Agricultural land has not, during the past 20 or 30 years, appreciated in value in this country. In some parts it has probably gone down. I know parts of the country where the value has gone up. But there has been an enormous increase in the value of urban land and of mineral property. And a still more important and relevant consideration in examining the respective merits of these two or three classes of claimants to taxation is this. The growth in the value, more especially of urban sites, is due to no expenditure of capital or thought on the part of the ground owner, but entirely owing to the energy and the enterprise of the community. [Cries of "Oh."] Where it is not due to that cause, and where it is due to any expenditure by the urban owner himself, full credit ought to be given to him in taxation, and full credit will be given to him in taxation. I am dealing with cases which are due to the growth of the community, and not to anything done by the urban proprietor. It is undoubtedly one of the worst evils of our present system of land tenure that instead of reaping the benefit of the common endeavour of its citizens a community has always to pay a heavy penalty to its ground landlords for putting up the value of their land. There are other differences between these classes of property which are worth mentioning in this connection, because they have a real bearing upon the problem. There is a remarkable contrast between the attitude adopted by a landowner towards his urban and mineral properties, and that which he generally assumes towards the tenants of his agricultural property. I will mention one or two of them. Any man who is acquainted with the balance-sheets of a great estate must know that the gross receipts do not represent anything like the real net income enjoyed by the landowner. On the contrary, a considerable proportion of those receipts are put back into the land in the shape of fructifying improvements and in maintaining and keeping in good repair structures erected by them which are essential to the proper conduct of the agricultural business upon which rents depend. Urban landlords recognise no obligation of that kind, nor do mineral royalty owners. They spend nothing in building, in improving, in repairing or in upkeep of structures essential to the proper conduct of the business of the occupiers. The urban landowner, as a rule, recognises no such obligations. I again exclude the urban landowner who really does spend money on his property; that ought to be put to his credit. The rent in the case with which I am dealing is a net rent free from liabilities, or legal obligations. Still worse, the urban landowner is freed in practice from the ordinary social obligations which are acknowledged by every agricultural landowner towards those whose labour makes their wealth.

It is true in the rural districts that there are good landlords and there are bad landlords. But in this respect there are so many good landlords in the country to set up the standard that even the worst are compelled to follow at a greater or a less distance. But the worst rural landlord in this respect is better than the best urban landlord in so far as the recognition of what is due to the community who produce the rent is concerned. [Cries of " Oh !"] I will point out what I mean. First of all the rural landowner has the obligation to provide buildings and keep them in repair. The urban landowner, as a rule, has neither of these two obligations. There is that essential difference between the two. The urban landlord and the mineral royalty owner are invariably rack-renters. They extort the highest and the heaviest ground rent or royalty they can obtain on the sternest commercial principles. They are never restrained by that sense of personal relationship with their tenants which exercises such a beneficent and moderating influence upon the very same landlord in his dealings with his agricultural tenants. And the distinction is not confined merely to the rent. Take the conditions of the tenancy. I am not here to defend many of the terms which are included in many an agricultural agreement for tenancy. I think many of them are oppressive, irritating, and stupid. But compared with the conditions imposed upon either a colliery owner or upon a town lessee they are the very climax of generosity. Take this case.—and it is not by any means irrelevant to the proposals which I shall have to submit to the Committee later on. What agricultural landlord in this country would ever think of letting his farm for a term of years on condition, first of all, that the tenant should pay the most extortionate rent that he could possibly secure in the market, three, or four, or even five times the real value of the soil; that the tenant should then be compelled to build a house of a certain size and at a certain cost, and in a certain way, and that at the end of the term he, or rather his representatives, should hand that house over in good tenantable repair free from encumbrances to the representatives of the ground owner who has not spent a penny upon constructing it, and who has received during the whole term of lease the highest rent which he could possibly screw in respect of the site? Why, there is not a landlord in Great Britain who would ever dream of imposing such outrageous conditions upon his tenant. And yet these are the conditions which are imposed every day in respect of urban sites; imposed upon tradesmen who have no choice in the matter; imposed upon professional men and business men who have got to live somewhere within reasonable distance of their offices; imposed even on workmen building a house for themselves, paying for it by monthly instalments out of their wages for 30 years purely in order to be within reasonable distance of the factory or mine or workshop at which they are earning a living.

This is by no means an imaginary picture which I am drawing. If anyone thinks so I would invite him to examine for himself the evidence given before the Town Holdings Committees in 1888 and the subsequent Committee of the same character held later on—Committees appointed by the Unionist administration of that date. There was the case of the Festiniog quarrymen, who had to build on rocks which could not feed a goat, and upon swamps for which the landlord could not, and did not, receive more than, sometimes, 2s. an acre, and, at the outside, 7s. 6d. an acre. These were let to

[Mr. Lloyd-George.]

the quarrymen for building purposes at rents that amounted to £50 an acre. Leases were given for 60 years. All the improvements were effected either by the quarrymen themselves or by the local authority to whom they paid their rates. To build or buy their houses, most of these quarrymen generally borrowed money from building societies. As long as they were in good health and in full employment they were able to pay their monthly instalments. When either health or work gave out they were very hard pressed indeed. But they never got any assistance or sympathy from the landllord. As they paid, the property, instead of increasing in value for them, became of less and less value as it passed year by year into the possession of the landlord. There were many illustrations of that kind given before these Committees, though not all 60 years. Some were 70, some ran up to 90, other were for lives and 21 years.

You cannot put cases of this kind at all in the same category as that of an agricultural landlord who builds farmhouses and farm buildings, and generally incurs most, if not all, of the capital expenditure in and around a farm, and who by no means, if he is a fair-minded landlord, ever thinks of extorting these monstious rents out of the necessities of his tenants. I might give other cases where land in the neighbourhood of towns has appreciated in value owing to the growth of the population. I do not wish to multiply instances, because every hon. Member must have in his own mind illustrations, with the details of which he is cognisant, from his own experience and observation of what I am referring to. I might, perhaps, take another case, and I am not sure that you can find a better or a fairer one than that which is provided by the working class suburbs of London. I am referring to the case of Woolwich. Considerable population has been attracted there largely owing to the expenditure of public money upon the Arsenal. If there is any increase in the value of land there, not a penny of that increment is attributable to anything done by the local landowners. Now I would commend Members of the House to a speech delivered by the late Conservative Member for Woolwich, who in his day was one of the most striking figures in this House. This is what he says about Woolwich :—

"In the parish of Plumstead land used to be let for agricultural purposes for £3 an acre. The income of an estate of 250 acres in 1845 was £750 per annum, and the capital value at 20 years' purchase was £15,000. The Arsenal came to Woolwich; with the Arsenal the necessity for 5,000 houses. And then came the harvest for the landlord. The land, the capital value of which had been £15,000, now brought an income of £14,250 per annum. The ground landlord has received £1,000,000 in ground rents already, and after 20 years hence the Woolwich estates, with all the houses upon them, will revert to the landowner's family, bringing another million, meaning altogether a swap of £15,000 for a sum of £2,000,000."

There are many cases of a similar character which will readily occur to the memory of every hon. Member who is at all acquainted with the subject. Take well-known properties in Lancashire and Cheshire in regard to which evidence was given. And yet, although the landlord, without any exertion of his own, is now in these cases in receipt of an income which is ten or even a hundred-fold of what he was in the habit of receiving when these properties were purely agricultural in their character, and although he is in addition to that released from all the heavy financial obligations which are attached to the ownership of this land as agricultural property, he does not contribute a penny out of his income towards the local expenditure of the community which has thus made his wealth, in the words of John Stuart Mill, "whilst he was slumbering." Is it too much, is it unfair, is it inequitable, that Parliament should demand a special contribution from these fortunate owners towards the defence of the country and the social needs of the unfortunate in the community, whose efforts have so materially contributed to the opulence which they are enjoying?

LAND KEPT OUT OF MARKET.

There is another aspect of this matter which I should like to say a word upon before I come to the actual proposals of the Government. I have dwelt upon the fundamental difference in the demeanour of landowners towards their urban tenants and that which under the inspiration of more high-minded and public-spirited principles guide their conduct towards their agricultural tenants. There is no doubt that the spirit of greed is unconsciously much more dominant and unrestrained in the former case. One disastrous result of this is that land which is essential to the free and healthy development of towns is being kept out of the market in order to enhance its value, and that towns are cramped and their people become overcrowded in dwellings which are costly without being comfortable. You have only to buy an ordnance survey map and put together the sheets which include some town of your acquaintance and the land in its immediate vicinity, and you will see at once what I mean. You will find, as a rule, your town or village huddled in one corner of the map, dwellings jammed together as near as the law of the land will permit, with an occasional courtyard, into which the sunshine rarely creeps, but with nothing that would justify the title of "garden." For it is the interest of the landlord to pile together on the land every scrap of bricks and mortar that the law will allow. And yet outside square miles of land unoccupied, or at least unbuilt upon; land in the town seems to let by the grain, as if it were radium. Not merely towns, but villages (and by villages and towns I mean the people who dwell in them) suffer extremely from the difficulty which is experienced in obtaining land, and by the niggardliness with which sites are measured out.

You cannot help feeling how much healthier and happier the community could have been made in these towns and villages if they had been planned on more spacious and rational principles, with a reasonable allowance of garden for every tenant, which would serve as a playground, as vegetable and flower garden, for the workman and his family, and which would even, in many districts, help materially to solve the problem of unemployment.

MINING ROYALTIES.

The same observations apply to the case of mineral royalties. There all the expenditure is incurred by the capitalist, who runs the risk of losing his capital, while the miner risks his life; and I do not think it is too much to ask the royalty owner, who has contributed no capital and runs no risk, to contribute in this emergency to bear the large burden that is cast upon us for the defence of the country, and to help to pay the large sum of money needed to make provision for social needs, for the aged, and for those who have been engaged in digging out mining royalties all their lives.

UNEARNED INCREMENT.

My present proposals are proposals both for taxation and for valuation. Although very moderate in character, they will produce an appreciable revenue in the present year and more in future years. The proposals are three in number.

First, it is proposed to levy a tax on the increment of value accruing to land from the enterprise of the community or the landowner's neighbours. We do not propose to make this tax retrospective.

It is to apply to future appreciation in value only, and will not touch any increment already accrued. We begin therefore with a valuation of all land at the price which it may be expected to realise at the present time, and we propose to charge the duty only upon the additional value which the land may hereafter acquire. The valuations upon the difference between which the tax will be chargeable will be valuations of the land itself—apart from buildings and other improvements—and of this difference, the strictly unearned increment, we propose to take one-fifth, or 20 per cent., for the State.

We start with the valuation of the present moment. No increment that has accrued before the date of the valuation will count. We value the land at its present value, and then count the increment from that point. You get the increment on two bases. You get at it when the land is sold. Then it will be discovered what the actual increment is. We propose to charge 20 per cent. on the increment which the landlord receives, ascertained by comparing what he receives with the valuation to be made immediately after this Bill. It would be also made on the passing of the property upon death, so that there will be an increment of estate duty; and if there is any increment which is not due to expenditure by the landowner himself on improvements, but is due merely to the appreciation of land in the neighbourhood owing to the growth of population or some other cause, then the same charge would be made on that increment. Corporations (which do not die) will pay upon property owned by them at stated intervals of years, being allowed the option of spreading the payment of the duty upon the increment accruing in one period over the following period by annual instalments.

An HON. MEMBER: What number of years?

Mr. LLOYD-GEORGE: I will give the particulars later on. Upon the creation of a lease or upon the transfer of an interest in land only such proportion of the increment duty will be payable as the value of the lease or of the transferred interest bears to the value of the fee simple of the land, and increment duty once paid will frank the increment or the portion of the increment in respect of which it has been paid from any further charge of the duty. As regards the duty payable on the occasion of the grant of a lease, provision will be made for payment by instalments, inasmuch as in such circumstances no capital

[Mr. Lloyd-George.]

sum is available for payment of the duty. As the standard of comparison is the value of the land at the present date, and the tax will be levied only upon the increment subsequently accruing, the yield in the first year will necessarily be small, and I do not think it safe to estimate for more than £50,000 in 1909-10. The amount will increase steadily in future years, and ultimately become a fruitful source of revenue.

DUTY ON UNDEVELOPED LAND.

The second proposal relating to land is the imposition of a tax on the capital value of all land which is not used to the best advantage. The owner of valuable land which is required or likely in the near future to be required for building purposes, who contents himself with an income therefrom wholly incommensurate with the capital value of the land in the hope of recouping himself ultimately in the shape of an increased price, is in a similar position to the investor in securities who re-invests the greater part of his dividends; but while the latter is required to pay income tax both upon the portion of the dividends enjoyed and also upon the portion re-invested, the former escapes taxation upon his accumulating capital altogether, and this, although the latter by his self-denial is increasing the wealth of the community, while the former, by withholding from the market land which is required for housing or industry, is creating a speculative inflation of values which is socially mischievous.

We propose to redress this anomaly by charging an annual duty of ½d. in the £ on the capital value of undeveloped land. The same principle applies to ungotten minerals, which we propose similarly to tax at ½d. in the £, calculated upon the price which the mining rights might be expected to realise if sold in open market at the date of valuation. The tax on undeveloped land will be charged upon unbuilt-on land only, and all land of which the capital value does not exceed £50 an acre will be exempted, as also any land exceeding that value with respect to which it can be shown to the satisfaction of the Commissioners of Inland Revenue that no part of the value is due to the capability of the land for use for building purposes. Under these provisions all land having a purely agricultural value will be exempt.

Further exemptions will be made in favour of gardens and pleasure grounds not exceeding an acre in extent, and parks, gardens, and open spaces which are open to the public as of right, or to which reasonable access is granted to the public, where that access is recognised by the Commissioners of Inland Revenue as contributing to the amenity of the locality. Where undeveloped land forms part of a settled estate, provision will be made to enable a limited owner who has not the full enjoyment of the land to charge the duty upon the corpus of the property. The valuation upon which the tax will be charged will be the value of land as a cleared site, deductions being allowed for any expenditure necessary to clear it, and likewise for any value attributable to works of a permanent character executed by, or on behalf of, any person interested in the land within a specified period of the date of valuation, for the purpose of fitting the land for building purposes. Until a valuation has been obtained it is impossible to estimate the yield of the tax with any precision, and the yield in the first year is made still more doubtful by the fact that, pending the completion of the valuation, the tax must be collected provisionally upon the basis of declarations by owners—arrears (if any) to be collected later when the valuation has been completed. But as these declarations will also form the basis for the charge of increment value duty until the valuation is completed, with respect to which an under-declaration may have serious consequences, it may be expected that they will be sufficiently reliable to allow at any rate, a large proportion of the whole amount due to be obtained within the year. I therefore feel justified in estimating that the duty of ½d. in the pound on undeveloped land and ungotten minerals will produce not less than £350,000 in the current financial year.

REVERSION DUTY.

My third proposal under the head of land is a 10 per cent. reversion duty upon any benefit accruing to a lessor from the determination of a lease, the value of the benefit to be taken to be the amount (if any) by which the total value of the land at the time the lease falls in exceeds the value of the consideration for the grant of the lease, due regard being had, however, for the case of the reversioner whose interest is less than a freehold. The reversion at the end of a long building lease having no appreciable market value at the time the lease is granted is, when the lease falls in, of the nature of a windfall, and can be made to bear a reasonable tax without hardship. Some consideration must, however, be shown to the purchaser of an approaching reversion where the purchase has taken place before the imposition of such a duty was contemplated. I therefore propose to have special provision to deal with that case. Special provision will also be made to meet the case of an increment value, in respect of which increment duty is payable under my first proposal, being included in a reversion. Another case in which special consideration should, I think, be shown is that of a lease determined by agreement between lessor and lessee before its expiration for the purpose of renewal. Towards the termination of a lease the lessee may be willing and even anxious to make improvements in the premises, provided that he can obtain a decent security of tenure at a reasonable rent. His business may be crippled for want of proper accommodation, but he is at the mercy of the ground landlord, who, in many cases, wrings out of him the uttermost farthing before agreeing to a renewal, which is to the interest of both parties. If the parties fail to come to terms the opportunity for an improvement, possibly of great public utility, is at any rate postponed, and perhaps irretrievably lost. The importance of facilitating such renewals to the interests of lessees, of the building trade, of the public generally, and even of the ground landlord himself, can scarcely be exaggerated. Accordingly in cases where a reversion is anticipated in circumstances of this character, and comes under taxation at an earlier date than would have happened in ordinary course, by reason of an agreement entered into with the lessee to enable him to improve the premises, I propose to make a special abatement of duty proportionate to the unexpired period of the original lease which is surrendered, and I have great hopes that this allowance, coupled with the fact that the value of the reversion for the purpose of the duty, will be calculated upon the difference between the consideration for the old and the consideration for the new lease, will induce owners to grant renewals more readily and upon more favourable terms than at present, and so tend to remove one of the most mischievous effects of the leasehold system.

There are no official statistics of the value of leasehold property, or of the dates upon which existing leases determine, and I am therefore not in a position to give more than a conjectural estimate of the annual yield of this duty. There is, besides, reason to believe that the num-ber of leases falling in from year to year is by no means a constant quantity, and this makes the task of estimating for a particular year still more difficult. On the whole, I do not think that I can in the present year rely on a larger revenue than £100,000 from this source, and I propose, therefore, to estimate the yield of the three land taxes for the current year at £500,000, an amount which, however, must not, as I have already explained, be regarded as any indication of the revenue they will ultimately produce.

Mr. W. W. RUTHERFORD: What is a lease? How long is a lease?

Mr. LLOYD-GEORGE: It is perfectly obvious that a tenancy from year to year would not be a lease.

Mr. RUTHERFORD: But what is?

VALUATION OF REAL PROPERTY.

Mr. LLOYD-GEORGE: These proposals necessarily involve a complete reconstruction of the method of valuing property. The existing taxes upon real property are levied upon the annual value of such property as a whole without distinguishing between the value which resides in the land itself and that which has been added to it by the enterprise of the owner in erecting buildings or effecting other improvements. Even apart from this, the methods of valuation vary in different localities, with the result that the incidence of existing burdens is very uneven. The intensely complex character of British land tenure introduces a further complication. There are no official records of the various interests in land, existing rates and taxes being charged upon the occupier, who is left to recover from the other interests (if any) either by a rough-and-ready scheme of statutory deductions from rent or by making such bargain as he is able with his landlord. It now becomes necessary for the purposes both of the increment value duty and of the undeveloped land duty to distinguish between the two elements in the value of real property, while, as the increment value duty and the reversion duty will both of them have to be collected from the particular interests to which those accretions respectively accrue, a complete register of the owners and other persons interested in land, with full details of the various interests, will ultimately be required.

The preparation of such a register will be a lengthy task which must in the main be proceeded with as each separate pro-

[Mr. Lloyd-George.]

perty comes under taxation, but the question of valuation is of greater urgency. The existing valuation lists on an annual value basis (even if they represented the true annual values which in many cases they do not) would be of little use for the purpose of determining capital values— the basis of the new duties—and it will therefore be necessary to provide machinery for a complete valuation on a capital basis of the whole of the land in the United Kingdom. I do not think I will enter into particulars now of the method which we propose to follow in valuation. I shall do that when we come to discuss the Resolution in Committee. Now I have disposed of direct taxation.

INDIRECT TAXATION.

I am not going at this late hour to enter into any discussion of the principles which ought to guide a Finance Minister in the imposition of indirect taxation. But one thing I am sure will be accepted by every Member of this House, and that is that we ought at any rate to avoid taxes on the necessaries of life. I referred some time ago, in the course of a discussion in this House, to the old age pension officers' reports. There was one thing in those reports which struck me very forcibly, and that was that they all reported that the poorer the people they had to deal with, the more was their food confined to bread and tea, and of the price of that tea, which of course was of the poorest quality, half goes to the tax gatherer. That is always the worst of indirect taxation on the people. The poorer they are the more heavily the tax falls upon them. Tea and sugar are necessaries of life, and I think that the rich man who would wish to spare his own pocket at the expense of the bare pockets of the poor is a very shabby rich man indeed, and therefore I am sure that I carry with me the assent of even the classes upon whom I am putting very heavy burdens, that when we come to indirect taxes, at any rate those two essentials of life ought to be exempt.

INCREASE OF SPIRIT DUTY.

There are three other possible sources— beer, spirits, and tobacco. An increase in the beer duty, sufficiently great to justify an addition to the retail price, would produce a very large sum—larger, indeed, than I require for my present purposes—and would have, besides, in all probability, the effect of diverting the consumption of alcohol from beer to spirits—a change

which would certainly not conduce to the social health of the country. The incidence of a small duty, on the other hand, would, to a large extent, at any rate in the first instance, be upon the liquor trade rather than upon the consumer; and I should not feel justified in imposing such a burden in a year when so considerable an additional contribution is being called for from that trade under the head of licence duties.

The case of spirits is, however, somewhat different. I am aware that the small increases in the spirit duties which were made by Lord St. Aldwyn during the South African war were disappointing in their financial results, and that any further increase would undoubtedly result in a considerably diminished consumption, which would to a very large extent at any rate nullify the benefit to the revenue which might otherwise be expected to accrue from it. It does not, however, follow from the result of this small experiment that we have reached the absolute limit of the profitable taxation of spirits, or that a substantial increase in the rates of duty would not, in spite of its effects upon consumption, produce an appreciable amount of revenue. I am disposed, at any rate, to try the experiment, which, even if it ends—to take the most pessimistic view—in no larger revenue being raised from the higher rate upon a diminished consumption, than by the existing rate upon the present consumption, will still, in my view, be conducive to the best interests of the nation. It is perfectly true that the small duties imposed up to the present have not been productive. The reason for that was that the publican, or the retailer, found that, probably by changes in the character of the whisky, or by other means, he was able to get his money in another way, and the consumption decreased by a considerable amount. It is idle, therefore, to put on anything except a fairly heavy tax, and I impose a duty which the publican will find it to his interest to charge. I propose to raise the present duties (Customs and Excise) on spirits by 3s. 9d. per gallon, an amount which will, on the one hand justify an increase in retail prices, and on the other hand, assuming such an increase to be at the rate of a halfpenny per glass, will leave a margin to the publican to recoup himself for loss of profits arising from decreased consumption, and have something over towards mitigating the pressure of the new licence duty. The mere paper increase of a duty of that sort would be very considerable, but I do not expect to get anything approximating to that. The right hon. Gentleman knows perfectly well the possibilities of getting more out of spirits. This year there are exceptional circumstances. First of all, the forestalments are very heavy. It is not merely forestalments up to the end of the last financial year, but they have been going on since, so that the wholesale people have got in hand sufficient stock to carry them on comfortably for a good many weeks at any rate. Therefore, we do not get the increase for some weeks, possibly for some months. That will make a very considerable hole in the estimate which I should otherwise have made of the yield of those taxes. Not only that, but I have not the faintest doubt that it will have the effect of decreasing consumption; that will be the inevitable effect. It may drive a good many from spirits to try beer and to expedients of that sort. It will involve a very considerable increase in the price of the commodity, and therefore, I think, must have a very considerable effect in diminishing the actual consumption. Taking all these influences into consideration, I do not feel safe in counting upon receiving more than £1,600,000 additional revenue as the result of the change in 1909-10.

INCREASE OF TOBACCO DUTY.

I have still nearly two millions more to find, and for this I must turn to tobacco —from a fiscal point of view, a much healthier source of revenue. The present rate of duty on unmanufactured tobacco containing 10 per cent. or more of moisture is 3s. a pound, and the increase I propose is 8d. a pound, with equivalent additions to the rates for cigars, cigarettes, and manufactured tobacco. Now, one pound of unmanufactured tobacco as imported, produces, after allowance has been made on the one hand for waste in manufacture, and on the other for the moisture which is added in preparing it for sale, nearly 1 1-5 pounds of the tobacco of retail trade, so that an addition of half an ounce to the retail price leaves the tobacco trade with an ample margin to finance the increased duty.

In estimating the additional yield from the increased rate of duty, regard must be had, as under the spirit duty, to the considerations that one month of the year has already passed, and that the duty-paid stocks are inflated by forestalments. Allowance must also be made—but in this case a comparatively small allowance—for decrease of consumption consequent upon the higher rate of duty. My estimate, therefore, is £1,900,000 for 1909-10, and £2,250,000 for a full year.

FINAL BALANCE SHEET.

I am now in a position to present my final balance sheet for 1909-10.

The Revenue, on the present basis of taxation, being...	£148,390,000
And the Expenditure, on the basis of the Estimates already presented to Parliament	164,152,000
The Account, before adjustment, shows, as I have already explained, an anticipated deficit of	£15,762,000

To the Revenue side of the Account must be added:—

Under Customs and Excise:—

New duty of 3d. a gallon on petrol	£340,000
Increase of spirit duties	1,600,000
Increase of tobacco duties ...	1,900,000
Revision and increase of liquor licence duties ...	2,600,000
Motor-car licences	260,000
Making a total addition under the heads of Customs and Excise of	£6,700,000

Under the various Inland Revenue duties the new proposals are estimated to produce:—

Estate duties ...	£2,850,000
Stamps	650,000
Income tax (net) .	3,500,000
And the new land taxes	£500,000
Or a total from new and increased Inland Revenue duties of	£7,500,000

These amounts (namely, £6,700,000 from Customs and Excise and £7,500,000 from Inland Revenue) added together give as the total estimated yield of new taxation £14,200,000

8

[Mr. Lloyd-George.]

Adding these sums to the estimated Revenue on the existing basis 148,390,000

We arrive at £162,590,000

as the estimated Revenue of the year.

To the expenditure side of the account must be added:—

Under the head of Consolidated Fund Services:—

The proceeds of the petrol duty and motor car licences, which will be paid to the new fund for improvement of roads £600,000

Under Civil Services:—

The amount required for the first year's giant to the new Development Fund £200,000
For labour exchanges 100,000

Making a total addition under Civil Services of... ... 300,000

and under Customs and Excise and Inland Revenue 50,000

for the payment of valuers and other administrative expenses arising in connection with the proposed taxes on land.

Adding these sums together we arrive at a total additional expenditure of ... £950,000

which, with the expenditure on the basis of the Estimates already presented 164,152,000

increases the total estimated expenditure for the year to £165,102,000

Deducting, under the head of Consolidated Fund Services, the amount of the proposed reduction of the Fixed Debt Charge 3,000,000

We arrive at £162,102,000

as the final figure on the Expenditure side of the Account.

The Total Estimated Revenue thus being £162,590,000

and the Total Estimated Expenditure 162,102,000

there remains a margin for contingencies of £488,000

There will be a very considerably increased demand upon the yield of those taxes for the coming year. If the Navy expenditure is at the maximum, which I anticipate, most of the increased expenditure will be absorbed by naval expenditure. The balance will be appropriated to those schemes of social reform which I sketched at the beginning of my observations.

I have to thank the House for the very great indulgence which they have extended to me and for the patience with which they have listended to me. My task has been an extraordinarily difficult one. It has been as disagreeable a task as could well have been allotted to any Minister of the Crown. But there is one element of supreme satisfaction in it. That is to be found in contemplating the objects for which these new imposts have been created. The money thus raised is to be expended first of all in ensuring the inviolability of our shores. It has also been raised in order not merely to relieve but to prevent unmerited distress within those shores. It is essential that we should make every necessary provision for the defence of our country. But surely it is equally imperative that we should make it a country even better worth defending for all and by all. And it is that this expenditure is for both those purposes that alone could justify the Government. I am told that no Chancellor of the Exchequer has ever been called on to impose such heavy taxes in a time of peace. This, Mr. Emmott, is a War Budget. It is for raising money to wage implacable warfare against poverty and squalidness. I cannot help hoping and believing that before this generation has passed away we shall have advanced a great step towards that good time when poverty and wretchedness and human degradation which always follow in its camp will be as remote to the people of this country as the wolves which once infested its forests.

The right hon. Gentleman resumed his seat at three minutes before eight of the clock.

Motion made and Question put.

SPIRITS.

1. That in addition to the duties of customs now payable on spirits imported into Great Britain or Ireland there shall on and after 30th April, 1909, be charged the following duties (that is to say):—

Enoch Powell demonstrates on Hola camp scandal he was far from a racist bigot

Denis Healey's political career began while he was still in uniform after having served in the Army in the second world war. He went on to become one of the most prominent figures in British politics for much of the second half of the 20th century.

He became known affectionately as the "old bruiser", a reputation based on the robust style that he brought to bear in dealing with his political opponents. It was an approach that was to stand him in good stead as, often in the face of opposition from all sides, he wrestled with some of the most serious problems to confront Britain's post war Governments. His policies earned him as many enemies as it did friends, which may have explained why he never became the leader of the Labour party.

He was born in 1917, the son of an engineer, an Irishman whose family hailed from County Antrim. His father idolised Winston Churchill, and young Healey was given Winston as his middle name, a fact that did not pass without comment in the Labour community in later years.

At the age of five he and his family moved to the West Riding of Yorkshire, his father having been appointed principal of the technical school in Keighley. Young Denis was educated at Bradford Grammar school and won an exhibition in classics that took him to Balliol college, Oxford where he took a double first. At Oxford he became involved in Labour politics, and in 1937 he joined the Communist party. He quit in 1939 in protest at the Molotov-Ribbentrop pact.

After graduation he joined the Army, serving with the Royal Engineers in North Africa, Sicily and Italy, where he was mentioned in dispatches and awarded the MBE. At the end of the war he left the service with the rank of major and, as an introduction to national politics, addressed the Labour party conference in 1945. At the general election soon afterwards, he stood for the Conservative seat of Pudsey and Otley, but, despite doubling the Labour vote, failed to win.

It was to be seven years before he entered Parliament, as the member for Leeds, South-East at a by-election in 1952. In 1959 he was appointed shadow Foreign Secretary. With Labour's victory in the 1964 general election he became Secretary of State for Defence.

It was a job he was to hold for the next six years, during which he implemented the withdrawal of Britain's military presence East of Suez, and cancelled the TSR2, but gave the go-ahead for the Nimrod, the Harrier and, in a collaborative deal with European partners, the Tornado multi-role combat aircraft.

With Labour's general election defeat in 1970, he was back in the shadow Cabinet, once more as shadow Foreign Secretary. Four years later, when Ted Heath's dispute with the mineworkers led to a general election and a knife-edge Labour victory, Harold Wilson appointed him Chancellor of the Exchequer. For five years he battled with inflation, sometimes in double figures, the balance of payments and an incomes policy that at the time dominated his life.

With the trade unions in open revolt, Britain embarked in 1978 on the so-called "Winter of Discontent". It was to cost Labour the next general election, to put Margaret Thatcher in Number 10 Downing Street and to see Denis Healey back in the shadow Cabinet.

Eighteen months later, Jim Callaghan resigned as Prime Minister. Denis Healey stood for the leadership but was beaten by Michael Foot. To those who offered him commiseration he offered them a saying from American politics – that he would rather people asked why he was not the leader than why he was. The position of deputy leader was still to be filled, and in an often bitter battle he narrowly defeated Tony Benn to take the job.

After the 1987 general election he stood down from the shadow Cabinet and in 1992 resigned his Leeds, East seat. He was given a peerage as Baron Healey of Riddlesden.

During his career he became as well-known for what he did not say as for what he did. Contrary to popular belief, he did not say that he would "squeeze the rich until the pips squeak". He did not initiate the expression "silly Billy". But he did say, on one memorable occasion, that being attacked by Geoffrey Howe was like being "savaged by a dead sheep."

He married Edna, now Lady Healey, in 1945, and is a prolific writer and an accomplished photographer.

Outstanding and surprising speech demanded adherence to British standards in Africa

I have chosen the speech made by Enoch Powell about the Hola Camp affair on 27 July 1959 because it was one of the best speeches he ever made, worthy of Demosthenes himself.

This was the time of the Mau Mau emergency in Kenya. It had its beginnings as early as 1951, the Mau Mau being a secret society among the Kikuyu tribe and its aims being to drive the white man from Kenya. In 1952 British troops were sent to Kenya and within weeks a state of emergency was declared and Jomo Kenyatta, destined 12 years later to become independent Kenya's first President, was arrested. Within six months he was sentenced to seven years' hard labour.

The Hola Camp affair was one of many unpalatable incidents in a terrorist campaign that lasted for seven years. It burst on to the front pages of Britain's newspapers, and in the House of Commons we attacked the Government's methods in dealing with the uprising.

Hola Camp was an internment camp for suspected Mau Mau terrorists. In March 1959 the internees were beaten for refusing to work. Ten of them were killed in the violence. A clumsy attempt to cover up what had happened by suggesting that the victims had died from drinking contaminated water was soon dispelled.

Powell's speech was not only outstanding, it was surprising because he agreed completely with the views expressed by two left-wing Labour MPs, Barbara Castle and Leslie Hale, who spoke immediately before and after him.

The camp had been established with the knowledge of the Governor, and the 10 men were killed by the warders. Powell told the House that we could not have inconsistency in our standards. We could not have African standards in Africa, Asian standards in Asia and British standards at home in Britain. That choice was not available to us.

He concluded his speech with the statement:

> "We must be consistent with ourselves everywhere. All Government, all influence of man upon man rests upon opinion."

What we could do in Africa where we still governed:

> "depends upon the opinion which is entertained of the way in which this country acts and the way in which Englishmen act. We cannot, we dare not, in Africa of all places, fall below our own highest standards in the acceptance of responsibility."

It was some years later that Powell was to make his famous – perhaps his most famous – speech at the Midland Hotel in Birmingham in which he said that the immigration of coloured people from the Commonwealth to Britain would produce "rivers of blood".

His speech about Hola Camp shows that he was far from being the sort of racist bigot so many have called him.

[MRS. CASTLE.]

Hola had had a bath. What was really happening was that dying men were vomiting water that they had drunk, and any person fit to hold the office of medical officer in charge of detainees ought to have enough medical knowledge to be aware of that fact.

Of course, perhaps he did, but perhaps like everybody else he was " covering up ". The most significant words of all in this business were spoken by Mr. Marsden, the District Officer, at the inquest. He said:

"There was a general attitude amongst all Europeans not to say anything".

This is our indictment. Yet we have here a whole network of responsibility and a picture of administrative callousness which shocks us, whatever it may do to right hon. and hon. Members opposite.

We have also here the violation of the constitutional principle which I should have thought this House would have gone a long way to defend ; and that is that if orders are given to subordinates and things go wrong the men who give those orders should have the decency to say that the responsibility is theirs.

The right hon. Gentleman the Colonial Secretary stands in the dock just as much as the Minister of Defence, the Governor of Kenya, or anybody else associated in any way with this shocking affair, because he has been asked in this House time and again if he approved of the Cowan plan and whether it was being operated anywhere else. We were told in the last debate we had that it would all be all right in future because the Governor was drawing up new directives as to the use of force. All I can say is that there must then have been something wrong with the present ones. This promise was given six weeks ago, and we were told that, when the new directives were ready, a copy would be put in the Library of the House. Yet I have been asking all afternoon if anything is yet available and it is not. After all this time, after eleven men have died, the new instructions are not available. At that rate, Mr. Lipson would be in his job for life. When this terrible shame comes upon the Colonial Secretary, whether he willed it or not, and he does not act, he shows he does not deserve to hold his office.

1.15 a.m.

Mr. J. Enoch Powell (Wolverhampton, South-West): Many aspersions have been cast and many imputations made by hon. Members opposite in the course of this debate with which I could not for an instant associate myself. And yet I cannot regret that even at this hour the House is once again considering the affair of Hola Camp. For the further documents relating to the deaths which were issued as a White Paper last week confirm what was already pretty clear from the earlier evidence, that it could be to the credit neither of this House nor of this country that the matter should rest where it now stands.

The affair of Hola Camp was a great administrative disaster, and to that administrative disaster there were three aspects. There was the authorisation of an operation which in its nature was likely to have fatal results ; there was the failure to see that that operation, such as it was, was at least carried out with the minimum of risk ; and, finally, there was the incident, which it is difficult to find a word to describe, of the water cart communiqué. The new documents show that the responsibility for all three aspects of this administrative disaster goes higher than can be discharged by the premature retirement of the officer in charge of the camp or by the retirement, accelerated by a few weeks, of the Commissioner of Prisons.

The central document in the White Paper of last week, and it has often been referred to in this debate, is the minute of 17th February addressed by the Commissioner of Prisons to the Minister of Defence. That Minute enclosed two other documents, Folios 9 and 10 on the file. Folio 9 was the Cowan Plan as drafted and intended by Cowan and put up by him as a proposal to his senior officers. Folio 10 was the extraordinary message which Sullivan had sent to Cowan on the 14th which can hardly be described otherwise than as a *cri de coeur*. It is impossible to read that document without sensing through it the state of mind of the man who wrote it or being aware of the risks which were attendant upon the situation which it reveals.

I will only remind the House of the ominous facts which it disclosed, that the Ministry of Works on the site had asked to be " disassociated entirely from any such operation" and the request for a senior superintendent, "with appropriate powers of summary punishment", to "be present when the policy outlined is implemented". It was clear evidence, among other things, that the Cowan Plan, Folio 9, was not what Sullivan, *vide* Folio 10, thought he was expected to implement. Incidentally, therefore, if there is blame for the failure to implement the Cowan Plan accurately, that responsibility must rest on all those who should have become aware, through seeing Folio 10, that Sullivan had misunderstood the Cowan Plan. With these two documents underneath, went this Minute, Folio 11, from the Commissioner of Prisons to the Minister of Defence. The Commissioner of Prisons had not yet taken a decision on the Cowan Plan. Indeed, when he saw it he gave instructions that "no action should be taken until authority was given" by his office. When he looked at 9 and 10 together, he decided that he, on his responsibility, could not authorise any action to be taken, and submitted it to his Minister, saying—and I am sorry to quote these words again, but they are essential—

"The plans Mr. Cowan worked out at (9) could be undertaken by us, but it would mean the use of a certain degree of force, in which operation someone might get hurt or even killed. I think this situation should be brought to the notice of the Security Council and a direction given on what policy should be adopted."

He then again referred to the

"action as planned at (9), with the risk of someone getting hurt or killed."

Those were not idle words, the reference to someone getting hurt or killed. He said in evidence to the Committee of three that the risk he had in mind that someone might get killed or hurt included "warder staff as well as detainees." Since the Commissioner of Prisons knew that in the Cowan Plan the numerical superiority of the warders to the detainees was to be overwhelming, the fact that he regarded the likelihood of being killed as applying to warders as well as to detainees is evidence of the degree of risk and danger which he associated in his mind with the Cowan Plan—the original, correct Cowan Plan, Folio 9. This was apart from the evidence in Folio 10 that things were going wrong, that it would not be that plan which would be put into effect, and that Sullivan had misunderstood.

He considered the responsibility for putting this into effect was not only one that he could not take, but it was one he could not advise his Minister to take alone, without reference to the Security Council.

Incidentally, the action of the Commissioner of Prisons disposes of the notion that the Cowan Plan for Hola was, as has often been said—and I quote the expression in the leading article in the *Daily Telegraph* yesterday—

"the application of a long-standing and highly successful technique of rehabilitation."

The truth is that it was the application of a modification, and a very important modification, of the technique which had elsewhere yielded good results.

When my right hon. Friend spoke in the debate on 16th June last, he was careful to put that correctly. He said:

"The proposals were the adaptation of a proved and successful technique to the circumstances of Hola."—[OFFICIAL REPORT, 16th June, 1959; Vol. 460, c. 280.]

They were, in fact, as proposed now in the Cowan Plan, something which represented such a serious departure from anything attempted before, something so dangerous in themselves, that he could not envisage the responsibility to carry them out being taken otherwise than by the Security Council itself.

The Minister of Defence decided that it was not necessary, and the Minister of Defence and the Minister of African Affairs took upon themselves the responsibility for authorising an operation which they had been warned involved the risk of death, in a minute accompanied by a paper which showed to anyone who cared to read it that not even that operation, dangerous as it was, was the one which Sullivan contemplated carrying out.

The hon. Lady the Member for Blackburn (Mrs. Castle) was a little too kind to the Minister for African Affairs. She overlooked the fact that he as well as the Minister of Defence had all the relevant papers in front of him. Those two men took upon themselves, with their eyes open and with full knowledge, not only the responsibility for the Cowan Plan but the responsibility for allowing the deformed version of it to go forward. It was authorised—now we come to the second phase, the execution—with the indication that it should go forward

[MR. POWELL.]

" subject to the proviso that " the Commissioner

" should first ensure that he has a sufficient number of warders at Hola to cope with possible eventualities."

So, warned of the danger implicit, aware from the S.O.S. that all was not well, the Ministers responsible, the Ministers who had given the decision, left the matter there and just sent it down the line.

Those two men, who knew that they had authorised—without reference, as advised by the Commissioner of Prisons, to the Security Council—an operation involving the risk of death, learnt on the afternoon of 3rd March that on the day on which that operation was carried out ten men had died at Hola Camp ; and on 4th March, after—and these are the words of the publicity officer :

" a good deal of discussion as to whether violence was the cause of the deaths of these men "

in a meeting presided over by His Excellency the Governor, they were parties to the issue of the water cart communiqué.

Those documents, that evidence, prove to me conclusively that the responsibility here lies not only with Sullivan and Lewis, but at a level above them. It lies with those to whom they actually appealed for help, whom they warned of the danger, from whom they received indeed a decision which transferred responsibility upwards, but no other help or guidance. That responsibility, transcending Sullivan and Lewis, has not been recognised ; but it cannot be ignored, it cannot be burked, it will not just evaporate into thin air if we do nothing about it.

I am as certain of this as I am of anything, that my right hon. Friend the Secretary of State from the beginning to the end of this affair is without any jot or tittle of blame for what happened in Kenya, that he could not be expected to know, that it could not be within the administrative conventions that these matters should be brought to his attention before or during the execution. When I say my right hon. Friend was in this matter utterly and completely blameless, that is of a piece with his administration of his high office generally, which has been the greatest exercise of the office of Colonial Secretary

in modern times. It is in the name of that record, it is in the name of his personal blamelessness, that I beg of him to ensure that the responsibility is recognised and carried where it properly belongs, and is seen to belong.

I have heard it suggested that there were circumstances surrounding this affair at Hola Camp which, it is argued, might justify the passing over of this responsibility—which might justify one in saying, " Well, of course, strictly speaking, that is quite correct ; but then here there were special circumstances."

It has been said—and it is a fact—that these eleven men were the lowest of the low ; sub-human was the word which one of my hon. Friends used. So be it. But that cannot be relevant to the acceptance of responsibility for their death. I know that it does not enter into my right hon. Friend's mind that it could be relevant, because it would be completely inconsistent with his whole policy of rehabilitation, which is based upon the assumption that whatever the present state of these men, they can be reclaimed. No one who supports the policy of rehabilitation can argue from the character and condition of these men that responsibility for their death should be different from the responsibility for anyone else's death. In general, I would say that it is a fearful doctrine, which must recoil upon the heads of those who pronounce it, to stand in judgment on a fellow human-being and to say, " Because he was such-and-such, therefore the consequences which would otherwise flow from his death shall not flow."

It is then said that the morale of the Prison Service, the morale of the whole Colonial Service, is above all important and that whatever we do, whatever we urge, whatever we say, should have regard to that morale. " Amen " say I. But is it for the morale of the Prison Service that those who executed a policy should suffer—whether inadequately or not is another question—and those who authorised it, those to whom they appealed, should be passed over? I cannot believe that that supports the morale of a service.

Going on beyond that, my hon. Friend the Member for Leicester, South-Eeast (Mr. Peel) reminded the House how proud the Colonial Service is of the integrity of its administration and its record. Nothing could be more damaging to the morale of such a service than that there should be a breath or a blemish left upon it. No, Sir ; that argument from the morale of the Prison Service and the Colonial Service stands on its head if what we mean is that therefore the consequences of responsibility should not follow in this case as they would in any other similar case.

Finally it is argued that this is Africa, that things are different there. Of course they are. The question is whether the difference between things there and here is such that the taking of responsibility there and here should be upon different principles. We claim that it is our object—and this is something which unites both sides of the House—to leave representative institutions behind us wherever we give up our rule. I cannot imagine that it is a way to plant representative institutions to be seen to shirk the acceptance and the assignment of responsibility, which is the very essence of responsible Government.

Nor can we ourselves pick and choose where and in what parts of the world we shall use this or that kind of standard. We cannot say, " We will have African standards in Africa, Asian standards in Asia and perhaps British standards here at home." We have not that choice to make. We must be consistent with ourselves everywhere. All Government, all influence of man upon man, rests upon opinion. What we can do in Africa, where we still govern and where we no longer govern, depends upon the opinion which is entertained of the way in which this country acts and the way in which Englishmen act. We cannot, we dare not, in Africa of all places, fall below our own highest standards in the acceptance of responsibility.

1.35 a.m.

Mr. Leslie Hale (Oldham, West): When an hon. Member has spoken with the effect and the sincerity which the hon. Member for Wolverhampton, South-West (Mr. Powell) showed, I realise that felicitations from the other side of the House are, sometimes, a little tactless. I beg the hon. Member to believe that I convey them with the same spirit that, I am sure, many hon. Members on both sides feel, and I am perfectly sincere when I say that I have sufficient respect for many hon. Members opposite to

realise that he was expressing views which quite a number of them would like to express. The hon. Member spoke so well and so clearly that there is not much for me to add, and, after the very brilliant speech, one of the most effective speeches I have ever heard in the House, from my hon. Friend the Member for Blackburn (Mrs. Castle), who dealt with principles first and with some of the important issues of practical detail later, much of what I wanted to say has been said. I had not intended to intervene at all until I heard the first speech from the benches opposite.

I have no wish to raise the temperature, but the fundamental issue here is not what happens to Mr. Sullivan. It is not whether somebody gets away with it, or whether somebody " carries the can." All those are matters of importance, and we have gone into the detail of some of the deplorable history of these events in which, it is quite clear, one of the persons whose conduct comes up for investigation is the Governor of Kenya himself. In these circumstances, any inquiry by subordinates of the Governor of Kenya is obviously inadequate. An inquiry into the homicide of eleven Africans by three Europeans is not, on the whole, the best way of conveying the impression of sincerity.

The important matter is that this House is still looked to all over the world because it has been associated with almost every fight for justice, liberty and freedom of significance for the Western Hemisphere. When we faced the post-war situation, we found that we were not, perhaps, in some ways, the great nation we had been. Our foreign policy is made in Washington, and our colonial policy, necessarily now, has to be dictated by world events and cannot be planned in isolation from world events. We cease to rank as a great Power, but moral power we still have. As a moral Power, there is still no country in the world, with the possible exception of one or two Scandinavian countries, which is regarded as we are, and there is hardly a country in the world which does not envy this House its democracy, the incorruptibility of our Civil Service, and the independence of our judiciary.

In the course of the events of the last fortnight, whether it be the direct responsibility of the right hon. Gentleman or not, all those things have come

Barbara Castle secures her greatest achievement with Bill on equal pay for women

Patricia Hewitt's political career and eventual rise to senior Cabinet status mirrored the fortunes of New Labour and Tony Blair, of whom she became a strong Cabinet ally. It was he who appointed her to her first ministerial job, and when he stepped down in 2007 she relinquished her post as Secretary of State for Health and returned to the Back Benches.

During her time at the helm of the Department of Health the Labour Government continued to inject substantial levels of funding into the NHS, but her policies for controlling spending and securing value for money set her at odds with an often hostile medical profession.

The disastrous implementation of a recruitment system for junior doctors, which led to calls for her resignation, the pay and hours of general practitioners, job losses among health workers and an enhanced role in the NHS for the private sector were among the major issues with which she was required to deal.

Notwithstanding the criticism, before she left office the number of patients being treated was running at an unprecedented level, waiting times were at their lowest ever, and she managed to balance the health service books. One of her significant achievements was to introduce, in the face of opposition from elsewhere in the Cabinet, a ban on smoking in public places.

Patricia Hewitt is an Australian by birth, the daughter of a senior civil servant who in retirement became a successful businessman. She was educated in Australia, but won a place at Newnham College, Cambridge where she was awarded a master's degree.

She became the press officer for Age Concern in 1971 before moving to the National Council for Civil Liberties two years later. In 1974 she moved up to become the council's general secretary, a position she held for nine years. It was during this time that she and her colleague, Harriet Harman, then the NCCL's legal officer and later Labour's deputy leader, were subjected to surveillance by MI5. The action was ruled by the Council of Europe to have breached their human rights in contravention of the European human rights convention. It resulted in the security services being put on a statutory footing for the first time and the British Government having to foot the legal bill.

Her first job in Parliament came in 1983 when, having failed to win the Leicester, East seat at that year's general election, she was appointed press secretary to Neil Kinnock when he became leader of the Labour party. Subsequently, she became his policy co-ordinator and led the review that radically reshaped Labour's policy thinking.

In 1989 she left to take on the role of deputy director of the Institute for Public Policy Research, the Labour think tank. While there, she wrote "About Time", an analysis of working hours that helped to shape Labour's policy on working families, and became deputy chair of the Commission on Social Justice, established by John Smith after the 1987 election. Her final job before being elected for Leicester, West at the 1997 election was as Director of Research for Andersen Consulting, now Accenture.

Once in Parliament, she made rapid progress in her ministerial career. A year after the election she was appointed Economic Secretary to the Treasury. A year later she was promoted to Minister for Small Business and e-Commerce, and two years after that, after the 2001 general election, she moved up to Cabinet rank, being appointed Secretary of State for Trade and Industry and Cabinet Minister for Women.

A lifelong feminist, she extended maternity pay, introduced paid paternity leave and created a new right to flexible working for parents of young children. After Labour's third election triumph in 2005, Tony Blair gave her the job of Secretary of State for Health.

Speech by women's heroine marked an end to a century of debate and delay

By Rt hon Patricia Hewitt MP

The Equal Pay Act was the greatest achievement of one of the greatest Labour women parliamentarians of the 20th century. A brilliant speaker, a lifelong campaigner for social justice and an unabashed feminist, Barbara Castle was a heroine for millions of women – including the women trade union members at Ford's at Dagenham whose 1968 equal pay strike helped mobilise support for the Labour Government's Equal Pay Bill.

Equal pay had been a 1964 election manifesto promise. But behind Castle's Second Reading speech was a hundred years of debate and delay, promises to end the injustice but precious little action. As Castle reminded the House of Commons, 'as far back as 1888 the TUC first endorsed the principle of the same wages for the same work – a very courageous *avant garde* thing to do in those days ... when women who worked in industry were certainly not considered respectable, even if they were regarded as human beings at all.' One hundred and twenty years after that first TUC resolution, women workers may be considered respectable – but the pay gap is still there, particularly for part-time workers, despite the dents inflicted by Castle's Act.

Getting the Bill introduced was not straightforward, as Castle's diaries reveal. In January 1966, as the Government wrestled with rising inflation, Castle was trying to persuade the unions to open discussions on 'how equal pay could be applied within the prices and incomes policy.' In June 1968, faced with the prospect of a Government defeat on a rebellious Back Bencher's equal pay amendment to the Prices and Incomes Bill, she used 'a carefully worded formula promising immediate discussions with the CBI and the TUC on a timetable for phasing in equal pay'. By September the following year, she stressed to Cabinet 'that we had run out of delaying excuses though we had behaved with an inertia worthy of the Northern Ireland Government'!

But it was Castle's passionate commitment to righting wrongs – not these earlier frustrations – that was on display as she moved the Second Reading. In words that would be echoed by a new generation of feminists, she proclaimed that 'this afternoon we are witnessing another historic advance in the struggle against discrimination in our society' and attacked the Conservatives for willing the end, but refusing to will the legislative means.

Women's earnings would need to increase faster than men's, Castle explained. Bad firms should not be allowed to undercut good. Fair pay would not destroy women's jobs; indeed it would improve productivity. Exactly the same arguments had to be deployed with the Blair Government's minimum wage.

Amidst so much that is familiar, however, I was struck by Castle's almost macho claim that 'we women Members would scoff at the idea that we were too frail to do all-night sittings. Indeed, we usually look fresher than the men at the end of them.' I'm sure Barbara Castle did! But a later generation of Labour women MPs would rebel against those all-night sittings, while building upon Castle's achievements for working women.

I first met Barbara Castle in the early 1970s, when I was a very young campaigner with Age Concern, appearing on television for the first time in a discussion about the then Conservative Government's pension proposals. She was a star – looking wonderful, as always; denouncing the Tory plans; and, after the programme, staying behind to talk to an adoring audience. Like so many other Labour party women, I wish she had become Britain's first woman Prime Minister.

ORDERS OF THE DAY

EQUAL PAY (No. 2) BILL

Order for Second Reading read.

Mr. Speaker: I wish to inform the House that I have not selected the Amendment standing in the name of the hon. and learned Member for Buckinghamshire, South (Mr. Ronald Bell) and some of his hon. Friends:

That this House, while accepting the general desirability of equal payment for work of equal value, does not believe that legislation is appropriate in this field and declines to give a Second Reading to a Bill which wholly conflicts with the view of the Royal Commission on Equal Pay.

That, however, will not affect the debate at all. The point of view expressed in that Amendment, and, indeed, any other point of view for or against the Second Reading of the Bill, may be expressed by any hon. Member I call.

Many hon. Members of both sexes wish to speak in this debate. I hope, therefore, that as we debate equal pay speeches will be of equal brevity.

3.35 p.m.

The First Secretary of State and Secretary of State for Employment and Productivity (Mrs. Barbara Castle): I beg to move, That the Bill be now read a Second time.

In our debates last week the right hon. Member for Mitcham (Mr. R. Carr) said of me:

"I bet that the right hon. Lady will be speaking when we come to the Second Reading of the Equal Pay Bill. She likes being in the kitchen when the sun is shining, but when the heat is on she gets clear."—[OFFICIAL REPORT, 3rd February, 1970 ; Vol. 795, c. 218.]

I found that a rather surprising statement, not only because I do not think that many hon. Members would recognise that image of me, but because I thought that the right hon. Member for Mitcham prided himself on having turned the heat on me successfully during those stormy debates on prices and incomes and industrial relations policy. But obviously I was wrong and he did not turn on the heat at all.

Be that as it may, on one thing I agree with the right hon. Gentleman. It is that the sun is certainly shining from these benches this afternoon. Indeed, I think that his rather uncharacteristic outburst of petulance was due far more to envy than to anger. He knows perfectly well that if he were occupying my post under a Tory Government he would never have been allowed to introduce equal pay at the present time, if ever. His industrial paymasters would have seen to that. I can only hope that if his better nature has had time to reassert itself, he will share my delight on this occasion.

There can be no doubt that this afternoon we are witnessing another historic advance in the struggle against discrimination in our society, this time against discrimination on grounds of sex. In introducing the Bill, I hope that there will be no difference between the two sides of the House about the principle. The only difference is that the present Government have had the will to act.

While other people have talked—lots of people have talked—we intend to make equal pay for equal work a reality, and, in doing so, to take women workers progressively out of the sweated labour class. We intend to do it, if the House will back us, in ways which will give a lead to other countries whose governments have left us behind in adopting the principle but who are still striving for effective ways of implementing it.

The concept of equal pay for equal work is so self-evidently right and just that it has been part of our national thinking for a very long time. Here, as in other things, it was the Trade Union Movement which gave the lead. Indeed, as far back as 1888 the T.U.C. first endorsed the principle of the same wages for the same work—a very courageous *avant garde* thing to do in those days, long before Queen Victoria's Diamond Jubilee, when women who worked in industry were certainly not considered respectable, even if they were regarded as human beings at all.

Since then the struggle against discrimination against women in rates of pay has had a chequered course. There was that great moment during the war when Mrs. Thelma Cazalet Keir, with strong Labour support, led a successful revolt against the Government on the issue of sex discrimination in teachers' pay, and the great man himself, Winston Churchill, had to come down to the House the next day to make the reimposition of sex discrimination a vote of confidence.

[MRS. CASTLE.]

Since then, the cause of equal pay has had its partial victories: the non-industrial Civil Service, non-manual local authority workers and teachers all got the first of seven instalments towards equal pay in 1955, and full equality in 1961. But its extension to that far greater number of women in industry for whom the T.U.C. fought so long ago has so far eluded us. The trade union movement has realised that this can be done only by legislation, and previous Governments have refused to legislate. Up to now, the extension of equal pay in industry has always foundered on three arguments: how should we define equal pay for equal work? How can we enforce it? And: "The economic situation is not right." It is a tremendous credit to this Government that they have found the answer to all three.

First, let me take the question of definition as we have embodied it in the Bill. When my predecessor in this job, the right hon. Gentleman the Member for Southwark (Mr. Gunter), first started his discussions with both sides of industry on the implementation of equal pay in fulfilment of our election promise, it seemed as if this problem of definition might prove insoluble.

The C.B.I. was all in favour of the definition embodied in the Treaty of Rome:

"Equal pay for the same work"

but the T.U.C. emphatically rejected this as inadequate. The T.U.C. wanted the I.L. Convention definition:

"Equal pay for work of equal value"

which the C.B.I., in turn, rejected as being far too open ended and indefinite. I think that they were both right: "Equal pay for the same work" is so restrictive that it would merely impinge on those women, very much in the minority, who work side by side with men on identical work, while, equally, the I.L. definition is far from satisfactory.

What does one mean by "work of equal value"? What does one mean by "equal value" in that context? The Convention is not very helpful on this matter, but merely says that its phrase refers to

"rates of remuneration established without discrimination based on sex."

That is fine. This is what we are seeking to achieve. But how does one estab-lish whether and in what forms discrimination has taken place?

The phrase "Equal pay for work of equal value" is too abstract a concept to embody in legislation without further interpretation. Is it suggested that some one should set a value on every job a woman does? Even if that were practicable it would not solve the problem, because what we are concerned with is the relationship between men's pay and women's pay, and men, of course, have never had equal pay for work of equal value. One could only establish the relative value of men's and women's work by evaluating the work, not only of all women but of all men in the population, which is something we have never attempted in our wildest dreams of prices and incomes policies.

The I.L. Convention does not require anything remotely like this. Indeed, it is pretty off-hand about this whole approach to job evaluation. All it says is:

"Where such action will assist in giving effect to the provisions of this Convention, measures shall be taken to promote objective appraisal of jobs on the basis of the work to be performed."

So the I.L. definition does not make job evaluation mandatory. Besides, the Convention leaves open whether the principle of equal pay shall be applied by legislation or through collective bargaining.

Sir Robert Cary (Manchester, Withington): I think that, in the sense in which the right hon. Lady is discussing the matter, equal pay for work of equal value referred merely to the length of time an individual was at work, and one could not evaluate the individual job done.

Mrs. Castle: That is certainly not the sense in which those who advocate that we should incorporate that definition in the legislation interpret the words.

The definitions that we have been offered so far have been too restrictive or too vague, while methods of enforcement have varied widely. Some countries have embodied the right of equal pay in their constitutions in general terms, and the detailed interpretation and enforcement of this right has depended on individuals raising cases in the ordinary courts. In other countries, the approach has been to encourage negotiations to incorporate suitable provisions in collective agreements. It is, therefore, hardly surprising that there are many countries which have ratified the I.L. Convention or signed the Treaty of Rome which have not yet effectively applied the principle in practice.

It is for this reason that the Government decided that they must look at the old definitions afresh and try to work out methods of enforcement which would have an effective practical impact on inequality. I think that in the Bill we have succeeded. Its aim is to eradicate discrimination in pay in specific identifiable situations by prescribing equally specific remedies.

The Bill deals with three different situations. The first situation is where men and many women are doing the same or " broadly similar " work, not only in the same establishment but in different establishments of the same employer where these are covered by common terms and conditions. The second is where they are doing jobs which are different but which have been found to be equivalent under a scheme of job evaluation. The third is where their terms and conditions of employment are laid down in collective agreements, statutory wages orders or employers' pay structures.

This three-pronged approach does all that can be done in legislation, and goes beyond anything in the law of other major countries. It gets away from abstractions like " equal pay for work of equal value ", and brings equal pay out of the debating room and into recognisable situations in factories, offices and shops, and into the black and white of pay agreements.

Clause 1 deals with the first two of the situations I have mentioned. It establishes that where a woman is doing work which is the same or broadly similar to that of men, or work which has been established as being equivalent to that of men by a job evaluation exercise, she qualifies for equal pay, whatever her contract of employment may have said before and whatever any collective agreement may say about her work.

The formula

" . . . the same or broadly similar work . . ."

covers not only the situation where men and women do identical work but also the situation where there are differences between the work of women and men but the differences are not of practical importance. The Clause provides that in deciding whether work is broadly similar regard shall be had to the frequency with which the differences occur in practice as well as to the nature and extent of the difference.

The other limb of the Clause deals with job evaluation. There will be no obligation on employers to carry out job evaluation, but where it has been done or is done in the future discrimination in pay on grounds of sex between jobs of equivalent value will be prohibited. Job evaluation schemes cover probably 30 per cent. of the working population, so that this provision will have a wide impact, particularly as there is nothing to prevent unions pressing for the extension of job evaluation schemes. The Clause also removes the effect of any blatant discrimination there may have been in the actual process of job evaluation.

There are two other things to notice about the Clause. The first is that discrimination against men is equally prohibited. Secondly, it applies to all Crown employment, except the Armed Forces. This exception does not mean that we do not intend to apply equal pay in the Services. Indeed, the Prices and Incomes Board Report of last June on pay in the Armed Forces recommended equal pay for men and women where they could be shown to be doing equal work, and we shall honour this. It is merely that the method of enforcement we propose in the Bill would not be appropriate to people in the Services.

The enforcement procedure for those two limbs of our equal pay policy is outlined in Clause 2. The aim here is to provide a means of redress which is speedy, informal and accessible and in the industrial tribunals, set up in 1965 to deal with industrial training levies and later with appeals about redundancy payments and S.E.T., we have the ideal machinery to hand. It is ideal because the tribunals are experienced in dealing with employment matters, they include representatives of workers and they sit at various centres scattered throughout the country.

Where a dispute has arisen as to whether a woman worker is receiving

[MRS. CASTLE.]

equal pay for broadly similar work or under a job evaluation scheme, she or her employer can take the dispute to the tribunal which, if it finds in the woman's favour, will be able to award her arrears of pay for a period up to two years before the start of proceedings. Where a woman should have received payment in kind as well, such as accommodation or the use of a car, it will be able to award her compensatory damages in respect of this as well, though not punitive damages against the employer.

Mrs. Renée Short (Wolverhampton, North-East): Can my right hon. Friend say how the woman would be able to take her case to a tribunal if a job evaluation exercise had not been carried out? I understand that it is one of the basic provisos that a job evaluation exercise must have been carried out. What happens if the firm concerned refuses to do this?

Mrs. Castle : It is not only in the case of a job evaluation exercise having been carried out, but in a case where the woman claims to be doing a job equivalent to the men concerned, but where we are trying to measure the value of work done, it must be through job evaluation. This is why it is important to realise that 30 per cent. of the population are covered by job evaluation schemes. There is nothing to prevent unions asking for their extension, which would be very much in keeping with all that is best in the development of pay structures at present. The Clause removes the effect of any blatant discrimination there may have been in the process of job evaluation

Incidentally, if there is any reason why the woman cannot take the case to the tribunal herself, I can take it for her. In the normal way her union would take up the case, but she may not belong to a union : she may be afraid of victimisation or be frightened at the thought of going before a tribunal. If so, she can go to her local employment exchange and explain the situation and if there seems to be validity in her complaint, I can act on her behalf.

Clause 2 also contains a concept which is crucial to the whole intention of the Bill. This is the concept of " a material difference " between a woman's case and that of comparable male workers. The

intention of the Bill is not to prohibit differences in pay between a woman and comparable male workers which arise because of genuine differences other than sex between her case and theirs. If an employer wishes to make additional payment to people employed on like work, in respect of matters such as length of service, merit, level of output and so on, the Bill will do nothing to hinder him, provided that the payments are available to any person who qualifies regardless of sex. But such payments must be related to actual differences in performance of service. It will not be permissible for an employer to discriminate between men as a class and women as a class, because he believes that in some way women generally are of less value to him as workers than men.

I now come to Clause 3, which deals with the third set of circumstances I have already mentioned—discrimination in collective agreements and in employers' pay structures which are not the subject of an agreement. The effect of this Clause is twofold. Where, on the operative date, a collective agreement or pay structure specifies a class of work or workers, however defined, to which separate men's and women's rates are attached, the women's rate must be raised to the level of the men's rate. And where an agreement or structure contains a women's rate as such—that is, without any description of the jobs that women do—that rate must be raised to the level of the lowest men's rate in the agreement. The effect of this on the women concerned is that none would get less than the lowest male rate and some might get more, depending on the jobs they actually perform. This achieves just what the women's organisations in their conference last Saturday were demanding. It prohibits different basic rates for men and women in collective agreements. I entirely agree that it is right that we should do this.

Disputes about collective agreements may be taken by any of the parties to an agreement, or by myself, to the Industrial Court. The Industrial Court is clearly the body best qualified to deal with disputes about collective agreements because of its considerable expertise in this field. The action of the Court will be confined to removing discrimination which appears on the face of the agreement in the way I have described. To that extent the court will redraft the agreement and the terms and conditions of workers covered by the agreement will be changed accordingly and become part of their contract of employment.

There is yet another way in which we can have a direct impact on discriminatory rates. As we know, some of the industries which employ a large proportion of women pay low rates of pay because trade union organisation in them is weak. It is for this reason that they have been brought under the protection of wages councils designed to reinforce the inadequacies of voluntary collective bargaining. We estimate that some 3,800,000 workers are covered by these wages councils, or by the Agricultural Wages Board, 2,375,000 of them women, and under Clauses 4 and 5 statutory wages orders embodying the agreements reached in these bodies will have to be brought in line with the principles I have outlined. Either side of the council or board concerned may complain that an order is discriminatory—so may I—and if the Industrial Court upholds the complaint, a fresh order must be made.

I would draw the attention of the House particularly to Clause 6. Unlike the legislation of some countries, our Bill provides that employers shall give equal treatment to women not only in remuneration, but in " terms and conditions of employment "—and here again we go further than the I.L. Convention. What do we mean by this? We mean that women must get equal treatment, not only in rates of pay, but in sickness and holiday schemes, payments in kind and any type of bonus rates. But we also say—and Clause 6 spells this out—that while being entitled to equal treatment in all these respects, a woman shall still retain the right to any favourable treatment accorded by law in respect of hours of work or to any special treatment accorded her by law or through negotiated agreements in connection with childbirth. In other words, we do not consider it preferential treatment for a woman to be given time off to have a baby, or to be paid while she is off— we would do the same for men if they had the courage to have babies, and I am sure the House will agree that this provision is right.

The hours of work question is more controversial. There are many who claim that the special restriction on women's hours of work contained in Part VI of the Factories Act, 1961, is out of date. The C.B.I. argues—so do many women—that now that we are legislating for equal pay all restrictions on women's hours of employment, including night work, should be removed.

I am the first to agree that there are a number of absurd anomalies in our present treatment of women over this. No one rushes in to protect nurses from night work—heaven help the rest of us if they did. We have women working nights on buses, as computer programmers, as air hostesses, in hotels and catering, without giving a second thought to it.

We women Members would scoff at the idea that we were too frail to do all-night sittings. Indeed, I have noticed that we usually look fresher than the men at the end of them.

Conditions in some parts of industry are more onerous ; but, even so, only 25 per cent. of women workers are covered by the Factories Act regulations, and I am frequently asked to make exemptions in their case with the consent of the women concerned. Only the other day an agreement was negotiated by the unions in a motor company giving women equal pay, and I have been asked to exempt them from the restrictions on night work as part of it.

Where the women agree and I am satisfied that there is nothing prejudicial to their welfare, I am always prepared to consider exemptions. However, I think that it would be quite wrong to make the introduction of this legislation conditional on the blanket removal of the hours restrictions. There are some unions which still argue very strongly that the restrictions should be retained, and I know employers who are against night work for women on social grounds. It will be necessary to reassure them that the removal of statutory restrictions would not mean that women would be compelled to do night work if they did not want to do so. It is also necessary to show that we are really on the road to equal pay. I myself believe that the need for these restrictions is disappearing fast, but the right way is for me to continue my consultations with both sides of industry on

[MRS. CASTLE.]

this as a separate matter in the hope of reaching an agreement.

Mr. Nicholas Ridley (Cirencester and Tewkesbury): When women get equal pay with men for equal work, will the Selective Employment Tax for women be raised to the same level as that for men?

Mrs. Castle : No, certainly not ; that has nothing whatsoever to do with the Bill.

There is one further point arising on Clause 6. I have given a great deal of thought to the question whether the Bill should also cover employers' pensions schemes. On the face of it, it seems just that pensions, as part of remuneration, should be covered by the Bill, but in practice there are a number of difficulties, and as far as I can ascertain no other major country has included pensions in the scope of its provisions for equal pay.

When men and women are both covered by an employer's pension scheme at the present time, their pension usually differs in a number of important respects—incidentally, often in the woman's favour. For one thing, her age of retirement is usually lower than the man's yet on average she lives longer. So if we insisted on exactly equal treatment, the woman employee might find herself worse off.

There is another point of considerable importance. Employers with pensions schemes now face a transitional period when they will have to adjust those schemes to the Government's new proposals for earnings-related pensions, and they would not welcome this additional complication and burden at the present time. For all these reasons, I think that it is better for all concerned not to include pensions in the Bill.

So much for the scope of equal pay. How quickly should it be implemented? Clause 8 provides for the Act to come into force on 29th December, 1975, the last Monday of that year. This will give industry over five years to adapt itself to these far-reaching changes. As the House knows, the T.U.C. has urged me to make the period two years, while the C.B.I. has argued that five years is too short: it has claimed that in view of the economic effect of equal pay on certain woman-intensive industries I ought to allow a period of seven years. Here again, I believe that our proposals are about right.

Mr. Michael Foot (Ebbw Vale): What interval has been demanded by Selsdon Park?

Mrs. Castle : I assure my hon. Friend that I have received no such demand, and I am awaiting with interest the contributions from hon. Members opposite this afternoon.

I was saying that I believe that our proposals are about right. Seven years is too long for women to wait for this basic act of justice. Besides, if we were to enter the Common Market, we would be expected to catch up more quickly than that with the other members of the Community which have been making progress in this direction over the past 13 years.

On the other hand, I believe that it is quite unrealistic to imagine that industry —or, incidentally, the workers in industry—could adapt themselves to these changes in a mere two years. The Government believe that, given reasonable time, industry can adjust itself to these additional costs. Overall we estimate that equal pay will add about $3\frac{1}{2}$ per cent. to the national bill for wages and salaries over the five years—something we can certainly assimilate at a time of rising productivity. Moreover, we believe that by making employers pay economic rates for their women workers we shall be giving a boost to higher productivity.

For this is a Bill designed, not only to end injustice, but to stimulate efficiency. As long as women are paid below their economic value, there is no incentive to put their work and their abilities to the best use. Sweated labour is a soporific to management, not a stimulant.

At the same time, we recognise that the incidence of equal pay will fall much more heavily on some industries and firms than on others, because they are far more dependent on women's labour. That is why my Department carried out a survey recently, in conjunction with the T.U.C. and the C.B.I., into the cost of introducing equal pay in a number of firms in 13 selected industries, the results of which have been published in the January *D.E.P. Gazette.*

The industries were selected because they contained a high proportion or a large number of women. They were not intended to represent a complete cross-section of industry ; therefore, the results are merely illustrative. They indicate that the median direct cost of introducing equal pay in the industries concerned would range from 0 per cent. to 18 per cent. In engineering, for example, the median figure would be only 2 per cent., whereas in retail distribution it would be 13 per cent. and in clothing 18 per cent. The cost for individual firms would vary even more—from 0 per cent. to 32 per cent. It is clear, therefore, that we must give the industries and firms most affected reasonable time to adjust. We believe that five years is reasonable.

Mr. Keith Speed (Meriden) *rose——*

Mrs. Castle : I will give way, if the hon. Gentleman seeks to raise a relevant point.

Mr. Speed : On the question of timing, if the right hon. Lady had accepted the Amendment I moved on Report of the Prices and Incomes Bill in June, 1968, which would have exempted from her prices and incomes legislation pay rises to implement equal pay, would we not have been that much further along the scale now, so that these problems would not have arisen?

Mrs. Castle : As I feared, that was a point of opinion and not one of fact. I reject it as being inaccurate. I hope that hon. Members will not interrupt me to make debating points which they would do better to make in speeches, if at all.

We do not think that it is necessary, as the C.B.I. has suggested, to exempt particular firms or industries from this timetable to give them a longer breathing space on the grounds that the cost to them would be higher. I believe that it would be particularly undesirable to exempt some firms and not others in the same industry. A moment's thought will show how unfair this would be to the firms not exempted, which would be placed at a competitive disadvantage because they had already introduced equal pay, were paying their women more, or were employing more men than the exempted firms. It is important that the firms which have the most catching up to do should not be allowed to drag their feet to the detriment of firms which are facing up to their social obligations. That

is why Clause 8 gives me power by Order, subject to the approval of Parliament, to provide an interim stage at the end of 1973 if I find it necessary. This would enable me, if I thought progress towards the implementation of equal pay was too patchy or too slow, to require all firms to have achieved a given percentage of the target of full implementation—say 90 per cent. of the men's rates—by 31st December, 1973.

There are two other thoughts that I want to leave with hon. Members who think that five years is too long. The first is that there is nothing to prevent any firm which can afford it from negotiating the earlier introduction of full equal pay—and nothing to prevent any union from pressing it, as some already have. If the unions are prepared to give women higher priority in their wage claims, no one will be more delighted than I.

However, we should also remember that the commitment in this Bill to achieve equal pay by the end of 1975 means that, by definition, pay increases for women will have to exceed those for men over the next few years if women are to catch up in the time allowed. This is what we are committing ourselves to do in the Bill. We have got to give men on the shop floor time, just as we have got to give their employers time, to adjust themselves to the practical consequences of this commitment to equal pay on their wage negotiations. I believe that it would be asking too much of them to try and concentrate those consequences in a period of two years.

Mr. Edward M. Taylor (Glasgow, Cathcart): Would the right hon Lady give way?

Mrs. Castle : If it is on a point of fact.

Mr. Taylor : The right hon. Lady has referred to every provision in the Bill except Clause 7, which relates to the police. Will she say something about the police and the special problems of rent allowances for men and women?

Mrs. Castle : I have made it clear already that the police are covered in this Bill. I have gone into it in as much detail as the House will require, in view of the fact that I do not want to take up too much time and so prevent other hon. Members from contributing to the debate.

[MRS. CASTLE.]

This, then, is the Bill that I commend to the House. I expect that, as we debate it during the coming months, we shall hear the usual range of conflicting arguments about the consequences of equal pay. On the one hand, we shall be told that the cost of these proposals will be crippling, that it will push up the cost of living, threaten our exports and damage our economic recovery. On the other, we shall be told that the proposals are so modest, that they will not help large numbers of women who are most exploited and that, in any case, men and their employers will successfully conspire to evade them. Yet again, we may be told that the proposals will be so effective in putting up women's rates of pay that they will put a large number of women out of work and damage the interests of women themselves.

Obviously these arguments cancel each other out. But let us look at them more closely. I believe that the country can afford this measure, that it will stimulate the more efficient use of labour, and that the effect on the cost of living will be marginal—far less than some of the tax proposals and proposals for import levies on food put forward by hon. Gentlemen opposite.

Will it, then, have the effect of throwing women out of work by forcing firms to automate or employ men instead? I accept that there are bound to be changes in a firm's workforce in specific instances. But I do not accept for a moment that the overall effect will be to create unemployment among women, any more than the introduction of equal pay in the non-industrial public services did—though we heard the same blood-chilling arguments put forward then as we are hearing now. Women form one-third of the working population, and they do so, not just because they are cheap labour or in it for the pin money, but because they need work and are urgently needed by their employers. Indeed, as we all know, there are innumerable jobs where women are employed because they are better at them than men, and in most areas of the country that I visit I find that employers are crying out for more women's labour. A number of employers, indeed, hope that equal pay will attract more women back into the labour force, where they are so badly needed.

How effective will the coverage of the Bill be? There are at the moment $8\frac{1}{2}$ million women in employment, over one million of whom already receive equal pay. Of the rest, we estimate that some three million women are probably engaged on the same or broadly similar work as men or likely to benefit through the adjustment of collective agreements; others are covered by job evaluation schemes and, as I have said, nearly $2\frac{1}{2}$ million women will be covered by the wages councils provisions.

There is also the fact that, if a number of women in a firm have their rates brought up to the men's rates, it is bound to have an effect on the pay of other women in the firm. Some of these categories, of course, overlap, but we believe that some six million women will be directly affected by this legislation, and that includes women who are engaged in what are traditionally " women's jobs ". But there is also what I call the " halo effect ".

Some of the firms surveyed in our inquiry told us that, although they believed that none of their women workers qualified directly for equal pay, they expected that they would have to increase their wages if increases were paid to women by other firms in the locality. Engineering, pottery and food firms in particular expected this to happen. I think that there can be no doubt that the introduction of equal pay along the lines of this Bill will lead to a general rise in women's earnings relative to men's.

What, then, of evasion? Again I have no doubt that some employers will try it on, and the T.U.C. has pointed out some ways in which it might be done; for example, by employers " phasing out " men from certain jobs in order to continue paying women a lower rate without being guilty of discrimination, or substituting job descriptions for women's rates that appear to make the men's and women's work different. I believe that extensive evasion along these lines can be prevented by the kinds of action that I have outlined earlier: the extension of job evaluation, properly drawn collective agreements, and the " halo effect ". But, undoubtedly, pockets of discrimination will remain—unless women organise to put a stop to it.

Legislation cannot cover every possible development, and, in any case, it is no part of my job to make it unnecessary for women to join a trade union. Their failure to do so is one of the reasons for their present plight. This Bill does all that the law can do. It is for women to call the trade union movement in aid to see that they get the maximum benefit out of it, and it is for the trade union movement to seize the biggest opportunity that it has ever had to organise women, by showing them what it can do to help them to see that this law is not evaded. If the trade unions will seize this opportunity—and if women will respond—there is no reason why this Bill should not be the means of bringing to an end an era of financial exploitation of women's work. There will be other forms of discrimination against women that we shall have to deal with in due course, but this Bill is an essential starting point.

There is just one thing I would like to say in conclusion. It is to pay a tribute to all those who have argued and striven over the past years for equal pay for women, and in particular to those hon. Members on both sides of the House who have championed the cause which is coming to such happy fruition today. I hope that we can unite enthusiastically behind this Bill.

4.19 p.m.

Mr. Robert Carr (Mitcham): I can assure the right hon. Lady that we were genuinely very glad to see her at the Dispatch Box today moving the Second Reading of the Bill. Since she referred to the matter, however, let me also reiterate that we were equally genuine last week in being censorious that she should be the first Minister responsible for labour, certainly in modern history, to fail to speak and defend the record of her Government and her Department in a major debate on unemployment in the House.

An Hon. Member: What has this to do with the Bill?

Mr. Carr: Just as much as the right hon. Lady thought it had to do with it this afternoon.

She said that she thought I might have said this out of envy because had I been in her place I should not have been able to do anything to promote equal pay. As she said that, I could not help looking at HANSARD of 11th June, 1947, which I happened to have by me. I had no idea that the right hon. Lady would say what she did and that the passage in question would therefore be so appropriate. On 11th June, 1947, the late Mr. Hugh Dalton, then Chancellor of the Exchequer, made a statement in the House about the reaction of the then Labour Government to the Report of the recent Royal Commission on equal pay. My right hon. and learned Friend the Member for St. Marylebone (Mr. Hogg), then Member for Oxford, put this question to the Chancellor:

" Is the right hon. Gentleman aware that, not for the first time, he has claimed the credit for a number of social improvements agreed to during the time of the Coalition, and does not his answer mean that the principle of equal pay for equal work, like other social advances, will have to wait for the return of a Conservative Administration?"—[OFFICIAL REPORT, 11th June, 1947; Vol. 438, c. 1072.]

And so it did.

Mr. Christopher Norwood (Norwich, South): As the right hon. Gentleman and his colleague had a considerable period in which to enact a similar Measure, why did this never happen?

Mr. Carr: I do not think that the hon. Gentleman can be very well informed on the historical facts of the matter. The Conservative Party commitment to equal pay goes back about a quarter of a century to " The Industrial Charter ".

An Hon. Member: The garden of Eden.

Mr. Carr: I believe that the T.U.C. was first committed to it about 100 years ago. The T.U.C. has taken a long time to get down to it.

In our " Industrial Charter ", published in 1947, we said in the section on incentives:

" In this connection we have examined carefully the claim for equal pay for men and women. It seems to us that payment by results ought to give equal pay for equal value whether the work is done by a man or a woman. We believe that there should be one rate for the job provided that the services rendered and the results achieved by men and women are the same. We commend this principle to those engaged in industrial wage negotiations as the right one to adopt. In non-industrial occupations we should wish to move forward on the same

Winston Churchill offers nation grim prospect as he sets tone for his wartime leadership

Michael Howard was elected leader of the Conservative party and became Leader of the Opposition in 2003 after 20 years in the House of Commons, having been a Cabinet Minister under both Margaret Thatcher and John Major.

Only a year after his election to Parliament for the seat of Folkestone and Hythe, he had his foot on the ladder to a ministerial career when in 1984 he was appointed Parliamentary Private Secretary to the Solicitor-General. Within a year he was on the Front Bench as Under-Secretary of State for Trade and Industry, with responsibility for corporate and consumer affairs.

In career terms it was an important role. He oversaw the regulation of the City of London and took responsibility for the Financial Services Bill, subsequently enacted, the first major measure to tackle regulation of the financial services industry.

A further promotion in 1987 took him to Minister of State rank, first for Local Government and subsequently for Water and Planning, in which job he implemented the privatisation of Britain's water industry.

Michael Howard is a lawyer by profession. At Cambridge, he read, first, economics and, subsequently, law, and in 1962 was President of the Cambridge Union. His contemporaries at university included Kenneth Clarke, Norman Lamont, Leon Brittan and John Gummer.

By 1970, they were all either in Parliament or trying for it. Michael Howard stood unsuccessfully for Liverpool, Edge Hill in 1966 and 1970, in which year he was elected chairman of the Bow Group. In the meantime he was pursuing a successful legal career, specialising in employment and planning law, having been called to the Bar in 1964. He was appointed a QC in 1982.

A year later, after the Falklands war, Margaret Thatcher called a general election and romped home with a landslide majority of 144. One of those seats was won by Michael Howard, who had been selected to replace the outgoing Sir Albert Costain at Folkestone and Hythe.

After his steady progress in Government, Mrs Thatcher gave him his first Cabinet appointment, in 1990, as Secretary of State for Employment, in which role he piloted through the Commons the Employment Bill, which outlawed the closed shop. He was also appointed a Privy Counsellor.

When Mrs Thatcher's grip on the party faltered after Sir Geoffrey Howe's resignation speech, Michael Heseltine mounted a leadership challenge. Michael Howard took an active role in campaigning for her re-election, but the Thatcher era was over, and John Major moved into No 10 Downing street. Under the new leader, Michael Howard retained his job and, after the unexpected Major victory at the 1992 general election, he was appointed Secretary of State for the Environment.

In the wake of the withdrawal of sterling from the European exchange rate mechanism and adverse publicity, Norman Lamont was sacked from the Major Government. In the ensuing reshuffle Michael Howard was promoted to Home Secretary, where he took a tough line on crime. He held the job for four years, at the end of which the statistics showed that crime had fallen by an unprecedented 18 per cent. with nearly a million fewer crimes a year being committed than when he took over.

John Major's resignation after Tony Blair's historic victory in 1997 resulted in the Tories looking for a new leader. Michael Howard put himself forward as a candidate. He was unsuccessful, but he was appointed shadow Foreign Secretary by the new leader, William Hague. After two years on the Opposition Front Bench, he resigned, but he was back again under Iain Duncan Smith's leadership when William Hague stepped down after the 2001 election defeat. This time he was appointed shadow Chancellor. When Duncan Smith was ousted by a vote of no confidence, Michael Howard was elected leader of the party unopposed.

He was to hold the job for over two years, taking the Conservatives into the 2005 general election. Although Labour secured an unprecedented third term of office, the Howard-led Tories severely dented Tony Blair's majority, cutting it from 167 to 66, and increasing the Conservative share of the vote.

In the aftermath, however, Michael Howard announced that he would be standing down, but only after the party had debated its future direction. Six months on, he resigned and, in due course, handed over to David Cameron.

He has announced that he will not be standing at the next general election, which must be called by May 2010.

Speech that brilliantly captured spirit of the man as Britain faced its finest hour

By Rt hon Michael Howard QC, MP

On 13 May 1940 the German army entered France. It had met little resistance in Holland and Belgium. On the afternoon of that day it began to cross the River Meuse. At just about that time in London, Winston Churchill rose in the House of Commons to deliver his first speech as Prime Minister.

He had become Prime Minister three days earlier, on Friday 10 May – the very day the German army had begun its advance. And his position was far from secure. He was regarded with widespread suspicion, not least on his own side. Many thought that his Administration would not last.

Jock Colville, soon to become one of Churchill's most loyal aides, wrote in his diary on 11 May,

> "There seems to be some inclination in Whitehall to believe that Winston will be a complete failure and that Neville (Chamberlain) will return."

On the same day, Lord Davidson, a very senior Conservative, wrote to former Prime Minister Stanley Baldwin,

> "The Tories don't trust Winston. After the next clash of war is over it may well be that a sounder Government may emerge."

When, in the afternoon of the 13th, Neville Chamberlain, the deposed Prime Minister, entered the Chamber of the House of Commons he had been greeted by long and noisy cheering from the Conservative Benches. When Churchill entered, a few minutes later, his reception was much more muted and what cheering there was came from the Labour Benches.

That was the background against which Churchill began his speech.

After describing the steps he had taken to form his Administration, he set the tone, in the concluding paragraph of the speech, for the whole of the five years of his wartime leadership.

He said:

> "I have nothing to offer but blood, toil, tears and sweat."

275

He described his policy and his aims and he ended with that call "to go forward together with our united strength."

It was one of his shortest speeches. It was not greeted with universal acclaim. It was not broadcast to the nation, though the BBC summarised it in its regular news bulletins and, in particular, quoted the reference to blood, toil, tears and sweat. It is not clear just how much impact it had on the days that immediately followed its delivery.

And it must, of course, be considered in the context of Churchill's other great speeches of the time – the speech of 28 May in which he asked the House to prepare itself for "hard and heavy tidings"; the speech of 4 June which contained the sentence:

> "We shall fight on the beaches, we shall fight on the landing grounds, we shall fight in fields and in the streets, we shall fight in the hills; we shall never surrender",

and the speech of 18 June – the "finest hour" speech.

Together the impact of these speeches was enormous. By the autumn of 1940 they were circulating in print throughout the country and beyond. Their effect on us, nearly 70 years on, is just as powerful.

They brilliantly capture the spirit of the man who led us through that finest hour. It is safe to say that as long as the English language lives, they will never be forgotten.

HIS MAJESTY'S GOVERNMENT.

2.54 p.m.

The Prime Minister (Mr. Churchill): I beg to move,

" That this House welcomes the formation of a Government representing the united and inflexible resolve of the nation to prosecute the war with Germany to a victorious conclusion."

On Friday evening last I received His Majesty's Commission to form a new Administration. It was the evident wish and will of Parliament and the nation that this should be conceived on the broadest possible basis and that it should include all parties, both those who supported the late Government and also the parties of the Opposition. I have completed the most important part of this task. A War Cabinet has been formed of five Members, representing, with the Opposition Liberals, the unity of the nation. The three party Leaders have agreed to serve, either in the War Cabinet or in high executive office. The three Fighting Services have been filled. It was necessary that this should be done in one single day, on account of the extreme urgency and rigour of events. A number of other positions, key positions, were filled yesterday, and I am submitting a further list to His Majesty to-night. I hope to complete the appointment of the principal Ministers during to-morrow. The appointment of the other Ministers usually takes a little longer, but I trust that, when Parliament meets again, this part of my task will be completed, and that the administration will be complete in all respects.

I considered it in the public interest to suggest that the House should be summoned to meet to-day. Mr. Speaker agreed, and took the necessary steps, in accordance with the powers conferred upon him by the Resolution of the House. At the end of the proceedings to-day, the Adjournment of the House will be proposed until Tuesday, 21st May, with, of course, provision for earlier meeting, if need be. The business to be considered during that week will be notified to Members at the earliest opportunity. I now invite the House, by the Motion which stands in my name, to record its approval of the steps taken and to declare its confidence in the new Government.

To form an Administration of this scale and complexity is a serious undertaking in itself, but it must be remembered that we are in the preliminary stage of one of the greatest battles in history, that we are in action at many other points in Norway and in Holland, that we have to be prepared in the Mediterranean, that the air battle is continuous and that many preparations, such as have been indicated by my hon. Friend below the Gangway, have to be made here at home. In this crisis I hope I may be pardoned if I do not address the House at any length to-day. I hope that any of my friends and colleagues, or former colleagues, who are affected by the political reconstruction, will make allowance, all allowance, for any lack of ceremony with which it has been necessary to act. I would say to the House, as I said to those who have joined this Government: " I have nothing to offer but blood, toil, tears and sweat."

We have before us an ordeal of the most grievous kind. We have before us many, many long months of struggle and of suffering. You ask, what is our policy? I will say: It is to wage war, by sea, land and air, with all our might and with all the strength that God can give us; to wage war against a monstrous tyranny, never surpassed in the dark, lamentable catalogue of human crime. That is our policy. You ask, what is our aim? I can answer in one word: It is victory, victory at all costs, victory in spite of all terror, victory, however long and hard the road may be; for without victory, there is no survival. Let that be realised; no survival for the British Empire, no survival for all that the British Empire has stood for, no survival for the urge and impulse of the ages, that mankind will move forward towards its goal. But I take up my task with buoyancy and hope. I feel sure that our cause will not be suffered to fail among men. At this time I feel entitled to claim the aid of all, and I say, " Come then, let us go forward together with our united strength."

3.1 p.m.

Mr. Lees-Smith (Keighley): I have been asked by my colleagues on this occasion to follow the Prime Minister because it is fitting that there should be a response to the striking, stirring and noble words which he has addressed to the nation. I have also been asked to do so in order to say immediately that, of course, we support this Motion. May I say as a result of one observation which the Prime Minister made, that we give our most sin-

Harold Macmillan announces his fateful and courageous decision to knock on Europe's door

Sir Geoffrey Howe was Margaret Thatcher's longest serving Cabinet Minister, but his service came to a dramatic end when, on 1 November 1990, he resigned and, 13 days later, in one of the most memorable speeches heard by the House of Commons, told his fellow MPs that he had had enough of Mrs Thatcher's policies and her style of leadership.

As he delivered his resignation speech to a tense and silent House, sitting at his side was Nigel Lawson, also one of Mrs Thatcher's former Cabinet Ministers. He, too, had quit in not dissimilar circumstances.

So significant was Sir Geoffrey's departure, and the tone and content of his speech, that the event marked the end for Mrs Thatcher. Within days she was to face a leadership challenge which culminated in her resignation and her departure from Downing street.

Sir Geoffrey was a barrister, having been called to the Bar in 1952. However, politics was to become his dominant career, and it was a career that kept him in the top echelons of Government and Opposition. In his resignation speech, delivered from the Back Benches, he observed that it had been 25 years since he had last addressed the House from that position. It was a remarkable achievement that for all of his time in the House until then, apart from a short period when he first entered, he had spoken from one Front Bench or the other.

He entered Parliament as the Member for Bebington at the 1964 general election. He lost the seat when Harold Wilson went to the country to secure a bigger majority in 1966. He was back again, however, representing Reigate, after the 1970 Conservative election victory. After boundary changes in 1974 it became Surrey, East, which he represented for the ensuing 18 years until he retired from the House in 1992.

His first ministerial appointment was in 1970 when he was knighted and given the job of Solicitor-General in Edward Heath's Government. In 1972 he was promoted to the Cabinet as Minister for Trade and Consumer Affairs.

The general election of 1974 put the Conservatives back in Opposition, but when they returned to power five years later, Mrs Thatcher made Sir Geoffrey her Chancellor of the Exchequer in which post he brought about a whirlwind of change in the nation's finances aimed at cutting inflation and liberalising the economy. He shifted the emphasis from direct to indirect taxation, introduced the medium-term financial strategy, with its strict monetary discipline, and abolished exchange controls. Many of his policies were to characterise the phenomenon that came to be known as Thatcherism.

With her second election victory in 1983, Mrs Thatcher appointed Sir Geoffrey to the post of Foreign Secretary, which he held for longer than anyone since Sir Edward Grey. Top of the agenda was Europe, and it was on this topic that the cracks in their relationship finally appeared. With Nigel Lawson, who succeeded him as Chancellor, Sir Geoffrey, in preparation for the EU Madrid summit in July 1989, pressed the case for joining the European exchange rate mechanism, threatening, with Mr Lawson, to resign unless Mrs Thatcher committed herself to that course of action.

Reluctantly – and, indeed, to their surprise – she did just that. But within a month, Mrs. Thatcher proceeded – equally to their surprise – to reshuffle her Cabinet. In what was perceived as a humiliating demotion, Sir Geoffrey was moved to become Leader of the House of Commons and Deputy Prime Minister. The message emanating from No 10 Downing street was that the role of deputy to Mrs Thatcher was of less significance than might appear to be the case.

Eighteen months after his resignation speech, at the 1992 general election, Sir Geoffrey stood down from the House of Commons. He was given a peerage as Baron Howe of Aberavon.

A decision for the House, not for the people

BY RT HON LORD HOWE OF ABERAVON CH, QC

"Perhaps the most fateful and forward-looking policy decision in our peace-time history". With those words, presented in October the following year in the Conservative Central Office pamphlet "Britain, the Commonwealth and Europe" under his own name, Prime Minister Harold Macmillan underlined the importance of the debate, which he had opened on 2 August 1961.

He emphasised to the House of Commons on that day that "the problems involved in the future of our relations with Europe are among the most difficult and the most important that the nation has ever had to face".

Never were truer words spoken. For in almost every week that Parliament has been sitting since then, we have been witnessing, and, indeed, experiencing, the repercussions of Macmillan's courageous decision and of our eventually successful accession to the European Community, as it then was.

It has often been suggested – and still is – that successive Governments failed to present the nation with a candid and comprehensive picture of the consequences of that decision. And least of all, it is sometimes said, was it foreshadowed that the venture would involve any partnership in the fields of foreign or defence policy – or in any purely "political" relationships.

Certainly, in this speech, Macmillan made plain that the Rome treaty itself did not touch upon defence or foreign policy questions but only on economic or trade issues. But he stressed that "The Community has developed a dynamic of its own" and that existing members were contemplating wider, political partnership.

So he spelt out very plainly the need for us to "bring our influence to bear", by membership of the Community, upon "the future structure of Europe" and thus upon "the future of our national influence in world affairs". And that theme has echoed and re-echoed, in theory at least, but often less in practice, throughout the subsequent half century.

Macmillan himself restated the dilemma even more clearly in his 1962 pamphlet: "One thing is certain. As a member of the Community, Britain would have a strong voice in deciding the nature and the timing of political unity. By remaining outside, we could be faced with a political solution in Europe which ran counter to our views but which we could do nothing to influence...To lose influence both in Europe and Washington, as this must mean, would seriously undermine our international position".

Small wonder then that Macmillan advised the Commons, in this speech, that "the failure of these negotiations would be a tragedy. Of course, it would".

He could certainly not have foreseen, as he said those words, the brutality with which, on 29 January 1963, his old companion-in-arms, President Charles de Gaulle, was to bring those negotiations sharply to an end – in ostensible response to Macmillan's own Nassau/Polaris deal with President Kennedy.

"Bad. Bad for us, bad for Europe and bad for the whole Free World", was Macmillan's immediate, shocked reaction.

Four years then had to elapse before Prime Minister Harold Wilson, in "a historic decision", as he himself described it, on 2 May 1967, was able to renew Britain's application to join the Community. After five more years, it was Prime Minister Edward Heath who was able to bring the process to a successful conclusion.

The ideal outlook at that time was, in my view, best described by the man who had served both Macmillan and Heath as Foreign Secretary – and had, in the interval between the two, himself served as Prime Minister, Sir Alec Douglas-Home. For him, as he stated in a speech delivered to and published by the Conservative Group for Europe in September 1971 under the title "Our European Destiny", our accession to the Community was "a step of the utmost political significance", in a "modern world which calls for real European unity" and in which "it is only as part of a strong and determined Europe that Britain's own character, personality and individuality can thrive."

Macmillan himself would, as I believe, have come to share that view. How different the world might be today if only Britain had, in the last decade, been acting as a leading member of a "strong and determined Europe" – a Europe, which had succeeded in warning the United States away from the crass unwisdom – even from their own point of view – of their crudely retaliatory reaction to the horrors of 9/11.

The final sentence of Macmillan's speech also deserves a glance. He asked the House "to give Ministers the authority – not to sign a treaty – but to find out on what honourable basis such a treaty could be put forward for the decision of the House."

And we may be sure that, not for one moment, did the word "referendum" enter, still less trouble, his mind. For it was for "the House" to decide.

Mr. Speaker : The answer to the first part of the submission of the hon. Member for Nelson and Colne (Mr. Silverman) is that in applying the rule against anticipation I am required to take into account the reasonable prospect of the matter being further debated. I am in some difficulty in imagining that the hon. Member's Motion has much reasonable prospect in the circumstances.

Selection is a matter for me, and I propose to select the Amendment which stands in the names of the right hon. Gentleman the Leader of the Opposition and other right hon. and hon. Members. I am in the happy position that, so far as I can see, everything that is is desired to be said in support of the other Amendments can be said upon the issues then arising. I will not blackmail myself in any way, but I will bear in mind the fact that the hon. Member has an Amendment on the Order Paper.

EUROPEAN ECONOMIC COMMUNITY

3.42 p.m.

The Prime Minister (Mr. Harold Macmillan) : I beg to move,

That this House supports the decision of Her Majesty's Government to make formal application under Article 237 of the Treaty of Rome in order to initiate negotiations to see if satisfactory arrangements can be made to meet the special interests of the United Kingdom, of the Commonwealth and of the European Free Trade Association ; and further accepts the undertaking of Her Majesty's Government that no agreement affecting these special interests or involving British sovereignty will be entered into until it has been approved by this House after full consultation with other Commonwealth countries, by whatever procedure they may generally agree.

We must all agree that the problems involved in the future of our relations with Europe are among the most difficult and the most important that the nation has ever had to face. The moment of decision, however, has not yet come. What the House is now asked to do is to support the Government's proposal to initiate negotiations on the Common Market within the terms of the Motion. When those negotiations are completed one way or the other, the House will have to pass judgment.

The underlying issues, European unity, the future of the Commonwealth, the strength of the free world, are all of capital importance, and it is because we firmly believe that the United Kingdom has a positive part to play in their development—for they are all related—that we ask the House to approve what we are doing.

After the last war, the process of reconciliation in Europe was itself a deliberate and positive act in which forbearance and even forgiveness played their part. It first took, I remember, a dramatic form when, in 1950, the German delegates were admitted to the Council of Europe. At that time, my right hon. Friend the Member for Woodford (Sir W. Churchill) conceived the notion of what he called the three interlocking groups, Britain and the Commonwealth, Europe, and the New World. He spoke of them, I remember, as three leaves of a piece of clover, or, again, as three intersecting circles. Of course, he was right in his analysis, but ever since then we have been, in one way or another, trying to find a practical solution to the problem of their interconnection.

N.A.T.O. brought together thirteen nations of Europe, one great Commonwealth country—Canada—and the United States in an alliance partly military, partly political. The other Commonwealth countries took no part, not because they did not sympathise with our purpose—many of them certainly did—but because they were distant from the Atlantic area. Some nations of Europe, like Sweden, remained neutral, partly through their tradition and partly through their position. In the O.E.E.C., the European group was somewhat widened to include countries such as Switzerland. Again, in the Council of Europe, we had another slight variation.

Meanwhile, there has grown up the practical application of the aspirations towards unity in continental Europe by the formation of the European Economic Community. I ask hon. Members to note the word " economic ". The Treaty of Rome does not deal with defence. It does not deal with foreign policy. It deals with trade and some of the social aspects of human life which are most connected with trade and production.

Whatever views are held of what should be our relations with the E.E.C., everyone will readily acknowledge the tremendous achievement involved. Its most striking feature, of course, is the reconciliation of France and Germany. That is on the moral side. But on the political side these countries have made remarkable economic progress in recent years. Of course, that is not all due to the European Economic Community. Nevertheless, the Community has imparted an impetus to the economic growth of the Six. The Community has developed a dynamic of its own. Above all, it is an idea which has gripped men's minds.

At the time when E.E.C. was being discussed, most people felt that it would be dangerous to split Europe in this way, and a great effort was made for two years, during negotiations in which my right hon. Friend the President of the Board of Trade played a conspicuous part, to form a free trade area upon an industrial basis, excluding agriculture,

thus allowing almost all European countries to take part.

This negotiation, which, at one time, seemed to have encouraging prospects of success, finally broke down. After this setback, some of the countries outside the Six formed the European Free Trade Association and one of its declared objects was to work for wider trading arrangements in Western Europe, and E.F.T.A. has steadfastly pursued that objective ever since its inception.

I am myself convinced that the existence of this division in Europe, although it is superficially of a commercial character, undoubtedly detracts from the political strength and unity of Western Europe. If we are to be involved in Europe at all, then we have a duty— and so have all the other countries in Europe—to seek some means of resolving the causes of potential division.

In this country, of course, there is a long tradition of isolation. In this, as in most countries, there is a certain suspicion of foreigners. There is also the additional division between us and Continental Europe of a wholly different development of our legal, administrative and, to some extent, political systems. If we are basically united by our religious faith, even here great divisions have grown up.

Nevertheless, it is perhaps worth recording that in every period when the world has been in danger of tyrants or aggression, Britain has abandoned isolationism. It is true that when the immediate danger was removed, we have sometimes tried to return to an insular policy. In due course we have abandoned it. In any case, who could say today that our present danger had been removed, or will soon disappear? Who doubts that we have to face a long and exhausting struggle over more than one generation if the forces of Communistic expansion are to be contained?

I have sometimes heard it asked, " What would happen if one of the countries with which we might be associated in Europe fell into political difficulties, even went Communist? Would not this have a grave effect on us if we were members?" Of course, but the effects would be equally grave whether we were members of the Common Market or not. If a member of

[THE PRIME MINISTER.]
N.A.T.O. or W.E.U. went Communist or semi-Communist, what would be the position of the other member States? If all the countries of Western Europe became satellites of Moscow, what would be the position of this island?

We have only to pose the question to answer it. We shall not escape from the consequences of such a disaster by seeking in isolation a security which our geographical position no longer gives us. Surely, from this point of view, it will be better for us to play our rôle to the full and use the influence we have for the free development of the life and thought of Europe.

There is also a feeling, and I share it, and it is a serious danger felt by many people, that it would be very dangerous if the United Kingdom, by helping to create a truly united Europe, united in every aspect of its life, were to join in a movement tending to isolate Europe from the world and turn its back on the world and look inwards only upon itself. It may, of course, be that there are some people in Europe who believe that this small but uniquely endowed continent can lead a rich, fruitful and prosperous life almost cut off from contact with the rest of the world.

But I do not believe that such people, if they exist, are to be found among the leading men or the Governments of Europe. Certainly, this island could never join an association which believed in such medieval dreams, but if there are little Europeans, and perhaps there are, is it not the duty of this country, with its world-wide ties, to lend its weight to the majority of Europeans who see the true prospective of events? I believe that our right place is in the vanguard of the movement towards the greater unity of the free world, and that we can lead better from within than outside. At any rate, I am persuaded that we ought to try.

Before I come in detail to the various problems, and there are many—the Commonwealth, British agriculture, and E.F.T.A.—I should like to say something about the method which we will follow. It is contained in the Motion before the House, but I think that it should be somewhat elaborated.

The first and most important point is that any agreement, if reached, will have to receive the approval of the House of Commons. The second is equally important. There will be full consultation at every stage with the interests affected. The consultation must take somewhat different forms. Some of the E.F.T.A. countries may be negotiating themselves in their own right, but we will all work closely together.

With regard to British agriculture, we shall keep very close to the representatives who can speak for this great industry. We shall consult the Commonwealth countries at every level and at all stages. If it is desired by the Commonwealth, we will have a meeting at the appropriate stage either of Ministers or of Prime Ministers, as they may wish. This is really for them. As I said on Monday, no difficulty presents itself here. I said:

" I have made it quite clear, and so have my right hon Friends: if, at some point, it were thought desirable to have a meeting of Commonwealth Prime Ministers, at the right moment, probably when the negotiations had reached a certain stage, before any final decisions were put before Parliament and this country, then I can only say that I would be the first to welcome such a meeting."—[OFFICIAL REPORT, 31st July, 1961 ; Vol. 645, c. 932-3.]

That is the method.

I now pass to the wider issues involved. It is, of course, argued, and with deep sincerity, that by associating more closely with Europe in this new economic grouping we should injure the strength of the Commonwealth. If I thought this, I would not, of course, recommend this Motion to the House. But let us examine the Commonwealth position. We make no binding decisions at the Commonwealth Prime Ministers' meetings. We follow no agreed foreign policy. We have no agreed defence policy. Some members of the Commonwealth are in the various defensive pacts of the free world, and some are unaligned. Yet, for all this diversity, the Commonwealth, although not strictly a political unit, has real life and unity. It is something precious and unique.

I ask myself the question: how can we best serve the Commonwealth? By standing aside from the movement for European unity, or by playing our full part in its development? By retaining our influence in the New World, or by allowing it to decline by the relative shrinking of our own political and economic power compared with the massive grouping of the modern world? Britain in isolation would be of little value to our Commonwealth partners, and I think that the Commonwealth understand it. It would, therefore, be wrong in my view to regard our Commonwealth and our European interests as conflicting. Basically, they must be complementary.

If it is vital not to destroy the influence of the Commonwealth in the political field, and I use it in its broadest sense, it is equally vital to do nothing that would damage it economically. What the Ottawa agreements did was to recognise and to strengthen a pattern of trade which had grown up naturally. It was trade between the old country and the new territories; Colonies in the strict sense of the word, opened up by British settlers as in Canada, Australia and New Zealand. The new countries provided the raw materials and agricultural products; the old country provided manufactured goods. The new countries opened up the territories; the old country provided the capital with which to build the harbours, the railways, and the rest, and sold the manufactured goods necessary to develop the new life. That was the system, and Ottawa formally regularised it.

The system of free entry and preferences has been of great advantage to all the partners although over recent years its impact has been reduced. But at the same time there have been important changes in these last thirty years. First and foremost, British agriculture has been revived and now supplies our country with two-thirds of its temperate foodstuffs and with one-half of all its foodstuffs. All the Commonwealth countries have also developed a wider diversity of manufactured goods, partly for sale at home and partly for export.

As the House knows, this changing pattern of trade has presented us with certain difficulties in certain quarters and they will have to be dealt with whether we enter the Common Market or not. Nevertheless, we recognise to the full our duty and our obligations to the Commonwealth. In the words of the Motion, our aim in these negotiations is to make satisfactory arrangements to meet the special interests of the Commonwealth, particularly, of course, in the economic field.

The same applies to our own agricultural industry, about which I will speak later. I frankly admit that if the structure of the European Economic Community had been going on for a generation or more this task would be not only difficult, but well-nigh impossible. But it has not. It is very new. The Treaty lays down a number of principles, but the working out of detailed policies, especially so far as agriculture is concerned, is only just beginning.

Before I come to consider the particular interests of the United Kingdom, I should give the House an account of the position of E.F.T.A. Our partners in the European Free Trade Association, of course, share our objective of bringing to an end the economic division of Western Europe. They have shown much understanding and sympathy during our consultations during recent weeks, and hon. Members will have noted the communiqué issued by the E.F.T.A. Council at Geneva last Monday. The Council considers that the decision of the United Kingdom to take the initiative which I announced to the House on Monday, and which was followed by a similar statement by the Danish Government, provides an opportunity to find an appropriate solution for all the E.F.T.A. countries and thus promote the solidarity and cohesion of Europe.

For our part, we have stated that arrangements which will meet satisfactorily the legitimate concerns of our fellow-members of E.F.T.A. must be among the conditions for our own entry into the E.E.C. Moreover, all members of E.F.T.A. will co-ordinate their actions and remain united throughout the negotiations. E.F.T.A. will remain in being until the objective of its members has been achieved through the creation of a wider European grouping.

I have spoken of the Commonwealth interests, which are mainly though not wholly in the field of raw materials and agricultural production. In referring to the special needs of this country in the Government's Motion we have very much in mind our own agricultural industry. We have always made it clear that any decision to join the European Economic Community depended upon satisfactory arrangements being made with the Community which would

[THE PRIME MINISTER.]

assure the continued well-being of British agriculture. Our objective is to have a prosperous, stable and efficient agricultural industry, organised to provide a good life for those who live and work in the countryside. This represents the fixed decision of the nation. I think that we are all agreed as to purpose. How this is to be achieved is a matter of method.

Methods have changed. In the war and for the period immediately afterwards we operated on the basis of a controlled market and the bulk purchase by the Government of the products of British farmers. We moved later into a different method, of a free market for imports, so as to obtain the advantage of cheap prices, coupled with a system of Exchequer support for the home producer. But even within this scheme there have been variations in emphasis, as in the case of milk, and deviations from the pattern of deficiency payments by the Exchequer.

Our system of agricultural support is basically different from the methods which are being employed on the Continent, and which seem likely to give the pattern of the common agricultural policy when it is decided. We shall have to see what sort of changes will have to be made over a period to bring the systems into line. It may mean that we shall ultimately have to shift from the system where much of the farmers' support comes from the Exchequer to one in which arrangements are made to secure that the market itself provides a fair return to the producer. Such a development would mean much more substantial adaptations in our methods than we have been accustomed to, at any rate in recent years—although our methods have never been static.

I believe that there is a growing realisation that with changing world conditions we are faced with the possibility of changes anyway. But such major changes could be made only gradually, and we should need to see at each stage how they could be so effected as to avoid the risk of prejudice to our main purpose. We are determined to seek such arrangements as will adequately protect the vital interests of our agriculture, but in this we shall not be in opposition to the Governments, still less of the peoples, of the Six countries : nor

to the declared aims of the Community respecting agriculture. In our country those engaged in agriculture represent an important—I would even say vital--part, but still a numerically small part of our population. In many European countries they are a very large part of the population, and it is in their interests as well as ours to make sure that agriculture is prosperous.

But objectives and principles are not enough ; we shall have to be satisfied that the actual policies adopted can successively achieve what is desired. The purpose of our negotiation will be to see how this can be achieved within the Community. Our view that we cannot carry matters further without formal negotiation applies with special force to agriculture. The common agricultural policy is not spelt out in the Treaty for all to see ; it is in process of being worked out by the Six, and by engaging ourselves in discussions with them we should be able to take a hand in shaping it.

We have given a pledge to maintain the 1957 Agriculture Act for the lifetime of this Parliament, and we stand by that. As I have said, our continuing purpose is to have a prosperous, stable and efficient agricultural industry. But we must be ready to examine carefully and dispassionately all methods of achieving that purpose, and if there is the will I do not think that the working out of satisfactory arrangements to meet our requirements should prove an impossible task.

Mr. George Craddock (Bradford, South): All that the Prime Minister has said applies to all countries throughout the world. Why should we not have this development through the United Nations? That was not set up because nations agreed on the question of peace and war, but because they disagreed. Therefore, why not have its complement in an international authority regulating international trade?

The Prime Minister : However great these dreams may be we must deal with the situation as we find it. We may get a second lift one day, or even a third ; meanwhile, let us travel in the lift that is available.

I must now turn to the needs of British industry. The development of the European Economic Community, the opportunity of the mass market which this has created for European industrialists, and the spur that this has given them to competitiveness and efficiency, present the British economy with a great challenge. Whether or not we go into the Common Market we shall have to face the competition of very efficient industries throughout Western Europe, sustained in some cases by populations not yet wholly industrialised. This competition will be severe. The test will be in the straight competition of brains, productive capacity and energy per man. Costs—that will be the test.

The protective tariffs set up before the war have given us some shelter from this competition in the home market. Many people feel that we have perhaps had too much shelter. However that may be, in the long run an island placed as ours is, where our need to export to other people which will always be greater than their need to export to us, cannot maintain the high standards of life that we want for our people in an isolated protective system.

An even more important question is: what would be the loss or gain, not merely of entering a competitive field but of having a common market to develop? In other words, what are the possibilities on the production side? In industries requiring heavy capital investment unit costs are determined by the extent to which the equipment can be used continuously at maximum capacity. With some modern industries, of which the petro-chemical and plastic industries are good examples, the economic scale of production and the capital expenditure involved are so large that the industries can be established and developed economically only with a mass market. It is also true that advanced industrial techniques, such as automation production lines, which can bring great savings in unit costs, are economic only with really large-scale production.

The scale of a potential market also has an important bearing on industrial research. We cannot draw up a precise balance sheet of the prospects for our industries—how much they would gain and how much they would lose—but I think that the weight of opinion among British industrialists is that the balance of advantage for them lies in joining a unit which will be of a size comparable,

let us say, to the United States or Soviet Russia.

There are some other aspects with which I wish to deal. The first is what might be called the social implications of the Treaty, such things as movements of population, equal pay and all the rest. At present, the countries of the Six are only beginning what we might call the harmonisation of their social policies. There are very different circumstances in the various countries and, naturally, each one must take into account its own circumstances. So if we joined at a formative stage, as it were, we should be able to bring our own ideas into the common pool with, I hope, mutual benefit.

Meanwhile, it is quite unreal to suppose that we could be compelled suddenly to accept a flood of cheap labour, or to alter the basis of our social security overnight. It is well understood, for instance, that movements of workers would be related by administrative control to actual offers of employment. These apprehensions about the social implications of joining the Treaty are really aspects of a wider constitutional anxiety about what has often been called " sovereignty."

I must remind the House that the E.E.C. is an economic community, not a defence alliance, or a foreign policy community, or a cultural community. It is an economic community, and the region where collective decisions are taken is related to the sphere covered by the Treaty, economic tariffs, markets and all the rest. Of course, every treaty limits a nation's freedom of action to some extent. Even before the First World War there were certain international conventions to which we bound ourselves. Before the Second World War they grew in character and affected both political and social questions, like the conventions agreed at the International Labour Organisation. Since the war this tendency has grown and our freedom of action is obviously affected by our obligations in N.A.T.O., W.E.U., O.E.E.C. and all the rest.

A number of years have passed since the movement began which culminated in the Treaty of Rome and I am bound to say that I do not see any signs of the members of the Community losing their national identity because they have

[THE PRIME MINISTER.]

delegated a measure of their sovereignty. This problem of sovereignty, to which we must, of course, attach the highest importance is, in the end, perhaps a matter of degree. I fully accept that there are some forces in Europe which would like a genuine federalist system. There are many of my colleagues on both sides of the House who have seen this at Strasbourg and other gatherings. They would like Europe to turn itself into a sort of United States, but I believe this to be a completely false analogy.

The United States of America was originally born out of colonists with only a few generations of history behind them. They were of broadly the same national origins and spoke the same language. Europe is too old, too diverse in tradition, language and history to find itself united by such means. Although the federalist movement exists in Europe it is not one favoured by the leading figures and certainly not by the leading Governments of Europe today. Certainly not by the French Government.

The alternative concept, the only practical concept, would be a confederation, a commonwealth if hon. Members would like to call it that—what I think General de Gaulle has called *Europe des patries*—which would retain the great traditions and the pride of individual nations while working together in clearly defined spheres for their common interest. This seems to me a concept more in tune with the national traditions of European countries and, in particular, of our own. It is one with which we could associate willingly and wholeheartedly. At any rate, there is nothing in the Treaty of Rome which commits the members of E.E.C. to any kind of federalist solution, nor could such a system be imposed on member countries.

Here again, unless we are in the negotiations, unless we can bring our influence to bear, we shall not be able to play our part in deciding the future structure of Europe. It may be, as I have said, that we shall find that our essential needs cannot be met, but if they can I do not feel that there is anything on the constitutional side of which we need be in fear and which cannot be resolved to our satisfaction.

I have mentioned the main considerations which are involved in this great problem, the long-term view of British industry and British agriculture; our responsibilities to our partners in the Commonwealth, our obligations to our fellow members of E.F.T.A.; the future of our national influence in world affairs and the strengthening of the Western Alliance.

These considerations are so important that I do not accept the view that we hesitated too long in reaching our decision. It was absolutely necessary to have the preliminary contacts both on the official and on the ministerial levels and with our friends in the Seven and with our friends in the Six. That has taken some time. It was also absolutely necessary to have thorough consultation with the Commonwealth. Equally, I think that everyone would agree that merely to postpone the decision until the autumn on some excuse or other would be mere temporising.

I have always said frankly to the House that I think that the failure of these negotiations would be a tragedy. Of course it would. If I am asked whether the prospects are now improved, I can only repeat that I am more hopeful than before. The very deterioration of the situation in Europe must tend to increase the forces of unity. There is an old fable of the rivalry between the sun and the wind, as to which could make the traveller discard his coat. As the East wind blows, nations tend to draw together under a common cloak of unity.

It has also been suggested that we should make application on a different basis, perhaps under Article 238, with the object of becoming associates of the Treaty rather than members—" country members " so to speak. We have thought about this and we have found that it would raise all the same problems for British agriculture and Commonwealth trade without giving us any position in which we could share in the decisions of the Community in all its aspects. We have, therefore, come to the conclusion, in the light of the informal discussions, which, as the House knows, we have had over a lengthy period, that the only practicable way to put the question to the test would be to apply for membership under Article 237 of the Treaty of Rome.

I feel sure that European countries realise that there are special problems affecting our position which must be dealt with by special provisions. Indeed, that was their experience when they formed the Six. For instance, special arrangements were made for France's large overseas interests. There were special protocols for Italy, for Holland and for Germany. These were all the subject of negotiation and debate. We must hope that the Six will regard the special arrangements which we require as negotiable in principle and in that case negotiations will begin.

These must, of their very nature, be protracted, detailed and technical. For as well as any matters of principle there is a question of dealing with a large number of separate commodities and reaching agreement on them. No one can be sure that these negotiations will succeed. We hope that the Six will recognise that our decision opens out wide perspectives for future co-operation which could be to our mutual benefit and to the benefit of many other countries, not least those in process of development. We have much to gain from membership of the Community and we have also much to contribute.

A great responsibility lies on the Six as well as on ourselves. Hitherto, although there has been this economic division in Europe, while the rift was there, there has also been the hope of closing it and thus the position has been tolerable. But if it should become clear that this rift will continue and perhaps deepen then I fear that the consequences will be grave. As I said in the United States earlier this year

" . . . it will be a canker gnawing at the very core of Western Alliance."

I am sure that this consideration is in the minds of our Continental friends.

To sum up, there are, as I have said, some to whom the whole concept of Britain working closely in this field with other European nations is instinctively disagreeable. I am bound to say that I find it hard to understand this when they have accepted close collaboration in even more critical spheres. Others feel that our whole and sole duty lies with the Commonwealth. If I thought that our entry into Europe would injure our relations with and influence in the Commonwealth, or be against the true

interest of the Commonwealth, I would not ask the House to support this step.

I think, however, that most of us recognise that in a changing world, if we are not to be left behind and to drop out of the main stream of the world's life, we must be prepared to change and adapt our methods. All through history this has been one of the main sources of our strength.

I therefore ask the House to give Ministers the authority—not to sign a treaty—but to find out on what honourable basis such a treaty could be put forward for the decision of the House.

4.22 p.m.

Mr. Hugh Gaitskell (Leeds, South) : I beg to move, to leave out from " House " to the end of the Question and to add instead thereof :

" notes the decision of Her Majesty's Government to make formal application under Article 237 of the Treaty of Rome in order to initiate negotiations to see if satisfactory arrangements can be made to meet the special interests of the United Kingdom, of the Commonwealth and of the European Free Trade Association ; regrets that Her Majesty's Government will be conducting these negotiations from a position of grave weakness ; and declares that Great Britain should enter the European Economic Community only if this House gives its approval and if the conditions negotiated are generally acceptable to a Commonwealth Prime Ministers' Conference and accord with our obligations and pledges to other members of the European Free Trade Association ".

I must begin with a personal explanation. Some time ago I accepted an engagement in Canada this week and I was to have flown there on Monday. In view of this debate, I managed to postpone this visit, but I do not think it right to cancel it altogether. If the House, as I hope, does not think me too discourteous, I shall leave for Canada tonight. Therefore, I am afraid that I shall not be available for the rest of the debate.

There are those who see the problem of whether or not we should enter the Common Market as a clear-cut and simple one. They have no doubts. Some are passionately in favour of our entry and others are equally passionately against, unconditionally in both instances. The pictures they present of what will happen if we follow the one course or the other are so different as to appear to be related to something totally different.

Harold Wilson's resolve crumbles over "In Place of Strife"

Bernard Ingham reached the height of his career when Margaret Thatcher appointed him her chief press secretary, five months after she became Prime Minister in 1979. He remained in the post until she left Downing street in 1990.

Mrs Thatcher described him as "indispensable", and although he came from a Labour background she liked him for the "tough, blunt, humorous Yorkshireman" that he was. To her, loyalty was one of the most important qualities she sought in a colleague. Bernard Ingham "never let me down," she said.

He was a journalist by profession, having started his career as a reporter in his home territory with the *Hebden Bridge Times*. He then moved on to the *Yorkshire Post* and the *Yorkshire Evening Post*, becoming the northern industrial correspondent for the former in 1961. Subsequently he joined *The Guardian* in Leeds before becoming a member of its labour staff in London in 1965.

In 1967 he left the world of newspapers to become a civil servant as press and information officer for various Government Departments. His first job was intended to be a short-term contract as chief press officer for the National Board for Prices and Incomes. However, it was to be 24 years before he returned to journalism.

His next post was as speech writer to Barbara Castle at the Department of Employment and Productivity, then director of information at the Department of Employment, and, finally, before the Downing street appointment, at the Department of Energy, where, subsequently, promoted to under-secretary level, he headed a new division on energy conservation.

In addition to working for Barbara Castle, he served as director of information for Robert Carr, Maurice Macmillan, Lord Carrington, Eric Varley and Tony Benn.

He calculates that he travelled half a million miles with Mrs Thatcher, dealing with the press at more than 40 summit conferences and half a dozen Commonwealth conferences. He was at her side when she met world leaders including Ronald Reagan, George Bush senior, Mikhail Gorbachev, Helmut Kohl and many more.

He was made head of the Government Information Service in 1989.

He retired when Mrs Thatcher left office, but his retirement was packed with work. His first task was to write his best-selling memoirs "Kill the Messenger", but he also took on both regular and intermittent newspaper writing as well as extensive public relations work.

He was knighted in 1990.

Surrender to Solomon Binding on the volcano's edge

By Sir Bernard Ingham

"Well, they will lose the election now". That was the view in the Department of Employment and Productivity when in 1969 the Labour Cabinet ditched Barbara Castle's heroically misnamed White Paper "In Place of Strife." And so it came to pass the following year, even though it seemed unlikely that the Conservatives would succeed where Labour had failed.

Nor did they. Ted Heath's Industrial Relations Act 1971 was a dead letter after the Official Solicitor we did not know we had was discovered and activated to release a handful of recalcitrant trade unionists from jail.

I was the Department of Employment's chief information officer during both these seismic events. I was also Margaret Thatcher's press secretary in No 10 when she faced down Arthur Scargill's "insurrection". What, you may ask, did I do to deserve this trial by ordeal – of conciliation in smoke filled rooms into the early hours, of coping with the media circus, of consummate union manoeuvring and inept employer dumbness and, not least, political frenzy in the Whitehall and Westminster jungles?

Never before or afterwards during my Civil Service career did I know panic and its close-bosomed friend, intrigue, as when "In Place of Strife" crumbled. It was like living on the edge of a volcano looking fearfully into the heaving crater while everybody simultaneously watched their backs.

The problem was the British propensity to go on unofficial, unsanctioned strikes usually called by shop stewards who conducted an immensely successful – in their terms – guerrilla war against public and private companies and industries. Who could solve it? Harold Wilson set that leftie firebrand Mrs Castle to work on the unions.

It took her only a few months to discover that male chauvinism was alive and well in Congress House and her inability to make any useful impression on them. She promptly – and courageously – embarked on complementing their power with responsibility in what now seem very inoffensive ways.

Much beer (and even more whisky) and sandwiches were consumed during negotiations – or more accurately on eroding the Government's resolve – with the Prime Minister in the lead. The Government's position was simple: there would be no legislation if the unions could come up with something equally effective. They did, of course. It was "a solemn and binding undertaking" by the TUC to intervene in serious unconstitutional stoppages.

I must say that Harold Wilson's exchanges with a "sniggering", entirely sceptical Opposition who likened him to the Grand Old Duke of York read far better than they sounded on 19 June 1969 when he announced surrender in the House. The cheek, chutzpah and ingenuity of the man! Solomon Binding, as the agreement was personified, became a national joke.

The following decade the Department of Employment recorded 25,924 strikes and 128,040,000 working days lost. During the 1980s union membership fell by more than half. At the Trades Union Congress on 12 September 2006 Jonathan Baume, the Civil Service union leader, dated the unions' long term decline to the destruction of "In Place of Strife."

Mr. Brian Parkyn : Would not my right hon. Friend agree that, as long as the Government of Hong Kong puts Chinese citizens in prison and holds them in detention without trial, the tragedy of Anthony Grey and many others in China could well be repeated?

The Prime Minister : No, Sir. I am afraid that the cases referred to by my hon. Friend are not in any sense on all fours with the treatment of Mr. Grey. Indeed, when there have been complaints from the Chinese Government, they have been about persons who have been found guilty by the courts of actions contrary to law and order, which I think would have been the subject of charges in any country. I do not think that it is right to put these on a parallel with the treatment of Mr. Grey.

Mr. Humphrey Atkins : When the right hon. Gentleman asks the Chinese Government about Mr. Grey, will he please also make equally strong representations about the many other British residents illegally detained in China?

The Prime Minister : That is a very fair point. My right hon. Friend has done that.

Mr. Whitaker : Is my right hon. Friend aware that those who have been working and pressurising for the release of all British subjects detained in China hope that there will be equally vociferous pressure from the Opposition on behalf of the two British subjects detained without trial in South Africa?

The Prime Minister : That is a very fair point, but, I think, a different question from that on the Order Paper.

Mr. Hastings : When may we expect a statement on negotiations for the release of Gerald Brooke? Is the Prime Minister aware that there is a great deal of apprehension that the Government may be weakening over the question of exchange for the Krogers, and that this could have the most serious consequences?

The Prime Minister : If I were wrong in saying to my hon. Friend the Member for Hampstead (Mr. Whitaker) that developments in South Africa were a different question from that on the Order Paper, I could certainly say that the

hon. Gentleman's supplementary question is similarly different.

Mr. Hugh Jenkins : Is my right hon. Friend aware that the Krogers are now getting very old ; and would it not be better if the British taxpayer ceased to pay for their upkeep?

The Prime Minister : I cannot answer any question except the Question on the Order Paper, which is about Mr. Grey. I know that the whole House is anxious about Mr. Grey, as it is about Mr. Brooke, but it would not help if, in trying to answer. I were to link the reply to one Question with the answer to another.

INDUSTRIAL RELATIONS

The Prime Minister (Mr. Harold Wilson) : With permission, I will now answer Questions Nos. Q1, Q5, Q8 and Q10 together.

Further to my interim report to the House in answer to Questions on Tuesday, together with my right hon. Friend the First Secretary of State I again met the General Council of the T.U.C. yesterday.

The House will recall that in the previous discussions the First Secretary and I made clear that the Government would not proceed with their proposals for legislation on industrial relations in this Session of Parliament if the T.U.C. took steps which the Government regarded as equally effective—[*Laughter.*] This is what I said on Tuesday ; I did not hear a snigger then—and that while the Government accepted the proposals adopted by the T.U.C. Special Congress on 5th June as satisfactory in relation to inter-union disputes, they had doubts about certain aspects of the proposals for dealing with unconstitutional strikes.

In the course of yesterday's discussions the General Council unanimously agreed to a solemn and binding undertaking which set out the lines on which the General Council will intervene in serious unconstitutional stoppages. In the light of this undertaking, the Government now regard the T.U.C.'s proposals as satisfactory. A copy of the undertaking has been placed in the Library, and will be circulated in the OFFICIAL REPORT.

In these circumstances, the Government have decided not to proceed with proposals for legislation involving financial penalties for those involved in inter-union and unconstitutional disputes. An interim Industrial Relations Bill will not, therefore, be introduced this Session. Consultations about the legislation to be introduced in the next Session of Parliament will continue with the T.U.C., the C.B.I. and the other organisations concerned.

In answer to Questions Nos. Q1 and Q5, I shall be making a Ministerial television broadcast on these matters tonight.

In answer to Question No. Q8, I would remind my hon. Friend the Member for West Ham, North (Mr. Arthur Lewis) that between us my right hon. Friend and I have attended several trade union conferences in recent months, and have been in close touch with trade union opinion.

In answer to Question No. Q10, I am not aware of any evidence of unauthorised disclosure of official information.

Mr. Heath: What will happen should unofficial strikers ignore the trade union leaders, and go on striking?

The Prime Minister: I am surprised that that is all the right hon. Gentleman could manage—[HON. MEMBERS: "Oh."] If that is the sum total of 13 years—[HON. MEMBERS: "Oh."] Perhaps I can enlighten him.

The T.U.C. has given us this binding declaration. On Tuesday, the right hon. Gentleman said that the reason his Government did not even introduce a Royal Commission was that they were negotiating with the T.U.C. They negotiated with the T.U.C. for 13 years—[HON. MEMBERS: "Answer."] Indeed, I will. We have negotiated with the T.U.C. for two months.

In the declaration, which I should have thought that the right hon. Gentleman would have read, he will see that in cases where the T.U.C. believes that strikers are unconstitutional and wrong in remaining on strike, it will place an obligation on the union or unions concerned to get them back to work—[HON. MEMBERS: "Answer."] I am trying to answer the question—[*Interruption.*] In cases where the unions flout the instruction of the T.U.C., action will be taken under Rule 13. This is what has come out of two

months' negotiations—[*Laughter.*] I am surprised that right hon. Gentlemen, who secured nothing out of their negotiations —[*Interruption.*]—who refused to take action because they said—[*Interruption.*]

Mr. Speaker: Order. The right hon. Gentleman must be heard reasonably.

The Prime Minister: I am quoting their words. They refused to take action because they said that it was a matter for the T.U.C. We have now got the T.U.C. to act while they did not.

Mr. Heath: Will the Prime Minister now answer my specific question: what will happen when unofficial strikers ignore the advice of their union leaders, and go on striking? This was the crux of the matter, and the reason for the right hon. Lady the First Secretary of State putting forward proposals for imposing a conciliation pause, with sanctions to enforce it against unofficial strikers.

The Prime Minister says that he must have something effective in its place. What will happen when unofficial strikers ignore the union leaders, and go on striking?

Mr. James Johnson: On a point of order, Mr. Speaker. When will the hon. Gentlemen be called who put down the Questions on the Order Paper?

Mr. Speaker: The hon. Gentleman must be patient.

The Prime Minister: The right hon. Gentleman the Leader of the Opposition has the answer I have given. In the cases I have mentioned, the T.U.C. will place an obligation on the unions concerned to get their members back to work. It will then be the duty of the unions concerned to do this, including, where appropriate, the use of their rule books—[*Laughter.*] I have heard enough—[*Interruption.*]

Mr. Speaker: Order. We must have reasonable order.

The Prime Minister: I have heard enough from hon. Gentlemen opposite about the power of union rule books— they have complained only too often about them in the past.

In this case there is an obligation, where it is needed, to use the rule book,

[THE PRIME MINISTER.]
including fines, suspensions and expulsion—which is a very serious punishment in a closed shop industry—where this is not carried out and the unions are not taking effective action. I have told the House what the T.U.C. powers are in respect of individual unions. This is in marked contrast to the literally nothing the party opposite did during 13 years of power.

Mr. Marten *rose——*

Mr. C. Pannell : On a point of order, Mr. Speaker. These answers are in reply to questions put on the Order Paper. While I recognise that the Leader of the Opposition has a unique position in the House, to which I bow, in the matter of Questions, it is a fact that Mr. Speaker Clifton Brown even ruled against Sir Winston Churchill and said that he must not muscle in to exclude the original questioner. Mr. Speaker Clifton Brown then called the original questioner. I should be glad, with all due deference to the undoubted rights of the Leader of the Opposition, to know whether that is still the position of back benchers.

Mr. Speaker : Order. There is some substance in the historical recollection of the right hon. Gentleman, who is an expert in the history of Parliament. If he reads the incident very carefully, he will, however, find that the circumstances were altogether different. Mr. Marten.

Mr. Marten : If the T.U.C. fails to discipline unconstitutional strikes in the months ahead, will the right hon. Gentleman then introduce a Bill with penal sanctions? Does this agreement need to be ratified by the Trades Union Congress in the autumn? If so, will it not be operative until then?

The Prime Minister : The first part of the hon. Gentleman's supplementary question is hypothetical. [HON. MEMBERS: " Answer."] I am surprised that hon. Gentlemen opposite are not aware of that. It was a fair question, but the mirth that greeted it makes me wonder whether hon. Gentlemen opposite really are refusing to take on trust a solemn obligation made by men with whom they dealt when they were in office, whom they trusted and who, after 12 years, they told should be handling this question of un-

official strikes. It is, therefore, a hypothetical question. I accept not only the sincerity but the determination of the General Council of the T.U.C. when it makes a declaration of this kind, which is unanimous.

The hon. Gentleman is right in suggesting, in the second part of his supplementary question—this is a binding declaration ; it is as binding as the Bridlington declaration which played such an important part in trade union history —that it requires to be approved by the Trades Union Congress. However, the General Council said yesterday, in relation to this and to the rule changes that it proposed at Croydon, that it will proceed to act within the spirit of them, even without waiting for Congress to pass the necessary legislation.

Mr. Eldon Griffiths : Since Mr. Victor Feather and not the Prime Minister now seems to be in charge of issuing dog licences, would it not be better for the Prime Minister to make his broadcast not from No. 10 Downing Street but from T.U.C. headquarters?

The Prime Minister : I am sorry to see that the hon. Gentleman is now having to get even his jokes as well as his opinions from the Tory Press this morning. To answer what he no doubt thought was the serious part of his supplementary question, I have said today and yesterday and we said it two months ago, both in this House and elsewhere——

Sir Knox Cunningham : What about last week?

The Prime Minister :—and last week as well, that if the T.U.C. was able to produce something effective and was determined about its use, not only in relation to unofficial strikes but in inter-union disputes, we would accept it as a substitute for ours.

That is what we have done and the hon. Gentleman, who used to write his own Prime Minister's speeches for him, should remember that at the time when he was writing them it was official Conservative policy to leave unofficial strikes to the T.U.C.

Several Hon. Members *rose——*

Mr. Eldon Griffiths : On a point of order. What the Prime Minister has just said and what he has frequently said is a lie and he should retract it.

Hon. Members: Withdraw.

Mr. Speaker: Order. I do not need help. The hon. Gentleman will withdraw the word " lie ".

Mr. Eldon Griffiths: I am sorry, Mr. Speaker, but you have placed me in a difficulty.

Hon. Members: Name him.

Mr. Speaker: Order. The Chair is equally sorry, but the Chair must protect the rules of the House and the conduct in it. It is not in order for one hon. Member to accuse another hon. Member of uttering a lie. The hon. Gentleman must withdraw the word " lie ".

Mr. Eldon Griffiths: With the greatest respect, Mr. Speaker—[HON. MEMBERS: " Withdraw."]—I quite deliberately used the word—[HON. MEMBERS: " Oh."]— which I knew to be outside the normal rules of the House. I did so because I felt it right to draw attention——

Hon. Members: Withdraw.

Mr. Speaker: Order. For the last time, I ask the hon. Gentleman to withdraw the word " lie ".

Hon. Members: Name him.

Mr. Eldon Griffiths: In response to your request, and yours alone, Mr. Speaker, I withdraw the word " lie "— and replace it with the phrase a terminological inexactitude in respect of something which the Prime Minister knew to be untrue.

Hon. Members: Oh.

Mr. Speaker: Order. The hon. Gentleman has withdrawn the word.

Mr. Arthur Lewis: Is the Prime Minister aware that, unfoundedly, some hon. Gentlemen opposite are casting doubt on the ability and veracity of the T.U.C.? Would my right hon. Friend agree that we should pay tribute to Victor Feather who, during these discussions, has proved the ability of the T.U.C.—[HON. MEMBERS: " Hear, hear."]—in that within a few hours of being asked by the Prime Minister so to do, the T.U.C. resolved the unofficial strike at the Pressed Steel factory?

Perhaps hon. Gentlemen opposite will now cheer that, as they cheered my earlier remark, and perhaps my right hon. Friend will pay tribute to the T.U.C. for the excellent work that it did in connection with that strike.

The Prime Minister: Yes, Sir, and I thank my hon. Friend for his remarks. I certainly did what he asks on that occasion. A matter which has not received much attention is the valuable demarcation agreement which has been concluded in the shipyards and which should make possible the end of the large number of strikes that have bedevilled that industry in the past generation.

As for hon. Gentlemen opposite, I am sure that when they have got over their little fit of instant opposition, to which we have become so used, they, too, will wish to pay tribute to the fact that the T.U.C. has really moved further forward in all these matters in the past two or three months than in the past 40 years. I do not think that even hon. Gentlemen opposite will grudge that tribute to the T.U.C. and that they will also recognise that this would not have happened but for our White Paper and the negotiations. I believe that they may one day pay tribute to that, too.

And considering their 13 years of negotiations with the T.U.C., I would now like one of them, perhaps one of their ex-Ministers of Labour, to tell us what was achieved during those 13 years of negotiation, apart from a lot of No. 10 talks about sherry and unemployment at Stockton-on-Tees.

Mr. Ashley: Is my right hon. Friend aware that in view of the Government's achievements in persuading the T.U.C. to act, the Opposition's hostility is predictable and understandable? Is he further aware that many of us would like to see the Government exercising similar persuasion on the employers to induce them to co-operate in the fundamental task of improving the collective bargaining machinery and changing industrial attitudes, a matter which is vital to the future of Britain?

The Prime Minister: Yes, Sir. I entirely agree with what my hon. Friend said about the predictability of the Opposition in this matter. I could understand their attitude if they had supported the White Paper, but they did not. They abstained in the White Paper debate. In

[THE PRIME MINISTER.]
connection with the Bill which we said would follow the White Paper, they made it very clear that they would do everything possible to hold up debate on it.

Mr. Mawby : Is the Prime Minister aware that congratulations are due to him for the greatest confidence trick of the century? [*Interruption.*] Is he also aware that this probably explains the attitude of the Opposition to his White Paper? As he explained to the Parliamentary Labour Party that the Bill to which he referred was essential for the Government to remain in office, will he now do what he should have done months ago—go to the country?

The Prime Minister : The hon. Member for Totnes (Mr. Mawby), who, I think, claims to be one of that extraordinary group known as Tory trade unionists, has enough experience of industry and of his own union as well as of the T.U.C. to know how inaccurate is his judgment of this matter. As a loyal trade unionist, for such I understand him to be, he will, I am sure, understand what it has meant that the T.U.C. has been able to make this declaration.

As for the quotation he made from a speech which I made in a Committee Room upstairs on, I think, 17th April, I noticed that he did not quote the other relevant part of that speech.

Mr. Atkinson : During the last two months the idea that workers could be exposed to prosecution by their employers in the event of a dispute was thoroughly rejected by the Government's advisers, by the D.E.P. and by the T.U.C. Would my right hon. Friend therefore agree that the proposals contained in the document " Fair Deal at Work " are now thoroughly rejected by every authority in Britain, and that the whole of the advice tendered to the Government means that those proposals made by the party opposite are now a non-starter?

The Prime Minister : They certainly always were a non-starter. However, I do not think that it would be appropriate for me, by way of question and answer, to attempt to comment adequately on the total irrelevance of the Opposition's proposals. I would prefer to invite the Leader of the Opposition to use his next Supply day to let us have a debate on these matters, when we can exchange our courtesies across the Floor of the House.

After all, last November the right hon. Gentleman called for an urgent Bill before Christmas. I am sure, therefore, that he would not grudge us one of his Supply days to debate this subject. We can then compare his record at the Ministry of Labour and the Tory record generally with what we have achieved in these past few months.

Dr. Winstanley : May I welcome the fact that even if the Prime Minister has not diagnosed the complaint, he has at least stopped prescribing the wrong medicine? Are we not misleading ourselves in describing the T.U.C. undertaking as binding and in assuming that the trade unions, as at present constituted and without reform, will be able to accomplish this task? Do not we now need positive legislation to attack the causes of industrial unrest and implement the more constructive parts of the White Paper?

The Prime Minister : I would not attempt to compete with the hon. Gentleman about medicine and prescribing. What we put forward in our White Paper was, in our view, the only means of dealing with this matter by Government action in a situation where industry was not prepared to make the necessary changes for us to be able to entrust it with, at any rate, part of the task.

I agree with the hon. Gentleman—and this is a central theme of the White Paper—that in addition to action to deal with unconstitutional strikers we must get at the basic causes of strikes, grievances, negotiating procedures, agreements, and so on. That is why we have set up the C.I.R. ; and that inspired a large section of " Programme for Action ". He is right to draw attention to that, but this alone will not deal with the urgent problem we face.

Mr. James Griffiths : Does my right hon. Friend appreciate that many hon. Members with experience of these matters are glad that the Government have abandoned the penal clauses, for our experience shows that they do not promote industrial harmony but industrial strife? Is he further aware that many of us with years of experience in the trade unions wholeheartedly welcome the steps which have been taken by the

T.U.C., in agreement with the Government, remembering that industrial peace is not possible against hostility from the T.U.C.?

May I, therefore, tell my right hon. Friend that it is now our duty to give every possible help to the T.U.C. in this matter; and, on a personal note, may I express my appreciation, as one who has known him for many years, for the efforts that my right hon. Friend has made and that have been made, also, by Mr. Victor Feather?

The Prime Minister: I thank my right hon. Friend. His long experience in industry on the trade union side as a national leader in this matter will, I hope, put to shame some of the sniggers and giggles from hon. Members opposite who are not capable of appreciating the importance of this step forward by the T.U.C. even though when they were in office they said that the T.U.C. must do the job themselves. That I find difficult to understand.

No one wanted to propose penal clauses. On the other hand, I do not think that anyone underrated the importance of the problem we had to deal with. That is why the Government were not, and would not have been, afraid to carry legislation on this despite the fact that hon. Members opposite would not have had the guts to support us. We were prepared to do that, but always we said that if the T.U.C. would propose an effective solution we would adopt it, and we have done so.

Mr. Boyd-Carpenter: Reverting to my right hon. Friend's two unanswered questions about the handling of unofficial strikes, which up to yesterday right hon. Gentlemen opposite were taking with desperate seriousness, may we have an assurance from the Prime Minister that as a result of this transaction beneficial results will appear in weeks rather than months?

The Prime Minister: I should have thought that even for the right hon. Gentleman these matters are too important in industrial relations for remarks of that kind, particularly since he seems entirely to have failed to see that already we have had some substantial results, as pointed out by my hon. Friends, in ending one or two serious strikes as a result

of the powers given by the Croydon conference to the T.U.C. The right hon. Gentleman is not satisfied with my answer, but, of course, he is a lawyer——

Sir Harmar Nicholls: Withdraw.

The Prime Minister: I do not think that that is a word one has to withdraw.

The right hon. Gentleman will be able to understand how totally irrelevant to the problems are the solutions which leave the whole matter in the arid atmosphere of a court decision when dealing with the basic problems of strikes, which is, of course, what we set out to do in our White Paper. That is why, when he asks, " What will you do with unions who do not ensure that strikers go back to work? ", this is the question which we have to put to the right hon. Gentleman the Leader of the Opposition.

Mr. Shinwell: Do I understand from my right hon. Friend that, despite the profound disappointment of the Opposition at the outcome of the Government's discussions with the trade unions, they have not yet requested a debate on this important and fundamental topic? Would it not be desirable that there should be an early debate to enable the Opposition to express in rational terms their opinion of the trade union movement, particularly the T.U.C., and also to indicate to the House and the country what would happen to the trade union movement and the workers if, by any mischance, members of the Opposition ever became the Government?

The Prime Minister: No, Sir. My right hon. Friend did not quite get the point I made about a debate. It is not a question of the Opposition having to request it, for they have a Supply day open to them next week and they can take it.

Mr. Heath: Is the Prime Minister aware that the Opposition have no Supply day next week? [*Interruption.*] Is the Prime Minister aware that in any case the House will have ample opportunity to debate the Government's conduct in this matter on Wednesday, when there is to be a debate on the Letter of Intent, because the Chancellor of the Exchequer gave a solemn undertaking that we would have industrial legislation of this kind as a result of abandoning

[MR. HEATH.]
the compulsory prices and incomes policy?

The Prime Minister : I accept, of course, what the Chief Whip said and I have confirmed that there is no Supply day next week. [HON. MEMBERS : " Withdraw."] I have done so ; I have accepted that, but I still believe that after last November, when the Opposition demanded an immediate Bill, they might have taken one Supply day. We shall be glad to give them a day at the earliest opportunity if they will take it. I do not know whether this is what the right hon. Gentleman was suggesting, but he was quite wrong to say that in the Letter of Intent there was a pledge that we would introduce legislation.

Mr. Heath : I said nothing of the sort. I said that it was in the Chancellor's Budget speech.

Mr. Dunn : On a point of order. Mr. Speaker. Did I hear the Leader of the Opposition state the business for next week, for Wednesday, although the House is not yet in possession of that information?

Mr. Speaker : Order. I have no control over leaks, even inside the House.

Mr. Heath : May I again correct the Prime Minister? He was quite wrong in what he said about my remarks. I did not say that it was in the Letter of Intent. I have no knowledge of that, but I said that it was in the Budget speech in reference to the Letter of Intent.

The Prime Minister : Yes, Sir, and it was said by my right hon. Friend the Chancellor that if we had an adequate alternative from the T.U.C. we would accept that. [*Interruption.*]

Mr. Speaker : Order. We ought to hear both sides equally fairly.

The Prime Minister : I have the text of it. I myself said on 17th April during the debate—[*Interruption.*] The right hon. Gentleman can sit back now. The right hon. Gentleman got out of the question of a debate on industrial relations by referring to the Letter of Intent which has nothing to do with the case and now he drags in the Budget debate. If the right hon. Gentleman—[*Interruption.*]

Mr. Speaker : Order. Hon. Members must be willing to hear what they do not agree with. [*Interruption.*] Order. The Prime Minister.

The Prime Minister : It is necessary to follow a rather difficult path to deal with the right hon. Gentleman's wriggles on what he said—on his refusal to deal with the question of a debate which led him by a corkscrew path, *via* the Letter of Intent, to my right hon. Friend's Budget speech. [*Interruption.*]

Mr. Speaker : Order. I must insist that the Prime Minister be heard. [*Interruption.*]

The Prime Minister : I therefore return to the suggestion that the right hon. Gentleman should use a Supply day to debate industrial relations, the first Supply day he gets. Then he can make a short speech, telling us what hon. Members opposite did during 13 years.

Sir T. Brinton : Mr. Speaker, could we get back to facts? The Prime Minister made it perfectly clear that the powers granted to the T.U.C. on 5th June were, in his opinion, insufficient for it to carry out the job he asked it to do as an alternative to legislation. What powers has the T.U.C. since been granted which makes the Prime Minister believe that it can now do something which he himself said it could not do on 5th June?

The Prime Minister : The answer to that is in the annexe to the statement issued yesterday, namely, the power to place an obligation on individual unions to get unofficial strikers back to work in the cases described in the document. There was no such power whatever in the statement from Croydon.

Mr. Houghton : In view of the display of political bias and ignorance that we have had from the benches opposite this afternoon, will my right hon. Friend now cease to treat the Opposition seriously in this matter? Has he not noticed that hon. Members opposite can scarcely conceal their fury because the Parliamentary Labour Party is not going to tear itself apart to provide a Roman holiday for the enemies of the Government?

The Prime Minister : No, Sir. I would not go so far as that. I acquit them, of course, of bias. I do not acquit them of ignorance. I think that their attitude arises from a sense of shame at their total inability to do anything themselves.

Mr. Hastings : On a point of order. Is there any point in the Prime Minister being heard further? [*Interruption.*]

Mr. Speaker : Order. Dame Irene Ward.

Dame Irene Ward : Will the Prime Minister inform the House how he enjoys being the Grand Old Duke of York?

The Prime Minister : I am genuinely flattered by the hon. Lady by her use of an old crack that I once made about her own Front Bench. I take it in the same spirit as it was then offered, but in our case we said that we would not introduce legislation if we had an effective alternative, and we have, but their attitude was different.

Mr. Ogden : Will my right hon. Friend agree that if the attitude of the Opposition this afternoon really were to represent the attitude of employers it would be amazing that there are not more unofficial strikes than fewer? Will my right hon. Friend now confirm that in his broadcast tonight he will put equal pressure on the C.B.I. to improve its procedures in industrial relations as he puts on the T.U.C.?

The Prime Minister : I have no reason at all to think that anything we have heard from the benches opposite this afternoon represents the view of at any rate progressive employers. My right hon. Friend and I hope to meet the C.B.I. later this afternoon to discuss these serious problems. Whatever differences there are between the C.B.I. and the Government about prescriptions for dealing with them, the C.B.I. and the Government take these problems very seriously indeed.

Several Hon. Members *rose*——

Mr. Speaker : Order. I must protect the business of the House.

Following is the undertaking :

The General Council has unanimously agreed that in operating Congress Rule 11, as recommended by the General Council and approved by the Special Congress on 5th June:

(*a*) Where a dispute has led or is likely to lead to an unconstitutional stoppage of work which involves directly or indirectly large bodies of workers or which, if pro-

tracted, may have serious consequences, the General Council shall ascertain and assess all the facts, having regard to paragraphs 20 to 27 of "Programme for Action".

(*b*) In cases where they consider it unreasonable to order an unconditional return to work, they will tender the organisation or organisations concerned their considered opinion and advice with a view to promoting a settlement.

(*c*) Where, however, they find there should be no stoppage of work before procedure is exhausted, they will place an obligation on the organisation or organisations concerned to take energetic steps to obtain an immediate resumption of work, including action within their rules if necessary, so that negotiations can proceed.

(*d*) Should an affiliated organisation not comply with an obligation placed on it under (*c*) above, the General Council shall duly report to Congress or deal with the organisation under Clauses (*b*), (*c*), (*d*) and (*h*) of Rule 13.

18*th June,* 1969.

BUSINESS OF THE HOUSE

Mr. Heath : Will the Leader of the House kindly state the business of the House for next week?

The Lord President of the Council and Leader of the House of Commons (Mr. Fred Peart) : Yes, Sir. The business for next week will be as follows:

MONDAY, 23RD JUNE and TUESDAY, 24TH JUNE—Remaining stages of the Development of Tourism Bill.

WEDNESDAY, 25TH JUNE—Supply [23rd Allotted Day] :

Debate on the Letter of Intent.

This will arise on a Motion for the Adjournment of the House.

Motion on the Civil Aviation (Navigational Service Charges) (Third Amendment) Regulations.

THURSDAY, 26TH JUNE—Completion of the remaining stages of the Housing Bill.

FRIDAY, 27TH JUNE—Motions on the Hosiery and Knitwear Industry (Scientific Research Levy) Order, the Cereals (Guarantee Payments) (Amendment) Order, on the Agricultural Lime Scheme (Extension of Period) Order, the Small Farm (Business Management) Schemes, the Bacon Curing Industry Stabilisation (Variation) Scheme and on the Milk (Extension of Period of Control of Maximum prices) Order.

Geoffrey Howe electrifies the Commons with a courageous Budget to transform Britain

As political editor of *The Sun* newspaper, Trevor Kavanagh became one of the best known names in political journalism. He was even once described as the most influential man in British politics, a compliment that he eschews, explaining that it is the newspaper that has the influence, not the person who is writing for it.

Nevertheless, with 10 million to 11 million people reading *The Sun* every day, Trevor Kavanagh could well have been the most widely read political correspondent of his time. He is now an associate editor of the newspaper.

Leaving his grammar school in Reigate, Surrey, his first job in journalism was on his local newspaper. He left there to take up the position of agricultural correspondent for the Hereford *Evening News* before moving to Australia. It was there, after working on a number of newspapers, that he joined the Rupert Murdoch empire, becoming political correspondent for the Sydney *Daily Mirror*.

Based in Canberra, he covered a turbulent period in Australian politics that was good for political journalists but not for Gough Whitlam's Labour Government, which collapsed after the unprecedented sacking of Whitlam by the Governor-General.

His good fortune in being in the right place at the right time persisted. In 1978 he returned to England to work for *The Sun* as its industrial correspondent just as the country descended into the "Winter of Discontent". It was a time that was good for journalists, especially for those whose job was to cover the strikes that were crippling Britain, but not for James Callaghan's Labour Government, which was voted out of power the following year, giving way to the Thatcher years.

In 1983, under Kelvin MacKenzie's editorship, Trevor Kavanagh took over from Walter Terry as the political editor of *The Sun*, a job he held until 2006 when, with the move to associate editor, he became responsible for a weekly column and the role of chief leader writer.

During his 25 years as a Lobby correspondent at Westminster he covered six general elections, witnessed the earth shattering changes under Margaret Thatcher's premiership and her eventual demise, and reported on the ascent of New Labour and Tony Blair's accession to Number 10 Downing street.

Among the awards he received for his work were the British Press Awards "Journalist of the Year" and "Reporter of the Year" in 1997. He also received the "What the Papers Say" "Scoop of the Year" award for making readers of *The Sun* the first to know the outcome of the Hutton inquiry into the death of the scientist Dr David Kelly.

Mrs Thatcher tells Sir Geoffrey "either borrowing gets the chop or you do."

By Trevor Kavanagh

Budget speeches are frequently long and boring. Geoffrey Howe was probably the most unexciting Chancellor in modern history. But on 10 March 1981, Sir Geoffrey – now Lord Howe – electrified the Commons and the nation with a Budget speech that began transforming Britain from the "Sick Man of Europe" to one of the world's leading economies.

Not so long ago, after 15 years of unbroken economic growth, stable inflation and strong employment, it would have hard to recall the crisis facing the Thatcher Government in 1979.

Those days of high unemployment and low growth have been brought back into sharp focus by the catastrophe that has overtaken the world economy – perhaps especially Britain's.

Yet even Thatcher's 1980s opponents, Tony Blair and Gordon Brown, now pay homage to the remarkable transformation in UK prosperity that flowed from her courageous decisions.

The economy was in a slump with state spending out of control and, by 1981, inflation at a dizzying 15 per cent – and rising fast. In 1980, output crashed by 2.5 per cent, manufacturing by 9 per cent to its lowest since the 1921 slump – and unemployment was up by 1 million in just 12 months.

This, according to the best economic brains of the day, required a pump-priming Budget, with gushers of extra taxpayers' money to get Britain back to work. Sir Geoffrey did precisely the opposite, He raised taxes, clobbered pay perks such as company cars, and hit banks with a windfall tax. Most painful of all, he slashed state borrowing, just as everyone expected it to rise.

The Chancellor came under ferocious attack, not least by Labour leader Michael Foot who claimed: "This is a no-hope budget delivered by a no-hope Chancellor." The unions were in uproar. Even the Tories started to panic, with Christopher Brocklebank-Fowler quitting the party to join the SDP.

And, in one of the most spectacular acts of professional misjudgment of all time, 364 economists signed a letter to *The Times* predicting the Budget would "deepen the depression, erode the industrial base of our economy and threaten its social and political stability".

They were all wrong.

The 1981 Budget, an act of great courage, paved the way for the transformation of Britain and laid the foundations for the strong economy that we enjoyed in the years that followed. Yet this was not entirely a Geoffrey Howe Budget. Behind the scenes, a struggle was raging between the Chancellor and Prime Minister Margaret Thatcher over state borrowing, with her economic guru, the late Sir Alan Walters riding shotgun.

It culminated in a stand-off in Mrs Thatcher's Downing street flat as she packed for an official trip to the States.

She insisted that borrowing must be slashed by more than 10 per cent – from £11.25bn to £10bn, a colossal sum in those days. The Chancellor was hard as nails when it came to public spending and borrowing. But even he blenched at the thought of such a dramatic belt-tightening exercise in the depths of recession.

As he reached for some hat boxes on top of the wardrobe, Sir Geoffrey told the Prime Minister: "You realise this means I either rewrite my Budget or .."

"Yes, Geoffrey," said Mrs T, ".. or you get the chop."

The Chancellor went away and thought about it. And agreed to amend his Budget.

In her memoirs, Baroness Thatcher says: "This was the turning point. I was glad Geoffrey had accepted the argument and I was pleased he had found a way of increasing tax revenues that did not run counter to our long term strategy of reversing Labour's high tax rates.

"Our budget strategy was now set. And it looked as if we would be able to announce a reduction of 2 per cent in MLR in the budget the following Tuesday."

WAY AND MEANS

Budget Statement

Mr. Deputy Speaker (Mr. Bernard Weatherill): Before I call the Chancellor of the Exchequer, it may be for the convenience of hon. Members if I remind them that at the end of the Chancellor's speech, as in past years, copies of the Budget Resolutions will not be handed around in the Chamber but will be available to hon. Members in the Vote Office.

INTRODUCTION

3.31 pm

The Chancellor of the Exchequer (Sir Geoffrey Howe): The annual presentation of the Budget is rightly regarded as the principal economic act of Government. But every Chancellor—indeed, every Member of the House—very well understands that the economic well-being of the nation owes more, at the end of the day, to the spirit and vitality of its people than to any single act of Government. I do not seek, in saying that, in any sense to undervalue the proper role of Government, but simply to set it in perspective. What is the essential duty of Government is to provide responsible management of the financial framework within which the nation has to live. That duty must start from a sober and realistic assessment of the nation's economic condition. It is with that that I begin.

First, there is the fight against inflation. We have made real progress. Prices are now rising only about half as fast as they were last summer. In the last year we have had the most rapid fall in inflation of any major country. Living standards in the personal sector as a whole are estimated to have risen in 1980 by a further 2 per cent. There have been fewer industrial disputes than at any time in the last 40 years. In 1980 Britain's exports increased in value, and held up in volume, and we achieved a record current account surplus of £2¾ billion. Many British companies are clearly facing the challenge with much more success than might have been expected.

However, there are sharp contrasts. In 1980 total output in the United Kingdom fell by about 2½ per cent. and that of manufacturing industry by no less than 9 per cent. Interest rates have remained high. Many parts of industry have been extremely hard pressed. Although the latest figures suggest that the rise in unemployment may be slowing down, there are almost 1 million more people out of work than there were a year ago. For individuals, families, and sometimes for entire communities, this can mean real hardship. The Government share the nation's deep concern.

WORLD DEVELOPMENTS

But Britain is not alone in facing these problems. In the spring and summer of last year, output fell sharply in six out of seven of the major economies. Unemployment rose by about 3 million in the OECD countries during 1980. In the American motor industry alone, almost 200,000 workers lost their jobs. The average OECD inflation rate remains in double figures. This year the output of the European Community as a whole is not expected to show any improvement over 1980.

A major cause of this world-wide setback is the enormous rise in oil prices in the last two years. The oil-producing countries of OPEC last year collected about 150 billion dollars more in export receipts than they did in 1978. That huge increase, and the surpluses that it created, mean that the rest of the world has had less to spend on other goods and services. At the same time, Governments have had to act firmly to counter the inflationary spiral set in motion by higher oil prices.

Those are the main reasons why the OECD has estimated that the national product of the industrial countries this year will be at least 6 per cent. lower than it would have been without the latest oil price increases. That represents a very large enforced reduction in sales and output. It has inevitably meant a big jump in unemployment. Because we are a trading nation, the fact that we have our own oil cannot protect us from the slowdown in many of the markets to which we sell around the world.

THE UNITED KINGDOM ECONOMY

There are still many businesses in Britain that lead the world. But the obstacles to recovery are none the less greater here than in other countries. Many parts of our industry have long been less dynamic than theirs. Years of high inflation, low productivity and delayed change have made our economy especially vulnerable, and reduced its ability to compete in both home and overseas markets. And so we are suffering more than others.

Those firms which have lagged behind have often been encouraged to do so in the misguided belief that change can be postponed indefinitely. Eventually, the combined pressures of competition and recession have compelled long-overdue moves to tackle these deep-seated weaknesses. They have been essential to the creation or preservation of secure jobs for the longer term. But, of course, the immediate effect has been to add to unemployment. Thus, nearly 300,000 jobs have been lost in the motor industry, steel, textiles and shipbuilding over the past 18 months.

As a nation we have carried the process of weakening our own economy a long stage further in the three years before the recession started. In each of the last three pay rounds, earnings in manufacturing industry rose by over 14 per cent. while the underlying improvement in productivity has been little more than 1 per cent. British unit labour costs have risen more than twice as fast as those of our foreign competitors.

Industry has had to adapt to a second huge increase in the price of energy. The world oil price is now three times what it was three years ago. Because of that, the North Sea has had the consequence of contributing to the sharp rise in sterling since 1977. Various other factors have also influenced the position of sterling, including changes in the fortunes of other major economies. Although the strong pound has conferred some benefit on British industry through cheaper imported materials, it has, of course, imposed real difficulty on businesses that sell against international competitors. That has been particularly true of those industries that were still seriously overmanned.

So, as consumers, we have benefited greatly from the strong pound and very often from large pay increases as well, while many companies have been hard pressed. Between 1977 and 1980, the real after-tax income of individuals rose by about one-sixth. But the real disposable income of industrial and commercial companies fell by one-quarter. And output rose by only 2 per cent. This contrast between the fortunes of individuals and businesses marks a striking imbalance. There is also a sharp difference—within the business sector itself—between the fortunes of the oil and banking sectors, on the one hand, and most manufacturing companies on the other.

In these circumstances, many manufacturing businesses have had to take drastic action in order to survive and they have sharply reduced the number of jobs that they were able to provide. Many factories had already gone a long way towards pricing themselves out of the market by earlier pay settlements. Many of those who secured big pay increases may have improved their own standard of living, but only at the cost of pushing their fellow workers out of a job.

Recently, however, there has been an increasingly constructive approach to these problems, at least in the private sector. The level of pay settlements has been falling significantly. Pay bargainers have begun to face up to the harsh truth that excessive pay is a major cause of unemployment. Most settlements in manufacturing since November have been below 10 per cent. That is in sharp contrast to the years that went before. Management and work force are at last joining together to tackle the problems of overmanning, restrictive practices, and out-of-date working methods. They understand that cutting unit labour costs is the way to become competitive again and to price themselves back into markets and jobs.

But the nationalised industries, many of them monopolies, are not subject to the same market disciplines as the private sector. They have often been slow to adapt. And when eventually they do adjust, the financial and social costs can be very heavy. But the cost of delaying change has often been even greater, in terms of markets lost and jobs destroyed. It is the need to make nationalised industries more responsive to market disciplines which lies behind the Government's vigorous programme to increase competition in, for example, transport and telecommunications, and wherever possible to return parts of the State-owned sector to private enterprise.

Nor have other parts of the public sector learnt these lessons at all quickly. Thus, the overall cost of the public sector has continued to grow in relation to the rest of the economy. Total spending programmes in 1980-81 are now expected to cost approaching £94 billion, compared with last year's Budget forecast of about £91½ billion. In addition, debt interest has cost £1 billion more than expected. The increase in the overall total would have been still greater had it not been for the notable success of my right hon. Friend the Prime Minister in negotiating refunds from the European Communities of some £600 million. The burden of public expenditure will be a recurrent theme in my speech.

393

BUDGET STRATEGY

It is against this background that I turn to the central objectives of my Budget.

Some have urged that I should abandon the battle against inflation as our top priority and look instead for ways of expanding the economy. If this were the way to sustained recovery for British Industry, and so to the creation of more long-term jobs, I should certainly be ready to consider a change of course, because the well-being of our people and the health of our economy are more important than any Government's commitment to a particular strategy.

But to change course now would be fatal to the whole counter-inflation strategy. Our problem in recent years has not been a lack of final demand. Since 1977, spending in the whole economy, in money terms, has risen by no less than 50 per cent. Most of the impact of that increase has been dissipated in higher prices. In so far as the volume of spending has increased, a large share of the extra has gone on imports. In the end, there has been very little effect on United Kingdom output.

Just boosting demand would do nothing to remedy that problem. Rather, it would risk throwing away the real achievements that we have secured, without winning any compensating gains. In the past, Governments have too often deprived themselves and the British people of the success that they deserved because they abandoned the policies when the going got rough—when the sacrifices, in fact, had largely been made, but before the long-term benefits had begun to arrive. It would, indeed be a tragedy to inflict on ourselves a further dose of crippling inflation just at the time when, with resolution, our industry can be helped to take advantage of the more stable conditions, which should follow the easing of the present recession.

I am, therefore, determined to sustain the firm action that is necessary to maintain our success in the battle against inflation. It is also essential this year to respond to the two imbalances in our economy that I have described: the imbalance between consumers and industry and the imbalance between the public and the private sectors. Moving towards a better balance must be the central purpose of this Budget.

THE MEDIUM-TERM FINANCIAL STRATEGY AND 1981-82 MONETARY TARGET

There is now world-wide recognition that inflation is the enemy of growth and employment. And it is just as widely recognised that sustained monetary restraint is necessary if inflation is to be kept permanently under control. Of course, there is not a rigid relationship between money and prices. Of course, there are other influences on inflation, particularly in the short run. We always made that absolutely clear. But monetary policy is of fundamental importance. These principles apply to this country just as much as to any other.

THE MEDIUM-TERM FINANCIAL STRATEGY

It is time for us to start thinking ahead to the advantages that can accompany a permanent reduction in inflation, for to live once again in a world that has banished the spectre of accelerating inflation must be our objective. We reaffirmed our commitment to that objective last year when we published the medium-term financial strategy. I am reaffirming it again today by taking the measures necessary to strengthen and carry forward that strategy.

I have no doubt that the House will expect me to spend a little time on monetary matters. As the recent report from the Treasury and Civil Service Select Committee has shown clearly, this is an absorbing area of policy.

Thanks to the tight financial conditions of the past 18 months, including the effects of the strong pound, we are well ahead in the battle against inflation. We have achieved that while reducing controls rather than by imposing them. But for a number of reasons related to the special circumstances of last year, the growth of sterling M3—the measure of money used to express the strategy—has been well outside the first year target range of 7-11 per cent. I said in November that I expected it to slow down in the new year. Recent figures, including the preliminary figures for banking February, published today, are fully consistent with that.

MONETARY GROWTH IN 1980-81

The first reason for rapid monetary growth over the year is the abolition of the so-called corset. That was long overdue. All that the corset achieved was to make the published figures artificially low. since its removal last summer those distortions have been reversed, and the figures have been artificially high. By their very nature, such distortions are impossible to measure accurately. They are likely to have been substantial. But purely statistical changes have no implications for future inflation. The distortions have now largely worked their way out of the system. In that respect, sterling M3 will from now on be a better measure.

Again, the growth of sterling M3 was increased last year by the special nature of the recession. Public borrowing increases in a recession, but that is normally offset by lower private sector borrowing. Over the past 12 months public borrowing has been exceptionally high. But on this occasion bank lending did not fall away as quickly as might have been expected.

Because of the exceptional imbalance between business and personal incomes, both sectors, for different reasons, have borrowed heavily. Faced with an unexpectedly severe recession and the consequences of previous pay increases, businesses borrowed to tide them over while they reduced costs. Many people, on the other hand, have seen their living standards rise to an extent unusual in a recession, and have been willing and able to borrow as well. The combined effect of that borrowing has been an important expansionary influence on sterling M3.

At the same time, there has been a high level of private investment in financial assets. That can be seen as an attempt by the private sector to rebuild its holdings of such assets, whose purchasing power had been sharply eroded by inflation. It has included an increase in holdings of interest-bearing money. But to the extent that it merely involves returning towards a more normal level of financial assets it need not fuel inflation.

Other indicators also suggest that the underlying financial conditions have, as the Government intended, been tight. Our Green Paper on monetary control, published a year ago, stressed the need to watch a range of measures of monetary conditions. Over the past 18 months the narrower measures of money have not grown at all rapidly. The pound has certainly been higher than would be expected from the behaviour of the money supply. That external pressure has reinforced the monetary squeeze and contributed to the fall in inflation. And inflation has fallen so much relative to interest rates that the real cost of borrowing has risen significantly.

Financial behaviour should now revert to a more normal pattern. The private sector has been moderating its borrowing from the banks, and the exceptionally rapid build-up of personal sector liquidity should come to an end as the growth of prices and incomes continues to slow down.

THE MEDIUM-TERM STRATEGY AND THE TARGET FOR 1981-82

It is important to express the medium-term strategy in terms of a wide measure of money, because it has close links with public spending and borrowing. So I am maintaining continuity by keeping sterling M3 as the yardstick for medium-term policy. The aim remains to reduce monetary growth to 4-8 per cent. by 1983-84. The new target range for next year, based on the actual figure for sterling M3 in banking February, will be an annual rate of 6-10 per cent. over the 14 months to April 1982.

The special factors at work last year are unlikely to be repeated. In any event, they should have no adverse implications for future inflation. But we cannot be certain that they were the only causes of the rapid growth in the money supply. So it may be desirable to recover some of the past year's high monetary growth in the form of lower growth over the medium term. But the most important requirement is a lower growth of the broad measures of money in the years ahead.

However, the short-term response of sterling M3 to interest rate changes is particularly uncertain and the full effect can be spread over many months. The narrower measures, which we also monitor, include fewer interest-bearing types of money and are more sensitive to changes in interest rates. But because they are so sensitive they can overstate the effect of interest rate changes on underlying monetary conditions. Moreover, their relationship to other aspects of policy is less clear.

I am taking steps, therefore, to improve the information available about the narrower measures. Publication of figures for monetary base will begin later this month.

Arrangements for a new statistical series for the retail deposits of the banking system, M2, are also well advanced. That will be publishted later this year.

We shall continue to monitor M1. In doing so, we shall take account of its normal tendency to grow quickly as nominal interest rates come down with inflation. For this reason we may now find M1 growing rather faster, for a time, than it did last year.

PUBLIC SECTOR BORROWING

I turn next to the public sector borrowing requirement, the PSBR. Some people, I know, are tempted to regard the PSBR as something mystical, of interest only to economists. How I wish that they were right. But, alas, that is not true. The size of public borrowing is, as it must be, a critically important constraint, for Governments are no different from individuals. The PSBR, in plain language, is broadly the difference between what the Government spend, or lend to others, and what they collect in revenue, mainly through taxation. It necessarily includes what the nationalised industries borrow. Most of that comes from the Government, and where they borrow from other sources the Government stand behind them. So the PSBR is the amount central and local government and the public corporations have to borrow. It is the experience of Governments around the world that if they try to borrow too much, either interest rates or inflation, or both, begin to soar.

Britain's experience tells the same story. If we are to stay on course for lower inflation and lower interest rates, we must borrow less. Public borrowing, as a proportion of national income, must be brought down. This is why the medium-term financial strategy envisages a downward path for borrowing, as well as for the growth of the money supply. These remain two essential prerequisites for a lasting grip on inflation.

Against that background, the House will understand my anxiety at the way in which borrowing has actually developed. For 1980-81, the year which is drawing to a close, the PSBR is now forecast to emerge at £13½ billion, or 6 per cent. of the gross domestic product. That compares with the 1980 Budget forecast of £8½ billion. The lion's share of the £5 billion excess in 1980-81 was accounted for by higher expenditure. There has also been a net shortfall of tax revenue of about £1 billion, with receipts from indirect taxes and North Sea oil below expectations—only partly offset by higher receipts from the other Inland Revenue taxes.

For the year now approaching, 1981-82, our published strategy suggested an illustrative PSBR of some 3 per cent. of the gross domestic product. Translated into today's prices that would be about £7½ billion. In 1981-82 output is expected to be lower, and unemployment higher, than envisaged a year ago. The effect of the recession on the PSBR is likely to be even greater this year. It is therefore clear that a £7½ billion PSBR for next year would be unduly restrictive.

Moreover, I must tell the House that this year's Budget-making exercise has started from the basis of a forecast for the PSBR in 1981-82 of no less than £14 billion. I am in no doubt that to begin the year with the intention of borrowing as much as £14 billion would be irresponsible in itself and unacceptable to the House.

We must consider what should be the objective for next year's PSBR. I have already ruled out £7½ billion as unduly restrictive. Taking everything into account, I have concluded that it would be right to provide for a PSBR in 1981-82 of some £10½ billion, which is a little more than 4 per cent. of the gross domestic product. This is still a high figure, but I believe it to be consistent with the monetary target that I have just announced. I also believe it to be a sum that can be financed without placing undue strains upon the capital markets.

But, as the House will understand, if the figure is to be brought down to £10½ billion from £14 billion, some harsh decisions are inescapable. The figure of £14 billion which I have just quoted incorporates the spending plans for next year that have already been announced—but it is otherwise based on unchanged tax rates and unchanged allowances. It allows for the increases in national insurance contributions that I announced last November—which the House has now approved. That leaves a net sum of around £3½ billion to be secured in this Budget: £1 billion of that will come from the new North Sea taxation that I foreshadowed last November. I shall be outlining other proposals later in my speech.

These tax changes should enable us to achieve our monetary objectives without having to face intolerably high interest rates. But we are determined to maintain the monetary and fiscal framework necessary for the reduction and defeat of inflation—even at the cost of departing, for the time being, from our commitment to lower personal taxes. The tax increases that I am announcing today are a measure of that determination. Equally, they reflect the bill that we as a nation must meet if we are to pay for the high level of public spending that we have chosen to support. I will return to the detailed proposals shortly.

METHOD OF BORROWING AND MONETARY CONTROL

Meanwhile, it is necessary not only to reduce Government borrowing but to finance it in a non-inflationary way. By drawing more efficiently on possible sources of savings it should be possible to control the growth of sterling M3 more effectively.

NATIONAL SAVINGS

Imaginative use of national savings can help to reduce pressure on the capital markets. Thanks to the initiative announced last autumn we have already achieved our national savings target of £2 billion for 1980-81.

For 1981-82 we have set the still more ambitious target of £3 billion. New measures are needed for that. We therefore propose two important changes to the second issue of index-linked certificates or "granny" bonds. From the beginning of next month the age of eligibility for these certificates will be reduced from 60 to 50—[Hon. Members: "Maggie bonds".] I am glad that the House is willing to join with me in recognising the declining age of grandmothers. From the beginning of next month the age of eligibility will be reduced from 60 to 50 and a minimum bonus of 4 per cent. will be provided for all holders, both new and existing.

A reduction in the interest rate on the national savings investment account from 1 May will be announced later this month. That will be compatible with keeping interest rates on national savings instruments competitive enough to achieve our target.

In October last year my right hon. Friend the Secretary of State for Energy announced plans for a bond which

395

[Sir Geoffrey Howe]

would allow the public to share in the benefits of the nation's North Sea oil resources. The Government intend to issue such a bond later this year. It will be aimed at small savers and will be a non-marketable certificate, administered by the Department for National Savings. Its capital value will be fixed, but the return on the bond will be linked to the value of the British National Oil Corporation's North Sea oil.

MARKETABLE SECURITIES

We also propose an important extension of the structure of Government borrowing by introducing an indexed gilt-edged security. This will be sold to pension funds and to life insurance companies and friendly societies in respect of their United Kingdom pension business.

Restricting the right to buy this indexed gilt will help to avoid the risk of attracting unwanted inflows of foreign funds. It will give those institutions that are eligible a new choice between indexed and conventional securities. The Bank of England is announcing this afternoon details of an issue of long-dated indexed stock worth £1 billion.

This innovation demonstrates the confidence that we have in our strategy for bringing inflation down. It will also reduce uncertainty about future real rates of return, thus helping borrowers and lenders alike. Those are important advantages for monetary control. We will have more flexibility in the market place and thus greater assurance of meeting the Government's borrowing needs.

We are also considering the introduction, later in the year, of new short-term marketable Government securities.

SMOOTHING THE FLOW OF REVENUE

I am proposing some new measures which will help short-term monetary management by smoothing the uneven flow of tax revenue. The most important area is that of North Sea oil taxation, to which I shall come later. Other proposals will be described by my hon. and learned Friend the Minister of State later in this debate, if he is fortunate enough to catch your eye, Mr. Speaker.

MONETARY CONTROL

These initiatives will be accompanied by other improvements in monetary control. Following extensive consultations based on last year's Green Paper, I outlined last November some changes that were desirable in their own right and would be consistent with a gradual evolution to monetary base control. These will come into effect during the coming financial year.

The reserve asset ratio has complicated monetary control. The first step in phasing it out was made in January. In the next month or two, at the conclusion of talks now to be undertaken with the banks, the ratio will cease to be a minimum requirement. Thereafter it will be adapted to have a transitional role as a prudential norm round which there will be variation, until the detail of the new arrangements has been settled.

The Bank of England has already made some useful changes in its money market operations. In its dealings with the discount houses it now relies mainly on buying and selling bills. Direct lending to the market has been greatly reduced. The interest rate on this lending is also now generally somewhat above comparable market rates,

while the rates at which the Bank conducts its open market operations have become more flexible. In conducting its operations in bills the Bank no longer quotes rates for more than one month ahead. Instead, it responds to bids and offers. This has the great advantage of allowing the market a greater role in determining the structure of short-term interest rates.

Discussions are now to take place with the financial institutions about these and other changes, including the future of the cash ratio. When they are complete, the Bank will aim to keep very short-term interest rates within an unpublished band, and in due course suspend altogether the practice of having an announced MLR, which would by then have lost its operational significance.

Decisions about short-term interests rates will continue to take account of the whole range of monetary indicators referred to earlier and other factors that affect the significance of the numbers, especially the progress of inflation. Modest reductions in interest rates were made in the second half of last year. Progress in reducing inflation, strongly positive real interest rates, a noticeable slackening in the growth of sterling M3 in recent months, and a marked fall-off in bank lending point towards a further reduction in rates. The increases in taxation that I am proposing in the Budget will make it possible to have an immediate reduction. Accordingly, the Bank of England is today, with my approval, reducing its minimum lending rate by two percentage points.

PUBLIC EXPENDITURE

Further progress towards lower inflation and lower interest rates does not depend primarily on improvements in funding techniques or in managing the money markets, important though these are. The overriding need is for more effective restraint of public spending. In the last year public expenditure has put a severe strain on the budget. Much of the increased spending has been caused by the effects of the recession being worse than expected. There has been an increase of £¾ billion in spending on unemployment benefit and on special employment measures, notably the temporary short-time working scheme. On many central Government programmes the expected shortfall in expenditure has not happened, and so the total has been higher than expected.

The recession has also—inevitably—had an adverse effect on the financial situation of most nationalised industries. It has meant an increase in the total of these industries' external financing limits for 1980-81 of some £900 million, over half of which has been for the steel industry. Some of the nationalised industries are now taking steps to reduce the overmanning and inefficiency which have built up over the years. But that, too, can cost more money initially.

These, however, have not been the only sources of upward pressure. On defence there has been substantial overspending—to the tune of £260 million—over and above a cash limit that had already been increased by £200 million. Local authorities' total cash spending appears to have been a good deal higher than allowed in my last Budget—and the position would have been much worse without the firm action taken by my right hon. Friend the Secretary of State for the Environment.

Because of all these developments we have not been able, in the course of 1980-81, to secure the full 5 per cent. cut at which we were aiming in our predecessors' planned volume of expenditure. We have nevertheless achieved a reduction of about 3½ per cent.—or £3½ billion. Moreover, since the Government came into office numbers employed in the Civil Service have fallen by 35,000, and by the equivalent of about 40,000 full-time staff in local government.

THE COMING YEAR

In the coming year, some of the upward pressures on public sector spending are bound to remain with us. I have in mind, for example, last November's decision to spend more on industrial support and on special employment measures to ease the effects of recession. Next year the cost of special employment measures will be no less than £1 billion. This will make it possible to offer every unemployed school leaver a place on the youth opportunites programme by Christmas. And we hope to offer other 16 and 17-year-olds, unemployed for three months, places within a further three months. In all, 440,000 opportunities will be offered—twice as many as in 1979-80. In addition, the temporary short-time working compensation scheme is currently supporting nearly 700,000 people.

However, this need to spend more on some programmes cannot justify accepting the wrong fiscal balance. That is why we took the decisions that I announced last November to reduce most of the Government's other programmes by £1,400 million cash. Those substantial cuts will go a good deal of the way to offset the other increases that I have described. But they have not gone far enough to avoid the need for substantial increases in taxation.

It is worth recalling that this Government have not been alone in having to cut planned and actual public expenditure. Our predecessors had repeatedly to do the same. Such reductions are necessary if the burdens on the rest of the economy are not to become intolerable. They are essential to the fight against inflation. That has been the recent experience of almost every other industrial democracy. The economic conditions that call for lower public spending are a world-wide phenomenon.

Today's new public expenditure White Paper shows a planned volume of public expenditure next year that would be much the same as this year's expected outturn. Various developments since the White Paper went to print, including the withdrawal of the plans for accelerated pit closures, have made it prudent to increase the size of the contingency reserve. I shall also be announcing later in my speech additional expenditure to help with industrial fuel costs. Altogether, these will add about one-third of 1 per cent. to the volume of expenditure next year, 1981-82. The resultant planning total is more than 3 per cent. higher than we had intended. But despite the much larger claims of employment support and of social security it will still be nearly 5 per cent. less than our predecessors had planned.

Our decisions for the future are designed to ensure that the volume of spending falls after 1981-82. The public expenditure White Paper shows a planned fall of 4 per cent. by 1983-84. Whether we can spend even on that scale must depend on how far we can afford to do so. During the annual review later this year we shall be looking hard at the possibilty of further reductions in those plans.

The House will find that the sheer size of public spending becomes much easier to grasp if one thinks not just in terms of the so-called volume of spending but in terms of actual cash paid out. The difficulty of controlling it also becomes clearer.

Last year—1979-80—we spent on programmes £77 billion in cash. This year—1980-81—the corresponding figure will be nearly £94 billion. Next year—1981-82—we will spend about £104 billion, cash. If debt interest is included, the rise is even greater.

An important part of the rise in total expenditure between last year and this has been due to the increase in the public services pay bill resulting from the Clegg commission and similar catching-up exercises, many involving staged settlements. The Clegg awards and staged settlements alone accounted for an increase of £2½ billion between the two years.

We have had to make provision for those consequences of the previous Government's incomes policies. But the significance of those consequences and the extent of the problem that they present have still not been widely recognised or understood. The pay bill for the public services in 1980-81 of about £30 billion is aout 25 per cent. higher than in the previous year. This is twice as fast an increase as in the pay bill of the private sector. Much of the overall cost of pay settlements in the private sector has been offset by a reduction in numbers of people employed, or in hours worked. So the cash cost of Government has been growing much faster than the cash income of the rest of the economy that has to support it.

The immediate lesson is simple, but vital. After the recent large increases it is now both fair and essential that public service pay should grow more slowly. Pay, after all, accounts for as much as 60 per cent. of the major public expenditure programmes, such as education and health. This is why it is so important to work out improved ways of settling public service pay. Any new system must take proper account of all the relevant factors; the balance of supply and demand for particular skills as well as comparisons with terms and conditions in outside employment and—inescapably—the limits of finance available. Due weight will also need to be given to the expectation and intention of a continuing decline in the rate of inflation.

Experience over a number of years shows clearly the need for a system for the control of public expenditure generally which displays the consequences of spending decisions as plainly as possible. The present system certainly does not do that. This year, as for many years past, the figures in our White Paper are expressed mainly in volume terms at "constant" prices. But there is something inherently unreal in trying to plan and measure things in terms of what is rightly described as "funny money". Goods are not bought and people are not paid in the money of last year or the year before. They are paid in cash.

When the community, acting through the Government, decides to buy goods and services, it has to pay in money of the day, just like any private individual. There is, of course, a case for planning in volume terms as well. There is a clear need to plan the number of hospitals or roads or frigates that we are aiming to have in future years. But there is great danger in planning in volume alone. For there is then an inevitable tendency to assume that a given quantity of goods or services will definitely be available,

397

[*Sir Geoffrey Howe*]

however much their costs may have risen. For this reason, it is essential that the control and planning systems should focus much more closely on the money actually spent.

I am accordingly making some important changes in the control and planning of public expenditure. These changes cannot be a substitute for the hard political decisions that have always to be taken. But they will enable those decisions to be taken with a much clearer appreciation of what is involved. They will help to displace the automatic assumption that what was once planned can always be afforded.

We have decided to make a major shift in the planning and control of spending from volume to cash. The introduction of cash limits by the last Government paved the way for this change. We now need to go a great deal further down that road.

In the first instance we shall, from the coming year onwards, change the way in which we operate the contingency reserve. This will now be a cash control. Previously, only decisions that increased the volume of spending during the year were charged to the reserve. Next year the control will be extended so that decisions to increase cash limits—in respect of pay or prices as well as in respect of volume—will be treated as a charge on the reserve. The reserve will be set at £2½ billion cash—about 2½ per cent. of the total of programmes. This allows both for the wider coverage resulting from the switch to a cash basis and for the increased provision, which I have already mentioned, to allow for developments since the White Paper.

Even more fundamental is the change that we shall be making in the way we go about future annual reviews of public spending. In planning public spending for 1982-83 we shall, from the outset, conduct our examination and discussions in terms of the cash that will be available for that year. This will change the whole framework and spirit within which decisions are taken. In some ways, it will make things more difficult for those who have to manage spending programmes—harder, indeed, for the Government as a whole. Departments will be obliged from the outset to form a view as to what their money will buy. That is bound to be less easy than just deciding what they want and then simply looking forward to receiving all the money needed to pay for it.

This is precisely the same problem as that which every family in the land has to face in planning their own spending. They may have to adjust plans, according to the way costs move and according to the availability of finance. For them, the focus must always be on how much cash is actually going to be available. It is high time for public spending to be subjected to similar discipline. This change to taking decisions in terms of cash will make a major contribution to improving financial management and will do much to support our other efforts to increase cost consciousness and accountability throughout the public sector.

398

SOCIAL SECURITY

I turn now to my specific tax and spending proposals. Even in a lengthy speech they cannot all be covered in detail, and more information about a number of them will be found in a series of press notices issued by the Departments concerned, copies of which are available in the Vote Office.

I have stressed already the huge total of public expenditure. Far and away the biggest element within it is the social security programme. It accounts for more than one-quarter of the total. In the last decade it has grown very fast. Partly, this is because of the increasing number of beneficiaries and the replacement of child tax allowances by child benefit. But it also reflects real increases in rates of benefit. Thus, over the decade the retirement pension has gone up by about 30 per cent. in real terms. That is about twice as much as the increase in the national income as a whole.

The cash cost of the social security programme in 1981-82 comes to a staggering £27 billion. This is about £1,000 per year for every worker in the country. We cannot, therefore, avoid considering this programme as closely as any other.

I estimate that prices will rise by 10 per cent. in the year to next November. The increase in pensions and other benefits made in last year's uprating proved to be 1 per cent. more than required to keep pace with last years' inflation. This is because prices rose more slowly than expected between November 1979 and November 1980. State retirement pensions, public service pensions, and most other benefits, including supplementary, unemployment and sickness benefits will, therefore, be increased next November by about 9 per cent. This reflects the expected rise in prices and at the same time adjusts for the over-provision made last year. The increase in the benefits will be substantial. The retirement pension for a married couple will go up by £3·90, to £47·35 per week, and for a single person by £2·45, to £29·60 per week. Unemploment and sickness benefits will be increased to £36·40 and £22·50 per week respectively.

Full details of the November increases will be announced tomorrow by my right hon. Friend the Secretary of State for Social Services. We shall be giving further consideration to policy towards public service pensions in the light of the report of the Scott committee. I shall myself have something more to say about child benefit in a few moments.

THE DISABLED

There is one group to whom we should pay special attention this year, despite the economic constraints that we face. I refer to the disabled, for this is the International Year of Disabled People. My right hon. Friend the Secretary of State will be announcing tomorrow an increase in the mobility allowance. I shall mention some other measures now.

The special income tax allowance for the blind has stood at its present level since 1975. I propose to double it to £360. I hope that this will be of some help to blind people in tackling the very real problems they have to face.

Many representations have been made to me for relief from value added tax on all purchases made by charities. I have regretfully concluded that such relief would be impossible to administer fairly or economically and would, in any case, cost too much. However, I do propose to extend existing value added tax reliefs for the disabled and the charities serving them. For example, the present zero rating for articles given to hospitals will, in future, cover ambulances and wheelchairs. The benefit of this zero rating will also be extended to institutions caring for the handicapped. Car adaptations for disabled drivers will also be relieved from VAT. The necessary Treasury order is being laid today.

I am also proposing changes that will widen the scope of the reliefs from capital taxation for trusts for the disabled. To encourage unemployed people to work for voluntary bodies, the amount that a person can earn without affecting unemployment benefit will be increased from 75p per day to £2 per day.

The total cost of these measures is relatively modest. But, if put alongside the tax reliefs that I announced last year in respect of covenanted gifts to charities, the overall amount is substantial. The House may like to be reminded that tax relief on covenants at the higher rates of tax becomes effective from 6 April this year at a revenue cost of £20 million. These reliefs should greatly improve the fund-raising ability of charities. I shall be arranging to publicise these reliefs, and the opportunities that they offer, much more widely.

There is one other matter to which I should refer. I announced last year that we planned to bring into tax the invalidity, sickness and other incapacity benefits. We had expected that this might be from April 1982. In part because of pressures on civil service staff numbers, we propose to postpone this. I confirm however, that when invalidity benefit comes into tax the 5 per cent. deduction made from the November 1980 uprating will be restored.

RAISING THE REVENUE: BUSINESSES

OIL COMPANIES

I come now to the range of measures that are necesary to raise the extra revenue for this year. First, the North Sea. In deciding on particular measures I have had to take into account recent developments and future prospects for North Sea oil and the implications that these have for Government revenues. In 1980 production in the North Sea, at 80 million tonnes of oil, was less than predicted—only four-fifths what had been expected two years before. The production difficulties experienced in the past year have led to a major revision of output levels over the next few years. My right hon. Friend the Secretary of State for Energy has just published reduced forecast ranges for North Sea production in the years to 1984.

While oil production is likely to be lower than once expected, oil prices are much higher. Increases since 1978 in the real price of oil have brought substantial benefits to the oil companies, which face a very different prospect from that when the present tax regime was introduced. Such has been the rise in the oil price in recent years that I believe that the Exchequer should properly look to this area for additional revenue beyond what will accrue from existing taxes. However, even after the measures that I am about to announce, the increase over the medium term in Government revenues from the North Sea will be smaller than was once expected.

In my statement last November I foreshadowed the measures that I had in mind for increasing the Government's share of these revenues while maintaining

incentives for further exploration and development. Consultations with the oil industry have taken place and I can now announce detailed proposals.

I intend to introduce a new tax—the supplementary petroleum duty—broadly as outlined last November. The new tax will be at a rate of 20 per cent. on the total value of oil and gas produced, after deduction of an allowance of 1 million tonnes a year for each field. It will be deductible in computing liability to petroleum revenue tax and corporation tax. In response to representations by the industry, gas supplied to the British Gas Corporation from earlier North Sea fields will be exempted, and there will be provision for the new tax to be refunded where fields do not fully recover their initial development expenditure.

The new tax will be payable in monthly instalments. This will make a useful contribution to achieving a smoother public sector cash flow through the year. I shall also invite the industry to consider with the Inland Revenue how a broadly similar pattern of payments may be introduced for PRT.

I also announced in November last year that the special reliefs devised for PRT were under review. I now have proposals to make involving some restriction of these reliefs. I hope that my hon. and learned Friend the Minister of State, Treasury will have the opportunity of covering them in more detail in the debate.

There are a number of other minor changes to improve the oil taxation regime—partly made in response to the industry's own views.

The new tax, together with changes to the PRT reliefs, will raise an extra £1 billion in 1981-82. There will be a substantial continuing yield in later years.

The oil companies have urged that my objectives of more revenue and a more efficient and economical pattern of tax relief could be better secured by a thoroughgoing reform of PRT, which would make it unnecessary to introduce a permanent new tax. Officials have over several months given exhaustive consideration to that possibility, but without success, and no other proposals that I could regard as satisfactory have been put forward from any other source. But I do not close my mind to the possibility that modified proposals producing a broadly similar yield might be forthcoming. I propose, therefore, that the new tax, SPD, should in the first instance have legislative effect only for the 18 months ending on 30 June 1982. That will allow ample time for further study and consultation before permanent arrangements are introduced in next year's Finance Bill.

BANKS

Apart from oil, one other business sector has largely been protected from the effects of the recession, and that is banking. Indeed, bank profits in recent years have increased sharply, both absolutely and by contrast with the experience of most other businesses. A substantial part of these profits is the direct consequence of high interest rates in recent years: this applies in particular to the so-called "endowment profit" on current accounts on which no interest is paid.

Recent levels of bank profits are partly, of course, a cyclical recovery from the low level to which they fell in the mid-1970s. Also, the banks have needed to make provision against the effects of inflation and to rebuild the

[*Sir Geoffrey Howe*]

reserves needed to underpin the valuable support that they give to businesses in difficult times. That is why I took no action last year.

However, I undertook to keep developments under review. The past year has seen further high banking profits, probably at a level not very different from the record profits of 1979. Certainly the contrast with the sharply reduced profits of industrial companies is, if anything, more striking. In present difficult circumstances, I cannot avoid the conclusion that I should require the banks to make a special fiscal contribution.

This will take the form of a special once-for-all tax on deposits of banking businesses that are in operation today. The tax will be charged by reference to non-interest bearing sterling deposits in excess of £10 million, averaged over the final three months of 1980. The rate of tax will be 2½ per cent. It will not be deductible against corporation tax. I estimate that the clearing banks will be the source of about 90 per cent. of the revenue, but the tax will apply to banking businesses generally. Altogether, an estimated £400 million will be raised in three instalments over the second half of 1981-82. This revenue will make it possible for me to give some help to the rest of industry this year which otherwise I could not afford.

RAISING THE REVENUE: INDIRECT TAXES

Even so, for the reasons that I have already explained, it is necessary to look principally to the personal sector for the additional revenue needed. People in employment have in general had more money to spend. Extra tax will have to be levied on that expenditure.

I do not propose any increase in the 15 per cent. rate of VAT. As last year, most of the extra revenue needed must come from the Excise duties. Increases would be necessary again this year simply to keep the rates of duty in line with the general movement of prices. Even when that had been done, however, many of the duties would be lower in real terms than they used to be. For example, since April 1975 the beer duty has risen by only about half as much as prices generally. I am proposing to increase the Excise duties to produce, in total, about twice as much additional revenue as would be required to compensate for one year's inflation.

ALCOHOLIC DRINKS, TOBACCO, ETC.

First, the duties on alcoholic drinks and tobacco. From midnight tonight I propose to increase the duties on drinks by amounts which, incuding VAT, represent about 4p on the price of a typical pint of beer, 12p on a bottle of table wine, 25p on a bottle of sherry, and 60p on a bottle of spirits.

On tobacco, I propose from midnight on Friday to increase the duty by an amount which, including VAT, will represent 14p on a typical packet of 20 cigarettes.

There will be consequential increases for other alcoholic drinks and tobacco products but a little less for pipe tobacco, which is used particularly by pensioners. I estimate that the increase on alcoholic drinks will yield £500 million in 1981-82 and £515 million in a full year. The increases on tobacco will raise almost exactly the same.

The duties on matches and mechanical lighters, which have not been raised since 1949 , will be increased substantially—to raise an extra £15 million a year.

ROAD FUEL DUTIES

Road fuel must also make a substantial contribution. The duties on petrol and derv will be increased from 6 pm tonight by the equivalent, including VAT, of 20p a gallon. These increases should yield an additional £910 million from petrol and £270 million from derv in 1981-82 and the same in a full year.

VEHICLE EXCISE DUTY

I propose to increase the vehicle excise duty on all vehicles by about 15 per cent. The annual duty on cars will thus increase by £10, to £70. As the duty on derv is being increased in line with that on petrol I do not propose any differential increase on heavy lorries. The VED increase should yield £225 million in 1981-82 and the same in a full year.

CAR TAX

Finally, I propose extending the car tax to motor cycles, scooters and mopeds. This tax is charged at 10 per cent. on the wholesale value and is in addition to VAT. There is no longer any reason why these machines should be treated any differently from motor cars. The change is estimated to raise about £10 million in 1981-82 and £15 million in a full year.

SUMMARY

In all, these changes to the indirect taxes should raise about £2,400 million in 1981-82 and about the same in a full year.

With the partial exception of the road fuel and vehicle excise duties, the increases fall on those products which are bought by private consumers. Had all these excise duties simply been increased in line with inflation this would have added one percentage point to the RPI. The increases that I propose could add up to a further point. This is the maximum impact effect on prices. But in the longer run, by reducing public borrowing they will help to bring inflation down and ensure that it stays down.

RAISING THE REVENUE—DIRECT PERSONAL TAXATION

I come now to income tax. Once again I must have the main priority in mind—the need to contain public borrowing so as to make it possible to secure lower interests rates and ease the conditions in which the trading sector of the economy has to operate.

Inflation raises the real burden of income tax. This is because allowances and rate bands are fixed in money terms. As the value of money falls so, too, does the value of these allowances and bands.

It was in order to counteract this effect that the House in 1977 carried a measure that required Governments to raise the tax allowances by each year's inflation unless Parliament explicitly decided to the contrary.

To implement this formula now would mean increasing allowances by about 15 per cent. In the circumstances of this year that simply is not possible. The incomes of most people have been rising in both money and real terms, but many companies have seen their profits virtually

400

disappear, with serious implications for jobs and investment. In these circumstances it will not be possible this year to make any increase in the income tax allowances or rate bands. As hon. Members will realise, the House will be asked to approve a resolution to this effect.

A Treasury order is also being made today, following the procedure laid down in the 1980 Finance Act, setting out what the increases would have been in the thresholds and allowances if indexation had been possible. The House will wish to know that full indexation of the allowances and bands would have reduced the full year yield of income tax by £2½ billion.

This decision has not been lightly taken, and I share the disappointment that everyone will feel. It enables us to avoid, as I am sure is right, the need for any change in the basic or other rates of income tax. And it enables me to tell the House, as I am glad to be able to do, that we propose that child benefit and one-parent family benefit will both be fully price-protected, in line with the forecast of inflation. Next November child benefit will, therefore, go up by 50p a week per child, to £5·25. The one-parent family benefit will go up by 30p, to £3·30 per week.

FRINGE BENEFITS

At a time when the real burden of income tax has to be increased it is all the more important that it should be fairly shared.

The benefit of a company car is already subject to tax but the tax scales fall well short of the true value. The amounts assessed to tax are less than half the AA's estimate of the annual costs of running a car. Last year we prescribed an increase of 20 per cent. in the scales from this April—just about enough to keep them rising in line with the costs of motoring. I now propose that they should be increased by a further 20 per cent. in April 1982. For company cars that have little or no business use there is a higher schedule of taxation. I propose to raise the business mileage below which this charge applies from 1,000 to 2,500 miles a year, with effect from this April.

Last year I referred to the growing practice of employers providing free petrol and said that I should be bound to contemplate action if it continued to spread. This warning has largely been ignored. I propose, therefore, to take action that will ensure that tax is chargeable in all cases where petrol is provided for the private use of a higher-paid employee or director. The Inland Revenue will consult employers' organisations over the administrative implications of the various possible methods of achieving this.

Most people have to pay for their own travel to work, whether by rail or by road. Some people have their travel costs met by their employers. Most of these pay tax on that benefit. There is, however, one small but growing group—not more than one commuter in 10—who get their travel costs tax-free. When an employer contracts with a transport authority for the provision of a season ticket to his employee the benefit is not, under the present law, within the general liability to tax. This is a clear anomaly. And it is plainly right to bring this group into line with everyone else.

Similarly, a minority of employees are provided with credit cards, which they use to obtain a wide range of goods and services that are charged to the employer. The

employee may thus avoid paying tax on part of what is truly his income. This, too, is quite wrong. I shall ensure that all employees pay tax on benefits of this kind.

Following consultations that took place last year, I have decided for now to leave in place the earnings threshold below which the taxation of fringe benefits does not, in the main, apply. Company cars and other such benefits will therefore continue not to be taxed in the hands of those earning less than £8,500 a year. Consistently with this approach, I propose to remove the charge to tax on medical insurance premiums paid by employers for the benefit of their employees earning less than this amount.

One pre-war anti-avoidance measure needs to be brought up to date following the decision in the Vestey case. This has shown that, among other imperfections, the rules dealing with avoidance of tax by way of transfers of assets abroad do not affect an individual who benefits from such a transfer but did not make or procure it. I propose changes in these complex and technical rules, to take effect from today, which will ensure that the individual pays tax on any benefit he receives. I propose also to amend the rules governing the taxation of capital sums paid by trusts.

Mr. J. Grimond (Orkney and Shetland) *rose——*

Sir Geoffrey Howe: Not even for the right hon. Gentleman do I wish to break the tradition of an uninterrupted Budget Statement.

HELPING BUSINESSES

So far I have been dealing almost entirely with a group of measures that will have the disagreeable but necessary effect of increasing the revenue.

In order to secure the reduction in interest rates most of that revenue must go to reducing the PSBR. But some can go, as it should, to lightening directly the tax burden on business and enterprise.

There is not enough for across-the-board measures. It is important to concentrate relief where it will be most effective. I cannot, for example, find room for a reduction in the national insurance surcharge, at a full year cost to the PSBR of £700 million for each percentage point. Nor would a general reduction in corporation tax be appropriate, since it would not help companies that are so hard pressed that they are making no profit. I therefore propose to bring help to business and to encourage enterprise in the following ways.

The first measure is one announced, subject to further consultation on the details, last November: the reform of the stock relief scheme.

This reform will tackle certain abuses of the old scheme that have attracted legitimate concern. It will also lift the threat of clawback—the withdrawal of tax relief when businesses reduce their stocks. This was jeopardising the financial position of industry in the current recession. It was, above all, this problem of clawback that made it essential for the details of a new scheme to be announced, as they were in our consultative document last November.

I have considered very carefully the representations that have since been made in response to my original proposals. As a result, I propose to make certain detailed changes, including improvements in the transitional arrangements.

In particular, I have considered very carefully the concern that has been expressed to me by many businesses

[*Sir Geoffrey Howe*]

about how they would be affected by the proposed credit restriction—that is, the arrangement under which relief should be restricted to the extent that a business may finance its stocks by trade credit or other borrowings. I have sought to balance the case in principle for the credit restriction against the fact that the other changes that I am making will in themselves reduce the scope for abuse under the old stock relief scheme. In the light of the severe difficulties which many businesses are now facing. I have decided not to legislate for the credit restriction. This will be reviewed in the context of other possible changes in the promised corporation tax Green Paper.

These changes will increase the cost of the new scheme to the Exchequer. The fall in the rate of inflation would by itself have reduced that cost. But as a result of the changes I now propose, the cost in respect of profits earned in the present calendar year, 1981—tax on which will mostly be paid in 1982-83—will be £450 million. This includes the cost of dropping the credit restriction, of about £75 million in the first full year. Only a part year cost—about £180 million—will fall in 1981-82. There will be a continuing revenue cost for some time to come and equally a substantial benefit to industry.

I also propose a limited extension of consortium relief to enable consortium members to pass relief downwards to a consortium company.

ENERGY PRICES

Another area of concern to industry has been energy prices.

I recognise the strength of the representations put to me to bring the level of fuel oil duty in this country more closely into line with that of our major European competitors. I have carefully considered the case for doing so.

The direct benefits to industrial costs are obvious. But there are also other consequences, arising particularly from arrangements entered into some years ago for gas purchases. I understand that the overall effect of those arrangements would be to put up the cost of gas purchased by the British Gas Corporation and, with it, the United Kingdom's gas import bill.

We shall keep the position under review. But in present circumstances I had to conclude that the wider national interest would be best served by not reducing that duty, but keeping it at its present level.

I am, however, able to announce measures which will assist industry on energy prices. The National Economic Development Council last Wednesday discussed the report of its task force on energy prices. The report showed that, while prices for the vast majority of industrial customers in this country remain in line with Europe, a limited but important number of large users of electricity and gas pay more for supplies than competitors in Europe.

In these circumstances, the electricity supply industry in England and Wales will, in addition to the action it has already taken, introduce new flexibility into its pricing arrangements, providing further scope for large high load factor industrial consumers to reduce their electricity coats.

The British Gas Corporation has already relaxed its industrial pricing policy to help its industrial customers. In addition, the corporation will now hold renewal prices for gas sold under contract to the present renewal levels until 1 December 1981. Furthermore, the normal quarterly price escalation arrangements for gas provided on a continuous basis will not be applied during this period. The action which is to be taken in this area by the Scottish electricity boards will be announced by the Scottish Office later today.

These moves will give direct benefit to British industry. Accordingly, I am increasing the external financing limits for the gas and electricity industries by some £120 million in 1981-82. That cost will add to the public expenditure total.

The NEDC task force also drew attention to industry's difficulties in the recession of finding the capital to convert equipment from oil to coal use. To help here we shall commit £50 million over the next two years for grants towards the cost incurred in converting from oil-fired boilers to coal. The expenditure will be offset, at least in part, by greater coal sales. Any net cost will be met from the contingency reserve.

CONSTRUCTION

DEVELOPMENT LAND TAX

The construction industry is particularly hard pressed and it is in any case sensible to remove unnecessary obstacles to development. We have identified three helpful changes to development land tax which will stimulate activity, and so employment, particularly this year and next.

First, under the present law, if industrial development is undertaken by the owner for his own use, tax is deferred until the property is sold or put to other use. I propose that for two years this relief should be extended to other types of development for the owner's use, including commercial and hotel development. If a development is begun by 1 April 1983 there will be no DLT for an owner to pay on any part intended for his own use until the property is sold or otherwise disposed of.

Secondly, where property is extended there will in future be no charge if the extension does not increase the size of the building by more than one-third. The current limit is one-tenth.

My third proposal will reduce the burden of DLT on builders who acquire land for residential development and will be of particular benefit where land is released by local authorities and others for building homes. The cost of these measures is put at up to £5 million in a full year but the benefit to the economy could be much greater.

INDUSTRIAL BUILDINGS ALLOWANCE

As I have said, I am concerned that businesses should continue to invest for the future. Our tax system already provides generous incentives for investment in new machinery. But modern machines will seldom yield their full potential if they are housed in obsolete and inefficient factories. I therefore propose to increase the initial allowance for expenditure incurred after today on the construction of new industrial buildings, from 50 per cent. to 75 per cent. The cost will rise to £25 million by 1984-85. This will benefit not only manufacturing but also employment in the construction industry.

402

317

CAPITAL TAXES

The measures I have just announced will in total be worth about £300 million next year. And the tax measures alone will be worth over £400 million in 1982-83.

But if we are to build a strong and vigorous economy, we must do more to encourage and reward the creation of new enterprises, new wealth and new jobs. I turn, therefore, to the subject of capital taxation, which bears especially heavily on the owners of small businesses.

CAPITAL TRANSFER TAX AND CAPITAL GAINS TAX

In a year in which we can give no income tax relief, I cannot make major changes in capital taxation. I do, however, propose to continue the process of making more sense of the structure of capital taxes.

First, there is capital transfer tax. One new concept introduced as a feature of that tax was the idea of cumulating gifts made at any time in a person's life. Some allowance was made for the earlier payment of tax on transfers during life than on death, but only at the bottom of the scales. As a result, people are deterred from transferring their property during their lifetime. This is undesirable. Business property, in particular, should be permitted to pass more freely from one generation to another.

I propose therefore to recast the lifetime scale. At the bottom the charge on gifts will remain half that on death; at the top it will become two-thirds. I also propose limiting cumulation to 10 years and extending the capital gains tax roll-over relief to gifts into trust, to avoid a double charge. I hope that, by encouraging gifts, the Exchequer will benefit as well as the taxpayer. I also propose to increase the annual exemption to £3,000.

Capital transfer tax is also holding back the supply of land for new entrants to the farming industry. Tax is not the only factor, of course. But it is important to maintain a proper balance between owner-occupied and let land, allowing for their different value. I have in mind the unequal treatment of let land. At present, no relief is normally given on let land. In future relief will be available at 20 per cent. Agricultural land not subject to a lease will continue to receive relief at 50 per cent. The difference in the rate of relief recognises the lower value that let land commands and the lower tax burden it attracts as a result. The facility to pay CTT by interest free instalments will be extended to let agricultural land and the limit of £25,000 will be removed.

Next, I turn to trusts. I am grateful to all who responded to our consultative paper. I propose to tackle some matters this year, but on discretionary trusts draft clauses will be prepared for further discussion and we shall legislate next year. Meanwhile, there will be a final extension of the transitional period to 31 March 1983, or 31 March 1984 where an application has to be made to a court.

I also propose dealing with certain avoidance devices which centre on the market value rule for capital gains tax purposes, and aligning the caital gains tax rules with the new income tax rules developed following the Vestey case.

The net affect of all these proposals in the capital tax field will be a cost of £5 million this coming year but a gain of £15 million in a full year—the saving from the anti-avoidance measures exceeding the cost of the reliefs I have proposed.

403

STAMP DUTIES

I intend to include one stamp duty provision in the Finance Bill which will help those buying council houses. This will ensure that stamp duty will be payable only on the discounted price that the buyer actually pays and not on some higher figure.

ENTERPRISE

Last year, I introduced a number of measures to help small firms. In addition to the major new initiative to establish enterprise zones, these included a venture capital scheme, improved tax relief for small workshops, and a reduction in the rate of corporation tax for small companies.

All these measures have been widely welcomed. The 11 proposed enterprise zones have stimulated intense interest among investors and the private sector has begun to respond even before the zones are formally established.

Meanwhile, provision of private finance for small factory units has grown rapidly. The continuing strong demand for small workshops shows the strength of the small business sector.

But we can and must do more to help existing small businesses to grow, and to encourage new businesses to start up. This remains an essential key to new jobs.

VALUE ADDED TAX

First, VAT. I propose that, as last year, the registration threshold should be increased in line with prices—on this occasion from £13,500 to £15,000. This change will take effect from midnight tonight.

SMALL COMPANIES CORPORATION TAX

Secondly, I propose to increase from £70,000 to £80,000 the limit up to which the lower 40 per cent. rate of corporation tax is payable by small companies. I also intend to respond to one of the long-standing complaints from small companies, which is the relatively high marginal rate of tax which they have to pay when profits exceed that limit. The limit at which the full corporation tax rate of 52 per cent. becomes payable will be raised from £130,000 to £200,000. This will make for a gentler progression from the small companies' rate to the full corporation tax rate. The cost of these changes will be £12 million in 1981-82 and £21 million in a full year.

INDUSTRIAL CO-OPERATIVES AND PARTNERSHIPS

Thirdly, new businesses depend on ready access to fresh capital. Last year I relaxed the conditions governing tax relief for interest on money borrowed to invest in close companies. That was good for small companies. I intend this year to relax the conditions for industrial co-operatives and partnerships.

PURCHASE OF OWN SHARES

Fourthly, as the House knows, the Government will shortly introduce new clauses in Committee on the Companies Bill, to enable companies to purchase their own shares. Corresponding changes are needed in the present tax structure to help with a number of problems arising in small and family businesses. I am, therefore, asking the Inland Revenue to issue a consultative document on this subject this summer, with a view to legislation in next year's Finance Bill.

VENTURE CAPITAL SCHEME

Fifthly, I intend to extend the venture capital scheme introduced last year. This scheme encourages investment in small businesses by allowing capital losses on shares in unquoted trading companies to be set off against income. At present, it is confined to investment by individuals. I propose to extend the scheme now to investment by companies, some of which may be able to provide funds for expanding small firms.

POSITIVE USE OF REDUNDANCY MONEY

Sixthly, we have looked at ways of encouraging people who are unemployed, particularly those who have just become redundant, to help themselves, and the economy, by setting up in business. Redundancy payments and other payments made on termination of employment are at present taxable if they exceed £10,000. I am raising that threshold to £25,000 with effect from 6 April. In addition, the rules for the taxation of these payments will be simplified.

Furthermore, we are looking at the suggestion that the existing social security rules act as a deterrent to initiative. We are considering whether they could be altered, or other arrangements made, so as to encourage people who have been declared redundant, or who have been unemployed for some time, to start their own new small business.

All these measures will be of significant help to small businesses. But I intend to go further and have two new measures to announce.

LOAN GUARANTEE SCHEME

First, as the House knows, I have been considering the introduction of a loan guarantee scheme. There are some people who, for one reason or another, have difficulty borrowing money to start or develop a business. They may, for example, not have the necessary collateral security. I am pleased to be able to tell the House that agreement in principle has been reached with the major clearing banks and the ICFC on the introduction of a pilot loan guarantee scheme.

The scheme will run for three years initially, subject to an overall maximum limit of £50 million to be lent in each year. Individual term loans of up to £75,000 will be available for periods of between two and seven years. Government guarantees will be available for 80 per cent. of each loan. The scheme will be administered by the Department of Industry. Further information will be given by my right hon. Friend the Secretary of State for Industry.

The scheme is intended to be self-financing. Lenders will make a full commercial charge for their loans, part as an interest payment to the lender, part as a guarantee premium payment to the Department of Industry. Receipts from premium payments will be designed to cover the cost of claims made under the guarantee provisions.

BUSINESS START-UP SCHEME

My second new proposal breaks entirely fresh ground.

One of the biggest problems faced by people thinking of starting their own business is the difficulty of attracting sufficient risk capital to finance it during its critical early years. The amounts of additional money needed can be modest—at least as compared with the sums in which the big financial institutions commonly deal. But in individual cases they can be crucial.

The individual private investor has for many years had little encouragement to help fill that gap in the capital market. I propose to change that. The private investor can often contribute not only risk capital but direct personal business experience. The opportunities are certainly there. What is needed is to make it more attractive and more rewarding for private investors to take advantage of them.

I am, therefore, introducing an entirely new tax incentive to attract individual investors to back new enterprises. It is designed for the outside or minority investor in certain new small trading companies, as distinct from the owner of the business, his close family and associates. I am calling it the business start-up scheme. Under the scheme an investor will be able to obtain relief against income tax on up to £10,000 invested in any one year. The relief will be given in addition to the range of tax reliefs already available to the company itself, provided the investment is maintained for at least five years.

The scheme will relate only to genuine new business enterprises of the kind I have in mind. There will be strict rules to ensure that it is not used for investment in financial or passive operations, or for tax avoidance.

I am introducing the new scheme in the first instance for a three-year period, beginning with the coming financial year 1981-82.

This business start-up scheme will be unique in not only this country but among our main trading competitors. It will be a striking new incentive to channel investment into small businesses.

BUSINESS OPPORTUNITIES PROGRAMME

These measures to encourage enterprise and risk-taking are essential if we are to replace the jobs that are disappearing elsewhere in the economy. There must be a healthy flow of new enterprises. We must be ready to set aside the resources to encourage them. They are the real future hope for absorbing and redirecting the people and resources at present squeezed out of employment by economic adjustment.

As I have said, this is the second Budget in which I have included measures to help and encourage small businesses. The measures I have just announced, together with those last year, constitute a formidable range of incentives. The tax system is now geared significantly in favour of enterprise, risk-taking and investment.

Much has also been done by this Government to ease the problems of small businesses in other ways—for example, by relaxing employment and planning rules. All this represents a complete change in the climate within which the small business operates. It is vital that these measures be widely known and that people be encouraged to take advantage of them.

The Government recognise the need to give a lead in that. We shall, therefore, be launching a business opportunities programme to publicise the help, advice and incentives available to small business. We shall be improving the advisory service available to small businesses in urban areas in England and to co-ordinate the advisory services provided by the Council for Small Industries in Rural Areas and the small firms service of the Department of Industry. The opportunities have been provided by this and earlier legislation and we must now do all that we can to see that they are taken advantage of.

CONCLUSION

This Budget has been designed to sustain the fight against inflation, and to help redress the balance of the economy in favour of business and industry. It is only by giving priority to those objectives that we can strengthen the basis for sustained economic advance.

We shall continue to pursue our strategy for the defeat of inflation with determination.—*[Interruption.]*

Mr. Deputy Speaker: Order. The Chancellor of the Exchequer must be allowed to complete his statement.

Sir Geoffrey Howe: That strategy will be fortified by the changes that I am proposing today. These changes will reinforce the progress that has already been made and for which the nation can take credit.

In the year ahead the burden of income tax and Excise duties has to rise in order to secure lower interest rates and thus improve the prospects for industry and employment.

The downturn in the present economic cycle has been unusually severe. But it should now be coming close to its end. When recovery does start, the country will be better fitted than for many years to take advantage of the new opportunities, for important lessons have been painfully learnt. A greater sense of realism has been restored.

So, as we look further ahead, we can reasonably expect lower inflation and, in due course, lower unemployment and a reversal of the upward trend in the burden of taxation.

My present proposals are designed to secure our steady progress in that direction, and I commend them to the House.

Mr. Deputy Speaker: Order. Under Standing Order No. 94, the first motion, entitled "Provisional Collection of Taxes", must be decided without debate.

PROVISIONAL COLLECTION OF TAXES

Motion made, and Question,

That pursuant to section 5 of the Provisional Collection of Taxes Act 1968 provisional statutory effect shall be given to the following Motions—

(a) Spirits (Motion No. 2).
(b) Beer (Motion No. 3).
(c) Wine (Motion No. 4).
(d) Made-wine (Motion No. 5).
(e) Cider (Motion No. 6).
(f) Tobacco products (Motion No. 7).
(g) Matches and mechanical lighters (Motion No. 8).
(h) Hydrocarbon oil etc. (Motion No. 10).
(i) Vehicles excise duty (Motion No. 11).
(j) Value added tax: registration (Motion No. 13).—*[Sir Geoffrey Howe.]*

put forthwith, pursuant to Standing Order No. 94 (Ways and Means Motions), and agreed to.

Mr. Deputy Speaker: I shall now call the Chancellor of the Exchequer to move the motion entitled "Amendment of the Law". It is on that motion that the Budget debate will take place today and on succeeding days. The remaining motions will not be put until the end of the Budget debate next week and they will be then decided without debate.

Budget Resolutions and Economic Situation

AMENDMENT OF THE LAW

Motion made, and Question proposed,

That it is expedient to amend the law with respect to the National Debt and the public revenue and to make further provision in connection with finance; but this Resolution does not extend to the making of—

(a) any amendment with respect to value added tax so as to provide—
   (i) for zero-rating or exempting any supply;
   (ii) for refunding any amount of tax;
   (iii) for varying the rate of that tax otherwise than in relation to all supplies and importations; or
   (iv) for any relief other than relief applying to goods of whatever description or services of whatever description; or

(b) any amendment relating to the surcharge imposed by the National Insurance Surcharge Act 1976 and applying to some only of the persons by or in respect of whom the surcharge in payable.—*[Sir Geoffrey Howe.]*

[Relevant European Community documents: No. 10444/80 and the annual report on the economic situation in the Community (1980) and the economic policy guidelines for 1981.]

5.3 pm

Mr. Michael Foot (Ebbw Vale): It is the custom of the House for the first speaker after the Chancellor of the Exchequer has delivered his Budget speech to offer congratulations to him on the manner in which he has delivered his speech, whatever may be the criticisms which may follow on the matter and on kindred questions. I am glad to follow that tradition.

I have been a Member of the House for a considerable number of years, together with the right hon. and learned Gentleman. On a number of occasions, I have heard him introducing various measures. We all know that he has high professional skills. He has a full capacity to make his case clear to the House. I am sure that he is still capable of doing so when he wishes. Therefore, when the right hon. and learned Gentleman lapses into opacity, obliquity or even direct obscurity, I am sure that he always does so on purpose. There may have been some passages in his speech when I thought that he treated his listeners to the range of objectivity and somnolence which he hoped to achieve, but I believe that all Chancellors of the Exchequer have had to resort to such means. That was all the more necessary for the right hon. and learned Gentleman in view of some of his previous speeches.

I cordially welcome some features of the right hon. and learned Gentleman's statement. I offer no satirical aside in doing so. We shall examine the detail of the closing of the Vestey loophole. I congratulate the right hon. and learned Gentleman on doing so. I hope that he had the full co-operation of Lord Thorneycroft in carrying forward that proposal. We recall that Lord Thorneycroft, at the time of the exposure of the loophole, seemed to take a rather different view of the matter.

We welcome the right hon. and learned Gentleman's proposals for the disabled, particularly as this is the International Year of Disabled People. We shall closely examine his proposals, but from what he seems to indicate, it is an advance which we welcome.

We listened carefully to what the right hon. and learned Gentleman said about child benefit. He has properly improved the position this year, although he has not made up for his failure in the previous year. Therefore, although

405

Tony Benn achieves victory for Members' rights in emergency debate on Zircon affair

After a journalistic career of more than 30 years during which he wrote for some of Britain's best known newspapers and news publications, **Peter Kellner** switched from expressing opinions to soliciting them. In 2001 he took an interest in, and became chairman of, the internet-only opinion polling organisation, YouGov.

While in his early 30s he had stood as a Labour candidate in the local council elections in Westminster. It was, as he describes it "to make up the numbers", and his career took him into writing about, not practising, politics.

As a journalist he has been the political editor of the *New Statesman* but has also written for *The Times*, *The Sunday Times*, *The Observer*, *The Independent*, and the *Evening Standard*. He has been a regular contributor to radio and television including the BBC's Newsnight, Channel 4's "A Week in Politics" and "Powerhouse" and various election night analysis programmes.

Beyond his media and YouGov interests, he has been a visiting fellow at Nuffield College, Oxford and the Policy Studies Institute at the University of Westminster where in 2007 he was awarded an honorary degree for his contribution to political analysis and debate.

He has served as an adviser on polls and public opinion to the Bank of England, the Foreign Office, the Corporation of London, the National Westminster Bank and the Trades Union Congress.

In 2007, having served as Chairman of YouGov for over five years, and in that year winning the Chairman of the Year award from the Quoted Companies Alliance, he became the company's President. He is responsible for YouGov's polls for media clients and for developing the company's methodology.

He holds an MA in Economics and Statistics from Cambridge University and is a member of the British Polling Council's committee on disclosure. He has written or contributed to a range of pamphlets and books and he compiled the "Journalists' Guide to Opinion Polls" for the European Society for Opinion and Marketing Research. He is a regular speaker at industry conferences and seminars.

Speech that swung the argument and secured a vital principle

BY PETER KELLNER

When I arrived for work on the morning of 19 of January, 1987, I was confronted by a shocking sight. My desk was tidy. I grant that neatly piled papers, in place of the usual array of randomly spread letters, reports, notes and documents, should normally arouse pleasure, not horror. But this time I knew immediately what had happened. Special Branch had combed through everything I had left at the office.

At the time I was political editor of the *New Statesman*. The reason for the raid was that my colleague, Duncan Campbell, had made a film for the BBC about a British signals satellite, called Zircon, which was due to be launched the following year to intercept radio and telephone signals, mainly from the Soviet Union and Eastern Europe. The cost of the project was £500 million – but Parliament and the public had not been told about it.

Once the film was made, nervous BBC executives approached the Government and sought their advice. The Ministry of Defence demanded that the programme be shelved in order to protect national security. The BBC complied. The *New Statesman* acted differently. It decided to run Campbell's story about Zircon and not tell the Government in advance. The magazine reached London's news stands on the morning of Thursday 15 January. The Special Branch's raids on the *New Statesman* and the BBC's Glasgow offices – Campbell's film had been made for BBC Scotland – took place over the weekend.

A number of mainly Labour MPs were outraged and planned a viewing of a tape of the programme in a Committee Room at the House of Commons. The Speaker, Bernard Weatherill, banned it. An emergency debate on this ban was held on January 27. Because events had moved quickly, Labour MPs had not had time to put down on the Order Paper an amendment to the Government motion, which backed the Speaker's decision.

Tony Benn, whose views on most things to do with socialism, economics and Europe are far from mine, was virtually alone at first in believing that the Government could be defeated. He submitted a manuscript amendment – so-called because he simply wrote it down on a piece of paper – which called for the issue to be referred to the Committee of Privileges. To his credit, and to some surprise, the Speaker accepted Benn's amendment for debate. Benn then delivered the speech which is published here. Years later, Weatherill said that Benn's "single speech totally swung the House of Commons on that issue. It is my best example of a single speech totally changing the view of other Members."

By the end of the debate, such was the mood of MPs in all parties that both the Labour and Conservative Front Benches accepted Benn's amendment. Thus Benn secured a vital principle: that the House should decide for itself what it can and cannot find out, and that court injunctions cannot automatically be used to keep information from MPs. That principle survived, even though the Committee of Privileges subsequently ruled that the film should not be shown at Westminster. It was, however, shown in a building nearby.

As for the BBC, its top management faced blistering criticism from the left for agreeing to shelve the programme, and from the right for allowing it to be made and then failing to keep it under wraps. Two days after the debate the BBC's director-general, Alasdair Milne, was summarily sacked.

The BBC eventually broadcast Campbell's film in September 1988 – after the Zircon project itself had been cancelled for being too expensive. Neither the broadcast nor the project's cancellation appeared to have altered the course of the cold war, which effectively ended in November 1989 with the fall of the Berlin Wall. What has endured, apart from the Special Branch's occasional appetite for tidying people's desks, is Benn's defence of the right of our elected representatives to decide their rules for themselves, and not to surrender those rights to kings, Governments or court injunctions.

am sure that, in making your ruling, Mr. Speaker, it was not your intention to inhibit the working of the Select Committees. That being so, I hope that the winding-up speech will be appropriately helpful and we can proceed accordingly.

6.10 pm

Mr. Tony Benn (Chesterfield): I am grateful to you, Mr. Speaker, for allowing me to put before the House the manuscript amendment standing in my name that would transfer the matter to the Committee of Privileges. The amendment is, in line 1, leave out from 'That' to end and add

'Mr. Speaker's ruling of 22nd January, relating to the showing of a film, be referred to the Committee of Privileges'.

Mr. Speaker: Order. The right hon. Gentleman may move the amendment at the end of the debate, but he may speak to it now.

Mr. Benn: If the motion proposed by the Leader of the House were passed today, even the Committee of Privileges would not be allowed to see the film upon which Mr. Speaker gave his ruling.

I think it is obvious to the House that the issues we are discussing go far beyond the immediate matters of controversy between the Government and the Opposition, the related question of the Campbell article in the *New Statesman* on the film or the project. I do not wish to go back over the issues of last week when you took a decision, Mr. Speaker, at very short notice, because it is today that we face the big decision.

Those of us who have anxieties about the implication of the decision that you took last week, Mr. Speaker, wish to make it clear that those anxieties are in no sense personally related to you. Nevertheless, those anxieties are clear and specific and can be set out in the following way. If the Government are asking that we should "confirm" your ruling, or if, as the amendment put down by my right hon. Friend the Member for Islwyn (Mr. Kinnock), states, we should "accept" that decision, the difficulties go far beyond the Opposition and extend to the Chairmen and members of the Select Committees. That is why I am moving that the matter should go to the Committee of Privileges, which was set up by the House many years ago to examine matters that require complex examination. We should not reach a decision until the Committee of Privileges has reported.

The issue that we are discussing is a fundamental constitutional one of the relationship of the Commons, Members of Parliament and the electors on the one hand; and the Executive and the judiciary on the other. Although you quite properly said, Mr. Speaker, that you did not wish your ruling of last Thursday to be treated as a precedent, if we confirm or accept it tonight it will appear in "Erskine May" and will be quoted in future Parliaments and have a profound effect upon Parliament.

I do not believe that there is any precedent for the ruling that you gave, Mr. Speaker. I have searched carefully through "Erskine May" and I can find no precedent, nor can I imagine that when the Committee on Accommodation was set up it was ever intended that the organisation of Committee Rooms of the House should be used to prevent the showing of a film on the provision of information that might assist hon. Members in the course of their work.

It is right that we should look at your role, Mr. Speaker, in this connection, because it is the highest office that we can bestow and you speak for us and defend us from the Executive. I have cited before, and will cite again, the words of Mr. Speaker Lenthall. On 4 January 1642 the King came to the Commons to seize the five Members. Mr. Speaker Lenthall, described as "a man of timorous nature", knelt and said:

"May it please your Majesty, I have neither eyes to see nor tongue to speak in this place but as the House is pleased to direct me, whose servant I am here."

That was the precedent. It could be argued that if it was not in relation to five hon. Members and King that precedent would not apply. However, we have taken it, ever since, as a statement of your role. Now when a new Speaker is elected he goes to the other place to claim the ancient privileges of the House.

I am sorry to go back to the texts, but people may not always appreciate their importance. In 1688 the 9th article of the Bill of Rights stated:

"That the freedom of speech, and debates or proceedings in Parliament, ought not to be impeached or questioned in any Court or place out of Parliament."

Hon. Members may ask whether a film shown somewhere else in the Chamber can be described as a proceeding in Parliament. Fortunately, we have a precedent for that as well. In 1938 Duncan Sandys, a Member of the House and also a member of the Territorial Army, received from a colleague in the Territorial Army information that there were defects in the air defence of London. He tabled a question and the person from whom he got the information was charged under the Official Secrets Act 1911. Duncan Sandys came to the House to appeal to the House to protect him by way of privilege and the person who gave the information.

I know about this matter because my father was on the Committee of Privileges or the Select Committee which reported on the case. I remember most vividly the debate in the House. The House upheld the view—I shall refer to it because it refers directly to the question as to what is a proceeding in Parliament—and did so in a case involving the Official Secrets Act. I shall quote from "Erskine May", page 93, commenting on the Committee that examined the Sandys case:

"cases may easily be imagined of communications between one Member and another or between a Member and a Minister, so closely related to some matter pending in, or expected to be brought before the House, that, although they do not take place in the Chamber or a committee room, they form part of the business of the House."

That was one of the most important judgments reached by the House, especially when one considers, to its credit, that it was in the middle of war. As far as I recall, the matter was discussed in the House in May 1940, when it may well have had other matters to consider. Nevertheless, it entrenched the right of its Members to receive information from someone who is not a Member of the House even when that information is in respect of the security of the country.

I give that historical and legal background only to underline the enormity of the decision that it is proposed we should take without any further examination of the issues at stake. My amendment does not prejudge any of those issues, but invites the House to put the matter to the Committee that is best qualified to judge.

It is an issue that is not just of historical and legal importance, but one which will have immediate, practical importance to the future workings of parliamentary democracy. I ask the House to ask itself these important

[*Mr. Benn*]

questions before hon. Members go into the Lobby to vote on any of the amendments, other than the one referring to the Committee of Privileges.

First, is it right for the Government to engage in major military projects without telling Parliament? This question, as my hon. Friends will know, points a finger of criticism at both Labour and Tory Governments. I think I am one of the few surviving Members who sat in this House when Mr. Attlee was Prime Minister and Mr. Attlee developed the atom bomb without telling Parliament. At the time, that may have been considered acceptable, but I do not believe that any hon. Member would accept that it would be right to do that today.

The House does not want technical details about the defence of secrets when the question of security arises. I have not read the article in the *New Statesman* and I do not particularly want to read what Duncan Campbell may say about a particular satellite. However, Parliament must know the general nature of major defence projects, their purpose and their cost. If Parliament does not know that it is abdicating its responsibilities.

The second question is whether it is right that Ministers should be able to go to any court and use the magic words "national security" as the basis for a court injunction. In a democracy it is for the House and electors to decide what is in the national interest. And when there is a general election, it is the people's judgment as to what is in the national interest that counts. It is not for civil servants, generals, scientists or Ministers to determine what is national security. The judges of the Cheltenham case have said that if the magic words "national security" are used they will not allow the matter to be raised.

Mr. Norman Buchan (Paisley, South) *rose——*

Mr. Benn: The third question that I would like the House to consider is whether it is right that any Speaker — so as not to personalise it — hearing news of an injunction that has been issued should be able, without the explicit and specific authority of the House, to prevent hon. Members from seeking available information that would assist Parliament in its work of holding Governments to account. As the court in question declined to grant an injunction against some hon. Members, it is clear that it recognised the limits of its powers. Page 204 of "Erskine May" states:

"the courts admit: That the control of each House over its internal proceedings is absolute and cannot be interfered with by the courts."

I do not know, and it is not my concern, to what extent that aspect was in your mind, Mr. Speaker, when you took what you feel to have been interim action, but that is the question that we have to ask today, because we are reaching permanent decisions.

The next question is whether we should accept and confirm a limit on our freedom as Members of Parliament that would assist the concealment of any matter by any Government of any Parliament — this is not just in relation to this matter—by the use of national security and injunctions. I worry greatly over the other implications of your ruling, Mr. Speaker. What if the police had gone to a magistrate and asked for a warrant to search the papers of my hon. Friend the Member for Livingston (Mr. Cook) at the time they were going to the home of Duncan Campbell? What would have been the

position? Is it the case that the House could ever allow the courts or a magistrate to send policemen into the Palace, where already a film may not be shown, to discover the sources of information of a Member who might be contemplating a parliamentary question?

If we accept the motion or the amendment, we would be placing the House of Commons and Members of Parliament for ever under the effective control of the Government, in that Ministers could bring an injunction, the court could accede to the injunction and—nobody would wish this less than you, Mr. Speaker — Mr. Speaker would become an agent of the Minister and his injunction and the court that upheld it, to enforce upon Members the denial of the rights for which we were elected. I cannot believe, knowing you, Mr. Speaker, that it would be your wish to be remembered as a "Counter-Lenthall" whose protection did not extend to hon. Members in this position.

I should like to make a final comment as an old Member of the House. We all take children and visitors round the House. I do and have done for many years. We tell them that we keep Black Rod out. We tell them about the Outlawries Bill, we tell them that the House decides on its own business before it gives attention to the Gracious Speech. We tell them about the Army and Air Force (Annual) Act and the order to prevent a standing Army being maintained and we tell them about the five Members. Those are not meaningless rituals. They are reminders of monumental struggles to build democracy against tyranny. It is important that we should not treat them simply as tourist attractions.

For all those reasons, I appeal to hon. Members of all parties to pass the amendment that refers the matter to the place where these implications can be fully considered. I appeal to the Leader of the House to recognise the importance of his role in granting a free vote to Conservative Members on the question of reference to the Committee of Privileges. If that is rejected, the matter will have to be dealt with by the motion on the Order Paper. In 36 years in the House I cannot recall a debate as important as this and I am grateful to you, Mr. Speaker, for allowing my manuscript amendment to be put on the Order Paper tonight along with the motion and the other amendments before us.

6.25 pm

Mr. Cranley Onslow (Woking): The right hon. Member for Chesterfield (Mr. Benn) is right in what he said about the importance of the debate. However, some of the considerations that he put before the House seem to be not quite as relevant as he supposed, and some of his arguments were not as complete as they might have been. When he told us how he conducts parties round the House, he might have added one other important piece of parliamentary law, which is the right of any hon. Member, when he feels it appropriate, to require that the House remembers its obligation to keep matters secret by "spying strangers". When we consider this important matter, we should not forget that we have that duty and that we have a procedure that has been used, rightly, in the national interest. I am glad to see that the right hon. Member for Cardiff, South and Penarth (Mr. Callaghan) appears to agree with me.

Mr. James Callaghan: I was agreeing with a remark made by my hon. Friend the Member for Midlothian (Mr. Eadie), not with the hon. Gentleman.

Michael Foot backs use of force to restore Falklands democracy

Robert Kilroy-Silk entered Parliament as the Labour MP for Ormskirk in 1974, having previously spent eight years as a politics lecturer at Liverpool university. After boundary changes, he went on to represent the seat of Knowsley, and served as shadow home affairs spokesman, although he resigned from that post in 1985 and quit the House altogether in 1986 to present the BBC talk show, "Day to Day", and subsequently the eponymous "Kilroy".

The show was pulled from the schedules in 2004, following the controversy provoked by the publication of a Kilroy-Silk article in *The Sunday Express* entitled, "We owe Arabs nothing."

As a Labour MP, he opposed Britain's membership of the EU, and he consolidated that position when he joined the UK Independence party in 2004, winning a seat in the East Midlands in the European parliamentary elections in June that year.

Buoyed by the success of UKIP in pushing the Conservatives into fourth place in the Hartlepool by-election in 2004, he told his party conference in October that the Conservative party should be "killed off". His bid for the UKIP leadership was launched in a television interview with David Frost the day after he addressed his party conference. He admitted that he was interested in taking over the leadership, and he criticised the then party leader, Roger Knapman.

The affair ended in acrimony, fuelled by his allegations that the Independence and Democracy Group in the European Parliament, which UKIP had joined, contained anti-semitic Polish members and Italian Members accused of racism, which he regarded as intolerable.

He quit UKIP in January 2005 to found his own Eurosceptic party, Veritas, and in the election that year he contested the seat of Erewash, coming fourth. Soon afterwards, he faced a challenge to his leadership, and resigned his position, claiming that "it would be virtually impossible for a new party to make a significant impact given the nature of our electoral system. We tried and failed."

He remains in the European Parliament, serving as a Eurosceptic Independent MEP, and has continued his broadcasting career: he has appeared on "Have I Got News for You?", "Any Questions?" and "Question Time", and featured in a Channel 4 documentary, "Kilroy and the Gypsies", in which he spent a week living with a Romany family in Bedfordshire.

Firm defence of Britain's interests leaves Back Benchers relieved and content

By Robert Kilroy-Silk MEP

This was not Michael Foot's finest speech. It was not even one of his best. It is not memorable for the thrilling oratory of which he was capable. There was none of that, just as there were no unforgettable lines, no amusing quips, none of his devastating wit or disarming, but politically effective, humour that usually characterised his performances.

But Michael Foot's oration as Leader of the Opposition at this specially summoned meeting of the House of Commons on Saturday 3 April 1982, after the invasion of the Falkland Islands by Argentina, was very important to me. It was a day of great drama and moment, and this was probably the most significant of all the speeches to which I listened in my thirteen and a half years as a Member of the House of Commons.

Along with a number of other Labour MPs who were members of the left-wing Tribune group, I was concerned to ensure that the Conservative Government of Margaret Thatcher was encouraged to regain the islands, by force if necessary, and that it would have the full support of the Opposition.

We were worried about Michael Foot. He was a supporter of CND. He exuded pacifism. It seemed likely that he would equivocate, want the matter handed over to the corrupt and inept United Nations, and maybe even play politics with the issue.

We wanted none of that. We conveyed that to him privately. We told him that we expected him to speak for us, for the Labour party at large, which wanted Britain to retake the islands, and for the overwhelming majority of our constituents who would support military action to do so.

We wanted no Hampstead-style pussyfooting, no equivocations, no wishy-washy "on the one hand this, and on the other that." We wanted to hear the leader of our party speak firmly and clearly – in support of the right of self-determination and of a country's right to use force to restore democracy. Whilst he had been reassuring, he had given no commitment.

We were, therefore, apprehensive when he rose to speak at 11.45am. I sat a few feet behind him and to his left. I listened to every word, weighing its meaning, analysing its nuances in a manner that I had never employed before or since. While I and my colleagues did not expect him to do a rallying "We shall fight them on the beaches," we wanted him to be firm and straightforward in defending British interests.

He was.

He began by setting out the rights of the islanders who wished "to be associated with this country...We have," he said, "a moral duty, a political duty and every other kind of duty to ensure that that is sustained."

I waited for the "but". None came. Instead he went on to say that they "were right to look to us" in the face of "naked, unqualified aggression."

That was it. That was enough. The meaning was clear. I was satisfied. But there was more. Anticipating Tony Blair in Bosnia and, later, Iraq, he argued that while it would be preferable to have the UN involved, he, nevertheless, made it clear that he was "determined" to "uphold the rights of our country throughout the world."

We left the Chamber for the buzz of the Members' Tea Room, relieved and content. The Falkland Islands would be safe in the Labour party's hands.

said nothing. On Friday, as the House knows, the Argentines invaded the Falklands and I have given a precise account of everything we knew, or did not know, about that situation. There were also reports that yesterday the Argentines also attacked South Georgia, where HMS "Endurance" had left a detachment of 22 Royal Marines. Our information is that on 2 April an Argentine naval transport vessel informed the base commander at Grytviken that an important message would be passed to him after 11 o'clock today our time. It is assumed that this message will ask the base commander to surrender.

Before indicating some of the measures that the Government have taken in response to the Argentine invasion, I should like to make three points. First, even if ships had been instructed to sail the day that the Argentines landed on South Georgia to clear the whaling station, the ships could not possibly have got to Port Stanley before the invasion. *[Interruption.]* Opposition Members may not like it, but that is a fact.

Secondly, there have been several occasions in the past when an invasion has been threatened. The only way of being certain to prevent an invasion would have been to keep a very large fleet close to the Falklands, when we are some 8,000 miles away from base. No Government have ever been able to do that, and the cost would be enormous.

Mr. Eric Ogden (Liverpool, West Derby): Will the right hon. Lady say what has happened to HMS "Endurance"?

The Prime Minister: HMS "Endurance" is in the area. It is not for me to say precisely where, and the hon. Gentleman would not wish me to do so.

Thirdly, aircraft unable to land on the Falklands, because of the frequently changing weather, would have had little fuel left and, ironically, their only hope of landing safely would have been to divert to Argentina. Indeed, all of the air and most sea supplies for the Falklands come from Argentina, which is but 400 miles away compared with our 8,000 miles.

That is the background against which we have to make decisions and to consider what action we can best take. I cannot tell the House precisely what dispositions have been made—some ships are already at sea, others were put on immediate alert on Thursday evening.

The Government have now decided that a large task force will sail as soon as all preparations are complete. HMS "Invincible" will be in the lead and will leave port on Monday.

I stress that I cannot foretell what orders the task force will receive as it proceeds. That will depend on the situation at the time. Meanwhile, we hope that our continuing diplomatic efforts, helped by our many friends, will meet with success.

The Foreign Ministers of the European Community member States yesterday condemned the intervention and urged withdrawal. The NATO Council called on both sides to refrain from force and continue diplomacy.

The United Nations Security Council met again yesterday and will continue its discussions today. *[Laughter.]* Opposition Members laugh. They would have been the first to urge a meeting of the Security Council if we had not called one. They would have been the first to urge restraint and to urge a solution to the problem by diplomatic means. They would have been the first to accuse us of sabre rattling and war mongering.

Mr. Tam Dalyell (West Lothian): The right hon. Lady referred to our many friends. Have we any friends in South America on this issue?

The Prime Minister: Doubtless our friends in South America will make their views known during any proceedings at the Security Council. I believe that many countries in South America will be prepared to condemn the invasion of the Falklands Islands by force.

We are now reviewing all aspects of the relationship between Argentina and the United Kingdom. The Argentine chargé d'affaires and his staff were yesterday instructed to leave within four days.

As an appropriate precautionary and, I hope, temporary measure, the Government have taken action to freeze Argentine financial assets held in this country. An order will be laid before Parliament today under the Emergency Laws (Re-enactments and Repeals) Act 1964 blocking the movement of gold, securities or funds held in the United Kingdom by the Argentine Government or Argentine residents.

As a further precautionary measure, the ECGD has suspended new export credit cover for the Argentine. It is the Government's earnest wish that a return to good sense and the normal rules of international behaviour on the part of the Argentine Government will obviate the need for action across the full range of economic relations.

We shall be reviewing the situation and be ready to take further steps that we deem appropriate and we shall, of course, report to the House.

The people of the Falkland Islands, like the people of the United Kingdom, are an island race. Their way of life is British; their allegiance is to the Crown. They are few in number, but they have the right to live in peace, to choose their own way of life and to determine their own allegiance. Their way of life is British; their allegiance is to the Crown. It is the wish of the British people and the duty of Her Majesty's Government to do everything that we can to uphold that right. That will be our hope and our endeavour and, I believe, the resolve of every Member of the House.

11.45 am

Mr. Michael Foot (Ebbw Vale): It was obviously essential that the House of Commons should be recalled on this occasion. I thank the Prime Minister for the decision to do so. I can well understand the anxiety and impatience of many of my hon. Friends on the Back Benches who voted in the Division a few minutes ago and who desire to have full and proper time to examine all the aspects of this issue. I shall return to that aspect of the matter in a few minutes.

I first wish to set on record as clearly as I possibly can what we believe to be the international rights and wrongs of this matter, because I believe that one of the purposes of the House being assembled on this occasion is to make that clear not only to the people in our country but to people throughout the world.

The rights and the circumstances of the people in the Falkland Islands must be uppermost in our minds. There is no question in the Falkland Islands of any colonial dependence or anything of the sort. It is a question of people who wish to be associated with this country and who have built their whole lives on the basis of association with this country. We have a moral duty, a political duty and every other kind of duty to ensure that that is sustained.

The people of the Falkland Islands have the absolute right to look to us at this moment of their desperate plight, just as they have looked to us over the past 150 years. They are faced with an act of naked, unqualified aggression, carried out in the most shameful and disreputable circumstances. Any guarantee from this invading force is utterly worthless—as worthless as any of the guarantees that are given by this same Argentine junta to its own people.

We can hardly forget that thousands of innocent people fighting for their political rights in Argentine are in prison and have been tortured and debased. We cannot forget that fact when our friends and fellow citizens in the Falkland Islands are suffering as they are at this moment.

On the merits of the matter, we hope that the question is understood throughout the world. In that respect I believe that the Government were right to take the matter to the United Nations. It would have been delinquency if they had not, because that is the forum in which we have agreed that such matters of international right and international claim should be stated.

Whatever else the Government have done—I shall come to that in a moment—or not done, I believe that it was essential for them to take our case to the United Nations and to present it with all the force and power of advocacy at the command of this country. The decision and the vote in the United Nations will take place in an hour or two's time. I must say to people there that we in this country, as a whole, irrespective of our party affiliations, will examine the votes most carefully.

I was interested to hear how strongly the President of France spoke out earlier this morning. I hope that every other country in the world will speak in a similar way.

If, at the United Nations this afternoon, no such declaration were made—I know that it would be only a declaration at first, but there might be the possibility of action there later—not merely would it be a gross injury to the rights of the people of the Falkland Islands, not merely would it be an injury to the people of this country, who have a right to have their claims upheld in the United Nations, but it would be a serious injury to the United Nations itself. It would enhance the dangers that similar, unprovoked aggressions could occur in other parts of the world.

That is one of the reasons why we are determined to ensure that we examine this matter in full and uphold the rights of our country throughout the world, and the claim of our country to be a defender of people's freedom throughout the world, particularly those who look to us for special protection, as do the people in the Falkland Islands.

I deal next with the Government's conduct in the matter. What has happened to British diplomacy? The explanations given by the right hon. Lady, when she managed to rise above some of her own party arguments—they were not quite the exclusive part of her speech—were not very full and not very clear. They will need to be made a good deal more ample in the days to come.

The right hon. Lady did not quote fully the response of Lord Carrington, the Secretary of State for Foreign and Commonwealth Affairs, at his press conference yesterday. She referred to the Minister of State, who, according to Lord Carrington,

"had just been in New York discussing with Mr. Ross, his opposite number, the question of resumption of talks with the Argentine Government about the problems of the Falkland Islands. And they had had a talk and come to an agreement. Mr. Ross went back to the Argentine and a number of things came up and they sent a message which"——

I emphasise the words——

"I have not yet had time to reply to."

Lord Carrington added:

"So there was every reason to suppose that the Argentines were interested in negotiations."

Those talks took place on 27 February. The right hon. Lady gave an account of these negotiations. But from what has happened it seems that the British Government have been fooled by the way in which the Argentine junta has gone about its business. The Government must answer for that as well as for everything else.

What about British communications and British intelligence? *The Guardian* states today in a leading article:

"This country devotes a greater proportion of its annual output to its armed forces than any other Western country, with the exception of the United States. It has extensive diplomatic and intelligence gathering activities. And all of that gave Mrs. Thatcher, Lord Carrington and Mr. Nott precisely no effective cards when the Argentine navy moved."

I should be very surprised to hear, because of some of the previous debates and discussions on the crises that have arisen with the Argentine, that the British Government did not have better intelligence than that. So good was our intelligence that, although the Prime Minister now tells us that the invasion took place at 10 am yesterday, the Lord Privy Seal—I know that he has apologised for some of his remarks—told the House of Commons and the British people:

"We are taking appropriate military and diplomatic measures to sustain our rights under international law and in accordance with the provisions of the United Nations charter."—[*Official Report*, 2 April 1982; Vol. 21, c. 571.]

When he was saying that, it was the Argentine Government who were taking appropriate military, not diplomatic, measures to enforce their will.

The right hon. Lady, the Secretary of State for Defence and the whole Government will have to give a very full account of what happened, how their diplomacy was conducted and why we did not have the information to which we are entitled when expenditure takes place on such a scale. Above all, more important than the question of what happened to British diplomacy or to British intelligence is what happened to our power to act. The right hon. Lady seemed to dismiss that question. It cannot be dismissed. Of course this country has the power to act—short, often, of taking military measures. Indeed, we have always been told, as I understand it, that the purpose of having some military power is to deter. The right to deter and the capacity to deter were both required in this situation.

The previous Government had to deal with the same kind of dictatorial regime in the Argentine, the same kind of threat to the people of the Falkland Islands, and the same kinds of problems as those with which the Government have had to wrestle over the past weeks and months. My right hon. Friend the Member for Cardiff, South-East (Mr. Callaghan) compressed the whole position into the question that he put to the Government only last Tuesday. I shall read his remarks to the House, and I ask the House to mark every word. This was no factious Opposition. This was an Opposition Member seeking to sustain the Government if the Government were doing their duty.

My right hon. Friend said:

"I support the Government's attempts to solve the problem by diplomatic means, which is clearly the best and most sensible way of approaching the problem, but is the Minister aware that there have been other recent occasions when the Argentinians, when beset by internal troubles, have tried the same type of tactical diversion? Is the Minister aware that on a very recent occasion, of which I have full knowledge, Britain assembled ships which had been stationed in the Caribbean, Gibraltar and in the Mediterranean, and stood them about 400 miles off the Falklands in support of HMS "Endurance", and that when this fact became known, without fuss and publicity, a diplomatic solution followed? While I do not press the Minister on what is happening today, I trust that it is the same sort of action."— [*Official Report*, 30 March 1982; Vol. 21, c. 198.]

The House and whole country have the right to say the same thing to the Government. The people of the Falkland Islands have an even greater right to say it than ourselves. The right hon. Lady has not answered that question. She has hardly attempted to answer it. It is no answer to refer to the matter so effectively disposed of by my hon. Friend the Member for Merthyr Tydfil (Mr. Rowlands), who has much knowledge of these matters. It is, of course, a very different question.

No one can say for certain that the pacific and honourable solution of this problem that was reached in 1977 was due to the combination of diplomatic and military activity. These things cannot be proved. There is, however, every likelihood that that was the case. In any event, the fact that it worked on the previous occasion was surely all the more reason for the Government's seeking to make it work on this occasion, especially when, according to the Secretary of State for Foreign and Commonwealth Affairs—I refer again to the diplomatic exchanges—it had been going on for some time. According to the diplomatic exchanges, the Argentine Government were still awaiting an answer from the Secretary of State on some of the matters involved.

The right hon. Lady made some play, although not very effectively, with the time it takes to get warships into the area. We are talking about events several weeks ago. All these matters have to be answered. They cannot be answered fully in this debate. There will have to be another debate on the subject next week. Whether that debate takes the form of a motion of censure, or some other form, or perhaps takes the form of the establishment of an inquiry into the whole matter, so that all the evidence and the facts can be laid before the people of this country, I have not the slightest doubt that, at some stage, an inquiry of that nature, without any inhibitions and restraints, that can probe the matter fully will have to be undertaken.

I return to what I said at the start of my remarks. We are paramountly concerned, like, I am sure, the bulk of the House—I am sure that the country is also concerned—about what we can do to protect those who rightly and naturally look to us for protection. So far, they have been betrayed. The responsibility for the betrayal rests with the Government. The Government must now prove by deeds—they will never be able to do it by words—that they are not responsible for the betrayal and cannot be faced with that charge. That is the charge, I believe, that lies against them. Even though the position and the circumstances of the people who live in the Falkland Islands are uppermost in our minds—it would be outrageous if that were not the case—there is the longer-term interest to ensure that foul and brutal aggression does not succeed in our world. If it does, there will be a danger not merely to the Falkland Islands, but to people all over this dangerous planet.

Several Hon. Members rose——

Mr. Speaker: Order. I remind the House that two hours remain for this debate. I appeal to those Privy Councillors who may be called not to take advantage of the fact that they are being called early because they are Privy Councillors. I ask everyone to bear in mind that almost all hon. Members have indicated that they would like to speak.

12.1 pm

Mr. Edward du Cann (Taunton): There are times, Mr. Speaker, in the affairs of our nation when the House should speak with a single, united voice. This is just such a time. The Leader of the Opposition spoke for us all. He did this nation a service when, in clear and unmistakable terms, he condemned what he called this brutal agression and when he affirmed the rights of the Falkland islanders to decide their own destiny. I warmly applaud that part of his speech. I resent and reject his charge of betrayal.

I have a single simple point to make and I can make it shortly. It is right that the House should also, at this moment of crisis for our nation and for the Government, pledge full support to my right hon. Friend the Prime Minister and her colleagues in their heavy and awesome responsibility. As the Leader of the Opposition said, we must do what is necessary and what is right. However, let us see that what we do is well done.

Undoubtedly, there will be questions to be asked. There will also be questions to be answered. I agree with the Leader of the Opposition that there will be a need for a full account of this affair. However, some of those questions can and should be listed shortly now.

It is astounding that, for all our defence expenditure, which in absolute and proportional terms is huge, and for all our capacity for diplomatic activity and intelligence, we appear to have been so woefully ill prepared. It is extraordinary that conventional forces were not deployed on standby against an occupation.

The rule should surely be that the defence of our realm begins wherever British people are. Defence of the realm begins wherever they travel on their lawful occasions and wherever they may be threatened. The apparent assumption that the problem could be resolved only by diplomatic means was surely fatuous. However, if we have no inquests as yet, it must surely be said now that this incident demands a revision of the United Kingdom's defence strategy, some aspects of which have made many hon. Members and others outside the House decidedly nervous.

However, let us declare and resolve that our duty now is to repossess our possessions and to rescue our own people. Our right to the Falkland Islands is undoubted. Our sovereignty is unimpeachable. British interest in that part of the world, in my judgment, is substantial. It is substantial in the Falkland Islands, however trivial the figures may appear to be. It is substantial in the sea, which has yet to yield up its treasures. It is also substantial in Antarctica. The British interest would be substantial even if we were discussing the affairs of just one fellow citizen.

We must rally support to our position and cause. I entirely agree with the Leader of the Opposition that this nation has always been prompt to condemn dictatorship, to ally ourselves and fight against it and fight against aggression. Of course, we must explore every diplomatic and legal means to recover what is legitimately ours.

Keir Hardie issues prescient warning of perils of all-white Government in South Africa

A Canadian by birth, **Anthony King** came to Britain as a Rhodes Scholar in 1956. He was a Fellow of Magdalen College, Oxford, during the early 1960s before moving to the then new University of Essex in 1966. He is now Essex County Council Millennium Professor of British Government at Essex.

He has taught in the United States at the University of Wisconsin-Madison and at Princeton. He has also been a visiting scholar at the Center for Advanced Study in the Behavioral Sciences, Palo Alto, California, and at the John F. Kennedy School of Government, Harvard.

He is a foreign honorary member of the American Academy of Arts and Sciences, a member of the Academia Europaea and an honorary life fellow of the Royal Society of Arts. In 2007 he received a lifetime achievement award from the Political Studies Association of the United Kingdom.

His many books include studies of the 1964 and 1966 general elections with David Butler, "Britain Says Yes: The 1975 Referendum on the Common Market", "The Birth Life and Death of the Social Democratic Party" with Ivor Crewe, "Running Scared: Why America's Politicians Campaign Too Much and Govern Too Little".

In 2008 he published "The British Constitution", which analyses the changes that have taken place in the United Kingdom's constitution over the past five decades and argues that, cumulatively, they have brought about a fundamental change in the character of the British political order.

As a freelance journalist and broadcaster, Professor King has written for a wide range of British and American newspapers and periodicals and since 1964 has appeared regularly on BBC radio and television election-night programmes.

Between 1994 and 1998 he served as a founder member of the Committee on Standards in Public Life (initially the Nolan Committee, latterly the Neil Committee), and in 1999-2000 he was a member of the Royal Commission on the Reform of the House of Lords. During the mid 2000s he chaired the Royal Society of Arts Commission on Illegal Drugs, Communities and Public Policy.

He is currently writing a book on the evolution of American politics and working with Sir Ivor Crewe on a study of major governmental failures in the UK.

Archetypal left-wing idealist and the prophecy ignored

By Professor Anthony King

Everyone interested in 20th-century political history has a picture of Keir Hardie in his or her mind. He is the archetypal left-wing idealist, bearded, cloth-capped, fiery of speech, flamboyant of gesture – a kind of home-grown Lenin. And certainly much of his career is consistent with that image.

He was a romantic, a passionate orator, with a temperament unsuited to the inevitable evasions and compromises of conventional parliamentary politics. However, as this speech shows, there was more to him than that. He was highly intelligent, with an ecumenical world view and a greater willingness to deal in political realities than he is often given credit for.

In 1909, only seven years after Britain's victory in the Boer War, the Liberal Government of H. H. Asquith struck a deal with the predominantly Boer leaders of Britain's four South African colonies. On the one hand, the four colonies would remain (and did remain during two world wars) loyal to Britain and the British Empire. On the other hand, Britain in return would promote a union of the colonies and, more important, would accord the new South African union the status of a self-governing dominion within the Empire.

In addition, the Asquith Government accepted, albeit reluctantly, that in South Africa self government would in practice mean white government.

To be sure, manhood suffrage would be introduced throughout the Union of South Africa, but the men in question would mostly be white. The only exceptions would be small minorities of black Africans and mixed-race 'Cape coloureds' who would still be allowed to vote for members of the Cape Colony and Natal provincial councils and even for members of the all-Union House of Assembly.

However, black Africans and Cape coloureds were barred from membership of the Union Parliament, and it would therefore be only a matter of time before they were deprived of the few voting rights they had. With the coming of full-blown apartheid, that time duly arrived.

Two features of Hardie's 1909 speech stand out. One is its moderation. Despite his reputation, Hardie was a genuine parliamentarian, not merely a mob orator. The other is its prescience. What Hardie predicted almost inexorably came to pass.

Long afterwards, on the occasion of the 50th anniversary of the passage of the Union of South Africa Act, voices could be heard asking whether what happened in the end could have been foreseen. The answer is that it was – by Hardie. 'Abandon hope', he said, 'all ye who enter here.' Perhaps there is a moral to be drawn: that ignorance of the future can be an excuse only when all alike are ignorant.

[Mr. Molteno.]

able arrangements. That is a striking illustration of the enormous advantage of not attempting to control native policy.

6.0 P.M.

In fact the history of South Africa is full of great warnings against any such attempt. We have had enormous success when we relied upon the proper policy, namely, that in regard to the control of native relations; the time has come when we must feel that our Colonies are capable of acting alone in this matter. Under this Bill you have every prospect that the natives, as a whole, will benefit very largely by the control of native affairs being placed in the hands of the central authority, and not left, as they are now, in the hands of the local authority. For all these reasons, it appears to me that it would be the height of unwisdom to interfere with this Constitution, however much we right some of its provisions. It still has the enormous advantage that it unites the white races, through whose disunion we have had the most terrible evils, and through whose disunion we may have in the future the most terrible evils again, and it is of great advantage that by means of it we should try to unite them. In the Cape Colony no disadvantage came from trusting the Cape Government, and the native relations are more satisfactory than they have ever been, and the arrangements which have been made will, I think, impress us with the conviction that it would be unwise to tamper with the solution which is brought before us, and which has brought about such good results in that part of the world. In conclusion, it appears to me that some of our proudest traditions are those of liberty, freedom, and self-government, which ensures their security and permanency. Never were those principles put to a severer test than in South Africa, and never has their success been more immediate, more striking, and more triumphant.

Mr. KEIR HARDIE: No one can speak in this Debate without feeling a sense of very great responsibility, because when this Bill has passed through this House, unlike others, it will be beyond recall or possibility of either repeal or amendment, and coming, as it does, with the full authority of the four Parliaments now existing in South Africa, it would be rashness carried to an extreme for the House of Commons, or any Member of the House of Commons, to seek to interfere with the matters affecting those representatives of the four Parliaments in South Africa. I want to preface my remarks by saying that any criticism which we on these benches have to offer to the Bill, or any proposals or suggestions we have to make, as Amendments, do not affect the white population of South Africa, but only those whom we are bound, as has been freely admitted both in another place and here, to regard as our wards, the coloured or native population, for whom we are more or less directly responsible. It was all to the credit of the Under-Secretary for Colonial Affairs (Colonel Seely) that he was laboured in his apology for certain portions of the Bill. It shows, as he frankly admitted, that those particular clauses were not there by his will, or even in accordance with his own feelings. A similar remark applies to the speech of the right hon. Gentleman the Member for St. George's, Hanover-sqaure (Mr. Lyttelton). No speech made yet has endeavoured to justify the appearance of certain clauses in this Bill. We have had those clauses apologised for; we have had attempts made to explain the reasons for their being there, but so far as the discussion has gone not one single speaker has sought to justify the presence of certain clauses, which I will deal with in a moment. The whole scheme of the Bill—and this will not, I think, be denied in any quarter—the whole scheme of the Bill is that of a white European South Africa, and that, under the circumstances, seems to some of us to be an impossibility. The method by which, for example, those who are to elect the representatives from the different provinces is to be ascertained is, after all, to consist of adult male Europeans.

For the purpose of the operation of this Act, there are two classes of people in South Africa who do not exist. First of all, the women of all races. They are ruled out, as are also the natives, who are in a proportion of six to one. The Kaffir man and the white woman of European descent are classed together in the Bill as not being fit to be counted, even in ascertaining what proportion of representation is to go to each of the provinces. May I say that none of us here are pressing that natives should get the franchise; neither are we seeking to enforce native representation or to remove the disqualification concerning natives in the Transvaal and Orange Free State. So far as we are concerned on these benches, what we seek to obtain—and in Committee stage we shall do our best to obtain—is that the *status quo* shall be continued, both in Cape Colony and Natal. At the present time in Cape Colony, out of 181,000 voters, 22,000 of these are coloured and native. There is no special native franchise in Cape Colony, but the law has been from the beginning that any person, no matter of what race, who is able to show the necessary qualifications shall *ipso facto* be admitted to the franchise, and the result has been that, out of a total electorate of 181,000, no fewer than 22,000 of those have been coloured or natives, who have raised themselves to the position of the necessary qualification. It may be said, it has been said, that this Bill does not interfere with the franchise in the Cape Colony. It has been said by the Under-Secretary that the framers of the Bill have taken special words to safeguard the continuance of the existing franchise in the Cape Colony. That may be so I confess, in regard to the franchise itself, but what about the disqualification of natives from being elected by the Cape Colony to a seat in the Union Parliament. What is the footing which the native or coloured people are put upon in Cape Colony itself, and what does it foreshadow? The right hon. Gentleman the Member for St. George's, Hanover-square (Mr. Lyttelton) said that in future the status would be enlarged, because they would have to elect a member not of the Provincial Parliament but of the South African Parliament, and therein rests an additional reason for attempting to get rid of this Cape Colony voting, for if the coloured man is so very objectionable that those who are to form this Parliament will not even run the risk of one of them being elected to sit by their side—if so, surely they will be unwilling to have the influence of the coloured men brought to bear upon them through their voting power in Cape Colony.

Besides that, the fact is that the existence of the franchise in the Cape Colony will be regarded as a reflection upon those other portions of the Union where no similar right and privilege has been secured, and for all these reasons there will be a strong inducement on the part of the statesmen and legislators outside the Cape Colony itself to endeavour to have the franchise equalised all over South Africa, not by bringing in the natives or coloured persons in the Transvaal or Orange Free State, but by excluding the native or coloured person where he now possesses the franchise, and this danger is not so very remote as may appear. As a matter of fact, we have several recent de-

claraticns on the subject from those who, in the future, will exert the determining influence in South Africa, which show that the apprehensions in the main of the natives are not without substantial foundation. On 24th February this year, for example, General Botha, speaking on this very subject, said:—

"The difficulty which we encountered was the native franchise. There is not a matter on which I have a stronger feeling than this of the native franchise, but do not let us blame our brothers of the Cape Colony. The native franchise was given to them at the time when they received responsible government. We know that it would be impossible for the Imperial Government to take back that which they have once given in the Cape Colony. We had a two-fold difficulty. How can you expect the Cape Parliament to pass this draft Constitution if it were to take away the native franchise? The only possible course for us to follow was followed in the draft Constitution and that was to create machinery which would enable the people of South Africa to settle this question."

The interpretation of that is that General Botha generously exonerated the white people of the Cape from all blame for having given the franchise to the natives, since that franchise was forced upon them by the Imperial Parliament at the time the Constitution was given. A phrase of that kind gives a fair indication as to the mind of General Botha on this subject. Speaking on the same day—and this dots the "i's" and crosses the "t's" of General Botha's statement—General Smuts says:—

"There was a vast majority of people in South Africa opposed to the native franchise. The Transvaal was very largely opposed to it and so were the Free States and Natal, and for that matter he supposed a large part of the Cape. As Mr. Merriman had said in his speech, the majority of the people of the Cape were opposed to it and on the first occasion that Parliament met it would be swept away. It was found necessary that there should be some check on such arbitrary action but it was not a powerful check. Perhaps it was not a check at all. It had been put in there but he did not think it meant much. At any rate it was a compromise which they had to accept or jeopardise the Union."

Speaking a month later, Dr. Kraus, also a member of the Transvaal Parliament, declared frankly that the white people in South Africa would be traitors to their colour if they did not take away the franchise from the coloured people so soon as the new Parliament met. These things constitute an element of fear in the mind of the native and the coloured people in Cape Colony and in Natal, and the Amendments which we shall ask the House to agree to will be that the European descent qualification shall only apply to the Transvaal and the Orange Free State, and that in Natal and Cape Colony the rights guaranteed to the coloured people by the Constitution granted to them by the late Queen and the Imperial Parliament shall be preserved and maintained, and their

[Mr. Keir Hardie.]

right to elect coloured people continued, as it is at the present moment. Then, in regard to the franchise, we shall ask the House to say that just as in the case of the liquor traffic and the supply to natives, so, too, in regard to the franchise, whatever Amendments will be made in the future shall not have the effect of worsening the position so far as the native is concerned, but shall reserve to him those rights he at present enjoys, and thereby give a lead to South Africa to a further development along the line of progress. It is most interesting in this connection to remember that the heads of nearly all the religious organisations in South Africa support this contention, that the native franchise and native eligibility to be elected should not be interfered with or in any way restricted. But, in addition to religious organisations and bodies, practically the whole of the labour organisations take the same view, but the declared intention of a very large section of opinion in South Africa is to prevent the natives coming into serious competition with the white man, either in the learned professions or as property owners, or in any other sphere except that of a low-paid worker in connection with industry. It is a common-place to have it alleged of a large section of opinion in South Africa that the one interest it has in the coloured peoples there is to reduce them to the position of a landless proletariat, where they will be compelled to accept wages at anything that is offered to them in order to maintain body and soul together. Already that policy has advanced a considerable way in more than one of the States. In the Orange River Colony the restrictions are numerous and vexatious. No coloured man may engage in trade without a permit, for which he has to pay 5s. a month. The permit may confine his work to jobs within the location. He is prohibited from making bricks for sale within the town, and in a variety of ways restraints and restrictions are placed upon the educated skilled native artisan. If he desires to become a contractor, as some were during, and since the war, he is prohibited from taking contracts and so on, a clear indication being given that the object of the rulers of the Orange Free State is to prevent the natives rising into the ranks of skilled workers or into those of the educated classes. Children must leave school when they are 16, and parents will be fined £2 for each child over 16 who is not found at work.

In Cape Colony matters are considerably better in these respects than they are in the Orange Free State or the Transvaal, and the reason is the different policy they pursued towards the coloured races, but even there there are indications of a change for the worse. The higher grade schools, I am informed, are closed against native children, even in Cape Colony, and now a well-to-do native desiring his child to receive higher grade or University education must perforce send him to this country or to America before the education can be received. So, too, in regard to the owning of land. The land laws of the Transvaal and the Orange Free State are well known. Their object has been to prevent natives from holding land even for cultivation, and even in Cape Colony—and this shows a tendency which I am advised exists all through South Africa—a law has been passed to prevent natives owning land near to the white townships. At present the law confines them in locations where the area which the natives may acquire for the building of houses is 40 feet square, and recently some of the more well-to-do and better educated natives have desired to obtain sites for building outside the locations. There was a case in which a gentleman had agreed to sell some 500 sites for building purposes to natives, 186 of these sites were sold, and the Government stepped in and prevented the sale of the others on the plea that, being so near to the white townships, sanitation and police management would be difficult. The interesting fact is that the laws and restrictions and limitations are new.

A further indication of the same spirit is to be found in the fact that the Bar Association of Cape Town made an attempt to pass a regulation to prevent people other than those of European descent from qualifying to practice in the law courts. These things indicate a change coming over South African opinion, even in Cape Colony, in regard to native rights and native opportunities. In the old days, when the missionaries were practically the dominant factor, they undoubtedly stood for giving natives the chance of occupying the best positions for which their talent and education fitted them. Nowadays, under the competition that exists, and with the growth of education and of ability, the competition between white and coloured is becoming more keen, and, as a consequence, there is a very natural feeling on the part of the white that he may prevent the native from rising, lest he compete him out of existence, and for that reason, as much as for any other, the provisions of this Bill should be carefully safeguarded, so as to prevent the coloured people and the natives of South Africa from being subjected to injustice at the hands of this House after the measure has become law. Both in Cape Colony and Natal equal rights were guaranteed under the charters and the Constitution granted to those places by the House, and quite recently the Under-Secretary himself made the proud boast that if anyone is admitted under the British flag he must be a potential citizen and must sooner or later be given equal rights with all men. That is the claim we make from these benches, and seek to enforce.

I will not deal with the question of native reservations, except to say that I am one of those who entirely agree that the Schedule is both wise and desirable. At the same time it will require amendments in several important particulars if it is to prove satisfactory for the natives of the different reservations and territories. We shall ask the franchise rights to be preserved where they exist against the possibility of being tampered with except in this House; that the qualification with respect to European descent shall be removed from the Cape Colony and from Natal; that the native territories and reservations shall not be under the control of the South African Parliament save with the consent of the peoples affected. We have no right, I submit, to compel these peoples who have voluntarily come under our protection to sever themselves from the Crown and put themselves under the protection of a Parliament which has yet to justify its existence and prove to those peoples that they may safely trust themselves to its care and to its guidance.

I regard this Bill as being a vital step in connection with the policy for which this country has hitherto stood. I venture to say that there is no Member of the House of Commons, no matter where he sits or to which party he belongs, who will rise in his place and justify the provisions of this measure. No one has done so yet, and I do not think that anyone will do so, and if it be said that to alter the measure will be to wreck the prospects of union, I do not believe it. I refuse to believe that the Dutch people in South Africa value union so little that they would wreck the whole scheme because the House of Commons insists upon protecting the franchise for the natives in Cape Colony and removing the colour disqualification which the Bill contains. To say that the Bill would be wrecked because of these Amendments is almost an insult to the zeal with which these men have worked to bring about Union in that vast territory. But the point is that, for the first time we are asked to write over the portals of the British Empire: "Abandon hope all ye who enter here." So far as colour is concerned, this Bill lays it down that no native or person of other than European descent can ever hope to aspire to membership in the Parliament of South Africa, and if a native or a person of colour cannot hope to aspire to membership in that Parliament, to rob them of the franchise is a very short and very small step. I hope, therefore, that if only for the sake of the traditions of our dealings with natives in the past, this Bill—before it leaves the House of Commons—will be so amended as to make it a real unifying Bill in South Africa. At present it is a Bill to unify the white races, to disfranchise the coloured races, and not to promote union between the races in South Africa, but rather to still further embitter the relationships. If only from that point of view, it ought to be amended before it leaves the House.

Mr. ELLIS J. GRIFFITH: If Members of the House will refer to the preamble of the Bill, they will see that it is to secure "the welfare and the future progress of South Africa." There are 36 million natives and coloured people in South Africa, and I shall address the House from that point of view. It is, I think, a little illuminating to know how this draft Bill was prepared. The South African Convention sat from October last year until February this year. It sat with closed doors. There was no native representative at it; there was no representative of the Imperial Government present, and, although I have no doubt they would know from time to time what was going on, it was not until 9th February this year that the first draft was published, and that the native and coloured population of South Africa knew anything of this draft Constitution I take that as an important aspect of the case, because directly the draft Constitution was published the native and coloured population met in congress after congress, to which hundreds of delegates were sent from throughout South Africa. At each conference they unanimously passed resolutions directed against the objectionable clauses of this Bill. Therefore, so far as

2 I

Aneurin Bevan introduces the Bill to create the National Health Service

Neil Kinnock began his political life as a left winger who went on to lead his party, take on the hard left and defeat them, and by his reforms open the door through which, a few years later, Tony Blair would pass to take Labour into Government with an unprecedented series of election victories.

By the time of the Labour landslide in 1997, the party had been in Opposition for 18 years, but it was Neil Kinnock who was credited by many with putting it on the road to recovery and electability. In frustration at losing to John Major at the 1992 general election, he resigned from the leadership after which his career finally took him to vice-presidency of the European Commission and then the House of Lords.

He was born in the south Wales town of Tredegar where his father was a miner and his mother a nurse. After leaving school he won a place at University College, Cardiff – famously describing himself in later years as "the first Kinnock in a thousand generations" to go to university. Education was his passion, which he regarded as the way out of poverty and under-achievement, and after university he worked for four years until 1970 as a tutor for the Workers' Educational Association.

In that year's general election, which Labour unexpectedly lost, he was returned for the mining constituency of Bedwellty, a few miles from the community where he had been born and grew up. He spent the next nine years on the Back Benches during which time he successfully led the opposition to Welsh devolution, which was overwhelmingly rejected in the 1979 referendum.

In 1974 he was appointed Parliamentary Private Secretary to Michael Foot, the Secretary of State for Employment, and in 1978 he was elected to the party's National Executive Committee. After Labour's defeat to Margaret Thatcher in the 1979 election, he was appointed to the Front Bench as shadow Education Secretary.

Under Michael Foot, Labour went into the 1983 general election with a strongly socialist manifesto promising unilateral nuclear disarmament, renationalisation and pulling out of the European Community. It was described by Gerald Kaufman as "the longest suicide note in history." Labour was fighting a Margaret Thatcher who was buoyed up by victory in the Falklands war. She romped home with a majority of 144, the largest of any party since 1945.

The Labour party was in disarray and looking for a new leader. Neil Kinnock was put up against Roy Hattersley and won decisively. Among his early appointments once in post were to give two young and up and coming MPs named Tony Blair and Gordon Brown their first jobs on the Labour Front Bench.

Barely five months after taking over, he was confronted with the 1984-85 miners' strike. He supported the miners in their fight to sustain Britain's coal industry, but he publicly opposed the tactics embarked upon by the mineworkers' leader, Arthur Scargill, not least in calling a strike without conducting a ballot of his members.

His speeches to the party conference in 1985 were among his most memorable. He launched a vehement attack on the NUM and its leaders and a blistering and humiliating assault on Militant Tendency councillors in Liverpool, led by Derek Hatton, who, he said, had orchestrated a situation of "grotesque chaos" in the city. The following year, Hatton was expelled from the party.

He led the party into the 1987 general election and cut the Tory majority to 102. It gave him the mandate to continue the process of modernising Labour. In 1990, the Conservatives ousted Margaret Thatcher and he faced John Major across the Dispatch Box. He took the party into his second general election as leader in 1992 with a reasonable expectation of victory. It was to elude him. In spite of cutting the Tory majority to 21, he felt unable to carry on and he resigned, convinced that the influence of the Conservative press had secured for that party a victory that it could not have achieved for itself "on the basis of its record, its programme and its character."

In 1995 he resigned his House of Commons seat – since the 1983 election renamed Islwyn – and was appointed a member of the European Commission. He became the Vice President in 1999, a post he held until 2004 when he was made chairman of the British Council. In January 2005 he became a member of the House of Lords as Baron Kinnock of Bedwellty, from which platform he vowed to campaign in the cause of education and democratic reform of the Lords.

Sparkling Bevanisms in a speech that was the model of calm reasoning

BY RT HON LORD KINNOCK OF BEDWELLTY

My choice of Aneurin Bevan's speech moving the Second Reading of the 1946 National Health Service Bill was determined by its substance and its style and my unreserved admiration for Bevan as a democratic socialist, a parliamentarian, an orator and a Minister.

The substance is there in the practical miracle wrought by applying the principles that "money ought not to be permitted to stand in the way of obtaining an efficient health service..." and "a person ought not to be financially deterred from seeking medical assistance at the earliest possible stage..."

Bevan's intimate understanding of the machinery and method of health care; his mastery of technical detail; his pragmatism, which ensured that doctors retained – indeed, gained further – clinical independence whilst becoming coherently organised for service to the community, are all demonstrated in a speech that is longer on informed argument than flowing rhetoric.

But there are sparkling Bevanisms, too: "I would rather be kept alive in the efficient if cold altruism of a large hospital than expire in a gush of warm sympathy in a small one" is a vintage example.

The references to the "caprice of private charity", the absurdity of thanking colliery companies for financing hospitals when the funding actually came from the workers, the contempt for the "vaulting ambitions" of those cottage hospital bosses who valued status above patient care, are all lacerating references to just some of the pre-NHS deficiencies familiar to Bevan and his contemporaries.

Nye's tone was not always temperate, but this speech was a model of calm reasoning. He could afford that. There was revolution enough in the purpose and the effect of the legislation that he was introducing "to universalise the best", to "lift the shadow from millions of homes", to relieve suffering and to save life.

Bevan and the Government to which he belonged were using the process of law, supported by democratic majority, for the purposes of human emancipation.

That, most of all, is what Parliament is for. Aneurin Bevan called the House of Commons "an arsenal for progress." No warrior of freedom ever used it to better effect.

ORDERS OF THE DAY

NATIONAL HEALTH SERVICE BILL

Order for Second Reading read.

3.47 p.m.

The Minister of Health (Mr. Aneurin Bevan): I beg to move, '' That the Bill be now read a Second time.''

In the last two years there has been such a clamour from sectional interests in the field of national health that we are in danger of forgetting why these proposals are brought forward at all. It is, therefore, very welcome to me—and I am quite certain to hon. Members in all parts of the House—that consideration should now be given, not to this or that sectional interest, but to the requirements of the British people as a whole. The scheme which anyone must draw up dealing with national health must necessarily be conditioned and limited by the evils it is intended to remove. Many of those who have drawn up paper plans for the health services appear to have followed the dictates of abstract principles, and not the concrete requirements of the actual situation as it exists. They drew up all sorts of tidy schemes on paper, which would be quite inoperable in practice.

The first reason why a health scheme of this sort is necessary at all is because it has been the firm conclusion of all parties that money ought not to be permitted to stand in the way of obtaining an efficient health service. Although it is true that the national health insurance system provides a general practitioner service and caters for something like 21 million of the population, the rest of the population have to pay whenever they desire the services of a doctor. It is cardinal to a proper health organisation that a person ought not to be financially deterred from seeking medical assistance at the earliest possible stage. It is one of the evils of having to buy medical advice that, in addition to the natural anxiety that may arise because people do not like to hear unpleasant things about themselves, and therefore tend to postpone consultation as long as possible, there is the financial anxiety caused by having to pay doctors' bills. Therefore, the first evil that we must deal with is that which exists as a consequence of the fact that the whole thing is the wrong way round. A person ought to be able to receive medical and hospital help without being involved in financial anxiety.

In the second place, the national health insurance scheme does not provide for the self-employed, nor, of course, for the families of dependants. It depends on insurance qualification, and no matter how ill you are, if you cease to be insured you cease to have free doctoring. Furthermore, it gives no backing to the doctor in the form of specialist services. The doctor has to provide himself, he has to use his own discretion and his own personal connections, in order to obtain hospital treatment for his patients and in order to get them specialists, and in very many cases, of course— in an overwhelming number of cases—the services of a specialist are not available to poor people.

Not only is this the case, but our hospital organisation has grown up with no plan, with no system; it is unevenly distributed over the country and indeed it is one of the tragedies of the situation, that very often the best hospital facilities are available where they are least needed. In the older industrial districts of Great Britain hospital facilities are inadequate. Many of the hospitals are too small—very much too small. About 70 per cent. have less than 100 beds, and over 30 per cent. have less than 30. No one can possibly pretend that hospitals so small can provide general hospital treatment. There is a tendency in some quarters to defend the very small hospital on the ground of its localism and intimacy, and for other rather imponderable reasons of that sort, but everybody knows today that if a hospital is to be efficient it must provide a number of specialised services. Although I am not myself a devotee of bigness for bigness sake, I would rather be kept alive in the efficient if cold altruism of a large hospital than expire in a gush of warm sympathy in a small one.

In addition to these defects, the health of the people of Britain is not properly looked after in one or two other respects. The condition of the teeth of the people of Britain is a national reproach. As a consequence of dental treatment having to be bought, it has not been demanded on a scale to stimulate the creation of sufficient dentists, and in consequence there is a woeful shortage of dentist the present time. Furthermore, about 25 per cent. of the people of Great Britain can obtain their spectacles and get their eyes tested and seen to by means of the assistance given by the approved societies, but the general mass of the people have not such facilities. Another of the evils from which this country suffers is the fact that sufficient attention has not been given to deafness, and hardly any attention has been given so far to the provision of cheap hearing aids and their proper maintenance. I hope to be able to make very shortly a welcome announcement on this question.

One added disability from which our health system suffers is the isolation of mental health from the rest of the health services. Although the present Bill does not rewrite the Lunacy Acts—we shall have to come to that later on—nevertheless, it does, for the first time, bring mental health into the general system of health services. It ought to be possible, and this should be one of the objectives of any civilised health service, for a person who feels mental distress, or who fears that he is liable to become unbalanced in any way to go to a general hospital to get advice and assistance, so that the condition may not develop into a more serious stage. All these disabilities our health system suffers from at the present time, and one of the first merits of this Bill is that it provides a universal health service without any insurance qualifications of any sort. It is available to the whole population, and not only is it available to the whole population freely, but it is intended, through the health service, to generalise the best health advice and treatment. It is intended that there shall be no limitation on the kind of assistance given—the general practitioner service, the specialist, the hospitals, eye treatment, spectacles, dental treatment, hearing facilities, all these are to be made available free.

There will be some limitations for a while, because we are short of many things. We have not enough dentists and it will therefore be necessary for us, in the meantime, to give priority treatment to certain classes—expectant and nursing mothers, children, school children in particular and later on we hope adolescents. Finally we trust that we shall be able to build up a dental service for the whole population. We are short of nurses and

we are short, of course, of hospital accommodation, and so it will be some time before the Bill can fructify fully in effective universal service. Nevertheless, it is the object of the Bill, and of the scheme, to provide this as soon as possible, and to provide it universally.

Specialists will be available not only at institutions but for domiciliary visits when needed. Hon. Members in all parts of the House know from their own experience that very many people have suffered unnecessarily because the family has not had the financial resources to call in skilled people. The specialist services, therefore, will not only be available at the hospitals, but will be at the back of the general practitioner should he need them. The practical difficulties of carrying out all these principles and services are very great. When I approached this problem, I made up my mind that I was not going to permit any sectional or vested interests to stand in the way of providing this very valuable service for the British people.

There are, of course, three main instruments through which it is intended that the Health Bill should be worked. There are the hospitals; there are the general practitioners; and there are the health centres. The hospitals are in many ways the vertebrae of the health system, and I first examined what to do with the hospitals. The voluntary hospitals of Great Britain have done invaluable work. When hospitals could not be provided by any other means, they came along. The voluntary hospital system of this country has a long history of devotion and sacrifice behind it, and it would be a most frivolously minded man who would denigrate in any way the immense services the voluntary hospitals have rendered to this country. But they have been established often by the caprice of private charity. They bear no relationship to each other. Two hospitals close together often try to provide the same specialist services unnecessarily, while other areas have not that kind of specialist service at all. They are, as I said earlier, badly distributed throughout the country. It is unfortunate that often endowments are left to finance hospitals in those parts of the country where the well-to-do live while, in very many other of our industrial and rural districts there is inadequate hospital accommodation. These voluntary hospitals are, very many of them, far too small! and, therefore, to

[Mr. Bevan.]
leave them as independent units is quite impracticable.

Furthermore—I want to be quite frank with the House—I believe it is repugnant to a civilised community for hospitals to have to rely upon private charity. I believe we ought to have left hospital flag days behind. I have always felt a shudder of repulsion when I have seen nurses and sisters who ought to be at their work, and students who ought to be at their work, going about the streets collecting money for the hospitals. I do not believe there is an hon. Member of this House who approves that system. It is repugnant, and we must leave it behind—entirely. But the implications of doing this are very considerable.

I have been forming some estimates of what might happen to voluntary hospital finance when the all-in insurance contributions fall to be paid by the people of Great Britain, when the Bill is passed and becomes an Act, and they are entitled to free hospital services. The estimates I have go to show that between 80 per cent. and 90 per cent. of the revenues of the voluntary hospitals in these circumstances will be provided by public funds, by national or rate funds. [An Hon. Member: "By workers' contributions."] And, of course, as the hon. Member reminds me, in very many parts of the country it is a travesty to call them voluntary hospitals. In the mining districts, in the textile districts, in the districts where there are heavy industries it is the industrial population who pay the weekly contributions for the maintenance of the hospitals. When I was a miner I used to find that situation, when I was on the hospital committee. We had an annual meeting and a cordial vote of thanks was moved and passed with great enthusiasm to the managing director of the colliery company for his generosity towards the hospital; and when I looked at the balance sheet, I saw that $97\frac{1}{2}$ per cent. of the revenues were provided by the miners' own contributions; but nobody passed a vote of thanks to the miners.

Major Guy Lloyd (Renfrew, Eastern): What was the right hon. Gentleman doing?

Mr. Bevan: I can assure the hon. and gallant Member that I was no more silent then than I am now. But, of course, it is a misuse of language to call these "voluntary hospitals." They are not maintained by legally enforced contributions; but, mainly, the workers pay for them because they know they will need the hospitals, and they are afraid of what they would have to pay if they did not provide them. So it is, I say, an impossible situation for the State to find something like 90 per cent. of the revenues of these hospitals and still to call them "voluntary." So I decided, for this and other reasons, that the voluntary hospitals must be taken over.

I knew very well when I decided this that it would give rise to very considerable resentment in many quarters, but, quite frankly, I am not concerned about the voluntary hospitals' authorities: I am concerned with the people whom the hospitals are supposed to serve. Every investigation which has been made into this problem has established that the proper hospital unit has to comprise about 1,000 beds—not in the same building but, nevertheless, the general and specialist hospital services can be provided only in a group of that size. This means that a number of hospitals have to be pooled, linked together, in order to provide a unit of that sort. This cannot be done effectively if each hospital is a separate, autonomous body. It is proposed that each of these groups should have a large general hospital, providing general hospital facilities and services, and that there should be a group round it of small feeder hospitals. Many of the cottage hospitals strive to give services that they are not able to give. It very often happens that a cottage hospital harbours ambitions to the hurt of the patients, because they strive to reach a status that they never can reach. In these circumstances, the welfare of the patients is sacrificed to the vaulting ambitions of those in charge of the hospital. If, therefore, these voluntary hospitals are to be grouped in this way, it is necessary that they should submit themselves to proper organisation, and that submission, in our experience, is impracticable if the hospitals, all of them, remain under separate management.

Now, this decision to take over the voluntary hospitals meant, that I then had to decide to whom to give them. Who was to be the receiver? So I turned to an examination of the local government hospital system. Many of the local authori-

in Great Britain have never been able to exercise their hospital powers. They are too poor. They are too small. Furthermore, the local authorities of Great Britain inherited their hospitals from the Poor Law, and some of them are monstrous buildings, a cross between a workhouse and a barracks—[An HON. MEMBER: '' And a prison.'']—or a prison. The local authorities are helpless in these matters. They have not been able to afford much money. Some local authorities are first-class. Some of the best hospitals in this country are local government hospitals. But, when I considered what to do with the voluntary hospitals when they had been taken over, and who was to receive them I had to reject the local government unit, because the local authority area is no more an effective gathering ground for the patients of the hospitals than the voluntary hospitals themselves. My hon. Friend said that some of them are too small, and some of them too large. London is an example of being too small and too large at the same time.

It is quite impossible, therefore, to hand over the voluntary hospitals to the local authorities. Furthermore—and this is an argument of the utmost importance—if it be our contract with the British people, if it be our intention that we should universalise the best, that we shall promise every citizen in this country the same standard of service, how can that be articulated through a rate-borne institution which means that the poor authority will not be able to carry out the same thing at all? It means that once more we shall be faced with all kinds of anomalies, just in those areas where hospital facilities are most needed, and in those very conditions where the mass of the poor people will be unable to find the finance to supply the hospitals. Therefore, for reasons which must be obvious —because the local authorities are too small, because their financial capacities are unevenly distributed —I decided that local authorities could not be effective hospital administration units. There are, of course, a large number of hospitals in addition to the general hospitals which the local authorities possess. Tuberculosis sanatoria, isolation hospitals, infirmaries of various kinds, rehabilitation, and all kinds of other hospitals are all necessary in a general hospital service. So I decided that the only thing

to do was to create an entirely new hospital service, to take over the voluntary hospitals, and to take over the local government hospitals and to organise them as a single hospital service. If we are to carry out our obligation and to provide the people of Great Britain, no matter where they may be, with the same level of service, then the nation itself will have to carry the expenditure, and cannot put it upon the shoulders of any other authority.

A number of investigations have been made into this subject from time to time, and the conclusion has always been reached that the effective hospital unit should be associated with the medical school. If you grouped the hospitals in about 16 to 20 regions around the medical schools, you would then have within those regions the wide range of disease and disability which would provide the basis for your specialised hospital service. Furthermore, by grouping hospitals around the medical schools, we should be providing what is very badly wanted, and that is a means by which the general practitioners are kept in more intimate association with new medical thought and training. One of the disabilities, one of the shortcomings of our existing medical service, is the intellectual isolation of the general practitioners in many parts of the country. The general practitioner, quite often, practises in loneliness and does not come into sufficiently intimate association with his fellow craftsmen and has not the stimulus of that association, and in consequence of that the general practitioners have not got access to new medical knowledge in a proper fashion. By this association of the general practitioner with the medical schools through the regional hospital organisation, it will be possible to refresh and replenish the fund of knowledge at the disposal of the general practitioner.

This has always been advised as the best solution of the difficulty. It has this great advantage to which I call the close attention of hon. Members. It means that the bodies carrying out the hospital services of the country are, at the same time, the planners of the hospital service. One of the defects of the other scheme is that the planning authority and executive authority are different. The result is that you get paper planning or bad execution. By making the regional board and regional organisation responsible both for the planning and the administration of the plans, we get a better result, and we

[Mr. Bevan.]

get from time to time, adaptation of the plans by the persons accumulating the experience in the course of their administration. The other solutions to this problem which I have looked at all mean that you have an advisory body of planners in the background who are not able themselves to accumulate the experience necessary to make good planners. The regional hospital organisation is the authority with which the specialised services are to be associated, because, as I have explained, this specialised service can be made available for an area of that size, and cannot be made available over a small area.

When we come to an examination of this in Committee, I daresay there will be different points of view about the constitution of the regional boards. It is not intended that the regional boards should be conferences of persons representing different interests and different organisations. If we do that, the regional boards will not be able to achieve reasonable and efficient homogeneity. It is intended that they should be drawn from members of the profession, from the health authorities in the area, from the medical schools and from those who have long experience in voluntary hospital administration. While leaving ourselves open to take the best sort of individuals on these hospital boards which we can find, we hope before very long to build up a high tradition of hospital administration in the boards themselves. Any system which made the boards conferences, any proposal which made the members delegates, would at once throw the hospital administration into chaos. Although I am perfectly prepared and shall be happy to cooperate with hon. Members in all parts of the House in discussing how the boards should be constituted, I hope I shall not be pressed to make these regional boards merely representative of different interests and different areas. The general hospital administration, therefore, centres in that way.

When we come to the general practitioners we are, of course, in an entirely different field. The proposal which I have made is that the general practitioner shall not be in direct contract with the Ministry of Health, but in contract with new bodies. There exists in the medical profession a great resistance to coming under the authority of local government —a great resistance, with which I, to some extent, sympathise. There is a feeling in the medical profession that the general practitioner would be liable to come too much under the medical officer of health, who is the administrative doctor. This proposal does not put the doctor under the local authority; it puts the doctor in contract with an entirely new body—the local executive council, coterminous with the local health area, county or county borough. On that executive council, the dentists, doctors and chemists will have half the representation. In fact, the whole scheme provides a greater degree of professional representation for the medical profession than any other scheme I have seen.

I have been criticised in some quarters for doing that. I will give the answer now: I have never believed that the demands of a democracy are necessarily satisfied merely by the opportunity of putting a cross against someone's name every four or five years. I believe that democracy exists in the active participation in administration and policy. Therefore, I believe that it is a wise thing to give the doctors full participation in the administration of their own profession. They must, of course, necessarily be subordinated to lay control—we do not want the opposite danger of syndicalism. Therefore, the communal interests must always be safeguarded in this administration. The doctors will be in contract with an executive body of this sort. One of the advantages of that proposal is that the doctors do not become—as some of them have so wildly stated—civil servants. Indeed, one of the advantages of the scheme is that it does not create an additional civil servant.

It imposes no constitutional disability upon any person whatsoever. Indeed, by taking the hospitals from the local authorities and putting them under the regional boards, large numbers of people will be enfranchised who are now disfranchised from participation in local government. So far from this being a huge bureaucracy with all the doctors little civil servants—the slaves of the Minister of Health, as I have seen it described—instead of that, the doctors are under contract with bodies which are not under the local authority, and which are, at the same time, ever open to their own influence and control.

One of the chief problems that I was up against in considering this scheme was the distribution of the general practitioner service throughout the country. The distribution, at the moment, is most uneven. In South Shields before the war there were 4,100 persons per doctor; in Bath 1,590; in Dartford nearly 3,000 and in Bromley 1,620; in Swindon 3,100; in Hastings under 1,200. That distribution of general practitioners throughout the country is most hurtful to the health of our people. It is entirely unfair, and, therefore, if the health services are to be carried out, there must be brought about a re-distribution of the general practitioners throughout the country.

Captain Crowder (Finchley): Does that mean the number on the panel or the population?

Mr. Bevan: The population. Indeed, I could amplify those figures a good deal, but I do not want to weary the House, as I have a great deal to say. It was, therefore, decided that there must be redistribution. One of the first consequences of that decision was the abolition of the sale and purchase of practices. If we are to get the doctors where we need them, we cannot possibly allow a new doctor to go in because he has bought somebody's practice. Proper distribution kills by itself the sale and purchase of practices. I know that there is some opposition to this, and I will deal with that opposition. I have always regarded the sale and purchase of medical practices as an evil in itself. It is tantamount to the sale and purchase of patients. Indeed, every argument advanced about the value of the practice is itself an argument against freedom of choice, because the assumption underlying the high value of a practice is that the patient passes from the old doctor to the new. If they did not pass there would be no value in it. I would like, therefore, to point out to the medical profession that every time they argue for high compensation for the loss of the value of their practices, it is an argument against the free choice which they claim. However, the decision to bring about the proper distribution of general practitioners throughout the country meant that the value of the practices was destroyed. We had, therefore, to consider compensation.

I have never admitted the legal claim, but I admit at once that very great hardship would be inflicted upon doctors if there were no compensation. Many of these doctors look forward to the value of their practices for their retirement. Many of them have had to borrow money to buy practices and, therefore, it would, I think, be inhuman, and certainly most unjust, if no compensation were paid for the value of the practices destroyed. The sum of £66,000,000 is very large. In fact, I think that every one will admit that the doctors are being treated very generously. However, it is not all loss, because if we had, in providing superannuation, given credit for back service, as we should have had to do, it would have cost £35 million. Furthermore, the compensation will fall to be paid to the dependants when the doctor dies, or when he retires, and so it is spread over a considerable number of years. This global sum has been arrived at by the actuaries, and over the figure, I am afraid, we have not had very much control, because the actuaries have agreed it. But the profession itself will be asked to advise as to its distribution among the claimants, because we are interested in the global sum, and the profession, of course, is interested in the equitable distribution of the fund to the claimants.

The doctors claim that the proposals of the Bill amount to direction—not all the doctors say this but some of them do. There is no direction involved at all. When the Measure starts to operate, the doctors in a particular area will be able to enter the public service in that area. A doctor newly coming along would apply to the local executive council for permission to practise in a particular area. His application would then be re-referred to the Medical Practices Committee. The Medical Practices Committee, which is mainly a professional body, would have before it the question of whether there were sufficient general practitioners in that area. If there were enough, the committee would refuse to permit the appointment. No one can really argue that that is direction, because no profession should be allowed to enter the public service in a place where it is not needed. By that method of negative control over a number of years, we hope to bring about over the country a positive redistribution of the general practitioner service. It will not affect

[Mr. Bevan.]
the existing situation, because doctors will be able to practise under the new service in the areas to which they belong, but a new doctor, as he comes on, will have to find his practice in a place inadequately served.

I cannot, at the moment, explain to the House what are going to be the rates of remuneration of doctors. The Spens Committee report is not fully available. I hope it will be out next week. I had hoped that it would be ready for this Debate, because this is an extremely important part of the subject, but I have not been able to get the full report. Therefore, it is not possible to deal with remuneration. However, it is possible to deal with some of the principles underlying the remuneration of general practitioners. Some of my hon. Friends on this side of the House are in favour of a full salaried service. I am not. I do not believe that the medical profession is ripe for it, and I cannot dispense with the principle that the payment of a doctor must in some degree be a reward for zeal, and there must be some degree of punishment for lack of it. Therefore, it is proposed that capitation should remain the main source from which a doctor will obtain his remuneration. But it is proposed that there shall be a basic salary and that for a number of very cogent reasons. One is that a young doctor entering practice for the first time needs to be kept alive while he is building up his lists. The present system by which a young man gets a load of debt around his neck in order to practise is an altogether evil one. The basic salary will take care of that.

Furthermore, the basic salary has the additional advantage of being something to which I can attach an increased amount to get doctors to go into unattractive areas. It may also—and here our position is not quite so definite—be the means of attaching additional remuneration for special courses and special acquirements. The basic salary, however, must not be too large otherwise it is a disguised form of capitation. Therefore, the main source at the moment through which a general practitioner will obtain his remuneration will be capitation. I have also made—and I quite frankly admit it to the House—a further concession which I know will be repugnant in some quarters. The doctor, the general practitioner and the

specialist, will be able to obtain fees, but not from anyone who is on any of their own lists, nor will a doctor be able to obtain fees from persons on the lists of his partner, nor from those he has worked with in group practice, but I think it is impracticable to prevent him having any fees at all. To do so would be to create a black market. There ought to be nothing to prevent anyone having advice from another doctor other than his own. Hon. Members know what happens in this field sometimes. An individual hears that a particular doctor in some place is good at this, that or the other thing, and wants to go along for a consultation. He gets a consultation and pays a fee for it. If the other doctor is better than his own all he will need to do is to transfer to him and he gets him free. It would be unreasonable to keep the patient paying fees to a doctor whose services can be got free. So the amount of fee payment on the part of the general population will be quite small. Indeed, I confess at once if the amount of fee paying is great, the system will break down, because the whole purpose of this scheme is to provide free treatment with no fee paying at all. The same principle applies to the hospitals.

Mr. Sydney Silverman (Nelson and Colne): Before we leave that point, I should like to ask whether we are to gather from the right hon. Gentleman that a doctor will be entitled to receive a fee for consultation from a patient who is on some other doctor's list?

Mr. Bevan: Yes.

Mr. Silverman: I always understood it was improper for a doctor to see a patient who was being treated by another doctor.

Mr. Bevan: He would not be treated by another doctor, but would be on the panel of the other doctor. We are hoping when our scheme gets going properly that everybody will be on somebody's panel, and unless an individual on someone else's panel is able to pay a fee no one will be able to pay a fee.

Mr. Logan (Liverpool, Scotland Division): If a patient can get specialist advice under the scheme what necessity will there be for him to pay for a consultant?

Mr. Bevan: I hope there will be very little necessity. Nevertheless, this is a field in which idiosyncrasies are prevalent. If an individual wishes to consult, there is no reason why he should be stopped. As I have said, the fact that a person can transfer from one doctor to another ought to keep fee paying within reasonable proportions.

The same principle applies to the hospitals. Specialists in hospitals will be allowed to have fee-paying patients. I know this is criticised and I sympathise with some of the reasons for the criticism, but we are driven inevitably to this fact, that unless we permit some fee-paying patients in the public hospitals, there will be a rash of nursing homes all over the country. If people wish to pay for additional amenities, or something to which they attach value, like privacy in a single ward, we ought to aim at providing such facilities for everyone who wants them. But while we have inadequate hospital facilities, and while rebuilding is postponed it inevitably happens that some people will want to buy something more than the general health service is providing. If we do not permit fees in hospitals, we will lose many specialists from the public hospitals for they will go to nursing homes. I believe that nursing homes ought to be discouraged. They cannot provide general hospital facilities, and we want to keep our specialists attached to our hospitals and not send them into nursing homes. Behind this there is a principle of some importance. If the State owned a theatre it would not charge the same prices for the different seats. [*Interruption.*] It is not entirely analogous, but it is an illustration. For example, in the dental service the same principle will prevail. The State will provide a certain standard of dentistry free, but if a person wants to have his teeth filled with gold, the State will not provide that.

The third instrument to which the health services are to be articulated is the health centre, to which we attach very great importance indeed. It has been described in some places as an experimental idea, but we want it to be more than that, because to the extent that general practitioners can operate through health centres in their own practice, to that extent will be raised the general standard of the medical profession as a whole. Furthermore, the general practitioner cannot afford the apparatus necessary for a proper diagnosis in his own surgery. This will be available at the health centre.

The health centre may well be the maternity and child welfare clinic of the local authority also. The provision of the health centre is, therefore, imposed as a duty on the local authority. There has been criticism that this creates a trichotomy in the services. It is not a trichotomy at all. If you have complete unification it would bring you back to paper planning. You cannot get all services through the regional authority, because there are many immediate and personal services which the local authority can carry out better than anybody else. So, it is proposed to leave those personal services to the local authority, and some will be carried out at the health centre. The centres will vary; there will be large centres at which there will be dental clinics, maternity and child welfare services, and general practitioners' consultative facilities, and there will also be smaller centres—surgeries where practitioners can see their patients.

Mr. Sidney Marshall (Sutton and Cheam): Will the executive councils have anything to do with the public health centres, or will the latter be managed entirely by the public health authorities?

Mr. Bevan: By the health authorities. The health centre itself will be provided by the local health authority, and facilities will be made available there to the general practitioner. The small ones are necessary, because some centres may be a considerable distance from peoples homes. So it will be necessary to have simpler ones, nearer their homes, fixed in a constellation with the larger ones.

Mr. Marshall: Will the executive councils have anything to do with it? That is the question I asked.

Mr. Bevan: The representatives on the local executives will be able to coordinate what is happening at the health centres. As I say, we regard these health centres as extremely valuable, and their creation will be encouraged in every possible way. Doctors will be encouraged to practise there, where they will have great facilities. It will, of course, be some time before these centres can be established everywhere, because of the absence of these facilities.

There you have the three main instruments through which it is proposed that the health services of the future

[Mr. Bevan.]

should be articulated. There has been some criticism. Some have said that the preventive services should be under the same authority as the curative services. I wonder whether Members who advance that criticism really envisage the situation which will arise. What are the preventive services? Housing, water, sewerage, river pollution prevention, food inspection —are all these to be under a regional board? If so, a regional board of that sort would want the Albert Hall in which to meet. This, again, is paper planning. It is unification for unification's sake. There must be a frontier at which the local joins the national health service. You can fix it here or there, but it must be fixed somewhere. It is said that there is some contradiction in the health scheme because some services are left to the local authority and the rest to the national scheme. Well, day is joined to night by twilight, but nobody has suggested that it is a contradiction in nature. The argument that this is a contradiction in health services is purely pedantic, and has no relation to the facts.

It is also suggested that because maternity and child welfare services come under the local authority, and gynæcological services come under the regional board, that will make for confusion. Why should it? Continuity between one and the other is maintained by the user. The hospital is there to be used. If there are difficulties in connection with birth, the gynæcologist at the hospital centre can look after them. All that happens is that the midwife will be in charge—the mother will be examined properly, as she ought to be examined—then, if difficulties are anticipated, she can have her child in hospital, where she can be properly looked after by the gynæcologist. When she recovers, and is a perfectly normal person, she can go to the maternity and child welfare centre for post-natal treatment. There is no confusion there. The confusion is in the minds of those who are criticising the proposal on the ground that there is a trichotomy in the services, between the local authority, the regional board and the health centre.

I apologise for detaining the House so long, but there are other matters to which I must make some reference. The two Amendments on the Order Paper rather astonish me. The hon. Member for Denbigh (Sir H. Morris-Jones) informs me,

in his Amendment, that I have not sufficiently consulted the medical profession——

Sir Henry Morris-Jones (Denbigh): That is not the wording on the Order Paper. I said there were no consultations.

Mr. Bevan: I intend to read the Amendment to show how extravagant the hon. Member has been. He says that he and his friends are

"... unable to agree to a measure containing such far-reaching proposals involving the entire population without any consultations having taken place between the Minister and the organisations and bodies representing those who will be responsible for carrying out its provisions...."

I have had prepared a list of conferences I have attended. I have met the medical profession, the dental profession, the pharmacists, nurses and midwives, voluntary hospitals, local authorities, eye services, medical aid services, herbalists, insurance committees, and various other organisations. I have had 20 conferences. The consultations have been very wide. In addition, my officials have had 13 conferences, so that altogether there have been 33 conferences with the different branches of the profession about the proposals. Can anybody argue that that is not adequate consultation? Of course, the real criticism is that I have not conducted negotiations. I am astonished that such a charge should lie in the mouth of any Member of the House. If there is one thing that will spell the death of the House of Commons it is for a Minister to negotiate Bills before they are presented to the House. I had no negotiations, because once you negotiate with outside bodies two things happen. They are made aware of the nature of the proposals before the House of Commons itself; and furthermore, the Minister puts himself into an impossible position, because, if he has agreed things with somebody outside he is bound to resist Amendments from Members in the House. Otherwise he does not play fair with them. I protested against this myself when I was a Private Member. I protested bitterly, and I am not prepared, strange though it may seem, to do something as a Minister which as a Private Member I thought was wrong. So there has not been negotiation, and there will not be negotiation, in this matter. The House of Commons is supreme, and the House of Commons must assert its supremacy, and not allow itself to be dictated to by anybody, no matter how powerful and how strong he may be.

Sir H. Morris-Jones: Would the right hon. Gentleman apply that doctrine to the Miners' Federation?

Mr. Bevan: Certainly. That is exactly what I did. The hon. Member was a Member of the House at the time, and he should remember it These consultations have taken place over a very wide field, and, as a matter of fact, have produced quite a considerable amount of agreement. The opposition to the Bill is not as strong as it was thought it would be. On the contrary, there is very considerable support for this Measure among the doctors themselves. I myself have been rather aggrieved by some of the statements which have been made. They have misrepresented the proposals to a very large extent, but as these proposals become known to the medical profession, they will appreciate them, because nothing should please a good doctor more than to realise that, in future, neither he nor his patient will have any financial anxiety arising out of illness.

The leaders of the Opposition have on the Order Paper an Amendment which expresses indignation at the extent to which we are interfering with charitable foundations. The Amendment states that the Bill

" gravely menaces all charitable foundations by diverting to purposes other than those intended by the donors the trust funds of the voluntary hospitals."

I must say that when I read that Amendment I was amused. I have been looking up some precedents. I would like to say, in passing, that a great many of these endowments and foundations have been diversions from the Chancellor of the Exchequer. The main contributor was the Chancellor of the Exchequer. But I seem to remember that, in 1941, hon. Members opposite were very much vexed by what might happen to the public schools, and they came to the House and asked for the permission of the House to lay sacrilegious hands upon educational endowments centuries old. I remember protesting against it at the time—not, however, on the grounds of sacrilege. These endowments had been left to the public schools, many of them for the maintenance of the buildings, but hon. Members opposite, being concerned lest

the war might affect their favourite schools, came to the House and allowed the diversion of money from that purpose to the payment of the salaries of the teachers and the masters. There have been other interferences with endowments. Wales has been one of the criminals. Disestablishment interfered with an enormous number of endowments. Scotland also is involved. Scotland has been behaving in a most sacrilegious manner; a whole lot of endowments have been waived by Scottish Acts. I could read out a large number of them, but I shall not do so.

Do hon. Members opposite suggest that the intelligent planning of the modern world must be prevented by the endowments of the dead? Are we to consider the dead more than the living? Are the patients of our hospitals to be sacrificed to a consideration of that sort?

Major Lloyd: Henry VIII did it.

Mr. Bevan: He was a good king, too; he had many good points. We are not, in fact, diverting these endowments from charitable purposes. It would have been perfectly proper for the Chancellor of the Exchequer to have taken over these funds, because they were willed for hospital purposes, and he could use them for hospital purposes; be we are doing no such thing. The teaching hospitals will be left with all their liquid endowments and more power. We are not interfering with the teaching hospitals' endowments. Academic medical education will be more free in the future than it has been in the past. Furthermore, something like £32 million belonging to the voluntary hospitals as a whole is not going to be taken from them. On the contrary, we are going to use it, and a very valuable thing it will be; we are going to use it as a shock absorber between the Treasury, the central Government, and the hospital administration. They will be given it as free money which they can spend over and above the funds provided by the State.

I welcome the opportunity of doing that, because I appreciate, as much as hon. Members in any part of the House, the absolute necessity for having an elastic, resilient service, subject to local influence as well as to central influence; and that can be accomplished by leaving this money in their hands. I shall be

[Mr. Bevan.]
prepared to consider, when the Bill comes to be examined in more detail, whether any other relaxations are possible, but certainly, by leaving this money in the hands of the regional board, by allowing the regional board an annual budget and giving them freedom of movement inside that budget, by giving power to the regional board to distribute this money to the local management committees of the hospitals, by various devices of that sort, the hospitals will be responsive to local pressure and subject to local influence as well as to central direction.

I think that on those grounds the proposals can be defended. They cover a very wide field indeed, to a great deal of which I have not been able to make reference; but I should have thought it ought to have been a pride to hon. Members in all parts of the House that Great Britain is able to embark upon an ambitious scheme of this proportion. When it is carried out, it will place this country in the forefront of all countries of the world in medical services. I myself, if I may say a personal word, take very great pride and great pleasure in being able to introduce a Bill of this comprehensiveness and value. I believe it will lift the shadow from millions of homes. It will keep very many people alive who might otherwise be dead. It will relieve suffering. It will produce higher standards for the medical profession. It will be a great contribution towards the wellbeing of the common people of Great Britain. For that reason, and for the other reasons I have mentioned, I hope hon. Members will give the Bill a Second Reading.

5.0 p.m.

Mr. Richard Law (Kensington, South): The right hon. Gentleman the Minister of Health has received an ovation from the Benches behind him for a speech as eloquent, as unconvincing, and as disingenuous as any I have ever heard from him. The right hon. Gentleman had a great opportunity with this Bill. He had the chance of bringing to the House of Commons proposals which would have been warmly welcomed by every party in the House and by every section of opinion, lay or medical, outside. Instead, he has preferred to bring to the House these proposals which are in fact feared and distrusted by the great majority of those who will be called upon to make them effective. The right hon. Gentle-

man might have done so much without doing this. He might have done so much more if he had been content to do a little less.

It is surely a most extraordinary thing that the right hon. Gentleman the Minister of Health, who has absolutely no administrative experience of a great Government Department, and who has no great knowledge, either practical or theoretical, of the very important subject matter with which this Bill is dealing, should have set his own intuition and judgment against all those best informed in the medical profession and in the hospital services outside the House. In fact, the right hon. Gentleman has done just that. The British Hospital Association and the British Medical Association are opposed to this Bill. [*Laughter.*] I do not know why hon. Members laugh at the mention of the British Medical Association. The British Dental Association is also opposed to this Bill, and the three Royal Colleges have criticised it with varying emphasis.

Mr. Bevan: Have the Royal Colleges placed anything on record against the Bill?

Mr. Law: The three Royal Colleges have criticised the Bill with varying emphasis—[Hon. Members: "Answer."] —and for various reasons. I think I am right in saying that the Royal College of Surgeons passed a resolution condemning aspects of the Minister's proposals in the most categorical terms. The Royal College of Obstetricians did the same. They said, if my memory serves me, that the Minister's proposals were likely to lead to a great increase in maternal mortality. [*Interruption.*] That was, I think, the purpose of a document which I have certainly seen and which emanated from the Royal College of Obstetricians. And even——

Dr. Morgan (Rochdale) *rose*——

Mr. Law: —the powerful advocacy of its President, Lord Moran, was unable to influence the Royal College of Physicians to give support to the Minister's proposals for taking over the voluntary hospitals.

Mr. Bevan: I must ask the right hon. Gentleman to amplify his statement, which otherwise might cause a great deal of alarm. Does he say that the Royal College of Obstetricians have placed on

Neil Kinnock launches attack over Westland as Mrs Thatcher faces her greatest challenge

At the time of his controversial departure from office, **Nigel Lawson** had been the longest serving Chancellor of the Exchequer since Lloyd George. During his time at the Treasury he was one of the principal architects of the Thatcher Government's policies.

Among his achievements, he was one of the protagonists of the policy of privatisation, which was to characterise the phenomenon that came to be known as Thatcherism.

After taking a first in philosophy, politics and economics at Christ Church, Oxford, he served as a conscript in the Royal Navy. On leaving the service, he worked on the editorial staff of the *Financial Times* before becoming city editor of *The Sunday Telegraph*. In 1963 he secured his first political job as special assistant to Sir Alec Douglas-Home during Sir Alec's brief tenure as Prime Minister.

With the Labour victory in the 1964 general election, he returned to journalism as a columnist for the *Financial Times* and a broadcaster with the BBC. Having unsuccessfully contested Eton and Slough at the 1970 general election, he worked as a special political adviser at Tory headquarters before winning the Leicestershire seat of Blaby when Ted Heath went to the country in February 1974. He held the seat for the ensuing 18 years before standing down when Parliament was dissolved for the April 1992 general election.

He became a Whip in 1976 and a Front Bench spokesman on Treasury and economic affairs a year later. When Margaret Thatcher swept into No 10 Downing street after her 1979 victory, she gave him the job of Financial Secretary to the Treasury under Geoffrey Howe as Chancellor. Within months they had removed controls on mortgages and abolished exchange controls. In the 1980 Budget, Geoffrey Howe unveiled the medium term financial strategy, the innovative framework for setting monetary and fiscal targets over a period of years, of which Nigel Lawson had been the principal author.

In 1981 he became the Secretary of State for Energy, in which role he anticipated the 1984 miners' strike and ordered the building up of coal stocks in preparation. In 1983 Mrs Thatcher made him Chancellor of the Exchequer to replace Sir Geoffrey Howe. It was to be a time of tax reform, with the emphasis on cutting income tax, recasting corporate tax, and simplifying the system as a whole.

Discord was eventually to surface, however, over exchange rate policy. He regarded the exchange rate as a key component of financial discipline and he advocated, in the face of Mrs Thatcher's virulent opposition, supported as she was by her personal economic adviser Sir Alan Walters, using it as such. With Walters insisting on making his opposition public, Nigel Lawson felt obliged to say, in effect, "Walters goes, or I go", but Mrs Thatcher refused to budge, and he resigned. It was the first crack in the edifice. Within a year, he was seated on the Back Bench next to Sir Geoffrey Howe while Sir Geoffrey delivered to the Commons the resignation speech that effectively marked the end of Mrs Thatcher's reign. John Major, whom Nigel Lawson had chosen as his Chief Secretary only two years before and who succeeded him as Chancellor would soon be moving into No 10 Downing street.

Out of front-line politics, as well as taking up a business career, he wrote his well-received memoirs, "The View from No 11: Memoirs of a Tory Radical". In 1992 he was made a life peer, and decided to address the question of his weight. He lost several stones and wrote a best-selling book about the diet he had followed. He subsequently used the upper House as a platform for his sceptical views on global climate policy, about which subject he also wrote a book – "An Appeal To Reason: A Cool Look At Global Warming".

Prime Minister on the ropes but no killer punch

BY RT HON LORD LAWSON OF BLABY

The emergency debate on 27 January 1986 was one of the more memorable and decisive occasions I attended during my time as a Member of the House of Commons and Cabinet Minister. Played out before a packed and excitable House, it featured a Government that appeared to have fallen apart, an Opposition leader, who launched the debate, equipped with an *embarras de richesse* of ammunition, and a hitherto dominant Prime Minister on the ropes. In the event, Mr Kinnock provided an object lesson in how not to do it.

Margaret Thatcher was subsequently to remark that, when she went to the House of Commons on the afternoon of Monday 27 January 1986 to reply to the emergency debate the Opposition had successfully called for, she was not sure that she would return to No 10 as Prime Minister.

More than 20 years later it seems astonishing that the fate of a west country helicopter manufacturer of at most only marginal strategic significance could have precipitated the greatest challenge to Thatcher's long premiership until the coup that finally unseated her almost five years later.

Indeed, it seemed pretty astonishing at the time. But it was a fact; and although in public her combative demeanour had not greatly changed, those of us working close to her had never seen her so mentally and physically drained and at such a low ebb.

Events had been moving thick and fast that January. On the 6th, a Thatcher-inspired letter from one of the Law Officers to the Defence Secretary, Michael Heseltine, suggesting that Heseltine had been guilty of "serious inaccuracies" in a letter that he had written to one of the merchant banks involved with Westland, was leaked to the press.

On the 9th, unconnected with the leak, Heseltine stage-managed his high-profile and acrimonious resignation over the Westland affair. The Law Officers made it clear that, unless there was a full inquiry into the leak, they too would resign.

On the 15th, the first available Opposition Day, the Labour leader, Neil Kinnock launched a debate on Westland, concluding with a suggestion that Leon Brittan, the Industry Secretary, who was widely believed to be the source of the leak, at Thatcher's implicit behest, should himself do the honourable thing and resign. Kinnock's speech was quite effective – certainly more so than Thatcher's somewhat subdued reply. On Friday the 24th, Brittan did indeed resign.

This was the (for him) promising background against which a triumphant and over-confident Kinnock launched the emergency debate on Monday the 27th. In the event, he got off to a poor start and never really recovered from it. He began with a slip of the tongue, accusing the Government of duplicity over, as *Hansard* recorded it, "the bids that were being made for Heseltine – *[Laughter.]* – for Westland".

Nettled by the Conservative laughter, he unwisely allowed himself to depart from his prepared indictment of Thatcher to accuse "Conservative Members of Parliament" of holding "a cavalier attitude towards dishonesty" – at which point an obscure Conservative Back Bencher raised a point of order, asking the Speaker whether it was in order to accuse Members of dishonesty. The Speaker then had to call on Kinnock on no fewer than three occasions to withdraw the accusation, before he gracelessly did so.

It was a disastrous, and wholly unnecessary, opening. It also inevitably lengthened the speech; which, given the widespread feeling in the House of Commons that Kinnock, although a natural orator, had an unfortunate tendency to go on too long, was additionally unhelpful. In fact, on a parliamentary occasion of this importance, the 25 minutes which his speech that day lasted might even then not have been too long had it possessed a rigorous structure and proceeded with remorseless logic to the inevitable concluding call for the Prime Minister to resign. But it lacked much in the way of structure, and the indictment was distinctly on the discursive side, reinforcing the unfortunate reputation Kinnock had acquired for being long-winded. Certainly, there was no killer punch.

Thatcher's reply, although a distinct improvement on her performance in the earlier debate, was not a great speech, either. But it did not need to be: Kinnock had already blown it.

A mere 16 months later, the Government she (still) led won a third successive election victory by a handsome margin; an outcome few would have predicted at the time of the Westland debate. But in one – albeit non-parliamentary – sense Thatcher had not escaped scot-free: it was Heseltine's leadership challenge, the best part of five years later, that was eventually to topple her.

NEW MEMBER

The following Member made the Affirmation required by law:

Seamus Mallon, Esq., for Newry and Armagh.

Teachers (Dispute)

3.32 pm

Mr. Clement Freud (Cambridgeshire North-East): I beg to ask leave to move the Adjournment of the House, under Standing Order No. 10, for the purpose of discussing a specific and important matter that should have urgent consideration, namely,

"the latest developments in the teachers' dispute."

The matter is urgent because the Secretary of State's weekend statement about not being able to find the money to pay for the ACAS-inspired agreement will cause further disruption and irrevocable damage to the education of children. It is specific because those seeking agreement have gone a long way down a flexible negotiating path, while the Secretary of State has remained obdurate. He has compounded his obduracy by undermining the ACAS deal before it has been ratified. The position has developed since Thursday's debate.

The matter is important because local authorities and parents now feel abandoned and deceived by the Government. A short period of calm after the 1985 settlement was needed, so that all could work towards a lasting solution. That is now threatened. Unlike Secretaries of State, who come and go, children are children and we are failing them.

Mr. Speaker: The hon. Gentleman asks leave to move the Adjournment of the House for the purpose of discussing a specific and important matter that he believes should have urgent consideration, namely,

"the latest developments in the teachers' dispute."

I have listened with care to what the hon. Gentleman said. He knows that my sole duty in considering an application under Standing Order No. 10 is to decide whether it should be given priority over the business already set down for this evening or for tomorrow. I regret that the matter that he has raised does not meet the criteria laid down in the Standing Order; I cannot, therefore, submit his application to the House.

Westland plc

3.35 pm

Mr. Neil Kinnock (Islwyn): I beg to move, That this House do now Adjourn.

Leave having been given on Thursday 23 January under Standing Order No. 10 to discuss:

The circumstances surrounding the publication of classified information relating to the future of Westland plc.

Mr. Kinnock: For all of the people in the Westland company, the affairs of that company are obviously vital. For most of us outside the company, the affairs of the company have become increasingly important in recent months. But no one inside or outside the Westland company would have considered four weeks ago that this matter could become one of such current critical significance.

As the Prime Minister said yesterday, it was a comparatively small thing. Now it is palpably a very big thing. It has grown in size because of the actions and the attitudes of the right hon. Lady and Members of her Administration. Of course, the Prime Minister says that it would never have assumed this proportion but for the fact that one member of the team was not playing like a member of the team. It is plainly true that we and the country would not have known what we know now but for the fact that the right hon. Member for Henley (Mr. Heseltine) kicked over the bucket of worms by resigning earlier this month. All the dishonesty, duplicity, conniving and manoeuvring would still have been taking place. We would not have known about it quite so quickly and quite so clearly.

Evasions, manoeuvrings and deceits nurtured this comparatively small thing until it became a very big thing. It was turned from an issue into a crisis by the dishonesty of people in this Administration. That dishonesty infected the Government's whole approach to the affairs of Westland plc. There was a basic duplicity of their public dispassion about the affairs of that company and their private partisanship in the bids that were being made for Heseltine—*[Laughter.]*—for Westland. I think that may be the last occasion on which Conservative Members of Parliament have cause to be amused in this debate. Clearly, they hold a cavalier attitude towards dishonesty, which may explain the attitude of many of them——

Mr. Tony Marlow (Northampton, North): On a point of order, Mr. Speaker. Is it in order for the Leader of the Opposition to accuse hon. Members of this House of dishonesty?

Mr. Speaker: I think the Leader of the Opposition would wish to withdraw any allegation of dishonesty against Members of this House.

Mr. Kinnock: I only withdraw allegations if the cap does not fit—*[Interruption.]*

Mr. Speaker: Order. This is a debate in which the House is taking a great interest. I ask the House to keep it on a level which is in keeping with our conventions. I am sure that the Leader of the Opposition, at the beginning of his speech, would wish to get us off to a good start.

Mr. Kinnock: You have that guarantee, Mr. Speaker, and it will continue like that——

Hon. Members: Withdraw.

334

Mr. Speaker: Order. I would ask the right hon. Gentleman to withdraw any allegations of dishonesty.

Mr. Kinnock: I said that hon. Members opposite have a cavalier attitude towards dishonesty. [HON. MEMBERS: "Withdraw."] On the point of order, Mr. Speaker. On the basis of the view that you take of affairs, I will certainly withdraw what I said earlier. I said that the Government's attitude was one of public dispassion and private partisanship. There are also the standing charges that still exist about moved meetings and minutes that were incomplete, and now we have the differing versions still existing of the meeting between Sir Raymond Lygo and the then Secretary of State for Trade and Industry. We know enough of the truth about the connivings of 6 January to understand that the dishonesty has run right through this whole episode. *[Interruption.]*

All dishonesty has to stop. We have had two dress rehearsals from the Prime Minister full of half-truths and concealments. Today the Prime Minister must come clean. That is not only my view; it is the view expressed throughout the country and expressed by the Home Secretary in the course of his interview yesterday. Today, the Prime Minister must answer the questions that she signally and significantly failed to answer six times last Thursday.

First, when did the Prime Minister find out about the decision to leak, how it was to be done and who was to do it? Secondly, how can the Prime Minister explain her claim that she did not know what action was being taken? Thirdly, did the Prime Minister establish an inquiry in response to the justifiable outrage of two Law Officers who felt that their integrity was being abused and compromised——

Mr. Churchill (Davyhulme) *rose——*

Mr. Kinnock: —or was there an additional reason for that? After seven days delay, did the Prime Minister establish an inquiry whose conclusions would not in the normal course of events be published, simply because she knew that demands for such an investigation would most certainly be made? Was that inquiry established for detection or was it established for deception? Was it set up to obscure the issues and to provide an excuse for silence? Was it set up by a Prime Minister who knew very well who had leaked, why they had leaked, when they leaked and what they did it for?

The Prime Minister must give clear and truthful answers to all of these questions. She must make no mistake. Today the Prime Minister is on trial. [HON. MEMBERS: "Rubbish."] The main testimony against the Prime Minister is provided by herself. It is provided by her own words to this House last Thursday, and testimony is further provided by the whole nature of her style of governing. How could it be that a Prime Minister who prides herself so earnestly on her involvement in detail; who prides herself so much on her knowledge of the minutiae of her Government; who has such a deep engagement historically in the Westland affair did not know of a supremely important decision, taken by those so very close to her, to manipulate events on 6 January?

How can it be——

Mr. Churchill: I am much obliged to the right hon. Gentleman for giving way, but before he accuses others

of deceit, will he explain whether it was deceit that led him to falsify his age when he first put himself forward for political candidature or did he just forget how old he was?

Hon. Members: Oh, no.

Mr. Kinnock: I think that that may be the best that Conservative Members will be able to do in the course of this afternoon. That was certainly the last time that I inadvertently added a year to my age.

On the testimony against the Prime Minister, provided by herself, we have to ask how it could be that seven days could pass before she recognised that the issue of the leak was so important that it warranted an inquiry. Who would expect us or the country to believe that 16 days could pass between the corrupt practice of that leak and the Prime Minister's discovery of the details when the plotters were her closest confidants—her most frequent companions?

Who would expect the House or the country to accept that in all that time the Prime Minister never asked her associates to venture even a guess about the identity of those involved in the leak? Who can expect us to believe that in all those endless hours of contact, through all those days of discussion and debate and questions and statements in the House and in the even closer quarters of No. 10 Downing street, the Prime Minister was really blundering around in blissful ignorance of the actions of 2 January? Who would expect us to believe any of that?

Well, obviously the Prime Minister expects us to believe that. It is clear that the Prime Minister expects the House, her party and her fellow citizens to suspend all normal standards of belief and to accept that it is strange but true. "Truth," she said on television yesterday, "is often stranger than fiction." When we heard that, as when we heard her last Thursday, many of us wondered whether the Prime Minister had lost the ability to tell the difference between truth and fiction.

We want to know truthfully now exactly when the Prime Minister first knew of the decision to send the Solicitor-General's letter. We want to know truthfully now exactly when she first knew of the decision to leak the Solicitor-General's letter. We want to know now exactly when she first knew of the involvement of the then Secretary of State for Trade and Industry and her office in the conspiracy. When did she first know that he had given his authority, as she put it, and when they had given their cover, as she put it, to act in good faith—act in good faith by making a furtive phone call to the Press Association for the specific and carefully contrived purpose of discrediting another member of her Cabinet?

We know that the right hon. Lady has not answered those questions. She has admitted that herself. Any statement, she said yesterday, is almost always a basis for further questions. That may be the understatement of the Prime Minister's lifetime. *[Interruption.]* But all we have had so far are excuses for the omissions and evasions of last week—no apologies for not answering questions with meticulous accuracy; just attempted excuses. All we have had is the propaganda about "toughing it out"—a phrase, Mr. Speaker, which you will recall first entered the British vocabulary when it came out of Richard Nixon's office.

We are told that last Thursday the Prime Minister was sheltering the Secretary of State for Trade and Industry. The Home Secretary told Mr. Brian Walden yesterday —*[Interruption.]* They are going to hear it all, Mr.

[*Mr. Kinnock*]

Speaker—that he could feel the courage going through the Prime Minister when she made her statement, as the Home Secretary put it, "protecting Mr. Leon Brittan". That excuse has palpably gone because the late Secretary of State for Trade and Industry has gone, although, interestingly, he went not without resistance. Even when the right hon. and learned Member for Richmond, Yorks (Mr. Brittan) wanted to do the right honourable thing and resign, the Prime Minister tried to talk him out of it and even invited him to apply for the next vacancy for "high office", as she put it.

But what of the Prime Minister's excuses for the omissions from last Thursday's statement and questions? *[Interruption.]* The Prime Minister said that the majority of the inquiry report — *[Interruption.]* Even the deliberate efforts, that will be heard by the nation, by Conservative Members to interrupt the House and to prevent someone from getting a fair hearing, will not stop the truth being heard. *[Interruption.]*

The Prime Minister said that the majority of the inquiry report was new to her. She said that, until the report was available, she did not have the full facts—what she called an "enormous number" of facts. As I listened to her then and to the Home Secretary yesterday, saying how much they wanted to be able to give the full facts, I began to think that it was the Government, not the Opposition, who had got the emergency debate today. *[Interruption.]*

The protest that there were just too many facts to be absorbed does not carry any weight at all. Of course, it is handy to have the full details for the historians—the dates, the times, the places, the footnotes. But only one fact was absolutely essential for the Prime Minister; one fact really mattered, and that was the fact that the Secretary of State for Trade and Industry and her office had conceived, organised and executed the leak. That was the fact which mattered and it was the fact which the right hon. Lady was forced to admit last Thursday. It was also the fact—the single salient fact—that the right hon. Lady was denied for over a fortnight.

Who were these people who decided to keep the right hon. Lady in the dark? Who were these merciless people who made the Prime Minister, in her innocent ignorance, go through the charade of the inquiry into the leak? *[Interruption.]*

Mr. George Foulkes (Carrick, Cumnock and Doon Valley): Do something about the giggling schoolgirls opposite.

Mr. Speaker: Order. I did not see anything going on.

Mr. Kinnock: Whatever anyone sees, the whole country will be able to hear what has been going on. Once again, Conservative Back Benchers have decided that, because they cannot take the truth, they will try to bury it. *[Interruption.]*

We want to know who were the people who prevented the Prime Minister from being able to gain access to the single fact about the involvement of the Secretary of State for Trade and Industry and her office in the decision to leak. Who were the cynics who let the Prime Minister be in the dark for 16 days? Who let her come here to tell truths so partial, so incomplete, that they began to look like untruths and who let her come to make a whole speech in this House on 15 January without telling her that they

knew who had leaked, how they had leaked and why they had leaked? Who were these callous people who caused the Prime Minister so many problems over the weeks?

Why, they were the Prime Minister's own Secretary of State for Trade and Industry and, strangest of all, her own office — the Prime Minister's very own office, her closest, most senior staff; her office which, in her own words, did not seek her agreement; her office, which, in her words,

"considered—and they were right—that I should agree with my right hon. Friend the Secretary of State for Trade and Industry".—[*Official Report,* 23 January 1986; Vol. 90, c. 450.]

That begs the question. If her office did not tell the Prime Minister, why did her office not tell the Prime Minister? There can be only two reasons. It was either because they did not want to tell the Prime Minister or because they did not think that there was a need to tell the Prime Minister. If they did not want her to be involved, that could be for only one reason—the simple, straightforward reason that they were doing wrong, that they knew that they were doing wrong and that they did not want the Prime Minister to be contaminated by the guilt.

Of course, it may be that they thought that the Prime Minister did not need to know about what was going on. They might have said to themselves, "There is no need to tell the Prime Minister. We know what her attitude is to Westland. We know her attitude to the turbulent Secretary of State for Defence. We know what her attitude is to his campaign and we know what her attitude would be to us using dirty tricks to defame and undermine the Secretary of State for Defence."

Were the people in the Prime Minister's office actually right about that? Do they really know the Prime Minister? Either they do know the Prime Minister and they think of her as a woman who would stoop to conquer, no matter how low, or they are totally mistaken and she is not the woman that they think.

From the Prime Minister's statement last Thursday it appears that they do not know the Prime Minister. We have the Prime Minister's own word for it. She told us that her office did know her well enough to guess accurately that she would agree to the attitude taken by the Secretary of State for Trade and Industry and that she did not and would not have consented, if she had been consulted, because she felt that there was a different way, a better way, to make the relevant details known.

Despite their years of close proximity and despite the deep mutual trust that has to exist between the Prime Minister and her office, it appears that they did not know the Prime Minister at all. There they were taking important decisions in her name—*[Interruption.]*

Hon. Members: Order.

Mr. Speaker: Order. May I say to the House that backchat does no credit to the House.

Hon. Members: It is deliberate.

Mr. Kinnock: Either they knew the Prime Minister or they did not know the Prime Minister. She says that they knew her well enough to understand that she agreed with the Secretary of State for Trade and Industry, but that, had she been consulted, she would have told them that there was a different way and a better way that must be found to make the relevant facts known.

336

That is all despite those years of close proximity and all that close contact. Despite all of that, there they were, taking important decisions for the Prime Minister as she busied herself yards away in Downing street.

They did not tell the Prime Minister, so we are told. All the time, they were outrageously miscalculating the Prime Minister's attitude towards the correct method of putting matters into the public domain. Having made that miscalculation, they then apparently compounded the fault by allowing her to set up an inquiry into a leak which they themselves had perpetrated.

They must have been wrong—practically wrong and terribly wrong; too wrong to enable them to endure in their present positions. At least that is what we would think. How can they continue to carry out the immense responsibilities and be the object of the Prime Minister's trust when they could be so terribly wrong, so we are told, about her attitude towards the way in which that information should be released?

If they are so wrong, why have they not gone? They have not gone, and they are not going. They are not going because the Prime Minister says that she has complete confidence in them. Why has she that confidence in them? Is it because the Prime Minister, who has the reputation for being ruthless with those who fail her, has suddenly gone soft? It cannot be that. It must not be because of charity. Can it be because of complicity by the Prime Minister? Can it possibly be that the Prime Minister is not innocent but that she is implicated and involved?

For the moment, we withhold our judgment while we wait for the Prime Minister to give her account. Last Thursday, in reply to my right hon. Friend the Member for Morley and Leeds, South (Mr. Rees), the Prime Minister said that she hoped that we would have the decency to accept her version of events. We have the decency; what we lack is the gullibility to accept the Prime Minister's version of events.

We want the facts. We want them now. We want only the one version that will be believed—the truth, the whole truth and absolutely nothing but the truth. If the Prime Minister cannot tell that truth, she cannot stay. If she will not tell that truth, she must go.

4 pm

The Prime Minister (Mrs. Margaret Thatcher): Before I come to the wider aspects of this debate, let us recall one thing clearly: the background is the future of Westland and its work force. We have to remember that that future still hangs in the balance. The Government's position throughout has been that it is for the company itself to take decisions about the course to follow in the interests of the shareholders and the employees, but the Government are a major customer of the company and the Government's policies and intentions in that capacity are very relevant to the decisions that the company has to take.

It is therefore of the first importance that any pronouncements by the Government that might affect the company's decisions are accurate, consistent and in no way misleading. It is largely because one member of the Cabinet could not accept arrangements designed to secure the accuracy and consistency of Government statements that we are debating the whole matter today.

I propose to deal at once with some questions that have arisen since my statement of 23 January. I shall do so under three headings: first, the circumstances leading up to the letter of 6 January by my hon. and learned Friend the Solicitor-General; secondly, the reasons for having an inquiry; and, thirdly, the outcome of the inquiry.

First, I shall deal with the circumstances leading up to the Solicitor-General's letter. The House will recall that I had cleared my own letter of Wednesday 1 January to Sir John Cuckney with the Departments concerned and with my hon. and learned Friend the Solicitor-General, for the reasons I have already given.

On Friday 3 January, there was an exchange of letters between Mr. Horne of Lloyds merchant bank, representing the European consortium, and my right hon. Friend the then Secretary of State for Defence. In his letter, Mr. Horne asked for amplification of a statement in my letter to Sir John Cuckney. As the House knows, my right hon. Friend went into considerable detail in his reply. His letter had not been discussed with my office before it was sent, even though it dealt with points arisng from my letter to Sir John Cuckney.

On the following day, Saturday 4 January, I saw copies of the exchange of letters. In view of the very careful steps that I had taken to clear my letter to Sir John Cuckney with the Departments concerned and with the Solicitor-General, I made inquiries to find out whether the Defence Secretary's letter had been cleared in the same way with the Department of Trade and Industry and with the Law Officers. It had not. In view of the continuing need for accuracy and consistency in Government statements on this subject, I asked that a message be sent to my right hon. and learned Friend the then Secretary of State for Trade and Industry, as the sponsoring Minister for Westland, to suggest that he should ask the Solicitor-General to consider—[Hon. Members: "Ah."]

Mr. Speaker: Order.

The Prime Minister: —the Defence Secretary's letter and give his opinion on whether it was accurate, and consistent with my own letter to Sir John Cuckney.

The Solicitor-General, on the basis of the evidence available to him, formed the provisional opinion that the Defence Secretary's letter contained material inaccuracies which needed to be corrected. This view was reported to me. The matter clearly could not be left there. I therefore, through my office, asked him to consider writing to the Defence Secretary to draw that opinion to his attention. I learned subsequently from the Solicitor-General that he spoke to the then Defence Secretary on the telephone that same evening and told him his provisional opinion about the letter and warned him that he would probably write to him on Monday 6 January, when he had checked the documents, and advise him to correct the inaccuracy.

The Solicitor-General further considered the documents on the morning of Monday 6 January. They confirmed him in his opinion. He therefore wrote to the Defence Secretary, advising him to write again to Mr. Horne correcting the inaccuracies. My right hon. Friend the Member for Henley (Mr. Heseltine) has asked for the further exchanges between himself and the Law Officers to be published. I have arranged for copies of the correspondence to be placed in the Library of the House.

It has been said that the letter to Mr. Horne has not been corrected. So far as the Government are concerned, we made it clear to the company—in the letter to Sir John Cuckney of 13 January from the permanent secretary to the

337

Lloyd George presents National Insurance Bill and lays foundation for welfare state

Elfyn Llwyd was elected the Plaid Cymru Member for Meirionydd Nant Conwy in 1992, and was made the leader of the party's Westminster group in 1999. His constituency contains the highest concentration of Welsh language speakers in the country, and his passionate support for the language is partly behind his attempts to secure local education authority funding for the London Welsh School, where the curriculum is taught through the medium of Welsh, the only such institution outside of Wales.

By profession he is a lawyer, having been a solicitor and then qualifying as a barrister when he was called to the Bar in 1997. He has been a keen supporter of the concept of children's rights. He proposed a number of amendments to the Family Law Bill, including the right of children to give evidence in court in divorce cases. He led the campaign for a Children's Commissioner for Wales, which office has now been introduced in Wales and throughout the United Kingdom.

A major area on which he has pressed for action has been the escalation in the number of second homes and holiday homes in Wales. A central plank of his party's policy has been control of second homes, and when, in 2001, the Exmoor national park authority drew up proposals for limiting second home ownership, he called for a similar approach in Wales where, he said, in addition to the impact for local people on house prices, the factors of language and culture also arose.

In August 2004, he supported his fellow Plaid Cymru MP, Adam Price, in an unsuccessful attempt to impeach the then Prime Minister, Tony Blair, for his conduct over the war in Iraq. With Scottish Nationalist leader Alex Salmond and two Conservative MPs, Elfyn Llwyd framed the impeachment motion, which covered issues including the question of the existence or otherwise of weapons of mass destruction and the legality of the war. The motion was never debated and the question remained undecided.

He has also called for the building of a prison to serve mid and north Wales, arguing that people from those areas being incarcerated in prisons in England at great distance from their homes and families and without Welsh language provision was challengeable on the grounds of basic human rights.

In August 2008 he calculated from statistics held by the National Association of Prison Officers that one in 10 of the prisoners held in United Kingdom jails were former members of the British armed forces. He claimed that a major contributing factor was the lack of support provided after service personnel had returned from war zones, and he pressed for more to be done to help them in dealing with the problems they encountered in the transition from military life in action to circumstances of civilian life.

He has been elected chair of the executive committee of the National Eisteddfod to be held in Bala in 2009.

One of the century's most important speeches set against backdrop of social revolution

BY ELFYN LLWYD MP

David Lloyd George's speech as Chancellor of the Exchequer on 4 May 1911 is, I think, one of the most important made in the last century. Lloyd George was introducing the National Insurance Bill thereby creating the foundation for the welfare state of the 20th century. Welsh men and women of my age group and upwards have been brought up on a diet of praising Lloyd George and many of us are aware of numerous examples of outstanding oratory on several and varied platforms, both through the medium of the English language and his mother tongue, and mine, the Welsh language.

I am aware that David Lloyd George's memory is sacred to many still and in particular in north and mid Wales where I come from. I am also aware that the great man did not deliver on all his promises. When the opportunities arose for a Parliament for Wales, a policy so central to the then Liberal Party and sacred to him personally, nothing came of it, and that remains a huge disappointment to many people. I also appreciate that in his dealings with the Irish nation he was not always as straight as he could have been, or worse, he behaved very badly. I therefore run the risk of offending my many Irish friends throughout the political spectrum.

In issuing that health warning I should also declare an interest. I left Aberystwyth University with a law degree and joined the solicitor firm Lloyd George and George of Porthmadog to undertake my articles of clerkship to qualify as a solicitor. On many an afternoon I looked up from my paperwork and glanced at a framed photograph of the great man and wondered if he had also sat at the same desk in his younger days before departing for London and a glittering political career.

Lloyd George's career was hugely significant in Welsh politics as it ushered in what was a new dawn. The old landed gentry who were habitually returned to Parliament unopposed were now being challenged and defeated by others on an agenda favouring the ordinary working classes and artisans as they were classed in those days. At long last these people had their voices heard and in time were represented by occupants of the highest offices of state. It was nothing short of a political and social revolution at a time when violent revolutions were taking place in several other countries.

It is against that particular backdrop that I view this speech. Though it has to be said that this is far from the best oratory from this politician, the huge significance of the speech and the Bill are still with us today, a century later. I wish to concentrate on the first section of the speech as reported in Hansard from columns 609 through to the top of column 614.

In the early section of the speech the plight of the poor is highlighted: "there is a mass of poverty and destitution in this country which is too proud to wear the badge of pauperism, and which declines to pin that badge to its children". Those are stirring words.

The speech goes on to refer to the efforts made by poor people to insure against the inevitable contingencies of life such as death, sickness and unemployment and describes how this groundbreaking Bill would deal with them.

The speech details the number of people who chose to insure against the contingencies and an astonishing figure of less than 10 per cent. of the "working class" were insuring against unemployment either because they chose not to do so, or, as is more likely, they simply could not afford it. I quote: "As a matter of fact, you could not provide against all those three contingencies anything which would be worth a workman's while, without paying at any rate 1s. 6d or 2s. per week at the very lowest. There are a multitude of the working classes who cannot spare that, and ought not to be asked to spare it, because it involves the deprivation of children of the necessities of life."

At column 613 Lloyd George refers to expectations from compulsory payment of what was to become national insurance. He refers to Army and Navy personnel. I quote: "It, is a crying scandal, I think, that at the present moment there are so many soldiers and sailors who have placed their lives at the disposal of the country, and are quite ready to sacrifice them…hundreds and thousands do actually leave the Army and the Navy broken through ill-health… These men leave the Army without any provision from either public or private charity, and they are broken men for the rest of their lives."

How prescient those words were within three years of the outbreak of the calamities of the first world war. They also have a contemporary ring to them when concern is expressed about the military covenant and its non-observance by the Government. Further, as I have discovered, many thousands of recent servicemen and women from the theatres in Afghanistan and Iraq end up in prison. Indeed, they represent up to 10 per cent. of the current prison population.

The Government would do well to revisit the sentiments expressed in this speech, delivered nearly a century earlier.

NATIONAL INSURANCE.

The **CHANCELLOR** of the **EX-CHEQUER** (**Mr. Lloyd George**): I ask leave to introduce a Bill " To provide for insurance against loss of health, and for the prevention and cure of sickness, and for insurance against unemployment, and for purposes incidental thereto."

In moving for leave to bring in the Bill of which I have given notice, I must thank the House for the great indulgence it has extended to me during the past two or three months. I am afraid I must plead for a little further indulgence during the time I am endeavouring to explain the provisions of this Bill. I shall do my best to make myself heard in all parts of the House, but I am sure I shall not appeal in vain to the kindness of my friends. I think it must be a relief to the Members of the House of Commons to turn from controversial questions for a moment to a question which, at any rate, has never been the subject of controversy between the parties in the State. I believe there is a general agreement as to the evil which has to be remedied. There is a general agreement as to its urgency, and I think I can go beyond that and say there is a general agreement as to the main proposals upon which the remedy ought to be based. In this country, as my right hon. Friend the President of the Local Government Board (Mr. Burns) said in his speech last week, 3) per cent. of the pauperism is attributable to sickness. A considerable percentage would probably have to be added to that for unemployment. The administration of the Old Age Pensions Act has revealed the fact there is a mass of poverty and destitution in this country which is too proud to wear the badge of pauperism, and which declines to pin that badge to its children. They would rather suffer from deprivation than do so. I am perfectly certain if this is the fact with regard to persons of seventy years of age, there must be a multitude of people of that kind before they reach that age.

The efforts made by the working classes to insure against the troubles of life indicate they are fully alive to the need of some provision being made. There are three contingencies against which they insure—death, sickness, and unemployment. Taking them in the order of urgency which the working classes attach to them, death would come first. There are 42,000,000 industrial policies of insurance against death issued in this country of small amounts where the

payments are either weekly, monthly, or occasionally quarterly. The friendly societies, without exception, have funeral benefits, and that accounts for about 6,000,000. The collecting societies are about 7,000,000, and those are also death benefits. Then the great industrial insurance companies have something like 30,000,000 policies. There is hardly a household in this country where there is not a policy of insurance against death. I will not stop to account for it. After all, the oldest friendly societies in the world are burial societies. All that I would say here is we do not propose to deal with insurance against death. It is no part of our scheme at all, partly because the ground has been very thoroughly covered, although not very satisfactorily covered, and also because this, at any rate, is the easiest part of the problem and is a part of the problem which is not beset with the difficulties of vested interests. Fortunately, all the vested interests which deal with sickness and unemployment are of a thoroughly unselfish and beneficent character, and we shall be able, I think, to assist them, not merely without interfering with their rights and privileges, but by encouraging them to do the excellent work they have commenced and which they are doing so well.

Sickness comes in the next order of urgency in the working-class mind. There are over 6,000,000 policies—that is hardly the word, perhaps, for friendly societies—but there is provision made by 6,000,000 people against sickness. Most of it includes a provision for medical aid. There are, I think, about 300,000 or 400,000 members who have insured for medical aid alone, but I think, almost without exception, the friendly societies include medical relief in the provision which they make. That is not, I think, the case with the trade unions. There are 700,000 members in the trade unions insured for sick benefits, but I do not think that includes medical relief. In addition to those, there are a good many unregistered assurances at works, where a man leaves a shilling a month at the office for the purpose of paying the works' doctor. I should say, therefore, that between 6,000,000 and 7,000,000 people in this country have made some provision against sickness, not all of it adequate, and a good deal of it defective. Then comes the third class, the insurance against unemployment. Here not a tenth of the working classes have made any provision at all. You have only got 1,400,000

U

[Mr. Lloyd George.]

workmen who have insured against unemployment. It is true that perhaps about half of the employment of this country is not affected by the fluctuations of trade. I do not think agricultural laoburers or railway servants are affected quite to the same extent. Then there is provision for short time in some of the trades. Taking the precarious trades affected by unemployment, I do not believe more than one-third or one-quarter of the people engaged in them are insured against unemployment. That is the provision which is made at the present moment by the working-classes: 42,000,000 policies against death, about 6,100,000 who have made some kind of provision against sickness, and 1,400,000 who have made some provision against unemployment.

Now comes the question, which leads up to the decision of the Government to take action. What is the explanation that only a portion of the working-classes have made provision against sickness and against unemployment? Is it they consider it not necessary? Quite the reverse, as I shall prove by figures. In fact, those who stand most in need of it make up the bulk of the uninsured. Why? Because very few can afford to pay the premiums, and pay them continuously, which enable a man to provide against those three contingencies. As a matter of fact, you could not provide against all those three contingencies anything which would be worth a workman's while, without paying at any rate 1s. 6d. or 2s. per week at the very lowest. There are a multitude of the working classes who cannot spare that, and ought not to be asked to spare it, because it involves the deprivation of children of the necessaries of life. Therefore they are compelled to elect, and the vast majority choose to insure against death alone. Those who can afford to take up two policies insure against death and sickness, and those who can afford to take up all three insure against death, sickness and unemployment, but only in that order. What are the explanations why they do not insure against all three? The first is that their wages are too low. I am talking now about the uninsured portion. Their wages are too low to enable them to insure against all three without some assistance. The second difficulty, and it is the greatest of all, is that during a period of sickness or unemployment, when they are earning nothing, they cannot keep up the

4.0 P.M.

premiums. They may be able to do it for a fortnight or three weeks, but when times of very bad trade come, when a man is out of work for weeks and weeks at a time, arrears run up with the friendly societies, and when the man gets work, it may be at the end of two or three months, those are not the first arrears which have to be met. There are arrears of rent, arrears of the grocery bill, and arrears for the necessaries of life. At any rate he cannot consider his friendly society only. The result is that a very considerable number of workmen find themselves quite unable to keep up the premiums when they have a family to look after.

Undoubtedly there is another reason. It is no use shirking the fact that a proportion of workmen with good wages spend them in other ways, and therefore have nothing to spare with which to pay premiums to friendly societies. It has come to my notice, in many of these cases, that the women of the family make most heroic efforts to keep up the premiums to the friendly societies, and the officers of friendly societies, whom I have seen, have amazed me by telling the proportion of premiums of this kind paid by women out of the very wretched allowance given them to keep the household together. I think it is well we should look all the facts in the face before we come to consider the remedy. What does it mean in the way of lapses? I have inquired of friendly Societies, and, as near as I can get at it, there are 250,000 lapses in a year. That is a very considerable proportion of the 6,000,000 policies. The expectation of life at twenty is, I think, a little over forty years, and it means that in twenty years' time there are 5,000,000 lapses: that is, people who supported and joined friendly societies, and who have gone on paying the premiums for weeks, months, and even years, struggling along, at last, when a very bad time of unemployment comes, drop out and the premium lapses. It runs to millions in the course of a generation. What does that mean? It means that the vast majority of the working men of this country at one time or other have been members of friendly societies, have felt the need for provision of this kind, and it is only because they have been driven, sometimes by their own habits, but in the majority of cases by circumstances over which they have no control—to abandon their policies. That is the reason why, at the present moment, not one half of the workmen of this country have made any provision for sickness, and not one-tenth for unemployment. I think it necessary to state these facts in order to show that there is a real need for some system which would aid the workmen over these difficulties. I do not think there is any better method, or one more practicable at the present moment, than a system of national insurance which would invoke the aid of the State and the aid of the employer to enable the workman to get over all these difficulties and make provision for himself for sickness, and, as far as the most precarious trades are concerned, against unemployment.

I come at once to the plan of the Government. The measure of the Government will be divided into two parts. The first will deal with sickness, and the second with unemployment. The sickness branch of the Bill will also be in two sections; one will be compulsory and the other voluntary. The compulsory part of the Bill involves a compulsory deduction from the wages of all the employed classes who earn weekly wages, or whose earnings are under the Income Tax limit. There will be a contribution from the employer and a further contribution from the State. There are exceptions from the compulsory clause. The first will be in the Army and Navy. We are making special provision for soldiers and sailors. It is a crying scandal, I think, that at the present moment there are so many soldiers and sailors who have placed their lives at the disposal of the country, and are quite ready to sacrifice them, as we know from past experience, not merely that they should be liable to but, that as a matter of fact, hundreds and thousands do actually leave the Army and the Navy broken through ill-health. I am talking now of ill-health not due to misconduct. These men leave the Army without any provision from either public or private charity, and they are broken men for the rest of their lives. I think it is a crying scandal that that should occur in a country like this, and I hope that this scheme will put an end to it. There will be special provision made for that. But these men will not be regarded as in the employed class for the purposes I am about to explain. The same thing applies to the teachers, and I hope to be able, with the assistance of my right hon. Friend the President of the Board of Education, to largely strengthen their present position. I think their provision is very inadequate, and, compared with the provision made in

other countries, I think a very paltry allowance is made for their superannuation.

Mr. JOHN REDMOND: Does that apply to Ireland?

Mr. LLOYD GEORGE: Certainly, I think the Irish case is a very bad case. I have had a number of Irish teachers before me, and some of them told me that they were getting about £1 a week. There are about 300 of them in the workhouses. They are doing their work for the Empire under very trying conditions, and I shall certainly consider it the duty of the Government, in any scheme of superannuation, to include the Irish teachers as well.

Mr. JOHN REDMOND: When?

Mr. LLOYD GEORGE: I hope it will be possible this year. We propose excepting all people employed under the Crown or under municipalities where, at the present moment, there is no deduction from their wages when they are ill, and where there is some superannuation allowance. There is no need to make provision for them because provision is already made. The same thing will apply to commission agents employed by more than one person. There is also an exception in the case of casual labour employed otherwise than for the purpose of the employer's trade or business. We think it is vital that casual labour should be included. Otherwise the same thing may happen here as I am told happens in Germany, where the exclusion of casual labour is rather encouraging its growth. That is a very bad thing in itself, and there is really no class which it is more important to include than casual labour.

Sir C. KINLOCH-COOKE: Does that include casual labour in dockyards?

Mr. LLOYD GEORGE: Casual labour at docks and in warehouses will be included. I think, too, that casual labour such as that of golf caddies should be brought in. I am making special provision for labour of that kind. Hotel waiters will be another difficulty. They are not paid salaries. I am told they very often pay for the privilege of waiting, and we have to make special provision for them. Cab drivers are another class we propose to include. All casual labour of this kind will be included, as well as casual labour of the kind referred to by the hon. Member opposite. The man who offers to carry your bag for sixpence you can never draw

υ 2

[Mr. Lloyd George.]

in, but it is our intention to attract all casual labour possible within the ambit of our Bill.

Mr. AUSTEN CHAMBERLAIN: Are we to understand that all the classes which the right hon. Gentleman has enumerated are exceptions to the compulsory provisions which he is about to describe?

Mr. LLOYD GEORGE: Certainly, they can come in the voluntary part if they like, so long as they answer to the definition which I have given. I think that is rather anticipating, but the right hon. Gentleman will later on find what class of persons will come in. I come to the amount of contribution. The workman now pays to his friendly society 6d. or 1s. The usual contribution to a friendly society is something between 6d. and 9d., as far as I have been able to discover, and anything under that produces benefits which are benefits I do not think it would be worth our while to include in an Act of Parliament. The House will be interested to know what German workmen have to pay, because that was the first great scientific experiment in insurance on a national scale. It has been enormously successful. That is the testimony borne by all classes of Germans. I have taken some trouble to inquire, and the German Government have been exceedingly kind and helpful in placing information at our disposal. They have shown every disposition to be helpful throughout, and their testimony is that all classes of the community are very much benefited by it. In Germany the payment is in proportion to wages, but the benefits are also in proportion to wages, so that the higher class of workman, who pays a very high contribution, gets a very substantial benefit. There are in Germany, I think, five classes of invalidity contributors, and for sickness every man pays according to his income. They divide their insurance into two separate branches of sickness and invalidity. There are two separate branches, but we propose to include them in one branch. In Germany a man who earns 30s. pays 10¾d. weekly for sickness and invalidity. There are not many of those. The man who is paid 24s. a week, which I think is about the average wage in this country, if you were to strike an average, which it is a difficult thing to do—the man who is paid 24s. a week pays 9d. a week. For that 9d. the benefits he gets will not be equal to the benefits we shall be able to give under our Bill twenty years hence.

The 20s. a week man pays 7¼d., the 18s. man 6¾d., the 15s. man 5¾d., the 12s. man 4¾d., and the 9s. man 3¾d.

That is what the workman pays in Germany, and when you come down to these lower classes the benefits are so small that the workmen in Germany say they prefer to resort to parish relief as the benefits are much too inadequate. For that reason we have decided in favour of one class, because if you have a scale which is proportionate it would be very difficult to give benefits to the lower class except by making special conditions which it would not be worth our while to make. It would certainly not give them a minimum allowance to keep their families from want. So we have decided to have one scale for all classes, with a provision for the lowest wages. Therefore, we have decided to propose a deduction of 4d. for men and 3d. for women. That is about a halfpenny a day and a penny on Saturday, or, as somebody told me, about the price of two pints of the cheapest beer per week, or the price of an ounce of tobacco. Now comes the difficulty of the man who is earning 15s. a week and under, and who finds it rather difficult to pay 4d. a week. We meet that case by saying that a man or woman who earns 2s. 6d. a day or less shall pay 3d., 2s. a day or less 2d., and 1s. 6d. a day or less 1d. a week. Let me make a very important exception. That would not include the cases where there is board and lodging in addition to the wage. These cases are excluded altogether. This is purely the case where the wage represents the whole payment. Who will pay the difference? If you make the State pay the difference, then it means that the employers who pay high wages to their workmen will be taxed for the purpose of making up the diminished charge for workmen of other employers who are paying less, and I do not think that would be fair. We have come to the conclusion that the difference ought to be made up by the employer who profits by cheap labour, and therefore in the lowest case (in the case of 15s. a week and downwards) the employer will pay more. I hope I have made it clear that our scale of deduction for the workmen is a uniform one, with the exception of that descending scale when you come to the very lowest wages and where you really cannot expect a man to pay 4d. a week. There is another difficulty. Are we going to include in the benefits of the scheme men of all ages at the present moment? If we are, on what scale? Are we going to charge the man of fifty more than the man of twenty-five? That is a question which, of course, presents itself the moment you begin to consider the actuarial position, because, after all, sickness doubles, trebles, and quadruples as you get along in life until when you get between sixty-five and seventy the average sickness in five years is fifty-two weeks. It begins with three or four days, then on to a week, then to a fortnight, and a man as he gets on in life becomes a heavier charge upon his friendly society and no society can possibly take a man at fifty or forty-five on the same terms as if he were only sixteen or twenty unless they make special provision.

Of course, we are now starting a new scheme, and the Government have decided to do this: to charge a perfectly uniform rate throughout, calculating the loss on older lives—because there will be a heavy initial loss as the result of that operation—calculating that loss, anticipating it, and making provision to wipe it out in so many years. We have made provision to wipe the whole of that loss out, charging a perfectly uniform rate in fifteen-and-a-half years. At the end of that time, of course, there will be a considerable sum that will have been realised for the purpose of increasing the benefits, and those who will come in early will then get the benefit of their thrift by having a considerable sum of money added to the sum which is available for increasing the benefits. The only difference we make is with regard to men over fifty. We then propose to pay them reduced benefits. Men who are over sixty-five at the present moment we do not propose should join the scheme at all, because that is an impossible undertaking; the burden would be much too heavy, and, after all, we must be fair to the man who comes in young with his money. He must be encouraged, he must get his reward for it, and if we take over too heavy a burden in the way of those who are at present very old, the young people will suffer. I am told that is the criticism in Germany that the young people do not get full value for their own money and the money of their employers. We propose to admit everyone up to sixty-five to insurance so long as it is done within twelve months after the passing of the Act. We are going to give twelve months' grace. If they come in after twelve months they will come in on the terms either of paying a rate appropriate to their age or of taking reduced

benefits, which comes to practically the same thing.

Mr. BALFOUR: Would not they come in at sixteen?

Mr. LLOYD GEORGE: A man may only start work at twenty-five, and if he comes in after the first twelve months he has to pay a rate appropriate to his age or to take reduced benefits for his life. There will not be very many such cases. The right hon. Gentleman is perfectly right the rule would be that everybody would come in at sixteen, but there may be people who come in after sixteen. In that case they will pay according to age or take reduced benefits. We make a certain exception about sixteen, because if a man has been training at a technical college, for instance, or in some other way, he is usefully employed in training himself for life, then we do not insist upon sixteen as a rigid limit. So much for the contribution by the employé. Now we come to the contribution of the employer. What interest has the employer in the matter? His interest is the efficiency of his workmen, and there is no doubt at all that a great insurance scheme of this kind removes a great strain of pressing burden and anxiety from the shoulders of the working classes, and increases the efficiency of the workmen enormously. The working men whom I met during the trades-union movement told me that many a time they used to go on working at their business because they dared not give it up, as they could not afford to, and it would have been better for them to have been in the doctor's hands. This procedure generally brings about a very bad breakdown, and not only that, when a man is below par neither the quantity nor the quality of his work is very good. I have taken the trouble to make some inquiry from the German employers as to their experience of insurance from this point of view, and I have got a number of answers which, perhaps, later on the House would be interested in having circulated. Here is one instance I had out of many. It is the opinion of an employer engaged in the steel industry. He said:—

"There can be no doubt that the Insurance Laws, together with the increase of wages, have exercised an enormously beneficial influence upon the health, standard of living, and the efficiency of workers."

Another great employer of labour says:—

"That from the employers' standpoint these laws pay, since the efficiency of the workman is increased."

And now there is this very curious position in Germany that the employers, and the

[Mr. Lloyd George.]

largest employers, are voluntarily offering to increase their contributions to national insurance for increased benefits. That is the view taken by the employer in Germany. What does he pay for sickness and invalidity insurance? He pays for a 30s. a week man 7¼d. For a 24s. a week man the employer would pay 5¾d. and for an 18s. a week man he pays 4¼d., then when it goes down below that the contribution is very much lower, and the benefits are very poor. We propose that the employer should pay 3d. a week, the workman will pay 4d., or 3d. for a woman, and the employer will pay 3d. for man and woman alike. That is our proposal.

I come to the contribution of the State. The advantage of the scheme to the State is, of course, in a happy, contented, and prosperous people. The German contribution is not a very large one. I believe it is about £2,500,000 and that includes Old Age Pensions. We have already got a burden of £13,000,000 a year for Old Age Pensions. But let me point this out to the House, that payment is equivalent to something like 5d. a week for employer and labourer under this scheme, and it makes matters very much easier. We certainly could not have offered the benefits which we are offering in this measure, 4d. for a workman and 3d. for an employer, had it not been that the whole burden of pensions over seventy years of age had been taken over by the State. That is the first actuarial fact which was borne in upon me the moment I came in contact with the actualities, what an enormous difference that made in the scheme, and how it eased matters. Had it not been for that I should have proposed very much dearer and sterner terms both for the employer and the employed. We do not propose that the State contribution should end with that £13,000,000. We propose that the State contribution shall be the equivalent—I will explain what I mean when I come to the finance of the scheme—of 2d. a member—4d. from a workman, 3d. from an employer, and 2d. from the State. I should like to point out to the House here how we are meeting the three difficulties experienced by contributaries in making provision for sickness. The first difficulty is the lowness of the wages. We are meeting that by a State contribution and a contribution from the employer which enables us to depress all round the amount of contribution demanded from the workman. More than that we have a special scale for those whose wages are lower. That is how we meet the case of low wages. I want to point out how we meet the case of the man who is unable to pay because of sickness and of unemployment, because really this is the most serious difficulty that the workman has to encounter, so therefore we propose special provisions for him. In the friendly societies, as everyone knows who is acquainted with their working, during sickness, whether you are sick or whether you are unemployed, you have to go on paying steadily. It is true that, not being societies working for profit, and being really quite worthy of their name of friendly societies, with a great sense of brotherhood, they make special efforts to spare their men the last dire necessity of expulsion, but still they have to get their money, and what they do is this. When a man is sick he may get a nominal allowance of 10s. a week, but his 6d. or his 9d. will be deducted from it, so that where he is nominally getting 10s. he is really getting 9s. 6d. That is the time when 6d. is worth more than 2s. 6d. when a man is in full wage. We propose to make no deduction at all from benefits, but where a man is receiving sick pay we do not propose that that should be counted against him at all. With regard to unemployment, there will be no deduction, and the mere fact that he has failed to pay from that time will not be reckoned against him when we come afterwards to compute the number of payments he has made.

Mr. BALFOUR: It will count exactly as if he had paid.

Mr. LLOYD GEORGE: That is a better way to put it. Now I come to unemployment. What is the workman to do when he is out of work? How is he to pay his contributions? We propose allowing a 6 per cent. margin for unemployment; that means three weeks a year. As long as a man is employed you deduct 4d., but we allow a margin of three weeks a year for unemployment. That means in a cycle, say of four years—bad times may come once every four years let us say—a margin of twelve weeks of unemployment. We propose to do more than that. After he has exhausted his twelve weeks, if he is still unemployed, then up to 25 per cent., that means thirteen weeks a year, we still allow him, but at reduced benefits. Up to three weeks there is no reduction in his benefit at all. He is allowed that free margin for unemployment. Beyond that, up to thirteen weeks a year, he is allowed, without expulsion or without his policy lapsing rather, to go on; but then there is a corresponding reduction in the benefits.

Mr. AUSTEN CHAMBERLAIN: The right hon. Gentleman has suddenly moved from sickness to unemployment.

Mr. LLOYD GEORGE: No, no.

Mr. AUSTEN CHAMBERLAIN: I beg pardon. I understood it. I am trying very hard to understand the right hon. Gentleman's statement. I thought he was now talking of unemployment.

Mr. LLOYD GEORGE: I am sorry if I have not made my point clear. I am still dealing with the difficulty of a man paying his contribution during sickness and unemployment, and I am just showing how the Government make special provision for the payment of contributions in these periods. I hope that is clear to the House. Later on I will point out that it is also proposed that what is called a Distress Fund in friendly societies should be set up which will help the workman to pay arrears of contribution for unemployment or for some other reason. That is the compulsory Clause as far as contributions are concerned. I now come to the voluntary contributors. There are two classes of voluntary contributors. There are persons who, whilst not working for an employer, are engaged in some regular occupation and are mainly dependent on their earnings for their livelihood. Take the village blacksmith who is not working for any employer, but is depending on his earnings for his livelihood. The same thing will apply to the small tradesman. I find looking through the lists of the friendly societies, in some of them there is a very high percentage of men who do not belong to the employed class in the ordinary sense of the term. For instance, in rural districts, you will find that all the publicans, all the tradesmen, the schoolmaster, the village blacksmith, and the man who is joinering on his own, who is not anybody's man, are members of friendly societies. We propose that they should be allowed to be members of this insurance scheme. They are really a great source of strength to the friendly societies. They help them in the management, and their business knowledge is of infinite value. It would be a great accession of strength to any scheme of this kind

that we should still retain in it men of that type. Then there is the other class of men, those who have been employed working for others and have ceased to do so, and are working on their own account. So long as they have been contributors for five years we allow them still to join. With regard to this class, there is a difficulty in allowing them to come in at any age and at all ages. With an employed class, you have always the test of employment for wages, but with this class, if a man is a trader, or is working on his own account, doing as little or as much as he likes, there is no test of that kind, and unless there is some sort of check you might have a rush of people who are fairly old coming in at the last moment to get benefits which are quite out of proportion to the contribution which they pay. Therefore, as far as the voluntary class is concerned, we are bound to put a limit to the age at which they can be allowed to join at the uniform rate. Therefore, we propose that all those of that class who wish to join within six months, and who are forty-five years of age and under, can join at a rate which covers the 4d. or 3d. as the case may be, whether they are men or women, they themselves paying the employers' contribution. That would mean that they would pay 7d. for men and 6d. for women, and they, of course, get the benefit of the State contribution. Those over forty-five join at rates appropriate to their ages, but they also get the benefit of the State contribution for what it is worth to them, and, of course, it is worth a good deal.

Another exception we are bound to make to this class of voluntary contributors. I do not think it would be advisable to allow married women who are not workers to join. It would be very difficult to check malingering—almost impossible, I am told by those who are working friendly societies and insurance work. There is no real test except the medical certificate, and that is not always conclusive. It is very difficult, doctors tell me, in these cases, and it would be very dangerous to allow them to come in unless you have something like the test of work. You have, I think, about 700,000 married women who are workers and come into the compulsory scheme as workers, but I do not think we can possibly agree to married women unless they are workers. I will give the numbers which, of course, must be approximate numbers, for we have not the latest Census returns, and therefore we have only to guess at what these

[Mr. Lloyd George.]

figures should be. The estimate of population has been falsified in the case of Scotland, and we cannot tell at present how the estimates will be falsified both in England and Ireland. I have, therefore, to state the figures which have been arrived at by the actuaries, who have given a great deal of thought to the subject. We have had very able actuaries at our command, but the figures must, of course, be estimated according to the details which they have had at their disposal, and if it is found subsequently that the figures are wrong because the Census returns do not substantiate them, it will not be their fault. First of all, as to employed contributors, we anticipate that 9,200,000 men will be in the compulsory class, and there will be 3,900,000 women, making a total of 13,100,000 in that class. Then the voluntary contributors will number 600,000 men, and 200,000 women, making a total of 800,000. Of course, here again I have to say that we can only guess at the number of people likely to come in.

Sir C. KINLOCH-COOKE: Are young persons included?

Mr. LLOYD GEORGE: Certainly; everybody who is employed in this country on wages of whatever age will come in. There will be a deduction in the case of young persons. I will state later on how we are going to deal with the deduction, but they will all come in. Otherwise there would be a premium on boy labour to that extent. If an employer got off without paying in respect of a boy of fifteen it would be an advantage to have boy labour, and therefore we propose that everybody should come in. With the 800,000 voluntary contributors, the total will be 9,800,000 men, 4,100,000 women, making 13,900,000 altogether. But to that has got to be added 800,000 persons under sixteen years of age, consisting of 500,000 boys and 300,000 girls. That makes a grand total of 14,700,000 persons who shall, we hope, enjoy the Insurance scheme.

Now I come to benefits. These will be distributed under three or four different heads. There will be medical relief. There will be the curing side of the benefit, and there will also be allowance for the maintenance of a man and his family during the time of his sickness. I will deal first of all with the medical side of relief. There is no doubt that there is great reluctance on the part of workmen to resort to the Poor Law medical officer. That is

admitted on all hands. It was stated both in the Majority and the Minority Reports of the Commission. He has to prove destitution, and although there is a liberal interpretation placed on that by boards of guardians, still it is a humiliation which a man does not care to bear among his neighbours. What generally happens is this. When a workman falls ill, if he has no provision made for him, he hangs on as long as he can and until he gets very much worse. Then he goes to another doctor and runs up a bill, and when he gets well he does his very best to pay that and the other bills. He very often fails to do so. I have met many doctors who have told me that they have hundreds of pounds of bad debts of this kind which they could not think of pressing for payment of, and what really is done now is that hundreds of thousands—I am not sure that I am not right in saying that millions—of men, women, and children get the services of such doctors. The heads of families get those services at the expense of the food of their children, or at the expense of good-natured doctors. Doctors are very great sufferers indeed. One of them said to me: "A man fell ill and wanted my attendance. Well, I asked myself, What am I to do in this case? Here is this poor fellow, who owes me already £9 or £10, which he can never pay, but how can I refuse to go?" He could not refuse, and he went. I do not think it right that we should do our charity at the expense of the medical profession. What we propose to do is this. If one of the 14,700,000 persons, who practically include all the industrial population of this country, falls ill, he can command the service of a competent doctor, and command it with the knowledge that he can pay. But not only that, the doctor whose service he commands will know also that he will be paid. That is going to make a very great difference in the doctoring of these people.

I come now to a rather delicate task, because the doctors and the friendly societies are at variance on the subject. The doctors say that they are underpaid. Well, we all say we are underpaid. On the other hand, the friendly societies say, "No, it is just your greed." That is really the quarrel that is going on at the present time, and it has become very acute. In some districts—they are rural districts—the doctor is paid half a crown per head per annum for members of friendly societies. In other districts the amount runs up to 6s. per head per annum, but on the average the doctoring for members of friendly societies is done at 4s. per head per annum. The doctors say, "We cannot do it," and I am inclined to agree with them. This is not the opinion of the friendly societies that I am putting before the House. I have information from independent inquiries I have made of men who have really no interest in the matter—men who have passed through the stage of doing friendly societies' work, and who are very good judges. They say that no doctor can possibly afford to give expensive drugs, and some of these are essential to the cure of certain diseases. These drugs cannot be purchased at the price paid to the doctor if he is to get anything for his professional services. I am on the whole inclined to agree that the doctors have got a case for increased payment, not as much as they ask, something far short of that, but at the same time something very substantial, and the first thing which I think should be done is to separate the drugs from the doctors, because a patient, so long as he gets something discoloured and really nasty, is perfectly convinced that it must be a very good medicine. Therefore there ought to be no inducement for underpaid doctors to take it out in drugs. I am not sure but that the Majority Report of the Commission recommended that change.

I suggest that there should be a separation of drugs from the doctor whose business should be confined to prescribing. It should be for the chemist to dispense. At any rate, there should be a compulsory separation of the two. I believe in Scotland that is the practice at the present moment. There are only a few exceptions on the West coast where there are no chemists available, and where the doctor has to do the whole thing. There may be cases of that kind now, for you cannot expect a man to start a chemist's shop in a Highland glen. There the doctor would have to do both the doctoring and the supplying of the drugs he prescribes. Therefore we propose to make provision that, if there is no chemist available, the doctor should be allowed to go on as at the present moment, but wherever there is a chemist available there should be separation. In addition to that, I think there ought to be provision for an improvement in the standard of payment to the doctors. Sometimes, no doubt, they are quite adequately paid, but sometimes they certainly are not, and I think financial provision ought to be made in the scheme for raising the level to 4s. I have done so, and I hope

that will meet the views of the House. So much for doctoring. There will be free doctoring for everybody who is a contributor to the scheme.

The second branch of medical attention will be in cases of maternity. There are only one or two friendly societies at the present moment which allow any maternity benefit, but they are all alive to the necessity for it, and they are gradually going on to establish branches for maternity benefit. Undoubtedly there is no more urgent need. Women of the working classes in critical cases are neglected sadly, sometimes through carelessness, but oftener through poverty, and that is an injury not only to the woman herself, but to the children who are born. A good deal of infant mortality and a good deal of anæmic and rickety disease among the poorer class of children is very often due to the neglect in motherhood. We propose to take the maternity benefit of the Hearts of Oak Society which, I think, has established a most successful benefit scheme in this respect. We propose that there should be a 30s. benefit in those cases which would cover the doctoring and the nursing, but only conditional upon those who are women workers not returning to work for four weeks, for I am told that in the mills you have very often cases where the women work up to the last moment and the maternity is over in a comparatively few days. I believe we ought to make some provision in the interests of humanity to prevent that from taking place.

I have now to refer to another branch of medical benefit. We propose to do something to deal with the terrible scourge of consumption. There are, I believe, in this country about four or five

5.0 P.M. hundred thousand persons who are suffering from tubercular disease. From the friendly societies point of view that is a very serious item, because of the dragging length of the illness. The average illness of patients of the Foresters, I think, was fifty-eight weeks. They received fifty-eight weeks' allowance on an average. Out of the total sick pay of the Foresters about 25 per cent. was due to tuberculosis. There are 75,000 deaths every year in Great Britain and Ireland from tuberculosis and, a much more serious matter, if you take the ages between fourteen and fifty-five among males, one out of three dies of tuberculosis between those ages in what should be the very period of greatest strength and vigour and service. It is a

[Mr. Lloyd George.]

very sinister fact that at the very period which is responsible for the continued life of the race one out of three between those ages is stricken down by tuberculosis. It kills as many in this kingdom in a single year as all the zymotic diseases put together, and a very terrible fact in connection with it is that the moment a man is attacked and compromised he becomes a recruit in the destructive army, and proceeds to injure mortally even those to whom he is most attached and to scatter infection and death in his own household.

There are forty-three counties and towns in Great Britain, with a population of 75,000, and there are 75,000 deaths each year from this disease. If a single one of those counties or towns were devasted by plague so that everybody, man, woman and child, were destroyed there and the place were left desolate, and the same thing happened a second year, I do not think we would wait a single Session to take action. All the resources of this country would be placed at the disposal of science to crush out this disease. I do not say that they can cure it, but doctors think they can cure it. They are confident they can. Men who have devoted a great deal of attention to the subject, and are the most confident of all those who have engaged in experiments, are full of bright hopes that they can stamp it out. But they can only do it if they have the means, and I propose to ask the House to give them. In Germany they have done great things in this respect. They have established a chain of sanatoria all over the country, and the results are amazing. The number of cures that are effected is very large. In this country there are practically only 2,000 beds in sanatoria for tubercular patients. There are only 4,000 beds in sanatoria altogether and half of those are occupied by other patients, so that there are only 2,000 beds when there are four or five hundred thousand people suffering from the disease. I really think it is about time that the nation as a whole, that the State, should take the matter in hand, because the State has suffered. The proposal of the Government is that we should first of all assist local charities and local authorities to build sanatoria throughout the country. We propose to set aside £1,500,000 of a capital sum for the purpose of aiding local people in building sanatoria throughout the country.

We have already, through the munificence and zeal of my hon. Friend the Member for Montgomery (Mr. David Davies), raised a very considerable sum of money, which enabled us to build a succession of them right across Wales. If the same thing were done throughout England and Wales, Scotland and Ireland, I believe we would soon stamp out the most heartrending and painful disease that ever afflicted the human race. We have got to provide maintenance for that. This is our proposal: that we should take a contribution of 1s. per member per annum for the whole of those who are insured compulsorily and voluntarily, and that in addition to that the State should find fourpence, so that there would be 1s. 4d. per member for the purpose of raising a fund for the maintenance of these institutions. This is not an additional contribution. I am done with contributions. There are no more contributions—not for management or anything. This is purely a benefit. What we propose is that out of that fund a shilling should be taken for each member, and that the State should add fourpence. That will mean a fund of a million a year for the purpose of maintaining these institutions, and I am assured by those who have taken the matter carefully into consideration, including the President of the Local Government Board and his very able staff, that that sum will enable us at any rate to do something for the purpose of stamping out this terrible scourge.

I come next to the sick allowance for the purpose of maintaining the families of the sick persons who are insured. In the friendly societies I think the allowance is six months, then it is dropped again to half. In some societies it is still further dropped, generally at twelve months. I propose that the first stage should be a three months' grant, because the real reason why six months' allowance is given is because of tubercular patients. They are the people who take over three months on the fund. Outside of them a man is generally either cured or off the fund before that period. I propose that in the first three months there should be an allowance of 10s. per week. Power will be given to the society to extend that to twenty-six weeks if they think it necessary. I point out later on that there are funds for that purpose, but, perhaps, at any rate, a start should be made with three months at 10s. Afterwards the allowance will be reduced to 5s. for another three months. After that, at the end of the six months, if a man is broken down altogether, there is a permanent disablement allowance of 5s. as long as he is unable to earn his living in any way. That is for men. For women the contribution is lower, and as we are keeping the accounts separate the actuaries say we would not be justified in giving more than 7s. 6d. per week for the first three months, and then 5s. We do not propose to make the allowance less in that case.

There will be a waiting period of six months in the case of sickness. No man will be allowed to get his sickness allowance within six months after he has joined the society. No man is entitled to claim for a disablement allowance unless he has paid for two years. In Germany that has been extended to five years. The allowance is conditional in every case on the patient obeying the doctor's orders—a very difficult thing to do. But at any rate you cannot allow a man artificially to perpetuate his sickness at the expense of the community by defying every rule that is laid down for his cure by the professional gentleman who is in charge of him. In Germany they have this power. They give instructions as to what a man is to do, and if he does not obey them his allowance is docked and I think it is a very salutary rule. I have no doubt it will be very liberally interpreted, but still it is a very necessary rule. There is another rule. The friendly societies do not admit sick allowance to any man whose illness is due to his own misconduct. What we have done in that case is this. If a man's illness is due to his own misconduct we do not allow him sick pay, but he is entitled to a doctor, not merely for his own sake, but for the sake of the community, and because eventually he will come back again, and he will fall on the sick fund and the burden will be much heavier. Now I come to the exceptions. In the case of persons over fifty years of age at the date of insurance the men will only be entitled to 7s. a week and the women to 6s. a week, unless they have paid 500 contributions. Men and women over sixty years of age will only be entitled to 5s. Persons under twenty-one years of age, if unmarried, males will be entitled to 5s., and, if females, to 4s.

There is another very important exception from the point of view of checking malingering. When you come to the lower rate of wages you must not give a sick allowance which would make it more profitable for a man to be sick than to be working. Therefore, we propose that where the sick benefit is more than two-thirds of the wages the amount shall be reduced. But seeing that with the low wages, the insured person is either, through himself or through the employer, paying exactly the same contribution, we propose that in that case there should be an alternative scheme of benefit which would be the exact equivalent in actuarial value. For instance, you might give a pension at sixty-five or sixty-six, as the case may be, but they must submit our scheme, which will be the actuarial equivalent of the amount by which their benefits are reduced. Now I come to the person under sixteen, and with regard to him we propose that he should get no sick pay allowances, but that he should get medical attendance and the benefit of the sanatorium, and that the rest of the money should be invested, in order to accelerate the period of his getting increased benefits. That is to pay off the loss which is due to your taking on men of older ages, and the money will be applied for the purpose of wiping off that loss. The sooner you do that the sooner will the young person come to increased benefit, so that you are really investing it for his own future advantatge.

An HON. MEMBER: Is that for girls also?

Mr. LLOYD GEORGE: Oh, yes. After paying for the doctor, after paying for the sanatorium, after paying maternity benefit, after paying 10s. a week and 5s. sick allowance, and 7s. 6d. for women, there will be left a balance of £1,750,000 in the hands of those who administer the funds. That is the actuarial calculation. We do not propose now to distribute those benefits, because we want to give an interest to those who are administering the funds, to administer them economically, and to declare alternative benefits, if they save the amounts which we anticipate they can save. We propose, therefore, to have a list of alternative benefits, optional benefits, and additional benefits. The first benefits, as I have indicated, will be the compulsory minimum benefits. They will be in every scheme. I now come to the additional benefits from which the society may choose, with this surplus at their disposal. This surplus will be £1,750,000 immediately the scheme begins to work, but at the end of fifteen years and a-half, when the loss on the older persons has been wiped out, you will then have an addition of something like £5,500,000 to the fund, and, of course, that will involve a

[Mr. Lloyd George.]

further contribution from the State of £1,500,000 per annum. That means £7,000,000, which will be added to the income of the scheme after this initial deficit has been wiped out—a surplus now of nearly £2,000,000 for additional benefits; a further surplus of £7,000,000 after declaring those benefits which I have mentioned, and which will be available for the declaration of additional benefits. What is the kind of additional benefit we have in mind? The first is medical treatment, not merely for the working man himself, but for his family. If the societies who administer the funds like to pay for that they have the money at their disposal. An increase of the sickness and disablement benefit and convalescent homes are other additional benefits. I have a long list of additional benefits of that kind from which they can choose, but I think the most interesting of all would be that, when the fifteen years and a-half have elapsed, when the loss has been paid off, and when you have released a fund of £7,000,000 between the State and the contributors, we shall then be within sight of declaring either a pension at sixty-five, or, what I think would be better still —and I propose this as an alternative—if a man does not choose to take his pension at sixty-five, but prefers to go on working, he shall increase his pension at a later stage in proportion to each additional year he goes on working. So much for the benefits.

I now come to the machinery of the Bill we have got to work. Collection is the first thing. We shall collect our funds by means of stamps. That is purely the German system. A card is given to a workman; he takes it to his employer at the end of the week, the employer puts on the workman's 4d. stamp and his own 3d. stamp; he deducts the 4d. out of the wages of the man, and he pays the 3d. himself; the card is in the possession of the man, who takes it to the post office, whence it is transmitted to the central office. The employer does not necessarily know—there is nothing on the face of the card to say— what society the man belongs to. It is entirely a matter for himself. The card is sent along to the central office, and the whole of the money is paid to the central office. Then comes the question, who is to dispense the benefits. In this country we have fortunately a number of very well-organised, well-managed, well-conducted benefit societies who have a great tradition behind them, and an accumulation of

experience which is very valuable when you come to deal with questions like malingering.

We propose, as far as we possibly can, to work through those societies. We propose that all the benefits shall be dispensed through what the Bill would call "approved societies." What are the conditions attaching to an approved society? It must be a society with at least 10,000 members; otherwise, it becomes a matter of very great complication which is much more difficult to manage from the actuarial and financial point of view. It must be precluded by its constitution from distributing any of its funds otherwise than by way of benefits, whether benefits under this Act or not, amongst its members. It must not be a dividing society; it must be a benefit society which provides for sickness and for old age. Therefore it cannot be a society that divides its profits at the end of each year. It cannot be a society that allows anybody to make a profit out of this branch of its business, and it must be mutual so far as this branch of its business is concerned. Its affairs must be subject to the absolute control of its own members; it must be self-governing, and its constitution must provide for the election of its committees and representatives and officers. There are other conditions. It must provide a reasonable security that the funds will be dispensed in the way the Act provides. It must have local committees. There are several societies, as hon. Members know very well, which have branches. There are other societies which are purely central. Both are very excellent societies in their way. The Hearts of Oak, I believe, is a centralised society. The Foresters, I believe, is a society with branches, and the Oddfellows the same. But the societies which have central control and no branches must have some sort of local committees and management; otherwise it will be quite impossible to distribute the benefits, and it will be very difficult to arrange about doctoring and other matters.

There are other things about keeping books and so forth, and there must be a valuation. We do not propose to interfere in the slightest degree with the funds of these friendly societies, funds which they have voluntarily collected, except to this extent: The moment you have a scheme which brings in 3d. from an employer and 3d. from the State for purposes which are identical with the purposes for which these other funds have been accumulated, you release enormous funds for other purposes. You cannot allow those sums to be distributed in cash amongst the members; they must be used for kindred purposes; and we propose that the friendly societies should submit schemes for the purpose, with additional benefits, but of a kindred character. That is the only interference we propose with the present funds of the friendly societies. We propose to allow them to have the most absolute right to admit members or to refuse them. It is a matter I considered for a very long time, whether you should compel them to take members, and I came to the conclusion that it is far better to leave it to ordinary free competition amongst them.

A good many more societies, I have no doubt, will spring up the moment we have a scheme of this character, and it is far better to leave it to competition amongst them. They pride themselves a good deal upon the right to choose their own associates, as most people do, and there are some people they would not care to have forced upon those societies, and I think they have a right to say, "We do not want them." Not only that, some of these societies have purposes which are sectarian, or let us say religious, and some of them are political. Gloucestershire, I find, is split up into Conservative friendly societies and Liberal friendly societies, both of them more or less actuarially sound. I need hardly say that if there are any sectarian or political societies anywhere you cannot exclude them from Ireland. I think there are one or two there which have purposes which are not either actuarial or altogether financial, but which I think are partly, perhaps, political. Then, of course, there are the trades unions. Their purpose is not altogether that of friendly societies. We propose—I will say later on how there shall be no abuse of the power—to give them absolute freedom. It would be quite impossible for the State to administer some of their rules. Take the Hearts of Oak. The Hearts of Oak take power to exclude men of a quarrelsome disposition. I have been watching events in Parliament from the solitude of Kent for some time, and I have wondered how many of my comrades and colleagues would survive the Hearts of Oak test if it were rigidly imposed on them. Then there are rules with regard to exclusion on grounds of conduct, and they interpret rules of that kind, I think, very largely according to the regularity with which a man pays his subscriptions. After all, they are

clubs, and they want to have the right to prevent a man who is objectionable to them entering their club. I do not propose to interfere with that at all. I will come later on to deal with persons who are not fortunate enough to get admission to any of those clubs. They have got to be dealt with by themselves. We propose that the societies should administer and manage their business in this respect exactly as they are doing at the present moment.

You come, then, to the question of age, and that is a difficult question. You are now allowing men to enter those societies who are giving benefits at all ages, and you must not give any sort of inducement to any society to depress its age limits. Otherwise you might have, say, the Hearts of Oak with an average age of forty years, and you might have the Foresters with an average of thirty, and unless you make special provision to equalise that matter by a system of credits, you will find that those societies whose ages are very young will gain an enormous advantage over those whose members are of all ages. We have got an adjustment, which is rather a complicated one. I think, for the moment, I had better let it wait until the Bill comes on. We propose to equalise the ages by a system of credits, so that there shall be no inducements for any society to exclude any man, nominally on the ground of a quarrelsome disposition, but really because he is sixty years of age. We come now to valuation. How do we propose that they shall administer the fund, and what is our check? We propose a valuation for so many years of their funds. Then we have credit for their account in the centre of all money paid in by their members, and paid in by the employers in respect of their members, and, of course, they will have the credit of the 2d. contributed by the State. I propose that there should be a valuation of their assets upon this basis. If there is a surplus then they will have power to declare additional benefits, and so that surplus will be an inducement to them to manage economically and carefully, because a society that manages carefully and economically can declare larger benefits for its Members, and therefore will attract larger custom, and will have a larger number of Members than a society that manages its affairs badly and uneconomically.

For valuation it is very simple to take the Hearts of Oak, as you there simply reckon up the whole of the value of their assets—but take a society with branches,

[Mr. Lloyd George.]

the branches you value separately which is more or less what is done now. If there is a surplus you cannot allow that branch to take the whole of the surplus, otherwise you would find a very healthy neighbourhood in one district declaring enormous benefits; while other neighbourhoods not so healthy would be very badly off indeed, and people would not bear each others burdens, as I think they ought to do in a system of this kind. At the same time there must be an inducement for the branch to be administered economically, and I propose they should get half of their surplus and pay the other half to the centre, because, on the other hand, when there is a deficiency, as I shall point out later, the centre must come to their rescue. Suppose there is a deficiency, what happens? If the insurance office finds there is a deficiency, and that they are not in an actuarial position to pay even minimum benefits, then the central insurance office will have power to do one of two things, either to compel them to reduce their benefits or to increase their levy, to make a special levy. That is the real check on malingering. You cannot check malingering by doctors' certificates. There is no doctor but will tell you that there are certain diseases in which it is quite impossible to say whether a man is shamming or not. Therefore you must depend really upon each member being almost a detective to spy on his associates. That is really the only way to do it. If a society has such a number of malingerers that it becomes insolvent or bankrupt, what happens is that there is an additional levy, or the benefits are depressed. Then the members would say: "Why is this? It is because 'So-and-so' is always sick. He is no more sick than I am." There is no more effective method for suppressing vice than to make it unpopular amongst the man's associates, and the same thing applies to malingering. In a very short time you would soon get a real stop put to the malingerer, because the workmen themselves would not stand it, and would begin to report on those they considered malingerers.

Now comes the question, what are we to do with the residue? You will get men who have been either rejected by the societies or who have left their societies through their carelessness. You may find men who say, "we will not join any society." You cannot compel a man to join a society. If he chooses to remain outside he can do so, but he does it at his own cost. Every inducement is offered to a man in this scheme to join a society, and I will show how that works. We propose that all the men in a county who have not joined a society should be collected together in a body called Post Office Contributors. You will form a fund of those people. Most of the people who remain outside will be uninsurable lives, men who would be rejected by all sorts of societies, because really they are ill at the time, or display symptoms of illness, and they are therefore quite uninsurable, or they may be drunkards. Those are the sort of reasons for which a society now excludes them. That must necessarily make it impossible for us to pay the same benefits to the Post Office Contributors as would be paid to men who are in the friendly societies, because they contain pretty well all the bad lives. It will be largely a temporary difficulty and a dwindling one, for the simple reason that in future men will be taken on at the age of sixteen, and at that age the vast majority of people have not developed any kind of fatal disease. Therefore it will dwindle almost to nothing in the future, and this difficulty is purely temporary. It will be a body of people who are not a very good insurable proposition.

What shall we do with them? We shall distribute the funds first of all in medical needs. They have paid their own contribution, and there is the contribution from the State, and the contribution of the employer. You will make a deduction for medical relief, and for sanitoria, and you will distribute the balance on purely deposit principles. There are societies in this country which do this thing now, and which is really a kind of banking transaction. You pay an amount in and you draw to the extent you paid in. With this condition in these cases you will get a number of lives that will drop, and still a balance who will not withdraw the whole of their deposits. I propose that that should go to swell the fund. Therefore those who are inside the Post Office Society will be able to draw to that extent upon the fund, and will get that additional advantage. It is quite clear there is no inducement to join the Post Office contribution, and we do not want that there should be. We want to give all inducements we can to the societies to govern themselves and take responsibility, and as they have taken the whole of the responsibility the government must be left in the hands of the societies. If you put on a State representative, or if you put on an employers' representative, you are dividing responsibility, and they will always come back to you and say the employer or the State ought to pay an extra penny as the whole responsibility is cast on them.

The only other thing I will say about the Post Office contributors is this. We propose that they should have to wait for fifty-two weeks after paying contributions before they get any relief at all. That is by way of having some kind of test, at any rate, when they enter into the Post Office Society that they are fit for labour. How are you to administer this fund. The Post Office cannot administer it because they certainly cannot go on appointing doctors, and checking malingering, and managing the funds generally. We propose therefore to set up Committees that we will call county health committees. There will be a membership between nine and eighteen, chosen in three batches, a third by the county councils, a third by the approved societies in the districts and failing agreement amongst them by the Insurance office, and a third by the Post Office insurers. We propose that the State should also have a fourth of the whole body to represent its interests in the county health committee. This county health committee we propose shall administer the whole of the sanatorium fund. We do not propose that the sanatorium funds should be left to the societies, because, after all, that has got to be done in the districts where there are no societies. We propose that the whole of the shilling, or, rather, 1s. 4d. per member, which goes to create the fund to establish sanatoria shall be entirely in the hands of the county health committee. Instead of a sanatorium for each county we propose that there should be grouping for the purpose of sanatoria. We propose that the whole of the funds of the Post Office insurers, including medical relief, shall also be administered by the county committee. We are also putting forward another proposition. If any approved society chooses to come to terms with the county health committee to do its medical work for it we propose that they shall have the power to do so, and to make arrangements for that purpose. But if they agree the county health committees can take over the medical part of the work of approved societies if they choose to do so. It is purely a matter of arrangement on both sides. There will be a further power. If a county health

committee are anxious to spend more money than they have funds at their disposal upon either the medical side or the sanatoria side, the county councils have power to agree to sanction further expenditure, provided the Treasury also agree. One-half the additional expenditure will come out of the rates, and the other half out of the Treasury. I want to make it quite clear that the county health committees have no right to incur expenditure and then pass it on to the ratepayer. They must submit the expenditure before it is incurred both to the Treasury and to the county council. If both those bodies approve the expenditure, then the county health committees may, if they choose, incur that extra expenditure.

There are one or two other functions, to which I attach great importance, which the county health committees will have to discharge. They will have to consider generally the needs of the county and borough with regard to all questions of public health, and to make such reports and recommendations in regard thereto as they may deem fit. I shall point out later on that they have power beyond that of merely making reports and recommendations; otherwise those reports and recommendations would be thrown into the wastepaper basket. There is already a plethora of reports and recommendations, and there must be some power of that kind. They will have power also to make provision for the giving of lectures and the publication of information on questions relating to health. This has been a very important power in Germany, because there is appalling ignorance of the most elementary conditions of health—diet, air, and fresh air especially, light, and the danger of the excessive use of alcohol and narcotics. All these questions affect the health of the community. It has been of enormous advantage in Germany to have lectures of this kind and other means of disseminating information upon these points. We also hope that the doctors will assist by imposing conditions which will improve the health of the community.

What are the further powers of the county health committees? The societies, as I have pointed out, are responsible for their own sickness. It is not fair to make them responsible for the cost of sickness that is due to somebody else's fault. Sometimes there is excessive sickness in a district, due to bad sanitation, to bad housing conditions, and generally to the neglect on the part of the local authorities to enforce such powers as they have got, either

[Mr. Lloyd George.]

through ignorance, through incapacity, or very often through a combination of interests. What we propose is that the county health committee shall have power to go to the Local Government Board whenever there is excessive sickness coming on the funds of the society, and apply for an inquiry into the cause of that sickness. Wherever the Commissioners of the Local Government Board find that it is due to neglect by the authority to discharge functions imposed by an Act of Parliament for the housing of the people, or for improved sanitation, they shall have the power of imposing that excess, not on the societies who are not at fault, but upon the local authorities who are at fault. That will be a much more effective check than the old obsolete form of *mandamus.*

I come now to the finance of the scheme. In the first year the sums paid by all classes of contributors will amount to nearly £20,000,000, of which employers will contribute nearly £9,000,000, and the employés £11,000,000. The expenditure on benefits and administration will, in consequence of the waiting periods, be only £7,000,000 in 1912-13, but will have risen to £20,000,000 in 1915-16, when the additional benefits begin to be granted. By 1922-3 the State contribution will also have risen. In the first year there will be no charge, because the Act does not come into operation until 1st May next year. There must be time to make arrangements. There will be only a charge for the necessary expenses of making preparation. But in 1912-13 the charge on the State will be £1,742,000; in 1913-14, £3,359,000; and in 1915-16—a full year—£4,563,000. That is the expense as far as the State and the contributors are concerned of that part of the scheme.

I will now briefly outline the unemployment insurance. My explanation will be considerably curtailed, owing to the fact that the Home Secretary very fully explained to the House the year before last the principles upon which the Government intended to proceed. The scheme only applies to one-sixth of the industrial population. We propose to apply it only to the precarious trades, which are liable to very considerable fluctuations. The benefit will be of a very simple character; it is purely a weekly allowance. The machinery is already set up, therefore it will not be necessary to explain that. The machinery will be the Labour Exchanges and the existing unions which deal with unemployment. I will not say anything about the suffering caused by unemployment. All I will say is that, whoever is to blame for these great fluctuations in trade, the workman is the least to blame. He does not guide or gear the machine of commerce and industry; the direction and speed is left almost entirely to others. Therefore he is not responsible, although he bears almost all the real privation. I think it is about time we did something in this matter, because it is not something which has happened once or twice, but something that comes regularly every so many years. We know it will come, and we know that distress will come with it; therefore we ought to take some means to alleviate the misery caused by phenomena which we can reckon on almost with certainty to within a year or two of its advent.

No real effort has been made except by the trades unions. That, of course, is a purely voluntary matter, and the burden is a very heavy one. It only applies, in their case, to very few trades, and I think to only about 1,400,000 workmen altogether. The others cannot afford it. Other trades have attempted it, but have laid it down because they could not afford the expense. On the Continent many efforts have been made, mostly failures, because they were all on the voluntary principle. In Cologne there was a great effort. It ended in about 1,800 people being insured out of a population of 200,000 or 300,000. There it meant people who knew they would be out of work, and who insured against almost certain unemployment in the winter. That is very little good. I came back, after examining some of these schemes, with the conviction that you must have, at any rate, three or four conditions. You must have a trade basis. to begin with. A municipal basis will not do; it must be a trade basis, because the fluctuations are according to trades. You must start with the more precarious trades. The scheme must be compulsory. I also came to the conclusion that the workmen's unsupported efforts are quite useless. These are the principles that we have incorporated in our Bill. We have started, first of all, by taking two groups of trades, and we propose to organise them individually—the engineering group and the building group. They include building, construction of works, shipbuilding, mechanical engineering and the construction of vehicles. These are the trades in which you have the most serious fluctuations—I think for a very good reason. The depression seems to fall more heavily on these trades; it seems to concentrate upon them, because they produce the permanent instruments of industry. We propose that in these trades a fund shall be raised for the purpose of paying an unemployment distress allowance. I ought to say here that you have not the same basis for actuarial calculation that you have in reference to sickness. It is very necessary to warn, not merely the House, but rather more especially the workmen upon this point. You cannot say with the almost certainty that you can in sickness that a certain fund will produce such and such benefits. In the case of sickness you have nearly 100 years' experience behind you, and you have the facts with regard to sickness and death. You have not got the facts with regard to unemployment, and the question is very difficult. All we know is that in certain branches of trade unemployment is prevalent and appalling. Some trades meet it by short time, but in other trades you cannot do that. As a matter of fact, in the building trade you may get men working overtime in one place at the very time when 20 per cent. of the workmen are out of work in another.

We propose that the workman should pay 2½d. per week and the employer 2½d., and that the State should take upon itself one-fourth of the total income. We propose that there should be an abatement to those employers who choose to pay for their workman by the year. I will show the extent of that abatement; it is very considerable. If you take the two contributions of employers and workmen at 2½d., they come to 21s. 8d. per annum; we propose that the employer who will undertake to insure a workman for the whole of a year can do so for 15s. He will get the whole benefit of the reduction. It is proposed that the workman shall pay the full 2½d. but that the employer should get the whole benefit of the abatement. It seems a very serious abatement. It is practically telling him that he can take one-half if he undertakes to insure the workman for a year at a time. It is an inducement to him to give regular employment; it is a discouragement of casual labour; it is a reward to the employer who keeps his workmen for a whole year. It is a very heavy one, but I think it worth while.

6.0 P.M. That is the only exception made by the employer. We propose, by way of benefits, to give, in the engineering trade, 7s. per week unemployed pay, and in the building trade 6s. for a maximum of fifteen weeks. The number of weeks is limited to fifteen, because, I again say here, there is no basis of actuarial calculation, and you will have to watch the thing. Now, you will have a huge distress fund, to which the employers will contribute very nearly £1,000,000 and the State £700,000 or £800,000 for the purpose of relieving the distress, and to enable the workmen to insure where otherwise they could not do it. But you cannot guarantee that it will work out at these figures. All we can say, having consulted the very best actuaries at our disposal, is that we are firmly convinced that the fund will work out in this way. What will happen? The workman who is out of work will go to the Labour Exchange. We want someone there to check him, so that you will not have a man who is not genuinely unemployed getting unemployed pay. Therefore you have to do this through the Labour Exchanges. The man will take his card and they will offer him a job. If he refuses a job, then comes the question who will decide whether he is unemployed or not? We have appointed an impartial court of referees to decide this; we cannot leave it to the Labour Exchanges entirely, or to the workmen, to decide whether the man is to take a job or the 7s. unemployed benefit. There will be no payment for a workman dismissed through his own misconduct. There will be no payment under this scheme where there is unemployment by reason of strikes or lock-outs, because this scheme has absolutely nothing to do with them. It is purely a relief scheme for unemployment which is due to fluctuations of trade.

I now take the trade unions which insure themselves against unemployment. We propose that in that case that they should reap the benefit, but we cannot possibly hand over State funds—certainly not employers' funds—to an organisation, the object of which, in the main, is to fight out questions of wages and conditions of labour with the employers. What we propose is this that the trade union shall pay its unemployed benefit to the men and claim from the fund repayment in respect of the amount which the men would have been entitled to draw had they gone direct to the Labour Exchanges. The State in effect allows trade unions to spend this money, and at the same time it protects against the unfairness of subsidising what after all is a war-chest—as the trade unions admit. There is no payment for the first

x

[Mr. Lloyd George.]

week of unemployment. In addition to that no man can draw more than one week's employ for five weeks of contribution, so that the real loafer soon drops out. The meshes of the Labour Exchange net might not catch him at first, but eventually and automatically he will work himself out, owing to the fact that he is not a regular contributor, and therefore he will come to an end of his right to obtain benefits. We also propose that where there is a society established on the Ghent model for the purpose of providing unemployed pay generally for the people, say, in the neighbourhood, to give a contribution of one-sixth to that fund for the purpose of enabling them to dispense unemployed pay. If any other trade wishes to come in they are to have, what I think they call in the Court of Chancery, "liberty to apply." If they make out their case and are prepared to make their contribution it will be possible to include them in our scheme. But for the moment we propose to begin to work the experiment with these trades, which are the very worst trades from the point of view of unemployment. This scheme will apply to over 2,400,000 workmen. The contributions of the workmen will be £1,100,000. The contributions of the employers will be £900,000. The cost to the State——

Mr. AUSTEN CHAMBERLAIN: But you said the contribution from the workmen and the employers are to be the same.

Mr. LLOYD GEORGE: I thought I had made it quite clear that there is a very considerable abatement to the employer. It is equivalent to £200,000 on the whole scheme—to the employers if they undertake the responsibility of insuring the whole of their workmen by the year. The cost to the State will be approximately £750,000 a year. The expenditure will undoubtedly fluctuate with the state of trade, and a fund will therefore have to be created for the purpose of dealing with times of very great distress. That is the position as far as both of these branches are concerned. The total sum to be raised in the first year is £24,500,000, of which the State will contribute £2,500,000. By the fourth year the State's contribution will have risen to nearly £5,500,000. That is the finance of the scheme.

I have explained to the House as best I could this great matter, and I thank Members for the courtesy with which they have listened to me. I have explained as best I could the details of our scheme— the system of contributions and of benefits and the machinery whereby something like 15,000,000 of people will be insured, at any rate against the acute distress which now darkens the homes of the workmen wherever there is sickness and unemployment. I do not pretend that this is a complete remedy. Before you get a complete remedy for these social evils you will have to cut in deeper. But I think it is partly a remedy. I think it does more. It lays bare a good many of those social evils, and forces the State, as a State, to pay attention to them. It does more than that. Meantime, till the advent of a complete remedy, this scheme does alleviate an immense mass of human suffering, and I am going to appeal, not merely to those who support the Government in this House, but to the House as a whole, to the men of all parties, to assist us. I can honestly say that I have endeavoured to eliminate from the scheme any matter which would cause legitimate offence to the reasonable susceptibilities of any party in the House. I feel that otherwise I would have no right to appeal, not only for support, but for co-operation. I appeal to the House of Commons to help the Government not merely to carry this Bill through but to fashion it; to strengthen it where it is weak, to improve it where it is faulty. I am sure if this is done we shall have achieved something which will be worthy of our labours. Here we are in the year of the crowning of the King. We have got men from all parts of this great Empire coming not merely to celebrate the present splendour of the Empire, but also to take counsel together as to the best means of promoting its future welfare. I think that now would be a very opportune moment for us in the Homeland to carry through a measure that will relieve untold misery in myriads of homes—misery that is undeserved; that will help to prevent a good deal of wretchedness, and which will arm the nation to fight until it conquers "the pestilence that walketh in darkness, and the destruction that wasteth at noonday."

Mr. AUSTEN CHAMBERLAIN: The right hon. Gentleman is quite assured of a cordial welcome back to-day. We have missed him from our Debates, and we have sympathised with him in the cause that has kept him absent. We are glad to see him here to-day, and are glad that he has

Sir Hartley Shawcross moves repeal of trade union law harking back to the general strike

When **Richard Marsh** was elected to the House of Commons for the Greenwich constituency in 1959 he was the youngest member of the parliamentary Labour party. His oratorical skills from the Back Benches were highly regarded and he became a Cabinet Minister before he was 40. His abilities marked him out for high office, but in 1970 he was sacked by Harold Wilson and he subsequently and successfully took his talents elsewhere – to the world of business.

The epitaph of more than one unfulfilled political career is "the best Prime Minister the country never had", and it is one that has been written for Richard Marsh. He was elevated to Lord Marsh in 1981.

He was born in 1928, the year after the legislation about which he has written became law. His father was a foundryman and his mother was a waitress. He studied engineering at Woolwich polytechnic and economics at Ruskin college, Oxford. In 1951 he became a health services officer with the National Union of Public Employees and in the general election of that year unsuccessfully stood for Labour at Hertford. He was the youngest candidate in the election.

He remained with NUPE for eight years until he won the Greenwich seat. Having served his time on the Back Benches, he was promoted to Parliamentary Secretary, Ministry of Labour by Harold Wilson after the 1964 election victory. After a year he was moved, still as a junior Minister, to the Ministry of Technology, and a year later he moved into the Cabinet as Minister of Power. Two years later, to the day, Wilson appointed him Minister of Transport. He took over from Barbara Castle, who became Secretary of State for Employment.

Wilson and Castle, were struggling to get their "In Place of Strife" trade union reforms through the Cabinet, eventually giving up in 1969. Richard Marsh had been one of the group of Cabinet Ministers who opposed them. A year later, Wilson sacked him in a reshuffle, and he returned to the Back Benches. He observed at the time that all politicians were sacked at some point. "It is one's political coming of age," he said.

After the 1970 general election defeat, Wilson reinstated him to the Front Bench, but it was to be a short-lived appointment. The newly-victorious Prime Minister, Edward Heath, recognised his talents and offered him the job of running British Rail, which he took in 1971. He was the chairman of the BR board for five years, after which he was given a knighthood. He then moved on to become chairman of the Newspaper Publishers Association. Subsequently he held a wide range of business appointments as the chairman or director of a succession of companies, many related to finance and investment.

Currently, he sits in the House of Lords as a Cross Bencher.

Profound analysis of basis of Britain's stability and tolerance

BY RT HON LORD MARSH OF MANNINGTON

On 12 February 1946 I was at the first of many crossroads in my life. At the age of 14 I had started work in a south London factory, making tea and sweeping the floor. Four years later, I had decided that there had to be more to life than making widgets until retirement at 65, and I decided to join the Army.

I had a few days' holiday owing and, for reasons long forgotten, I made my first visit to the House of Commons on the very day that Sir Hartley Shawcross moved the repeal of the highly controversial 1927 Trade Disputes and Trade Union Act.

I cannot claim that I can remember how I felt at the time, but, when I was invited, over 50 years later, to contribute to this volume, I read the original Hansard report for the first time. I have to confess that I was ready for disappointment. In the event, and I have now read and re-read it many times, I was most certainly not disappointed.

What could have been a good old party knockabout, so familiar to us all, was instead a quite profound analysis of the basis of this country's extraordinary history of political stability and tolerance by one of the great advocates of that period.

The 1926 General Strike was, and still is, regarded as a seminal episode in the unique history of the 20th-century development of the British trade union movement. However, as is so often the case, the reality fails to live up to the folklore, and it was a peculiarly British and completely peaceful demonstration, which ended in a humiliating climbdown by the unions after only nine days.

The 1926 dispute, however, followed major strikes in 1919 and 1921 and had demonstrated to the establishment the potential power of organised labour should it decide to use it against the political and industrial establishment. All of this was against the background of the Russian revolution and the emergence of the European communist parties. The 1927 Act was designed to remove that threat for all time.

One section in particular posed a threat to the new and rapidly growing Labour party, which was directly funded by a political levy on all trade union members unless they individually opted out – a brave move, indeed, in unionised industries such as coal, steel or transport. The Act required trade union members to opt in to the political levy with serious consequences for the Labour party's finances. Sir Hartley was moving the Second Reading of a Bill that would repeal this adverse provision.

389

The Labour Government had been returned in 1945 and the division between the Labour and Conservative parties over the 1927 legislation was as wide and bitter as it had been 20 years earlier. However, the tables were now well and truly turned. Labour had a majority of over 200 and the Government were led by confident and high calibre Cabinet Ministers, many of whom were well known and respected as a result of their membership of Churchill's War Cabinet.

Shawcross, as chief prosecutor of the Nazi leaders at the Allied War Crimes Tribunal, had received massive publicity and was a household name. No other Law Officer was ever such a star.

The end of this story is ironic for, almost exactly 20 years later, a Labour Cabinet of which I was a member was completely divided by an attempt to introduce legislation to control the unions in many ways not dissimilar to those which Shawcross had defeated 20 years earlier.

The argument raged in the Cabinet and the parliamentary Labour party for several weeks, but, in the event, a majority of Ministers, of whom I was one, forced the Prime Minister to withdraw the proposals. To my great chagrin, Lord Shawcross chose that moment to announce that he thought that his great speech in 1946 had been completely misguided.

Emergency Allowances, Repair of Furnishings) Order, 1946, copies of which were presented on 4th February, and the Electoral Registration Regulations, 1946, a copy of which was presented on 7th February, and are of the opinion that there are no reasons for drawing the special attention of the House to them, on any of the grounds set out in the Order of Reference of the Committee.

To lie upon the Table.

MESSAGE FROM THE LORDS

That they have agreed to—

Local Government (Financial Provisions) Bill,

Emergency Laws (Transitional Provisions) Bill, without Amendment.

That they have passed a Bill, intituled, " An Act to repeal the Straits Settlements Act, 1866, and to make further provision for the government of the territories heretofore known as the Straits Settlements." [Straits Settlements (Repeal) Bill [*Lords*].

BUSINESS OF THE HOUSE

Proceedings on Government Business exempted, at this day's Sitting, from the provisions of the Standing Order (Sittings of the House) for One hour after a quarter past Nine o'clock. — [*The Prime Minister.*]

ORDERS OF THE DAY

TRADE DISPUTES AND TRADE UNIONS BILL

Order for Second Reading read.

3.31 p.m.

The Attorney - General (Sir Hartley Shawcross): I beg to move, " That the Bill be now read a Second time."

In view of what has just been said about the acoustics of the House, I think I must begin by way of apology for my voice. I shall try to make it heard in every quarter of the House, but it is still suffering a little from the effects of influenza. I must ask the House to bear with me in that respect.

I learn from the evening newspapers which settle policy for hon. Members opposite, that this Bill is to be the subject of fierce and bitter contest at every stage. I certainly do not complain of that. There may be some who think that hon. Members on the opposite side of the House might be more prudent to reserve such intellectual powder and shot as they have got for the more fundamental matters which the House has to consider from time to time, but I would not presume to advise on a matter of that sort.

Mr. Prescott (Darwen): May I interrupt the hon. and learned Gentleman? If this Measure is not fundamental, why is it being introduced?

The Attorney-General: If the hon. Gentleman will wait and listen, if he understands he will see why. The language of hyperbole has been so lavishly used about this Bill; the campaign which has been conducted against it by the Conservative Party in the country outside has been so characterised by political misrepresentation and chicanery, and so divorced from the facts relating to this matter, that I think I ought, at the very outset, to try to put the

[The Attorney-General.]

matter in its proper perspective and explain, if I can, in a sentence or two, what this Bill does not do, and what it does. Those who say, as Conservative propagandists outside this House have said—we shall wait to hear whether they repeat it here—that this is a Bill which is intended to legalise and encourage the general strike are saying that which is completely false. This Bill will legalise nothing that was illegal in 1927.

In so far as this Bill improves, as it undoubtedly will improve, the atmosphere in industry—[*Interruption*]. Hon. Members should try to view this matter with detachment, and free from political prejudice, and they would do well to remember that for 20 years the Act of 1927 has been a sore, a small sore, it may be, but a running sore, which has debilitated our industrial body politic, and, to the extent that we remove it and improve the atmosphere in industry, this Bill will make strikes even less likely than they are at the present time. If this country should ever be faced—and I hope it will not—with the misfortune of a recurrence of a general strike, then at least this Bill will avoid a conflict with the law which, in existing circumstances, the law would inevitably lose with grave constitutional results.

Those who say, as Conservative propagandists outside this House have from time to time been saying, that this Bill is an attack upon the freedom and liberty of the individual, are saying something which they must know to be completely untrue. This Bill, in fact, restores certain hard-won and important individual freedoms, and it does so without threatening the liberty of any one in the slightest degree. Those who pretend, as Conservative propagandists outside this House have pretended, that this Bill is designed to compel people to contribute to political funds when they do not desire so to do, are saying that which is a grotesque travesty of the facts as established by previous experience. On the other hand —and let me say this quite frankly—this is really quite a modest little Bill. I am not going to pretend to the House—and I give hon. Members opposite the point at once—that this Bill is intended to make any great contribution to the building up of a new Heaven and a new earth. Of course it is not. This Bill plays only an indirect, and, in some senses, a psycho-logical part in the Government's programme, but what it will do—and at least it will do this—will be to remove from the Statute Book an Act of Parliament, the perpetuation of which, in existing circumstances, is an undoubted and historical injustice.

Quite frankly, looking back at the 1927 legislation now, one can see that it very largely failed to achieve the purposes for which its supporters hoped and which many of its opponents feared. It had no practical effect whatever on the exercise of the right to strike—not a scrap. It imposed some inconvenience on the organisation of the trade unions. Also, although it resulted in what I suggest to the House was a wholly unjustifiable but not really significant diminution in the political funds of the trade unions, it did nothing to prevent the trade unions and the Labour Party going on from strength to strength. What it did do—and this is its importance, because we must get rid of this, if we are to maintain and strengthen the better feeling between both sides of industry which manifested itself during the war—was to create among the great mass of the working people of this country a bitter sense of injustice, a feeling that the courts of their country had been turned against them, a belief that the law had been vindictively manipulated to their disadvantage, and a feeling that their hard-won right to withhold their labour if they chose, which, after all, is the inalienable right of every free man, had been whittled away. It is to remove that sense of injustice, to do away with these unwarranted restrictions upon the rights of individuals as individuals, or in association together, that this Bill is presented to the House.

May I very diffidently express a view and a hope about the conduct of our discussion of this Bill? We all look forward to many important contributions from hon. and learned Members of this House, but I hope the fact that I, as Attorney-General, am moving the Second Reading of this Bill will not give a legal complexion to the whole of our proceedings. This discussion, if I may say so, ought not to become a kind of lawyers' holiday as did the Debates in 1927 and 1931. Never was so much legal advice given by so many at so small a cost, unless, indeed, it was to the professional reputations of those who give it, for never was confusion worse confounded, or obscurity more obscured than it was at the end of the 22 or 27 days of the discussion of the original Act in 1927. The House is, of course, entitled to be advised on the legal implications of this Bill, and, for my part, I shall do my best, as I am sure will other hon. and learned Members, to advise the House on the legal aspects of the matter, with complete detachment. But, at bottom, the matters involved in this legislation are matters of common sense and of policy. I am very conscious of the fact that a legal qualification gives one no particular or special right to speak about these matters.

May I, then, at the outset, refer to matters which are of a non-legal nature? I shall do so quite shortly, with regard to the circumstances in which the 1927 legislation came to be passed. I do it not intending for a moment to revive old and, I hope, out-worn antagonisms, nor to discuss the merits of the matter as at that time, but in order to show the House, if I can, that the reasons, if any there were, which supported the 1927 legislation have long since ceased to have any kind of practical reality. So much so, indeed, that anybody who looks at this matter now with detachment, objectively, unbiased by any preconceived theories, must realise that the 1927 Act is as clear and as iniquitous a piece of discriminatory class legislation as was ever placed upon the Statute Book. What were the reasons and the motives behind the 1927 legislation? There were, I suggest, three. Each one—they may be none the worse for this—was, in some sense, a motive of fear. There was, first, the very natural, right and proper fear of a repetition of that tragic occurrence——

Mr. W. J. Brown (Rugby): On a point of Order, Mr. Speaker. I am sorry to interrupt, but my capacity for following the hon. and learned Gentleman in his important speech is being heavily impeded by the muttering of a group of political nondescripts on my left.

Hon. Members: Withdraw.

Mr. Speaker: The hon. Member is entitled to complain that he is unable to hear because of the chatter of other hon. Members, but it does not entitle him to refer to them as a group of political nondescripts.

The Attorney-General: I was saying that the first motive behind the Act of 1927, and what was put forward as the primary motive then—it will be very interesting to see whether, in this Debate, it will be a matter to which primary importance is attached—was the general strike of 1926 and the fear of a repetition of that occurrence which had caused such damage to the community. People were, very properly, naturally and rightly anxious to ensure that there should be no repetition of a general stoppage of that kind in this country, and, accordingly, the Conservative Government at that time took the view, rather I suppose on the King Canute principle, that the proper way to prevent a general strike occurring in future, was to prohibit it by Statute, by an Act of Parliament.

That was the main reason. It was not the only reason. There were other reasons and motives behind the 1927 legislation which were, perhaps, less laudable; certainly they had nothing whatever to do with the general strike. I think the House will agree with me when I say that there were probably two of them of main importance. One was the fear which may have been right or wrong—I am not attempting to discuss the merits of the matter—of the growing power, both in political and in industrial matters, of the trade unions. There were those at that time, though I do not suppose there are many now, who had not perhaps fully recognised that, with the growing economic complexity of our national life, with the increasing intervention of Parliament in economic and in industrial matters, it was inevitable that the trade unions should concern themselves more and more with political problems; and there were those who disliked the growing interest of the trade unions in political matters.

Then there were those who were afraid of the increasing power of the trade unions in industry—their amalgamations, their increasing membership, and so on. I think it is right to say that there were not many important industrialists who took that view, but there were at that time in this House not a few who believed in liberty, not the liberty in which we believe, but the liberty of the employer at a time of great unemployment to exploit as he chose the unorganised workmen whom he might choose to employ. Those people, rightly or wrongly, feared the growth of the trade unions in those respects. Then, of course, there were the others, who

[The Attorney-General.]
viewed with some dismay the increasing power of the political Labour Party. They laboured under the odd delusion that the Labour Party was being built upon the hard-earned pennies of honest Conservatives, who were too timid to declare their true political colours and were being bullied by horrid, nasty trade unionists into supporting the political funds of the Party to which they were so much opposed.

Those were, as many hon. Members will remember far better than I do, the three main reasons and motives behind the 1927 legislation at the time it was introduced. Where are they now? Where is a single one of them? I suggest to the House that they have all disappeared into the same kind of oblivion which surrounds most of the lawyers and most of the politicians who were responsible for putting this piece of shameful legislation on the Statute Book. One has to realise, as, indeed, the right hon. Gentleman the Member for Woodford (Mr. Churchill) said about this matter, that the atmosphere today is very different from the atmosphere on the morrow of 1926, or the atmosphere on the morrow of 1927. It is not only that the trades unions and the trade unionists have demonstrated, if any demonstration were needed, their essential loyalty to the State. Only the other day, the right hon. Gentleman the Member for Woodford was referring to the inestimable debt which we owe to the trade unions for what they did for the country during the war.

Squadron-Leader Sir Gifford Fox (Henley): What about the dock strike?

The Attorney-General: I will deal with the dock strike. It is also the case that we have realised, because of our experience of unofficial strikes during the war, that it is utterly impossible to prohibit strikes and prevent them by processes of the criminal law. Because of that very fact, and many others, most people nowadays realise that it is in the interests, not only of industry but of the State to have strong and powerful trade unions of which all the workers in industry are members, and which are able to guide and to lead their members. I would have thought it would be difficult to find any stronger argument against the continuance of the 1927 legislation than

our experience of unofficial strikes during the war. I shall come back to this matter in connection with the actual legal implications of this Bill.

As for the other reasons for the 1927 legislation, I can pass them by in a word. There was, indeed, some reduction in the political funds of the trades unions. I will give some more information about that in a few minutes. The trade unions have increased their membership enormously, and increased—and it is very fortunate that they have increased—their influence and their power both in industry and in political matters. So far as the growth of the Labour Party is concerned, well, here we are and here we are going to remain for a very long time to come. There is this final circumstance which hon. Members opposite may find it impossible completely to disregard, however much they seek to divorce themselves from the facts of this situation. Since 1927, this matter has been submitted to the verdict of the people. I am not going to use the word " mandate ". It was the right hon. Gentleman the Member for Woodford himself who said, shortly before the General Election, that this very matter ought to be submitted to the verdict of the people—that was at a time when he took the view that the verdict was going another way—and that the verdict of the people ought to govern the way in which it was dealt with in the new Parliament. Well, here we are, in the new Parliament, and it will be, perhaps, for hon. Members on this side of the House to see that the view which the right hon. Gentleman then expressed is implemented, and that the verdict of the people is fulfilled by the repeal of this Statute.

I come at once to the legal effect and the legal implications of this Bill. It is a repealing Bill, and it may be for the convenience of the House if in dealing with it, as I shall try to do, in as non-technical a way as I can, I take each of the material Sections of the 1927 Act, and try to indicate what their effect was, and what the position of the law will be when they are, as they will be, swept away. The main object, or what was alleged to be the main object or purpose of the Act —I am far from committing myself to the view that it was the main purpose of the Act—as it was presented to the House in 1927 was achieved by the first Section which prohibited certain kinds of strikes.

Although at that time Lord Birkenhead, Sir Douglas Hogg, the then Attorney-General, Sir Walter Greaves-Lord and others who advised the Government, took great pride in this Section, said that it was one of the most carefully considered and carefully drafted Sections that had ever been presented to Parliament—and I am mentioning this merely to explain my difficulty in telling the House the effect of it —one of our greatest Lords Chief Justice, Lord Reading, said of it:

" The language used is more vague and indefinite than the language of any Bill I ever remember seeing."

Therefore the House will bear with me if I am not able to make the effect of this legislation very clear. The general effect was this. It made a strike illegal if it had any object other than or in addition to the furtherance of a trade dispute in the industry immediately affected by the strike, and was intended or likely to coerce the Government, either directly or by inflicting hardship on the community. It further made illegal any primary strike—I am using the word " primary " in contradistinction to a sympathetic strike—which was not in furtherance of a trade dispute but was intended to coerce the Government. That was the short effect of the Section. In practice, its effect, of course, was that it prohibited not simply a general strike —although no doubt it prohibited that— but went far further and it prohibited any sympathetic strike on a considerable scale. Nowadays one has to realise— and that is why one is so anxious to avoid strikes of any kind, whether they be general strikes or limited strikes—that any strike is likely to inflict a degree of hardship on the community. The effect of the Section, therefore, was. to confine legal strikes to those which were in furtherance of a trade dispute in the industry immediately concerned.

That was the legal effect, but let me say at once, and I think the whole House will really be with me on this matter, that that Section is so much dead wood upon the Statute Book, and the sooner we get rid of it, the clearer our law will be and the more easy will it be to deal by law with such strike situations as may arise. If we could not enforce the far more specific prohibitions against strikes which are contained in the war-time legislation, at a time when the unions are not merely not behind the strikers but are opposed

to them, and when the whole community is united in hostility to the strikers—that is the point referred to by the hon. and gallant Member who spoke of the dock strike, and one could call to mind a number of other instances which, unfortunately occurred during the war—if we cannot prohibit unofficial strikes of that kind by the processes of the criminal law, it is, I venture to suggest, manifest that we cannot prohibit a general strike, when, *ex hypothesi,* the unions would be behind the strikers, as would a very large section of the population, because after all trade unionists and their families and friends do represent a considerable section of the population. You might as well try to bring down a rocket bomb with a pea-shooter, as try to stop a strike by the processes of the criminal law. The way to stop strikes is not by a policeman but by a conciliation officer, not by the assize courts but by the arbitration tribunals. It is a striking commentary upon this Section that in the only case in which it has been sought to apply it to an actual strike, the decision of the judge and jury at the assizes was upset by the Court of Criminal Appeal on a point of law, with the result that the strikers were able to go away and laugh at the law. As this Section is a piece of mere dead wood upon the Statute Book, we propose to get rid of it.

From one point of view it is quite academic to discuss what the law will be in regard to this matter when this particular Section is repealed, but the House is entitled to know our view upon it, and I will endeavour to explain it. Let me say at once, quite frankly, that it is a matter which is not free from doubt. [Hon. Members: " Hear, hear."] Hon. Members say " Hear, hear," but the learned advisers of the Conservative Party in 1927 had no doubts about the matter. They had no doubt in 1926; there was no lack of confidence then. Lord Birkenhead, Sir Douglas Hogg, the then Attorney-General, and Sir Walter Greaves-Lord all pledged their professional reputations that the strike was illegal. Sir John Simon, as he then was, in the notable series of speeches which he delivered, took the same view, and one should add that that great lawyer, so much respected in our profession, Sir Frederick Pollock, also adhered to the view, without any doubt at all, that the general strike of 1926 was illegal. Confronted with those great

[The Attorney-General.] names, I speak about this matter with a great deal of hesitation and diffidence, and I hope that the House will not consider me guilty of impertinence if, in the face of those very eminent opinions, I suggest that there is an element of doubt about the matter. I think myself that a question of fact is involved. A revolutionary strike always was, and always will be, illegal. Nobody has any doubt about that; an industrial strike may, in certain circumstances, be illegal under the 1927 Act, but, when that Act is repealed, will be legal. The difficulty or doubt arises in regard to the intermediate field, and it is there that I think the question of fact is involved.

Mr. Henderson Stewart (Fife, East): Would the hon. and learned Gentleman mind explaining what he means by the words " revolutionary strike "?

The Attorney-General: I should have thought that the word " revolution " was sufficiently understood in the House. I am talking about a matter which I should have thought would be within the competence of any Member of this House. A revolution, as I understand it, is an attempt to overthrow the constitutional Government of a country by force. A strike which has that purpose and effect, is quite clearly, illegal; nobody doubts it.

Mr. Stewart: I hope I may be allowed to intervene further, for we are at the very crux of the matter here. Surely the hon. and learned Gentleman does not suggest that we are to understand by a revolutionary strike, a bloody revolution with arms? What I have understood to be a revolutionary strike was a strike like the late general strike. If the hon. and learned Gentleman has a different interpretation, let him say so. I should have thought that a revolutionary strike was like the last general strike, namely, a challenge to the authority of the State.

The Attorney-General: It will be of interest to the House to know what the hon. Member thought about the matter, but I am not going to follow him into any discussion of the general merits of the 1926 strike. I cannot think that that would be a very useful pursuit at this time.

When we approach the circumstances of the general strike of 1926 we get, as I think, into that intermediate field between, on the one hand, the obviously revolutionary strike, which is intended to overthrow the Government by force or by non-constitutional means, and, on the other hand, the normal industrial strike. Let me repeat that I am only putting forward my own view; I am very conscious of the fact that lawyers may take different views and my view may very easily be wrong, but I am putting it forward for what it is worth. It is when we get into that intermediate field that I think some doubt arises, because it is a question of fact in each case. If, examining the circumstances of a particular strike, you find, as a matter of fact and looking at the substance of the matter, that the real object of the strike is not to further a trade dispute—and I am using now the language which Lord Loreburn used in one of the cases—but that the trade dispute is being used as a kind of camouflage or cloak for sectarian or political ends, then, in my view, the protection created by the legislation of 1875 and 1906 goes, and the ordinary law as to breach of contract, and so on, applies to the matter.

That is not to say that the strike is illegal, far less that it is criminal, but that is the first stage. If, after that first stage, looking at the actions and intentions of any particular body of men involved—the leaders perhaps or any other men taking an active part in it—you find, again as a question of fact, that the object is to overthrow the Government, to coerce the Government, or to obtain a change in the law by unconstitutional means, then I think that an indictment lies against those men for criminal conspiracy. But these are questions of fact. These are not questions for the Attorney-General or any single one of His Majesty's judges to settle. These are questions that, according to the great and very wise and safe tradition of English law, are best submitted to the good judgment and common sense of the 12 men on the Clapham omnibus—in other words, to a common jury of the common people. They are the people who should decide ultimately whether or not particular persons indicted before them have had criminal intentions in regard to a strike or not.

Mr. Henderson Stewart *rose——*

The Attorney-General: I am very conscious of the fact that I am taking too much time already, and I do not want to keep the House too long. Will the hon. Member forgive me if I do not give way? I have expressed my view of the law. I have said that if the facts are as I have indicated, a criminal prosecution would lie.

Of course, I do not want to suggest for a single moment, that any Government in their senses would attempt to suppress a strike by means of a criminal prosecution. Mr. Baldwin's Government in 1926 did not do so. They had no doubt the strike was illegal; they did not attempt to suppress it by the processes of the criminal law. Looking back on it now, it is difficult to imagine anything that would have done more to exacerbate the situation. You cannot settle these great human movements, wrong and misguided as they may be, by putting a few people into prison. That only makes martyrs of those people. That is not to say, of course, that it is not the duty of the Government to deal with any strike situation which may arise. Of course it is. And it is a duty which the present Government will loyally discharge. In 1920, in contemplation, as a matter of fact, of the possibility that a general strike situation might arise, Parliament passed the Emergency Powers Act of that year, giving the Government all necessary powers to deal with any such situation, short of this: that the Government were not to be allowed to declare that the strike itself was illegal. Those powers were operated in 1927, and they continue to exist. If the Government of the time, faced with any emergency of this kind, found that their existing powers were not adequate to deal with the situation, then they could come back to Parliament and ask for whatever additional powers were necessary in the circumstances of that situation.

That is the genius of our flexible Constitution. We can adapt it to meet any situation as it arises. It is only when you have a rigid system, rigid laws in regard to such matters as are provided for by the 1927 legislation, and you have to operate a law, the operation of which is going to bring the law into conflict with the people against whom it is directed, and the operation of which will inevitably result in a defeat for the law, that constitutional danger arises. I be-

lieve, myself—though I do not know whether hon. Members will agree with me about this—that it is a principle of great and vital constitutional importance that the respect for the law in this country, the maintenance and strengthening of the rule of law in this country, does in very large measure depend on excluding from the Statute Book laws which are manifestly unenforceable, in the circumstances with which they purport to deal, and which at the same time cause resentment, rightly or wrongly, on the part of a large section of the population. We commend the repeal of the first Section and the consequential Sections of the 1927 Act dealing with the right to strike. We commend the repeal of those Sections to the House in the confident belief that they would do nothing to make a general strike or any strike more possible or more probable, and that they will certainly do nothing to weaken the respect for the law and the maintenance of the rule of law in this country.

Now may I pass at once to the third Section of the Act—the second as I have said is consequential—to that part which deals with intimidation? Let it be said at the very outset—because, if hon. Members will forgive me for saying so, propaganda outside the House has sedulously sought to obscure the fact—that intimidation always was, and always will remain illegal. Under the law as it stood before 1927, under the law as it was laid down in 1875 and 1906, you had to have something concrete, something tangible; you had to have actual violence, or a threat of violence against a man or his family likely to cause a breach of the peace. That was the criterion, and that was the law as it was operated from 1906 to 1927. But the 1927 Act interfered with the law, which had been operated quite easily, quite clearly, quite effectively up to that time, by introducing a new definition of intimidation. It was quite an artificial definition, as I shall invite the House to say. It was this: intimidation was to " cause in the mind of a person "—I pause for a moment there to indicate the obvious legal difficulty of applying that subjective test in the criminal courts of this country

" to cause in the mind of a person a reasonable apprehension of injury,"

including injury to his business, occupation, or other source of income. Hon. and learned Members on the other side of the

[The Attorney-General.]

House will agree with me about this, that the text writers who study these matters—perhaps it is of more interest to the text writers than to any practical lawyer—have been able to make very little of this Section, and I do not profess to make much of it myself.

Let me take a few examples of how I think the thing would work in practice, though it has not been much operated. Suppose you had a strike in which some men stay out. Suppose one of the strikers going along to a friend; going along, at all events, in a perfectly friendly and peaceable way to a man who had thought it right to remain in work; and suppose he said, " Look here, Tom, if you stick out we shall be beaten, and if we are beaten they will bring all our wages down, and you will lose money in the end, the same as the rest of us." Perhaps hon. Members may think there is nothing very terrible in that, but that is intimidation under the terms of the 1927 Act, and that conduct would be punishable on indictment. [HON. MEMBERS: " No."] It often happens—hon. Members opposite may think it wrong; I am not discussing the merits of the matter, whether it be right or wrong—that members of a trade union, finding that they are being called upon to do a particular kind of work with a non-unionist, object. They are perfectly entitled to object. If they go on strike about the matter, it is perfectly legal for them to do so. Strikes have been occasioned by circumstances of that kind. But if before they go on strike one of them, the secretary of the union or an official of the union, goes along to see the non-unionist, and says, in a perfectly friendly and peaceful way, " Look here, Bill, come and join us," and points out the advantages of trade unionism to the industrial worker, and says, " Come along and join us, and become a member of the union, for if you don't we shall refuse to work for old Tom Noddy, the employer," that would be intimidation. [HON. MEMBERS: " No."] It would. Hon. Members opposite are surprised, which goes to show that they do not really know the implications of this Act. They have not bothered to acquaint themselves with the law which they are so anxious to support. That was the Chester case, decided at Chester quarter sessions.

I am not dealing with hypothetical matters. It is astonishing that it should be legal to strike about such a matter, and not legal to seek to avoid a strike by peaceful persuasion of a man. It is perfectly legal to boycott a man who is staying in, and not striking with his pals, by refusing to speak and associate with him—leaving the pub when he comes in to have a drink and so forth. It is perfectly lawful to do that, but to go up to him beforehand, and say to him, in a perfectly friendly and peaceful way, " Look here, George, if you don't come in with your pals and join us in this strike, which is so vital to our interests; if you stand out against the lot of us the result is going to be that we are not going to have anything to do with you; we shall no longer be your friends," that may be an indictable offence at assizes under this law.

One could go on giving lots of examples of this kind, but I am not going to take up the time of the House, except to give one which is outside the industrial field, because I think that it ought to be remembered that this law laid down in 1875, and amended in 1906 and extended in 1927, does not deal only with matters connected with trade disputes. Anybody who, in order to compel someone else to do or not to do something which he is legally entitled to do, intimidates him, is guilty of an offence, whatever the thing may be. It need not have anything to do with a trade dispute at all. The intimidation Section of the Act of 1927 uses the words, " to cause a reasonable apprehension of injury." Take the case, if hon. Members opposite can imagine such a shocking case happening, of someone who wanted to influence votes in a General Election, who, speaking with all the authority of a great political leader over the wireless system of this country, said: " The Gestapo will get you if you don't watch out. There will be a political police, I assure you of it, if you vote Socialist." Such a man, if there were such a man, would be liable to be fined 40s. at the instance of some timid housemaid who had been caused a restless night. [*Laughter.*] Hon. Members may laugh, but this really is a serious matter. I do not think hon. Members on this side of the House ought to allow politicians on the opposite side of the House to be exposed to danger in that way. Let them say what they like on the wireless system of this country; it only makes more people vote for us.

So we propose to repeal this Section of the Act. We propose to repeal also the provision of the Act which would prevent people, it may be political canvassers, attending at a man's home in order to communicate information to him, or peacefully to persuade him. Let this be quite clear. When this Section of the Act is repealed, the law will be amply strong enough to deal with any question of improper pressure or intimidation which may arise. I am going to read now the language of one, who spoke with far more authority than I can do—the Conservative Home Secretary at the time. He said on 2nd June, 1926, in the middle of the general strike—he had referred to the words of the Statute, but I will not bother the House by reading them all out. [An Hon. Member: "The 2nd June was not in the middle of the strike."] I am sorry, it was about that time. This was after the strike, but the mining strike, I think, was still going on. Sir William Joynson-Hicks, a lawyer, and Home Secretary, speaking, no doubt. with all the advice and authority of his Department responsible for the administration of the law in this particular, read out the words of the Section of the relevant Act. He said:

"These are the words which are the charter, so to speak, of peaceful picketing. They are limited, and much more closely limited than has been thought to be the case by a good many people, sometimes lawyers and sometimes not lawyers. Any person, even today, who attempts to prevent any person from working by using violence or by intimidation either of him or his wife or children, or who injures his property, is guilty of an offence, and so is anybody, in spite of the Act of 1906, who persistently follows a workman from place to place or follows him with two or more other persons in a disorderly manner. Those are still offences under the Act of 1875, and they are in no way excepted by the Act of 1906. I hope that hon. Members will realise the seriousness of what I am saying. The law is that you cannot compel a man to listen. If a workman does not choose to listen, you have no right to stop him. You have no right to compel a man to listen. That is continued under the Act of 1906. If he likes to listen you may impart information, or try to persuade him to strike or not to work. But if he says, ' I do not want to speak to you or to listen to you,' and you continue to do it, it is an offence under the Act of 1875."—[Official Report, 2nd January, 1926; Vol. 196, c. 819.]

Speaking some time later he said:

"If a person watches or besets the house or other place where such other person resides, or works, or carries on business."—[Official Report, 30th August, 1926; Vol. 199, c. 19.]

it was a criminal offence and he added if a number of men persistently beset the house of a miner who desired to work, and watched his house from time to time, watching him going in and watching him coming out, that was an offence under the law as it stood. Of course, the fact is that up to 1927, the law had stood unaltered since 1906. During those 20 years there had been, unhappily, many strikes, some of them large, some of them small, many of them serious; but I think I am right in saying—I am certain that I shall be corrected if I am wrong—that no Home Secretary responsible for the peace, order and good government of this country has ever come to the House of Commons and said, " These powers are inadequate; I must have additional powers in order to deal with this intimidation which is taking place." I think that we ought to remember that this attempt to extend the law relating to intimidation was not only inept, as I have ventured to suggest, but entirely unjustifiable. I want to remind the House of what Sir John Simon said about this matter at that time. No one can suggest that Sir John Simon was taking a view especially marked by any particular favour towards the trade unionists. He said:

"Everybody here who remembers the events of a year ago must take pride in remembering that the feature of the general strike which impressed foreign observers beyond any question was the general orderliness of the whole operation.

"That is certainly the feature which particularly impressed foreign observers and it was not due solely to the police or to public-spirited members of the public who lent their aid; it was due also to the counsel and guidance of trade union leaders and it was due to the general spirit of reasonable orderliness among the men who were out themselves."

Then he said this, and I hope we shall remember it when discussing the matter at this particular time:

"We really do a very grave injury to our own national reputation if we do not always remember that that was the feature of the general strike which particularly impressed the world at large."—[Official Report, 4th May, 1927, Vol. 205, c. 1643.]

There was not a shred, not a tittle, not a rag of evidence to support the enactment of these new rules and this new definition of intimidation.

Let me come at once to Section 4 of the Act, which deals with the political levies. This is the Section over which

[The Attorney-General.]

hon. Members opposite have tried with indifferent success—if they will permit me to say so—to work themselves up into a political frenzy. Hon. Members know that that Section was never intended to protect the workmen against having to pay a farthing per week. That is the amount involved, and that that Section was ever intended to protect the workmen against having to pay that political contribution is really the purest political bunkum. Nobody believes it now, and nobody believed it in 1927 and it is manifestly not so. If the number of those who do not wish to subscribe to political funds is as large as hon. Members opposite invite us to believe, then clearly they are numerically strong enough to protect themselves and to come out in their true political colours without fearing any improper pressure or bullying by trade unionists of different political views. The figures of the Registrar of Friendly Societies demonstrates that there is not a rag of evidence to support the view that anyone was being compelled to contribute to political funds against his will. The truth is, of course—and I confess it quite frankly—where you have any large body of people you come up against a certain degree of human inertia, which prevents certain numbers taking any particular action. They just cannot be bothered filling in a form, whether it is a form to contract in or contract out. They cannot be troubled doing it, they cannot be bothered and they let the thing go.

The question here is very simple, whether the trade unions, which by a majority have decided to have a political fund, should benefit if you like from that human inertia, as I have called it, to the extent of throwing the onus on the dissentient minority to declare their objection to contribute to particular political funds, or whether the onus should be put the other way, and whether the majority, who have already voted in favour of the political fund, should be required to go further, and fill in a form showing they wish to make a particular contribution. In any ordinary organisation like a club or a company—a company having power under its articles to devote money to particular purposes—the minority have to toe the line. They do not get any opportunity of contracting out at all, but in any organisation where the minority are entitled to exemption from the view of the majority,

the normal practice—I would almost say the invariable practice—is to throw the onus on the minority to claim the benefit.

What are we to do next? Are we to say that it is the law of this country, if people have not got a conscientious objection against being vaccinated, that before vaccination takes place everybody has to fill in a form to say they want to be vaccinated? I do not see any difference, in principle, between the two cases in that analogy. This Statute which we are inviting the House to repeal put the onus the other way—on the men who wanted to pay a political contribution. Let me say at once that that Section is the only Section of this Act which, in part, did achieve its purpose. We did lose the benefit of that particular element, the inertia element who could not be bothered to fill in a form, and, as a result, the contributions to the political funds went down. The position differed in the different unions, and it is very difficult to compare a position like that, because the membership of the unions has increased very greatly, on the one hand, and, on the other, during the past six years, there has been little political organisation and canvassing. [*Interruption.*] Hon. Members mistake me. I was referring to political canvassing on the trade union and Labour side, not on the Conservative side. Hon. Members will find, if they look at the figures—and I am not going to bother the House with more than two or three cases—that the position differs greatly in the different unions, and I tried to see why from the figures themselves. As far as one can judge, where there is a union with a membership widely dispersed, and where there is not active political organisation, canvassing and so on, subscriptions go down. Where there is a well-knit union, with the members closely associated, and the political organisation is good, the subscriptions keep up. The figures differ very greatly in different unions. Because I want to be quite fair with the House, I will give three instances and show the net result.

The Locomotive Engineers' and Firemen's Union had a membership of 48,000 in 1927—I am leaving out the odd figures for the sake of convenience—19,000 of whom contributed to the political fund. In the year 1945—I think the latest figures are for that year—it had a bigger membership at 68,000, but the political fund did not go up in proportion to the numbers, though it did go up almost in proportion, for it increased to 23,000. Another case, and it is quite an interesting one, is that of the Shop Assistants. They had a membership of 34,955—and I am giving the odd figures here because it is a rather remarkable case—and there were no fewer than 33,950 subscribers to the political fund in 1927. Why? Surely, not because they were being coerced to give. I cannot think of any way in which a large trade union could really effectively bring pressure upon persons so widely spread out over the country as the shop assistants. Yet that was their subscribing membership, and the reason for it was this: They just would not be bothered, if they did not want to contribute, to fill in the form to contract out. There was that high figure of contribution to the political fund, and there is a drop there. The membership has gone up by 97,000 in the last year, but the contributors to the political fund have only gone up to 40,000. The reason for that is exactly the same. Here is a union which is widely dispersed, the members of which cannot be canvassed and invited to fill in a form to contract in, so that they do not bother and the subscription is not paid.

Another rather interesting instance is that of the Agricultural Workers' Union. They had astonishing figures in 1927, when they had a membership of 29,591, of whom 29,590 contracted in, leaving only one who took the trouble to fill in the contracting out form. The membership went up to 110,000, but contributions went up only to 72,000, not in complete proportion to the increase in membership. There, again, it is obvious that that cannot be accounted for by pressure upon, or by intimidation of, members of an industry which is so widely dispersed as the agricultural industry. What was the reason, what was the excuse, for providing this system of contracting in instead of contracting out? It was said that when you had contracting out you had a list of those who were in political disagreement with the majority of the union. and that they became marked men. That is equally possible when you have contracting in. You can have a list if you want one, and you can still mark your men if you want to mark them. Therefore, there is not the slightest validity, if that is the reason, for this difference in

procedure. I do not know whether the right hon. Gentleman opposite is indicating that that was not the reason, but at all events that was the reason which was put forward in 1927—that you had a list, that men were marked, and that they could be intimidated. The right hon. Gentleman who now sits for West Bristol (Mr. Stanley) said at that time—as one would have expected him to say, fairly and frankly—this about that argument:

" Let us see what alteration it is that the Government propose. Does it meet the case? Does it, in fact, take away from those who may have the will to intimidate the power to do so? In my opinion, I must confess it does not. You still have the knowledge, which is the essential preliminary to intimidation—you may change people and you may mark them in instead of out; you may tick them off with a red pencil, instead of a blue pencil—that, in fact, there are two lists still there—the list of those who pay and the list of those who do not pay. Although, in some cases, there may be intimidation, and although men may have to come up for examination, yet the opportunity does still exist, and there are many ways in which the trade union leaders, if they want to intimidate, can still do it."—[OFFICIAL REPORT, 25th May, 1927; Vol. 206, c. 2080.]

On that ground the right hon. Gentleman refused to vote for the particular Clause under discussion in the 1927 legislation. We propose to invite the House to go back to the old method, which is the logical and normal method. In future, if anybody prefers not to contribute to the political funds of his union, all he has to do is to sign a form, and once and for all he is free from the obligation to contribute. If pressure is brought to bear upon him he has the right to go to a very powerful, independent and impartial tribunal in the form of the Registrar of Friendly Societies.

Now I come to Section 5, which prohibits established civil servants from belonging to trade unions. By that Section established civil servants were not allowed to belong to trade unions of which outside persons were members, or which were themselves affiliated to outside bodies like the Trades Union Congress. There was not a shadow of justification for it, so far as the general strike was concerned. The right hon. Gentleman the Member for Woodford (Mr. Churchill) made that perfectly clear. The civil servants made their position clear. They sympathised with the strikers, and did what they were legally entitled to do.

[The Attorney-General.]
They contributed to funds for the miners' wives and their children, but they took no active part. On this point, I want to emphasise that the right of civil servants to strike is not in point in this legislation at all. The 1927 Act did not forbid civil servants to strike, and nothing that we propose to do now will make it any more legal than it is today for civil servants to take strike action. It is true that civil servants perform, in their various degrees, services which are essential to the State, and that some of them stand, by reason of the very nature of their employment, in a particular relation to the community. I take the opportunity of making it quite clear that this Government, like any Government as an employer, would feel itself perfectly free to take any disciplinary action that any strike situation that might develop demanded. To take a completely hypothetical case—supposing a special section of the Civil Service, for instance, prison officers, disregarding the machinery of the Whitley Council, went on strike, the Government would undoubtedly take disciplinary action by exercising their right, as an employer, of instant dismissal without hope of reinstatement. But it is no good laying down prohibitions of that kind by Statute——

Mr. W. J. Brown: The point that the Attorney-General is making is that the first recourse of a public servant should be to the recognised conciliation and arbitration machinery existing in his profession, and that that ought to militate against the strike weapon ever being employed. But would the Attorney-General recognise the corollary to that, and give to the police, who are now denied it, the right to have a union and proper conciliation and arbitration machinery?

The Attorney-General: The police stand in a different position. They are a disciplined service. Their position has been considered, and the proposals we now make do not involve any alteration in that position. I am dealing now with the ordinary civil servant who has recourse to the Whitley machinery, just as police officers have recourse through their Association, to other means by which they can make representations in regard to conditions of their employment. I was saying that we cannot deal with these matters by statutory prohibition, but if we could, the 1927 Act clearly ought to apply to non-established, as well as to established, civil servants. There are now far more non-established civil servants than established civil servants; even in normal times, they are almost as numerous as the established civil servants, and perform equally important functions. But we do not think that statutory prohibition is the right method; we do not think we can secure loyalty and allegiance from the Civil Service by the device of cutting them off from association with others with whose terms and conditions of employment their own are often closely related.

Now I come, finally, to Section 6. This was the Section which made it illegal for local or public authorities to make membership of a trade union a condition of employment. It is sometimes of advantage—many industrialists find it so—especially where you have negotiating machinery of a particular kind, to ensure that all employees are represented by a union which is on the opposite side on the conciliation machinery. Many ordinary employers take that view. We see no reason why democratically elected local authorities, or responsible and statutory public authorities, should be discriminated against by the law in this matter. Their position is not different from the position of any other employer, except perhaps to this extent: that their responsibilities to the electors in so far as local authorities are concerned, and to the Government in so far as public authorities are concerned, makes it more likely that they can properly be entrusted with discretion in this matter which is left, apparently, without disadvantage to the ordinary private employer.

Nor do we think it right that the mere fact that a man is employed by a public authority or by a local authority should make it a criminal offence if he breaks his contract, even though such breach of contract may result in serious inconvenience to the public. The question is not one as to the character of the employer, but as to the nature of the employment. Parliament has provided that in the cases of gas, water and electricity, a breach of contract may in certain circumstances result in a criminal offence. If it is necessary to extend those provisions to other services, that can be done. but we do not see that there is any reason to make this question depend upon whether the employer concerned is a local or a public authority. We propose to ask the House to repeal Section (6) and go back to the ordinary law as generally applicable in industry as a whole.

That is the whole matter. I am conscious of the fact that I have taken up the time of the House too long, and for a good deal longer than I had intended to do. I shall not hide from hon. Members that two views seem to be taken on the other side of the House about the 1927 Act. One hon. Member opposite permitted himself, if I may respectfully say so, in a most friendly way, the grotesque extravagance of calling the 1927 Act the charter of the working man in his home; and Mr. Strauss, whose services were lately so regrettably rejected by the electors of Norwich, has improved the shining hour in the meantime by preparing a brief for hon. Members opposite—I confess I have found it exceedingly useful myself— the tone of which is perhaps characterised by the statement that, if we repeal the 1927 Act, the state of the law of this country will be unworthy of any civilised country. On the other hand, " The Times," taking, one may think, a more objective view of the matter, referred to the 1927 Act as being admittedly a punitive Measure. It is not a good thing to have punitive Measures on the Statute Book. It is a good thing that political parties which seek to put them on the Statute Book should know that in the due course of time they will be taken off. So we are to take this one off, and we are to restore the law to the condition in which it was as the result of a century of orderly, deliberate, constitutional growth, as the result of the decisions of Parliament, usually after inquiries by impartial Royal Commissions, the decisions 'of Liberal Parliaments and Conservative Parliaments, Parliaments which, like this Parliament, but perhaps unlike the Parliament of 1927, are not afraid of the industrial liberties and the personal freedoms which, by this Bill, we invite the House to restore.

4.54 p.m.

Mr. Eden (Warwick and Leamington): The hon. and learned Gentleman the Attorney-General, in his opening observations, expressed the hope that the discussions on this Bill would not be carried on throughout by members of the learned profession of which he is such an ornament. I have done my best to respond to his suggestion, and I offer myself, a mere layman, to make some observations upon the hon. and learned Gentleman's speech and upon this Bill. I would, however, like to re-echo his appeal and express the hope that our discussion will not all of it be in the legal stratosphere, but will be upon the issues as they seem to the layman who attempts to apprise himself of this problem.

The hon. and learned Gentleman's statement that this is not a fundamental Measure which the Government are bringing forward at the present time will, I should imagine, cause the country the very greatest surprise. At this time innumerable problems are pressing upon the Government. The right hon. Gentleman the Lord President of the Council, most reluctantly, I am sure, is obliged to refuse us Debates every day on almost every subject. The Coal Bill has to be sent to a Standing Committee. At this time of great difficulty, we are given only Thursday to discuss the food situation. Yet the hon. and learned Gentleman says that this is not a fundamental Bill; it is not really awfully important, he says, but we may as well get rid of the 1927 Act now, and get it over. If that is the position, there could not be a worse time than the present to bring a Measure of this kind before the public.

Mr. Sydney Silverman (Nelson and Colne): Why did the right hon. Gentleman ask for two days to discuss it?— [*Interruption.*]

Mr. Eden: Because I do not happen to agree with the Attorney-General, as I hope to have an opportunity of showing the hon. Member for Nelson and Colne (Mr. S. Silverman) in the course of my relatively brief remarks.

Mr. Bechervaise (Leyton, East): On a point of Order, Mr. Deputy-Speaker. Is it in Order to use the phrase " silly ass " on the Floor of the House?

Mr. Eden: I did not say that.

Mr. Deputy-Speaker (Major Milner): I did not hear the phrase used. It would certainly not be an acceptable expression.

Michael Foot makes a great speech but fails to secure a great victory

During a political career that spanned more than 50 years, **Ian Paisley** mounted an implacable opposition to any action or policy that he deemed damaging to the Protestant majority in Northern Ireland and to the Province's union with Great Britain.

In 1970 he was elected to the House of Commons to represent Antrim, North, and for most of his career thereafter he was regarded by many as the most dominant figure in Northern Ireland politics. Controversy was his constant companion, and compromise was rarely a word that featured in his vocabulary.

His stance earned him the reputation for always saying no, and his powerful vocal opposition to those he regarded as the enemies of both causes frequently prompted an equally powerful reaction, but not one that would ever silence him. He was thrown out of the European Parliament and the Stormont Assembly. He was arrested and imprisoned. He came close to being disciplined in the House of Commons when, with fellow MP Peter Robinson, he mounted a demonstration from the Side Gallery – not from the Floor of the House – when Prime Minister Margaret Thatcher rose to make a statement on the Anglo-Irish agreement in November 1981.

They left the Gallery before the Serjeant at Arms could reach them to eject them, but they were ordered by the Speaker, Mr George Thomas, to appear in the Chamber and answer for their actions. When they did not appear, the Speaker gave them until the following Monday to present themselves. On the intervening Saturday, Rev Robert Bradford, the Unionist Member for Belfast, South, was murdered by the IRA while meeting his constituents.

When the House met on Monday, moving tributes were paid to Rev Bradford from all sides of the House. Ian Paisley reminded MPs of the chilling fact that "those of us in Northern Ireland who have been elected to office walk with death."

The Speaker told the House that, in view of the "tragic events" he proposed to take no further action over the demonstration, but he asked the two Members to reflect on the consequences of their action for the good name of Parliament.

Ian Paisley was born the son the Rev James Kyle Paisley, an ordained minister, in 1926. He was ordained as a minister himself at the age of 20, and after five years founded the Free Presbyterian Church of Ulster.

He became active in politics in the mid-1950s, and in 1970 he was elected on the Protestant Unionist Party ticket to both the Stormont Parliament as the Member for Bannside and to Westminster for the Antrim, North constituency. The following year, he co-founded the Democratic Unionist Party, which he was to lead both in Northern Ireland and Westminster for the next 37 years, finally stepping down in 2008.

In 1979, he was elected to the European Parliament, where he served for 25 years until 2004 when, at the age of 78, he stood down. He had served for five terms, and at each election he received the highest vote of any MEP. It was in the Hemicycle of the European Parliament that he had staged a demonstration during a speech by Pope John Paul II which resulted in his being forcibly ejected from the Chamber.

Throughout his political life he had opposed any move towards closer links with the Republic of Ireland and any easing of the position against Sinn Fein and the Irish Republican Army. He opposed the Sunningdale agreement, with its power-sharing executive. He said no to the Anglo-Irish agreement, resigning en masse with his fellow Unionist MPs in protest. They stood in by-elections in opposition to the agreement and were overwhelmingly re-elected.

He was to say no again, this time to the Belfast agreement in 1998, holding out against participation by Sinn Fein. He was elected to the new Northern Ireland Assembly, which was set up under the agreement. After four years, with little to show, the Executive and the Assembly were suspended. There was to be no real progress until the parties met in Scotland and hammered out the St Andrews agreement in October 2006. It provided for fresh elections to a resurrected Northern Ireland Assembly and a new Northern Ireland Executive.

In the ensuing election, Ian Paisley's DUP increased its share of the vote and its number of seats from 30 to 36. On 8 May 2007 power was once more devolved to Stormont and Ian Paisley was endorsed as the First Minister. His old enemy Martin McGuinness of Sinn Fein became his deputy. In the spirit of the time, they put their past behind them and established a good working relationship.

In his inaugural speech he declared that the Province was starting – he emphasised "starting" – on the road to lasting peace.

He had appeared in *The Official Report* over the years as the Rev Ian Paisley. He was also known as Dr Paisley for his doctorate of divinity. When he became the leader of the fourth largest party in the Commons, he was made a Privy Counsellor and *Hansard* now records him as "The rt hon Rev Ian Paisley."

In March 2008 he announced that he was standing down as leader of the DUP and First Minister of Northern Ireland. He was succeeded by Peter Robinson, the man who had stood beside him during that Commons protest 27 years earlier.

Every word a dagger point, but not enough to give the Government the edge

By Rt hon Rev Ian Paisley MP

Hansard is to the dedicated Member of Parliament what the King James (Authorised Version) of the Bible is to the Bible-believing preacher – the final court of appeal in all matters of record.

"Thus saith *Hansard*" puts an end to all argument about what is said, or not said, in Parliament. It is the great silencer, the authority of finality. The story of *Hansard* is marvellous history, and its columns are either enchanting or disenchanting according to the political creed of the reader.

Since 1970 I have been a Member of Parliament, except for a brief period when my Unionist colleagues, including Mr Enoch Powell, resigned in protest against the Anglo-Irish agreement and stood again in a series of by-elections. The Anglo-Irish agreement met its Boyne water immersion from which it never recovered, and it was laid to rest in a Sadducee's grave – a grave without resurrection.

Alas *Hansard* cannot convey the moods of the House of Commons, and what moods it has! The moods of all its Members are as numerous as liquorice allsorts and dolly mixtures.

One of the most outstanding debates I ever attended was the one in March 1979 on a motion of no confidence that led to the downfall of the Labour Administration by one vote. I claimed it was mine! The Labour Lord President of the Council and Leader of the House, the great orator and parliamentarian Michael Foot, wound up the debate with a speech that deserves inclusion in any collection of great House of Commons speeches.

One sentence in that momentous speech was his reference to the leader of the Conservative party, Margaret Thatcher. "What the Rt hon Lady has done today is to lead her troops into battle snugly concealed behind a Scottish Nationalist shield, with the boy David holding her hand," he declared.

The reference was to the fact that the motion of no confidence, although tabled by the Conservatives, sprang from Scottish National party dissatisfaction after Labour had failed to proceed with Scottish devolution. The Liberal party, led by David Steel, had been in alliance with Labour but it had withdrawn from the deal in the previous October, and now Mr Steel had agreed to go with the Conservatives. All this had left Prime Minister Jim Callaghan isolated. He had just come through the so-called "winter of discontent", and his standing with the electorate had reached a low point.

Each word in Michael Foot's speech was a dagger point. However it was he and Prime Minister Callaghan who were to fall and it was Margaret Thatcher who went forward to be crowned.

The greatest speeches in Parliament do not always end in the greatest victories, but, often, in the greatest defeats for those who made them.

Hansard, that historic record of the Mother of Parliaments, is always available, a Mother Book indeed, with an amazing progeny. Long live Mother *Hansard*, and may her children be many!

[Mr. Whitelaw.]

background, we have an opportunity tonight to assert the power of the House of Commons in the best interests of democracy. By supporting the motion, we can bring to an end a disastrous Government and a Parliament which has nothing more to contribute to the well-being of our nation. In doing so, we shall be acting in the best interests of all our people in all parts of the United Kingdom.

9.28 p.m.

The Lord President of the Council and Leader of the House of Commons (Mr. Michael Foot): The right hon. Member for Penrith and The Border (Mr. Whitelaw) was good enough at the beginning of his speech to make a few kindly references to myself. Therefore, it would be churlish if I did not comment upon them. I had intended to start my speech by making a few remarks on the speeches of the representatives of the smaller parties. However, let me say at once to the right hon. Gentleman that I was especially gratified that he quoted—accurately for a change—my words at the Moss Side by-election. So effective were my words on that occasion, and so overwhelming was the force of my argument, that a good Labour Member was returned to the House of Commons. I am not saying that it was entirely due to my words on that occasion, but it shows that the right hon. Gentleman has not picked on the most damning of all indictments against me for what I might have said.

I shall return later to the speeches of the right hon. Gentleman and the right hon. Lady the Leader of the Opposition. First, I should like to refer to some of the extremely important speeches that have been made by representatives of the smaller parties in the House. I do not know whether all hon. Members understand that this is a House in which smaller parties have rights. [HON. MEMBERS: " Hear, hear."] I do not know why Conservative Members should jeer so readily. It would be discourteous of me not to reply to those speeches.

I refer first to the speech of my hon. Friend the Member for Belfast, West (Mr. Fitt). I am glad that there were a considerable number of hon. Members in the Chamber for my hon. Friend's speech. All those who heard it, whatever their views, would have been deeply moved.

My hon. Friend proved again what we on this side of the House have always recognised—that he is a man of great courage and great honour. The House is wise to heed what he says.

I did not agree with everything that my hon. Friend said about the Government and our conduct in Northern Ireland. My hon. Friend is one of my oldest friends in the House, and I believe that when he comes to review everything that he said he will recognise that there were some unjust comments on what has been done by my right hon. Friends. Nevertheless, I respect his speech. Of course, I would have preferred that my hon. Friend could have made a peroration in which he said that he would come into the Lobby with us, but even though that peroration was absent it does not detract from the admiration felt by every hon. Member who heard his speech.

The hon. Member for Antrim, South (Mr. Molyneaux) also speaks for Northern Ireland. He is well aware that my right hon. Friend the Secretary of State for Northern Ireland made a statement just under a year ago on many of the matters that the hon. Gentleman touched on. We are pursuing those policies faithfully and properly. Anyone who reviews what the Government have done in that area cannot doubt the straightforwardness and honesty with which we have approached the problems. I do not believe that the hon. Members who represent Northern Ireland, on both sides of the House, can question what I am saying.

I believe that the right hon. Member for Western Isles (Mr. Stewart) and his party have made an error in the way that they propose to vote. However misguided the right hon. Gentleman may be if he adheres to his apparent resolution to vote in the Lobby with those who are most bitterly opposed to the establishment of a Scottish Assembly, hon. Members who heard his speech must acknowledge the remarkable allegiance that the right hon. Gentleman commands from his followers. It is one of the wonders of the world. There has been nothing quite like it since the armies of ancient Rome used to march into battle. It is only now that we see the right hon. Gentleman in his full imperial guise.

" Hail Emperor, those about to die salute you."

Which brings me to the Leader of the Liberal Party. He knows that I would not like to miss him out. I am sure that I shall elicit the support and sympathy of the right hon. Lady when I say that she and I have always shared a common interest in the development of this young man. If the right hon. Lady has anything to say about the matter, I shall be happy to give way to her. I should very much like to know, as I am sure would everybody else, what exactly happened last Thursday night. I do not want to misconstrue anything, but did she send for him or did he send for her—or did they just do it by billet-doux? Cupid has already been unmasked. This is the first time I have ever seen a Chief Whip who could blush. He has every right to blush. Anybody who was responsible for arranging this most grisly of assignations has a lot to answer for.

That brings me to the right hon. Lady. I have never in this House or elsewhere, so far as I know, said anything discourteous to her, and I do not intend to do so. I do not believe that is the way in which politics should be conducted. That does not mean that we cannot exchange occasional pleasantries. What the right hon. Lady has done today is to lead her troops into battle snugly concealed behind a Scottish nationalist shield, with the boy David holding her hand.

I must say to the right hon. Lady—and I should like to see her smile—that I am even more concerned about the fate of the right hon. Gentleman than I am about her. She can look after herself. But the Leader of the Liberal Party—and I say this with the utmost affection—has passed from rising hope to elder statesman without any intervening period whatsoever.

I hope that the House will excuse me if I refer to some of the speeches made by representatives of the smaller parties. Although there have been occasional mischievous attacks made on politicians in this House, and sometimes occasionally on myself, I believe that, especially in a Parliament where there is no absolute majority, it is the duty of the Leader of the House to be prepared to enter into conversation with representatives of all parties. What is more, there is not one spokesman or representative of any smaller party in this House who can say that I have misled him on any occasion in any conversation I have had with him. I believe that that process assists the House in transacting its business, and I believe that the House of Commons will come to learn that.

Let me turn to the central theme of the right hon. Lady's speech. She quoted a book which was written by Anthony Crosland, who was a good friend of hon. Members who sit on the Labour Benches. I hope that she will not mind if I quote from a book, published not so long ago, by Reginald Maudling. I do not do this as a taunt, but I believe that it is of major significance to the House in deciding the vote and to the country at large in the more general debate over the coming weeks and months. It concerns a matter of major significance to our country over the past seven or eight years. Mr. Maudling wrote of his experience in the Shadow Cabinet:

"From the start, there was a tendency in the Shadow Cabinet to move away from the Heath line of policy further to the Right: to this I was totally opposed. In particular, I could not support the arguments of Keith Joseph, who was inclined to say that all we had done in the Government of 1970-74 was wrong and not true Conservatism. I totally disagreed with this, because it seemed to me that Keith was fully entitled to measure himself for a hair shirt if he wanted to, but I was blowed if I could see why he should measure me and Ted at the same time."

I am sorry that we do not have the assistance of the right hon. Member for Sidcup (Mr. Heath). That was just a prelude, and Mr. Maudling continued:

"I could not help recalling Selsdon Park, and the swing to the Right in our policies which occurred then, and how long it had taken in Government to get back to the realities of life. I feared that the same thing was beginning to happen again."

I believe that that is an authentic account of what happened in the Shadow Cabinet when the right hon. Lady, out of passionate conviction, led her party back to the Selsdon Park policies. That is the reality of the matter and the reason why the right hon. Lady has never succeeded in securing full political cooperation with the right hon. Member for Sidcup. There is still a great gulf between Selsdon Park Conservatives and those who learnt, in the words of Mr. Maudling, "the realities of life". That comes from someone with great experience in the 1970-74 Government.

Some of us believe that a major purpose in politics is to ensure that our country shall not again have to live

[Mr. Foot.]

through the situation in the period 1970 to 1974. What the right hon. Lady is proposing, which is confirmed by Mr. Maudling's experience inside the Shadow Cabinet, is retreading that path. Nothing more disastrous could happen to our country, not only in industrial relations, which is perhaps most strongly branded on the public's mind, but in almost all areas. It was part of the Selsdon Park policy to abandon support for British industry, drive us into the Common Market on the most disadvantageous terms, and return to the naked *laissez-faire* policies of the right hon. Member for Leeds, North-East (Sir K. Joseph). Those are the policies to which the right hon. Lady has led her party. I give her full credit. She does it because she believes in it. She would hardly deny it. Or will she deny it and pretend that on this issue she has some special new policy of her own?

The Leader of the Opposition has not been able to explain very successfully to the House her special policy for dealing with devolution. We have made a proposal, but the Leader of the Opposition said in reply to my hon. Friend the Member for West Lothian (Mr. Dalyell) that she proposed—and I think that this is a fair summary of what she said—talks about talks about talks about talks. That is her proposal for devolution. In fact, I think that my summary of her reply is rather complimentary because what she really proposes is to do nothing at all—[HON. MEMBERS: "Good."] Conservative Back Benchers shout "Good" and the hon. Member for Halesowen and Stourbridge (Mr. Stokes) shouts louder than anyone, but the Leader of the Opposition has, on the devolution question, torn up all the original policies of her party —the ones on which they fought the last general election—and now she proposes to do nothing. She has no proposals for a Scottish Assembly or any form of devolution or progress in that direction.

If that is her course, she has come round in a big circle. I will not say full circle, because she has never been very much in favour of devolution. She has torn up the proposals that her party put forward in "The Right Approach" not so many years ago. At that time she said:

"in our view the Union is more likely to be harmed by doing nothing than by responding to the wish of the people of Scotland for less government from the centre."

What the right hon. Lady is doing is what she said a few years ago she was not prepared to do.

We believe that if this House says that it will wipe the Scotland Act off the statute book without proper consideration, very serious injury could be inflicted on the United Kingdom and on the Union itself. This House of Commons should pay resepect to the referendum, even if it does not comply with the full requirement of 40 per cent. laid down in the Bill. It was on that basis that we made our proposal to the right hon. Lady and to the other parties. If we win the vote tonight, we will renew these proposals. I hope that every section of the House, whatever its preliminary views on the matter, will be prepared to discuss these issues afresh, otherwise there will be a deep gulf and breach, which will grow in years to come, between Scotland and the rest of the United Kingdom. That would be a highly dangerous development. I hope that Conservatives will have second thoughts on the subject.

In her speech today, the right hon. Lady sought to make us forget what happened in the years of the previous Conservative Government. She also sought to give a very peculiar impression of the kind of legacy the Conservatives left behind for the Labour Government who came to power in 1974. It is interesting to note the things that she did not mention at all. She did not say a word about the balance of payments. I do not know whether she regards that as a matter of any significance. The fact is that the deficit in our balance of payments in the year that she and her right hon. Friends left office was the biggest in our history—even bigger than the deficit that the Tory Party left us in 1964. But of course she wants all that to be wiped away from the public memory. She wants to have wiped away from the public memory also the real figures of the rate of inflation when the Conservatives left office—what is more, a rising rate of inflation. There was a rate of inflation of 14 per cent. in February, with 15 per cent. and more in the pipeline, and a prophecy then of 20 per cent.——

Mr. Rost : What about 8·4 per cent.?

Mr. Foot: We have heard the old parrot cry from all the right hon. and hon. parrots before, and I dare say that they will utter it again. We shall hear it all through the general election campaign, but it will not alter the fact that the Conservatives left us a rising rate of inflation, zooming upwards, with threshold payments inbuilt to make the rate of inflation continue upwards. That is what they left us, and what we have done is to bring the rate down to less than half what it was when the right hon. Lady and her right hon. and hon. Friends were put out of office. That is another of the major aspects of what has occurred that the Conservatives wish to leave out of the reckoning.

Worst of all, perhaps, the greatest disservice that the right hon. Lady does to the country in the way in which she presents the argument is that she seeks to pretend that all the burdens and problems that we have had to contend with in the past four years—and nobody can say that the storm has not been a fierce one—[HON. MEMBERS: "Ah."] The Conservatives think that there is no storm blowing outside. So ignorant are they of the outside world that they think that there is a storm blowing only here. So incompetent and ill equipped are they to try to put things right that they do not even trouble to know what is happening in other parts of the world.

When my right hon. Friend the Prime Minister goes to conferences to meet the leaders of the United States, Japan and other countries, all that the right hon. Lady and her friends can do in the House is to jeer and sneer as if those were matters of no significance. Moreover, the right hon. Lady does something worse. She says that in some way or other this country has been demeaned in the councils of the world during these past four years. There is no basis for that. It is not what the leaders of the other countries say; it is only what the Leader of the Opposition in this country says. That is not what the other countries have said about the policies that we have advocated at the summit meetings.

Why does not the right hon. Lady say whether she agrees or disagrees with the propositions that we have put at those summit meetings? It is because she wishes to mislead the people of this country into thinking that there is a problem only here, that there is no problem in the wider world. We have had this from the Conservative Party on many occasions before. It has happened so often in our history, and I believe that it will happen again in the coming months when the public go to the polls to decide the issue. The argument must be lifted from the levels where the right hon. Lady would have it to the level of seeing what is happening to our country as a whole. Anyone who looks can see a very different story from the one told by the right hon. Lady today.

It is not the case that we have failed to grapple with all the problems in the past four years. We have started to deal with them, even with the limited power that we have had in this House. We have also, despite all the storms, despite all the setbacks, despite all the hardships, carried out major programmes of social reform at the same time. It is because we were determined to carry out those social changes, those social reforms, those improvements in the social services, despite all the difficulties, determined to share better the wealth produced by this country, even if that wealth was not as great as we wanted to it to be, that we have been able to weather the storm and prepare for other times.

So what will happen? What will once again be the choice at the next election? It will not be so dissimilar from the choice that the country had to make in 1945, or even in 1940 when the Labour Party had to come to the rescue of the country —[HON. MEMBERS: "Oh."]

Mr. Michael Brotherton (Louth) *rose——*

Mr. Foot: It was on a motion of the Labour Party that the House of Commons threw out the Chamberlain Government in 1940. It was thanks to the Labour Party that Churchill had the chance to serve the country in the war years. Two-thirds of the Conservative Party at that time voted for the same reactionary policies as they will vote for tonight. It is sometimes in the most difficult and painful moments of our history that the country has turned to the Labour Party for salvation, and it has never turned in vain. We saved the country in 1940, and we did it again in 1945. We set out to rescue the country —or what was left of it—in 1974. Here

[Mr. Foot.]

again in 1979 we shall do the same—[*Interruption.*]

Mr. Speaker : Order. The noise in the Chamber prevents me from hearing what the Lord President is saying.

Mr. Foot : They are trying to stop me from getting your vote as well, Mr. Speaker. [HON. MEMBERS: " Shame."] I do not know why Conservative Members are saying that this is shameful. I think that it is high time that the Tory Party recovered some sense of humour, even if it has lost everything else—[*Interruption.*] Conservative Members really ought to have had plenty of practice at laughing at themselves over these recent years, and they should make a better effort on this occasion.

I repeat—and I hope within your hearing, Mr. Speaker—that over the coming weeks and months the British people will make the decision. If the debate is any test, if argument counts for anything, and if overwhelming support from the Government Benches counts for much, it will of course be a very good election and there will be a thumping Labour majority, too.

We are quite prepared to have an election, but the Conservative Party has always had the idea that it was born to rule, although I should have thought that the country had been cured of that impression long since. It has always thought that everything must be decided according to the desires and whims of Conservative Central Office, that everything else is unpatriotic. Well, we say that this House of Commons should decide when an election takes place, and that the people will decide which Government they will have to follow this one.

We believe that once the record is fully put to the country we shall come back here with the real majority that the Labour Government require to govern for the next five years.

Question put :—

The House divided : Ayes 311, Noes 310.

Division No. 109]　　　　　　AYES　　　　　　10.00 p.m.

Adley, Robert
Aitken, Jonathan
Alison, Michael
Amery, Rt Hon Julian
Arnold, Tom
Atkins, Rt Hon H. (Spelthorne)
Atkinson, David (B'mouth, East)
Awdry, Daniel
Bain, Mrs Margaret
Baker, Kenneth
Banks, Robert
Beith, A. J.
Bell, Ronald
Bendall, Vivian
Bennett, Sir Frederic (Torbay)
Bennett, Dr Reginald (Fareham)
Benyon, W.
Berry, Hon Anthony
Biffen, John
Biggs-Davison, John
Blaker, Peter
Body, Richard
Boscawen, Hon Robert
Bottomley, Peter
Bowden, A. (Brighton, Kemptown)
Boyson, Dr Rhodes (Brent)
Bradford, Rev Robert
Braine, Sir Bernard
Brittan, Leon
Brocklebank-Fowler, C.
Brooke, Hon Peter
Brotherton, Michael
Brown, Sir Edward (Bath)
Bruce-Gardyne, John
Bryan, Sir Paul
Buchanan-Smith, Alick
Buck, Antony
Budgen, Nick
Bulmer, Esmond
Burden, F. A.
Butler, Adam (Bosworth)
Carlisle, Mark
Chalker, Mrs Lynda
Channon, Paul

Churchill, W. S.
Clark, Alan (Plymouth, Sutton)
Clark, William (Croydon S)
Clarke, Kenneth (Rushcliffe)
Clegg, Walter
Cockcroft, John
Cooke, Robert (Bristol W)
Cope, John
Cormack, Patrick
Corrie, John
Costain, A. P.
Craig, Rt Hon W. (Belfast E)
Crawford, Douglas
Critchley, Julian
Crouch, David
Crowder, F. P.
Dean, Paul (N Somerset)
Dodsworth, Geoffrey
Douglas-Hamilton, Lord James
Drayson, Burnaby
du Cann, Rt Hon Edward
Dunlop, John
Durant, Tony
Dykes, Hugh
Eden, Rt Hon Sir John
Edwards, Nicholas (Pembroke)
Elliott, Sir William
Emery, Peter
Ewing, Mrs Winifred (Moray)
Eyre, Reginald
Fairbairn, Nicholas
Fairgrieve, Russell
Farr, John
Fell, Anthony
Finsberg, Geoffrey
Fisher, Sir Nigel
Fletcher, Alex (Edinburgh N)
Fletcher-Cooke, Charles
Fookes, Miss Janet
Forman, Nigel
Fowler, Norman (Sutton C'f'd)
Fox, Marcus
Fraser, Rt Hon H. (Stafford & St)
Freud, Clement

Fry, Peter
Galbraith, Hon T. G. D.
Gardiner, George (Reigate)
Gardner, Edward (S Fylde)
Gilmour, Rt Hon Sir Ian (Chesham)
Gilmour, Sir John (East Fife)
Glyn, Dr Alan
Godber, Rt Hon Joseph
Goodhart, Philip
Goodhew, Victor
Goodlad, Alastair
Gorst, John
Gow, Ian (Eastbourne)
Gower, Sir Raymond (Barry)
Grant, Anthony (Harrow C)
Gray, Hamish
Grieve, Percy
Griffiths, Eldon
Grimond, Rt Hon J.
Grist, Ian
Grylls, Michael
Hall-Davis, A. G. F.
Hamilton, Archibald (Epsom & Ewell)
Hamilton, Michael (Salisbury)
Hampson, Dr Keith
Hannam, John
Harrison, Col Sir Harwood (Eye)
Harvie Anderson Rt Hon Miss
Haselhurst, Alan
Hastings, Stephen
Havers, Rt Hon Sir Michael
Hawkins, Paul
Hayhoe, Barney
Heath, Rt hon Edward
Henderson, Douglas
Heseltine, Michael
Hicks, Robert
Higgins, Terence L.
Hodgson, Robin
Holland, Philip
Hooson, Emlyn
Hordern, Peter
Howe, Rt Hon Sir Geoffrey
Howell, David (Guildford)

Alan Duncan applies quiet reasonableness to turn tide with a brave and skilful speech

Matthew Parris is one of the few people to have left the Floor of the House for a career upstairs in the Press Gallery. He had been the Conservative Member for West Derbyshire for seven years, but left politics for a career in television and to write the parliamentary sketch for *The Times*.

He was born in Johannesburg and attended school in Swaziland. His father's work took the family to various countries including elsewhere in Africa. On leaving school, he won a place at Clare college, Cambridge, where he studied law, taking a first-class degree. He then attended Yale university to study international relations, and in 1974 he joined the Foreign Office where he remained for two years before leaving to pursue a career in politics.

He took a job initially in the Conservative research department before moving on to become press secretary to Margaret Thatcher. As Prime Minister, she presented him with an RSPCA medal for rescuing a dog from the Thames. He fought Michael Howard and Peter Lilley for the Conservative candidacy for West Derbyshire, a seat that he represented from 1979 to 1986.

As an MP, he took part in a "World in Action" programme in which he tried to survive for a week on £26.80—the supplementary benefit payment for a single unemployed man set by the Conservative Government. The experiment failed when he ran out of money for the electricity meter but, as he acknowledged, it was the making of him:

"A couple of months later I was famous, and I never really looked back, quitting politics the following year for television and journalism. That programme made me."

He left Parliament to host "Weekend World" on ITV. When the series ended, he became parliamentary sketch writer for *The Times* from 1988 to 2001.

He currently presents "Great Lives" on Radio 4, and writes twice weekly for *The Times* and fortnightly for *The Spectator*.

He has received numerous accolades for his journalism, including the British Press Awards columnist of the year in 1991 and 1993, the "What the Papers Say" writer of the year in 1992 and 2004, and the George Orwell prize for 2006.

He has been a determined fighter for gay rights, a keen marathon runner with a personal best of 2:32, and an intrepid traveller, twice climbing Mount Kilimanjaro, making numerous expeditions to Africa and South America, and spending part of 2000 on the French sub-Antarctic territory of Kerguelen or Desolation Island.

Speech that took the wind from the sails of moral reaction

By Matthew Parris

There are speeches which themselves change their times, and there are speeches which are indicative of changing times. There are speeches which help alter Parliament's mood, and there are speeches which help alter one party's mood.

Alan Duncan's personal speech on the Second Reading of the Civil Partnership Bill in October 2004, though made from the Opposition Front Bench, probably made no critical difference to the parliamentary arithmetic in the vote that followed, and is perhaps most honestly assessed as following, rather than leading, the spirit of the times.

But in the context of the Conservative party at that moment in history it was ground-breaking, it was skilful, and in its very steadiness and sense of no-nonsense practicality, it was personally brave.

Sitting in the Gallery, any shrewd observer will have sensed the turning of a tide. Though the ink was hardly dry on the repeal of what had been known as "Section 28" – a Conservative Government's attempt to prohibit the "promotion" of homosexuality in schools and elsewhere – homosexual rights were now heading for an effective consensus between all major parties. It took an uncompromising yet good-natured speech from a prominent Tory Front Bencher who was at the same time openly gay himself, yet in no sense a "wet" or left-wing Conservative, to set the seal on this consensus.

On re-reading and re-hearing, what distinguishes Mr Duncan's speech is how relaxed it was, and how relaxed he was – how amiable – towards his tormentors from the moral right of his party. This was no Joan of Arc at the stake as the flames licked higher, no valiant, against-the-odds stand against the howling mob, no confessional appeal for sympathy and understanding. It might have made for more memorable rhetoric if it had been.

But instead, the tone is low-key: one of quiet reasonableness in pursuit of obvious good sense. Duncan was assisted in spreading this mood by the fact that, though often teased, he was liked in the House, and his openness about his own homosexuality was thought admirable. In this speech he is refusing to give Edward Leigh, Gerald Howarth or Ann Widdecombe the fight for which they are obviously spoiling, and they finally give up. These three last-named represent the intelligent and thoughtful end of right-wing spectrum, and my impression is that they had the wit to steer away from unpleasantness, and recognise defeat. The speech to which they were listening did not lack earnestness of purpose, but the sincerity was quiet, convinced – and astonishingly confident.

It can fairly be said that as Alan Duncan sat down at 2.51pm on Tuesday afternoon, 12 October 2004, a door silently closed behind him – the door back into decades of sour 20th-century moralising over an issue that had, rather suddenly, become a matter of quiet common sense.

Inside he may have been shaking; but around him he had helped create an air of calm, of functionality, and of good humour. The wind had gone from the sails of moral reaction. This was now a debate that had changed, and changed for good.

[Jacqui Smith]

areas of legislation that must be amended to reflect the existence of the new legal relationship of a civil partner. For example, schedule 24 will ensure that income-related benefits rules treat same-sex couples in the same way as opposite-sex couples. Child support rules will assess civil partners in the same way as married people, and civil partners will be entitled to most state pension benefits from the date of commencement of the Bill. The Bill also contains powers to require that pension benefits provided to married people are made available to civil partners from the date of the Bill's commencement, notwithstanding the commitment that I made earlier.

I must inform the House that the Government will move several amendments during the Bill's passage through this House. Most of them will be minor and I will write to hon. Members with detailed explanations of them. The great majority were tabled for consideration in the other place, but because of the impact on the Bill of the amendments passed on Report, which would fundamentally change the nature of civil partnerships, it was impossible for us to proceed with them.

Mr. Alan Duncan (Rutland and Melton) (Con): Will the Minister clarify the reference that she made earlier to survivor benefits? Is she saying categorically today that equal rights will be retrospectively applied for public sector pensions?

Jacqui Smith: I made a comment at the behest of my hon. Friend the Member for Wallasey (Angela Eagle). She and other hon. Members have rightly emphasised the Bill's objectives on equality and the possible inequality that could arise with survivor benefits under pensions. I undertook to examine her representations and those of others in more detail.

The Bill has commanded widespread support and I would like to offer the House just two examples of that. A fortnight ago, I was able to visit the registration department of Brighton and Hove city council. It opened a pink wedding waiting list in July and people came from all over the country and queued around the block to express their personal wishes to register their relationships and support the Bill. I commend Brighton for that initiative.

Chris Bryant: I join the Minister in commending Brighton, but what will happen if a council such as Kent county council, a Conservative council that has reintroduced its version of clause 28, chooses not to co-operate?

Jacqui Smith: The Bill makes clear the process that registration authorities will need to put in place to ensure that civil partners have the opportunity to have that civil partnership recognised.

Support has also come from across the political spectrum. In November last year, a leader in *The Daily Telegraph* said:

"The time has come to give homosexual couples some legal recognition . . . It is perverse that existing law should actively discourage any two people in a lifelong relationship from enjoying legal and financial security . . . Allowing gay people to affirm their relationship within a civil contract does not undermine the institution of marriage. It might even reinforce it".

I do not often agree with *The Daily Telegraph*, but I do in this respect. The support recognises that the Bill offers a reasonable and principled solution to the disadvantages that same-sex couples face because they cannot gain legal recognition of their relationships. Amendments passed in another place do not weaken our resolve to see the end of that unfair treatment and exclusion.

The Bill sends a clear and unequivocal message that same-sex couples deserve recognition and respect. It is a crucial step on the road to a fair and inclusive society, and I look forward to the House restoring it to its original purpose. I commend it to the House.

2.21 pm

Mr. Alan Duncan (Rutland and Melton) (Con): I thank the Minister for her opening remarks and explanation of the Bill. It is a pleasure for me to give it my personal support and to do so on behalf of my party from the Front Bench.

Mr. Gerald Howarth: I well recognise that my hon. Friend speaks in a personal capacity and from the Front Bench, but I take it that he is not speaking on behalf of the entire Conservative party.

Mr. Duncan: My hon. Friend should show a little patience. My right hon. Friend the leader of the Opposition has stated openly many times that he supports civil partnerships and will vote for their introduction. I am pleased to repeat and share that commitment. However, as my hon. Friend the Member for Aldershot (Mr. Howarth) rightly and forcefully points out, Conservative Members have a free vote. The Bill is not whipped. It is up to my hon. Friends to vote as they choose, from the position of principle that they will undoubtedly argue, although I am confident that a large number will share my view that supporting the Bill provides a timely opportunity to show that the party understands the world in which we live and that, as my right hon. Friend the leader of the party has said, we are a party for all Britain and for all Britons.

Miss Widdecombe: Will my hon. Friend clarify, in the same way as the Minister did—I have to say, with some honesty—that the Bill is actually about homosexual marriage?

Mr. Duncan: I do not accept that, but I will try to clarify the situation. In anticipation of my right hon. Friend's assessment of the Bill, I intend to devote a lot of time to answering that question, which it is fair and reasonable to ask. I hope that I might even be able to allay her concerns to the extent that she might approach the Bill differently.

Miss Widdecombe: I do not think so.

Mr. Duncan: I live in hope.

The demand for the Bill is far greater than many people realise. One of the facts about people's attitudes to gay people in the modern world is that essentially they are relaxed—utterly unexercised—about the phenomenon until the time when which they detect intolerance, at which point they become deeply and profoundly indignant. That is the climate in which the Bill is sought, not just by those who benefit from it, but by those who see the benefits it confers on others. It has much wider support than from those who are directly affected by it.

In passing, perhaps the Minister will confirm in the wind-ups that there is no danger, as highlighted in the report in *The Independent on Sunday,* that the passage of the Bill is under threat from the compression of time as we reach the end of the Session. I do not think that that many amendments will be tabled in Committee.

Mr. Chope: Does my hon. Friend think it reasonable that the Committee will have only two days to discuss this detailed Bill, plus all the Government amendments?

Mr. Duncan: I thought for a moment my hon. Friend said two gays in Committee.

Chris Bryant: Take a roll-call.

Mr. Duncan: Indeed.

I am not aware of how many days are proposed for the Committee, but I am sure that that will be discussed by the usual channels. I am sure that the Committee stage will be extended appropriately if amendments are tabled so that the Bill can be properly discussed.

I shall deal first with the Bill as the Government introduced it in another place, before turning to the amendments passed there. The need for the Bill is obvious to anyone who has seen and felt some of the heart-rending injustices that can occur when a committed gay couple are denied the basic rights that a married heterosexual couple would take for granted. Despite sharing their lives together, too many of these people find that their mutual love and commitment count for absolutely nothing in the eyes of the law. As the Minister mentioned, practical matters such as pension rights and financial issues are on one side, but more serious still are cases—sadly, all too common—in which the partner of a terminally ill patient is denied the right to make key medical decisions, or even the right to visit the ill person. On death, the surviving partner can be crippled by inheritance tax and evicted from the home they have both shared for years.

To illustrate that I shall quote just one of the examples, which is vivid, contained in a briefing from Stonewall. It says:

"Rex is 76. His partner, John, died after they had spent 45 years together. Their house was in both names and John left everything to Rex in his will. Rex faced a huge tax bill in order to be able to stay in his own home. He also lost John's pension. Had he been married to a woman for just one day, no tax would have been payable, and Rex would have had a survivor's pension."

I hope that those reasons alone are enough to convince hon. Members that the Bill is needed.

Rob Marris: Do the hon. Gentleman and his Front-Bench colleagues support, as I and many of my colleagues do, retrospective survivorship benefits on pension schemes for registered gay couples?

Mr. Duncan: We will consider that in Committee. I am not clear about the likely cost. If it is minimal, the

public sector might give serious consideration to retrospectivity. Shifting actuarial calculations is much more difficult in personal and private schemes because other people in a similar scheme could be disadvantaged by the retrospectivity applied to same-sex couples. That needs to be discussed properly in Committee in a responsible way.

Gay men and women are a fact of life in our country, in our communities and in the House. There are some who wish it were not so, but it is. Gay couples live together in committed relationships across the land and are accepted as couples by their friends and families. The Bill's purpose is to say that continuing to use the law to penalise them cannot be justified. It is designed to recognise same-sex relationships while applying the same restrictions as marriage regarding consanguinity—the bloodline links—thereby excluding partnerships between son and father, daughter and mother, siblings and so on. It is also designed, as the Minister said—I share her view personally—to apply equally across the country, so as to leave no pockets of discrimination within our United Kingdom, and to avoid the absurdity of people rushing from Gretna Green or Belfast to avoid it.

Civil partnerships have already been introduced in different forms around the world. Denmark introduced the first registration scheme in 1989. Today, eight EU members have some form of civil partnership, as do Norway, Iceland, Canada, Australia and some states of the United States. All have recognised the need for such provisions and have legislated for them.

One argument, brought up by my hon. Friend the Member for Gainsborough (Mr. Leigh), is that civil partnerships create "gay marriage" and thus damage and undermine the institution of marriage. Some may see it that way; the House may wish to see it otherwise. First, although there are of course many similarities between the two institutions, they remain distinct in several important respects. While marriage is an ancient institution with special religious significance, civil partnership is a secular legal arrangement. That difference is made clear in the drafting of the Bill. Registration is given effect by the signing of the register rather than by the verbal affirmation, and a religious service is specifically banned during the signing of the register; in both such important respects, civil partnership is very different from marriage.

Even taking into account the elements of the proposed partnerships that are similar to marriage, the argument that they will damage the institution of marriage still does not stack up. If we preach that the values inherent in marriage—love, mutual commitment and responsibility—strengthen and enrich society, how can we claim that the replication of such values for gay couples will cause damage? Imitation is, after all, the sincerest form of flattery.

True, the two institutions are designed on similar lines, but they are designed on parallel lines; and parallel lines, as we all know, never meet. They are separate institutions for different groups of people. Gay men and lesbians are different precisely because of who they love, so the formal recognition of that love will itself create differences. One can therefore argue strongly that the Bill does not undermine or compete with marriage. After all, we are not exactly fishing in the same pool.

[Mr. Duncan]

Many practical issues will need to be dealt with as civil partnerships become accepted. For example, what does one call one's civil partner? It is a problem of modern manners that the term "partner" has many meanings these days: it can mean a business partner, a casual boyfriend, a girlfriend, or someone in a longer-term relationship. As developments take place, we may well find that we need to find new etiquette and new manners to enable us in our changing civil society to describe others in a form that makes people comfortable. I invite hon. Members to try to think of an appropriate word. As a prize, I offer a bottle of pink champagne. *[Laughter.]*

Mr. Leigh: I disagree with my hon. Friend. He supports the creation of an institution that is formalised in a register office, has all the attributes of marriage and can be terminated only by a form of divorce. Marriage does not need to be a Christian contract; it can be carried out in a register office, just like the proposed partnerships. Why will he not simply be honest and say that what we are creating is a form of gay marriage? He is entitled to that view, and he should be honest about it.

Mr. Duncan: The honesty emerges from a clear difference in respect for religious institutions. If we were forcing partnerships on a Church or religious institution, my hon. Friend would have a valid argument that they would conflict with what is now regarded primarily as a religious or religiously blessed institution. It is up to Churches, not up to Parliament, to decide what happens in future, but the clear distinction between a civil secular partnership and the institution of marriage will, in my view, be preserved. If my hon. Friend does not agree, he can vote against the Bill.

Chris Bryant: The hon. Gentleman is making a very good speech. In fact, the Bill prohibits Churches from taking such a step, despite the fact that many lesbian and gay Christians and ministers might want to do so.

Mr. Duncan: It is up to the Church. Yes, the Bill prohibits any sort of ceremony for the purpose of these partnerships in a religious institution. By the way, the Bill is flawed in that respect: it refers to any religious institution "so designed", but on Charing Cross road there is a gay club in an old church—a building designed as a religious institution. That might have to be dealt with in Committee. However, I repeat that it is for the Church to decide. That reinforces the point that I made in response to my hon. Friend the Member for Gainsborough: the Bill establishes a clear distinction between secular civil partnership and the existing institution of marriage.

Mr. Paul Goodman (Wycombe) (Con): I am following my hon. Friend's argument about parallel lines with great interest. If one accepts that that argument is correct, does it not follow that heterosexual couples who do not want to marry might feel that the terms of the Bill unreasonably exclude them from entering into a civil partnership?

Mr. Duncan: The answer is clearly no, because such couples have the option of marriage, in either a church or a register office, and under the law as it stands they can use other legal means to register their interdependency, so to apply civil partnerships to such couples would undermine marriage. That is why such a provision should not be made in the Bill.

Miss Widdecombe: I, too, have been following my hon. Friend's parallel lines with great interest. Citing the religiosity of the institution, he makes a distinction between marriage and the proposed partnerships, but what is the distinction under the Bill between a civil marriage carried out in a register office and a civil partnership? Will he admit that there is none?

Mr. Duncan: No. I admit that there is not a massive difference, except in terms of the ceremony itself: in marriage, the verbal vow is the contract, whereas in a civil partnership it is the written signature. In that sense, there is a legal distinction. Although I want to stick religiously—if I can put it that way—to the geometry of my parallel lines, I acknowledge that they appear to get ever so slightly closer together in that respect.

David Cairns: The hon. Gentleman is making an excellent speech. Earlier, he read out a long list of countries that have civil partnerships, some of which have had them for years. Has his research revealed any shred of evidence that the existence of partnerships has in any way undermined heterosexual marriage?

Mr. Duncan: In my personal view, no. In many respects, their creation has introduced in those countries' societies a degree of stability that is currently prohibited in ours by the law as it stands.

Rev. Martin Smyth (Belfast, South) (UUP): The hon. Gentleman said that consanguinity is applicable in civil partnerships as it is in marriage. Why, when the partnerships signify a secular relationship but the degree of prohibition comes from religious teaching?

Mr. Duncan: Because the proposed partnerships are a recognition of loving couples in stable relationships, not an endorsement of incest—something that I am sure the hon. Gentleman would not want to see in any legislation. I shall address those points when I discuss the amendments made in another place.

Concern is frequently expressed that civil partnerships will undermine the family. Let us consider those arguments. Today's families come in many shapes and sizes and people face many challenges. Marriages break up, parents remarry and the structure of the family changes. Many families no longer fit perfectly into the traditional two-parents-and-2.4-children framework, but are extended families in which there has been remarriage and same-sex relationships. The latter are increasingly acknowledged and accepted, even by grandparents, who 25 years ago would have found such relationships abhorrent. No one suggests that the absence of traditional arrangements within those new family units has led to the absence of bonds of loyalty, commitment and support that hold families together. Despite the difficulties of modern life, those values have shown a reassuring durability.

Mr. Gerald Howarth: I must challenge my hon. Friend on that point. All the Office for National Statistics surveys illustrate that children brought up in a married household do better than those brought up in a cohabiting household, let alone in a homosexual household. The question that my hon. Friend has to answer—I am sure that he will do so elegantly, if not persuasively—is, is he not setting up yet another alternative lifestyle, which young people will consider equally valid, and will not the nuclear family be destroyed?

Mr. Duncan: What the Bill does is recognise what already is, and it tries to introduce a measure of permanence and stability into those relationships. I agree wholeheartedly with my hon. Friend that a mother and a father together in a happy marriage are the best forum in which to bring up children, but I disagree with his suggestion that the Bill undermines that in any way. I do not think that it does.

Pete Wishart: I am enjoying the hon. Gentleman's speech. May I contrast it with some of the clarion calls from Conservative Back Benchers, which confirm the view that theirs is very much the "nasty party"? What does he say in response to the illiberal and intolerant attitude that has been demonstrated by some of his hon. Friends?

Mr. Duncan: I say simply that the hon. Gentleman is wrong. We should dignify the House by accepting one another's differences in a proper way that puts arguments in an honest and direct context, which my right hon. Friend the Member for Maidstone and The Weald (Miss Widdecombe) does on so many issues, many of which I do not find myself in agreement with. There we are. Difference in the House, as a form of democracy, should be respected.

Let me follow on from what has been said. The fact that the bonds of relationships have endured is due in no small measure to the way in which our predecessors in the House have adapted the law to allow it to keep pace with social change. We have seen reforms of property rights, tax arrangements, divorce law and child care, which have all played their part. We have always accepted that ordered change is the best way to conserve those things that we value. The issues of child care and work-life balance are a growing item on the political agenda and are becoming increasingly important.

Measures such as those before us today are a way of protecting the family in changed times, not of damaging it. As I have said, gay couples are a fact of life. Rather than ignoring their existence, perhaps the House can now take a positive stance on their position in society.

I am sure that the issue of child care, which often causes strong feelings, will arise during the debate. It will be argued, rightly, that the best environment for bringing up a child is with two loving, married parents. However, that is not always possible, for a host of reasons, and children are now raised in many different circumstances. What is most important is that love is given to the child and that there is stability in his or her home life.

We had these debates at length two years ago during the passage of the Adoption and Children Act 2002, which legalised joint adoption by gay couples. I openly admit—the Minister was the judge of this—that even I

was not entirely comfortable with the concept for a number of reasons. I was largely undecided. I had some qualms about whether it was the right way in which to proceed, but we passed the legislation. In many ways, that was a far more emotive issue than the one that we are discussing today. Having passed such measures into law, it makes even more sense now to approve civil partnerships. If we are concerned that children should be brought up by a stable, loving couple, these measures when seen in conjunction with gay adoption, make a positive contribution to the family, rather than detract from it.

There is much in the Bill that I believe can be seen as deriving from the values in which Conservatives believe. It promotes responsibility and removes the intrusive hand of the state from people's personal relationships. As a whole, the Conservative party has always been welcoming of people from different backgrounds, and does not pigeonhole people from different backgrounds. It does not pigeonhole people into restrictive categories. I may be the first openly gay Conservative Member, but history will show that gay men and women have played leading roles in our party for many years, and I am pleased to say that many are among our candidates in winnable seats at the next election. So I do not accept that the Bill is in some way incompatible with conservatism. I personally welcome the measure, but it is up to my right hon. and hon. Friends to decide how they wish to vote.

I shall deal with the concerns that exist over the consideration of the Bill in another place and the amendments that were passed there. I begin from the basis that although the issues of discrimination and unfairness which the original Bill was aimed at tackling are, in my view, the most widespread—in many ways they are damaging and pernicious—they are sadly not the only ones that exist. Other groups are still disadvantaged, and the Bill as introduced does not, or did not, assist them.

It is profoundly unfair that carers and siblings who cohabit are disadvantaged on the death of one or other of them by being forced out of their home by their tenancy terms or by the burden of inheritance tax. So it was right for these issues to be raised in debate, and in doing so the plight of those who are disadvantaged in this way has been drawn to a wider audience. That is one of the purposes of our parliamentary system of scrutiny, and I am glad that the efforts and effective advocacy of colleagues in another place resulted in the Government promising—they did so, and I remind the Minister of this—to take further action to address these issues.

In another place, the Minister of State at the Home Office, Baroness Scotland, said in Grand Committee:

"I shall certainly undertake . . . to give the House the more mature reflection of the Government in relation to how to respond to that issue".

That is, the issue of siblings and carers. The Minister then said that

"these issues have percolated to the top of the discussions on a number of occasions. They are issues with which the Government have grappled and they will wish to continue to do so."—[*Official Report*, 10 May 2004; Vol. 661, c. GC31.]

As they have now had since May to grapple and to percolate, I look to the Government, as I think all Opposition Members do, to fulfil that undertaking. I

[*Mr. Duncan*]

seek a clear guarantee from the Minister of State of the Government's firm intent to bring forward measures to address these issues at an early opportunity.

Angela Eagle: Does the hon. Gentleman agree that it is highly inappropriate, regardless of the merits of argument about home sharers, to think that the solution somehow lies in civil partnership arrangements? Will he be voting to take out the provisions in section 2(1) and schedule 1, which so disfigure the Bill?

Mr. Duncan: The hon. Lady's timing is impeccable. I was coming on to that issue and I can assure her that I think she is right. I accept that the Bill was not the appropriate vehicle for such action. When those in another place supported the Back-Bench amendment to widen the scope of the Bill, I believe that they did so with good intent. However, in doing so they fundamentally changed the Bill's nature and effect. They created a Bill that is at best bad legislation, and at worst unworkable and damaging.

As the Minister has said, the Carers Association has stated its opposition to the changes made in the other place, stating:

"We foresee many potential negative impacts"—

I think that this is the same quote—

"on the cared for person and the carer with the amendments to the Bill . . . The changes could have a devastating impact on the income of the carer and the person for whom they care."

So we are not doing a favour to carers if we move an amendment about carers that they do not want.

As the Minister said, many other anomalies and rather absurd unintended consequences arise. For example, a woman who formed a civil partnership—the Minister said with her grandfather, but I can equally say with her grandmother—would, following the amendment, have her own mother as a stepdaughter. That is clearly absurd and unworkable. On a more serious point, by allowing the degrees of prohibitive blood relationships within the existing family to be breached—I hope that this is persuasive to my right hon. and hon. Friends—to form a partnership with one another, the amendment does a great deal to destabilise and compromise the traditional family unit.

Their Lordships' amendment destroys what it sets out to protect. As my right hon. Friend the Leader of the Opposition has said in a letter to people who have written to him on this issue, if

"two sisters were to register their partnership, they would have to pool all their assets. If later on, one of them wanted to get married, the only way they would be able to terminate this partnership would be through complicated legal proceedings."

That would be divorce. Imagine Doris and Violet, aged 80, going through a divorce. All that they would really need would be inheritance tax deferral so that one partner would not have to sell their home when the other dies.

Whatever the good intent, the Bill, as amended in another place, is now unworkable. The impression has been given that the Conservative party has sought to wreck the creation of civil partnerships, which I can assure the House is certainly not the case. That is why my right hon. Friend the Leader of the Opposition has

said explicitly that he would like to see the amendment reserved—[*Interruption.*]—reversed. I can give that guarantee. We have a free vote, but I am confident that that is likely to happen.

I urge my right hon. and hon. Friends to use the time that we have available during the debate to discuss other issues of detail, of which there are many. The issues of carers and siblings deserve their own bespoke legislation. If right hon. and hon. Members want to advance this cause, I hope that they will join me in demanding that the Government bring forward any such Bills at an early opportunity. I hope also that the Minister will now withdraw her rather abrupt refusal to do so in response to the intervention of my right hon. Friend the Member for Wokingham (Mr. Redwood). In a sense, what she said starkly contradicts the comments of Baroness Scotland in another place.

The Bill is not, as some have argued, about giving an extra set of rights to gay couples and thereby discriminating against other couples. On the contrary, it is about removing a discrimination that already exists in law against them. For this reason, it is a case not of greater state intrusion, but of less intrusion, which is to be welcomed. As far as I am concerned, the duty of the state is to intervene where two people are hurting each other and not where two people just happen to love each other. As a Conservative, I believe in encouraging committed long-term relationships that strengthen society. That is one of the best reasons that I can give for supporting the Bill.

For too long there has been perpetuated a negative stereotype of gay love as less committed, less stable and less valid than that between heterosexuals. That has been at the root of much homophobia, and has been used by otherwise rational people to argue for the retention of discrimination. "I am not homophobic," they say, "but gay people, are promiscuous and do not want long-term relationships." That argument is not only insulting but inconsistent. How can people argue, as the Christian Institute does, that the proposals

"create a counterfeit moral standard that is imposed on all"

while also claiming that there is no demand for them? If we refer to our personal experience, I suspect that most of us can see at once how wrong that contention is. Most of us know at least one gay couple who live together in a loving, committed relationship. Many of us also know of at least one heterosexual couple whose relationship may not be so healthy or committed. The simple fact is that love comes in many forms, and so do the relationships that give expression to that love. It would be odd indeed if those who espouse and defend traditional values of commitment and faithfulness opposed giving gay couples the choice to live their lives according to those values. There is a long way to go in eroding the homophobia that still exists in certain places in Britain today. Gay people still face many barriers to full acceptance, but eliminating discrimination from our laws is an essential first step to eliminating discrimination from our hearts and minds.

2.51 pm

Mrs. Barbara Roche (Hornsey and Wood Green) (Lab): It is a privilege to follow the hon. Member for Rutland and Melton (Mr. Duncan), whose speech was

104 CD0135-DEB1/30

Michael Heseltine delivers masterful speech on General Belgrano to sink Ponting's reputation

Michael Portillo joined the Conservative research department in 1976, and went on to become a Government adviser after the Conservative election victory of 1979. He won the seat of Enfield, Southgate in 1984, in the by-election caused by the death of Sir Anthony Berry in the Brighton bombing. He held a succession of ministerial posts from 1987, and developed a reputation as a right winger, urging the Tories to separate their policies from those of their rivals with "clear blue water".

He was born in London in 1953. His father, Luis, had come to Britain as a refugee at the end of the Spanish Civil War, and his mother, Cora, was brought up in Fife. She met Luis while she was an undergraduate at Oxford.

After grammar school, Michael Portillo went to Peterhouse, Cambridge, where he gained a first class degree in history. After working for a shipping company, he joined the research department at Conservative headquarters. Three years later, in the 1979 general election, he had the job of briefing Margaret Thatcher for her press conferences.

Two years after entering Parliament, Margaret Thatcher gave him his first job as a Government Whip. Thereafter he became Under-Secretary of State for Social Security, Minister of State for Transport and Minister of State for Local Government and Inner Cities. He became a Cabinet Minister when he was appointed Chief Secretary to the Treasury in 1992, and rose in the Major Government to become Employment Secretary in 1994 and Defence Secretary from 1995 to 1997.

In a shock defeat at the 1997 election, he lost his seat and turned to journalism, writing about walking as a pilgrim on the Santiago Way and working as a hospital porter. He also contributed a weekly column to *The Scotsman*.

425

He returned to the Commons in 1999 as MP for Kensington and Chelsea, becoming shadow Chancellor in 2000. He moved to the centre right, announcing, for example, that the Tories would keep the national minimum wage introduced by Labour. Beaten in the leadership contest held after the Conservative election defeat of 2001, he stepped down as an MP in 2005.

He has developed a successful broadcasting career. In 2002, he presented a programme about the trip from Granada to Salamanca in the "Great Railway Journeys" series that was partly a biography of his late father. In 2003, he stepped into the shoes of a single mother living on benefits in "When Michael Portillo Became a Single Mum". He is a *Sunday Times* columnist, a panellist on "The Moral Maze" on Radio 4, and he appears in the politics show, "This Week", with Andrew Neil and his old friend, Labour MP Diane Abbott. He was a theatre critic for *The New Statesman* from 2004 to 2006, and he chaired the judges panel for the Man Booker prize in 2008.

Relentlessly factual and logical delivery forced House to hang on every word

BY RT HON MICHAEL PORTILLO

As the Royal Navy task force sailed towards the Falkland Islands to recover them from Argentina, the submarine HMS Conqueror detected the cruiser General Belgrano. The submarine's captain sought permission to sink the warship, and did so on 2 May 1982.

Tam Dalyell, the Labour MP for Linlithgow, had been an opponent of the war, and after it hotly pursued the Prime Minister Margaret Thatcher, accusing her of ordering the sinking even though the cruiser was headed away from the Royal Navy fleet, with a view to scuppering efforts at peace.

A Ministry of Defence civil servant, Clive Ponting, was found to have leaked material to Mr Dalyell during 1984. He was prosecuted under the Official Secrets Act, but acquitted by the jury on 11 February 1985. A week later the Commons debated the sinking of the General Belgrano, and the debate was opened by Michael Heseltine, the Secretary of State for Defence.

The speech had been remarkably well prepared. Heseltine had a complicated task, because he needed to cover several different aspects of the issue, and to be very precise about the sequence of events. He described what happened when the warship was sunk, how ministers had set about responding to letters and questions on the issue in 1984, what Ponting's roles had been, both as a key adviser to Ministers and as the leaker of information to the Opposition, and how the Government had responded to the House of Commons Foreign Affairs Committee.

A less skilfully drafted speech would have bored the House or lost it as Heseltine quoted documents and stressed the importance of particular dates in his chronology of events. A less adept Commons performer might have allowed a highly charged House to deflect him or break his flow. Heseltine avoided all those dangers.

It was all the more remarkable because Heseltine did not have a reputation for being a man for detail. He was also thought a swashbuckler, and it was a surprise to me listening to him that he was so relentlessly factual and logical. The speech lasted an hour and eleven minutes with relatively little interruption. I found it riveting. The House was forced to hang on every word for fear of missing the sequence of the argument.

Essentially Heseltine argued that Ponting had advised Ministers that much of the information sought by Dalyell and by others about the sinking could not be supplied because it would breach national security. Ponting had then apparently changed his mind, and then began to suggest questions to Dalyell through anonymous communications.

Ponting was later to claim that he had been driven to leak because he was outraged at the Government's failure to provide the Select Committee with information regarding changes to the rules of engagement that occurred in May 1982. Heseltine argued that Ponting had begun leaking long before the Government made its submission to the Select Committee, and in any case the civil servant had made no objection to the form in which the Government decided to make that submission.

The most devastating paragraph in Heseltine's speech refers to his leaking of information to Dalyell and reads:

"The constitutional novelty that the House is expected to support, if the Opposition have their way, is that the most trusted civil servants, in the most secure parts of our defence establishments, should be free anonymously to draft questions for Opposition Back Benchers to submit to Ministers on which the selfsame leaking civil servants may then brief the Ministers on the answers which they consider appropriate. The Opposition may perhaps be beginning to wonder whether they have been any better served by Mr Ponting than I was."

Ponting's acquittal and his accounts of what had happened – which filled the newspapers before the debate – led to an expectation that the Government would be on the defensive. However, in my judgment, Heseltine destroyed Ponting's arguments and reputation, a feat which Ponting witnessed from the Public Gallery. So much so, that I really wondered whether the Opposition spokesman Denzil Davies would continue to press the Opposition's amendment to the Government's motion. He did, of course.

Heseltine's speech was masterful. It marshalled the facts precisely and arrived at devastating conclusions about Ponting's behaviour. I heard it at the start of my parliamentary career. Perhaps I was impressionable then, but I still believe that it was an outstanding parliamentary performance.

Sinking of the General Belgrano

3.38 pm

Mr. Speaker: Before we enter upon this important debate, I quote some wise words from "Erskine May":

"Good temper and moderation are the characteristics of parliamentary language. Parliamentary language is never more desirable than when a Member is canvassing the opinions and conduct of his opponents in debate."

Today's debate raises very important issues on which hon. Members feel strongly. I hope that they can be fully discussed within our long-established rules governing orderly debate.

I have selected the amendment standing in the name of the Leader of the Opposition. I propose to apply the 10-minute limit on speeches between 7 pm and 8.50 pm.

3.39 pm

The Secretary of State for Defence (Mr. Michael Heseltine): I beg to move,

That this House recognises that the sinking of the General Belgrano was a necessary and legitimate action in the Falklands Campaign; and agrees that the protection of our Armed Forces must be the prime consideration in determining how far matters involving national security and the conduct of military operations can be disclosed.

The House will understand that I must make a lengthy and detailed speech on what is an important issue involving the rights of Parliament and the duties of Ministers, our national security, and the relationship between Ministers, their colleagues, and civil servants.

It may be helpful if I summarise at once the ground that I intend to cover and the approach that I intend to adopt. I intend to outline the background that led to the decision to sink the Belgrano. I shall set out rather more fully the events that surrounded the decision itself.

I was not involved in the decision to prosecute Mr. Ponting. Neither I nor my right hon. Friend the Minister of State for the Armed Forces had any contact, directly or indirectly, with the Law Officers or their officials in that context. In general, with one exception, we were not consulted about the case or the papers submitted to the court. The Attorney-General has set out the position to the House in the clearest language. I have nothing to add to his statement.

My only involvement in the conduct of the case came many months later, when it was necessary to consider requests from Mr. Ponting's lawyers that classified documents belonging to my Department should be disclosed to the court. I was consulted over the disclosure of one of those documents—the one now known as the "Crown Jewels". After consultation with senior colleagues and the Government's security advisers, it was decided to provide that document under special conditions.

The disclosure of a number of internal Ministry of Defence documents to the court creates a most unusual situation. Advice to Ministers on policy matters is disclosed to this House only in carefully defined areas, such as the outcome of studies related to efficiency. It is a wholly necessary position carefully to restrict such disclosures.

If civil servants are to have confidence that they can put their views fully and honestly to Ministers, if the concept that advice given to one Government is not made available to another is to be maintained, and if the proper accountability of Ministers—and not civil servants—to Parliament is to be preserved, we must maintain that

position. Failure to do so would change fundamentally the position of the Civil Service. Particularly, it would rapidly lead to the politicisation of the Civil Service, which very few would want. *[Interruption.]*

The essence of the debate centres on the allegations made by a civil servant about the behaviour of Ministers. Mr. Ponting has made the most serious allegations—many of them repeated yesterday—about my conduct in discharging my responsibilities as the Secretary of State for Defence. Most extreme and unfounded allegations have been made about the Prime Minister and about my right hon. Friend the Minister of State for the Armed Forces. *[Interruption.]* In those quite deplorable circumstances, the Government have decided—exceptionally—to reveal the advice given to Ministers by officials. I have no option but to quote from the advice that Mr. Ponting gave me. When I do so I shall make available the full text of his advice to the Select Committee on Foreign Affairs and place copies in the Library of the House.

I further intend to enable members of the Foreign Affairs Committee to have access to the document known as the "Crown Jewels", under appropriate security arrangements, and I propose to discuss with the Chairman of that Committee how best that can be done.

The House will want to judge Mr. Ponting's claims in the light of the advice that he gave to Ministers at the time. I shall deal specifically with the events associated with the letter written on behalf of the shadow Cabinet by the right hon. Member for Llanelli (Mr. Davies), the letter that I received in March from the hon. Member for Linlithgow (Mr. Dalyell), the preparation, in the light of those letters, of the document known as the "Crown Jewels", and the subsequent handling of the questions of the hon. Member for Linlithgow. I shall refer in particular to the suggestion that has been made, quite wrongly, that Ministers misled the House in May in answer to parliamentary questions.

I shall want to deal also with the events that occurred later, when the Foreign Affairs Committee requested a note of all changes in the rules of engagement issued to Her Majesty's forces in the South Atlantic in the Falklands campaign. Our response to that request, which has become known as the "Stanley Memorandum" — although the request and the reply were approved personally by me— is that specific subject of the Opposition amendment today. It is that memorandum which, until yesterday, Mr. Ponting appeared to argue had finally persuaded him to leak documents and breach the trust of a civil servant to Ministers. For him, that memorandum was apparently the straw that broke the camel's back. On that basis the Opposition have been persuaded, I presume, to draft their rather narrow amendment. We shall see whether the House believes that it was any better served by Mr. Ponting than I was.

When I first became personally involved in this matter I had no first hand knowledge of the events that had taken place in the South Atlantic in 1982, save as a member of the Cabinet involved in general policy discussions, or as a result of media coverage. I recall that the decision to send the task force was given all-party support by the House in 1982. However, the House will also remember that the hon. Member for Linlithgow never agreed with that judgment. Some would regard that independence of mind on his part as an act of personal courage. No one would question his right to reach such a view, however much one disagreed with it, and no one could disagree with it more profoundly that I did, and still do.

The views of the hon. Member for Linlithgow were clear from the outset. On 7 April 1982 he told the House:

"Some of us believe that the fleet should turn round and come back to Portsmouth and Rosyth as soon as possible."—[*Official Report*, 7 April 1982; Vol. 21, c. 1037.]

On 19 April the hon. Gentleman told the House:

"Is it not an illusion to think that the Amercans will be less than evenhanded".—[*Official Report*, 19 April 1982; Vol. 22, c. 25.]

On 13 May the hon. Gentleman told the House:

"The Argentines have a very tough marine corps of at least 6,000 officers and men who are highly regarded by professional marines in this country. The conscripts will fight as if they are fighting in a holy war. There will be massive casualties; that fact should be faced."—[*Official Report*, 13 May 1982; Vol. 23, c. 983.]

On 8 June the hon. Gentleman suggested that Britain was "slithering into a British Vietnam in the South Atlantic."—[*Official Report*, 8 June 1982; Vol. 25, c. 32.]

By 21 December 1982 the hon. Gentleman was telling the House:

"The sinking of the Belgrano, when the right hon. Lady knew what she did about peace proposals, was an evil decision of an order that it would not have occurred to me to attribute to any other . . . politician of any party since I have been in the House".—[*Official Report*, 21 December 1982; Vol. 34, c. 901.]

During my earlier days as Secretary of State for Defence, from the beginning of 1983, it was the hon. Gentleman alone who pursued a campaign based upon that hostility and with changing centres of attack. The Government's position was clear. Towards the end of April 1982 the first elements of the task force were moving towards the Falkland Islands. As they moved southwards from Ascension Island, they were vulnerable to attack. While an exclusion zone had been established around the Falkland Islands to avoid Argentina consolidating her illegal occupation, measures to defend our own forces had overriding priority.

On 23 April the Government issued a warning to the Argentine Government which was conveyed to them by the Swiss. I shall read it in full. It was as follows:

"In announcing the establishment of a maritime Exclusion zone around the Falkland Islands, Her Majesty's Government made it clear that this measure was without prejudice to the right of the United Kingdom to take whatever additional measures may be needed in the exercise of its right of self-defence under article 51 of the United Nations Charter. In this connection, Her Majesty's Government now wishes to make clear that any approach on the part of Argentine warships, including submarines, naval auxiliaries, or military aircraft which could amount to a threat to interfere with the mission of British Forces in the South Atlantic will encounter the appropriate response. All Argentine aircraft including civil aircraft engaging in surveillance of these British Forces will be regarded as hostile and are liable to be dealt with accordingly."

That was the end of the warning.

Mr. Tam Dalyell (Linlithgow): From that time on, why were the rules of engagement changed at all if they were so clear?

Mr. Heseltine: The rules of engagement govern the orders and discipline within which the British Fleet operates. The warning that I have read was given to the Argentines.

At the end of April the task force was close to the Falkland Islands. It had limited defences against attack, particularly from the air. It was operating 8,000 miles away from home against forces operating close to their own mainland. Argentina could bring to bear both land-based aircraft and those on the aircraft carrier the 25th of May, which greatly increased the reach and flexibility of the Argentine air threat. Argentine ships could move quickly from the safe haven of areas close to the Argentine coast to positions where they could threaten our forces. The Royal Navy had no such easy options.

The first hostilities around the Falkland Islands took place on 1 May. That day Vulcan and Sea Harrier aircraft attacked Argentine positions on Stanley airfield to enforce the total exclusion zone. The task force itself came under attack for the first time from the Argentine air force and some Argentine aircraft were shot down. There was no doubt in Argentina about what was happening. Argentine radio on 1 May claimed that they had attacked the task force.

On 2 May there were clear and unequivocal indications that the task force was under further threat from a strong and co-ordinated pincer movement by the major units of the Argentine navy, including the cruiser General Belgrano and the aircraft carrier. The Prime Minister and her War Cabinet were advised of the threat in the light of the best military and intelligence assessments and were advised by the Chief of the Defence Staff that the rules of engagement should be changed to permit attacks on Argentine warships outside the exclusion zone.

No Prime Minister could have hesitated in the face of that advice. The rules of engagement were changed, not only to cope with the threat from the Belgrano but to cope with that from other Argentine warships on the high seas. Argentina had been clearly warned on 23 April that a threat to interfere with the mission of British forces would encounter the appropriate response.

On 4 May, Sir John Nott described to the House the circumstances of the attack on the Belgrano, saying that she had been detected at 8 pm on 2 May when the group of ships of which she was a part was closing on elements of our task force. Both the Falkland campaign White Paper and Admiral Sir John Fieldhouse's official dispatch also referred to detection on 2 May. We know that, in fact, she was sighted on 1 May. I will explain how the Prime Minister and I came to address this error in March of this year. The Prime Minister in her letter to the right hon. Member for Plymouth, Devonport (Dr. Owen) has fully explained the background to Sir John Nott's statement on 4 May.

Interest in these and other questions was heightened by the publication of a book on the sinking of the General Belgrano by Messrs Gavshon and Rice. From the time of publication in March 1984 a range of detail was available that raised a host of issues and questions. Two particular issues emerged: first, the date on which the Belgrano was detected; secondly, the course of the Belgrano and the orders under which she was operating from the time when she was first picked up by HMS Conqueror to that when she was sunk.

The right hon. Member for Llanelli wrote on behalf of the shadow Cabinet to the Prime Minister on 6 March 1984. His letter focused mainly on the issue of when the Belgrano had first been located and sighted, but also asked about the ship's course when it was sunk. His letter was referred to Mr. Ponting as the head of the appropriate division for advice and for a draft reply. I personally gave no guidance to Mr. Ponting about the advice that he should provide. My right hon. Friend the Minister of State for the Armed Forces went further and asked that the option of

[Mr. Heseltine]

admitting for the first time that the Belgrano was sighted on 1 May and not 2 May should be addressed. Mr. Ponting submitted his advice through my right hon. Friend the Minister of State for the Armed Forces and it reached my office on 21 March. I intend to quote from Mr. Ponting's advice and also from the manuscript note written on that advice by my right hon. Friend the Minister of State for the Armed Forces. I will, as I have said, make these documents available.

Mr. Ponting wrote:

"You asked for a draft reply to send to No. 10 for the Prime Minister to send to Denzil Davies and the Shadow Cabinet. Minister (AF) asked me to prepare a draft admitting for the first time that the Belgrano was sighted on 1st May and not 2nd May, this is draft 2 attached. I have however prepared an alternative reply, draft 1, which maintains the existing public line. There are no operational or intelligence reasons for withholding the 1st May date and the choice between the drafts is therefore essentially political".

Mr. Ponting went on to set out the advantages and disadvantages of each alternative course, but left the issue to me. He said in his advice that the choice was "essentially political". My right hon. Friend added a manuscript note making it clear that it was he who had sought drafts on both bases in referring the matter to me.

It is plain beyond doubt that my right hon. Friend was determined that I, not he, should be able to make a proper judgment about how the Prime Minister should be advised to reply to the shadow Cabinet. It is also clear that the Minister of State for the Armed Forces was the first person whose name is associated with a policy of more, not less, disclosure. The Minister of State for the Armed Forces did not seek to take the decision, and merely ensured that I had the options in front of me.

In practice, I did not put either of Mr. Ponting's alternative drafts to the Prime Minister. The explanation is simple. On 19 March the hon. Member for Linlithgow wrote me a letter asking nine questions. In one respect the hon. Gentleman repeated the question about the date of the detection of the Belgrano, as had the letter from the right hon. Member for Llanelli. But the hon. Gentleman went on to ask a number of other questions concerning the course followed by the Belgrano, the details of the attack on her, and others relating to the Argentine aircraft carrier.

I decided that, as a result of the events that I have described, I could not properly discharge my duty to Parliament unless I had before me an account of events in the South Atlantic in a detail that no one until that time had considered necessary. Mr. Ponting was asked to prepare that document—the document known as the "Crown Jewels".

I must now read to the House the instructions that were sent to Mr. Ponting about what was required. The House will remember that the central issue of this debate is whether Ministers sought to cover up the events that we are discussing. My private secretary, Richard Mottram, wrote to Mr. Ponting on 22 March. I quote two passages of his minute:

"The Secretary of State wishes to know the substance of what happened at the beginning of May 1982 in relation to the Belgrano and the Argentine aircraft carrier in order to judge how much of this can properly be made public without security implications. For the purpose of considering the substance, he would be grateful for a detailed chronology of the events leading up to the sinking of the Belgrano. This should cover the answers to the questions raised by Mr. Dalyell in his latest letter together with those to the following questions."

382

Having listed a range of other questions that might be worth exploring, Richard Mottram went on:

"This list of questions"—

that is, his list of questions—

"is simply those which occur to me and is not meant to be exhaustive. What the Secretary of State is seeking is a comprehensive account of events which covers all the information and not just that which underpins the main defensive line we have used hitherto. I would be happy to have this in log form with the relevant documents enclosed — given the possible sensitivity of some of the information involved there would be no need of course to copy it widely within the Department.

Additionally, I should be grateful for a draft reply to Mr. Dalyell's latest letter together with advice on whether the line proposed to be taken with Dalyell affects the line proposed to be taken with Denzil Davies."

Mr. Ponting's reply — *[Interruption.]* The House is fully aware that it would be inconceivable if the Civil Service were not to ensure that, if the Prime Minister is answering specialist questions, what she says is consistent with the advice from the specialist Department concerned. Mr. Ponting's reply to the minute is the document which is publicly known as the "Crown Jewels". It consists of Mr. Ponting's advice, an unclassified draft reply to the letter of the hon. Member for Linlithgow and a log, and supporting documentation, dealing with highly sensitive operational and intelligence aspects of the sinking of the Belgrano. The document is classified "Top Secret. Codeword". That classification would have been applied by Mr. Ponting, reflecting the classification of some of its source material.

Mr. Eric S. Heffer (Liverpool, Walton): What is the difference between determining the line and telling the truth?

Mr. Heseltine: "Determining the line" is simply the language that is commonly used in the Civil Service to describe the advice that Ministers are given for public disclosure. The hon. Gentleman will remember those words from his experience as a Minister in the Labour Government.

I should like to deal first with the conclusions which Mr. Ponting reached. He concluded that, on the basis of the information in the "Crown Jewels", the arguments put forward by the hon. Member for Linlithgow and his supporters could be refuted, but, because of the classification of the material, it was not possible to use it in public to refute detailed allegations.

As to what should be said to the hon. Member for Linlithgow, Mr. Ponting's advice was that the draft reply was simple because, whatever general line was taken, these issues related to detailed operational and intelligence information. He therefore submitted a draft reply to the hon. Member for Linlithgow, which read as follows:

"Thank you for your letter of 19th March.

As I expect you know the Prime Minister has, in a letter to Denzil Davies, confirmed that the Belgrano was sighted on 1st May. However, the other questions you have raised in your letter all concern detailed operational and intelligence matters on which I am not prepared to comment."

Those are not my words, but Mr. Ponting's. They represent Mr. Ponting's considered advice to me on 29 March as to how I should reply to the hon. Member for Linlithgow. That advice presented me with difficult problems in carrying out my responsibilities to Parliament for the defence interests of the country and my responsibility to Parliament to provide it with as much information as is compatible with that security.

Mr. Ponting's role in the "Crown Jewels" is clear. He informed me that the long running arguments of the hon. Member for Linlithgow did not stand, that an effective negation of his case was incompatible with national security and that the hon. Gentleman should be sent a six-line reply closing down that line of inquiry. I could simply have accepted Mr. Ponting's advice that day and sent a reply on the basis that he proposed, but I refused to accept his advice.

I was scheduled to leave for a NATO meeting the following Monday, so there was therefore great urgency. I called a series of meetings on Friday 30 March and Sunday 1 April. Their purpose was to address how far information could be disclosed in answer to the right hon. Member for Llanelli and the hon. Member for Linlithgow without security implications. We had before us Mr. Ponting's advice, which leaned towards disclosure on when the Belgrano was sighted, but which was categorically opposed to answering the questions asked by the hon. Member for Linlithgow, on grounds of operational and intelligence security.

The first meeting ended inconclusively. I decided that I would report matters to the Prime Minister. However, after the meeting broke up, I discussed further the form of my advice to the Prime Minister with my permanent secretary, Sir Clive Whitmore. My private secretary was also present. The conclusion that was reached was recorded and I am making available a copy of that record. My problem was to define as responsibly as I could the line up to which I could reveal information to Parliament, but beyond which I could not go without damaging national security.

The conclusion that I reached provisionally was that it might well now be possible to reveal that the Conqueror first detected the Belgrano group on 30 April 1982, and first sighted the Belgrano itself on 1 May, but that the Government should not allow themselves to be driven beyond that point, whatever the pressures. Those conclusions were made known to Mr. Ponting at that time. He never queried them. They are totally inconsistent with Mr. Ponting's account in *The Observer* yesterday.

Mr. Dalyell: If this is the line that the Secretary of State is taking in relation to Mr. Ponting, as counsel said in court, he was not counsel for Mr. Dalyell but counsel for Mr. Ponting. Nevertheless, if this is the line, does the Secretary of State not think that he ought to have gone to court No. 2 at the Old Bailey himself, rather than send Richard Mottram, and submitted himself to examination by counsel?

Mr. Heseltine: I think the hon. Gentleman will understand on reflection that, as I and my right hon. and learned Friend the Attorney-General have made clear, I had no part to play in the conduct of the case against Mr. Ponting. With the sole exception of the question arising out of the release of the "Crown Jewels" on security grounds, if it had been considered necessary or desirable by those conducting the case to have called me to the court, I should, of course, have been prepared to go. They did not ask me to go or consult me about whether they should ask me to go, and I was not called. I believe that that is a complete answer to the hon. Gentleman's question.

I reported my preliminary conclusions that Friday afternoon to the Prime Minister, but I was still not wholly

satisfied. I was determined to talk to the head of the appropriate intelligence agency and other intelligence experts outside the Ministry of Defence, in addition to my own advisers on these matters. That I did on the afternoon of Sunday 1 April. That meeting addressed in full the intelligence background to the action taken by the Government on 2 May 1982 and what might be said in response to the claims which were being made by the hon. Member for Linlithgow, Messrs. Gavshon and Rice and others about the interception of Argentine orders to its fleet. The House will appreciate that the information then appearing in the British press and in the books that I have mentioned was largely the product of Argentine sources, which were anxious, no doubt, to probe the scale of our understanding of their activities.

It was obvious that once the Government had confirmed that the Belgrano had reversed course at 9 am on 2 May and had headed for a number of hours in a westerly direction, the focus of attention would be on the intelligence assessment which led to the decision to sink the ship and upon allegations about Argentine orders to recall the fleet to port, and whether these had any connection with the so-called Peruvian peace initiative.

It is possible to answer a question on a matter of fact which is not of itself classified, but if that single answer then becomes, as one would anticipate that it might, a precedent for a series of similar questions, that series could lead rapidly into matters that are classified. As events have shown, the disclosure of information about the movements of the Belgrano has led precisely to detailed questions, the answers to which would breach national security. The advice put to me by the Government's intelligence authorities at the time was that it would not be possible safely to comment on these matters. They gave me their reasons, which were compelling, and Mr. Ponting was present. I concluded, therefore, that the preliminary judgment that I had reached on Friday 30 March should stand—that we should not enter into a debate with the hon. Member for Linlithgow about events at the beginning of May 1982. That judgment reflected Mr. Ponting's advice.

It has now been alleged that that decision was to do with political embarrassment. I deny that allegation utterly. At that time I recommended that we should face political embarrassment involved in correcting the date when the Belgrano had been detected. I concluded that to maintain the statement made originally to the House by Sir John Nott was no longer right. I therefore advised the Prime Minister, who immediately and without qualification agreed.

Consequently, the Prime Minister replied to the right hon. Member for Llanelli on 4 April essentially on the basis of the advice that I had given the previous Friday. I had a further brief word with my right hon. Friend on Monday 2 April, at which my right hon. Friend the Minister for State for the Armed Forces was present. That was the only occasion on which he discussed these matters with the Prime Minister. He did so at my invitation and in my presence. The Prime Minister's reply was in much fuller terms than Mr. Ponting had originally recommended and along the lines that I had suggested.

The dispatch by the Prime Minister of her letter to the right hon. Member for Llanelli opened the way for me to deal with the original nine questions of the hon. Member for Linlithgow in his letter to me of 19 March. I was about to do that when the hon. Gentleman wrote to the Prime

[Mr. Heseltine]

Minister pursuing issues raised in her letter to the right hon. Member for Llanelli. The hon. Member for Linlithgow wrote a four-page letter which covered the Belgrano's course, our intelligence capability, the motivation behind the decisions and issues concerning the rules of engagement. When referring to the Prime Minister's letter the hon. Gentleman said:

> "You stressed that on 2nd May we had indications about the movements of the Argentine fleet which lead to Admiral Woodward's request for a change in the Rules of Engagement. What precisely were those indications? . . . My information is that the Argentine fleet was by that time under orders to return to base and you knew that. Gavshon and Rice in their book set precise times (2007 hours on 1st May and 0119 hours on 2nd May) when those orders were sent by Admiral Allara, and by the Naval Command in Buenos Aires. The text of one of those messages is included in their book."

The hon. Member for Linlithgow, within one day of the Government's response to the shadow Cabinet, was attempting to draw us precisely into those areas of security which we had anticipated he would and on which we knew we would not be able to comment. We could not have had a speedier or clearer vindication of our judgment that the hon. Gentleman would not rest until our security and intelligence protection was stripped away.

In line with the approach that I had previously discussed with the Prime Minister, it was suggested that my right hon. Friend should reply very briefly to the hon. Member for Linlithgow, making it clear that his purpose in asking these questions was to establish his contention that the attack on the Belgrano was related to Peruvian peace proposals—all of the allegations appeared yet again in his letter. In those circumstances, it was not useful to prolong the exchanges. That was what Ministers decided. The Prime Minister replied along those lines on 12 April, but before she did so, Mr. Ponting, as one of the responsible officials, was invited to comment on the approach that she was considering. On 10 April he said that he would not dissent from the suggestion that the Prime Minister should avoid detailed exchanges with the hon. Member for Linlithgow and that a general reply would be sufficient.

The House will realise that, because the hon. Member for Linlithgow had written on 5 April to the Prime Minister and attention was focused on her reply, I had at this stage yet to reply to the nine questions in the hon. Gentleman's earlier letter of 19 March, which had been at the heart of the "Crown Jewels" exercise, during which Mr. Ponting had already submitted to me one draft reply, which I have read to the House.

On the same day that the Prime Minister sent her general reply to the hon. Member for Linlithgow — 1 April — Mr. Ponting submitted further advice on the questions put to me on 19 March.

Mr. Robert Sheldon (Ashton-under-Lyne) *rose——*

Mr. Heseltine: The advice that Mr. Ponting gave me was diametrically opposed to that in his earlier draft. Although he told me on 29 March that it was not possible to answer the questions of the hon. Member for Linlithgow because they touched on operational and intelligence matters, on 12 April he told me that the answers were not classified and should therefore be given.

My right hon. Friend the Minister of State for the Armed Forces, having read Mr. Ponting's advice, minuted

me to point out that it was inconsistent with the line that the Prime Minister had just taken with the agreement of all involved, including Mr. Ponting, in her reply to the hon. Member for Linlithgow.

Mr. Sheldon *rose——*

Mr. Heseltine: I shall give way, but not in the middle of a sequence of events which it is important for the House to hear in one piece.

My right hon. Friend the Minister could not have behaved more properly or more speedily. But it would not have made any difference if he had not sent me a minute, because I was already fully aware of the background to these issues and that for no apparent reason Mr. Ponting had changed his advice and now sought to reverse my earlier decision.

Mr. Sheldon: The right hon. Gentleman is making a great deal of the fact that Mr. Ponting was giving advice of a kind that fitted in exactly with what the right hon. Gentleman wished. Is the right hon. Gentleman not aware that civil servants do that all the time? When I was on the Fulton committee, I saw that happening all the time. Parliamentary secretaries always provide the sort of information that they know will be required by a Minister. That happens all the time and is not a cause for surprise.

Mr. Heseltine: That is one of the most scurrilous attacks on the Civil Service that I have ever heard. *[Interruption.]*

Mr. Speaker: Order. I call the Secretary of State.

Mr. Heseltine: The House has heard me read my private secretary's instructions to Mr. Ponting to provide me with the truth. There was no possible, conceivable pressure on Mr. Ponting to do anything but to tell me the whole story at the time.

As I said, Mr. Ponting, for no apparent reason, had changed his advice and sought to reverse my earlier decision based on that advice. I therefore replied in general terms to the hon. Member for Linlithgow on 18 April in line with the decision which the Prime Minister and I had taken on the basis of the advice of our most senior advisers on matters affecting national security, and in conformity with Mr. Ponting's earlier advice and agreement. Mr. Ponting made no protest about my answer, either to me or to his superiors through the established channels of complaint open to members of Her Majesty's Civil Service.

Neither I nor my right hon. Friend the Minister ever had a coherent explanation for Mr. Ponting's change of advice, until yesterday. In *The Sunday Times* Mr. Ponting gave his explanation. He stated:

> "When the 'Crown Jewels' were actually written, I had four days to do it in. It was very complex and I did not have time for analysis. It was only later that I realised that much of the information was not classified and could be released."

For the House to judge the credibility of this explanation, I shall set out the actual time scale of Mr. Ponting's involvement. Mr. Ponting had been looking into some of these issues since the letter of the right hon. Member for Llanelli was referred to his division at the beginning of March. Certainly he had been the head of the division only since 9 March, but he was an experienced official and could draw on the advice of other experienced officials. He had far more time to analyse these matters than the Ministers who had to account to Parliament and to draw on his advice and the advice of the other experts concerned. In any case, on 10 April, after about five weeks in the job, he was advising that the Prime Minister should send a general reply, and two days later he proposed that I should do the exact opposite.

We should now move on to the heart of the Opposition's amendment—that my memorandum to the Foreign Affairs Select Committee provided a misleading account of changes in the rules of engagement during the Falklands campaign. We should move on, not only because it is specifically referred to in the Opposition's amendment, but because until very recently it was said to have been Mr. Ponting's shock at Ministers' handling of that evidence to the Foreign Affairs Select Committee that forced him to overturn all the instincts, after 14 years in the Civil Service, that told him that loyalty was to Ministers and to the Department. Those words came from *The Observer* yesterday. We should move on if we accept Mr. Ponting's version of events—that is, his version of events until a week ago.

Far from acting in protest against the Foreign Affairs Select Committee memorandum, we were still 11 weeks away from the submission of that memorandum. Far from being driven to near breaking point by ministerial consideration of the handling of parliamentary questions in mid-May, Mr. Ponting began the process of breaking his loyalty to Ministers and to the ethics of Her Majesty's Civil Service on 24 April, when he sent an anonymous letter to the hon. Member for Linlithgow. As I have told the House, I had replied to the hon. Member for Linlithgow on 18 April in line with the policy advice that Mr. Ponting himself had originated, and which the Prime Minister and I had accepted. For no good reason, Mr. Ponting later tried to persuade me to change that position. He failed. Within days of receiving a copy of my letter to the hon. Member for Linlithgow, he began the process of feeding ideas and questions to the hon. Member for Linlithgow anonymously.

Mr. Dalyell: The ideas on the rules of engagement came from me, as will be witnessed by the discussions that I had with Professor John Erickson of the University of Edinburgh. As we are on this subject, let me quote a letter from the hon. Member for Stroud (Sir A. Kershaw), Chairman of the Foreign Affairs Select Committee— [HON. MEMBERS: "When?"]—1 June 1984. It stated:

"Dear Tam, Thank you for your letter of 19 May, to which I am sorry not to have been able to reply sooner. I will certainly keep confidential the letter you were kind enough to send me. I would doubt whether it really alters the situation. That situation will be reflected in the answers to your questions and I regard the letter as more in the nature of an encouragement than a breach of any confidence."

That was the view of a senior member of the Conservative party.

Mr. Heseltine: In no way would I wish to misrepresent the hon. Gentleman. I think I heard him say that the letter he wrote was dated 19 May, but the anonymous letter that he received was on 24 April. I think the hon. Gentleman said that the ideas about the rules of engagement were his. I hope the House will remember that the hon. Gentleman has claimed those ideas for his own, when later I explain certain factual contributions. I shall take the opportunity to remind the House of that precise intervention later in my speech.

Mr. Dalyell: The right hon. Gentleman should get his officials to phone Erickson.

Mr. Heseltine: As I said, within days of receiving a copy of my letter to the hon. Member for Linlithgow, Mr. Ponting began the process of feeding ideas and questions to the hon. Gentleman anonymously.

On 19 August 1984 the hon. Member for Linlithgow was quoted in *The Observer* as having received three documents, the first of which was dated 24 April and sent to him at the House of Commons in a plain envelope similar to that containing the other papers which he subsequently received in mid-July. When this article appeared in August, there was little that those concerned with security in my Department could be expected to do. No one knew at the time where that anonymous letter had originated.

On the night of Mr. Ponting's acquittal—a week ago today, on Monday 11 February—"News at Ten" carried an interview with Mr. Ponting which was, I believe, a shortened version of one shown earlier that evening on Channel 4. The film showed Mr. Ponting typing a letter. It showed the envelope in which it was sent, addressed to the hon. Member for Linlithgow and postmarked 24 April. I shall place in the Library of the House a copy of the contents of that letter transcribed from the copy shown on the television screen.

I shall now read the contents of that letter — *[Interruption.]* I should alert the House to the fact that the envelope on the screen was clearly dated 24 April. Again, I do not want to misrepresent the hon. Member for Linlithgow. He says that the letter was undated, but the envelope was dated by the post officials, and I think I am right in saying that the hon. Gentleman later admitted that he had the letter on 24 April. I do not think that there is any difference between us on the technical question of when he got the letter, although there may be differences between us about what happened as a consequence.

In reading this letter I must now fulfil my undertaking to remind the House of what the hon. Member for Linlithgow said a few minutes ago—that the ideas about the rules of engagement originated with him. The letter stated:

"Dear Mr. Dalyell, For what I hope will be obvious reasons I cannot give you my name but I can tell that I have full access to exactly what happened to the Belgrano. You have probably seen by now that Michael Heseltine has not covered any of the questions that you posed in your letter in March. This was against the advice of officials but in line with what John Stanley recommended. None of the information is classified and to get answers you should put the questions down as PQs. The answers will be quite interesting. In addition you might like to consider another linked question. Did the change in the Rules of Engagement on 2nd May refer only to the Belgrano or did they go wider? When were the Rules of Engagement changed to allow an attack on the 25 de Mayo? Was this on 2nd May or was it earlier. If so, when?

You are on the right track. Keep going."

It will be seen that this letter was sent on 24 April. If Mr. Ponting is the author, as he claims he is, it is not consistent with his argument that he was driven to leak by my behaviour or by the behaviour of my right hon. Friend the Minister of State for the Armed Forces in May or July. In the news programmes in which it was shown, the impression was created that he was forced to write anonymously because of the exchanges that he had had with the Minister of State for the Armed Forces in May about the handling of parliamentary questions. I shall come to that issue in a moment. The only problem with this version of events is that not even my right hon. Friend can take actions in May which provoke a civil servant to

385

[*Mr. Heseltine*]

write anonymously in April. I know that my right hon. Friend is regarded in some quarters as having the most extraordinary powers. He was even accused two weeks ago by the hon. Member for Linlithgow of managing to doctor Admiral Fieldhouse's official dispatch in 1982, while at the time he was serving the Government as a highly successful Minister for Housing and Construction.

Mr. Dalyell: Remember his Royal United Services Institute for Defence Studies' connections.

Mr. Heseltine: We have the highest regard for my right hon. Friend, but even we do not think that he has powers of this supernatural quality.

What was the true sequence of events? As I have said, Mr. Ponting appears to have written anonymously to the hon. Member for Linlithgow very soon after he had seen the terms in which I had written to the hon. Member. There was not much time devoted to agonising. As we know, since the full text of the letter became available a week ago, he suggested that the hon. Member for Linlithgow should do two things: first, that he should put down for answer in Parliament the unanswered questions from his letter of 19 March; secondly, that he should ask some new questions about changes in the rules of engagement.

As we now know, the hon. Member for Linlithgow acted on the first suggestion separately from the second. He put down as questions to me some of those left over from his earlier letter. He also asked a related question to the Prime Minister about how many times contact was made and lost between Conqueror and the Belgrano on 1 and 2 May, what were the reasons for the loss of contact on each occasion, and if she would make a statement. At the same time, on 1 May, he wrote me a further letter asking me to answer his questions.

The answers to the parliamentary questions were addressed first and came in the normal way to my right hon. Friend the Minister of State for the Armed Forces. All but one of the questions in the event fell by the wayside because the hon. Member for Linlithgow was suspended from the House. The one that remained was to the Prime Minister. Not surprisingly, my right hon. Friend the Minister of State for the Armed Forces was in touch with No. 10 Downing street about it.

My right hon. Friend the Minister of State for the Armed Forces asked for Mr. Ponting's views on 9 May on the suggestion that the Prime Minister should reply in part:

"It is not our practice to comment on military operational matters or the details of military operations."

Those who regard that phrase as sinister might reflect that Mr. Ponting himself had recommended some six weeks previously that the hon. Member for Linlithgow's questions should not be answered because:

"all concerned detailed operational and intelligence matters on which I am not prepared to comment."

The hon. Member's question, if answered in full, would have gone to the heart of our submarine capability. An answer, if given, would add nothing to the essential story about why and how the Belgrano was sunk. Mr. Ponting put up advice on 9 May saying that the formula suggested by my right hon. Friend could not be sustained and recommended again that I should answer the hon. Member for Linlithgow's questions.

There was no reason to change the approach agreed earlier. It misled no one—certainly the hon. Member

for Linlithgow was under no illusions about what it meant. It was not necessary to deploy the sentence to which Mr. Ponting objected. It is ridiculous to suggest that there was no operational sensitivity about disclosing details of Conqueror's sonar stalk of the Belgrano. Therefore, when my right hon. Friend the Prime Minister answered the question on 17 May, she followed the strategic approach which I had agreed with her, but the sentence to which Mr. Ponting objected was not in the answer. In other words, the real lesson of these events is that I and my right hon. Friend the Minister of State for the Armed Forces went to some lengths to consult Mr. Ponting and to try to take account of his views. He, meanwhile, was conducting an argument with us, having already started writing anonymously to the hon. Member for Linlithgow.

Before we leave the anonymous letter of 24 April, it is worth recalling the second of Mr. Ponting's suggestions. This is the point at which the hon. Member for Linlithgow was telling us that he had originated the process of interrogation. Mr. Ponting offered the hon. Member for Linlithgow some new questions on rules of engagement. When the hon. Gentleman wrote to me again on 27 May, there, as large as life, were Mr. Ponting's anonymous questions repeated word for word. So much for the suggestion that it was the hon. Gentleman who conceived that these were questions that should be asked.

The constitutional novelty that the House is expected to support, if the Opposition have their way, is that the most trusted civil servants, in the most secure parts of our defence establishments, should be free anonymously to draft questions for Opposition Back Benchers to submit to Ministers on which the self-same leaking civil servants may then brief the Ministers on the answers which they consider appropriate. The Opposition may perhaps be beginning to wonder whether they have been any better served by Mr. Ponting than I was. I now come, finally, to the issue of the memorandum that I submitted to the Foreign Affairs Committee on rules of engagement.

I say "I submitted" deliberately, because that memorandum has come to be called the "Stanley Memorandum". The memorandum was presented to Ministers by Michael Legge, head of defence secretariat 11, and his minute is known as the "Legge Minute."

Mr. Dennis Skinner (Bolsover): Is the right hon. Gentleman sure about him?

Mr. Heseltine: If it helps the hon. Gentleman in his characteristic attempts to denigrate everything that is said in the House, I must tell him that Michael Legge is an exemplary and talented civil servant.

I made it clear to the Foreign Affairs Committee, when I gave evidence to it, that it was a memorandum which I approved and which is therefore my responsibility. My right hon. Friend the Minister of State for the Armed Forces certainly advised me—that is what he is there to do—but I decided to send in the memorandum, and I am wholly responsible for what happened.

So what did happen? The Foreign Affairs Committee was not investigating the sinking of the Belgrano. The terms of reference of its inquiry are clear. They were:

"To examine progress towards the restoration of diplomatic and commercial relations between the United Kingdom and Argentina since June 1982; to examine the future constitutional and economic development of the Falkland Islands; and to examine the prospects for a negotiated settlement of the UK/ Argentine dispute over the Falkland Islands in the light of the establishment of a democratic regime in Buenos Aires and in the light of previous failures to secure such a settlement."

In his letter of 28 June the Clerk of the Foreign Affairs Committee——

Mr. Ian Mikardo (Bow and Poplar): Surely the right hon. Gentleman is aware that the Select Committee decided to conduct two inquiries, one with the terms of reference that he has just quoted, and the other on the events arising out of the happenings on 1 and 2 May. There were two separate inquiries.

Mr. Heseltine: If what the hon. Gentleman says is the case, I unreservedly accept that point. *[Interruption.]* However, that does not change the significance of the letter that we received in the Department from the Clerk of the Foreign Affairs Committee. This letter set the terms upon which the original advice and memorandum were placed. It asked for:

"A note of all changes in the Rules of Engagement issued to HM Forces in the South Atlantic between 2nd April and 15th June 1982 and confirming the accuracy of Mr. Pym's statement to the Committee on 11th June that changes in the Rules of Engagement: 'happened quite a number of times in the course of the war.'"

This request presented my Department with a difficulty. A comprehensive list of all the changes in the rules of engagement would have been classified, but we were advised that the Committee would prefer the note to be unclassified. Ministers therefore received a draft addressing the issue which had provoked the original inquiry, but in a document which was not in itself classified.

The memorandum was not misleading. It never purported to be a comprehensive list of all the changes in the rules of engagement, and it could never have been read as such. If the Foreign Affairs Committee wished, in the light of our advice, still to receive a comprehensive list, it had a simple remedy open to it, and that was to ask again for such a list. I would have supplied it on a classified basis and, indeed, subsequently I did.

The House will realise that I discussed the matter with the Foreign Affairs Committee when I appeared before it. It would be quite wrong of me to anticipate its views, but I must provide for the House my views on the significance of the so-called Legge minute advising me how to respond to the Select Committee's request.

Paragraph 1 of that minute sets out the basis of the request from the Committee which I have read to the House. Paragraph 2 gives five reasons why I should not comply with the Committee's request in full. The first reason transcends all the others, and I shall read it to the House:

"Firstly, the rules of engagement themselves are classified and are drawn from the Fleet operating and tactical instructions, which is a classified document. The Committee has indicated that they would prefer the note to be unclassified."

The second reason leaves no responsible Secretary of State any discretion, and I shall read it to the House:

"Secondly, some of the rules of engagement are still in force for our Falklands garrison. We run the risk of undermining their effectiveness if they were published and debated openly by the Foreign Affairs Committee."

The third and fourth reasons are about the time involved and the problems of converting the rules to layman's language. They are not compelling.

The fifth reason is presumably that which motivates the Opposition today. It reads:

"In addition, a full list of changes would provide more information than Ministers have been prepared to reveal so far about the Belgrano affair."

Taken out of context by someone unaware of the circumstances, that sounds damaging. But in the context of the first two reasons it is clearly not the reason why I did not give the Foreign Affairs Committee a full list of rules of engagement changes. My duty, first and foremost, is to national security. The House will realise that in this case Ministers followed the official and expert military advice of the Department, and I have never doubted that it was right.

The House will know that as soon as the memorandum had been sent to the Select Committee, Mr. Ponting leaked it to the hon. Member for Linlithgow, who took to the Foreign Affairs Committee the document containing the advice of his, Mr. Ponting's, colleague, Michael Legge. Mr. Ponting's explanation is that this was the straw that broke the camel's back; that his sense of integrity no longer permitted him to hold back from sending papers that he leaked to a wider world. Of course, he had been writing anonymous letters before that, but that is the explanation about which we have been told.

Mr. Nigel Spearing (Newham, South) *rose*——

Mr. Heseltine: There is one small gap in the logic of Mr. Ponting's position. Perhaps it would have a momentary credibility if Mr. Ponting's first exposure of his colleague Michael Legge's work was when it was presented, beyond Mr. Ponting's influence, to the Foreign Affairs Committee. The facts are diametrically opposed to this version of events.

Mr. Spearing *rose*——

Mr. Heseltine: Michael Legge's name appears at the bottom of the Legge memorandum. Michael Legge was the head of defence secretariat 11 at the time. But the memorandum was not the sole product of Michael Legge's division. It was the joint work of two civilian divisions, together with military advice. Michael Legge was one of those divisions.

Mr. Gerald Kaufman (Manchester, Gorton): Michael's leg was pulled.

Mr. Heseltine: It was, by Mr. Ponting. But the truth is that the leg that has been pulled further and faster in this debate is the leg of the Opposition, and it is not surprising that they have not even one leg left on which to stand.

Mr. Dalyell *rose*——

Mr. Speaker: Order. The Secretary of State is not giving way.

Mr. Dalyell *rose*——

Mr. Speaker: Order. The hon. Member for Linlithgow (Mr. Dalyell) can see for himself that the Secretary of State is not giving way.

Mr. Dalyell *rose*——

Mr. Spearing: On a point of order, Mr. Speaker. It may be that you can see that the Secretary of State is not giving way to my hon. Friend the Member for Linlithgow, (Mr. Dalyell). But, through you, may I ask whether the Secretary of State has seen me seeking to intervene?

Mr. Speaker: I think that the Secretary of State saw the hon. Gentleman rise, but he can say that for himself.

387

Mr. Spearing: Will the right hon. Gentleman allow me to intervene?

Mr. Heseltine: No. I hope the House will feel that I have given way to hon. Members at points which have not interrupted the flow of what is a complicated explanation. It is very important that the House hears this critical analysis, because this is at the heart of the Opposition's amendment.

As I was saying, this memorandum was the joint work of two civilian divisions, together with military advice. Michael Legge's was one of those divisions. The other division was Mr. Ponting's. Michael Legge submitted his first advice to my right hon. Friend the Minister of State for the Armed Forces on 6 July. On the same day, he sent me a copy. He also sent a copy to Mr. Ponting, whose junior officials had co-operated in its production.

Ministers made no change to the basic approach in that draft memorandum. It was ready to be issued to the Foreign Affairs Committee on 16 July. Mr. Ponting, upon whom I was entitled to rely for advice, spent 10 days in absolute silence. He made no protest to my right hon. Friend the Minister of State for the Armed Forces. He made no protest to me. He made no protest to any of his senior colleagues, only some of whom had been involved in earlier discussions. If he had had this sense of outrage about what his own colleagues were advising, why did he not challenge their advice? Why did he not try to stop the memorandum from going to the Foreign Affairs Committee in the first place?

I was entitled to expect that a man in such a position of trust would give me his full and dispassionate advice, but he did not. Parliament is expected to believe that, before Ministers make statements to the House or its Committees, civil servants in senior positions will advise on the text of such submissions. Mr. Ponting did not.

So we have another constitutional novelty. A senior and trusted civil servant upon whom Ministers were entitled to rely for loyal and conscientious service claims it proper to sit in silence believing that Ministers are deceiving Parliament so that at the moment that it happens he may leak anonymously the advice of his own Civil Service colleagues which he has done nothing to counter.

The Government, the Prime Minister, my right hon. Friend the Minister of State for the Armed Forces and I, and those official advisers with whom we have worked in a spirit of trust and mutual loyalty, have fully discharged their duties and have misled no one. The House will judge whether Mr. Ponting can say the same.

What lay, and still lies today, at the heart of these issues is the safety of British service men serving in the South Atlantic. Ministers were faced over the weekend of 1-2 May 1982 with clear evidence that the Argentine navy was planning to attack the task force. A major part of that threat was the General Belgrano. The task force commander decided that he must respond by attacking the Belgrano and so remove that source of danger to his ships. Exactly when the Belgrano was first sighted and exactly where she was when sunk were not relevant to the starkly dangerous and uncertain situation that our forces were in.

Ministers would have behaved with the utmost irresponsibility if they had rejected the advice of the Government's military advisers and not given the task force commander the authority that he had sought. They gave me that authority. HMS Conqueror sank the Belgrano. The Argentine navy was effectively knocked out of the conflict. The Government have already published a great deal of information about these events of nearly three years ago. I should like to be able to give the House every single detail, but I cannot today, just as my predecessor could not at the time. Some of the crucial information came to us from the most sensitive sources. Those sources are as vital to us and to our armed forces now as they were in 1982.

I, as the Secretary of State for Defence, have to balance my responsibility to give information to this House with my duty to safeguard national security, and in particular the security of our forces. That is a difficult line to draw. But I and my right hon. Friend the Prime Minister have always made it clear that that was what we were doing. Ours have not been the actions of people engaged in a hole-in-the-corner cover-up, in an attempt to mislead this House. Ours have been the actions of Ministers exercising the highest and most difficult responsibilities of our office.

4.50 pm

Mr. Denzil Davies (Llanelli): I beg to move, to leave out from "House" to the end of the Question and to add instead thereof:

"believes that, by seeking to conceal information from, and to purvey distorted and misleading information to, the House of Commons and its Foreign Affairs Committee on the subject of the sinking of the General Belgrano, Ministers have betrayed their responsibility to Parliament.".

As was to be expected, the Secretary of State tried to carry out a character assassination of Mr. Ponting. Indeed, it was entirely to be expected because that, at the end of the day, is the only case which the Secretary of State can try to put at that Dispatch Box. He gave an account of a very unreal world in the Ministry of Defence. This terrible man Ponting, who had been given the Order of the British Empire on the recommendation of the Prime Minister, was trying to prevent information from being disclosed to Parliament when over a period of three years these innocent Ministers—the Secretary of State, the Minister of State for the Armed Forces and the Prime Minister—were desperately keen to let Parliament have all the information that they could about the Belgrano. That is the unreal world in which the Secretary of State seems to have been living, because the world at the Old Bailey a few weeks ago was quite different.

The Opposition do not condone breaches of trust by civil servants or by Ministers who have a duty to account to this House, but at the Old Bailey a civil servant, who had spent 14 years in the Civil Service, risked prosecution and a gaol sentence of at least six months. That was the kind of sentence that Sarah Tisdall received when she was prosecuted by the right hon. Gentleman's Government. This civil servant apparently did not want to disclose any information. He carried out the wishes of Ministers. Then, by some kind of magic catalyst, he ended up at the Old Bailey where his whole career and future were put in jeopardy. That is the kind of unreal and selective account which the Secretary of State has tried to put before the House this afternoon.

The Secretary of State referred to the trial. He could have challenged some of the evidence given by Mr. Ponting at his trial at the Old Bailey—[HON. MEMBERS: "How?"] How? By calling witnesses to refute that evidence. Is the Secretary of State saying that counsel for the Crown and the Treasury Solicitor did not know what

388

Denis Healey at his formidable best denounces GCHQ trade union ban

Described by John Major as "one of the more balanced observers" of the Westminster scene, **Peter Riddell** has been a political journalist since 1981 and is currently the chief political commentator and assistant editor of *The Times*.

In June 2007 he was elected chairman of the Hansard Society, the leading political research and education charity. He had been a member of the society's council since 1996.

On graduating from Sidney Sussex college, Cambridge, of which he is now an honorary fellow, he joined the *Financial Times* in 1970, writing for the Lex column and subsequently becoming its economics correspondent. In 1981 he moved to Westminster as the newspaper's political editor, a post he held for seven years until he took over as Washington correspondent and bureau chief.

In 1991 he returned to the United Kingdom to take up the job of political columnist and commentator for *The Times*. He was elected chairman of the Parliamentary Press Gallery in 1997.

In describing the changes at Westminster during the nearly 30 years that he has known it, he has commented on its transformation from an inward looking, mainly male, club to a much more open, if less coherent and cohesive body. He believes that one catalyst for the change has been the huge turnover of MPs, and the increased number of younger and women Members. Another significant factor has been the less discussed arrival of Portcullis House, the new parliamentary building in the shadow of the Clock Tower, which he sees as an open, democratic meeting place for MPs, their staff, visitors and even journalists in place of what he describes as the "exclusive and hidden" Members' Lobby.

He broadcasts regularly, presenting the "Week in Westminster" on Radio 4 and appearing in "Talking Politics". He has written six books including; "The Thatcher Decade", "Hug Them Close: Blair, Clinton, Bush and the 'Special Relationship'" and "The Unfulfilled Prime Minister: Tony Blair's Quest for a Legacy". "Hug Them Close" won the Channel Four Political Book of the Year award in 2004.

He has been awarded two honorary doctorates of literature at the Universities of Greenwich and Edinburgh. In November 2008 he became a part-time senior fellow of the new Institute for Government.

His work for the Hansard Society has included his membership of the Newton commission, which examined the question of parliamentary scrutiny, and of the Puttnam Commission on the Communication of Parliamentary Democracy. On his election as chairman, he pledged himself to ensuring that the society played a leading role in the public debate about how to reinvigorate and deepen parliamentary democracy in order to strengthen Britain's representative system.

Mrs Thatcher's decision, but Geoffrey Howe bears the brunt of audacious onslaught

By Peter Riddell

Most memorable parliamentary speeches I have heard in the Commons during nearly 30 years as a political journalist have been when the House was packed: Michael Foot's winding-up speech at the end of the no-confidence debate in March 1979 when the Labour Government were defeated by one vote; the Falklands debates in 1982; the dramas of Westland in early 1986; Budgets; resignation statements; the speeches by Robin Cook and Tony Blair ahead of the Iraq war in March 2003. But the single most vivid and effective exercise in invective was addressed to a half-empty House, even though the Prime Minister, the Foreign Secretary and his shadow were present.

The issue was the highly controversial one of the banning of trade union membership for workers at GCHQ, the Government Communications Headquarters in Cheltenham. This was very much Margaret Thatcher's personal decision following a day of action in 1981 during the bitter Civil Service dispute – although there had been no impact on operations.

The ban was announced by Sir Geoffrey Howe, the Foreign Secretary, who bore the brunt of the onslaught launched by Denis Healey, his shadow, in a Commons debate in late February 1984. I was sitting in the Press Gallery on the Opposition side of the House, so above the Labour Front Bench and, fortunately, looking down on the faces on the Conservative side.

Healey's 35-minute speech showed him at his formidable best. He set out the background, then gradually built up to his conclusion, brushing aside Howe with contempt.

The Foreign Secretary "is not the real villain in this case; he is the fall guy. Those of us with long memories will feel that he is rather like poor van der Lubbe in the Reichstag fire trial. We are asking ourselves the question that was asked at the trial: who is the the Mephistopheles behind this shabby Faust? The answer to that is clear..... I quote her own Back Benchers – the great she-elephant, she who must be obeyed, the Catherine the Great of Finchley, the Prime Minister herself".

The historical comparison from Healey was typically audacious, even outrageous, since the man behind van der Lubbe and the Reichstag fire of 1933 was, in fact, Joseph Goebbels, Nazi propaganda chief and then gauleiter of Berlin. Only Healey would, or even could, compare Thatcher to Goebbels. As Healey developed his onslaught, even Conservative MPs started laughing, led by Julian Critchley, author of the she-elephant phrase and enemy of Thatcher. Then, as Mark D'Darcy recalls in his book "Order! Order! 60 Years of Today in Parliament", the laughter spread to the Government Front Bench, first to John Biffen, the Leader of the Commons. Other, more loyalist Ministers could not suppress smiles, though the Prime Minister and Foreign Secretary remained unamused.

Healey then warned that Thatcher's "formidable qualities, a powerful intelligence and immense courage" could turn into "horrendous vices, unless they are moderated by colleagues who have more experience, understanding and sensitivity". This, he argued, had presented Cabinet Ministers with "the most damaging of all conflicts of loyalty". That turned out to be the key phrase of Howe's resignation speech in protest at Thatcher's policies a long six and a half years later (as well as the title of his autobiography). But that was another great speech.

4.17 pm

Mr. Denis Healey (Leeds, East): Let me begin by agreeing on one thing with the Foreign Secretary. No one with any knowledge of the matter can underestimate the importance of this issue. GCHQ has been by far the most valuable source of intelligence for the British Government ever since it began operating at Bletchley during the last war. British skills in interception and code-breaking are unique and highly valued by all of our allies. GCHQ has been a key element in our relationship with the United States for more than 40 years.

I am glad that, in his final words, the Foreign Secretary recognised the skill, loyalty and dedication of the men and women who work there. I have personal cause for gratitude as a result of my years as Secretary of State for Defence. Many other Government Departments benefit, although GCHQ is carried solely on the Foreign Office Vote. I shall come to an implication of that in a moment.

It is just over four weeks since the Foreign Secretary told the House that he had decided to rob those loyal and dedicated men and women of their right to trade union membership—a right that they have enjoyed throughout their employment there and which has been enjoyed by all employees ever since GCHQ was first set up. It is a right that is enjoyed by tens of thousands of other men and women who do work of equal secrecy and of equal national importance in other Government Departments and in private industry. It is a right that is enjoyed by more tens of thousands of men and women in the Post Office, the Health Service and in many other parts of the Government service on whose continuity of work lives might well depend.

The decision that the Foreign Secretary announced to the House just over one month ago was taken without consulting the representatives of the workers concerned and without consulting even his colleagues in the Cabinet. Since then, I must tell the Foreign Secretary, his daily contradictory statements have made him the laughing stock of the world. When reading through them this weekend I was reminded of nothing so much as the five press conferences given by President Reagan on the Lebanon. The Foreign Secretary has been attacked anonymously by fellow Ministers as basing his decision on emotional and not on intellectual judgment. He has been attacked publicly by Conservative Back Benchers, notably the hon. Member for Cheltenham (Mr. Irving), in whose constituency most GCHQ workers reside, and by the hon. Member for Hendon, North (Mr. Gorst) — Gorst of Grunwick as some of us have learnt to call him—who, on radio recently, described the Foreign Secretary's action as

"the nasty thin wedge of Fascism".

The Conservative newspapers have been even more outspoken. *The Daily Telegraph* described the behaviour of the Foreign Secretary and the Government as "little short of shambolic". The *Daily Express* described their decision as "highly illiberal and authoritarian". Moreover, they were condemned unanimously by the Select Committee of the House which has a majority of Conservative Members.

More important still, the Government's decision has already done immense damage to the morale, not only at GCHQ but of the Civil Service as a whole. It was condemned by Lord Bancroft in a letter to *The Times* as:

"Breathtakingly inept; a further exploration of the bloody fool branch of management science."

28

Lord Bancroft wrote as a former head of the Civil Service. The entire First Division Association, which represents the top rank of the Civil Service, is up in arms. The Cabinet Office members of the First Division Association have already formally complained to the Minister for the Civil Service, and middle and junior staff have walked out both at the Cabinet Office and the Treasury. The whole machinery of Government is now seething with discontent, partly because the Government's decision is seen as a precedent for attacks on union membership in other secret work—public and private—and in other areas where continuity of operation is regarded by the Government as important.

The Foreign Secretary told the House that he had no intention of using this precedent elsewhere. I remember him and the Prime Minister telling us at election after election that they had "no intention" of cutting Health Service provision. The fact is, however, that that phrase is used by members of the Government to disguise a decision to do something by not actually denying that they will do it. For the Government, the way to hell is paved with "no intentions".

The Government must recognise that their decision about GCHQ is a kick in the teeth for all those trade union leaders who have been prepared to develop a constructive relationship with the Government. Above all, it is a kick in the teeth for Mr. Lionel Murray.—*[Interruption.]*—Before Conservative Members sneer, I hope that they will recognise the significance—I am sure that the Foreign Secretary does and I hope that the Prime Minister does—of the fact that the opposition to the decision is led by Mr. Alistair Graham, who compared the Prime Minister to General Jaruzelski, and by Mr. Bill McCall. No one who knows them would describe them as mindless militants.

In the past month everyone has been asking why on earth the Foreign Secretary took the decision. It was not because he believed that trade unions were likely to be spies, because he knows, as we do, that most spies since the war have been public schoolboys, masons, scientists or service men. I have no doubt that the Government have in hand measures for dealing with that particular threat to our security. The Foreign Secretary told the House this afternoon that he took the decision because the disruption at GCHQ on certain occasions between 1979 and 1981 broke the continuity of work there and might have endangered lives. He concluded—he told us again this afternoon—that membership of the trade union produces an unacceptable conflict of loyalties.

Some hon. Members may have been impressed by some of the quotations that the Foreign Secretary read out in his speech from trade union leaders during those periods of industrial action. However, the trade unions have shown that there was no prejudice to the essential operations of GCHQ at the time, and the Foreign Secretary told the Select Committee that there was no evidence that any damage was done.

The most important statement by a Minister was made on 14 April 1981, after all those interruptions had taken place. Sir John Nott, the then Secretary of State for Defence, said in the House:

"I do not wish to discuss the difficulties surrounding the dispute, but up to now they have not in any way affected operational capability in any area . . . I have the highest praise for the great loyalty shown by the Civil Service to Governments of all kinds."—*[Official Report,* 14 April 1981; Vol. 3, c. 136.]

There was one another incident, in Hong Kong in 1982, that the Foreign Office quoted in its briefing shortly after the Foreign Secretary's announcement to the House. In that briefing the Foreign Secretary suggested that that incident might have affected our operational capability in the Falklands war. However, the then director-general of GCHQ, Sir Brian Tovey — I shall refer to him on several occasions in my speech—sent a telegram to all staff when the war was over. He said:

"High level praise. Never has so much praise been accorded. There can be no doubt that this praise has been well deserved. It has been earned by hard and dedicated work by you as individuals."

Against that background the Foreign Secretary's accusations today and during the past four weeks are an insult to dedicated men and women, and he should withdraw them.

I do not deny that Ministers said one thing at that time and say another thing now, and that some trade union leaders said one thing then and say another thing now. There has been an element of what psychologists call role reversal in recent weeks. The Foreign Secretary cannot have it both ways. If the action of the unions in 1979 was as dangerous as he told us it was this afternoon, it was a gross dereliction of duty for him not to have taken then the action that he is now proposing.

Since then there has been a series of international events, in which the continuity of operations at GCHQ was of vital importance to the country — for example, the Falklands war, the death of Brezhnev and the continuing trouble in the middle east. Five years have passed since those events which he described to us today. Hon. Members know only that GCHQ had informal discussions at official level in 1980. When the Foreign Secretary gave evidence to the Select Committee, he was unable to say what those discussions were and had to send a vague and unspecific letter about it later. He told the Select Committee that Lord Carrington had discussed the matter with a small group of Ministers, including himself, who was then the Chancellor of the Exchequer. The proposal for a ban on union membership, which was discussed by Ministers in 1982, was brushed aside so contemptuously by Lord Carrington that he could not even remember that it had been put to him when he was questioned by his friends, as reported in *The Times* a fortnight ago.

Two years after Ministers rejected a ban on union membership at GCHQ, the Foreign Secretary and the Prime Minister took a decision to ban the unions right out of the blue. Their only excuse was that the Government had not avowed the existence of GCHQ as an intelligence centre until they published the report of the Security Commission on the Prime affair. I have been in the House for more than 30 years and that is the daftest excuse I have ever heard a Government give for an act of policy. Paragraph 1.2 of that report, in describing in detail how GCHQ operates, points out:

"There has long been close and fruitful cooperation between the signals intelligence organisations of the United States, the National Security Agency (NSA), and the United Kingdom to the mutual advantage of both countries. Whilst this is generally known, and has certainly long been known to all hostile intelligence services, the methods by which their operations are carried out, the targets at which they are directed . . . are among the most important secrets".

The existence and function of GCHQ have been known to any interested person anywhere in the world since the end of the second world war. In 1960, two American defectors from the National Security Agency in Washington held a 90-minute press conference in Moscow describing the work of NSA and its foreign links. Mr. Krushchev joked about it in public when he visited the United States 25 years ago. Mr. Prime was recruited in 1968.

Moreover, the Government avowed the role and function of GCHQ when, in the so-called ABC trial in 1978, they prosecuted two journalists for an article which described in detail and which showed a plan identifying the sites of GCHQ and the NSA in Britain. That article was published in May 1976. The Government of the day prosecuted the journalists concerned for offences under the Official Secrets Act, but they had to drop the case when counsel for the defence, Lord Hutchinson, showed that all the facts in the *Time Out* article in 1976 were either available or deducible from public sources, mainly from the offical records of the Royal Signals Association and the Intelligence Corps, to which the journalists subscribed. Anyone else can subscribe if he so wishes.

As an ex-Secretary of State for Defence, may I say that Ministers and officials sometimes have the most peculiar ideas about what are official secrets. When I assumed office as Secretary of State for Defence in 1964 I was told that the configuration of the Polaris submarine was the most jealously guarded secret in my possession. On my next visit to New York I was able to buy a scale model of the Polaris submarine, produced by the Metal Toy Company, for my children. Anyone who is interested in the higher lunacies of Government should read the account of the ABC trial, where the former head of SIGINT in Britain, Colonel Hugh Johnson, admitted in a mood of gloomy confusion,

"I am not sure what is a secret and what is not."

For the Prime Minister and the Foreign Secretary to tell us in 1984 that no one had known — the Government had never admitted—until eight months ago that GCHQ was an intelligence headquarters is arrant nonsense, and they know it.

It is difficult to find any convincing reason for this sudden decision by the Government—eight months after the publication of the Security Commission report on Prime—except for their fear of staff reaction to the introduction of the polygraph, or lie detector, which is due to begin on an experimental basis in a few weeks' time. The lie detector has been described by a scientist who studied it as wrong on two thirds of the occasions on which it was used, and it was condemned by the Royal Commission on Criminal Procedure as unsuitable for use in court proceedings in Britain for that reason.

There is no doubt but that the Government were terrified of how staff might react if the use of the lie detector was made a ground for dismissal. Perhaps there was also American pressure—we were told that by the previous director of GCHQ, Sir Brian Tovey, who said in an interview with *The Sunday Times* in recent weeks that discreet pressure had been applied. He was so proud of his interview in *The Sunday Times* that in *The Times* the next morning he wrote a letter urging everyone to read it. Someone must have had a word with him within the next 24 hours, because he told a different story to the Select Committee. He said that what *The Sunday Times* had printed was not quite right, but he did not tell us what he said, and I understand from the journalists who conducted the interview that those were his precise words. General Keegan, a retired American general from the intelligence community, said in an interview just after the

29

[Mr. Denis Healey]

Government's announcement that subtle pressure would have been applied. I do not know whether there was such pressure. My experience is that the Government are quite capable of making their own mistakes without pressure from other sources.

The Government undoubtedly feared that staff at GCHQ might have recourse to industrial tribunals to protect themselves. However, it is interesting to note that the staff have never been interested in using industrial tribunals. In all but three cases during the past 40 years, when there has been a dispute they have taken it to the Civil Service appeals tribunal, and they are prepared to do so now. The only case which required any publicity of an industrial tribunal affecting GCHQ was one brought by Colonel Thwaite recently, because he was not a member of a trade union and was complaining about the effect of union activities on his personal prospects. However, I am glad to see that since the Government's announcement Colonel Thwaite said that if he was still a member he would join a trade union now like a shot.

We all agree that there is a powerful case for guaranteeing continuity of operation at GCHQ, but the unions have now offered that in terms of a contract which is legally binding on individual employees. In the evidence quoted at the end of the Select Committee report, Sir Brian Tovey says that had that offer been available when he was director-general, it would have satisfied him. Such an arrangement is far better than a yellow-dog union like a staff association. I regret having to say this, but the management of GCHQ has shown that it is not very good at managing on its own. Sir Brian Tovey told Ministers at the time, and expressed the view to the Select Committee, that not more than 20 of the 10,000 employees at GCHQ —10,000 was the figure given in Mr. Peter Hennessey's Foreign Office briefing in *The Times* immediately after the Foreign Secretary's statement—were likely to refuse the Government's offer. The quality of management seemed to be slightly in doubt because of what *The Sunday Times* called Sir Brian Tovey's two-faced behaviour when he boasted of his duplicity with the trade unions—"boasted of his duplicity" were the words used in the interview of which Sir Brian was so proud.

If the Government had a spark of common sense, they would have jumped at the offer made by the trade unions, and the next Labour Government will do so when the opportunity arrives. But the Prime Minister has behaved in this affair, uncharacteristically, like General Galtieri, who rejected her offer on the Falklands — a very favourable offer—preferred to fight, and lost. She is now gambling with people's lives. Sir Brian Tovey told us that if only 10 per cent. of the members of GCHQ in key areas refused to stay there, the operation would collapse. I put it to the Foreign Secretary that it is certain that many more than that will refuse, especially the radio operators at the outstations, which are the most important area of GCHQ operations. The Foreign Secretary told us, without giving figures, that two thirds of employees had already signed, but we know that 40 per cent. of employees are not trade union members, so they are taking the £1,000 and running. Some trade union members might also have signed, but there is no doubt that a very large number of dedicated men and women in key posts at GCHQ have not signed and will not sign.

30

The Foreign Secretary and the Prime Minister talk of conflicts of loyalty. They have forced on the staff in GCHQ the most damaging conflict of loyalty known to man—loyalty to principle as against loyalty to family. The staff know that in many cases, if they give up work at GCHQ, it will be impossible for them to find work anywhere else without breaking their family life.

One of the results of the Government's action has been to give more publicity to GCHQ in the last three weeks than it has had over the past 40 years. The Government's action is risking the disruption of the work of GCHQ at one of the most dangerous periods in the post-war world, when the Lebanon is in chaos, when the Gulf war is threatening oil supplies to the Western world, when the United States is warning of military intervention very close to the Soviet frontier, and when there is a new leadership in the Kremlin. What a wonderful moment for the Government to choose to put this vital operation in jeopardy.

Mr. John Browne (Winchester): The right hon. Gentleman regards the no-strike agreement as paramount, as if function were the only thing to be considered here, but surely security is also of vital importance. Is it not true that trade union practice and convention at Cheltenham prevent such things as briefcases being searched when people leave the premises? *[Interruption.]* Therefore, what is needed from the trade unions is a guarantee not just of function but of security operations at the site itself.

Mr. Healey: I made the point before that the threat to security in that sense, through espionage, in all Government establishments comes from former public school boys such as the hon. Gentleman. *[Interruption.]* The Government have never told us that they have raised these issues at any time in their discussions with the trade unions. The issue raised by the hon. Gentleman is a wholly false one.

Not everybody is unhappy at the Government's decision. The sharks are now circling round GCHQ in Cheltenham — notably, representatives of the Plessey company, of which Sir Brian Tovey is now a consultant. The company has put advertisements in the local newspaper asking members of GCHQ to leave their work on the grounds, as it is put in the advertisement, that

"it is difficult to feel dedicated at GCHQ, where prospects have clouded".

Who has clouded those prospects? They have been clouded by the Government.

I fear that many of the people who have taken the £1,000 will leave GCHQ and take the jobs on offer from private companies. But many others will refuse — at least one third, I suspect, according to the Government's own figures. Then what will happen? This is where the "resolute approach" is already fraying at the edges. The Prime Minister is unravelling her woollen statue very fast, because Sir Robert Armstrong has given the director at GCHQ freedom to delay action indefinitely against people who refuse to sign—a day, a week, a month, a year. *[Interruption.]* I have read the letter, and the Minister who replies to the debate may read the whole thing to us, but the director has been given freedom to act if and when he thinks fit. My right hon. Friend the Member for Cardiff, South and Penarth (Mr. Callaghan) quoted from a directive which I have not yet seen myself. I have no doubt that the Minister will later make his own speech in his own inimitable way, and I look forward to seeing the faces of Conservative Members when he does so.

It is possible that the Government may sack some members of the staff in order to encourage the others, but then they will find that staff pay is made up by the trade union movement, and the Government will face legal action. The Civil Service tribunal, as the Government know, can award unlimited damages if it finds against the Government in favour of an employee who has been unfairly treated.

The unions will also be going to the International Labour Organisation because they believe—and I share their belief, although I am not a lawyer—that the Government's decision is in flat violation of an ILO convention that the Government have signed.

I ask the Government to recognise that they have now embarked on a long-drawn-out campaign that they are bound to lose. The campaign will continue until the Government change their mind, or until the Government are changed by the British people, because there is deep feeling on this matter throughout the trade union movement.

The £1,000 bribe was deeply offensive to trade unionists throughout the country. The Permanent Secretary at the Foreign Office told the Select Committee on Foreign Affairs that the cost of the bribe, if successful, could amount to £10 million. I hope that we shall be told that it will not be carried on the Foreign Office Vote, but I understand that there is no other Vote on which GCHQ is carried, so will the Government take it out of the pockets of Cementation? *[Interruption.]*

Every trade unionist in Britain feels threatened by what the Government have done. The anger felt by trade unionists was felt deeply by everyone, not least Mr. Murray, who attended the meeting with the Prime Minister last week, because she was felt to be accusing trade unions of lack of patriotism, of being prepared to risk people's lives and to break their promises. The Foreign Secretary made it crystal clear in his speech that that, in his view, is what trade union membership at GCHQ must imply. I ask the Government to recognise that they really cannot talk in those terms to people such as Terry Duffy and Kate Losinska, who are now leading the campaign against the Government. What a miracle the Government have achieved in the trade union movement.

I remind the Government of the last time when anything such as this happened. It was when Mr. Chamberlain and his Home Secretary compared Ernie Bevin to Quisling. Within months they were out of office and Ernie Bevin was in office, helping to win the war for Britain.

I have not wasted time on the Foreign Secretary this afternoon, although I am bound to say that I feel that some of his colleagues must be a bit tired by now of his hobbling around from one of the doorsteps to another, with a bleeding hole in his foot and a smoking gun in his hand, telling them that he did not know it was loaded.

The Foreign Secretary, however, is not the real villain in this case; he is the fall guy. Those of us with long memories will feel that he is rather like poor van der Lubbe in the Reichstag fire trial. We are asking ourselves the question that was asked at the trial: who is the Mephistopheles behind this shabby Faust? The answer to that is clear. The handling of this decision by—I quote her own Back Benchers—the great she-elephant, she who must be obeyed, the Catherine the Great of Finchley, the Prime Minister herself, has drawn sympathetic trade unionists, such as Len Murray, into open revolt. Her pig-headed bigotry has prevented her closest colleagues and Sir Robert Armstrong from offering and accepting a compromise.

The right hon. Lady, for whom I have a great personal affection, has formidable qualities, a powerful intelligence and immense courage, but those qualities can turn into horrendous vices, unless they are moderated by colleagues who have more experience, understanding and sensitivity. As she has got rid of all those colleagues, no one is left in the Cabinet with both the courage and the ability to argue with her.

I put it to all Conservative Members, but mainly to the Government Front Bench, that to allow the right hon. Lady to commit Britain to another four years of capricious autocracy would be to do fearful damage not just to the Conservative party but to the state. She has faced them with the most damaging of all conflicts of loyalty. They must choose between the interests of their country, our nation's security and our cohesion as a people and the obstinacy of an individual. I hope that they resolve this conflict in the interests of the nation. If not, they will carry a heavy responsibility for the tragedies that are bound to follow.

4.52 pm

Mr. Charles Irving (Cheltenham): I am one of the few hon. Members who have lived and grown up with GCHQ since it arrived in Cheltenham. In the late 1940s I played a part as a councillor in encouraging the Government of the day to establish that important presence in Cheltenham. I know better than anyone else that from its arrival it was well known what GCHQ was doing. From its commencement, a trade union presence and a right of choice to belong to a trade union was established.

A communication circulated by the personnel and establishments officer on behalf of the director of GCHQ to all new employees states:

"The management has close relationsips with the Unions and the Departmental Trade Unions and you are encouraged to join the Union concerned with your grade. Advice on many aspects of your employment as a civil servant is available to you as a member of your association and, should the need ever arise, representation of your personal problems can be made at the highest level.

The names of officers of the various Unions and the Departmental Whitley Council are to be found in the pink pages of the GCHQ Telephone Directory."

That was hardly a discouragement from management. The advice was still operative until Wednesday 25 January. It was withdrawn only moments after the Foreign Secretary announced in the House that the terms and working conditions of GCHQ employees would be changed at a stroke.

I make a correction—I should like the Foreign Secretary to spare just a second to listen to me. GCHQ has not encouraged and certainly would not encourage any of the suggested strike steps being initiated for tomorrow. Neither I nor they are that type of person. The Foreign Secretary underestimates GCHQ employees. The Foreign Secretary's comments in his opening speech were completely wrong in that assumption. Having lived in Cheltenham for so long, I assure the House that it would be difficult to find a more noble, loyal, hardworking and sincere group than the 8,000 employees, plus all those who subcontract work from GCHQ. They seek only the opportunities to continue with their valuable services in

31

H. H. Asquith acts to assert Commons authority and curb the power of the Lords

Roger Sands who retired as Clerk of the House in 2006, joined the Clerks Department of the House of Commons in 1965 by the then conventional route of taking the Civil Service administrative grade tests during his final year at university.

His decision to opt for the House of Commons rather than the mainstream Civil Service was motivated partly by reading a book about the House at precisely the right psychological moment, and partly by realising, despite his notoriously poor mathematical skills, that as there was only one vacancy for a Commons Clerkship, there was no point in not making it a first preference.

He ended his career by serving from 2003 to 2006 as Clerk and Chief Executive of the House of Commons, a role which combined being the primary source of advice for the Speaker and other Members on parliamentary practice and procedure with being ultimately responsible for the administration and expenditure of the House – a staff of over 1,500 and an annual budget, including Members' salaries and allowances, of over £300 million. He was knighted in 2006.

During his time in the House he served in roles as varied as Clerk to the Scottish Affairs Select Committee from 1982-85 and Registrar of Members' Interests from 1991 – 94, the period when the "cash for questions" controversy was beginning to come to the boil. He was serving as Clerk of the Overseas Office, a job that involves taking charge of links with overseas parliaments, at the time the Berlin Wall came down.

As a result he made visits in successive years to the Parliaments of Poland, Hungary and Czechoslovakia, which were gradually reforming themselves after the years of communist repression. In 1998 he was privileged to attend the first sitting at Stormont of the new Northern Ireland Assembly as a behind-the-scenes adviser to the Assembly's Speaker.

His interest in the genesis of the Parliament Act 1911, the subject of his contribution, is readily explicable. From 1994 to 2001 he was head of the Public Bill Office. In that capacity he was responsible for the legislative process and oversaw the application of the Act's procedures to two statutes which were passed into law without the assent of the House of Lords during that period: the European Parliamentary Elections Act 1999 and the Sexual Offences (Amendment) Act 2000.

And as Clerk of the House he was in attendance throughout the turbulent day of 18 November 2004, when the Hunting Act received Royal Assent under the Parliament Act after 9pm on the final day of the 2003-4 session, amid scenes of some disorder both within Parliament and in Parliament square outside.

Beginning of the end for constitutional impasse – but issues still remain

BY SIR ROGER SANDS KCB

The British constitution is well known around the world both for being unwritten and for being unusually stable. But there have been constitutional crises along the way, and one such was taking place just at the time when the unofficial *Hansard* was changing its status to become the *Official Report*.

The general election of 1906 had seen the first electoral landslide of modern times. The Liberal Party (led by Sir Henry Campbell-Bannerman until his sudden illness and subsequent death in the spring of 1908, and thereafter by Mr H. H. Asquith) won a majority over all other parties of 129. Its normal majority over the Conservative Opposition was the even more impressive figure of 357, because the Irish Nationalists and the 53 newly elected Labour Members would generally support the Government.

Despite this triumph, the Liberal Government proceeded to experience three years of almost complete frustration, as much of its legislative programme – notably Bills on education and plural voting (to prevent owners of several properties from voting more than once in general elections) – was either amended out of recognition or rejected altogether in the House of Lords, where the Conservatives had a substantial majority.

The leader of the Conservatives in the House of Commons was the subtle but somewhat unprincipled Arthur Balfour; and the situation led to the famous remark by David Lloyd George, then Chancellor of the Exchequer, that "The House of Lords is not the watchdog of the constitution; it is Mr Balfour's poodle".

The parliamentary standoff continued throughout the first three Sessions of the 1906 Parliament. Apart from Money Bills, the only Bills to be allowed through the House of Lords in anything like their original form were those which the Conservatives had declined to vote against in the Commons. A very small elected Opposition was effectively determining the legislative programe of a Government elected by a popular landslide.

The crisis came to a head in 1909, when Lloyd George introduced a Budget which, although fairly moderate by subsequent standards, was regarded by land-owning peers and business leaders in the City as a vindictive and damaging attack on private property and successful commerce: a super tax at sixpence in the pound; an increase in death and estate duties; and, which was particularly inflammatory to the Lords, an array of new taxes on land.

The Finance Bill which embodied this "People's Budget" was contested every step of the way by the Opposition in the Commons and occupied the bulk of the House's time during 1909: 70 days of debate, many lasting right through the night; 554 Divisions; and sittings continuing through most of August and September. The Bill's Third Reading was finally carried on 4 November, by 379 to 149. Although the House of Lords had not rejected a Finance Bill for over 250 years, their blood was up. Ignoring all sober constitutional advice to the contrary, they rejected Lloyd George's Bill on Second Reading, by 350 to 75.

Baulked of the legislation necessary to finance state services, the Government had no option but to appeal to the country. The resulting general election, in January 1910, returned the Liberals to power, albeit with a reduced majority, and with a clear mandate to reform the House of Lords or, at least, to limit its powers of veto.

It was against that background that Mr Asquith made the speech printed below. The Prime Minister was moving the somewhat arcane motion: "That this House will immediately resolve itself into Committee to consider the relations between the two Houses and the question of the duration of Parliaments". The substance of his proposals, which, as his speech makes clear, were not novel, was contained in three Resolutions: to limit the Lords' power over Money Bills to one month's delay; to limit their power over other legislation to delay of just over two years, subsequently reduced to one year by the Parliament Act 1949; and to reduce the maximum duration of a Parliament from seven to five years.

These Resolutions formed the basis of the Parliament Bill 1910, introduced a few weeks later. After initial rejection in the House of Lords, a further general election in December 1910, and a threat by the King to create enough new peers to change the political balance of the House of Lords – a threat foreshadowed in columns 1171-2 of Asquith's speech, the Bill was finally enacted as the Parliament Act 1911.

The speech is not an example of great parliamentary oratory, although its final passages approach greatness. Its importance is that it represented the beginning of the end of a damaging and surprisingly long drawn out constitutional impasse, and that, in its wider reflection on the composition and role of a second Chamber, it raised issues which still await final resolution today.

Naval Strength.

Mr. BURGOYNE (for Mr. Yerburgh) asked what is the standard of naval strength now adopted by the Government?

The PRIME MINISTER: I must refer the hon. Member to the Debate on the standard of naval strength which took place on 26th May, 1909. I have nothing to add to the declarations then made on behalf of the Government.

French Tariff.

Mr. JAMES HOPE: May I ask the right hon. Gentleman the Secretary of State for Foreign Affairs a question, of which I have given him private notice, namely, whether the new French Tariff is at this moment law; and, if not, whether it is within the power of the President of the Republic to withhold his assent to the same or to delay its promulgation until a new Chamber shall have been elected and convoked?

Sir E. GREY: The answer to the first part of the question is in the negative. The President is required by Article VII. of the Constitutional Law of 1875 to promulgate laws within a month, and in urgent cases within three days, of their submission to him; but within these periods he can require them to be reconsidered.

Mr. JAMES HOPE: Is the right hon. Gentleman aware that the Tariff is now worse for British trade than when it passed the Senate?

Sir E. GREY: I have not had an opportunity of studying the matter.

BILLS PRESENTED.

The following Bills were presented, and read the first time:—

REPRESENTATION OF THE PEOPLE BILL.

"To provide for the better Representation of the People, and redistribution of seats in the House of Commons," presented by Sir HENRY KIMBER, supported by Sir John Bethell, Mr. Simon, Earl of Ronaldshay, Mr. Nield, and Mr. David Alfred Thomas; to be read a second time upon Friday, 8th April.

VEHICULAR TRAFFIC (REGULATION OF SPEED) (SCOTLAND) BILL.

"To secure the safety of pedestrians in public thoroughfares in populous places in Scotland," presented by Mr. MUNRO

FERGUSON; supported by Sir Henry Craik, Mr. Cathcart Wason, Mr. Dundas White, and Mr. George Younger; to be read a second time upon Monday next.

RELATIONS BETWEEN THE TWO HOUSES.

DURATION OF PARLIAMENT.

The PRIME MINISTER (Mr. Asquith) moved: "That this House will immediately resolve itself into a Committee to consider the relations between the two Houses of Parliament and the Question of the duration of Parliament."

It is less than three years since the late House of Commons carried, by a large majority, a Resolution declaring it to be necessary that the power of the House of Lords to alter or reject Bills passed by this House should be restricted by law. Since that date three events have occurred which may be regarded as landmarks in the development of the controversy which was then formally begun. The House of Lords, for the first time in our Parliamentary history, has taken upon itself to reject the whole financial provision of the year. A General Election has been held, in which the relations between the two Houses, having regard both to finance and general legislation, were, as I think everybody will admit, at any rate a leading issue. And we have seen, since we reassembled here at Westminster, action spontaneously taken by the other House, of which I will only say for the moment—I shall have to revert to it later on—that it constituted an admission that the wholehearted complacency with which that body surveys itself is not shared by the nation at large, and that by some process, as yet undefined, there must be at least a superficial transformation. Thus we have had within the last six months first, and by way of climax to a long series of acts by which the decisons of this House have been flouted and set at naught, an encroachment by the House of Lords upon a domain which has come to be regarded by universal consent as entirely outside their constitutional province. Next we have had an election in which, if our interpretation of it is correct, a large majority of the representatives of the people have come here with the direct and express authority of their constituents to bring this state of things, both as regards finance and legislation, to the earliest possible close; and, lastly, we have

[Mr. Asquith.]

the acknowledgment of the Lords themselves, that with all the virtues and all the wisdom which they are conscious of possessing, they are like a certain class of heroines in fiction, "not fully understood." At any rate, they are an item on the debit side of the electioneering account of the party opposite. These things mark a substantial and significant advance since the time of Sir Henry Campbell-Bannerman's Resolution; and, in the opinion of the Government, they not only warrant, but give imperious urgency to the Motion which I am about to make—that this House should immediately resolve itself into a Committee to consider the relations between the two Houses of Parliament and the question of the duration of Parliament.

The scope of subject-matter which we propose should be referred to the Committee are confined, as the House will observe, to these two topics. That assumes that in our view it is expedient we should have in this country —should continue to have in this country —two legislative chambers. Speaking for myself, I am ready to admit that is an opinion which I have not always held, or at any rate not always held with any great strength of conviction. It would be quite easy for an industrious person who wished to embark upon a singularly unattractive and unprofitable task to cite from speeches I have made in days gone by expressions, at any rate, of scepticism on that subject. I believe I once—and not in the extreme heat of political youth—went so far as to say that leaving upon one side Federal Constitutions like those of the United States and Germany, which stand entirely upon a footing of their own, I could find no country in Europe, or outside, in which it could be shown that the existing Second Chamber was in fact rendering indispensable service to the State. [MINISTERIAL cheers.] Hon. Members cheer. After longer experience, perhaps closer study of the facts, possibly that insidious and potent influence, the growing conservatism of age, have brought me to the conviction that whatever may be the case elsewhere, in this country there is both room and need for a Second Chamber. [OPPOSITION cheers.] Yes. Let me say there is no subject in which greater confusion of thought and speech exists, and I will try to make clear—I am told I am now a past master in the arts of ambiguity and evasion—I will try to make clear what I do, and what I do not, mean by a Second Chamber.

I deny entirely, and my opinion cannot be too strongly stated or too emphatically repeated, that we live in this country, except in name, under a bicameral system. We do not. When the party opposite is in a majority here only one Chamber counts, and that Chamber is the House of Commons. We are then, and I am speaking of a very recent experience—an experience which many of us went through between 1895 and 1905, a period of ten years—not a small period in the constitutional life of a nation—we are then, we were then, without any of the checks and safeguards in the way of delay, in the way of revision, still less of threatened reference to the people, which are commonly represented as among the primary and essential functions of the Second Chamber. When that state of things exist we are exposed, the country is exposed in the full blast, without screen or shield, to all the dangers and drawbacks of single Chamber Government. On the other hand, when we, who for the time being sit upon this side of the House, have a majority here again there is only one Chamber that counts, and that not the House of Commons, but the House of Lords. The experience of the last Parliament, which sat from 1906 to 1910, supplies frequent and almost continuous illustrations of that truth. We are told, I know, that even in that Parliament Liberal measures became law; they were allowed to pass. Yes, but why? They were allowed to pass into law on a purely tactical ground, boldly and plainly announced by Lord Lansdowne in the month of December, 1906, in regard to the Trade Disputes Bill—a measure which was offensive in the highest degree to the House of Lords, and which in the very same speech was denounced by Lord Lansdowne himself as fraught with danger to the community and inaugurating a reign of licence. And how did Lord Lansdowne then speak —I am going to quote his exact words— what did Lord Lansdowne say was the function of the House of Lords in the presence of a Bill which a large majority of them regarded as in the very highest degree pernicious in the best interests of the State?

"They were passing through a period when it was necessary for the House of Lords to move with great caution. Conflicts and troubles might be inevitable; but let their lordships, so far as they were able, be sure, if they were to join issue, that it was upon ground which was as favourable as possible to themselves."

Yes, favourable ground, favourable to what? Favourable to whom? Favourable to some great cause? Favourable to some vital principle? Nothing of the kind. Favourable to the maintenance of their own powers and privileges. The whole case against the claim of the House of Lords to be in any thing but in name a Second Chamber could not be better stated. What does it come to? You have a frankly partisan assembly, always ready to pass the Bills of one party, and always ready to reject and to maim the Bills of the other party, subject only to this restraining consideration, that it rests upon a purely hereditary basis and, as it is in the long run devoid of any other authority, it must be careful at all hazards not to risk its own skin. Speaking for myself, and I believe for a great many other people also, I would far rather live under the absolute and untempered autocracy of a Single Chamber which, after all, is elected by and responsible to the people of this country, than have superadded to it as a kind of constitutional appendage this simulacrum of a Second Chamber, which, on the avowal of its own leader, is ready at a pinch to sacrifice what it conceives the best interests of the nation if by so doing it can only renew its own licence under normal conditions to continue its habitual and mischievous intervention. I say then, first of all, that at present we have no Second Chamber system at all, but only a travesty and caricature of such.

What then do I desire? When I speak of the necessity or the expediency of a Second Chamber in this House, I do not accept the view — and I suspect very few people on either side accept it — which is put forward by advocates in the other place, like Lord Curzon, who seem to think that the whole function of a legislative assembly is to protect people primarily against their own representatives, and ultimately against themselves. I do not think my colleagues and I desire to see a Second Chamber which can be described as in any sense co-ordinate with the House of Commons. We do not desire to see a Chamber which can compete, or claim to compete, on even terms with this House as the authorised exponent of public opinion and the national will. We desire to see maintained in all its integrity, in the best interests both of the nation and of the Empire, the predominance of this House in legislation—a predominance which is the slowly-attained result of centuries of struggle and advance, and which we believe to be the sheet anchor of our representative system. But there are functions which can be usefully and honourably discharged, consistent with the predominance of this House, by a Second Chamber, questions of consultation, of revision, and subject, as I have more than once said before, to proper safeguards, of delay. The body which is to discharge these functions consistently with the maintenance of the predominance of this House must be a body which is relatively small in number. It must be a body, if it is to have any credentials whatever for the performance of its task, which rests upon a democratic, and not a hereditary basis. It must be a body which, by virtue both of its origin and of its composition, of its atmosphere, of its constitutional attitude, is not as the House of Lords is, governed by partisanship, tempered by panic, but a body which is responsive to, representative of, and dependent upon the opinion and will of the nation.

Holding these views, as I do, as to the need for a Second Chamber, and as to its proper basis and functions, it follows that I do not put forward the Resolutions, which, when we get into Committee, we shall submit to the House, as a final or as an adequate solution of the problem with which we have to deal. On the contrary, I admit to the full that, under these very proposals, the House of Lords will remain in possession of powers, which, as it is at present constituted, we believe it to be ill-qualified to exercise. A non-representative body, it will be able to interpose serious delays in the fulfilment of what may be the clearly expressed will of the electors. A partisan body, if past experience is any guide to the future, will be reasonably counted upon to decline to exercise even the suspensory Veto when its own Friends are in power in this House. The problem, therefore, will still remain a problem calling for a complete settlement, and in our opinion that settlement does not brook delay. But this problem is forced into the forefront of politics largely by the action of the House of Lords itself. It is true that the only practical contribution in the recent Debate which they have made towards its solution is an ambiguous Resolution, which may mean anything or nothing. Even that Resolution was passed in a thin House, in which at least two-thirds of the total membership of the House of Lords did not take the trouble

[Mr. Asquith.]

to attend. The "backwoods" have not yet disclosed their secret. They may still —under the guidance of those two distinguished veterans who told in the Division the other day, and in whose bosoms there still glows the unquenched fire, perhaps something of the untempered audacity of extreme and perpetual youth—they may still, under the guidance of those veterans, find themselves able to rout a half-hearted and divided attack. However that may be, in my opinion, and in the opinion of the Government, until you have substituted for the present House of Lords a body constituted on the lines, and limited to the functions which I have indicated, you cannot enjoy any of the advantages which a genuine Second Chamber is capable of bringing, under modern conditions, to a democratic State.

I pass from that to the immediate business of the hour. In the meantime, and as a necessary preliminary to the working out of our declared policy, we have, as a first and urgent step, to deal with things as they are, and, in particular, to deal with the House of Lords as it is, and to prevent a repetition of the unconstitutional raid of last year into the domain of finance. We have to secure, as against the House of Lords, that the wish of the people, as expressed by the mature and the reiterated decisions of their elected representatives, shall in all legislation be predominant. We have, as I think, at the same time, to provide by adequate safeguards that the elected House shall not outstay its authority and purport to act as the exponent of a public opinion which it no longer represents. These are all matters which were clearly brought before the constituencies at the last election, and on which we believe this House is prepared to pass an immediate verdict. The Resolutions for the consideration of which I am asking the House to go into Committee, are of necessity couched in general terms. They are not to be treated as clauses in a Bill. They are, on the contrary, the broad basis on which a Bill is to be built up. Let me briefly pass them in review.

The object of the first Resolution is to obtain statutory definition and protection for a well-established constitutional practice. I do not want to weary the House with matters of detail, or, more than is necessary, with matters of history, and I will not go back to the Report of this House in 1628 or to the Resolutions of 1671, 1678, and 1860. Those great Parlia-

mentary Acts and Declarations, constitute the ground work of our financial autonomy. I will cite two or three dicta drawn from the lips of the greatest Parliamentary authorities both of the past and of the present. I will begin with the Great Commoner, a title willingly accorded to him by his fellow countrymen, the first William Pitt. In language which is now very familiar, but which will bear repetition, used in this House in 1766, he declared that:—

"Taxation is no part of the governing or legislative power. Taxes are a voluntary gift, the grant of the Commons alone. In legislation the three estates of the realm are alike concerned, but the concurrence of the Crown and the peers to a tax is only necessary to clothe it with the form of law."

It is the fashion on the benches opposite now, I will not say to decry, but at any rate to deride, what are called "musty constitutional antiquarianisms." Let us come down to the present day. I will content myself with citing the language of three persons, two of whom are still living, who have been my predecessors in the office which I have now the honour to hold. I will begin with Lord Rosebery. This is as late as 1894, in the House of Lords:—

"I do not think it is necessary (speaking of the Finance Bill) that your Lordships should make themselves masters of it, because I deprecate altogether the idea that the House of Lords has anything to do with Money Bills."

I come to his successor, Lord Salisbury, speaking in the same House and at the same time, he says:—

"It is perfectly obvious that this House has not for many years interfered by amendment with the finance of the year. The reason why this House cannot do so is that it has not the power of changing the Executive Government, and to amend or reject the Finance Bill and leave the same Executive Government in its place is to create a deadlock from which there is no escape."

More wisely prophetic words have rarely been spoken. Again, only a year later, Lord Salisbury used this language in the same place:—

"This House, by custom, takes no share whatever in the votes by which Governments are displaced or inaugurated. It takes no share whatever in that which is the most important part—the annual constitutional business of every legislative body—the provision of funds by which the public services are to be carried on, and the determination of the manner in which those services are to be carried out. In regard to those matters, it takes no part whatever."

I finish my citations by quoting the authority of the right hon. Gentleman who sits opposite (Mr. Balfour). But there is a consentient and concurrent stream of authority in regard to this matter, or there was until last year. The right hon. Gentleman, in language which has often been cited, and which is still fresh and still true, less than three years ago in speaking on Sir Henry Campbell-Bannerman's Resolution in this House said:—

> "We all know the power of the House of Lords thus limited, and rightly limited, in the sphere of legislation is still further limited by the fact that it cannot touch Money Bills which, if it could deal with, no doubt, it could bring the whole executive machinery of the country to a standstill."

Finally, a year later, and precisely in the same sense speaking in the country in October, 1908, the right hon. Gentleman declared:—

> "It is the House of Commons and not the House of Lords which settles uncontrolled our financial system."

In the face of those authorities and that practice I should hope that we may have a practically unanimous assent to the first of the three Resolutions. The action taken by the House of Lords in the autumn of last year shows unhappily that we can no longer rely on unwritten conventions, however well established or upon the dicta of the weightiest and most illustrious Parliamentary authorities. Statutory protection has become necessary if this House is to continue to enjoy and to exercise the privileges it has claimed and exercised undisputed for more than two centuries.

In regard to the precise form of our proposal I would only say this. We recognise, as everybody must, that if you are going to put into statutory shape the declaration and assertion of the financial autonomy of this House, you must make some adequate provision against the possibility of what is called tacking—tacking to Finance Bills proposals which are not germane or relevant to their subject matter. I am not aware of any instance in the past where any such practice has been resorted to, but as we are scrupulously anxious in defining the rights of the House of Commons to circumscribe them within the area in which they have hitherto been exercised, and as there might come a time when an imprudent and unscrupulous Minister might, by the aid of, perhaps, a precarious and subservient majority, seek to annex irrelevant and extraneous matter to a Finance Bill—I only regard that as in the dim and distant future and as a purely speculative possibility—but as that time might come, we think it is right to guard against such a contingency in advance and to trust the Speaker, who at present exercises a precisely analogous function in regard to all matters of privilege in Bills which come back to us from the House of Lords; we entrust to him the power and duty of determining whether or not a Bill is a Money Bill.

I should deprecate very much entrusting any such power to any of our courts of law. It is not that I have any want of respect for courts of law. I have spent the greater part of my life within their walls, and I have the highest possible reverence for the great judicial traditions there adopted. I should deprecate, not from any want of respect for courts of law, but from conservative adherence to the constitutional traditions of this House—I should deprecate introducing here what you have in America, wherever you have a Federal Constitution, the intervention of the courts of law to determine whether or not the legislature has acted *intra* or *ultra vires*, and the submitting a question which is not a question really appropriate for judicial determination to a body properly charged with other functions. You have here an impartial representative of all parties in this House who sits judicially in our Chair, a functionary who by tradition, by experience, and from the universal respect with which his decisions are regarded and observed, is, in our opinion, a far better tribunal to determine such matters than the courts of law.

I pass now to the second and third Resolutions which, in a sense, should be taken together; that is to say, the second Resolution without the third is not a Resolution which the Government would submit to the House. I will deal more particularly with the second. I admit at once that, unlike the first of our proposals, it is not a mere reaffirmation with new safeguards of an old constitutional understanding. On the contrary, it proposes to provide a new remedy for an evil which, so long as the House of Lords remains as it is, only comes into being when there is a Liberal or progressive majority in the House of Commons. I mean a deadlock between the two branches of the legislature. If the House will bear with me, before explaining and discussing our proposals, I should like to answer two preliminary questions.

The first question is, What are our existing constitutional resources

4.0 P.M.   for dealing with such a situation? The second is what, if any, are the practical alternative proposals to the scheme of the Government? What are our existing constitutional resources in this matter? A deadlock between the two Houses can of course always be got rid of for the time being by the exercise on the part of the Crown

[Mr. Asquith.]

of the prerogative of dissolution. If that were the only way of escape we should have to admit that in existing constitutional circumstances the House of Lords, itself indissoluble, can, whenever it pleases, call for a General Election. But our Constitution, though by no means perfect, is not so lopsided as that. The remedy by way of dissolution obviously does not apply to the House of Lords, but the Constitution has provided a means by which the House of Lords, stubbornly bent on refusing to give effect to the will of the people as declared by their representatives, can be brought to reason. That is the exercise by the Crown of another of its prerogatives, the creation of new Peers. It is a Prerogative I agree which has been rarely either exercised or threatened.

Lord HUGH CECIL: Would the right hon. Gentleman say when it has been exercised?

The PRIME MINISTER: Perhaps the Noble Lord would restrain his impatience for a moment. It is a Prerogative which has been rarely exercised or threatened. Does he dispute that proposition?

Lord HUGH CECIL: It has never been exercised.

The PRIME MINISTER: It is a Prerogative which, I repeat for the third time, has been rarely exercised or even threatened, but it exists. That it is not dormant or obsolete is, I venture to say, the opinion of almost every one of our great constitutional authorities. I will cite one or two of them. They are people who are not partisans, and whose authority will command universal respect. I take first of all Sir Erskine May. In his "Constitutional History" he says:—

"It must not be forgotten that although Parliament is said to be dissolved, a dissolution in fact extends in fact no further than to the Commons. The Peers are not affected by it. . . . So far, therefore, as the House of Lords is concerned, a creation of Peers by the Crown on extraordinary occasions is the only equivalent which the Constitution has provided for the change and renovation of the House of Commons by a dissolution. In no other way can the opinions of the House of Lords be brought into harmony with those of the people."

I go on to cite another great living authority whose opinions will be received with the utmost respect by the party opposite, and who has provided them with a great deal of dialectical pabulum, I mean Professor Dicey, in his "Introduction to the Study of the Law of the Constitution."

After speaking of the "understanding and habit" in accordance with which the House of Lords are expected, in every serious political controversy to give way at some point or other to the will of the House of Commons—I wish it were more "habit"—he goes on to speak of that "further custom which, though of comparatively recent growth, forms an essential article of constitutional ethics." Will the Noble Lord observe that—"modern constitutional ethics," by which "in case the Peers finally refuse to acquiesce in the decision of the Lower House, the Crown is expected"—expected—"to nullify the resistance of the House of Lords by the creation of new Peers." That is the opinion of Professor Dicey on this matter of modern constitutional ethics. Finally, I may cite a great authority who, though he is not a lawyer, is, as everybody admits, one of the most brilliant, far-seeing and illuminating writers on British politics known in our time—the late Mr. Bagehot. In his "English Constitution" he said:—

"The very nature, too, as has been seen, of the Lords in the English Constitution shows that it cannot stop revolution. The Constitution contains an exceptional provision to prevent it stopping it. The Executive, the appointee of the popular Chamber and the nation, can make new Peers, and so create a majority in the Peers; it can say to the Lords, 'Use the powers of your House as we like, or you shall not use them at all.'"

In face of those authorities it is very difficult to maintain that this is not an integral and essential part of our constitutional practice. Indeed, if it were not so, there would be absolutely no escape except by means of either force or revolution out of a constitutional impasse.

Reference is sometimes made—and I shall have to speak a little later on of that—to the old Royal Prerogative of Veto over legislation. That prerogative, of course, could not be continued side by side with the development of real representative Government. They are contradictory one to the other. On the other hand, such an artificial bicameral system as ours makes the exercise of the prerogative of creation absolutely essential to the preservation of popular rights. Let me point out in this connection, and it cannot at this moment be too clearly borne in mind, that the Resolution passed the other day by the House of Lords to the effect that the possession of a peerage should not in itself give the right of sitting and voting in the House, deals a direct and fatal blow at this Royal Prerogative. If that Resolution were to be passed into law, if it were to acquire the power that can only be given to it by a statute, what would be the constitutional situation? The House of Lords would become, for the first time in our history, an autonomous and uncontrollable body beyond the reach of the Crown and its Ministers, and securely entrenched in a position of absolute and unassailable constitutional independence. That is as far as the House of Lords have yet gone. But both these prerogatives—the prerogative of dissolution which applies to this House and the prerogative of creation which applies to the other House—are, as everyone will admit, and no one more fully than I, grave and exceptional remedies, not to be resorted to except under the stress of urgent and extreme necessity. *Nisi dignus vendice nodus.* Neither of them is perfect, and neither of them is suitable for dealing with every day cases of difficulty and deadlock which, under our present system, occur from time to time between the two Houses when they are not of the same political complexion. So I come now to my second question. Apart from these prerogative powers, real, living, to be held in reserve, only to be exercised in case of need, but in case of need to be exercised without fear—apart from these prerogative powers standing in that position, what practical suggestions have been put forward other than the proposals which we are about to make, which are suitable to deal and appropriate to deal with what one may call the habitual and constantly occurring deadlock between the two Houses?

As far as I know there are only two. The first is what goes by the rather barbarous name of the Referendum. I admit that, speaking on Sir Henry Campbell-Bannerman's Resolution three years ago, I coquetted with the Referendum, and I say quite distinctly that I reserve the question of the appropriateness and the practicability of what is called the Referendum as possibly the least objectionable means of untying the knot in some extreme and exceptional constitutional entanglement. But I am now speaking of the Referendum as a mode of escape from what I call the ordinary or everyday deadlocks of our present Parliamentary system, and as an expedient for dealing with that situation I confess I think it altogether inadequate. In the first place, the Referendum in practice as it would be applied would be extremely uneven; if you are to have a Referendum when the two Houses differ what are you going to have when the two Houses agree? That is not such a foolish question as at first sight appears. That is what happened within our own experience. Supposing you have a House of Commons which, as the General Election shortly afterwards showed, completely perverted and misrepresented the mind of the nation; suppose you have that House passing by large majorities measures which have approved themselves to its Members for the time being, but which are condemned by the great bulk of the nation; suppose you have a sham or a dormant revising Chamber at the other end of the corridor, without demur and without reference to the people passing those measures *sub-silentio*; must you not give the great majority of the inhabitants of this country some power corresponding to the Referendum, some power of initiative, some power of submitting to the popular vote the question at issue? A Referendum which can only be exercised when the two Houses differ would be a very uneven constitutional system. The Referendum as a normal part of our constitutional machinery, in my opinion and that of my colleagues, and probably of the great majority of both sides of the House, would tend largely to undermine the independence and responsibility of this Chamber. So long as you have here the opinion of the vast majority of the constituencies, on their shoulders would rest the undivided responsibility for determining the policy of the Government, and saying what measures shall be put on the Statute Book. This House acts under a sense of restraint, but if the matter were left at large it could always be said, "It does not matter very much what we do, for, after all, it can always be referred to the people." In the interests of Parliamentary independence and responsibility the Referendum is not a normal part of our system. Let me point out one or two further considerations, if I am not taking the House too far into matters, because all these things really work into one another. It is said that by means of the Referendum, in case of a deadlock between the two Houses, you could do what you cannot do now when you have a General Election—you could disentangle and isolate the particular issue. I do not believe you could do anything of the kind; indeed, I am certain you could not. The Referendum might be nominally and ostensibly on some particular point, and everybody knows that the whole machinery of both parties in the State would be brought to bear on the determination of that issue. You would have the turmoil, the tumult, and a large part of the

[Mr. Asquith.]

expense of a General Election, and, while I have the highest possible respect for the intelligence and political instinct of my fellow-countrymen, I do not believe it would be possible for them, under these conditions, completely to segregate the particular issue on which the Referendum took place, and entirely to ignore the whole of the rest of the field of politics. On these grounds, which might be elaborated, I should deprecate the adoption of that solution of our difficulty. Let me now come to the other, and the only other solution, which, so far as I know, has been suggested, and that is a joint Session between the two branches of the Legislature. That is the remedy which has been accepted by two of our greatest self-governing dominions. We find it in the Australian Constitution and in the South African Constitution, to which we assented a year ago. In France, although there is no constitutional provision on the subject, yet both Houses have, I believe, by rules which they have made for themselves, provided that in the event of a deadlock the matter should be determined and, if possible, settled by a conference between them. This scheme of a joint Session has, I think, a great many recommendations, and I desire to say most distinctly here and now that if you have two Legislative Chambers composed upon a democratic basis, and related to one another somewhat after the fashion I indicated earlier in my speech, with a proper numerical relation one to the other, I think there is a great deal to be said for settling differences that might arise between them by means of a joint Session. I do not in the least prejudge it, and when it arises I think the hands of Parliament ought to be perfectly free with regard to it.

But is it applicable, can it be made applicable to our existing Constitution? It is apparent that it could not. In the first place, the House of Lords consists at present, I believe, of over 600 Members, and we are 670 Members; so that in a joint Session of the two Houses, quite apart from the unwieldiness of the body and the mechanical difficulties that might arise, you would have the non-representative House in the proportion of something like 50 per cent. of the whole body. That in itself is a fatal objection to a joint Session. Apart from that, taking the House of Lords as it is, you have got a body which is a partisan body in the proportion of something like ten to

one. Take the late House of Commons, which was a very good illustration. We had a majority larger than any Government has ever possessed in any House elected since the time of the Reform Act—a majority, I suppose, of over 300; yet, if we had gone into a joint Session with the House of Lords on a matter like the Education Bill or the Licensing Bill, it is at least extremely doubtful whether we could have carried either Bill. Of course, you may say it is the superior representative quality of the House of Lords. But assuming, as I am entitled to assume, for the purpose of my argument, that the House of Commons at that time represented the opinion of the country, and the House of Lords did not, it is perfectly clear that no way of escape from the deadlock would be found by a joint Session. Of course, you might attempt to solve the difficulty—I do not betray any secrets when I say that my colleagues and I in the days gone by thought of this, and entertained it, weighed it, and tried it—by a reduction of the panel, but then you get for a time an artificial combination. I do not believe, with the House of Lords as at present constituted, you could devise any method of joint-Session which would attain the result desired. I pass from those two alternative methods of dealing with the difficulty to the one which the Government are going to propose, namely, the limitation of the Veto. The proposal to convert the absolute Veto at present possessed by the House of Lords into a suspensory Veto, is not our proposal. It goes much further back. It is the proposal of the late Mr. John Bright. It was made by him in a more drastic form than we are now presenting it to Parliament, in a celebrated speech which he delivered on 4th August, 1884, at Bingley Hall, in Birmingham. I should like to call the attention of the House for a moment to that speech—I do not think it is irrelevant to the subject—and to the reception which it met with at the time in the country. Some people think that a novel and an evil practice has been introduced—I do not know whether by me, but certainly by some of my right hon. Friends—of using strong language about the House of Lords. I advise them to read Mr. Bright's speech at Birmingham in 1884. He made some very unpleasant quotations, which I do not venture to repeat, from the 73rd Psalm. He ventured on such language as this, speaking of the House of Lords:—

"Privilege everywhere tends to beget ignorance, selfishness, and arrogance."

That is what is called setting class against class. But although the speech is very well worth perusal and study, it is more important to see the reception with which it met from those who were then, as now, the accredited organs of Conservative, I will not say of timid, but more or less Conservative, and certainly of intellectual opinion in this country—I mean "The Times" and the "Spectator." [An Hon. Member: "It was Liberal."] I do not remember whether "The Times" was Liberal or not then. "The Times" said:—

"Mr. Bright's name and authority will bespeak for this scheme attentive consideration."

It goes on to say:—

"It is to be regretted that Mr. Chamberlain, at the same meeting, should have used language which anywhere but in Birmingham would certainly be regarded as somewhat vituperative."

That is a sort of apostolic succession of the whipping boys of "The Times." It goes on to say:—

"The case against the House of Lords under the present Government is sufficiently strong in itself to render it quite unnecessary to indulge in unmeasured invective and extravagant abuse."

Proceeding to deal with the suspensory Veto, it declared:—

"The question is rapidly coming within the range of practical politics. The suggestions are not very subversive, and on the whole are entitled to most respectful consideration."

That was the opinion of "The Times." But I must do myself the pleasure of quoting the opinion of that great weekly organ the "Spectator." The complaint of the "Spectator" was that the Bright proposals were "much too conservative." They got rid of deadlocks between the two Houses only by "the most prodigal waste of the time of the House of Commons." But a still more serious objection was the temptation, to which the Peers might succumb, of applying the limited Veto with greater readiness than they had been in the habit of resorting to the absolute Veto. Therefore, that great organ of opinion, rejecting as being too Conservative and too timid this way of dealing with the situation, suggested the less Conservative method of restricting the number of Peers summoned to the House of Lords under a scheme which would secure that the Ministry of the day would have a majority in the Upper as well as in the Lower House. I thought it interesting to recall the earlier stages of this proposal. It was adopted and revived by the late Government under the leadership of my lamented predecessor in a much less drastic form, and we now, in the proposals we submit to the Committee, have still further modified and, I think, improved them. What are the changes we have made in the proposals put forward by the last Parliament? They are, in substance, two. The first is that we have enacted that there should be an interval of two years between the first introduction of a Bill and its final passing into law. The next is—and I think this is a very solid and substantial improvement—that we have provided that the three Sessions referred to shall not necessarily be Sessions in the same Parliament, and we couple with that the proposal that the duration of the House of Commons shall not be longer than five years.

I should like now to deal with a suggestion which goes to the very essence of the matter. I will not deal with the details of the proposals—which are Committee matters—but with the suggestion which I believe is seriously entertained, and which is certainly urgently put forward, that the adoption of the suspensory in lieu of the absolute Veto, would bring us to the condition of a Single Chamber Government. I want to deal with this as a matter of principle.

We have in this country slowly but decisively adopted democracy as our form of Government. What is the essence of democratic Government? Surely it is, and here, I think, I shall carry with me universal assent, that the will of the people, by which we mean the will of the majority of the people for the time being, shall, both in legislation and policy, prevail. Further, we have come to the conclusion that, in common with all other democratic countries, the proper and only practical way of ascertaining that will and that opinion is by the process, the rude process, the imperfect process, in many ways the very unsatisfactory process, of periodical popular election. I say rude and unsatisfactory for this reason: On the one hand you have have growing constantly in number and complexity a mass of political questions which present themselves at popular elections simultaneously for solution; and, on the other hand, unsatisfactory also because of the perfection to which the science and art of electioneering has now been developed. For both those reasons it becomes more and more difficult to disentangle issues and assign, I will not say the relative predominance, but even the relative importance and influence to this or that issue in deciding the general verdict. The verdict of the country is pretty clearly, as a rule, though not always, in favour of one party as

[Mr. Asquith.]

against another. The verdict of the country is pretty clearly, as a rule, in favour of one set of measures and one line of policy and against the other. But when it comes to a particular case, the case of a particular measure or particular question, it falls open to a variety of constructions. These are the inevitable defects of the system of popular election, which we share and suffer from, in common with all other democratic countries. But it is the only practical way of ascertaining the national will.

What follows? If my premises are correct, there is at least a strong, nay, almost irresistible presumption, that a measure passed by a majority of the House of Commons still fresh, or relatively fresh, from the polls, is a measure which is approved in its main principles by the majority of the people, and which, therefore, in accordance with the principle of democratic government, ought to be allowed to pass into law. There are exceptions, I admit. It may be, as I have said, that representatives of the people in a particular case have mistaken the terms of their authority. It may, again, be that the majority by which a particular measure is passed through this House is so small, or so obviously casual and heterogeneous, that its verdict ought not to be treated as expressing the considered judgment of the nation. I admit these are both conceivable cases, and they show the possible uses of the Second Chamber, even such a Chamber as the House of Lords, and they suggest the wisdom of procuring delay, if that Second Chamber so desires, such as is procured by these Veto Resolutions. What is the object of delay? In the first place it affords an opportunity of consultation if it is a matter merely for revision. That is its real purpose. Still more it gives time and opportunity to the articulate expression of public opinion. Does any hon. or right hon. Gentleman suppose that a measure hurried through this House under closure or guillotine by what is called a scratch majority, could survive such an ordeal as that provided under this Resolution—the ordeal of having to be passed in three Sessions here, and having for two years to be submitted to the scrutiny and agitation of public opinion outside? Under this scheme in the first two years a fresh House of Commons will be constantly subject, and therefore legislation of the country would be subject to the operation of public opinion,

and during the last two years the time of the House will not be, as it would have been under the Campbell-Bannerman Resolution, to a large extent sterilised. It may go on, and if they have passed their measure once, they may pass it again: a general election will intervene, and the people will have an opportunity of pronouncing an opinion before the final resistance of the House of Lords is over borne.

Taking the House of Lords as it is, taking the two Houses as they are, that limitation of Veto, coupled with the shortening of the duration of the House of Commons, is the best and most practical means by which, under existing conditions, we can secure that the popular will shall not be either frustrated or perverted, but shall, with due opportunities for consideration and revision, be promptly and effectually carried into law. Let me add, what is often ignored, that nothing is more absurd than the notion that an Act of Parliament once put upon the Statute Book remains sacrosanct, and can never be touched. It is a ridiculous perversion of history. A large part of the time of the Parliaments since 1832 has been consumed in reversing the work of their predecessors. If a new Parliament, a new House of Commons thinks the work of the old House of Commons wrong, why cannot it undo it? We were engaged in the last Parliament during nearly two years to a large extent in trying to undo the work of our predecessors, and, but for the obstruction suffered from elsewhere, we should have undone it, and wiped out from the Statute Book two measures, the Education Act of 1902, and the Licensing Act of 1904, which, as we believe, ought never to have been put on the Statute Book.

I am sorry to have detained the House so long in dealing with the details of these Resolutions. We put them forward to deal with the emergency which confronts us, not as purporting to be a full or adequate solution of the whole problem, or, as exhausting the policy of the Government. We put them forward as the first and indispensable step to the emancipation of the House of Commons, and to rescue from something like paralysis the principles of popular government. Further, we put them forward as a demand, sanctioned as we believe by a large majority of the representatives of the people chosen at the recent General Election, themselves representing a large majority of the electorate. Fundamental changes in this country, as nothing illustrates more clearly than this controversy, are slow to bring into effect. There was a story current of the last Parliament, which in this connection bears repetition. It was told of a new Member of the then House of Commons that in 1906 he witnessed for the first time the ceremony of opening Parliament. He saw gathered in the other Chamber at one end the King sitting on his throne, at the other end Mr. Speaker standing at the Bar. In between there was that scene of subdued but stately splendour, bringing and making alive to the eye and the imagination the unbroken course of centuries during which we alone here, of all the peoples of the world have been able to reconcile and harmonise the traditions of the past, the needs of the present, the hopes and aspirations of the future. He was a man of very advanced views, and as he gazed upon that unique and impressive spectacle, felt constrained to mutter to a neighbour, a man of like opinions with himself, "This will take a lot of abolishing." So it will. It was a very shrewd observation. But I am not sure that he had mastered the real lesson of the occasion. So far as outward vision goes, one would seem, no doubt, in the presence of such a ceremony as that, to be transplanted to the days of the Plantagenets. The framework is the same ; the setting is almost the same. The very figures of the picture—King, Peers, Judges, Commons— are the same, at any rate, in name. But that external and superficial identity masks a series of the greatest transformations that have been recorded in the constitutional experience of mankind. The Sovereign sits there on the Throne of Queen Elizabeth, who, as history tells us, on one occasion, at the end of a single Session, opposed the Royal Veto to no less than forty-eight out of ninety-one Bills which had received the assent of both Houses of Parliament. That Royal Veto, then and for long afterwards, an active and potent enemy of popular rights, is literally as dead as Queen Anne. Yes, Sir ; and has the Monarchy suffered? Has the Monarchy suffered? There is not a man among us, in whatever quarter of this House he sits, who does not know the Crown of this Realm, with its hereditary succession, its Prerogatives adjusted from generation to generation to the needs of the people and the calls of the Empire, is held by our Gracious Sovereign by a far securer tenure than ever fell to the lot of any of his Tudor or Stuart ancestors. The liberties again of the Commons, which you, Sir, only a month ago once more claimed and asserted at the same Bar, in time-honoured phrases which carry us back to the days when those liberties were in jeopardy from the Crown— the liberties of the Commons, slowly and patiently won, in these days newly threatened and invaded—not, indeed, through the Crown, but from another quarter—are only in danger if, unlike our forefathers here, we refuse to take the necessary steps to make them safe. But there is one factor in the Constitution which, while everything else has changed, remains, sterilised in its development, possessing and exercising power without authority, still a standing menace and obstacle to progressive legislation and popular government. The absolute Veto of the Lords must follow the Veto of the Crown before the road can be clear for the advent of full-grown and unfettered democracy.

Mr. A. J. BALFOUR : There were phrases in the peroration of the right hon. Gentleman which suggested that he had approached the great constitutional issue which he has raised by these Resolutions in the spirit of a constitutional Minister ; but I confess that, neither in the proposals themselves nor in the arguments by which, in the main, he has supported them, do I see any of that wise power of adapting institutions to the changing needs of the community which has been the glory of this country in its great historical traditions, to which both parties in the House, I think, may justly lay claim, but which appear to have been abandoned by the present Government at the inspiration of new forces and new demands which certainly have nothing to do with democracy properly understood, and which suggest changes in the future to which true democratic opinion—by which I mean the settled opinion of this great community— will find itself wholly alien. The right hon. Gentleman, as I think was only proper, introduced his comments and explanations of the particular proposals which he means to bring before us by some observations upon Second Chambers in general and the position of the House of Lords in particular. On the position of Second Chambers in general I understand that there is not absolute unanimity either in the party which the right hon. Gentleman leads or in the Government of which he is a Member. He himself appears to have gone through a good many oscillations in connection with

Margaret Thatcher turns disaster into triumph in her farewell speech

After more than 30 years in newspaper and television journalism and over 20 years as a senior political correspondent at Westminster, **John Sergeant** came full circle and returned to light entertainment and comedy. It was the point from which he had begun.

On graduating from Oxford university, he was given a traineeship at Reuters. However, Alan Bennett saw him perform in the university's review at the Edinburgh festival and offered him a job. It was to be the first of many instances where he had to decide between serious news or light entertainment – a dilemma with which he continues to wrestle with his frequent appearances in quiz shows and current affairs programmes.

In 1966 the light entertainment option won the day and he sacrificed the Reuters job to appear in Bennett's award winning BBC series "On the Margin". He left the programme in 1967 after only a year to take up a news reporting career, joining the *Liverpool Echo* as a trainee reporter.

His chosen profession took him around the world to cover major news events and trouble spots. When he finally said farewell to news, he took up a successful career in light entertainment, appearing in television and radio programmes, touring with his own one-man show, and featuring on the public speaking circuit. He is also a successful author.

After three years with the *Liverpool Echo* he secured a reporting job with the BBC. He covered assignments in more than 25 countries including Vietnam, Rhodesia, Northern Ireland, Cyprus during the Turkish invasion, and Lebanon during the Israeli invasion. He was also a senior correspondent in Dublin, Paris and Washington.

In 1981 he was appointed political correspondent for the BBC. Seven years later he became the Corporation's chief political correspondent. It was a position he held for 12 years before leaving to join ITN as political editor. He stayed there for three years, leaving to concentrate on writing and other broadcasting work.

In 1990 he won a Press Guild award for the most memorable outside broadcast. He was awaiting Margaret Thatcher's appearance outside the British Embassy in Paris during the challenge to her leadership that was to end her premiership. During his live broadcast she suddenly appeared behind him, but as he offered her his microphone in an attempt to interview her he was elbowed to one side by her press secretary, Bernard Ingham.

His non-political broadcasting work has covered an extensive range of programmes. He is a regular contributor to the BBC's "One Show", was a guest on "Parkinson", has twice chaired "Have I Got News for You" and was the subject of an edition of "Room 101". He has also contributed to the "Culture Show" and "Balderdash and Piffle". He was the subject of headlines in every newspaper in 2008 when, regardless of the huge public support that had kept him in the competition, he voluntarily withdrew from the BBC dance competition, "Strictly Come Dancing."

On radio, he has presented "World at One", "Today" and "PM", and has been a guest on many other Radio 4 shows including "News Quiz", "Quote Unquote", "Just a Minute" and "X Marks the Spot".

In 2001 he published his memoirs "Give Me Ten Seconds", which was in the best-seller lists for six months and sold over 300,000 copies. His second book on the last part of Mrs Thatcher's career, "Maggie: Her Fatal Legacy", which was published in February 2005, also appeared in the best seller lists.

When the Prime Minister made water run uphill

BY JOHN SERGEANT

Margaret Thatcher's last speech to the House of Commons as Prime Minister may seem an unusual choice to those searching for the most significant or the most important speech in recent times. Plenty of others, full of policy and earnestness, would obviously take precedence.

But for those of us who were there it is hard to imagine a better example of the British love of politics as theatre. A political disaster, described by her wilder supporters as something close to a coup d'état, was, for a brief moment, transformed into a personal triumph.

Disbelief was suspended. Margaret Thatcher, one of the most dominant Prime Ministers this country has ever seen, was refusing to lie down, even though a stake had been driven through her heart.

After her 11 years at No. 10, her Cabinet had turned against her, and that morning she announced her resignation. By chance, within a few hours she had to defend her Government, and therefore her record, in a debate on a motion of no confidence in the House of Commons.

Not for her an abject apology or stumbling excuses. She grabbed the chance of a bravura display in front of the cameras, assuming correctly that it would be her last chance of this kind.

The Leader of the Opposition, Neil Kinnock, found himself in some difficulty. His fox had shot herself, and all those Labour MPs who had cursed the day that Thatcher was born had to decide whether it would be unseemly if they now too readily danced on her grave.

It would have been so much easier for them if Labour could credibly have claimed that Mrs Thatcher's fall was as a result of their efforts. But everyone knew that the Conservative civil war was the cause, and the regicides, as her supporters would call them, were such well known figures as Sir Geoffrey Howe and Michael Heseltine.

It was because Mr Heseltine had come so close to beating her in the first round of the leadership contest just a few days before that she had been eventually forced to conclude that the game was up.

The more thoughtful Labour MPs realised that her departure would give the Conservatives a chance to find a new leader and therefore improve their prospects in the election which would have to come within the next two years. But the name of John Major was not even being whispered.

For Margaret Thatcher it was a chance to make water run uphill, to defy the laws of gravity. She laid out in great detail all the reasons why her period in office had been such a resounding success. She managed to avoid the awkward point that her career was effectively over.

It was, I thought, her greatest moment.

Glory years end with blistering rebuke for Tory dissidents who had written off Mrs Thatcher

Norman Tebbit was regarded by Margaret Thatcher as one of those rare politicians who was able to combine good presentational skills with the ability to get the job done. He was a Front-Bench member of her team from the moment she became Prime Minister, and for much of the time he was one of her most trusted lieutenants. Of all her supporters in the Government, none, she declared, had the strength and acumen of Norman Tebbit.

He was elected Conservative MP for Epping in 1970, after serving with the RAF during his national service and subsequently working as a commercial pilot for BOAC. He had been a prominent member of the British Airline Pilots Association, in which body he occupied various offices.

Following boundary changes, he represented Chingford from 1974 to 1992. He was made a trade Minister by Mrs. Thatcher after the Conservative election victory of 1979, going on to become Employment Secretary in 1981. In that role, he took a tough approach to trade unions, notably in the Employment Act 1982, which he regarded as his "greatest achievement in Government".

The legislation completely recast the status of trade unions and their members under the law. When he put his proposals to the Cabinet in late 1981 they were seen to deal a severe blow to the closed shop, expose strikers to the risk of being sacked without recourse to the unfair dismissal procedures, tighten up the definition of a "lawful trade dispute", and lift the immunity trade unions had enjoyed in protecting their funds from actions for damages.

His declared aim was to put trade unions on the same legal footing as anyone else. In spite of some opposition from his Cabinet colleagues, within four months he introduced the Bill into the Commons with its provisions largely unchanged from his original proposals. It became law in December 1982.

In 1981, his speech to the Conservative party conference contained words which have been adapted into one of the most common everyday expressions. Responding to the suggestion that the Handsworth and Brixton riots were a reaction to the frustration of unemployment, he recalled the experience of his unemployed father in the 1930s: "He didn't riot. He got on his bike and looked for work, and he kept looking till he found it." This was soon truncated in the press and in popular usage into the slogan, "On yer bike" the meaning of which has evolved beyond what he originally intended.

He went on to become Trade and Industry Secretary in 1983. The following year he was seriously injured when, shortly before 3am on 12 October, the Provisional IRA detonated a bomb at the Grand hotel, Brighton during the Conservative party conference. It was seen as an attempt to assassinate the British Cabinet, many of whom were staying in the hotel at the time. He was fortunate to be pulled from the rubble alive. The blast left his wife, Margaret, disabled and confined to a wheelchair, and it was his determination to care for her that, in due course, spelled the end of his time in front-line politics. Mrs Thatcher was bitterly to regret his departure.

In 1985, he became chairman of the Conservative party, and organised the 1987 election campaign with the advertising firm, Saatchi and Saatchi. After the election, he acted on his warning to Mrs Thatcher that he would be leaving. He returned to the Back Benches so that he could spend more time caring for his wife.

He nevertheless remained a prominent, and controversial, figure. He was a vociferous opponent of the Maastricht treaty, and although he did not at the time advocate leaving the EU, he fervently believed in manipulating and controlling it. In 1990, he suggested that a "cricket test" – popularly known as the Tebbit test – be used as a measure of the degree of integration into British society of immigrants or first generation British of foreign descent. The test was whether they supported the team of the country to which they had come, or that of the country they had left.

He resigned his Commons seat at the 1992 election, but he was granted a life peerage and joined the House of Lords as Baron Tebbit of Chingford. He now supports the Better Off Out campaign, which proposes an end to Britain's EU membership, and is vice-president of the Conservative Way Forward group.

Anticipated wake becomes a carnival triumph

By Rt hon Lord Tebbit of Chingford CH

On 21 November 1990, following the failure of Conservative Members of Parliament to endorse by a sufficient majority her victory over the challenge for the party leadership by Michael Heseltine, Margaret Thatcher announced that she would resign both as Prime Minister and leader of the party.

Mr Kinnock, as Leader of the Opposition, put down a motion of no confidence in the Government, to which Margaret Thatcher was bound to reply. "Informed opinion" around Westminster had prepared both Parliament and the country for a Kinnock triumph and a wake for the Prime Minister.

In fact, it was a triumph for her, a non-event for the Opposition, and a blistering rebuke for the dissident Conservative minority who had claimed that Thatcher was "past her sell-by date".

As with all Margaret Thatcher's great speeches, a good deal of midnight oil had been burned in its preparation. I was one of a select few who had worked on the script until well gone midnight before leaving the Prime Minister to add her own mark to what we had drafted.

When the House assembled, the Opposition Benches were brimming over with glee at the prospect of the final humiliation of a Conservative leader second only to Churchill and even surpassing him in electoral success.

The Conservatives were muted: some were angry, ashamed at what their colleagues had done; some ashamed at what they had done; and some still triumphant at their iconoclasm.

Confounding almost all expectations, there was no hint of defeat in the words, nor the demeanour of the Prime Minister. At times her delivery could be stilted – but not on that day. Interventions were brushed aside, her fluency grew, she dominated the House. "I am enjoying this," she declared. And she was.

There are moments when the House of Commons is pure theatre – whether the theatre of tragedy, comedy or farce. But on 22 November 1990 it was more like opera. It was Margaret Thatcher's grand finale, her last great aria in the House.

Had it indeed been opera, no one but Maria Callas could have sung the role of Prime Minister – a solo role that turned the expected wake into a carnival triumph for Margaret Thatcher even as her party's glory years ended and the long dark night of electoral humiliation began for those who had encompassed her downfall.

Exit – con brio.

Mr. Kinnock: Everything that I have heard from the Conservative party in recent weeks shows that it has a surfeit of comedians.

The intergovernmental conferences approaching in a few weeks' time are clearly vital to Britain. The party of government is locked in civil war over the issue. That is one of the reasons for what we are hearing today. During recent weeks the Foreign Secretary and the Prime Minister have sent very different signals about the political process. We also know that during recent weeks the Chancellor and the Prime Minister have differed greatly on economic union. We can only assume that in the wake of the Prime Minister's departure there will be a degree of similarity between the views of the Foreign Secretary and the Chancellor. What is certain, however, is that a substantial body of opinion in the Tory party strongly disagrees with the Chancellor and the Foreign Secretary. That division is basic and unbridgeable.

All that Conservative Members have in common is their opposition to the social charter and the standards that it sets for youth training, social security, health and safety at work, and much else. All that unites them is their opposition to the opportunities for improvement that could be afforded to the British people by that charter. They are also against the extension of majority voting to secure greater protection for the environment.

The Labour party is for the social charter. We are for extending majority voting for proposals to improve social and environmental standards. We are for them because they are a means of gaining advantage for the British people; a means of ensuring that we are part of a community as well as part of a market.

I could not really care less what Conservative Members do to themselves and their party, but I do care about the damage that they have done, are doing and will do to the interests of our country. How can anyone have confidence in a Government whose former deputy Prime Minister admits that they have been pursuing the wrong policies for half a decade? Who can have confidence in a Government with Cabinet Ministers who in the past week have been privately telling the press that the Prime Minister is finished and minutes later in the television studio supporting her position, before going off to a private meeting to contrive a coup against her? What confidence can there be in a Government headed by anyone who has sworn allegiance to Thatcherism, as every one of the contestants in the leadership contest has? Who can have confidence in a Government split from top to bottom? If they have no confidence in one another, how can the country have confidence in them? Conservative Members on the Back Benches and on the Government Front Bench have no confidence in one another, as they have shown in everything that they have said about one another in recent weeks and everything that they have done about one another in recent weeks. They are unfit to govern and should go now.

In a democracy, there should be one fitting conclusion to today's dramatic events—a general election. Let the people decide and let Britain have a fresh chance with a Labour Government.

4.50 pm

The Prime Minister (Mrs. Margaret Thatcher): It is, of course, the right and duty of Her Majesty's Opposition to challenge the position of the Government of the day. It is also their right to test the confidence of the House in the Government if they think that the circumstances warrant it. I make no complaint about that. But when the windy rhetoric of the right hon. Member for Islwyn (Mr. Kinnock) has blown away, what are their real reasons for bringing this motion before the House? There were no alternative policies—just a lot of disjointed, opaque words.

It cannot be a complaint about Britain's standing in the world. That is deservedly high, not least because of our contribution to ending the cold war and to the spread of democracy through eastern Europe and the Soviet Union —achievements that were celebrated at the historic meeting in Paris from which I returned yesterday.

It cannot be the nation's finances. We are repaying debts, including the debts run up by the Labour party. It cannot be the Government's inability to carry forward their programme for the year ahead, which was announced in the Gracious Speech on 7 November. We carried that debate by a majority of 108.

The Opposition's real reason is the leadership election for the Conservative party, which is a democratic election according to rules which have been public knowledge for many years—one member, one vote. That is a far cry from the way in which the Labour party does these things. Two in every five votes for its leader are cast by the trade union block votes, which have a bigger say than Labour Members in that decision: precious little democracy there.

The real issue to be decided by my right hon. and hon. Friends is how best to build on the achievements of the 1980s, how to carry Conservative policies forward through the 1990s and how to add to three general election victories a fourth, which we shall surely win.

Eleven years ago, we rescued Britain from the parlous state to which socialism had brought it. I remind the House that, under socialism, this country had come to such a pass that one of our most able and distinguished ambassadors felt compelled to write in a famous dispatch, a copy of which found its way into *The Economist,* the following words:

"We talk of ourselves without shame as being one of the less prosperous countries of Europe. The prognosis for the foreseeable future",

he said in 1979, was

"discouraging".

Conservative government has changed all that. Once again, Britain stands tall in the councils of Europe and of the world, and our policies have brought unparalleled prosperity to our citizens at home.

In the past decade, we have given power back to the people on an unprecedented scale. We have given back control to people over their own lives and over their livelihood—over the decisions that matter most to them and their families. We have done it by curbing the monopoly power of trade unions to control, even to victimise, the individual worker. Labour would return us to conflict, confrontation and government by the consent of the TUC. We have done it by enabling families to own their homes, not least through the sale of 1·25 million council houses. Labour opposes our new rents-to-mortgage initiative, which will spread the benefits of ownership wider still. We have done it by giving people choice in public services—which school is right for their children, which training course is best for the school leaver, which doctor they choose to look after their health and which hospital they want for their treatment.

Labour is against spreading those freedoms and choice to all our people. It is against us giving power back to the people by privatising nationalised industries. Eleven million people now own shares, and 7·5 million people have registered an interest in buying electricity shares. Labour wants to renationalise electricity, water and British Telecom. It wants to take power back to the state and back into its own grasp— a fitful and debilitating grasp.

Mr. Martin Flannery (Sheffield, Hillsborough): The right hon. Lady says that she has given power back to the people, but more than 2 million of them are unemployed. Has she given power back to them? Inflation is 10·9 per cent. Is that giving power back to the people, compared with rates throughout the rest of Europe? Is the frittering away of £100 billion-worth of North sea oil, which no other country has had, giving power back to the people? Will she kindly explain that—and how pushing many people into cardboard boxes and taking power away from them is somehow giving power back to them?

The Prime Minister: Two million more jobs since 1979 represent a great deal more opportunity for people. Yes, 10·9 per cent. inflation is much higher than it should be, but it is a lot lower than 26·9 per cent. under the last Labour Government. Yes, we have benefited from North sea oil. The Government have made great investments abroad that will give this country an income long after North sea oil has ceased. We have provided colossal investment for future generations. Labour Members ran up debts, which we have repaid. We are providing investment for the future; we do not believe in living at the expense of the future.

Mr. Dave Nellist (Coventry, South-East): If things are as good as the Prime Minister is outlining, why are her colleagues not happy for her to continue in the job of defending that record?

The Prime Minister: These are the reasons why we shall win a fourth general election. We have been down in the polls before when we have taken difficult decisions. The essence of a good Government is that they are prepared to take difficult decisions to achieve long-term prosperity. That is what we have achieved and why we shall handsomely win the next general election.

I was speaking of the Labour party wanting to renationalise privatised industry. Four of the industries that we have privatised are in the top 10 British businesses, but at the very bottom of the list of 1,000 British businesses lie four nationalised industries. Labour's industries consume the wealth that others create and give nothing back.

Because individuals and families have more power and more choice, they have more opportunities to succeed—2 million more jobs than in 1979, better rewards for hard work, income tax down from 33p in the pound to 25p in the pound and no surcharge on savings income. Living standards are up by a third and 400,000 new businesses have been set up since 1979—more than 700 every week. There is a better future for our children, thanks to our hard work, success and enterprise. Our people are better off than ever before. The average pensioner——

Mr. Simon Hughes (Southwark and Bermondsey): Will the right hon. Lady give way?

The Prime Minister: If the hon. Gentleman will just listen, he might hear something that he did not know. The average pensioner now has twice as much to hand on to his children as he did 11 years ago. They are thinking about the future. This massive rise in our living standards reflects the extraordinary transformation of the private sector.

Mr. Hughes: There is no doubt that the Prime Minister, in many ways, has achieved substantial success. There is one statistic, however, that I understand is not challenged, and that is that, during her 11 years as Prime Minister, the gap between the richest 10 per cent. and the poorest 10 per cent. in this country has widened substantially. At the end of her chapter of British politics, how can she say that she can justify the fact that many people in a constituency such as mine are relatively much poorer, much less well housed and much less well provided for than they were in 1979? Surely she accepts that that is not a record that she or any Prime Minister can be proud of.

The Prime Minister: People on all levels of income are better off than they were in 1979. The hon. Gentleman is saying that he would rather that the poor were poorer, provided that the rich were less rich. That way one will never create the wealth for better social services, as we have. What a policy. Yes, he would rather have the poor poorer, provided that the rich were less rich. That is the Liberal policy.

Mr. Hughes: No.

The Prime Minister: Yes, it came out. The hon. Member did not intend it to, but it did.

The extraordinary transformation of the private sector has created the wealth for better social services and better pensions—it enables pensioners to have twice as much as they did 10 years ago to leave to their children.

We are no longer the sick man of Europe—our output and investment grew faster during the 1980s than that of any of our major competitors.

Several Hon. Members rose——

The Prime Minister: If hon. Members would be a little patient, it would allow me to get a little further.

No longer a doubtful prospect, when American and Japanese companies invest in Europe, we are their first choice. Britain no longer has an overmanned, inefficient, backward manufacturing sector, but modern, dynamic industries.

The right hon. Gentleman referred to the level of inflation. Yes, in 1987 and 1988, the economy did expand too fast. There was too much borrowing, and inflation rose. That is why we had to take the tough, unpopular, measures to bring the growth of money supply within target. Inflation has now peaked and will soon be coming down. Inevitably, the economy has slowed, but we firmly expect growth to resume next year. For the fundamentals are right. Our industry is now enterprising. It has been modernised and restructured. In sector after sector, it is our companies which lead the world—in pharmaceuticals, in telecommunications and in aerospace. Our companies have the freedom and talent to succeed—and the will to compete.

Mr. Sillars: The Prime Minister is aware that I detest every single one of her domestic policies, and I have never hidden that fact. *[Interruption.]*

Mr. Speaker: Order.

Mr. Sillars: However, it is always a greater pleasure to tackle a political heavyweight opponent than a lightweight Leader of the Opposition—*[Interruption.]*—who is afraid to explain why, after a lifetime of campaigning to get rid of nuclear weapons, he is going to plant three Trident missiles in my country.

Can I take the Prime Minister back to the question of the poor getting poorer? Does she not realise—even at this point, five minutes after midnight for her—that, because of the transfer of resources from the poor to the wealthy, the poll tax was unacceptable, and that it was because of the poll tax that she has fallen?

The Prime Minister: I think that the hon. Gentleman knows that I have the same contempt for his socialist policies as the people of east Europe, who have experienced them, have for theirs. I think that I must have hit the right nail on the head when I pointed out that the logic of those policies is that they would rather the poor were poorer. Once they start to talk about the gap, they would rather that the gap were that—*[indicating]*—down here, not this—*[indicating]*—but that—*[indicating]*. So long as the gap is smaller, they would rather have the poor poorer. One does not create wealth and opportunity that way. One does not create a property-owning democracy that way.

Can I now get back to the subject of industry and an industrial policy from which Scotland has benefited so much, and from which it could never have benefited under the Government that the hon. Member for Glasgow, Govan (Mr. Sillars) used to support, and under the political policy that he espouses now?

Yes, our companies have the freedom and talent to succeed, and the will to compete. And compete we must. Our competitors will not be taking a break. There must be no hankering after soft options and no going back to the disastrous economic policies of Labour Governments. No amount of distance lends enchantment to the lean years of Labour, which gave us the lowest growth rate in Europe, the highest strike record and, for the average family, virtually no increase in take-home pay. Labour's policies are a vote of no confidence in the ability of British people to manage their own affairs. We have that confidence. Confidence in freedom and confidence in enterprise. That is what divides Conservatives from socialists.

Our stewardship of the public finances has been better than that of any Government for nearly 50 years. It has enabled us to repay debt and cut taxes. The resulting success of the private sector has generated the wealth and revenues which pay for better social services—to double the amount being spent to help the disabled, to give extra help to war widows, and vastly to increase spending on the national health service. More than 1 million more patients are being treated each year and there are 8,000 more doctors and 53,000 more nurses to treat them.

Mr. Jack Ashley (Stoke-on-Trent, South) *rose—*

The Prime Minister: That is the record of eleven and a half years of Conservative Government and Conservative principles. All these are grounds for congratulation, not censure, least of all from the Leader of the Opposition, who has no alternative policies.

Mr. Ashley *rose—*

The Prime Minister: I shall give way to the right hon. Gentleman, but then I should like to move on to say something about Europe, because what the Leader of the Opposition said about it was, to say the least, opaque.

Mr. Ashley: The Prime Minister mentioned disabled people, and as she is always anxious to be honest with the House, would she care to give a wider perspective about what has happened to disabled people under her Government? Would she care to confirm the official figures, which show that, in the first 10 years of her reign, average male earnings rose by 20 per cent. in real terms, whereas benefits for disabled people in that period rose 1 per cent. in real terms? How well did disabled people do out of that?

The Prime Minister: The right hon. Gentleman is very selective indeed. He knows full well that, in the past 11 years, we have spent twice as much on the disabled, over and above inflation—not twice as much in cash terms, but twice as much in terms of what the benefits will buy— especially in the mobility allowance and the Motability scheme. This has been quite outstanding and has been brought about because, under our policies, we have been able to create the wealth which created the resources to do that, among other things.

During the past 11 years, this Government have had a clear and unwavering vision of the future of Europe and Britain's role in it. It is a vision which stems from our deep-seated attachment to parliamentary democracy and commitment to economic liberty, enterprise, competition and a free market economy. No Government in Europe have fought more resolutely against subsidies, state aids to industry and protectionism; unnecessary regulation and bureaucracy and increasing unaccountable central power at the expense of national Parliaments. No Government have fought more against that in Europe than we have.

We have fought attempts to put new burdens and constraints on industry, such as the social charter which would take away jobs, in particular part-time jobs. For us part of the purpose of the Community is to demolish trade barriers and eliminate unfair subsidies, so that we can all benefit from a great expansion of trade both within Europe and with the outside world.

The fact is that Britain has done more to shape the Community over the past 11 years than any other member state. Britain is leading the reform of the common agricultural policy, getting surpluses down, putting a ceiling on agricultural spending. We have been the driving force towards the single market which, when it is completed, will be the most significant advance in the Community since the treaty of Rome itself. We have done more than any other Government to resist protectionism, keep Europe's market open to trade with the rest of the world, and make a success of the GATT negotiations.

We have worked for our vision of a Europe which is free and open to the rest of the world, and above all to the countries of eastern Europe as they emerge from the shadows of socialism. It would not help them if Europe became a tight-knit little club, tied up in regulations and restrictions. They deserve a Europe where there is room for their rediscovered sense of nationhood and a place to decide their own destiny after decades of repression.

With all this, we have never hesitated to stand up for Britain's interests. The people of Britain want a fair deal in Europe, particularly over our budget contribution. We have got back nearly £10 billion which would otherwise have been paid over to the EC under the arrangements negotiated by the Labour party when it was in power.

Indeed, what sort of vision does the Labour party have? None, according to the Leader of the Opposition. Labour Members want a Europe of subsidies, a Europe of socialist restrictions, a Europe of protectionism. They want it because that is how they would like to run—or is it ruin?—this country.

Every time that we have stood up and fought for Britain and British interests, Labour Front Bench spokesmen have carped, criticised and moaned. On the central issues of Europe's future, they will not tell us where they stand. Do they want a single currency? The right hon. Gentleman does not even know what it means, so how can he know? —[*Laughter.*]

Mr. Kinnock: It is a hypothetical question.

The Prime Minister: Absolute nonsense. It is appalling. He says that it is a hypothetical question. It will not be a hypothetical question. Someone must go to Europe and argue knowing what it means.

Are Labour Members prepared to defend the rights of this United Kingdom Parliament? No, for all that the right hon. Gentleman said. For them, it is all compromise, "sweep it under the carpet", "leave it for another day", and "it might sort itself out", in the hope that the people of Britain will not notice what is happening to them, and how the powers would gradually slip away.

The Government will continue to take a positive and constructive approach to the future of Europe. We welcome economic and monetary co-operation: indeed, no other member state has gone further than Britain in tabling proposals for the next stage, including the hard ecu. But our proposals would work with the market and give people and Governments real choice.

We want the Community to move forward as twelve: and from my talks in Paris with other European leaders over the past few days, I am convinced that that is their aim too. Europe is strongest when it grows through willing co-operation and practical measures, not compulsion or bureaucratic dreams.

Mr. Alan Beith (Berwick-upon-Tweed): Will the Prime Minister tell us whether she intends to continue her personal fight against a single currency and an independent central bank when she leaves office?

Mr. Dennis Skinner (Bolsover): No. She is going to be the governor. [*Laughter.*]

The Prime Minister: What a good idea. I had not thought of that. But if I were, there would be no European central bank accountable to no one, least of all national Parliaments. The point of that kind of Europe with a central bank is no democracy, taking powers away from every single Parliament, and having a single currency, a monetary policy and interest rates which take all political power away from us. As my right hon. Friend the Member for Blaby (Mr. Lawson) said in his first speech after the proposal for a single currency was made, a single currency is about the politics of Europe, it is about a federal Europe by the back door. So I shall consider the proposal of the hon. Member for Bolsover (Mr. Skinner). Now where were we? I am enjoying this.

Mr. Michael Carttiss (Great Yarmouth): Cancel it. You can wipe the floor with these people.

The Prime Minister: Yes, indeed—I was talking about Europe and the socialist ideal of Europe. Not for us the corporatism, socialism and central control. We leave those to the Opposition. Ours is a larger vision of a Community whose member states co-operate with one another more and more closely to the benefit of all.

Are we then to be censured for standing up for a free and open Britain in a free and open Europe? No. Our policies are in tune with the deepest instincts of the British people. We shall win the censure motion, so we shall not be censured for what is thoroughly right.

Under our leadership, Britain has been just as influential in shaping the wider Europe and the relations between East and West. Ten years ago, the eastern part of Europe lay under totalitarian rule, its people knowing neither rights nor liberties. Today, we have a Europe in which democracy, the rule of law and basic human rights are spreading ever more widely, where the threat to our security from the overwhelming conventional forces of the Warsaw pact has been removed: where the Berlin wall has been torn down and the cold war is at an end.

These immense changes did not come about by chance. They have been achieved by strength and resolution in defence, and by a refusal ever to be intimidated. No one in eastern Europe believes that their countries would be free had it not been for those western Governments who were prepared to defend liberty, and who kept alive their hope that one day east Europe too would enjoy freedom.

But it was no thanks to the Labour party, or to the Campaign for Nuclear Disarmament of which the right hon. Gentleman is still a member. It is this Government who kept the nuclear weapons which ensured that we could never be blackmailed or threatened. When Brezhnev deployed the SS20s, Britain deployed the cruise missiles and was the first to do so. And all these things were done in the teeth of the opposition of the hon. Gentlemen opposite—and their ladies. [*Laughter.*] The SS20s could never have been negotiated away without the bargaining strength which cruise and Pershing gave to the west.

Should we be censured for our strength? Or should the Labour party be censured for its weakness? I have no doubt that the people of Britain will willingly entrust Britain's security in future to a Conservative Government who defend them, rather than to socialists who put expediency before principle.

Sir Eldon Griffiths (Bury St. Edmunds): May I offer my right hon. Friend one measurement of the immense international respect and affection that she enjoys as a result of her policies of peace through strength? An opinion poll published on the west coast of America last month—[*Laughter.*]

Mr. Speaker: Order. This takes up a great deal of time. The hon. Gentleman is seeking to participate in the debate. Will he please ask a question?

Sir Eldon Griffiths: The figures are Gorbachev 74 per cent., Bush 75 per cent. and Thatcher 94 per cent.

The Prime Minister: I am sure that they were quite right, too.

[The Prime Minister]

I wish to say a word or two about the situation in the Gulf, because it will dominate politics until the matter is resolved. It is principle which is at stake, as well as the rule of international law.

In my discussions with other Heads of Government at the CSCE summit in Paris, I found a unanimous and impressive determination that Iraq's aggression must not succeed. The resolutions of the United Nations must be implemented in full. That is the peaceful option, Mr. Speaker, and it is there to be taken, if Saddam Hussein so chooses. There was also a widespread recognition among my colleagues in Paris that the time was fast approaching when the world community would have to take more decisive action to uphold international law and compel Saddam Hussein to leave Kuwait.

No one can doubt the dangers which lie ahead. Saddam Hussein has many times shown his contempt for human life, not least for the lives of his own people. He has large armed forces. They are equipped with peculiarly evil weapons, both chemical and biological.

Mr. Tam Dalyell (Linlithgow): Will the Prime Minister give way?

The Prime Minister: No, not now.

Twice in my time as Prime Minister we have had to send our forces across the world to defend a small country against ruthless aggression: first to our own people in the Falklands and now to the borders of Kuwait. To those who have never had to take such decisions, I say that they are taken with a heavy heart and in the knowledge of the manifold dangers, but with tremendous pride in the professionalism and courage of our armed forces.

There is something else which one feels. That is a sense of this country's destiny: the centuries of history and experience which ensure that, when principles have to be defended, when good has to be upheld and when evil has to be overcome, Britain will take up arms. It is because we on this side have never flinched from difficult decisions that this House and this country can have confidence in this Government today.

Mr. Speaker: Before I call hon. Members to speak in this important debate, I must say that I have no authority to limit speeches in a debate of this sort, nor would it be right to do so. Nevertheless, this is a day on which right hon. and hon. Members should exercise self-restraint. I ask hon. Members who are not remaining to leave quietly, please.

5.24 pm

Mr. Paddy Ashdown (Yeovil): It is impossible to follow the Prime Minister without soberly reflecting for a moment that we have just heard what is probably the last of her important and considerable speeches from the Government Dispatch Box. It was a bravura performance of the sort which she has made her own. I cannot with honesty say that I shall miss it, but I shall certainly remember it and, as time intervenes, remember it with ever greater affection.

We have just heard a catalogue of the Prime Minister's achievements and to some extent a political will and testament to her party. I must warn whoever is successful in the leadership election to watch out for that one on the Back Benches. Whatever the right hon. Member for Old Bexley and Sidcup (Mr. Heath) did to her, she will be a powerful voice in months to come. We shall be interested to see how much that voice will be used to unite her party or, on the issue of Europe, to divide it.

It is impossible to have lived through last week without feeling that one is participating in a moment of history.

Mr. David Winnick (Walsall, North): Will the right hon. Gentleman give way?

Mr. Ashdown: If the hon. Gentleman will let me get further into my speech, I shall happily consider his intervention later.

In the past week we have seen the end of one era—the end of a decade to which the Prime Minister has in many senses given her name—and the beginning of another. What struck me as remarkable about the two speeches was that neither was about the future and both were about the past. Both were about what has happened in the past decade. If there is a reason to have a lack of confidence in this Government it is much more that they are not addressing the real agenda of the 1990s—a new agenda is opening up—than their terrible failures in the past.

I recognise that the Prime Minister's decision today was a difficult one. She took it in a way which was right for her remarkable reputation, right for her party's unity and right for the country. We can all understand what she went through. She is a fighter and must have been considerably tempted to stay on and battle it out—to go down like the Fighting Temeraire with all guns blazing. That would undoubtedly be a noble end for a great captain, but not best calculated to encourage enthusiasm in the crew, as we have seen during the past week.

The Prime Minister has opened the way for the new politics that Britain so badly needs. It is impossible to let the moment pass without having the smallest tinge of sadness about the end of an era. I do not want to underestimate her considerable achievements. I have never agreed with her politics. I have always felt that they are bad and wrong for Britain. I have never agreed with her style. I have not denied—nor can we deny—some of her achievements or the courage and skill with which she has done her job. Indeed, she has achievements.

Mr. Bob Cryer (Bradford, South): What achievements? Name one.

Mr. Ashdown: The Prime Minister's pre-eminent achievement, which is not welcome to Labour Members, and the one for which she will be remembered, is the democratisation of the trade union movement.

In 1979 we debated whether Britain would be run by the trade unions or the elected Government of the day—it is hard to remember that now. The Prime Minister, to her credit, answered that challenge. [HON. MEMBERS: "Get on with it."] I hear Opposition Members baying behind me; no doubt they do not like to hear that. It is important, however, to mark up what the Prime Minister has done. She is right to say that she has given this country a standing abroad that it did not have in the 1970s. The right hon. Lady has also given us some sense of the value of sound money, which is important. She has also highlighted the importance of the market in our economy.

Sir Jim Spicer (Dorset, West): Will the right hon. Gentleman say just a word of thanks to the Prime Minister on behalf of his constituents and mine who work——

Dennis Skinner devises a desperate plan to safeguard stem cell research

In his 38 years in the House of Commons, **Dennis Skinner** has built an almost unparalleled reputation as the forthright and outspoken voice in the House of the traditional working-class Labour party. The party may have moved to a new political point of view, but he has steadfastly remained a champion of the left. In his entry in "Who's Who" he describes himself as coming from good working-class mining stock.

His assiduous attendance in the Chamber harks back to his years as a miner where his rule was that one never missed a shift at the pit. He won the seat of Bolsover at the 1970 general election, but on the Monday after the poll, although by then officially a Member of Parliament, he turned up for work as usual at Glapwell colliery.

He was bitterly opposed to Margaret Thatcher, whom he believed was waging a class war. On one occasion, during typically acrimonious exchanges, he told the House "whether I am in Parliament or outside, I shall fight for the working class that sent me here, just as the Tories ... fight for their class day in and day out—including all those crooks in the City."

She described him as an old sparring partner, but his hostility towards her was brought to a new pitch by her fight with the miners under Arthur Scargill. Throughout the dispute Dennis Skinner's mining background and his roots in the Derbyshire mining community dictated where his loyalty lay. His support for Scargill and the miners remained unquestioning and unqualified.

His adherence to the policies of the left is uncompromising, but he was a stout defender of the achievements of the Blair Government. He is liberal on social issues. He has been strongly pro-choice on abortion, campaigned for stem-cell and embryo research, as his choice of speech demonstrates, and supported gay rights.

Although his academic abilities enabled him to go to grammar school, when he left school he went into the pit at Parkhouse colliery. He remained a miner until his election to Parliament in 1970. The trade union environment of the mines fired his enthusiasm for politics and he joined the Labour party in 1956. He entered local politics in Clay Cross in 1960, was elected to Derbyshire county council in 1964, and became president of the Derbyshire, North-East constituency Labour party in 1968. He was elected president of the Derbyshire branch of the National Union of Mineworkers in 1966, a position he relinquished on becoming an MP.

Although never holding a Front-Bench position – perhaps because he has been at odds with the leadership on too many occasions – he has always been popular in the party. He was a member of Labour's National Executive Committee for nearly 20 years. During that time he held the position of both vice-chairman and chairman of the party.

In the House, his uninhibited observations and allegations about the conduct of his political opponents often brought him into conflict with the Chair. He was "named" by the Speaker on several occasions for violating the etiquette of parliamentary debate and refusing to apologise for, or withdraw, what he had said. It was his blunt speaking and uncompromising attitude that earned him the title the "beast of Bolsover".

When Mrs Thatcher's Government banned trade unions at GCHQ and were told by the High Court that in one respect their action was invalid, she told the House that Ministers were lodging an appeal. He suggested that the Prime Minister would be prepared to bribe the appeal judges "to save her own neck." When he would not withdraw the comment, the Speaker named him and he was out.

If he reviled Margaret Thatcher, his feelings towards the Social Democratic party – "the party that dare not speak its name" – and the so-called Gang of Four – Roy Jenkins, Shirley Williams, Bill Rodgers and David Owen – whom he regarded as traitors to his party, ran a close second. A comment about David Owen's character was the reason for another expulsion from the Chamber.

He has customarily sat in the first seat below the Gangway, and, when in Opposition, it meant that he sat immediately in front of the SDP Benches. He was ideally placed to heckle throughout their speeches, and since they shared the same microphone his comments were picked up and usually appeared in *Hansard*. To stop the frequent appearance of "Skinnerisms" in the report, Speaker Bernard Weatherill, without mentioning any names, ruled from the Chair that forthwith only seated interventions that were taken up by the Member who had the Floor should be reported in the columns of the *Official Report*. It is a rule that operates to this day.

Unprecedented use of procedure results in a great and glorious day

BY DENNIS SKINNER MP

One of the great advances in medical science has been the advent of stem cell research and treatment. It offers relief to sufferers of a variety of conditions including Parkinson's disease, diabetes, cancer and leukaemia and other blood disorders. The great prize, however, remains in the field of embryonic stem cell research, which holds out the potential for treating some of the most devastating diseases. Work in this vital area is progressing in laboratories around the world, but it came within a whisker of being banned in Britain.

Enoch Powell, who was a very shrewd and accomplished parliamentarian, had introduced a Bill to ban embryo research. Those of us who supported the research had fought a long battle to stop him, both in the Committee stage and on the Floor of the House. We had forced his Bill to a standstill and he had run out of time. Any hope that we might have beaten him was shattered, however, when he devised an ingenious scheme to use parliamentary procedure to give his Bill all the time it needed to become law.

His friend and ally the Conservative MP Andrew Bowden secured the first place in the queue for Private Members' motions on Friday 7 June 1985. Most MPs who get that slot use it to raise a constituency topic or a major issue of the day. Instead, Enoch Powell persuaded Bowden to use it to table a business motion to provide open-ended time for his Bill.

I realised that desperate action was needed to stop Powell. If the motion were approved, the Bill, which in all other circumstances was dead, would suddenly get all the time it needed and spring back to life. Powell had let it be known that, if necessary, he would keep the House sitting all weekend. It would almost certainly have got through, and that would have been the end of such research in this country.

At the time, the Brecon and Radnor by-election was pending after the death in May of Tom Hooson, the Conservative MP. I realised that if I moved the writ for that by-election, my motion would take precedence over Bowden's motion and, if we could keep our debate going long enough, we could squeeze him out. The problem was no one had ever done what I planned. This was to be a first. When I eventually told colleagues my intention, they simply responded "That's impossible. It can't be done."

I told no one of my scheme until the last possible minute – the night of Thursday 6 June. The first person I told was the Speaker, Bernard Weatherill. When I said that I planned to move the by-election writ his instant reaction was "You can't do that." But when he checked with the Clerk of the House he was told that I could. My motion duly appeared on the Order Paper.

So, at just after 9.30 on that Friday morning, after Prayers, I moved the writ and made my speech. Others made theirs, and we kept the debate going. Of course, I never got the writ, and I did not want it, but we stopped Bowden and we stopped Powell and we stopped the Bill.

I have chosen my speech from that occasion, but the speech is largely irrelevant. The importance attaches to the occasion and its consequences.

For me, as a Back Bencher, this was one of the most significant moments during my time in the House. Every time I read of another advance in stem cell research I think back to that great and glorious day.

House of Commons

Friday 7 June 1985

The House met at half-past Nine o'clock

PRAYERS

[MR. SPEAKER *in the Chair*]

9.35 am

Mr. Speaker: Today is a Back-Bench motions day, and the hon. Member who has won the first place in the ballot has the right to have his motion put to the House. Equally, other hon. Members have the right to speak and vote for or against that motion. I am well aware of the strong feelings aroused by the motion. I remind the House that it is a procedural one, and not primarily about the merits or otherwise of the Unborn Children (Protection) Bill.

I have selected the amendment in the name of the right hon. Member for Blaenau Gwent (Mr. Foot) and 53 other right hon. and hon. Members. I have received notice, perfectly properly, of other business to come ahead of today's principal debate. I hope that proceedings on those matters will not be artificially prolonged, and that today's proceedings will be conducted in the best traditions of the House of Commons.

New Writ (Brecon and Radnor)

9.36 am

Mr. Dennis Skinner (Bolsover): I beg to move,

"That Mr. Speaker do issue his Warrant to the Clerk of the Crown to make out a new Writ for the electing of a Member to serve in this present Parliament for the County Constituency of Brecon and Radnor in the room of Tom Ellis Hooson, Esq., deceased."

I mention Tom Hooson, and I think that it would be appropriate at this stage to remind hon. Members of his untimely death and pay a tribute to the service that he gave to the House. I must admit that to me Brecon and Radnor does not immediately suggest Tom Hooson, because I had a great friend from that area, Caerwyn Roderick. I believe that the name of Caerwyn Roderick is synonymous with Brecon and Radnor, and that is how I managed to get to know a little bit about the place and about the magnificent service that he gave to our party, the Labour party, and to my right hon. Friend the Member for Blaenau Gwent (Mr. Foot), the then leader of the Labour party, in his capacity as parliamentary private secretary.

Therefore, when I heard that there was the possibility of the writ for Brecon and Radnor being delayed, and I read the usual outpourings in the press—it must have been about a fortnight ago—I thought that it would be a good idea to get the thing hurried along. It so happened that at that time there was the suggestion that other matters would be moved this Friday. I am not sure whether I was thinking of moving the writ early, before the shock waves of the suggestion of the right hon. Member for South Down (Mr. Powell) hit the House of Commons, or whether it came after that, but it was about that time. I must make that point, because I am trying to show that it is purely a coincidence that my application falls on the day when other matters might have been discussed.

Mr. Tam Dalyell (Linlithgow): Before my hon. Friend leaves the question of Caerwyn Roderick, may I also mention Tudor Watkins? Only three days ago, I visited Lady Watkins in Brecon. He gave great service to the House between 1945 and 1970, and anyone who is interested in agriculture and hill farming should respect the memory of Tudor Watkins.

Mr. Skinner: I, too, remember Tudor Watkins. He had left by the time I came to the House, but I used to see him at Labour party conferences. I know that my hon. Friend the Member for Linlithgow (Mr. Dalyell) went to see Tudor's widow the other day while on his tour of the Falklands, the General Belgrano and Miss Murrell. He goes all over the country on a solo campaign which is gaining ground, and I am pleased to say that the General Belgrano and all those other matters will become an issue in the by-election.

Mr. D. N. Campbell-Savours (Workington): Is my hon. Friend aware that Mr. Tom Hooson was a great advocate of life issues? He voted in all Divisions in favour of life issues. Does not my hon. Friend believe that the use of this procedure in this way does a great disservice to his memory?

Mr. Skinner: My hon. Friend has a bit of a cheek, because he is part of a small group in the House which proposed to change the business of the day in a way which many people—not me—thought was an abuse of the procedures. Now he is trying to chide me for doing something to which I plead not guilty. In any case, Mr. Speaker, I think you would agree with me—I know you would—that we should talk about the issues that will be discussed during the by-election campaign, and not become involved in genetic engineering and other matters. I should say in passing that it is a bit rich that there is all this complaint about genetic engineering, yet the right hon. Member for South Down is acting as the master scientist and pottering about with that young embryo, the hon. Member for Brighton, Kemptown (Mr. Bowden).

Mr. Speaker: Order. I am not sure that that has much to do with the writ.

Mr. Skinner: No, but I think that you would agree, Mr. Speaker, that that might become an issue in the by-election. It is fair to say that anything that can be discussed in the House of Commons will become an issue in the Brecon and Radnor by-election. The Labour party candidate, Richard Willey, is only too anxious to get on with the job of raising those issues——

Mr. Campbell-Savours: What solidarity.

Mr. Skinner: My hon. Friend suggests that Mr. Willey may not be the greatest Left-winger of all time, but I shall be down there campaigning for him because he is the Labour candidate. I rest in the knowledge that our standard bearer in Brecon and Radnor will do a first-class job in raising all the issues that I may mention later, including the economy, the welfare state, and the countless other matters that may affect that rural area. It is between 30 and 40 miles wide——

Mr. Robert Adley (Christchurch): It is perhaps nothing more than a coincidence, but I had a premonition that this might be a suitable day to raise the subject that the hon. Gentleman has raised, and I happened to come in armed with several books about the ralway history of

[*Mr. Robert Adley*]

central Wales. Will the hon. Gentleman refer during his speech to this vital consideration in the forthcoming by-election? If he does not, I hope that he will not consider it wrong of me to take up the point later in the morning.

Mr. Skinner: On page 6 or 7, I have a section dealing with transport, especially the Transport Bill and privatisation. I am not sure whether the hon. Member for Christchurch (Mr. Adley) voted with the Labour party against the Transport Bill, but I shall let that pass. I know that our candidate, Richard Willey, will be campaigning on the Transport Bill and its effects on rural constituencies.

I am looking forward to Richard Willey sitting here, because I will advise him, as others advised me when I entered the House, that what one must get to know in this place, apart from all the politics, is the procedure. I shall suggest to Mr. Willey that he reads "Erskine May", because it may help him one day. He may need some background knowledge one unusual Friday. He will no doubt be campaigning about rail cuts and rail closures. I have no doubt that he will not be so parochial——

Mrs. Elaine Kellett-Bowman (Lancaster): On a point of order, Mr. Speaker. Is it in order for the hon. Member for Bolsover (Mr. Skinner) to open the campaign of the Labour candidate?

Mr. Speaker: The hon. Gentleman should be, and I think he is, advancing his case as to whether I should issue my warrant in respect of this by-election. But I ask the hon. Gentleman not to go into too much detail of the issues in the campaign, and to stick to the writ and to the question whether I should grant my warrant.

Mr. Skinner: You are absolutely correct, Mr. Speaker. Today is not a day to become engaged in argument and hassle. It is a day on which we must consider this serious issue. It may be that, after I have heard comments on my motion from the Government and certainly from my right hon. Friend the Member for Bethnal Green and Stepney (Mr. Shore), who may advance other arguments about the nature of the writ and whether it should be accepted, on this rare occasion, I may take all those suggestions into account and come to a different conclusion myself. Today, I am ready to listen to alternative arguments.

Mr. Andrew F. Bennett (Denton and Reddish): As many hon. Members are not clear about the procedures involved in his application, will my hon. Friend make it clear that if we must vote on this matter we have a choice of setting a by-election date within 28 days or not setting a date for this Session since the Standing Orders state that the motion may be made only once? Therefore, will he make it clear that his application is not necessarily designed to be voted upon, but simply to persuade my right hon. Friend the Member for Bethnal Green and Stepney (Mr. Shore) to think of an alternative approach?

Mr. Skinner: My hon. Friend has read "Erskine May", and I, too, have studied the matter. There may be an opportunity for other hon. Members to move motions that could affect the issue. But it does not matter because, as the right hon. Member for South Down, who is an expert in procedure, would be the first to agree, whatever

happens today on a vote, the House is sovereign and it could, within the next few days, decide to overturn that decision.

This is one of the few areas, Mr. Speaker—I think that you will agree with me on this — where the Common Market has not ripped away our sovereignty. The House retains that power, and the Leader of the House could, if he wished, irrespective of the outcome of a vote today, decide to say that the House is sovereign and that we shall set a new date. The House has the power to do that, as it has power in many other areas, although sadly it is affected in many areas by Common Market regulations, which will no doubt become a feature of the by-election campaign, whenever it takes place.

A further reason why I believe that we can get this matter——

Mr. Norman Buchan (Paisley, South): My hon. Friend raised an important point about the Common Market. Will he bear in mind that there is a problem there in relation to majorities and the exercise of a veto? Has he considered whether he wishes to exercise a veto on matters coming from the Government side of the House, or to rely on a majority?

Mr. Skinner: I kept my eye firmly on you, Mr. Speaker, while my hon. Friend made that point, and I saw a little bit of a nod, which suggested that we should not travel down that road. There are areas where we should not tread today. We should keep to the straight and narrow. One thing is certain — the Common Market is not straight and narrow. It has gravy trains, but it is not straight and narrow.

Mr. Dave Nellist (Coventry, South-East): When my hon. Friend develops that argument about whether a by-election in Brecon should take place within the next 28 days, possibly after a decision today, will he take up the point which I raised twice yesterday? Within that period of 28 days, there will be several thousand 16 and 17-year-old school leavers in Wales. One hundred and forty-four school leavers will chase one vacancy at a careers office in Wales. In Brecon there are only 10 vacancies for the hundreds of school leavers there. Brecon is one of only four careers offices in Wales which has 10 or more vacancies. Only the offices in Cardiff and Shotton have 11 vacancies or more. In Wales, 38 of the 42 careers offices have fewer than 10 vacancies. Indeed, eight of them have not a single job for young people, and seven have only one job each. Will my hon. Friend develop the question of the need for a speedy by-election so that the Labour candidate can give hope to those thousands of young school leavers, and attack the Government for their mass unemployment policies?

Mr. Skinner: Although I am sure that others will do so, I intend to see to it that our friend in Brecon and Radnor will receive a copy of the report of today's debate while he advances the cause of our party in the election campaign. He will then be able to read all the comments made, including those of my hon. Friend the Member for Coventry, South-East (Mr. Nellist) in his description of what I have loosely termed on other occasions Yosserland. Young people in Brecon and Radnor and elsewhere cannot get a job when they leave school, even with all their O-levels, A-levels and other certificates. Unemployment will become a big factor in the campaign.

286

Mr. Doug Hoyle (Warrington, North): My hon. Friend referred earlier to Caerwyn Roderick. Will he bear in mind our friend's robust knowledge of the education needs of the Welsh people? Does he believe that, together with the problem of youth unemployment, education will figure largely in the by-election campaign? Does he agree that that needs to be brought to the fore?

Mr. Skinner: The Government's education policy will be a prominent issue in the campaign; no one can deny that. I have some figures for Brecon and Radnor, and they are more pertinent than the general arguments.

I was about to say that another reason why we can have a fairly early by-election is that the parties have already lined up their candidates. I believe that the Welsh nationalists are dealing with the selection of their candidate this weekend. The hon. Member for Caernarfon (Mr. Wigley), if he catches your eye later, Mr. Speaker, will probably tell us what the position is. I am told that the Social Democratic and Liberal parties are ready for the by-election.

Mr. John Home Robertson (East Lothian): Which one is standing?

Mr. Skinner: I am not sure, as I have not gone into that matter. However, I have told the people of Brecon and Radnor to ask the alliance candidate which party and leader he supports, and to ask him whether he is in favour of getting rid of cruise or keeping cruise, as the Liberals and Social Democratics think respectively. That will be an important factor in the campaign.

Mr. Donald Coleman (Neath): The people of Brecon and Radnor would give a simple answer to that if they remembered that at one time their Member of Paliament was Mr. Tudor Watkins. His advice would undoubtedly have been "No" to cruise.

Mr. Skinner: My hon. Friend, who represents a Welsh constituency, is better versed in these matters than I am. He keeps a close eye on all things Welsh—even the choirs. He also knows a bit about them. Perhaps my hon. Friend will be able to catch your eye, Mr. Speaker, and present the special Welsh considerations. I do not intend to use all the pages of my speech because the matter would be better debated. In view of the unusual number of hon. Members present this Friday, they should take part and make some additional points.

I know that the alliance has its candidate ready and, therefore, that is all right in terms of the general electoral considerations. I believe that it has transported people to Radnor on a semi-joint selection basis. I do not think that they voted on a one person, one vote system. The SDP sent representatives from the regions, but the Liberals adopted a different tactic. It was called joint selection, but those of us in the know understand how it works. I believe that the alliance bussed those people in with British School of Motoring money.

Mr. Jack Straw (Blackburn): Before my hon. Friend leaves that important point, can he say from his expert knowledge of the internal workings of the SDP and Liberal parties in Wales whether their candidate has the support of the leader of the SDP in Wales or of the leader of the SDP in the United Kingdom? As my hon. Friend knows, the leader of the SDP in Wales, Mr. Gwynoro Jones, has no confidence in the leader of the SDP in the United Kingdom as a whole. Indeed, he is on record as thoroughly

criticising the leader of the SDP in the United Kingdom. Does he agree that that is a crucial matter, of which the people of Brecon should become aware?

Mr. Skinner: That will blow up during the campaign. When the writ is issued, many people will jump on that bandwagon. There is a great deal of comment in the local press about Gwynoro Jones. I managed to get hold of some of it many weeks ago. He became a Member of the House at the same time as me—I mention that en passant. I remember him well. The problem, to put it crudely and simply, is that Gwynoro Jones was the satellite of the right hon. Member for Glasgow, Hillhead (Mr. Jenkins). When the right hon. Gentleman lost the job as leader, it created friction, and Gwynoro Jones cannot settle down with the new leader of the SDP. Sparks will undoubtedly fly, and I look forward to them because it will help our candidate.

Mr. Thomas Torney (Bradford, South): My hon. Friend has made several references to "Erskine May". Will he read the paragraphs of "Erskine May" which are relevant to the writ, and explain what they mean?

Mr. Skinner: I understand that a Conservative Member may deal with that matter.

Mr. A. J. Beith (Berwick-upon-Tweed): Allies!

Mr. Skinner: The hon. Gentleman says that we are allies, but there is plenty of evidence that I began the campaign for the writ many days ago purely in an attempt to accommodate the candidates down in Brecon and Radnor. If the hon. Gentleman listens carefully, he will find that that issue is dealt with. I know that he is upset because he is on the other side.

Mr. Campbell-Savours: In what?

Mr. Skinner: In nearly every respect. I have said from the outset that we are not involved in a game. This is a serious matter. We are debating this issue to give hon. Members an opportunity to discuss important topics on a Friday, when most hon. Members are around.

I have just seen where the Tory candidate was nominated.

Mr. David Alton (Liverpool, Mossley Hill): There are two of them.

Mr. Skinner: One of the Liberals behind me who keeps rabbiting on says that there are two Tory candidates. If there are, all well and good. No doubt the hon. Gentleman will justify that comment in the campaign. He will be able to say so in his *Focus* leaflet which floats under doors day after day—their content will probably change day after day. By and large, the candidates of the main parties are ready for action. Our candidate has his troops massed on the Black mountains and on the Brecon Beacons.

There is another point which I referred to earlier but which I should like to re-emphasise in case some of my hon. Friends are a little worried about my moving the writ. There is a motion on the Order Paper which refers to using Friday as suggested by the hon. Member for Kemptown and which says that it is an abuse to do such a thing. There are differences between some of us who take an alternative view about that matter. I have not signed that——

Mr. Speaker: Order. That comes when the hon. Gentleman has finished his submission. I welcome this new-found establishment figure. The hon. Gentleman is

287

[*Mr. Speaker*]

otherwise absolutely in order and I pay tribute to him for that. If other hon. Members who may be called to speak follow his example and watch me nodding or shaking my head, I shall not need to interrupt too often.

Mr. Skinner: I shall shortly finish to enable Liberals, Tories, Welsh Nationalists and some of my colleagues from Wales to speak. It is a good idea to keep the Government up all weekend, but I am not too keen on the idea of keeping Back Benchers up and not causing the Government any trouble.

Mr. Speaker *rose*——

Mr. Skinner: Yes, I am moving on now.

Mr. Speaker: Order. That has nothing to do with the motion.

Mr. Skinner: I have discussed the matter with my hon. Friend the Member for Bow and Poplar (Mr. Mikardo). We were talking about Friday. It has been a topic of conversation in the Tea Room and elsewhere. I asked him the other day, "What are the odds, Mik?" He said, "We have not got a book on it—the odds are so long that we shall be there all weekend." I said, "Well, I shall slip anchor on Friday." To which he replied, "That's running on Wednesday." Do not get me wrong, Mr. Speaker. I am not trying to score a victory by seven or eight lengths— a short head will do—but we need to have a little in reserve.

It will be a lively by-election. It will be about the fact that monetarism has failed—the Prime Minister's brand of monetarism, that is. There is a place for monetarism somewhere, but it is hardly likely to be developed in a highly technological country such as ours. I believe in my simple fashion that standing on one's own two feet went out with Robinson Crusoe—he had to get Man Friday to bail him out. The Government's philosophy and their record in the past six months will become a great feature of the campaign, as will their record on unemployment and the massive cost of it.

Mr. Roland Boyes (Houghton and Washington): I think that my hon. Friend will appreciate what I have to say. When talking of the Government's record, he will recall his activities during the coal miners' strike. I do not want to raise that matter, but my hon. Friend may not be aware that one of the leaders of the Durham Miners Association, Jimmy Inskip, died last night. In view of my hon. Friend's interest in the mining industry, perhaps he would like to pay a short tribute to the leadership of the Durham miners, including Jimmy Inskip, who I do not doubt would have been joining my hon. Friend in the by-election had he still been alive.

Mr. Skinner: I shall not make too much of that. My hon. Friend has got his name recorded and I suppose that that will suffice. Many miners will participate in the campaign, as they did in the county council election campaign. Many more than we expected participated and some of the results in the coalfields were exceptionally good. That includes parts of south Wales, of which Brecon and Radnor is a part.

I was discussing the main issues in the campaign and, as hurriedly as possible, mentioning the dole queues, education, state earnings-related pensions, the threatened abolition of wages councils and the Common Market, which is always a good runner in by-elections. We shall give our candidate some advice on that.

Mr. Laurie Pavitt (Brent, South): Another issue will be how the nurses are being short-changed on the phasing of their pay award as announced yesterday.

Mr. Skinner: My hon. Friend will be pleased to know that I have, in my notes, details about hospital closures in Powys. I am skipping across such information on hospitals and education, for example, so that others can go into more detail. My hon. Friend the Member for Brent, South (Mr. Pavitt) is a long-standing hon. Member who I believe will be going at the end of this Parliament. I hope that he catches your eye, Mr. Speaker, as he can speak on behalf of the disabled and others as he has done so well during his many years in the House. I am sure that he could shed some light on the problems of nurses and others. The election campaign will be about the Health Service, pensions and the closure of railways.

Dr. Norman A. Godman (Greenock and Port Glasgow): My hon. Friend has mentioned several substantial issues that will be debated in the election campaign. Does he believe that political devolution will also feature largely in the campaign?

Mr. Skinner: It has not done so for some years in Wales or Scotland. I shall not get involved in a matter which may not be significant in the campaign. I am sticking to the general issues. All the issues that I have mentioned will be debated at length. At the end of all that, we shall have a new Member of Parliament to represent that constituency.

Mr. Andrew F. Bennett: Will my hon. Friend give way?

Mr. Skinner: My hon. Friend may be about to ask some awkward questions, so perhaps I would do better to suggest that, as he knows so much about procedural matters and once nearly moved a writ himself, he may wish to catch your eye, Mr. Speaker, during this very lengthy debate.

The House of Commons is an unusual place. There are many heartaches and few blessings, but one thing is certain. This place, like life generally, is full of surprises. One comes here one morning and the unexpected happens. In a way, that is reinvigorating. Just as one is beginning to lose faith a little, something new happens. This Friday has been one of those unusual days. It was started by the right hon. Member for South Down, who put the cat among the pigeons. I know that the motion is in the name of the hon. Member for Kemptown, but I think that the right hon. Member for South Down will agree with me that there are days when we win and days when we lose and I have a sneaking feeling that this day will belong to those of us who are arguing for this writ and for an early by-election. That is the important point.

I am prepared to be flexible in these matters——

Mr. Beith *rose*——

Mr. Skinner: All right; I know that the hon. Gentleman has been trying.

Mr. Beith: Has not the hon. Gentleman ascertained whether his own Chief Whip and the Government Chief Whip have arranged to introduce a motion to prevent the

House from reaching a decision about the writ and thus to prevent the early by-election that we should welcome as much as the hon. Gentleman claims?

Mr. Skinner: When the current leader of the Liberal party in the House today starts talking like that, I worry about his position vis-a-vis you, Mr. Speaker, because I do not want any unnecessary trouble and what the hon. Gentleman has just suggested borders nigh on heresy. He has suggested that plans have been made when we know that everything today has been spontaneous. I must admit that I had a little help from the Clerks in the Table Office. I shall not name them because they did a good job and I do not want to hamper their promotion.

I look forward to the continuation of this debate, Mr. Speaker. Having spent a few moments making the argument, I bring you this little blue form and rest my case.

10.13 am

Mr. Gwilym Jones (Cardiff, North): I oppose the suggestions made by the hon. Member for Bolsover (Mr. Skinner) and perhaps two personal reasons qualify me to do so. I might easily have entered the House as a result of a by-election, because immediately before the last general election I was the Conservative candidate for Cardiff, North-West and a writ for a by-election would have been announced but for the calling of the general election. Therefore, I well understand what is involved in the organisation of a by-election and all the considerations that go with it.

I am somewhat appalled, however, that the hon. Member for Bolsover should proceed in this way today. It seems to have slipped his memory and that of certain other right hon. and hon. Members that our late colleague, Tom Hooson, who was an excellent Member of Parliament and a first-rate representative of the constituency of Brecon and Radnor, died only on 8 May. It was a sad, cruel and untimely death for a man who almost until the end worked extremely hard and assiduously on behalf of his constituents. That was just four short weeks ago. I suggest that in seeking this morning to move the writ for a by-election the hon. Member for Bolsover is proceeding with somewhat indecent haste.

I assure the hon. Member for Bolsover and the whole House that there is no reluctance on the part of the Conservative party to fight this by-election. As the hon. Gentleman has said, our candidate is already in place. Chris Butler is an excellent candidate and may be the only Welsh-speaking candidate to fight the by-election. He is also a constituent of mine, and I cannot speak too highly of him.

Mr. Andrew F. Bennett: Does the hon. Gentleman accept that it would be completely unacceptable if the electors in that constituency could not elect a Member of Parliament before September, as they would be left unrepresented for a long period? It is important that the election should take place before people start going away on holiday, as the new proposals for holiday voting are not yet in operation. Does the hon. Member accept that the sooner the election takes place the better will be the opportunities for most people in the constituency to participate?

Mr. Jones: I do not disagree entirely with the hon. Gentleman's suggestion. He intervened earlier to point out

the difficulties that would arise if the motion moved by the hon. Member for Bolsover were defeated. We do not want that to happen. As I have said, there is no reluctance on the part of the Conservative party to proceed to a by-election. I agree that it should take place relatively early, but I do not believe that today is the right time to pursue this. The hon. Member for Bolsover pointed out that the Welsh nationalists do not have a candidate in place yet. I have no brief to speak for Plaid Cymru, so I had better give way to its former leader.

Mr. Dafydd Wigley (Caernarfon): Our candidate will be in place by tomorrow night, so that is no reason for holding back the election. More important, if the writ is moved today the by-election could take place on, say, 4 July, before the main holiday period begins. That is important not just from the point of view of people in Brecon and Radnor going away on holiday, but because of the impact of the tourist industry on the constituency, which would be a major problem if the by-election were held towards the end of July. In practice, that would mean holding the by-election over until the autumn and leaving the constituency without representation for the intervening period.

Mr. Jones: I know the significance of the remarks of the hon. Member for Caernarfon (Mr. Wigley), for we were both in the Brecon and Radnor constituency recently when the Select Committee on Welsh Affairs was investigating tourism in Mid-Wales. That visit took place just before the sad death of Tom Hooson. I agree that an early by-election is needed, but this is not the right moment to pursue it. I assure the Opposition that the Conservative party has an excellent organisation locally as well as an excellent candidate who is looking forward to contesting the seat at an early date. If the writ is moved today, Plaid Cymru will inevitably be at a disadvantage if its candidate is not adopted until tomorrow, because the announcement will not filter out until next week. I know that Plaid Cymru has a very small party organisation and has to save up for the deposit, which it will certainly lose yet again.

I suspect the motives of the hon. Member for Bolsover. He has rightly referred to all the important issues which will be fully debated and explored during the by-election campaign. Attention will be focused upon who comes third in the by-election. Will the Labour party be able to keep the alliance in third place or will Labour go down to that place? Is the hon. Member for Bolsover seeking to take a mean advantage by jumping the gun on Plaid Cymru, which is at present in fourth place, and trying to make sure that Plaid Cymru stays below the Labour party?

Mr. Adley: A moment ago the hon. Member for Caernarfon (Mr. Wigley) mentioned tourism and holidaymakers. Does my hon. Friend the Member for Cardiff, North (Mr. Jones) believe that an issue at the forthcoming by-election should be the legislation passed by the House during this Session, which implements a pledge made by our party at the last general election to give votes to holidaymakers? Does that not demonstrate the serious intention of the Conservative party to increase the franchise and enable people to vote at elections?

Mr. Jones: My hon. Friend is quite right. That important reform of our electoral system is widely welcomed throughout the country, particularly in the

289

Enoch Powell makes uncompromising stand of principle on embryo research

Ann Widdecombe was born in 1947 and spent her childhood moving around with her family as her father, who was head of naval supplies in the Admiralty, was posted variously to Portsmouth, Singapore, Bath and Whitehall.

She attended La Sainte Union convent boarding school in Bath before winning a place at the University of Birmingham, where she read Latin for which she was awarded the first of her two degrees. Her second, in philosophy, politics and economics, was from Lady Margaret Hall, Oxford. While there, she was secretary and treasurer of the Oxford Union, which she described as a "political nursery with everyone toddling about in political nappies posturing as if already Prime Ministers."

She began her working life with Unilever and then took up a post as senior administrator with London University in which she remained until entering Parliament in 1987 as the Member for Maidstone. It was at her third attempt. She had fought Burnley in 1979 and Plymouth, Devonport in 1983.

The first step on her path to a ministerial career was taken three years after entering Parliament when Tristan Garel Jones, Minister of State at the Foreign and Commonwealth Office, appointed her his Parliamentary Private Secretary. Within weeks, John Major made her Under-Secretary for Social Security. In 1993 she moved to the Department of Employment as Under-Secretary before being promoted to Minister of State a year later. She was given her next job in 1995 at the Home Office as prisons Minister. Prime Minister Major never gave her a Cabinet post, which she humorously ascribed to having told him that she could not stand cricket

In the wake of the disastrous 1997 general election the Conservatives began the process of finding a new leader. Her former boss, Michael Howard, was one of the candidates, but during the campaign she famously said there was "something of the night" about him. He was knocked out at the first ballot,

William Hague went on to win, and, although he did not initially include her in his Front-Bench team, within a year he brought her back as shadow Secretary of State for Health. She took that year's Conservative party conference by storm, striding around the platform and speaking, without notes, for 40 minutes. A year later she was made shadow Home Secretary,

A second disastrous showing at the polls in 2001 left the Conservatives again seeking a new leader. Although popular with Conservatives in the country, at Westminster she was unable to summon sufficient support for a leadership bid and she returned to the Back Benches to pursue a successful career as a writer and broadcaster.

She has published four novels, two of which were best sellers, and has made a variety of television programmes, including acting as an agony aunt, a role she also briefly carried out for *The Guardian*. She currently has a weekly column with the *Daily Express* and a popular website, the Widdy Web.

Ann Widdecombe is a committed Christian who has campaigned and spoken extensively on moral issues. Soon after entering Parliament, she introduced the Abortion (Amendment) Bill, which was designed to give rights to unborn children. She was one of the few Conservatives to campaign for the abolition of fox hunting.

After representing the Maidstone constituency, renamed Maidstone and the Weald in 1997, for over 20 years, she announced her intention in 2007 not to stand at the next general election. At the time she was in the process of writing her fifth novel.

Defence of the human embryo meticulously delivered with eloquence and erudition

BY RT HON ANN WIDDECOMBE MP

In 1978 the first birth of a child produced by *in vitro* fertilisation took place, sparking a major ethical debate. Gradually it was realised that embryos could be grown in test tubes not just to be placed in a womb but to be used for research and then destroyed.

It was to be another 12 years before the Government were to introduce comprehensive law on the subject, but meanwhile the controversy raged and in 1982 an inquiry was established under Dame Mary Warnock. This reported in 1984 and in February 1985 Enoch Powell initiated a Private Member's Bill to outlaw the use of embryos created by *in vitro* fertilisation for any purpose other than to enable a woman to bear a child.

The speech was remarkable in several ways. It was probably the last to be founded on adherence to a single principle which allowed neither exception nor mitigation. Later attempts to reform the abortion laws, for example, sought to restrict but not to outlaw the practice. The debates around section 28 or civil partnerships or the age of consent have focussed on the need to protect children or to keep marriage unique, but have carefully avoided any discussion of morality.

"There is a difference," said Powell when he introduced his Second Reading debate, "between adopting a procedure hitherto not tested with a view to a greater prospect of success in enabling a woman to bear a child and on the other hand using a human embryo, normally to destruction, in order to increase the sum of knowledge."

Indeed the very title of his Bill was uncompromising: not the Human Fertilisation and Embryology Bill but the Unborn Children Protection Bill. In the course of the speech he argued that the House should accept that, by prohibiting the use of embryos for experiment, some scientific knowledge would be sacrificed but that could not outweigh the "moral, human and social costs" of obtaining information in such a way.

If the speech was remarkable in its principle it was even more so in its prose and Ciceronian construction, its sentences precisely drawn, its grammar meticulous, its vocabulary that of an age when language was still important. At one point Powell even quotes the Talmud in Hebrew, not a feat of learning often associated with modern political debate.

As man stood on the threshold of a biological revolution the age old struggles of science versus ethics and public versus private morality were being rehearsed in the House of Commons.

The arguments that surrounded the Powell Bill were to be heard many more times but probably never again would they be introduced with such eloquence and erudition. This speech marks the passing of such mode of debate.

487

Orders of the Day

Unborn Children (Protection) Bill

Order for Second Reading read.

Mr. Speaker: Before I call the right hon. Member for South Down (Mr. Powell) to move the Second Reading of his Bill, I must tell the House that more than 40 right hon. and hon. Gentlemen have have indicated their wish to take part in this debate.

I propose to apply the 10-minute limit on speeches between 11.30 and 1 o'clock, but I hope that those right hon. and hon. Members who are called both before and after that time will bear that limit broadly in mind.

9.48 am

Mr. J. Enoch Powell (South Down): I beg to move, That the Bill be now read a Second time.

The Bill has a single and simple purpose. It is to render it unlawful for a human embryo created by in vitro fertilisation to be used as the subject of experiment or, indeed, in any other way or for any other purpose except to enable a woman to bear a child.

Almost as important as what the Bill seeks is what the Bill does not seek to do. At this early stage in my speech I want to bring that firmly to the attention of the House. The Bill does not concern itself in any way with questions such as those of surrogacy, abortion, or the source of the gametes of a fertilised ovum. All that side of this great question lies outside the scope of the Bill, from which it is my opinion wholly capable of being separated.

The second thing which the Bill does not do is to interfere in any way with the procedures which are in use at present for enabling women who would not otherwise be able to do so to bear children. The Bill is deliberately and carefully drawn so as in no way to interfere with those procedures.

At this point I invite the attention of the House to the successive provisions of the Bill. It had been my original intention, as is the ambition of most hon. Members who are lucky in the ballot for private Member's Bills, to be able to frame a single-clause Bill which would outlaw the mischief at which the Bill is aimed. But both advice and reflection convinced me that that would be neither effective nor right. It is not possible for this House to proscribe as unlawful a particular action but to provide no means whereby its will can be carried out and the execution of its intentions subjected to surveillance and policing. It was necessary to set up under the Bill a mechanism which would ensure that the purpose of the House and its objective, if it accepts the Bill, is carried out.

That is not a difficulty which is unique to this Bill. Those who sought to frame legislation to carry out the recommendations of the Warnock report, to permit experimentation under licence upon a human embryo, would find themselves equally obliged to establish a system of notification in order that the licensing might be effective. In order to permit, it would also be necessary to prohibit. It is not a vice of this Bill that it is obliged for its purposes to create the machinery which is set out in the Bill. The Bill proceeds, then, by prohibiting the procurement of a fertilisation or the possession of a human embryo except under specific authority. The remainder of the Bill is concerned with the definition and the operation of that authority.

The authority is the authority given by the Secretary of State, subject to the conditions that are set out in the Bill.

Mr. Robert Jackson (Wantage): May I ask the right hon. Gentleman whether it is his intention, because it is not made clear in the Bill, that the provider of the ovum and the person who receives the embryo should be the same person? Does the right hon. Gentleman accept that if that were to be the case it would severely limit the range of infertility problems that could be treated?

Mr. Powell: I am much obliged to the hon. Member for Wantage (Mr. Jackson). I had hoped I made it clear in my introductory remarks that there was no question of the origins of the gametes from which the fertilised ovum proceeds being in any way controlled or regulated by the provisions of the Bill, nor is there any power in the Bill to do so.

The over-arching requirement of the authority is that it be given solely for the purpose of enabling a named woman to bear a child. The reason why the woman has to be specified is that if the authority were to be for the general purpose of promoting childbirth or fertility, it would not be possible for the intention of the House, if it accepts the Bill, to be seen to be carried out: the process has to be authorised as specifically for the benefit of a certain woman in order to enable her to bear a child. That is a condition which the Secretary of State has no power to limit or to modify. The law would lay that down as an overriding condition.

The Secretary of State's authority would automatically be given upon the application of two medical practitioners. This is essentially a trigger mechanism. It does not entrust to the Secretary of State, or impose upon him, any discretion to pick and choose between one such request and another. It is an automatic compliance with an application duly made.

However, the Secretary of State does have certain duties in respect of the authority which he gives, namely, to specify the persons by whom the operation is to be carried out and also the place or places where it is to be carried out and the persons who may have possession of the embryos produced by fertilisation. Those requirements are necessary for it to be possible to establish that the provisions and intentions of the Bill are being carried out.

Perhaps I should say at this stage that I accept that, if the will of the House and of Parliament is clearly made known in terms of legislation, I do not impute it to the medical profession that it would be looking for ways to evade the will of Parliament. The procedure laid down in the Bill is necessary so that it may be seen that the will of Parliament, if the Bill is enacted, is being carried out.

As to the duration of the authority, that is deliberately so chosen as not to intefere with the procedures at present being carried out to enable women who would not otherwise be able to do so to have children. But should the periods that are set out in the Bill not be satisfactory in a particular case — should, for example, a series of mischances make it impossible for the insertion to take place within the four or the extended six months—no limitation whatsoever, no inhibition, is placed on a renewed application *de novo* for a new authority.

The Bill proceeds to make provision for the details of the application for authority and of the granting of

[Mr. Powell]

authority—details that will need, in the terms of the Bill, to come before the House before effect is given to them. They are clearly necessary so as to ensure that the Secretary of State has the power to obtain the necessary particulars in order that his authority may be duly and appropriately given.

Subsection (5) is a penalty clause. Again I must confide to the House that my original intention was different from that which appears in the Bill. I had originally thought that a merely nominal penalty would be appropriate to what I have already said about my view of the attitude of the medical profession. But again, upon reflection and advice, I was convinced it would be inappropriate for this House to identify a matter of such great gravity that it should be prohibited by law without the infraction of that legislation attracting a penalty appropriate to such a serious offence. However, I say again that I do not regard the penalties as the real nature of the deterrent or of the authority which I am asking the House to give. It is in the opinion of the country, as I hope this House and Parliament will express it, that the real sanction and the real authority reside.

Of finance, hon. Members will understand that I had no alternative, unless I was to seek a money resolution from the Government, to make the Bill as it stands self-financing. I do not like this. If the House gives a Second Reading to the Bill, I shall ask the Government, in view of the decision of the House, to provide a money resolution so that the actions of the Secretary of State in implementing the Bill can be carried out under the same financial conditions as the other duties laid upon him by law.

Such, then, are the provisions of the Bill. Hon. Members will have seen that it has been drawn with a jealous care to ensure that it inhibits or prevents no one from obtaining the blessing of a child by means of in vitro fertilisation through any process which is at present in action. Indeed, it would be true to say that the Bill in no way inhibits the future improvement of those processess by those who are engaged in carrying them out.

If within his clinical responsibility the practitioner in charge decides, with a view to increasing the chance of success in enabling a woman to bear a child, to use a process which has not hitherto been used, in good faith and with the intention that it should increase the chance of the embryo surviving and of a child being born, there is nothing in the Bill which will prohibit it.

Mr. Dafydd Wigley (Caernarfon): I am grateful to the right hon. Gentleman for giving way. I declare an interest in the matter. Does the right hon. Gentleman accept that the Bill will prevent medical research into in vitro embryos of up to 14 days, research which is central to the overcoming of many genetic disorders which are transmitted down the female line, and in so doing will end the hopes and aspirations of countless thousands of families of disabled children and prevent doctors from undertaking research which can be accomplished successfully within the next few years?

Mr. Powell: I hope that it will be the hon. Gentleman's good fortune to catch the eye of the Chair later in the debate, but I trust he will credit me with not having intended to conclude my speech without referring to so substantial a matter as that which he has mentioned.

I was making it clear that no new methods, no alterations in procedure, which are adopted in order that the process of insertion may have a better chance of succeeding for the purpose of enabling a woman to bear a child are excluded in any way by the Bill.

Mr. Patrick Nicholls (Teignbridge) *rose*——

Mr. Powell: I am anxious not to take too much of the time of the House. May I ask for the patience of the hon. Gentleman, because I may clear his point? If I appear not to be doing so, I shall gladly give way to him at a later stage.

There is an essential and visible difference between what I have just described and the process of experiment. There is a difference between adopting a procedure hitherto not tested with a view to a greater prospect of success in enabling a woman to bear a child and on the other hand using a human embryo, normally to destruction, in order to increase the sum of knowledge. There need be no quibble or doubt about the boundary line between progress in the fertilisation procedures and what is meant by experimentation which the Bill intends to eliminate.

The question may now be asked — it has been anticipated in a sense by the hon. Member for Caernarfon (Mr. Wigley)—why should a Bill be brought forward to forbid the use of a human embryo thus produced from becoming the subject of experiment? If I may, I should like to begin to answer that question in personal terms.

When I first read the Warnock report I had a sense of revulsion and repugnance, deep and instinctive, towards the proposition that a thing, however it may be defined, of which the sole purpose or object is that it may be a human life, should be subjected to experiment to its destruction for the purpose of the acquisition of knowledge.

I formed that view and it was strengthened by my indignation at the suggestion that the House might be asked to surrender its judgment and powers in such a matter to the judgment of a body of persons, however eminent or distinguished, however expert or inexpert, who would, from case to case, decide whether a process inherently repugnant should be performed.

I soon discovered, having formed that opinion for myself, that it was widely shared. It came to my knowledge that it was shared inside as well as outside the medical profession, that it was shared among all classes and callings and throughout the people of this country. That early impression has been abundantly confirmed by the expressions of public opinion since it became known that there was a possibility of this legislation.

I do not appeal to some abstract principle from which such deductions can be drawn. I do not appeal to a definition of the embryo which would seek to settle the probably impossible question of the stage at which a human being becomes a human being. That question is unanswerable, because it goes to the heart of the great unanswerable question: what is man?

Many of those who wish the Bill well, many of the millions out of doors who we know want to see the Bill reach the statute book, believe that it is authorised by and in accordance with their religious beliefs. I have no complaint or criticism of that. On the other hand, I have a great envy of people who have that faith and certitude. Yet I must tell the House that I would make the plea that

I am making this morning exactly as I am doing if I were addressing an assembly of atheists in an atheist country. *[Interruption.]*

Mr. Deputy Speaker (Sir Paul Dean): Perhaps the right hon. Member will continue. This is an important debate and we do not want it to be interrupted if we can avoid it.

Mr. Powell: The repugnance with which those of many religious persuasions or none view the actions that the Bill would forbid is of a more fundamental character. It is an instinct implanted in a human society. This is the recognition by a human society of its obligation to itself, to future generations and to human nature.

It is argued — and this is the principal case as the hon. Member for Caenarfon said against the Bill — that to permit the use of the fertilised embryo for research would open the way to new and useful medical knowledge. I do not stand here as a layman to dispute that. True, I must admit I have a suspicion that the inquiring human spirit will, if denied one avenue of arriving at truth and information, speedily find other ways of doing so. I have also been impressed to see a profound difference of opinion on this very point among people apparently equally qualified in the medical profession and in the sciences.

Nevertheless, I do not ask the House to reject that proposition. On the contrary, I ask the House to face it. I ask the House, in coming to its decision, to make the assumption that by means of what the Bill will prohibit, useful and beneficial knowledge could in future be obtained. I ask the House to exercise a choice—it is indeed making a choice — and to decide that nevertheless the moral, human and social cost of that information being obtained in a way that outrages the instincts of so many is too great a price to pay.

There is at issue that sense in all of us which we inadequately describe as a sense of what is owed to the dignity of man. In that remarkable compilation of thought and wisdom known as the Talmud, I found a principle enunciated and argued that seemed to crystallise the very essence of that which this Bill asks—"Gadol kavod ha-beriot". Those three Hebrew words mean, "In case of doubt or difficulty, of conflict of authority or interest, let the dignity of man always prevail". I hope that the decision of the House on this Bill will accord with that principle. I believe that it is a principle which the country preponderently wishes to see affirmed by its representatives in Parliament. I ask them to uphold and assert the dignity of man by giving the Bill a Second Reading.

10.11 am

Ms. Jo Richardson (Barking): In some senses the right hon. Member for South Down (Mr. Powell) has put his finger on the essence of the debate in assuming that it concerns only the dignity of man. However, it also concerns the dignity of women, and that should not be forgotten. I am not being frivolous. At the beginning of the debate, Mr. Speaker announced that more than 40 hon. Gentlemen wished to speak, and in so doing ignored the fact that there were several women in the House who also wanted to contribute to the debate.

Mr. Ian Mikardo (Bow and Poplar): It may help my hon. Friend's case if I inform her that the word "beriot",

used by the right hon. Member for South Down (Mr. Powell), does not mean men but creatures, and thus includes women.

Ms. Richardson: I am not sure whether that intervention helps my case, but it shows that there is some difference of interpretation of the Hebrew words as between my hon. Friend the Member for Bow and Poplar (Mr. Mikardo) and the right hon. Member for South Down.

Today, the House could take a most serious step, and that is why it is so full. The private Member's debates that we hold on a Friday are quite different from the debates held on other weekdays. Unfortunately, we usually know the outcome of debates held on other weekdays, because they are predetermined, but on Fridays we all have an opportunity to make our individual view known, and the outcome is not certain. Nevertheless, we could take a very serious and retrograde step today, which would enshrine in law what the magazine *Nature*—not exactly a Leftist feminist magazine — described in its editorial of 7 February as
"home-made and half-baked legislation."

The right hon. Member for South Down, with his knowledge of the House, his command of drafting and his meticulously prepared speeches, is listened to with the greatest of respect, although we do not always agree with everything that he says. I am sure that he would be offended by that description in *Nature*, but it represents the views of many practitioners and laboratory researchers who have been working for years to help infertile women and to try to eliminate the miscarriages that cause so much physical and emotional suffering, and who have tried to make some progress towards the prevention of congenital malformations in future generations. They have also been working to help male infertility. Indeed, male infertility accounts for about half of the problems of infertility.

Although the right hon. Member for South Down and his supporters claim that the Bill will not interfere with research into infertility, that is not the opinion of distinguished men and women who are qualified in a way that we are not. Having read the Bill, they believe that it will have the effect of outlawing such research. Even if the right hon. Gentleman is right, and the Bill does not close the door on infertile couples, and the doctors are wrong, the Bill will impose the most serious and alarming procedures on the practice of in vitro fertilisation, under which the infertile woman will have to be named in advance by physicians and will have to await the Secretary of State's express permission.

That procedure, which is incredibly bureaucratic, represents a serious threat to the civil liberties of the women concerned. Hon. Members should note that yet again women are not to be allowed to decide for themselves, in conjunction with their doctors, but will have to await the Secretary of State's express consent.

Mrs. Elaine Kellett-Bowman (Lancaster): Will the hon. Lady give way?

Ms. Richardson: I shall give way in a moment.

The right hon. Member for South Down said that such consent would be absolutely automatic. I accept his word for that, and that was no doubt his intention, but that is not what the Bill says.

Mr. Leo Abse (Torfaen): Although the Bill states certain rules specifically, it does not withdraw discretion

333

Robin Cook resigns with a devastating analysis of the consequences of the Iraq invasion

Shirley Williams came from a social democrat family background, was a Labour Cabinet Minister and served for 10 years on Labour's National Executive Committee. But disillusionment at the growing influence of the left and at the party's 1980 decision to withdraw from the EEC, she resigned from the Labour party. As one of the so-called 'Gang of Four', she was instrumental in creating the Social Democratic Party.

She was the first member of the SDP to be elected to Parliament when, at a by-election in 1981, she shook the political establishment by taking the previously safe Tory constituency of Crosby. She overturned a Conservative majority of almost 20,000 to give the SDP victory by over 5,000 votes.

It was to be a high point. Less than two years later in the 1983 general election, with the constituency's boundaries redrawn, she lost the seat and was out of Parliament for 10 years, never again to return to the Commons. In 1993 she was made a life peer. She retained her position as President of the SDP, to which she had been elected in 1982. During her absence from Westminster the SDP, with her support, had merged with the Liberal party to form the Liberal Democrats and in 2001 she was elected leader of that party in the House of Lords.

She graduated from Somerville college, Oxford, where she was an Open Scholar in History and the first woman chairman of the university's Labour club, in 1951. After a year at Colombia University, New York as a Fulbright Fellow she began work as a journalist for the *Daily Mirror* and then the *Financial Times*. In 1960 she became the general secretary of the Fabian Society.

She first stood for Parliament as the unsuccessful Labour candidate at the by-election at Harwich in 1954 and again in the 1955 general election. In 1959 she was the Labour choice at Southampton, Test. She was finally to enter Parliament when she took the Hitchin seat in 1964. She was to hold it and the seat of Hertford and Stevenage for 15 years.

Barely had she crossed the threshold of the Commons when she took her first step towards a ministerial career. Health Minister Kenneth Robinson appointed her his Parliamentary Private Secretary. Within two years, she was appointed Parliamentary Secretary at the Ministry of Labour. A year later came promotion to Minister of State for Education and Science, followed two years later with the job of Minister of State for the Home Office.

In Opposition after Labour's 1970 general election defeat, she held a series of Front-Bench posts including Shadow Home Secretary. When Harold Wilson took Labour back into power in 1974, he appointed her the Secretary of State for Prices and Consumer Protection, a job she held for two years until she took on the joint roles of Secretary of State for Education and Science and Paymaster General. When Labour lost the 1979 general election, she was one of the casualties and her seat fell to the Conservatives.

After completing three terms as President of the SDP, she pursued an academic career, lecturing at Princeton, Cambridge and Berkley, and was Professor of Elective Politics at Harvard. She also did work at the Political Studies Association where she addressed questions of employment policy, a subject on which she produced a series of publications. She was appointed Acting Director of the Institute of Politics at Harvard in 1988, and then Public Service Professor of Elective Politics.

Among her books are "Politics is for People" (1981); "A Job to Live: The Impact of Tomorrow's Technology on Work and Society" (1987); "God and Caesar" (1993).

Extraordinary prophecy of brilliant debater who made an individual stand

BY RT HON BARONESS WILLIAMS OF CROSBY

The resignation of a senior politician still in office is a significant event, and can change the course of politics. The voluntary departure in November 1990 of Geoffrey Howe, who had been both Foreign Secretary and Chancellor of the Exchequer, was such an event. So was the resignation in March 2003 of Robin Cook, Leader of the House of Commons and himself also a former Foreign Secretary.

Both men made brilliant resignation speeches to a packed and intense House of Commons.

That of Geoffrey Howe was beautifully crafted. It was courteous and understated, and it was delivered more in sorrow than in anger. But through the courtesies and regrets he wove a lethal strand, one that was to lead to the collapse of the Thatcher Government.

Robin Cook's position was different. Unlike Geoffrey Howe, he was not one of a group of Ministers leaving a Government that was disintegrating. The Labour Government had been triumphantly re-elected in 2001, less than two years before, to its second term. It was riding high in the polls, and the Prime Minister, Tony Blair, was still popular.

I have therefore chosen Robin Cook's resignation speech because it was very much the stand of an individual, although there were certainly many other Labour MPs and even Ministers with doubts and concerns about the path the Government were taking in supporting the US invasion of Iraq.

Cook was a brilliant debater and a clever, ambitious man. He was widely admired, but not widely liked. He could be arrogant and abrasive; he suffered fools badly. But his colleagues recognised in him a man of strong commitment and radical views.

When he became Foreign Secretary in that new Government he outlined his ideas for his ethical foreign policy. A conscientious student of international affairs, with his own personal network of information and intelligence, Cook had learned a great deal from his worldwide sources. He was better informed than many of his predecessors. One of the things he had learned was the extraordinary success of the policy of containment against Iraq – the no-fly zones and the sanctions. The truth is that Iraq was forced into abandoning all its programmes to develop weapons of mass destruction in the late 1990s, five years before the invasion.

He also knew a good deal about Iraq – the competing and mutually hostile communities of Shias, Kurds and Sunnis – and the probable consequences of the country falling apart. But he was the Foreign Secretary for only a few months after the election of President George W. Bush before he was replaced.

During those months he would have discovered how deeply certain senior members of the new Bush Administration were committed to regime change in Iraq, how little they knew about the country, and how wildly optimistic were their assumptions about the reaction of the Iraqi people to an invasion and occupation. He doubtless passionately disagreed with them. Whether that was a factor in his replacement, we do not know.

What we do know is that Robin Cook in his resignation speech showed an almost uncanny prescience. After the requisite courtesies and a generous tribute to Tony Blair, he underlined the dangers of acting without the support of the international community or any of the international organisations of which the United Kingdom was a member.

He presented his own devastating analysis of the probable consequences of the Iraq invasion and commented acridly that there were some in the US administration who refused to allow more time for inspections just because those inspections might demonstrate that Iraq had no weapons of mass destruction.

Most chillingly, he referred to the disintegration of the coalition against terror forged by the atrocity of 9/11. "Only a year ago," he declared, "we and the United States were part of a coalition against terrorism that was wider and more diverse than I would ever have imagined possible. History will be astonished," he continued, "at the diplomatic miscalculations that led so quickly to the disintegration of that powerful coalition."

We who outlived him now understand better that extraordinary prophecy.

Mr. Bradshaw: The Government have bent over backwards to honour their commitments to the House and I am confident that they will do so again tomorrow by giving the House an unprecedented opportunity to express its will.

Chris Grayling (Epsom and Ewell): Will the Minister tell the House whether the Prime Minister will lead the debate tomorrow and how much time he will spend in the Chamber?

Mr. Bradshaw: Yes, the Prime Minister will lead the debate tomorrow. I do not know how much time he will spend in the Chamber, but I suspect that it will be a lot.

Mr. Speaker: I have a statement that may help the House.

The Secretary of State invited me in the course of his statement to specify a time by which amendments to the Government's motion on Iraq must be submitted. Members who want their amendment to appear on the Order Paper tomorrow morning must, of course, table it before the House rises tonight, but I will consider for selection any amendment that is submitted in good order before 10 am tomorrow.

Personal Statement

9.44 pm

Mr. Robin Cook (Livingston): This is the first time for 20 years that I have addressed the House from the Back Benches. I must confess that I had forgotten how much better the view is from here. None of those 20 years were more enjoyable or more rewarding than the past two, in which I have had the immense privilege of serving this House as Leader of the House, which were made all the more enjoyable, Mr. Speaker, by the opportunity of working closely with you.

It was frequently the necessity for me as Leader of the House to talk my way out of accusations that a statement had been preceded by a press interview. On this occasion I can say with complete confidence that no press interview has been given before this statement. I have chosen to address the House first on why I cannot support a war without international agreement or domestic support.

The present Prime Minister is the most successful leader of the Labour party in my lifetime. I hope that he will continue to be the leader of our party, and I hope that he will continue to be successful. I have no sympathy with, and I will give no comfort to, those who want to use this crisis to displace him.

I applaud the heroic efforts that the Prime Minister has made in trying to secure a second resolution. I do not think that anybody could have done better than the Foreign Secretary in working to get support for a second resolution within the Security Council. But the very intensity of those attempts underlines how important it was to succeed. Now that those attempts have failed, we cannot pretend that getting a second resolution was of no importance.

France has been at the receiving end of bucketloads of commentary in recent days. It is not France alone that wants more time for inspections. Germany wants more time for inspections; Russia wants more time for inspections; indeed, at no time have we signed up even the minimum necessary to carry a second resolution. We delude ourselves if we think that the degree of international hostility is all the result of President Chirac. The reality is that Britain is being asked to embark on a war without agreement in any of the international bodies of which we are a leading partner—not NATO, not the European Union and, now, not the Security Council.

To end up in such diplomatic weakness is a serious reverse. Only a year ago, we and the United States were part of a coalition against terrorism that was wider and more diverse than I would ever have imagined possible. History will be astonished at the diplomatic miscalculations that led so quickly to the disintegration of that powerful coalition. The US can afford to go it alone, but Britain is not a superpower. Our interests are best protected not by unilateral action but by multilateral agreement and a world order governed by rules. Yet tonight the international partnerships most important to us are weakened: the European Union is divided; the Security Council is in stalemate. Those are heavy casualties of a war in which a shot has yet to be fired.

I have heard some parallels between military action in these circumstances and the military action that we took in Kosovo. There was no doubt about the multilateral support that we had for the action that we took in Kosovo. It was supported by NATO; it was supported by the European Union; it was supported by every single one of the seven neighbours in the region. France and Germany were our active allies. It is precisely because we have none of that support in this case that it was all the more important to get agreement in the Security Council as the last hope of demonstrating international agreement.

The legal basis for our action in Kosovo was the need to respond to an urgent and compelling humanitarian crisis. Our difficulty in getting support this time is that neither the international community nor the British public is persuaded that there is an urgent and compelling reason for this military action in Iraq.

The threshold for war should always be high. None of us can predict the death toll of civilians from the forthcoming bombardment of Iraq, but the US warning of a bombing campaign that will "shock and awe" makes it likely that casualties will be numbered at least in the thousands. I am confident that British servicemen and women will acquit themselves with professionalism and with courage. I hope that they all come back. I hope that Saddam, even now, will quit Baghdad and avert war, but it is false to argue that only those who support war support our troops. It is entirely legitimate to support our troops while seeking an alternative to the conflict that will put those troops at risk.

Nor is it fair to accuse those of us who want longer for inspections of not having an alternative strategy. For four years as Foreign Secretary I was partly responsible for the western strategy of containment. Over the past decade that strategy destroyed more weapons than in the Gulf war, dismantled Iraq's nuclear weapons programme and halted Saddam's medium and long-range missiles programmes. Iraq's military strength is now less than half its size than at the time of the last Gulf war.

Ironically, it is only because Iraq's military forces are so weak that we can even contemplate its invasion. Some advocates of conflict claim that Saddam's forces are so weak, so demoralised and so badly equipped that the war will be over in a few days. We cannot base our military strategy on the assumption that Saddam is weak and at the same time justify pre-emptive action on the claim that he is a threat.

Iraq probably has no weapons of mass destruction in the commonly understood sense of the term—namely a credible device capable of being delivered against a strategic city target. It probably still has biological toxins and battlefield chemical munitions, but it has had them since the 1980s when US companies sold Saddam anthrax agents and the then British Government approved chemical and munitions factories. Why is it now so urgent that we should take military action to disarm a military capacity that has been there for 20 years, and which we helped to create? Why is it necessary to resort to war this week, while Saddam's ambition to complete his weapons programme is blocked by the presence of UN inspectors?

Only a couple of weeks ago, Hans Blix told the Security Council that the key remaining disarmament tasks could be completed within months. I have heard it said that Iraq has had not months but 12 years in which to complete disarmament, and that our patience is exhausted. Yet it is more than 30 years since resolution 242 called on Israel to withdraw from the occupied territories. We do not express the same impatience with the persistent refusal of Israel to comply. I welcome the strong personal commitment that the Prime Minister has given to middle east peace, but Britain's positive role in the middle east does not redress the strong sense of injustice throughout the Muslim world at what it sees as one rule for the allies of the US and another rule for the rest.

Nor is our credibility helped by the appearance that our partners in Washington are less interested in disarmament than they are in regime change in Iraq. That explains why any evidence that inspections may be showing progress is greeted in Washington not with satisfaction but with consternation: it reduces the case for war.

What has come to trouble me most over past weeks is the suspicion that if the hanging chads in Florida had gone the other way and Al Gore had been elected, we would not now be about to commit British troops.

The longer that I have served in this place, the greater the respect I have for the good sense and collective wisdom of the British people. On Iraq, I believe that the prevailing mood of the British people is sound. They do not doubt that Saddam is a brutal dictator, but they are not persuaded that he is a clear and present danger to Britain. They want inspections to be given a chance, and they suspect that they are being pushed too quickly into conflict by a US Administration with an agenda of its own. Above all, they are uneasy at Britain going out on a limb on a military adventure without a broader international coalition and against the hostility of many of our traditional allies.

From the start of the present crisis, I have insisted, as Leader of the House, on the right of this place to vote on whether Britain should go to war. It has been a favourite theme of commentators that this House no longer occupies a central role in British politics. Nothing could better demonstrate that they are wrong than for this House to stop the commitment of troops in a war that has neither international agreement nor domestic support. I intend to join those tomorrow night who will vote against military action now. It is for that reason, and for that reason alone, and with a heavy heart, that I resign from the Government. [*Applause.*]

Mr. Speaker: Order. I have motions to put before the House.

Defence Minister on the attack as the Callaghan Government teeters on the brink of defeat

As a child, **Robert Worcester** announced to his family in Kansas City that his ambition was to live in London. That ambition did not at the time encompass the creation of one of the best known and largest opinion research companies in the world. But his eventual arrival in the capital in 1969 at the age of 35 to found MORI – Market Opinion & Research International – marked a significant step towards that destination.

Before leaving the United States, he had worked for management consultants McKinsey and Company in Washington and New York and served as chief financial officer of the Opinion Research Corporation in Princeton, New Jersey.

In the nearly 40 years that he has resided in Britain he has become a prominent member of the academic and business communities. He took British citizenship in 2005 after his appointment as deputy lieutenant of the county of Kent. He was subsequently knighted by the Queen for "outstanding service to political, social and economic research and for his contribution to Government policy and programmes".

He is a past president of the World Association for Public Opinion Research.

However, his range of interests extends far beyond his immediate commercial activities. He is Chancellor of the University of Kent and a visiting professor and governor of the London School of Economics and Political Science. He is an honorary professor at the Universities of Kent and Warwick, holds five honorary degrees, and is a Fellow of the LSE and of Kings College, London.

He also maintains a close interest in Anglo-US relations, being chairman of the Pilgrims Society, a member of the Magna Carta Trust, and a governor both of the English Speaking Union and of the Ditchley Foundation. He has been a member of the US-UK Fulbright Commission. Formerly a member of the Board of the Institute of United States Studies of the University of London, he is also a vice president of the UK United Nations Association and of the European Atlantic Group.

As well as serving as a specialist adviser to the House of Commons Treasury Select Committee, he is now an advisor to the House of Commons Librarian's "Parliament and the People" initiative.

Environmental issues are a major area of interest to him. He was president of ENCAMS – the environmental campaign charity best known for its "Keep Britain Tidy" movement of which he was also the president. He is a vice-president of the Royal Society of Wildlife Trusts and was a trustee of the Worldwide Fund for Nature and the Wildfowl and Wetlands Trust.

As a deputy lieutenant of the county, his links with Kent inevitably extend well beyond Kent university. He lives in a 13th century castle overlooking the river Medway. He was on the board of the Kent Messenger newspaper group and has been chairman of Maidstone Radio. He is a Kent county council appointed "Kent Ambassador" and formerly held the post of non-executive director of the Medway Maritime Hospital NHS Trust.

To the general public he is well known as a television pundit analysing the results as they flow in on election night. In addition to his broadcasting activities, however, he is a regular contributor to national newspapers and has edited or written more than a dozen books, the latest of which – "Explaining Labour's Landslip: The 2005 General Election" – analyses the circumstances of that event.

Excitement mounts in the House on the eve of momentous events

BY SIR ROBERT WORCESTER KBE, DL

The House was packed on the night of 27 of March 1979, not so much for the defence debate itself, or to hear the Minister of State's winding up speech, but because everyone in the House, and most of the country, knew that on the following day the Government would fall.

For nearly a decade I had advised first Harold Wilson and then James Callaghan on the state of British public opinion, as the private pollster for the Labour Party. I had been invited to witness the tenor of the House in the closing days of the Government I had worked with for nearly a decade. I knew, and I knew the Prime Minister knew, every member of the Government knew, that they were doomed to defeat at the general election to come.

At 9:31 Dr. John Gilbert rose to speak, observing that "This is a sad occasion", as he bade farewell to Members he had served with who had announced that they would not be standing again, and that this was the eve of their departure from Parliament forever.

He commended the left-wing pacifist Frank Allaun for putting forward an alternative amendment, but then ridiculed it with irony and wit, observing the wish of Allaun for defence spending to be converted to peaceful production was shared by the British shipbuilding industry which would welcome any orders at all, warship or civilian, and that defence spending was alleviating problems of unemployment on the Clyde, Merseyside and the North-East, all Labour areas where seats were at risk.

It was a serious speech, listened to with attention, but as the time drew closer to the final 10 o'clock Division, the Benches grew rowdier, and the interruptions grew more frequent, Sir Ian Gilmour and Sir Geoffrey Pattie led the pack. Dr. Gilbert stood his ground, well prepared, quoting from speeches each had made in the House and even abroad.

He rebutted Sir Ian's previous speech in the debate, which criticised the Government for its reduction in defence expenditure by nearly £12 billion on his calculation. Assuming the Tories would restore the £12 billion he said, and with his eye on the clock as it neared the time for the Division, Dr Gilbert concluded above the clamour, that he assumed that the Opposition, if in office, would make the restoration over 10 years.

"I could tell him how he could find this figure of £1,200 million a year", Gilbert shouted. "He could get £400 million by doing away with 10,000 hospital beds (Order Papers waving). He could get another £300 million by doing away with 150,000 industrial training places. He could save another £300 million by cutting out 500,000 nursery school places; or he could...". I won't go on, but Dr. Gilbert did, for several more minutes, to a crescendo of support from the Labour benches, and at the stroke of 10, the Speaker called the Division.

Reading Hansard, I am struck at how little the atmosphere of the evening is conveyed on the pages. I'll never forget it.

Winchester (Rear-Admiral Morgan-Giles) at these debates. He reminded us that this week sees the final departure from the Service of the "Ark Royal". On Saturday, the Leader of the House goes to Malta to celebrate the withdrawal of the last British Service men from that island. What a symbol of national decline!

We also say farewell to the Secretary of State for Defence, for I do not know of any political commentator who believes that the Secretary of State can survive in his present post in any circumstances. In a few days or weeks he will be gently towed to some distant dockyard where he will undergo an extensive political refit. We wish him well. In previous posts, he has often shown courage and common sense. We recognise that it is a tragedy for him that he will be largely remembered in his present post for falling asleep during the Jubilee fly-past.

After all, everyone in public life runs the risk of having silly photographs taken. But these particular photographs stuck in the mind of the public, because there was a subconscious realisation that he had actually been sent to the Ministry of Defence to go to sleep. He was meant to lull the Left wing. He was meant not to bother the Treasury. He was meant to preside over a period of silent decline. Over the past five years, this Government have proved that they lack the policies, the resources and the will to provide for the adequate defence of this country. Tomorrow they must go.

9.31 p.m.

The Minister of State, Ministry of Defence (Dr. John Gilbert): I have no intention of following the latter remarks of the hon. Member for Beckenham (Mr. Goodhart).

Mr. Duffy: Let them roll in their own gutter.

Dr. Gilbert: This is a sad occasion, if only for the fact that this is the last defence debate in which the hon. and gallant Members for Winchester (Rear-Admiral Morgan-Giles) and Eye (Sir H. Harrison) will take part. I think I speak for every Labour Member when I say that we have all enjoyed their contributions over the years. I count myself privileged to have served under the hon. and gallant Member for Eye on the Defence and External Affairs Sub-Committee for about half the time during which he has been a distinguished Chairman of that body.

Possibly the most enjoyable speech during the debate came from my hon. Friend the Member for Hemsworth (Mr. Woodall). It was not only enjoyable but it showed us all insights into the life of the ordinary Service man and his family, about which we need reminding from time to time. It was an extremely healthy and helpful contribution.

This evening we face an Opposition in a quite extraordinary posture. They have no motion of their own on the Order Paper, so it is difficult to debate precisely what their views are. It could well be that the reason why they have no motion of their own is that they have no policy of their own, or, if they do, they wish to keep it concealed. They are reduced to opposing my right hon. Friend's motion, which bases British security on the collective effort to deter aggression while seeking every opportunity to reduce tension through international agreement on arms control and disarmament. I find it difficult to understand how any hon. Member could oppose sentiments of that sort. As my hon. Friend the Under-Secretary of State for Defence for the Army said yesterday, their policy is more interesting than ours because theirs is a complete mystery.

The attitude of my hon. Friend the Member for Salford, East (Mr. Allaun), and that of my other hon. Friends who signed the amendment, is much more comprehensible and candid than that of the official Opposition. At least my hon. Friend has tabled an alternative proposition which we can debate, and I propose to start by doing so. His amendment contained three basic propositions—that British defence expenditure was destabilising, that more should be done on converting defence industries to civil production, and some comments on nuclear policy. As my hon. Friend would expect, I propose to concentrate on the first two, because my right hon. Friend the Secretary of State dealt yesterday with the question of nuclear policy.

My hon. Friend's amendment refers to

"a massive increase in military expenditure to £8,588 million in the year 1979-80".

[Dr. Gilbert.]

Yesterday my hon. Friend said:

"The defence estimates show an increase from £7·1 billion last year to £8·6 billion this. That is an increase in cash terms of 24 per cent."—

I make that 20 per cent.

"We all know roughly the figure of inflation. It is nothing like 24 per cent. Despite explanations that I have secured from statisticians, I am not satisfied that the real increase is only 3 per cent."—[*Official Report*, 26 March 1979; Vol. 965, c. 72.]

That may well be a genuine misunderstanding, and there is a clear explanation on page 62 of the White Paper of what is apparently a considerable increase in defence expenditure.

In the previous White Paper the Vote was set out in terms of volume. This year we are taking the Estimates on cash limit terms, and inflation is built into this year's prices but was not last year. The 1979-80 Supply Estimates are being published for the first time on a forecast outturn basis, and are being based on prices prevailing in 1979-80. The difference between the two figures effectively represents two years' inflation and not one, as a result of the different conventions. I hope that that is clear to my hon. Friend the Member for Salford, East, who in a former more wicked existence was a chartered accountant. I am sure that he is quite at home with such matters.

My hon. Friend and I will never agree on whether our expenditure leads to instability. I respect his sincerity but agree far more with my hon. Friend the Member for Hornchurch (Mr. Williams). He pointed out that the 30 years of NATO's existence and the continuing peace of the Continent of Europe are not coincidences but cause and effect. My colleagues on the Front Bench and I share those sentiments.

The second point raised by my hon. Friend the Member for Salford, East also exercises my hon. Friend the Member for Keighley (Mr. Cryer), namely, the need to convert defence industries to peaceful production. That involves British Shipbuilders and also the Royal Ordnance Factory, Leeds. At present British shipyards will welcome any orders, including warship export orders. It is a proper function of the Ministry of Defence to give assistance in obtaining those orders and alleviate the serious problems of unemployment on the Clyde, Merseyside and the North-East that would result from the total drying up of civilian orders.

The Royal Ordnance Factory, Leeds, is more directly my responsibility. I am chairman of the board of the Royal ordnance factories. It has been suggested, for instance, that we turn the productive facilities there to making agricultural tractors, and such suggestions are wholly impracticable. We need the capacity to provide the British Army with its new main battle tank for the 1980s. If that capability is not preserved in the United Kingdom, we shall have to buy our tanks abroad. That is not in this country's interests or those of any constituent.

I have said many times at the Dispatch Box, and I resile from not a word, that I would much rather live in a world where defence sales were not so important to the economies of this country, the United States, Germany and France. Other countries, however, wish to buy the means of their self-defence. Manufacturers of civilian goods in this country are already selling all that they can abroad, and they have capacity to spare. They do not want more competition from British firms but more markets abroad.

The answer must come from the policies that were advocated by my right hon. Friend the Prime Minister at the United Nations special session on disarmament. My right hon. Friend's contribution to that session was applauded by my hon. Friend the Member for Oldham, East (Mr. Lamond), who, like my hon. Friend the Member for Keighley, spoke movingly about the need to combat hunger, poverty and disease in less-developed countries. I agree with everything that they said. It must be our objective to achieve detente between NATO and the Warsaw Pact Powers and between all areas of friction throughout the world.

I regret that the hon. Member for Chichester (Mr. Nelson) is not in his seat. He made an extremely thoughtful and constructive contribution. He asked some pertinent questions about the defence budget being allocated between individual Services. I regard the allocation between different functions as more significant. The hon. Member suggested that the balance had remained static over the years. He was misinformed on that point. There has been an appreciable redistribution in recent years. In the 1974-75 defence budget the RAF received an allocation that was 24 per cent. higher than that of the Royal Navy, but this year the two are about equal. However, it would be impractical to run the Services, or any other large organisations, on the basis of frequent and radical changes.

One must consider that the life of equipment from the project definition stage to the final phasing out of service existence can often be more than 30 years. Therefore, the changes must be gradual. We are constantly trying to improve the way in which we arrive at our major resource allocation decisions. We have made progress in recent years, but I am far from satisfied that we have the methodology right. We may well be making the right decisions, but occasionally we may make wrong decisions. That is true of any Government, faced with the complexity of decisions in defence procurement.

In my view, it is important that the decisions should be taken on the basis of explicit assumptions rather than implicit, imprecise ones. Any development of that sort will in no way absolve senior advisers from producing assessments based in the last resort on informed judgment. The important thing is that the assumptions are required to be explicit. Under my chairmanship we are studying at the highest level in the Ministry the way in which decisions are made and how this process can be improved.

One of the most difficult areas of resource allocation relates to our anti-surface ship capability. A lot has been said today about anti-submarine and anti-mine capability. If one takes the view that we are devoting too great a proportion of our resources to this capability or to any other, there is no simple means of dramatically changing the policy in a short period. All the weapons platforms that may operate against surface vessels need to be provided with effective weapons. Therefore, we need air-to-surface weapons to be fired from fixed-wing aircraft and helicopters, we need surface-to-surface weapons, and we also need submarine-launched weapons.

The difficulty is that weapons systems have become so specialised and so opti-

mised for a particular role that many different weapons are required, unfortunately in very small quantities. This worsens the ratio of development to production costs and makes decisions about changing the allocation of resources at the margin very much more difficult.

There are a couple of other areas in which we are trying to improve the decision-making machinery on resource allocation in the Ministry of Defence. We are looking at the spread of work on operation analysis which at present is distributed throughout the Services and the procurement executive. We are trying to eliminate any redundancy between these various activities and we hope that we shall be able to derive further benefits from some form of organisational change.

Another reform that we are trying to institute is a cutting down of the extremely long time scale for the completion of major works projects. At present a major project can take as long as seven years to complete and often construction time accounts for no more than half of that. Therefore, when short-term changes must be made in the defence programme, because of technological change or industrial difficulties, it takes a considerable time before the loss can be made good in other elements of the programme, and we lack a degree of flexibility which we would very much hope to acquire.

I shall deal with some of the specific questions asked today and with those which were raised in the debate yesterday. The hon. and learned Member for Colchester (Mr. Buck) asked about the dockyards. I am happy to tell him that there is a full work load for all four home yards. We are seeking to improve productivity through the development of a new productivity scheme. Progress towards an agreed scheme is well advanced. We are continuing our programme of capital investment in buildings and facilities in every yard.

The defence White Paper foreshadowed further orders this year for Type 42 destroyers. I am pleased to tell the House that today we have placed an order for the twelfth of these ships from Vosper Thornycroft Ltd. of Southampton. Subject to satisfactory contractual negotiations, we intend to place two further orders for Type 42s in the next three or four weeks. The tendering process for

[Dr. Gilbert.]

these orders was initiated many months ago.

Hon. Members will wish to know of the importance we place on the nuclear fleet submarine programme. In line with our current policy of multiple tendering and ordering of equipment, to achieve better performance and prices from our contractors, we are accelerating the fleet submarine ordering programme to reduce the interval between orders. Thus, we hope to be able to assist shipyards to maintain their sources of supply with sub-contractors who, until now, have suffered from time to time from insufficient work loads.

The hon. and gallant Member for Eye asked whether there would be a 3 per cent. increase in the budget next year. I take it he means 1980-81. My answer to that is an unambiguous " Yes ".

The hon. Member for Haltemprice (Mr. Wall), among many questions, asked about tankers and container ships. He said that it would not be necessary to spend much money in order to acquire many more platforms for Sea Harriers, thus enabling us to increase our anti-submarine warfare capability. This has been examined, particularly in the context of ordering some new RFA tankers. I have had discussions with senior naval officers more than once and I took the same view as he did, but I regret to tell him that I am now persuaded that we cannot achieve increased capability without spending a great deal more money. It might be possible eventually, but certainly not in the near future.

My hon. Friend the Member for Walsall, South (Mr. George) spoke at length about the Territorial Army Volunteer Reserve. My hon. Friend the Under-Secretary of State for Defence for the Army has a total commitment to the TAVR, since he has spent a number of weekends at work with them. He is grateful to my hon. Friend for his helpful and thoughtful speech. The recommendations of the Shapland report have been put in hand urgently and we expect to be able to announce decisions shortly.

Several hon. Members spoke about our capability in mine warfare and mine counter-warfare. The House will be interested to know that we propose to use the hovercraft in this role. It was always believed to have a potential as an MCM vessel because of its inher-ently low magnetic, acoustic and pressure influence signatures. We have investigated possible weapon equipment for any future MCM hovercraft but have not yet found any which is satisfactory. We have bought a medium-sized hovercraft and we propose to evaluate one operationally in the MCM logistic support role. The hovercraft will go out from the main port so that the MCM vessels can spend much longer on their task. We are optimistic about such developments.

I agree with the hon. Member for Haltemprice and the right hon. Member for Belfast, East (Mr. Craig) that we must look closely at our capability for defensive and offensive mining operations. We are doing that.

The hon. Member for Plymouth, Sutton (Mr. Clark) asked whether it was more costly to refit Leanders instead of building the new Type 22. It would probably be cheaper, but the question is whether it would be more cost-effective. The modernisation programme for Leanders is well in hand. We can see an end to it. The Type 22 is a more modern ship with a capability in anti-submarine warfare which is indispensable. There is scope in the fleet for both the Type 22 and the Leander class since each can perform its own role.

I agree that we should examine seriously the question of building ships with a shorter life. So far that proposition has not been thought to be economical. The idea is that we can move eventually to a greater cellularity in ships so that we can speed up refits—refit ships more frequently and more easily convert them from one role to another.

The hon. and gallant Member for Winchester suggested that we should build ships on spec. The Royal Navy is co-operating with British Shipbuilders in the Type 24 experiment. It is too early to say whether that ship will be suitable for Royal Navy work. We hope that it will be.

The hon. Member for Haltemprice asked me about AV8B. It is improbable that the RAF will want to order 25 AV8Bs and end up with a mixed fleet of British Harriers and United States Harriers to operate at the same time. There would be all types of operational difficulties and the logistic problems would be considerable.

I reaffirm that the RAF places great importance on the unique take-off and landing capabilities of the Harrier. Our experience with that plane has confirmed the high potential value of such aircraft when they can operate out of forward positions in close support of the Army. That is particularly important when conventional airfields are under attack. Our firm view is that an aircraft such as this will remain a major component of the Royal Air Force front line. Plans are in hand to modify the Harrier to improve its performance and to extend its useful life for many years.

I have dealt with as many contributions as I can from Back-Bench Members. I shall devote a few minutes to the speeches from the Opposition Front Bench. The hon. Member for Beckenham talked about comparability for the Armed Forces. The right hon. Member for Chesham and Amersham (Sir I. Gilmour) now talks of full comparability for the Armed Forces this year. That is an interesting change from the Opposition's official position this time last year.

Sir Ian Gilmour (Chesham and Amersham): Our position is the same.

Dr. Gilbert: Last year the hon. Member for Stretford (Mr. Churchill) said that the Opposition were asking for a return to full comparability in a time scale which was no less favourable than that accorded by the Government for the firemen. He asked for an undertaking to that effect. I gave that undertaking. We remain committed to that undertaking.

Sir Ian Gilmour: I am sorry to interrupt an interesting speech. I made it clear last year. I said that we would restore comparability next year—that is, this year. There has been no change in our policy.

Dr. Gilbert: If that is so, the right hon. Member for Chesham and Amersham and his hon. Friend the Member for Stretford were speaking out of different sides of their mouths last year. The evidence is clear. Of course the song now is "the lot, this year", which I am sure has nothing whatever to do with an election arriving; it is just a happy coincidence.

The hon. Member for Chertsey and Walton (Mr. Pattie) made a speech today which was not nearly so interesting as the speech he made in Chicago recently, which was the subject of quotation earlier today. The hon. Gentleman used some very strange language. He tried to justify what he said about Milan and Tow—I assume he was quoted correctly in the report in the " Defence and Foreign Affairs Daily "—in which he said they had been delayed, as though by act of this Government they had been delayed. He nods his head. That is what he thinks. I repudiate that totally. The House has been told repeatedly that the introduction of Milan into service has been accelerated, and the decision to buy Tow has been brought forward.

The hon. Gentleman talked about the delay in the introduction of the Chinook, which was a piece of impudence coming from a spokesman for a party three years in office which did nothing whatsoever to introduce the Chinook.

The hon. Gentleman talked about the Bloodhound being " virtually obsolescent ". When he was in Chicago he talked about it being " obsolescent " without any " virtually " in front of the word. There are a series of other complaints of which the hon. Member saw fit to deliver himself in Chicago. I regard the hon. Gentleman with considerable respect and affection, and I am very sorry that he chose to make so inaccurate and distorted an attack on his country's defences while he was abroad. [HON. MEMBERS: " Hear, hear."] I trust he will see fit not to repeat such activities again.

Mr. Pattie: The Minister of State must realise that I was invited to take part in a seminar that was involved with the Soviet challenge to Western Europe, and that inevitably had to do with the capability of this country's defence policies. I wished only to give what I considered to be an honest assessment of that position.

Dr. Gilbert: What I complain about is a series of distortions and inaccuracies in the hon. Gentleman's speech to a foreign audience.

I turn now with some relish to the speech of the right hon. Member for Chesham and Amersham, who yesterday stated that this Government have reduced defence expenditure by nearly £12 billion, and he went on to speak with all the authority of a former Secretary of State with 56 days in office, 21 days of which

[Dr. Gilbert.]

he spent electioneering. I do not know what he did with the other 35 days because history does not recall that. His last 21 days, of course, were not very successful in keeping himself in office. I know that he went to Devonport, where he said the Labour Government would close the dockyard. I shall go there on Friday to remind them how much reliance they can place on his statements inside and outside this House. He said that there was no conceivable justification for these defence cuts amounting to £12 billion. I assume, therefore, that he would restore them—I do not know whether he is going to restore them over 10 years. I may say that he is a little more ambitious than he was last year, when he was only talking about implementing expenditure by 1 per cent. in the defence budget ; that was about £80 million a year. Now he is talking of £12 billion. I assume that he would restore them over 10 years. That would amount to £1,200 million a year. I could tell him how he could find that figure of £1,200 million a year. He could get £400 million by doing away with 10,000 hospital beds. He could get another £300 million by doing away with 150,000 industrial training places. He could save another £300 million by cutting out 500,000 nursery school places ; or he could get £100 million by reducing grants for 30,000 private dwellings. For another £100 million—which would give him his £1,200 million—he could reduce social security benefits, old-age pensions and long-term social security benefits by 1 per cent. I do not know whether that is the right hon. Gentleman's policy. I do not know where else he will get the money from. In addition, he intends to cut taxation and reduce public sector borrowing at large.

The prospects of this country for the social spending which our people need will be grim indeed under policies of that sort.

Question put, That the amendment be made :—

The House divided : Ayes 52, Noes 228.

Division No. 107]   AYES   [10.00 p.m.

Allaun, Frank
Atkinson, Norman (H'gey, Tott'ham)
Bain, Mrs Margaret
Bennett, Andrew (Stockport N)
Bidwell, Sydney
Buchan, Norman
Canavan, Dennis
Carmichael, Neil
Crawford, Douglas
Cryer, Bob
Edge, Geoff
Ellis, John (Brigg & Scun)
Evans, Gwynfor (Carmarthen)
Ewing, Mrs Winifred (Moray)
Flannery, Martin
Fletcher, Ted (Darlington)
Fowler, Gerald (The Wrekin)
Heffer, Eric S.
Hooley, Frank

Hoyle, Doug (Nelson)
Jeger, Mrs Lena
Jenkins, Hugh (Putney)
Kelley, Richard
Kerr, Russell
Kilroy-Silk, Robert
Kinnock, Neil
Lamble, David
Lamond, James
Latham, Arthur (Paddington)
Lee, John
Litlerick, Tom
Loyden, Eddie
Madden, Max
Maynard, Miss Joan
Mikardo, Ian
Mitchell, Austin (Grimsby)
Parry, Robert
Pavitt, Laurie

Price, C. (Lewisham W)
Richardson, Miss Jo
Rodgers, George (Chorley)
Silverman, Julius
Skinner, Dennis
Stewart, Rt Hon Donald
Thomas, Dafydd (Merioneth)
Thomas, Ron (Bristol NW)
Thorne, Stan (Preston South)
Tilley, John
Torney, Tom
Wigley, Dafydd
Wilson, William (Coventry SE)
Wise, Mrs Audrey

TELLERS FOR THE AYES:
Mr. Ivor Clemitson and
Mr. Stan Newens.

NOES

Abse, Leo
Anderson, Donald
Archer, Rt Hon Peter
Armstrong, Ernest
Ashley, Jack
Atkins, Ronald (Preston N)
Bagier, Gordon A. T.
Barnett, Guy (Greenwich)
Barnett, Rt Hon Joel (Heywood)
Bates, Alf
Bean, R. E.
Beith, A. J.
Benn, Rt Hon Anthony Wedgwood
Bishop, Rt Hon Edward
Blenkinsop, Arthur
Boardman, H.
Booth, Rt Hon Albert
Boothroyd, Miss Betty
Bottomley, Rt Hon Arthur
Boyden, James (Bish Auck)

Bradford, Rev Robert
Bradley, Tom
Bray, Dr Jeremy
Brown, Hugh D. (Provan)
Brown, Robert C. (Newcastle W)
Buchanan, Richard
Callaghan, Rt Hon J. (Cardiff SE)
Callaghan, Jim (Middleton & P)
Campbell, Ian
Cant, R. B.
Carter-Jones, Lewis
Cartwright, John
Castle, Rt Hon Barbara
Cocks, Rt Hon Michael (Bristol S)
Cohen, Stanley
Coleman, Donald
Conlan, Bernard
Cowans, Harry
Cox, Thomas (Tooting)
Craig, Rt Hon W. (Belfast E)

Craigen, Jim (Maryhill)
Crawshaw, Richard
Crowther, Stan (Rotherham)
Cunningham, G. (Islington)
Cunningham, Dr J. (Whiteh)
Dalyell, Tam
Davidson, Arthur
Davies, Bryan (Enfield N)
Davies, Rt Hon Denzil
Davies, Ifor (Gower)
Davis, Clinton (Hackney C)
Deakins, Eric
Dean, Joseph (Leeds West)
de Freitas, Rt Hon Sir Geoffrey
Dell, Rt Hon Edmund
Dempsey, James
Dewar, Donald
Doig, Peter
Dormand, J. D.
Douglas-Mann, Bruce